The
BOOKER T. WASHINGTON
Papers

The
BOOKER T. WASHINGTON
Papers

VOLUME 2

1860-89

Louis R. Harlan
EDITOR

Pete Daniel
ASSISTANT EDITOR

Stuart B. Kaufman
ASSISTANT EDITOR

Raymond W. Smock
ASSISTANT EDITOR

William M. Welty
FELLOW IN HISTORICAL EDITING

University of Illinois Press
URBANA · CHICAGO · LONDON

vol. 2

cop. 1

To
Portia Washington Pittman

ACKNOWLEDGMENTS

THE BOOKER T. WASHINGTON PAPERS project is a team effort, and the editors appreciate the dedication of those who have worked on the project in the past five years. William M. Welty served with the project during the academic year 1970-71 as a National Historical Publications Commission fellow in editing. In all respects he functioned as one of the editors of this volume. Sadie M. Harlan, research assistant to the editors from the project's inception, has with deep interest and impressive stamina worked with the vast manuscript collection at the Library of Congress. She helped compile the preliminary selection of documents and served as a resource for other members of the staff, who relied on her close knowledge of the manuscripts. Virginia V. Molvar, project secretary, contributed her expert typing and grasp of stylistic matters. Barbara Adams served as project secretary during the first two years and also helped in preliminary selection of documents. Blanche Dixon and Janet Hearne also worked on the preliminary selection process at the Library of Congress. University of Maryland graduate assistants have dug into the resources of the Library of Congress and other major repositories searching for annotation material. Several of the following have been assigned to the project each year: Arlene Ehrlich, Michael Franch, Nancy Hornick, John L. King, Jr., John Lenihan, and Elaine Smith. University undergraduates who have handled clerical tasks, photocopying, and preliminary proofreading for the project include Delcina Cook, Charles D. Farmer, Jr., Marijeanne Lovaas, Maretha Martin, and Dianne Swann.

The editors could not have done their work without help and encouragement from many individuals and institutions, which they gratefully acknowledge. They particularly appreciate the following:

Members of the Board of Editorial Advisors for helpful advice in the operation of the project and for critical reading of the manuscript of the first two volumes: John Hope Franklin, Francis C. Haber, Milo B. Howard, Elsie M. Lewis, Arthur S. Link, August Meier, Haskell Monroe, Dorothy B. Porter, Benjamin Quarles, Willie Lee Rose, David A. Shannon, Charles H. Wesley, Daniel T. Williams, and C. Vann Woodward.

The University of Maryland for giving the Booker T. Washington Papers an institutional home and substantial financial support, and certain officers and staff members of the university who have been especially helpful: President Wilson H. Elkins, Vice-President R. Lee Hornbake, Dean Charles Manning, Vice-Chancellor George H. Callcott, Professor Walter Rundell, Jr., Linda Edwards, and Milton Goldberg.

Tuskegee Institute, and particularly President Luther H. Foster, Daniel T. Williams, Helen Dibble, and Raymond Jackson, for many helpful services.

The National Endowment for the Humanities, and particularly J. Saunders Redding and William Emerson, for their encouragement and for indispensable financial aid.

The National Historical Publications Commission for its part in initiating the Booker T. Washington Papers, its assignment of two fellows in advanced editing of documentary sources in U.S. history to the project, several grants-in-aid, and the friendly interest of Oliver W. Holmes, Handy Bruce Fant, Sara D. Jackson, and Fred Shelley.

The staff of the University of Illinois Press, particularly Richard L. Wentworth, the associate director, whose advice went beyond the publication aspect into all of the problems of initiating the editorial enterprise, and the copyeditor, Elizabeth Dulany.

The staff of the Manuscript Division reading room of the Library of Congress, under the direction of C. Percy Powell, John Knowlton, Horace F. Hilb, and Carolyn Sung.

The staff of the Stack and Reader Division of the Library of Congress, notably Dudley B. Ball, Herbert Davis, and William Sartain.

The staff of Hampton Institute, particularly Eleanor Gilman, Edward Graham, and Fritz Malval.

Members of the staff of the National Archives, notably Elaine Everly, Helen T. Finneran, and Robert Kvasnicka.

Many individuals who have helped in numerous ways, bringing our attention to documents, searching in their own archives or providing notes for information, or critically reading the manuscript. Helpful in these ways are some already mentioned, and the following: Harry Brown, Emma Dorsette Bunce, Helen Carr, Reverend Charles W. Carpenter, Frank P. Chisholm, Minnie W. Cooper, Daniel W. Crofts, Raymond Demallie, Donald S. Gates, John C. Harlan, V. Leslie Hebert, James L. Hupp, Carolyn E. Jakeman, Ernest Kaiser, Barbara Kraft, Gilbert Lusk, Barry Mackintosh, Ernest Rice McKinney, Leslie B. McLemore, J. Marcus Mitchell, Portia Washington Pittman, Marty Shaw, Edith Washington Shehee, John Sullivan, Ruth Tirrell, and Edwin T. Watters.

The Booker T. Washington Papers is under special obligation to the editorial staff of the Papers of Woodrow Wilson and to Haskell Monroe, editor of the Papers of Jefferson Davis, for their advice on editorial method and style. The editors have also taken advantage of the experiences of others engaged in similar enterprises by consulting the published papers of the Adams Family, Henry Clay, Benjamin Franklin, Ulysses S. Grant, Alexander Hamilton, Thomas Jefferson, Andrew Johnson, James Madison, Theodore Roosevelt, Woodrow Wilson, and the Wright Brothers.

The editors dedicate this series of volumes to the anonymous black participants in American history whose experiences need fuller documentation as a part of our national heritage.

CONTENTS

CONTENTS

CONTENTS

ILLUSTRATIONS

INTRODUCTION

H ISTORIANS HAVE GENERALLY RECOGNIZED Booker Taliaferro
Washington as the outstanding American black man of his day
and the supreme black example of the success hero. Washington
believed that his life, as related in his autobiography *Up from Slavery,*
was a model, not an exception, and that his famous Atlanta Compromise address in 1895 was the charter for racial peace, not an acceptance
of second-class status. As violence swirled around black southerners,
Washington remained strangely optimistic about race relations. Whites
could look to Washington for calming words, reassurance, accommodation; humble and oppressed blacks could vicariously share Washington's
success and power. The founder of Tuskegee Institute in Alabama
sought always to say what people wanted to hear, and except for a few
black and white critics, Americans accepted him as the spokesman of
his race, the Negro of the hour. His story, however, was a deeper and
more complex one. At one level of reality, there was indeed a struggle
to rise from slavery, to gain an education, to plant a school in the
Alabama Black Belt, to win powerful allies and raise money. In his
more ruthless struggle to fight off his critics and to retain his power,
however, Washington showed a different personality. Behind his
smiling eyes lurked a multifaceted essence with all the complications
of the human condition and the additional complexity of being black
in white America.

Washington began life about April 5, 1856, as a slave on the James
Burroughs farm near Hale's Ford, Virginia, the son of a house servant
and an unidentified white man. After emancipation in 1865, he went

with his mother to West Virginia, where his black stepfather had escaped during the Civil War. He labored as a miner and houseboy and secured a rudimentary education. Traveling to Hampton Normal and Industrial Institute in Virginia, he gained training which qualified him for teaching, while paying part of the cost of his education through "industrial" work. There he came under the spell of the founder of Hampton, General Samuel Chapman Armstrong, who gave Washington's career his guidance until his death in 1893, and whose social philosophy Washington adopted as the guiding principle of his life. This philosophy combined the paternalistic racialism of Armstrong's missionary parents, the Puritan work ethic of Williams College under Mark Hopkins, the Spartan regimen of the army, and conservative accommodation to the conditions of southern life.

After several years of experimentation with other careers, including politics and the Baptist ministry, Washington returned to Hampton in 1879 as a teacher and dormitory supervisor. In 1881 he went to Tuskegee, Alabama, to found Tuskegee Normal and Industrial Institute on the Hampton model. It was as principal that Washington combined all of his ambitions, for presiding over Tuskegee Institute called for shrewd politics and preacher-like oratory as well as teaching. As had been the case when he was a slave on the Burroughs farm, a youth in the West Virginia mining region, and a janitor at Hampton, Washington realized that in Alabama the whites possessed the power, and he tailored his words and actions to please the rulers.

Whether it originated from the slave heritage, the close experience with whites, or the difficult situation he faced by being black and ambitious in Alabama, deception became a part of Washington's style. Long before he became nationally famous he had learned that to survive in the South a black man had to assume a certain public role no matter what he believed. Any action that Washington thought would offend his white benefactors he did clandestinely. He withstood several political and economic challenges to his school in the eighties and early nineties. During these years the building of his institution absorbed much of Washington's energy and ambition.

In 1895, the year Frederick Douglass died, Washington was catapulted into a position of Negro leadership by the effects of a single speech. Douglass's death signaled the end of the old Reconstruction black leadership; Washington was standing in the wings eagerly awaiting a chance to launch a new approach to the race issue. His approach, which combined quietism and economic striving, would appeal more to whites than Douglass's political approach. At a time when lynchings, riots, and disfranchisement laws signaled a stormy era in race relations, accompanied by accelerating trends of economic discrimination and segregation, Washington delivered before the Cotton States and International Exposition his famous Atlanta Compromise address.

He urged the black man to remain in the South, to make friends with his white neighbor, and to work at the "common occupations of life." He reminded fellow blacks that "there is as much dignity in tilling a field as in writing a poem." If southern whites would give the black man a chance, Washington promised, "you can be sure in the future, as in the past, that you and your families will be surrounded by the most patient, faithful, law-abiding, and unresentful people that the world has seen." Nor did Washington challenge white supremacy. "In all things that are purely social we can be as separate as the fingers, yet one as the hand in all things essential to mutual progress." This image became famous immediately, for it at once allayed white fears of social equality and offered an opportunity for racial cooperation. "The wisest among my race," he further explained, "understand that the agitation of questions of social equality is the extremest folly, and that progress in the enjoyment of all the privileges that will come to us must be the result of severe and constant struggle rather than artificial forcing." Washington then pointed to the exhibits in the segregated Negro exhibition building as a sign of black progress. He hoped that whites would allow the black man a chance to prove himself, suggesting that his formula would "bring into our beloved South a new heaven and a new earth."

Washington's accommodationism became, for many reasons, the "conventional wisdom" of his day in race relations. The press carried his Atlanta message across the land, and he exploited his fame, emerging as the spokesman for black Americans. With strong white support, Washington became the outstanding black leader not only in the fields of education and philanthropy, but in business and labor relations, politics, and all public affairs. His best-selling autobiography, *Up from Slavery*, published in 1901, told the story of his success and further established his leadership. In the years between 1895 and his death in 1915, he constructed a network of organizations and personal ties, usually called the Tuskegee Machine, which sustained his leadership and philosophy. His power derived from his control of many Negro newspapers and fraternal, religious, professional, and business organizations, including dominance of the Afro-American Council, the Committee of Twelve for the Advancement of the Negro Race, and the National Negro Business League; strong influence on the philanthropic activities of John D. Rockefeller, Andrew Carnegie, Anna T. Jeanes, Robert C. Ogden, and Julius Rosenwald, and the foundations they established; a moderating private influence on many southern white leaders; and wide public influence through his many books, articles, interviews, and public lectures all over the country. Through these organizations and individuals and through the expenditure of his own energy in the endless details of his school — a model of black self-help — Washington hoped to point the way toward the solution of the race problem.

Despite his power and influence, Washington could never relax, for more outspoken blacks challenged his leadership and his claim to speak for his race. First William Monroe Trotter, a Harvard graduate and newspaper editor, and then William Edward Burghardt Du Bois, another Harvard man, attacked Washington's thinking on the race issue. They deplored Washington's accommodationism, his passivity in a time of worsening race relations, his emphasis on industrial training instead of intellectual pursuits, and his hold over the black press. Washington's critics, including whites who had formerly backed him, institutionalized their program in the National Association for the Advancement of Colored People. Using secretly methods that he publicly disapproved, Washington fought off their attacks by establishing a spy network in the enemy's camp, by controlling the black press, and by continuing to utter his platitudes of racial harmony.

Even as he fought the black intellectuals, Washington delved into civil-rights issues, clandestinely sponsoring a series of court suits against discrimination in voting, exclusion of blacks from jury panels, Jim Crow railroad facilities, and peonage. He did not use these secret efforts to answer his black critics, for they never learned and hardly suspected that he had participated in these cases. Perhaps he was lighting a backfire, hoping that by privately fighting for civil rights he could control the increasing oppression that he publicly ignored.

Washington emerges from the evidence of his private papers as a man who continually acted out a series of conflicting roles. At Tuskegee he was the master of his plantation, giving paternal attention to the smallest detail. When raising funds in the North he drew the admiration and the contributions of such men as Andrew Carnegie, for like the steel millionaire Washington had sprung from obscurity and by hard work and good management had achieved success. With southern whites Washington moved gingerly, courting favor with the rulers and the wealthy while convincing the poor that he was no threat to them. To southern blacks he was the hero, the wizard, the man who had risen from slavery to greatness. Washington tried through industrial training to free the black man from economic bondage to the white landowners of the rural South. But as his critics pointed out, many of the trades taught at Tuskegee had little efficacy in the changing world of the twentieth century.

Washington's ideas for racial progress, derived largely from General Armstrong in the mid-nineteenth century, never changed, but his methods of accomplishing his ends became ever more elaborate. The wealth of his papers guarantees him the detailed hearing his historical significance warrants.

THE PAPERS

Booker T. Washington's life and views found clearer expression in his private papers than in his deliberately conventionalized public writings and utterances. His frequent resort to secret and sometimes contradictory actions gives added interest to the study of his private correspondence. The central reason for publishing his papers, however, is Washington's historical importance and that of the events in which he was involved.

The principal collection of manuscripts of Booker T. Washington is the Booker T. Washington Papers in the Manuscript Division of the Library of Congress. These papers, numbering about a million items, extend from 1882 to 1942, but the bulk of the material dates within the period from 1900 to Washington's death in 1915. Washington and his able private secretary, Emmett Jay Scott, saved both incoming and outgoing correspondence of this extraordinarily rich collection. The collection contains significant material in black history, American education, national and local politics, Negro business, and international affairs as related to race questions. In addition to correspondence, the collection includes typescripts and notes of speeches, reports from Tuskegee departments, scrapbooks of clippings, copies of published works, and photographs.

There are many Washington letters also in other collections, and these are of particular value for the early volumes, for Washington was not careful to save copies of his outgoing correspondence before Emmett Scott became his private secretary in 1897. Other substantial collections are the archives of Tuskegee Institute and of Hampton Institute; the papers of Robert C. Ogden, Jabez L. M. Curry, Theodore Roosevelt, William Howard Taft, James S. Clarkson, Carter G. Woodson, Ray Stannard Baker, and the National Association for the Advancement of Colored People in the Manuscript Division of the Library of Congress; the Census Bureau, Freedmen's Bureau, and patronage correspondence in the National Archives; the Emily Howland Papers in the Schomburg Collection of the New York Public Library and at Cornell University; the Charles W. Chesnutt Papers, Fisk University; the Francis J. Grimké Papers, Howard University; the Walter Hines Page Papers and Oswald Garrison Villard Papers, Harvard University; the William Edward Burghardt Du Bois Papers, in custody of Herbert Aptheker of the American Institute of Marxist Studies, New York; the Seth Low Papers, Columbia University; and others. For a record of Washington's appearances before the public as a speaker and writer, the editors have searched in scrapbooks, newspapers, magazines, and the reports and proceedings of conferences.

The principal Washington collection originally was simply the files of the principal's office at Tuskegee Institute, and this explains the quantity of institutional administrative records in the collection. A separate series of family and personal correspondence supplements the family letters filed in the largest series, the Principal's Office Correspondence. Some of the most significant letters are in the series designated as Regular Correspondence, that is, letters to and from persons with whom Washington regularly corresponded. There is also the Local Correspondence between Washington and the Tuskegee department heads. Other series include correspondence regarding students, applicants for positions, donations, lecture engagements, the National Negro Business League, and miscellaneous. When the Washington Papers were moved from Tuskegee to the Library of Congress in 1943, the original order of the collection was preserved. Though the collection is poorly arranged, with much material misfiled under wrong dates and names, the Manuscript Division in 1958 prepared a published register of the Booker T. Washington Papers to assist users. Also helpful is E. Franklin Frazier's descriptive article, "The Booker T. Washington Papers," in the Library of Congress *Quarterly Journal of Acquisitions,* 2 (Feb. 1945), 23-31.

THE PROJECT

The Booker T. Washington Papers project had its origin in a poll of American historians conducted by the National Historical Publications Commission in 1965. Washington was ranked twelfth and was the only black American near the top of the historians' ratings of those whose papers should be published as a part of the national historical heritage. The editor was meanwhile at work on a biography of Washington. The editing project began in September of 1967. Unlike the subjects of most earlier enterprises in historical editing, Washington was neither a founding father nor a national political leader. Yet his importance in American history is firmly established, and his significance as a subject for an editing project stands securely on the wealth of social history revealed in his papers as well as the fact that Washington was a leading black American.

The Washington Papers project does not seek to build a monument to this controversial figure or his social philosophy but to reveal black culture in all its complexity and rich human interest and the story of American race relations, black and white, in the late nineteenth and early twentieth centuries. This critical approach to the central figure is not adopted because he was black or because he was Booker T. Washington, but because of the editors' belief that history should serve the cause of social criticism instead of exalting a people or an individual hero. Because Washington was a middleman between the white and black America of his day, his papers also shed light on interracial relations in the "age of accommodation." But the reader should be warned that there is an imbalance in the Washington Papers, for with the exception of occasional mention of the crop-lien system or lynching or discrimination, Washington rarely admitted that there were deep racial problems in America. He generally took the hopeful view on the ground that it was more constructive, an approach that soothed white southerners and loosened the purse strings of philanthropists. By including incoming correspondence the editors hope to broaden the focus of the papers beyond Washington's restricted perspective. This wealth of sources transcends Washington's private and public life, and the editors seek in the selection of documents to portray not only Washington's life but as far as possible his age as well.

In this volume the editors have been less selective than they will be in later volumes because of the paucity of available early material related directly to Washington. Later volumes, however, will probably contain no more than 5 percent of the total available documents. Many researchers will want to see also the documents not selected for publication here, and the editors make no claim to preempt the whole field of study of Booker T. Washington. They hope that some of the published documents will be merely suggestive leads to others. On the other hand, they have sifted and winnowed carefully to exclude repetitive and routine documents that abound in this collection as in many others. Some items that are in themselves of a rather trivial nature are included because they reveal something of the manner of life at the time or place. Items such as those dealing with admission of students, job applications, donations, interoffice memoranda, and forms have generally been omitted. It is possible, however, that just such documents may be useful to specialists in educational history. The daily reports of the swine herd and the poultry yard may be of interest to agricultural historians, for example, but the editors choose to cast only a few such pearls before our readers.

The editors have made an effort to annotate each correspondent, but names in lists are identified only if they assume importance in Washington's life. Standard biographical and reference works are rarely cited, nor is citation provided for matters of fairly general knowledge or for a subject previously identified. The length of an annotation is usually an index of the subject's importance in Washington's life, but at times the absence or brevity of an annotation results simply from sparse information, a comment on the obscurity of many figures and events of the period. White people, for example, more often appear in easily available biographical directories than their "invisible" black counterparts.

Explanatory footnotes are used to clarify obscure references in a document. The editors do not attempt, however, to explicate or interpret the documents exhaustively. They believe that their proper role in annotation is to illuminate the document in the context in which it was written, to identify persons and unclear references to places and events when necessary and possible, and to suggest, when appropriate and possible, the connection between the persons and events of the documents and the life and times of Booker T. Washington. The editors feel that editorial restraint in the interpretation of documents enhances their value as sources rather than diminishes their value, though this may occasionally cause annotation to be less complete than it could be.

The editors hope that their approach to document selecting and editing will give a faithful portrayal of Booker T. Washington as revealed in his papers. A further account of the Washington Papers project, its founding and methodology, is provided in Pete Daniel and Stuart B. Kaufman, "The Booker T. Washington Papers and Historical Editing at Maryland," *Maryland Historian*, 1 (Spring 1970), 23-29.

EDITORIAL METHOD

The papers of Booker T. Washington are organized and presented chronologically. The only exception to this is Volume 1, *The Autobiographical Writings*. Documents dated only by year or month follow those more precisely dated for that year or month. Documents covering substantial periods of time are placed at the date of earliest entry. When dates are the same, outgoing correspondence precedes incoming correspondence, except rarely, when considerations of transition or clarity dictate a different order.

Documents are presented faithfully as written except for silent correction of typed and printed errors. The first word in every sentence begins with a capital, and all sentences end with a period except in semi-literate letters, which are reproduced exactly as written in order to avoid an inordinate amount of editorial intrusion into the document. Words originally run together are separated by a space. Most documents are reproduced in full, but in rare cases editorial omission of a substantial body of material is shown by a four-dot ellipsis centered on the page. A shorter omission is shown by a four-dot ellipsis after the last word in the sentence. Superscripts are lowered, and antiquated renderings of dates, money symbols, fractions, and abbreviations when possible are made consistent with modern usage. Unnecessary dashes are eliminated, and dashes used to end sentences are converted to periods. Modern form is used with quotation marks. Underlining in handwritten letters appears as italics.

The editors incorporate interlineations and marginal notes at appropriate places. Only addenda or alterations seeming to reflect altered opinion or those of psychological importance are specially noted; deleted material, when both readable and relevant, is indicated by ~~deleted.~~ Obliterated letters of a word or phrase are supplied in brackets.

Editorial insertions of words omitted by the author appear in brackets: [this]. Words supplied by the editors but of which they are unsure are enclosed in brackets followed by a question mark: [this?]. Partly illegible words are followed by a bracketed question mark: this[?]. Material that cannot be deciphered is represented by ellipsis marks. Words with missing characters are corrected by the bracketed insertion of the omitted letters: th[i]s or t[ha]t, but no attempt has been made to correct complicated misspellings. Only in extraordinary cases do the editors employ *sic*. The reader should assume that the spelling in this printed text accurately represents the original spelling rather than a typographical error.

Attachments are generally printed with their covering letters; the less important ones are summarized or listed in notes to their covering letters. Docketing is not usually noted except when necessary to establish the identity of the correspondent. Enclosures deemed important are printed in chronological order with cross references between them and their covering letters, but less important enclosures are simply noted. Notations such as "Private," "Confidential," or "Secret" precede the document as in the original.

The endnote provides a technical description in symbols of the nature and location of the document. The symbols, in order, show the type of correspondence, folder number, container number and other information, collection, and repository. Other explanatory matter in endnotes provides further information about the document. For example, in the case of a letter addressed simply to "Dear General," an effort is made through study of internal evidence and related documents to determine which of several possible generals was the actual correspondent. Similarly, problems of location and dating sometimes call for explanation.

On rare occasions the editors include an excerpt rather than a complete document when particularly important material appears in a lengthy document most of which is unrelated to Washington's affairs. Stray documents that come to light during the course of the project will appear as addenda in later volumes. Each volume will contain an index, and the final volume will contain a general index for the series.

Washington's writing style presents some problems to editors and readers. He wrote rapidly, formed his letters and words poorly, and misspelled many common words though usually in consonance with their sound. His hasty scrawl may be attributed partly to his imitation of Samuel Chapman Armstrong, who wrote in the same way. His misspellings stemmed partly from the fact that he had little more than the standard secondary-school education, but also from his impatient disregard of form in his search for the substance of what he had to say. It was of a piece with his plainness of speech, homely anecdotes, and lack of pretension. He wrote in the same manner as many a brusque, self-made businessman to whom he frequently appealed for funds. Washington never learned to use a typewriter, and dictated most of his typed correspondence. There the spelling and punctuation peculiarities of the handwritten manuscripts were usually corrected.

For decisions about editorial style the editors have generally followed standard usage in the University of Chicago *Manual of Style*, 12th ed. (Chicago, 1969).

THIS VOLUME

The first volume of the letters of Booker T. Washington traces his career in the thirty-three years from his birth in 1856 to the death in May 1889 of his second wife, Olivia A. Davidson Washington. Because Washington was a product of slavery and its attendant illiteracy, sources revealing his early life are sparse and often tangential. Census material and other such incomplete documents put the young Washington in the context of public records of Virginia and later West Virginia. The editors hope to convey, prismatically, as it were, the shaping forces of his early life. After Washington entered Hampton Institute in 1872 his record unfolds more completely, though gaps in documentation remain. One of the more interesting series of documents shows the young Washington in an active if non-controversial role in West Virginia politics. His writings on Indian students also provide an insight into Hampton's mission and American white attitudes toward the darker races. Much material relates to the founding of Tuskegee Normal and Industrial Institute. Washington's life became so interwoven with his school that to illustrate his career is also to tell the story of the institution.

Washington's tremendous physical and psychic energy, his ability to raise funds, to oversee the school, to challenge any competition, all at the same time, emerge in this volume. His concern was with the blacks who sought an education, with those who would administer the lessons, and with the whites of the North and the South who could supply the funds for his dream. If his autobiography was embellished and somewhat mythological, the documentary record was even more amazing, for it told of a black man that white men and even his black critics never dreamed of. The talent that would later make Washington the spokesman for many black Americans emerges in this volume. Unlike the success hero of the autobiographical writings, Washington was in reality a complex man who played various social roles according to need. His black intimates did not call him "the wizard" for nothing.

CHRONOLOGY

1856   Ca. Apr. 5: Born a slave on the James Burroughs farm, near Hale's Ford, Franklin County, Va.

1861   July 24: Death of James Burroughs.

1865   April: Emancipation of the Burroughs slaves.

August or September: Journey to Malden, Kanawha County, W.Va.

1872   Oct. 5: Enrollment in Hampton Institute.

1874   Summer: Death of mother.

1875   June 10: Graduation from Hampton Institute.
Ca. September: Return to Malden to teach school.

1877   Summer: Campaign to make Charleston the state capital.

1877 or   Attendance at Wayland Seminary in Washington, D.C.
1878

1879   May 22: Postgraduate address at commencement exercises of Hampton Institute.

September: Teacher at Hampton and organizer of the night school.

1880-81   Resident supervisor of "The Wigwam," the Indian boys' dormitory at Hampton Institute.

1881   July 4: Opening of Tuskegee Normal School at Butler's Chapel A.M.E. Zion Church in Tuskegee, Ala.

1882   Apr. 15–July 14: First northern tour of BTW and Olivia A. Davidson.

Aug. 12: Marriage to Fanny Norton Smith of Malden.

November: Completion of Porter Hall, first large campus building.

1883   June 6: Birth of daughter Portia Marshall Washington.

1884   May 4: Death of Fanny Norton Washington.

July 16: Address before the National Educational Association at Madison, Wis.

1885   Apr. 24: Protest against discriminatory treatment on railroads.

May 28: First graduating class at Tuskegee Institute.

1886   Aug. 11: Marriage to Olivia A. Davidson.

1887   January–May: Struggle with William B. Paterson over the location of the Alabama State University for Colored Students.

May 29: Birth of son, Baker (later Booker) Taliaferro Washington.

Summer: Course in physical education at Harvard.

1889   Feb. 6: Birth of second son, Ernest Davidson Washington.

May 9: Death of Olivia A. Davidson Washington.

SYMBOLS AND ABBREVIATIONS

STANDARD ABBREVIATIONS for dates, months, and states are used by the editors only in footnotes and endnotes; textual abbreviations are reproduced as found.

DOCUMENT SYMBOLS

1. A — autograph; written in author's hand
   H — handwritten by other than signator
   P — printed
   T — typed

2. C — postcard
   D — document
   E — endorsement
   L — letter
   M — manuscript
   W — wire (telegram)

3. c — carbon
   d — draft
   f — fragment
   p — letterpress
   t — transcript or copy made at much later date

4. I — initialed by author
   r — representation; signed or initialed in author's name
   S — signed by author

Among the more common endnote abbreviations are: ALS — autograph letter, signed by author; TLpI — typed letter, letterpress copy, initialed by author.

REPOSITORY SYMBOLS

Symbols used for repositories are the standard ones used in *Symbols of American Libraries Used in the National Union Catalog of the Library of Congress,* 10th ed. (Washington, D.C., 1969).

A-Ar	Alabama Department of Archives and History, Montgomery, Ala.
ATT	Tuskegee Institute, Tuskegee, Ala.
DLC	Library of Congress, Washington, D.C.
DNA	National Archives, Washington, D.C.
LNHT	Tulane University, New Orleans, La.
MH	Harvard University, Cambridge, Mass.
MNS	Smith College, Northampton, Mass.
MWiW	Williams College, Williamstown, Mass.
MeB	Bowdoin College, Brunswick, Me.
MnHi	Minnesota Historical Society, St. Paul, Minn.
OFH	Rutherford B. Hayes Library, Fremont, Ohio.
PHC	Haverford College, Haverford, Pa.
RPB	Brown University, Providence, R.I.
Vi	Virginia State Library, Richmond, Va.
ViHaI	Hampton Institute, Hampton, Va.
WHi	State Historical Society of Wisconsin, Madison, Wis.

OTHER ABBREVIATIONS

BRFAL	Bureau of Refugees, Freedmen, and Abandoned Lands
BTW	Booker T. Washington
Con.	Container
EJS	Emmett Jay Scott
RG	Record Group

Documents, 1860-89

An Item from the Census:
The James Burroughs[1] Family

[Franklin County, Va., 1860]

The name of every person whose usual place of abode on the first day of June, 1860, was in this family	Description		Profession, Occupation or Trade of each person, male and female, over 15 years of age	Value of Estate Owned		Place of Birth, Naming the State, Territory, or Country	Attended School within the year
	Age	Sex		Value of Real Estate	Value of Personal Estate		
Jas. Burroughs	65	M	Farmer	3105	8200	Va	
Elizabeth W. "[2]	59	F				"	
Martha F. "[3]	30	F				"	
Ann E. "[4]	26	F				"	
Christopher "[5]	22	M	Farmer			"	I
Eliza J. "[6]	20	F				"	
Susan A. "[7]	18	F				"	
Newton E. "[8]	15	F				"	
Ellen D. "[9]	13	F				"	

Census of 1860, Free Inhabitants, Northeast Division of Franklin County, Va., p. 259, RG29 M-653 DNA. Columns left blank by the census taker were: color, married within the year, persons over twenty years of age who cannot read and write, and whether deaf and dumb, blind, insane, idiotic, pauper, or convict.

[1] James Burroughs (1794-1861) was born near Smith Mountain in the southern part of Bedford County, Va., one of the eleven children of Joseph Burroughs, a Baptist minister of French Huguenot descent. The name was usually pronounced Bur'rus. James Burroughs served in the War of 1812 and later drew a pension for this. In 1818 he married Elizabeth W. Robertson, and in the next year purchased 228 acres of farmland in Bedford County. In the census of 1830 he reported four slaves, of which the female under ten could have been Jane, mother of BTW, and a free black youth between ten and twenty-four living in the household. In 1850 he purchased from Thomas Burroughs a tract of 177 acres near Hale's Ford in Franklin County which the latter, probably a brother, had purchased in 1833. Four years later James Burroughs purchased an adjoining tract of 30 acres. It was on this farm of 207 acres that BTW was born in slavery in 1856. (For other details on the Burroughs family, see Mackintosh, *Burroughs Plantation 1856-1865*.)

3

[2] Elizabeth W. Robertson Burroughs (1802-95), daughter of Nicholas Robertson, a neighboring farmer in Bedford County, Va., married James Burroughs on Aug. 8, 1818. In twenty-eight years she bore him fourteen children. She lived on the Burroughs farm at least until after 1865.

[3] Martha Frances ("Mat") Burroughs (1829-1904), sixth child of James and Elizabeth W. Burroughs, married Charles R. Noell, a Franklin County farmer, in 1870.

[4] Ann Elizabeth Burroughs (1833-1903), eighth child of James and Elizabeth W. Burroughs, remained at home until her marriage in 1866 to John Cardwell Ferguson, eldest son of Josiah Ferguson, a substantial farmer and tobacco manufacturer who lived directly across the road from the Burroughs farm.

[5] Christopher Frank Burroughs (1838-65), tenth child of James and Elizabeth W. Burroughs, known as Frank, enlisted in the Confederate Army in 1861 at the first muster of the Franklin Rangers, which became Company D of the Second Virginia Cavalry. At about this time he married Fannie Cundiff, who remained at the Burroughs farm during the war. After discharge in August 1862 he re-enlisted. Captured by Union forces, he died in 1865 as a prisoner of war, perhaps at sea.

[6] Eliza Jane Burroughs (1840-1918), eleventh child of James and Elizabeth W. Burroughs, lived in 1870 with her mother at the home of her sister Ann Burroughs Ferguson. In 1877 she married David O. Witt of Bedford County. It was while visiting her in 1895 that Elizabeth Burroughs died. Both are buried near Body Camp, Va.

[7] Presumably Laura Angeline Burroughs (1842-1912), twelfth child of James and Elizabeth W. Burroughs. BTW was said by a nephew to be "quite a favorite of Aunt Laura." (James A. Burroughs to BTW, Nov. 7, 1903, Con. 251, BTW Papers, DLC.) Less credible are family stories that he rode behind her to her school in order to bring back her horse, and that she or her sister Ellen taught him to read. In 1873 she married Stephen R. Holland, presumably a relative of the prominent Holland family of Hale's Ford, and lived thereafter in Bedford City. In 1904 and 1910 she wrote detailed letters to BTW.

[8] Edwin Newton Burroughs (1844-1922), thirteenth child of James and Elizabeth W. Burroughs, enlisted in the Confederate Army and was wounded at Nance's Shop on June 24, 1864. Though his service record simply recorded a wound in the right thigh, family tradition more accurately described it as "in the rump." When teased about this, he confessed that, with bullets whizzing about him, he had been running away. (James, "Uncle Tom? Not Booker T.," 100.) In 1869 he married Mary Adeline Virginia Peters, and in 1870 the census reported him working as a farm laborer in Bedford County. Incorrectly reported as female.

[9] Ellen America Burroughs (1846-91), fourteenth and youngest of the children of James and Elizabeth W. Burroughs. In 1871 she married William Judson Goggin, Bedford County minister and farmer. He was the son of Thomas Clark Goggin, a Baptist minister of Bedford County who performed the marriage ceremonies for at least seven of the other Burroughs children.

An Item from the Census:
The Slaves[1] of James Burroughs

[Franklin County, Va., 1860]

Names of Slave Owners	Number of Slaves	Description			No. of Slave houses
		Age	Sex	Color	
Jas Burroughs	I	41	F	B[2]	
	I	40	F	B[3]	
	I	22	M	B[4]	
	I	12	F	B[5]	
	I	8	M	M[6]	
	I	4	M	M[7]	
	I	I	F	B[8]	2

Census of 1860, Slaves, Northeast Division of Franklin County, Va., p. 21, RG29 M-653 DNA. Columns left blank by the census taker were: fugitives from the state; number manumitted; deaf and dumb, blind, insane, or idiotic.

[1] Identities of the unnamed slaves are drawn from the inventory of the James Burroughs estate, Nov. 23, 1861.

[2] Sophia Agee (1819?-1900) was the half-sister of Jane. All or some of the other young slaves of the Burroughs family may have been her children. After emancipation she moved to West Virginia and in 1870 lived in Malden with her husband James Agee, a sixty-year-old foundry worker. In 1880 she had moved to Handley, W.Va., a coal-mining town across the river from Malden, where she lived with her daughter Sallie and son-in-law W. W. Poe. She listed her occupation as midwife. She was in bad health in her later years.

[3] Jane Ferguson (1820-74) was the mother of the two mulatto children John Henry and BTW, and then married, whether formally or not, Washington Ferguson, hired-out slave of neighbor Josiah Ferguson, by whom she had the black child Amanda. In the 1830 census of Bedford County, James Burroughs was reported to own a female slave under ten years old, which could have been Jane. The possibility that she might have been owned by the Burroughs family from a young age is strengthened by the claim of Silas C. Burroughs, a grandson of James, that he knew her birthplace near Stone Mountain in Bedford County. In August 1865 Washington Ferguson sent for her and the children to join him in Malden. She lived there until her death during one of BTW's summer vacations from Hampton.

[4] A twenty-three-year-old unnamed slave of James Burroughs was reported to have died on May 23, 1861. (Register of Deaths, Franklin County Courthouse, Rocky Mount, Va.)

[5] The twelve-year-old black girl may have been either Mary Jane or Sally [Sallie Poe], listed in the Burroughs inventory below.

[6] John Henry Washington (1852?-1924), BTW's older half-brother, was born

at Hale's Ford, Franklin County, Va. BTW remembered in *Up from Slavery* that his older brother had shared with him a rag pallet on the dirt floor and that John had volunteered to wear his stiff new flaxen shirt until it was broken in enough for the younger brother to wear. When BTW went to Hampton, John continued to work in the Malden salt mines, helping to support the family and occasionally sending money to BTW. Soon after BTW returned to Malden to teach, he convinced John to attend Hampton and aided him financially while he was there. John graduated in 1879 and returned to replace BTW in the school at Malden, but soon began working for the federal government in Charleston on a series of locks and dams on the Kanawha River.

In 1885 he came to Tuskegee as business agent, farm manager, and superintendent of industries and in the following years performed a variety of tasks for the school. In these early years John Washington's practical common sense and his jack-of-all-trades ability made him vital to the physical development of the school. He had BTW's practical gifts but lacked the same ability to work with others. He planned and supervised the building of all the early structures on the Tuskegee campus, devising ingenious schemes to cut costs and to use the willing but unskilled student labor force. To solve Tuskegee's water shortage in 1891, "Mr. J. H.," as he liked to be called, explored and found a large spring three-quarters of a mile from the school, bought pipe, and laid it himself to save the installation cost. When in the late 1880s it looked as if a gift of a cupola for the new Tuskegee foundry from Alabama Polytechnic Institute in Auburn would be lost because Tuskegee did not have the money to pay for its shipment, "Mr. J. H." impulsively hitched a team of oxen to a heavy cart used for hauling wood and made the thirty-mile trip to Auburn for the machinery. Besides establishing the trades and industries training and being responsible for the overall care and upkeep of the institution, he was the first drillmaster and commandant of cadets, started the band and the baseball team, began the record-keeping system of the institute, and introduced bee culture, poultry raising, and fruit canning.

Inevitably, as the school grew larger, men more expert than John Washington came to replace him in one after another of these early positions. For instance, Robert R. Taylor, an architect trained at M.I.T., replaced him in 1892 as head of the building program and director of the mechanical industries, and George Washington Carver relieved him of his farm-manager duties in 1896. According to one of Carver's biographers, Rackham Holt, John H. Washington protested his brother's decision to hire Carver. "We don't need what they call a scientific agriculturist. We need a dairyman," he told BTW shortly after Carver's arrival. (Holt, *George Washington Carver,* 154.) After 1902 John H. Washington was superintendent of industries and, whenever both BTW and Warren Logan were absent, acting principal. John H. Washington played a smaller role in the affairs of the institute after his brother's death. He retired in 1919 and died five years later.

⁷ Booker, later named Booker Taliaferro Washington (1856-1915). BTW's medium-brown skin, reddish hair, and gray eyes suggest that he was the son of a white man. He apparently never knew and was never particularly interested in the identity of his father, knowing only that the man was from the neighborhood. It is conceivable that the father was any one of the five older sons of James Burroughs or Burroughs himself; either Josiah Ferguson, who owned the farm across the road from the Burroughs, or his son Thomas Benjamin Ferguson; or Benjamin N. Hatcher, part owner of a tobacco factory and blacksmith shop in

the neighborhood. (For information on the evidence of paternity, see Harlan, *Booker T. Washington,* 3-5.)

[8] Amanda Ferguson Johnston (1859-1915) was Jane's daughter by her husband, Washington Ferguson. She received little education as compared with her half-brothers; in fact she was barely literate. She married Benjamin Johnston (d. 1902) and had four children, George Washington Albert (known as Albert), Benjamin H., Scovill, and Clara. After her husband's death, she struggled to support herself and sent her children to Tuskegee Institute to be educated. She remained in the Malden area, and her daughter Clara returned to live with her. For a time she operated a restaurant, and for many years raised chickens and garden vegetables for sale on a plot of land that BTW rented from Ernest H. Ruffner. She was active in the African Zion Baptist Church in Malden, serving as its clerk for several years. She suffered a stroke on April 21, 1915, and died on May 4, 1915. Her funeral brought so many black and white friends that it was conducted in the white Presbyterian church in Malden instead of her own smaller one.

An Item from the Census:
The James Burroughs Farm[1]

[Franklin County, Va., 1860]

Name of Owner, Agent, or Manager of the Farm	Jas Burroughs
Acres of Land	
Improved	107
Unimproved	100
Cash value of Farm	3,105
Value of Farming Implements and Machinery	75
Live Stock, June 1, 1860	
Horses	4
Asses and Mules	
Milch Cows	4
Working Oxen	
Other Cattle	5
Sheep	12
Swine	16
Value of Live Stock	535
Produce during the Year Ending June 1, 1860	
Wheat, bushels of	250
Rye, bushels of	
Indian Corn, bushels of	450
Oats, bushels of	100

Rice, lbs. of	
Tobacco, lbs. of	2,000
Ginned Cotton, bales of 400 lbs. each	
Wool, lbs. of	30
Peas and Beans, bushels of	1
Irish Potatoes, bushels of	5
Sweet Potatoes, bushels of	20
Barley, bushels of	
Buckwheat, bush. of	
Value of Orchard Products, in doll's	
Wine, gallons of	
Value of Produce of Market Gardens	
Butter, lbs. of	75
Cheese, lbs. of	
Hay, tons of	
Clover Seed, bushels of	
Grass Seeds, bushels of	
Hops, lbs. of	
Hemp	
Dew Rotted, tons of	
Water Rotted, tons of	
Other prepared Hemp	
Flax, lbs. of	10
Flaxseed, bush. of	23
Silk Cocoons, lbs. of	
Maple Sugar, lbs. of	
Cane Sugar, hhds. of 1,000 lbs.	
Molasses, gallons of, and from what made	
Beeswax, lbs. of	
Honey, lbs. of	
Value of Homemade Manufactures	15
Value of Animals slaughtered	120

Census of 1860, Productions of Agriculture, Northeast Division of Franklin County, Va., pp. 17-18, Vi.

[1] This and other reports indicating the nature of the Burroughs farming operation are analyzed and described in thorough detail in Bearss, *Burroughs Plantation.* It is clear from the census report that with only 107 acres of improved land and seven slaves reported, it was a farm rather than a plantation in the general usage of the terms. Those products which Burroughs did not raise were usually not produced by his neighbors, though some had orchards and beehives and produced hay. The 2,000 pounds of tobacco represented the principal cash crop and showed the commercial character of the farm. The farm was of such

diversity, however, as to supply most of its own basic needs. It was characteristic of most farming in Franklin County and elsewhere in the upper Piedmont, which is hilly but not mountainous country, with most landholdings about the size of the Burroughses' or smaller, and with fewer slaves than in the lower Piedmont and coastal regions. During most of their lives the Burroughs couple must have had about as many of their own children as they had slaves on the farm. Most of the crops and livestock needed for subsistence can be found in the census report.

An Inventory of the Estate of James Burroughs

[Rocky Mount, Va., Dec. 2, 1861]

Inventory & appraisement of the estate personal
of James Burroughs Decd. taken the 23d Day of November 1861.[1]

Articles		Value
1 Lot Scantling & plank	[$]	1.50
Shovel Digger & 3 forks		1.00
5 Turning plows & 3 double trees		10.00
7 Hilling hoes 3 grubbing hoes		2.50
6 plows (Shovel)		3.00
3 Coulters & Stocks		.75
1 Lot single trees & double trees		1.75
3 wedges & frow		1.00
1 Lot of old irons		.50
1 Jack screw, ox yoke & jointer		.50
1 Lot Barrels		.50
3 plough points		1.50
2 Scythes & cradles		2.50
1 Jack screw & Bolt pin & tar bucket		2.00
1 Lot flax		1.00
2 hides		7.50
1 harrow		3.00
1 Bell cow & calf		12.00
1 Muly cow whitish		10.00
4 yearlings 5$		20.00
3 Cows & calves 12$		36.00
1 Sow & 8 shoats		15.00
16 fat hogs		128.00
1 Top stack & shucks		10.00

1	Straw rick	[$] 5.00
1	lot blade fodder	15.00
1	Lot Cleaned oats & hogsheads	20.00
1	Fan mill[2]	2.50
1	Lot flax seed	1.50
120	bus. wheat	102.00
1	Lot Hay	8.00
1	cutting knife & barrel brand	1.80
1	Lot oats in tobacco house	30.00
85	barrels corn 2$	170.00
1	Wagon & log chain	15.00
1	Wagon	50.00
4	axes	2.25
1	Carriage & Harness	100.00
1	Lot old irons & Bell &c	1.00
1	Grind stone	1.50
1	Lot tools	2.00
1	Lot mowing blades	1.50
1	Loom	5.00
1	Reel & flax wheel	4.00
3	cotton wheels	3.00
1	Lot Sleighs & harnesses	2.50
3	bbls & lot corn & 1 box	2.50
1	½ bushel measure & 2 hammers	1.00
1	Bed & Furniture	25.00
1	*trunnel*[3] bed & Furniture	6.00
1	Gun & shot pouch	2.00
1	table & candle stand	1.25
1	Lot leather & shoe makers tools	20.00
1	Desk & clock 5 2½	7.50
1	Lot vials bottles &c	2.00
10	Windsor chairs	10.00
10	Split chairs	1.25
2	tables	7.50
2	settees	5.00
1	Waiter & pitcher	.50
1	pr Shears & hackle	1.25
1	Strainer jar soda &c	1.00
1	Lot coffee	4.00
1	Lot spun cotton & thread	1.50
1	Wash stand Bowl & Pitcher	2.25
1	chest	.50

1 Bed & furniture	[$] 25.00
1 Bed & furniture	12.50
1 Trunnel Bed & furniture	3.00
3 looking glasses	.50
1 Bed & furniture	25.00
1 Bed & furniture	20.00
1 Bed & furniture	20.00
1 *trunnel* bed & furniture	2.50
1 chair & lot counterpanes	20.00
1 Chest & box	1.50
1 trunk & contents	5.00
1 Bowl & pitcher & 6 bottles	.50
1 Looking glass	.50
1 *Loot*[4] cooking vessels	15.00
10 pcs water vessels	2.50
contents & smokehouse	5.00
1 Bay mare (Fan)	90.00
1 Sorrel horse (Jack)	140.00
1 bay horse (Sam)	130.00
1 Sett wagon & plough harnett[5]	30.00
2 flat irons trivit[6] baker & table	1.25
Cupboards & contents	40.00
1 Lot dining tables	4.00
2 sacks salt	7.00
Cupboard & contents	4.00
Lot bbls kegs &c	2.00
lot jars jugs & baker	5.00
1 negro man (Munroe)[7]	600.00
1 negro woman (Sophia)	250.00
1 negro woman (Jane)	250.00
1 negro man (Lee)[8]	1000.00
1 negro boy (Green)	800.00
1 negro girl (Mary Jane)[9]	800.00
1 negro girl (Sally)[10]	700.00
1 negro boy (John)	550.00
1 negro boy (Bowker)[11]	400.00
1 negro girl (Amanda	200.00
	$ 7083.80[12]

In accordance with an order of the County Court of Franklin made at its November term (4th November 1861) and directed to the undersigned we have taken the inventory & made the appraisement of the estate of James Burroughs Decd which is herewith submitted November 23rd 1861.

B. N. Hatcher[13]
James Wright[14]
T. Holland[15]

In the Clerk's Office of Franklin County Court the 2nd day of December 1861.

This Inventory and appraisement of the personal estate of James Burroughs Decd was exhibited into the said Office and admitted to record.

Teste Ro. A. Scott C.F.C.[16]

Will Book 12 (1861-63), pp. 148-51, Franklin County Courthouse, Rocky Mount, Va.

[1] James Burroughs died on July 24, 1861, of "lung disease." (Register of Deaths, Franklin County Courthouse, Rocky Mount, Va.)

[2] This is probably the contraption mentioned in BTW, *Up from Slavery*, chap. 1: "I was required to go to the 'big house' at meal-times to fan the flies from the table by means of a large set of paper fans operated by a pulley."

[3] Trundle.

[4] Lot.

[5] Harness.

[6] Trivet.

[7] Monroe Burroughs was a half-brother of Jane. He did not appear as a Burroughs slave in the census of 1860, but the report of him in the 1880 census put his age then as fifty-seven. He was probably born, therefore, in 1833. Some members of the Burroughs family spoke of him as a full blood relative of BTW, though that may have been in error. BTW referred to him as his uncle and reported in *The Story of My Life and Work* that Monroe was stripped naked and whipped with a cowhide one morning in his presence. Laura Burroughs Holland denied this, however, in a letter to BTW. After emancipation Monroe adopted the surname Burroughs and became a farm laborer in Bedford County. The Burroughs family kept in touch with him. Laura Burroughs Holland wrote to BTW: "Your uncle Monroe is looking badly, is quite feeble & most of his children have left him. He has moved off out of his old vicinity & is not getting on very well I learned." (Laura Burroughs Holland to BTW, Jan. 4, 1904, Con. 289, BTW Papers, DLC.)

[8] Nothing is known of Lee. He could have been a child of Sophia. Perhaps his comparative youth or a skill gave him a greater value to the owner than Monroe, then past his physical peak.

[9] Both Green and Mary Jane were possibly children of Sophia.

[10] This was almost certainly BTW's cousin Sallie Agee Poe, daughter of Sophia Agee. In the 1880 census Sallie was reported as being married to W. W. Poe, a Tennessee-born miner.

[11] This name was first written Bowker. Then in another hand and ink the letter *w* was changed to an *o*.

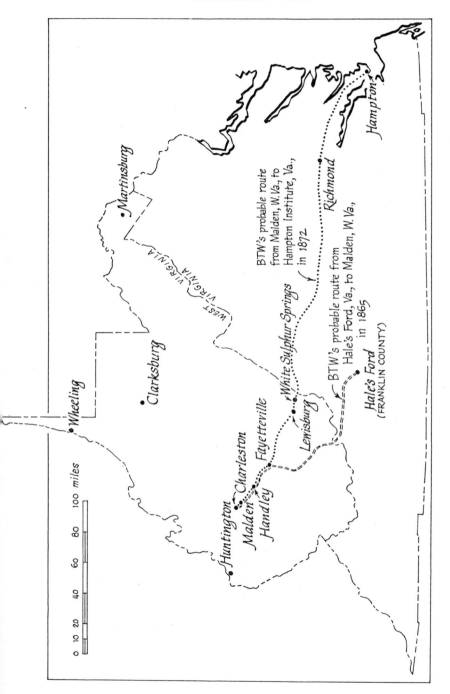

Map I. Virginia and West Virginia: scene of Booker T. Washington's early life.

Wheeling

Clarksburg

Martinsburg

WEST VIRGINIA

VIRGINIA

Richmond

Hampton

White Sulphur Springs

BTW's probable route
from Malden, W.Va., to
Hampton Institute, Va.,
in 1872

BTW's probable route from
Hale's Ford, Va., to Malden, W.Va.,
in 1865

Hale's Ford
(FRANKLIN COUNTY)

Lewisburg

Fayetteville

Handley

Charleston

Malden

Huntington

0 10 20   40   60   80   100 miles

[12] This computation is in error. The total is actually $7,078.80.

[13] Benjamin N. Hatcher, thirty-one years old in 1860, was a local manufacturer. He was a partner of John Cardwell Ferguson in the tobacco-manufacturing firm of Ferguson and Hatcher, reported in the census of manfactures in 1860. The firm hired forty slave men and four slave women and produced 160 pounds of chewing tobacco in the fiscal year 1859-60. The two partners also owned a black-smith shop.

[14] James Wright, a near neighbor, was listed as a sixty-five-year-old farmer in the 1860 census.

[15] This may have been Thomas M. Holland, a near neighbor, twenty-five years old in 1860, teacher of the local common school, or possibly Thomas Holland or Thomas N. Holland, members of the Halesford Sons of Temperance in 1851. (Minutes of meeting, Jan. 4, 1851, document in possession of Sarah Dinwiddie, Halesford, Va.)

[16] Clerk of Franklin County.

Charles Wheeler Sharp[1] to John Kimball[2]

Charleston, West Va., Sept. 20/67

J. Kimball, Esq., Supt of Schools:

.   .   .   .

Malden Township — The school districts, and the enumeration of scholars are as follows:

District No. 2 — Scholars — 11	These two districts
" " 3 — do — 16	lie near together
27	and could send
	scholars to the
	same school.

Tinkersville[3]   — District No. 4 — Scholars — 79
Oakes Furnace —   "   "   5 —   "   — 41
Camel's Creek[4] —   "   "   8 —   "   — 31
178 — Whole number.

I met the Board of Education in this township and submitted to them the proposition of the Bureau, and urged the matter as discreetly and forcibly as possible. I presented their own interest in building now, the necessity of some better provision than the present in order to [have?] good schools, the state and national policy of educating every class and condition, and met all their objections. The only point of any account which they made in reply was, that they had contracted for school houses for white children, to the amount of $4000, so that they were obliged to issue bonds, payable from the tax levy of 1868. I then proposed to get subscriptions from the freedmen. The Board favored this idea, and intimated that they would build at least two houses.

I visited and talked to the freedmen at *Camel's Creek* and got a subscription of $75, towards their house; also at *Tinkersville,* & got $110; also *Oakes Furnace* or Brook's Hollow, & got $107. I now made an appointment to meet the Board, but they failed to meet me. I saw them individually, presented the matter anew, and at length met them officially, and offered $200 from the Bureau towards each of the three houses proposed, as well as the subscriptions named above, which they considered reliable. They at once objected to the plan of the Bureau; said each house would cost $1000; they had no money to build this year; they could hire or rent for the present; log houses were good enough; they must provide for the white children first; they could not provide for both at once, their taxes were now more than they could bear, they would provide two houses some other time — next year, perhaps — they would not issue any more bonds. I offered the $275 towards the house at Camel's Creek, which might be built for $500. They thought a log house might be put up for $275, & that was good enough. At Tinkersville, they thought, no house was needed. I explained to them the importance of having desks, and other arrangements convenient for a school, but to no purpose. I would say, that by private conversation I usually dispose individual members favorably; but when together, as soon as a single objection is raised, they all give way, yielding to the slightest opposition. I may also say, in general, these School Boards are mostly ignorant, coarse-minded men; and while they are disposed to keep the letter of the law, are not willing to be at the slightest inconvenience in this matter. However, it is still possible to get $300 or $500 from the Board yet; if houses could be put up in any way.

A school is in operation at Tinkersville. The building used for a school cannot be made comfortable in winter, and is in no way suited to a school, though it is better than anything the School Boards have yet provided. The school at Brook's Hollow has been recently discontinued. The school at Camel's Creek is held is [in] a little room, part of a log hut. At the two latter places, the freedmen are anxious, and sorrowful, for fear they will not get houses for their schools, as well as houses in which to worship. They might give still more, if they could be assured they could use the school houses as places of worship on Sundays. They now have no places for that purpose. They are wide awake on the subject of schools, and their heart is in this matter. The same is true elsewhere.

At Brook's Hollow the freedmen own a plot of ground for a school house.

·   ·   ·   ·

Very respectfully,

Rev. C. W. Sharp
Agent R. F. & A. L.

ALS   District of Columbia Superintendent of Education, Reports of Sub-District, RG105 BRFAL DNA. Pages 4-7 of fifteen-page report.

[1] Charles Wheeler Sharp (1832-80) was born in Newton, Conn., and educated at Yale University, Union Theological Seminary, and Yale Divinity School. After holding several pastorates in the Congregational Church in New York State, he went to Charleston, W.Va., in 1867 under the auspices of the Freedmen's Bureau and the American Missionary Association to help erect schoolhouses for Kanawha Valley freedmen. Later he taught in freedmen's schools in Wilmington, N.C., superintended a school in Savannah, Ga., and taught blacks in Connecticut and in Boydton, Va.

[2] John Kimball (1831-97), born in Barton, Vt., attended Dartmouth and Union Theological Seminary. After graduating from Union in 1859 he served as a Congregational minister in New York City and in California. An army chaplain from 1863 to 1865, he was appointed superintendent of colored schools in Washington, D.C., after the war, holding the position until 1869. Later Kimball was an American Missionary Association agent on the West Coast and held a number of temporary pastorates in the following decades.

Kimball toured West Virginia with the state superintendent of schools in the summer of 1867 and reported to General Charles H. Howard in Washington after returning. About the Kanawha Valley he said: "The people appear to be doing very well. Among the mines and salt-works they receive good wages, and some of them are securing homes. There are already seven (7) schools in operation in the valley, five of which are taught by Colored persons from Ohio. Most of these schools have received some assistance from the local and State School tax." He said that a school of thirty pupils had been established at Tinkersville. "We met a very large Colored congregation at Tinkers[ville] on the Sabbath-day. They were gathered from all the country round about. Colored men from Tinkersville, Oakes Furnace, and Camels [Campbell's] Creek assured us that they would use their best endeavors to build houses and put the schools on a permanent footing with our help." Kimball recommended "that at Charleston a first class man be stationed who shall be the Principal of the school there, and also have immediate charge of the work throughout the Valley. He shall hold institutes for the instruction of the Colored teachers, and see that the schools are conducted in the most approved manner. He shall also engage the efforts now being put forth to secure suitable school-houses. I think that one of the Northern Societies will furnish such a man and I recommend that he be secured without delay in order that the work of house building may go on this summer." (State Superintendent of Education, Reports of Schools, District of Columbia, Delaware, Maryland, and West Virginia, Oct. 1865–June 1870, RG105 BRFAL DNA.)

[3] BTW attended the Tinkersville Colored School. It is not certain when he attended, but it was at various times between 1867 and 1872. Tinkersville was the neighborhood in Malden where most of the black inhabitants lived.

[4] Properly spelled Campbell's Creek.

William Davis[1] to John Kimball

Tinkersville, Kanawa Valley W.Va. [Nov. 20, 1868]

Dear Sir   I would have sent the reports[2] sooner ~~but as~~ I intended closing school in November   my school is now closed   I will send them all together   the one that was intended for december I send also blank   I remain Dear Sir   Yours truly

Wm Davis

ALS   Letters Received by Superintendent of Education, District of Columbia, 1868, D 45, vol. 1, RG105 BRFAL DNA.

[1] William Davis (1846-1938), a black man, BTW's first teacher, was born in Columbus, Ohio. He obtained the fundamentals of an education during the three years he resided in Chillicothe, Ohio (1861-63). Two years of service as assistant cook with the independent cavalry company known as "Lincoln's Body Guard" left him nearly deaf in one ear, the result of an abscess. After a mastoid operation he received his discharge. Working briefly on a boat running between Columbus and Gallipolis, Ohio, he went to Malden, W.Va., in 1865 and became the teacher at a private school established by black patrons under the leadership of Lewis Rice (d. 1902), a local minister. The school operated at first in Rice's bedroom, the bed being taken down and benches brought in each day for this purpose, but it moved shortly to a newly constructed church. Under the policy of state support for free Negro schools initiated by West Virginia in 1866, Malden, with a relatively large black population, qualified for support, and Davis was able to obtain space in a county schoolroom. Married at Charleston in 1869 to Hallie Ann Lewis, Davis had seven children. He remained at the Malden school until 1871, when he became principal of the black school at Charleston, whose two rooms at the start soon expanded to four. Until 1876 Davis lived with Lewis Rice at Malden, after which he resided in Charleston. Among his Malden students, in addition to BTW, were William T. McKinney, later principal at Huntington, W.Va., and Henry B. Rice. (Misc. documents in folder XC2573366, Veterans Administration, RG15 DNA; Service Record of William Davis, Bennet's Co. Union Light Guard, Ohio Cavalry, RG94 DNA.)

[2] Davis made seven reports between November 1867 and September 1868 that are still extant. These reveal the nature of the Tinkersville school that BTW at-

17

tended. The school was owned by the freedmen of the Malden area and was a one-room, one-teacher operation. The average day-school attendance in 1867-68 was twenty-seven pupils, generally more males than females except in the spring, when girls outnumbered boys. Most of the students were less than sixteen years of age and were learning the rudiments of reading and writing. Other courses included geography and arithmetic, but it is clear from the statistics of Davis's reports that less than half the students were "advanced readers" or arithmetic students. A greater number of students, averaging approximately forty during 1867-68, attended the Sabbath school held in conjunction with the regular day school. In 1867 Davis felt that the black schools in the Malden area were not well received by the whites. In November 1867 he reported to John Kimball that "General apathy prevails, where there is not decided prejudice and opposition." The following year Davis thought conditions were "very good." The Freedmen's Bureau encouraged students in the black schools to form temperance clubs, and Davis was proud to report that in August 1868 he had twenty pupils in the "Van Guard of Freedom No. 64." (Reports, William Davis to John Kimball, Nov. 1867–Sept. 1868, RG105 BRFAL DNA.) in 1868 there were eight day schools, one night school, and five Sabbath schools for black children in the Kanawha Valley. These schools ranged from run-down log cabins to small buildings erected and owned by local black school patrons. Charleston boasted the best facilities, valued at $1,300. The Tinkersville school used a small black church, which may account in part for the high attendance at the Sabbath school. (Sub-Assistant Commissioner's Report on the Education of Freedmen and Refugees in the 6th Sub-District, West Virginia, Jan.-June 1868, RG105 BRFAL DNA.)

An Item from the Census:
The Washington Ferguson[1] Family

[Malden, W.Va., 1870]

Dwelling-houses, numbered in the order of visitation	Families, numbered in the order of visitation	The name of every person whose place of abode on the first day of June, 1870, was in this family	Description			Profession, Occupation, or Trade of each person, male or female
			Age at last birth-day. If under 1 year, give months in fractions, thus, 3/12.	Sex — Males (M) Females (F)	Color — White (W), Black (B), Mulatto (M), Chinese (C), Indian (I)	
1	2	3	4	5	6	7
212	212[2]	Furgerson, Watt [Wall?]	50	M	B	Packs Salt
		Nancy[3]	59	F	B	Keeping house
		John[4]	17	M	B	Day labor
		Booker	14	M	M	Domestic Servant
		Amand[5]	12	F	M	At home
		James[6]	8	F[7]	M	

Census of 1870, Malden Township, Kanawha County, W.Va., p. 199, RG29 M-593 DNA. Columns left blank by the census taker were: parentage (father of foreign birth; mother of foreign birth); if born within the year; if married within the year; attended school within the year; whether deaf and dumb, blind, insane, or idiotic; male citizens of U.S. of twenty-one years of age and upwards, whose right to vote is denied or abridged on other grounds than rebellion or other crime.

[1] Washington Ferguson, whose name is misspelled in the document, was a slave of Josiah Ferguson of Hale's Ford, Franklin County, Va. He married Jane, the mother of BTW, about 1859 and was the father of Amanda. He gave trouble to his owner, who hired him out at the salt furnaces of Kanawha Salines, on the construction crew of a railroad, and to a tobacco factory in Lynchburg after the Civil War began. He seldom visited his family except at Christmas. Sometime during the Civil War, Wash Ferguson escaped into freedom, probably in June 1864, when the Union general David Hunter raided into Virginia as far as Lynchburg and then was forced to retreat. According to John H. Washington's recollection, Wash Ferguson was among the many slaves who escaped and followed Hunter. (John H. Washington to Asa L. Duncan, Aug. 20, 1913, Con. 934, BTW

| Value of Real Estate owned | | Place of Birth, naming State or Territory of U.S.; or the Country, if of foreign birth | Educa-tion | | Constitutional Relations |
Value of Real Estate	Value of Personal Estate		Cannot read	Cannot write	Male Citizens of U.S. of 21 years of age and upwards
8	9	10	16	17	19
	500	Va	1	1	1
		Va			
		Va			
		Va			
		Va			
		Va			

Papers, DLC.) He then made his way to the Kanawha Salines, renamed Malden, and in August 1865 sent a wagon, or money to secure one, to Jane and her family. Wash Ferguson exploited the labor of his stepchildren, working them beside him in the furnace and coal mine. When his wife died about 1874, he apparently drifted away from his child and stepchildren, but in the 1890s he was back in Malden in poverty and poor health. Henry B. Rice, perhaps at BTW's urging, employed Wash Ferguson as janitor of his school. His daughter Amanda may also have taken care of him in his old age.

[2] The census shows that the Ferguson household was surrounded by white families. Household 211, for example, was that of James Hall and his family of eight. He was a white man, a fireman in a salt furnace. In household 213, on the other side of the Fergusons, was John Ferrel, a white carpenter, and his family of nine.

[3] This presumably was Jane, but her age was probably fifty rather than fifty-nine.

[4] Should have been reported as mulatto rather than black.

[5] Should have been recorded as Amanda. She was eleven rather than twelve and black rather than mulatto.

[6] James B. Washington (1864-1938) was found abandoned in a stable in Malden, and the Fergusons adopted him into their family. When they took the surname Washington, so did he. BTW helped him to attend Hampton Institute, where he was not as serious a student as his brothers but graduated in 1882. He returned to West Virginia to teach school and worked between sessions in the coal mines. He lived at Fayette Station, married a local girl, Hattie Calloway, and named their first son Booker C. Washington. On their fiftieth anniversary a reporter observed, "Mrs. Washington has made a happy home for her family —

husband and four children — and her influence is a power for good in the community. No sorrowing or suffering home is without her encouraging word and her
ministering hand." (Chicago *Defender,* Apr. 18, 1936, clipping in James B. Washington Folder, President's Office Vault, ViHaI.) James B. Washington did not
prosper in West Virginia, and despite his education could earn only a No. 2
teaching certificate. That may have been a result of racial discrimination, since
in some areas of the South black teachers had difficulty getting the higher pay
scale that went with a No. 1 certificate. In January 1890 he moved to Tuskegee,
where he taught and coached the baseball team. When football became popular
he learned that sport and served as coach of the school's squad. He was also
clerk of the campus post-office substation, which through his efforts was raised to
a third-class and later a second-class post office. One observer suggested in 1936
that he was probably the only black postmaster serving at the second-class level.
(Ibid.)

[7] Male, not female as reported.

The Minutes of a Republican Rally
at Tinkersville

[Tinkersville, W.Va.] July 13, 1872

On motion, H. C. Rice[1] was called to the Chair, and Booker T.
Washington was chosen Secretary.

On motion, the following committee was appointed on Resolutions:
Musie C. Strother,[2] Frank Randolph,[3] Isaac McKinney,[4] John Teal
and Campbell Woodyard.

The committee, after a brief retirement made the following report:

Resolved, 1. That we will stand by and support the principles enun-
ciated by the Republican party.[5]

2. That we will not countenance or support any man who is in any
way hostile to the colored people.

3. That we will not support any candidate who comes out in opposition to the regular nominees of the Republican National, State, and
County Convention.

The resolutions were unanimously adopted.

After addresses by C. A. Brockmeyer, Wm. Davis, Wm. Wilson,[6]
Thos. Swinburn[7] and G. W. Atkinson,[8]

On motion, adjourned.

H. C. Rice, Ch'n.
Booker T. Washington, Sec'y.

Charleston *West Virginia Journal,* July 24, 1872, 2.

[1] Almost certainly Henry B. Rice, born in Malden, W.Va., in 1856, son of Rev. Lewis Rice. After graduation from Hampton Institute in 1877, he taught in Malden, Cannelton, St. Albans, Coal Valley, and Winifrede, all in Kanawha County, W.Va., and later for many years in Charleston. He was also ordained as a minister and worked for the Baptist state convention. He was living in retirement in Charleston in 1942.

[2] Presumably the Musey Strawder mentioned in the letter of William T. McKinney to BTW (Sept. 11, 1911, Con. 429, BTW Papers, DLC). The McKinney letter referred to Strawder as an active participant in the monthly meetings of Lewis Rice's African Zion Baptist Church in Tinkersville. He was reported in the 1880 census as D. Mucey Strauder, black male, age thirty, a hostler, able to read but not to write.

[3] Frank Randolph appeared in the census of 1880 as a mulatto laborer in Malden, age fifty-five, unable to read or write. He was married with six children. The 1870 census report showed discrepancies in the ages reported.

[4] Isaac McKinney was reported in the census of 1880 as a black "engineer," age forty-eight, unable to read or write, married with five children. The 1870 census reported him as a farmer.

[5] In the election of 1872 the Democrats swept the state, continuing a trend begun in 1870 when the Democrats gained the governorship and control of the legislature. The election of 1870 broke the control the Republican party had had in the state since its beginning in 1863. The Democrats dominated West Virginia politics for the rest of the century. The Republican party in West Virginia during Reconstruction was dominated by moderates rather than radicals, but was more friendly to black political rights than the Democrats.

[6] Probably William B. Wilson, a white miller in Charleston.

[7] Thomas Swinburn, born in Lancashire, England, in 1840, moved to the United States at the age of eleven and settled in Kanawha County, W.Va. He served for three and a half years in the Union Army and was wounded. He worked as a newspaper and magazine writer on political matters and in 1879 was clerk of the circuit court in Charleston.

[8] George Wesley Atkinson (1845-1925), Republican governor of West Virginia from 1897 to 1901. He served in many political positions in Charleston after 1870, being postmaster, internal revenue agent, and U.S. marshal. In 1889 he was elected to the U.S. Congress for one term. From 1905 to 1916 he was a judge in the U.S. Court of Claims.

The Catalog of
Hampton Normal and Agricultural Institute

[Hampton, Va., 1874-75]

CATALOGUE

OF THE

Hampton Normal & Agricultural Institute.

HAMPTON, VA.

For the Academical Year

1874-5.

~~~~~~~~~~~~~~~~~~

Incorporated by Special Act of the General Assembly of Virginia.

OPENED APRIL, 1868.

~~~~~~~~~~~~~~~~~~

HAMPTON:
PRINTED AT THE NORMAL SCHOOL PRESS,
1875.

HISTORY

The Hampton Normal and Agricultural Institute stands on the east shore of Hampton Creek, a little below the town of Hampton, and not far from Fortress Monroe, on an estate of one hundred and twenty acres, once known as "Little Scotland," and during the war, known as "Camp Hamilton."

The first slaves brought to America were landed a few miles off; and the earliest English civilization on this continent was established at Hampton.

In this neighborhood, during the war, a great number of "contrabands" were collected, and the first school for freedmen was established among them.

The beauty and healthfulness of the spot, its accessibility, by water and railroad communication, as well to Northern markets as to the region of the Chesapeake Bay, and to the whole of Virginia and the Southern Atlantic States, with the density of the colored population in its vicinity, marked it out as a suitable centre for a great educational work.

The American Missionary Association[1] having purchased the "Little Scotland" estate in the summer of 1867, fitted up the necessary buildings; and in April, 1868, the school was opened with twenty scholars, on a manual labor basis.

Through liberal grants from the Freedmen's Bureau, and donations from Northern friends, a large and durable school-house in which three hundred students can recite, has been erected, the farm has been supplied with buildings, stock and tools, and an industrial department for the manufacture of clothing has been built up. A boarding department is in operation with one hundred and seventy student boarders; and a printing-office has been established in which the various branches of the printing trade are taught, and the *Southern Workman* is published.

In June, 1870, the Institute received a charter from the General Assembly, creating a corporation, with power to choose their own successors, and to hold property without taxation. They now hold and control the entire property of the school by deed from the American Missionary Association.

In March, 1872, the General Assembly passed an act, giving it one-third of the Agricultural College land grant of Virginia; its share was one hundred thousand acres, which was sold on the 1st of May, 1872, for $95,000. Nine-tenths of this money has been invested in bonds bearing six per cent. interest; the other tenth has been expended in the purchase of additional land, increasing the size of the farm to one hundred and eighty-five acres. The land thus received is a portion of the "Segar" estate adjacent to the grounds of the Institute, and well adapted to the needs of the school.

In October, 1874, "Virginia Hall" was sufficiently completed to be occupied. It has sleeping rooms for one hundred and fifty young women, and boarding facilities for three hundred students. It contains a large Chapel and Sewing rooms, and is furnished with all needed appliances for right living.

There are about eighty full graduates, and twenty undergraduates, engaged in the work of teaching, chiefly in Virginia and North Carolina.

It is estimated that not over five per cent. of the graduates fail to devote themselves to the educational work. Nearly all are working under State auspices and the direction of Southern men, and apparently with good mutual satisfaction. There are no complaints from either side, and many signs of excellent feeling and of good hope for the future.

John F. Lewis,[12] Port Republic, Va.
Robert C. Ogden,[13] Brooklyn, N.Y.
Samuel Holmes,[14] Montclair, N.J.
Anthony M. Kimber,[15] Philadelphia, Pa.
Edgar Ketchum,[16] New York City
E. M. Cravath,[17] Brooklyn, N.Y.

INSTRUCTORS

S. C. Armstrong, Principal
Moral Science and Civil Government

J. F. B. Marshall, Treasurer and Acting Assistant Principal
Book-keeping

ACADEMIC DEPARTMENT

Edmund H. Sears, Jr.[18]
History and Natural Sciences

Mary F. Mackie[19]
Mathematics

Amelia Tyler[20]
Grammar and Composition

Elizabeth H. Brewer
Natural Philosophy and Physical Geography

Mary Hungerford[21]
History and Georgraphy

Helen W. Ludlow[22]
English Literature

Nathalie Lord
Writing and Elocution

Julia E. Remington[23]
Writing and Geography

Martha M. Waldron[24]
Physiology and Geography

MUSICAL DEPARTMENT

Thos. P. Fenner,[25] In Charge

GIRLS' INDUSTRIAL DEPARTMENT

S. H. FENNER,[26] In Charge

HOUSEWORK AND BOARDING DEPARTMENTS

MARY F. MACKIE, In Charge
SUSAN P. HARROLD,[27] Asst. Matron
C. L. MACKIE,[28] Steward

AGRICULTURAL DEPARTMENT

ALBERT HOWE,[29] In Charge

LECTURER ON AGRICULTURE

GEORGE DIXON[30]

PRINTING OFFICE

W. J. BUTTERFIELD,[31] In Charge

STUDENTS

SENIOR CLASS

Brown, Matilda J. — Bridgewater, Penn.
Davis, Laura E. — Norfolk, Va.
Farley, Delia — Petersburg, "
Ferribee, Maria — Portsmouth, "
Ferribee, Alice — " "
Gibson, Lizzie — Greensboro, N.C.
Gregory, Sallie P. — Pittsylvania C. H., Va.
Millon, Susan — Wrightville, Penn.
Morse, Lucy — Yorktown, Va.
Ross, Ann — Danville, "
* Stephens, Mary E. — Beaufort, N.C.

Bowen, Reese — Tazewell Co., Va.
Brown, Henry — Charlotte Co., "
* Canaday, Edward M. — James City Co., "
Cardwell, John — Greensboro, N.C.
Catus, William — Winton, "
Collins, John W. — Upper Trappe, Wicomico Co., Md.
Draper, Joseph W. — Newbern, Va.
Dungey, Robert — King William Co., "
Dyson, James A. — Quincy, Ill.
Evans, David — Lexington, Va.
Floyd, John — Montgomery Co., "
Green, Charles — Gates Co., N.C.
Harrison, George M. — Enfield, Halifax Co., "
* Harrison, John — Danville, Va.
Henry, William — Philadelphia, Penn.
† Holley, Alphonso — Lexington, Va.
Holt, John — Wilmington, N.C.
* Howard, George B. — Charlottesville, Va.
Hunt, Zachariah — Big Lick, Roanoke Co., "
Ivy, Frank B. — Jonesboro, Tenn.
Ivy, Lorenzo L. — " "
Jackson, George W. — Brooklyn, Halifax Co., Va.
Jackson, Godfrey R. — Darien, Ga.
Jacobs, Albert R. — Northampton Co., N.C.
Mebane, Joseph — Mebanesville, N.C.
Mendenhall, Madison M. — Greensboro, "
Merchant, Rollins — Lynchburg, Va.
Middleton, Maurice — Lexington, "

* Left before the close of term.
† Died October 27, 1874.

Newsome, John L.	Winton, N.C.
Reasoner, Howard R.	Trenton, N.J.
Ricks, Robert	Portsmouth, Va.
Scott, Thomas H.	Washington, D.C.
Smith, Timothy	Chambersburg, Va.
Towe, Joseph B.	Norfolk, "
Turner, Daniel Y.	Elizabeth City Co., Va.
Waddy, James M.	Richmond, "
Waring, Champion	Thetford, Vt.
Washington, Booker T.	Malden, W.Va.
* White, Ackrel	Windsor Station, Va.
Whiting, Robert W.	Alexandria, "

MIDDLE CLASS

Bray, Maria E.	Greensboro, N.C.
Brockette, Dora	Norfolk, Va.
Brown, Josephine	New York City
Carroll, Sarah	Alexandria, Va.
Chadwick, Della	Beaufort, N.C.
* Chaplain, Grace F.	Boston, Mass.
* Downs, Rosa	New Orleans, La.
Edmunds, Ann Maria	Charlotte C. H., Va.
Gray, Georgie	Norfolk, "
Gray, Mary A.	Greensboro, N.C.
Hays, Rhoda	Greensboro, N.C.
Holmes, Ellen	Hampton, Va.
Hunter, Henrietta	Norfolk, Va.
Lewis, Martha	New Kent Co., Va.
Moore, Ella	Greensboro, N.C.
Mosely, Mary E.	Pemberton, Va.
Patillo, Ada	Greensboro, N.C.
Poole, Sarah F.	Norfolk, Va.
Seaton, Constance G.	Alexandria, "
Shelton, Jennie	Buffalo Springs, "
Smoot, Sarah E.	Washington, D.C.
* Spottswood, Jennie	Mill Creek, Va.
Thomas, Anna	Augusta, Ga.
Thomas, Caroline	Philadelphia, Penn.
Washington, Margaret	Yorktown, Va.
Waters, Mary	Jenkintown, Penn.
Bacon, Jerome	Philadelphia, Penn.
Bailey, James	Danville, Va.

* Left before the close of term.

Bassette, Andrew	Hampton, "
Berger, Tapley S. D.	Christiansburg, "
* Boyd, William C.	Deep Creek, "
Bradley, George B.	Enfield, N.C.
Calloway, James	Danville, Va.
Calvin, Amos	High Point, N.C.
* Cole, George W.	Chattanooga, Tenn.
* Cole, James	Philadelphia, Penn.
Deans, David	Southampton Co., Va.
Fantleroy, Richard H.	Hampton, "
Garrette, Thomas	Newport News, "
Goode, George B.	Aspinwall, "
* Green, Robert	Danville, "
Hamilton, Robert	Philadelphia, Penn.
Hayden, Lindsay	Lynchburg, Va.
Harrison, Isaac	Danville, "
Hemmings, Gordon	Buckingham C. H., "
Ivy, Walter	Jonesboro, Tenn.
Jackson, Robert B.	Columbia, S.C.
Jones, James	Mill Creek, Va.
Kelser, Robert	Farmville, "
Logan, Warren	Greensboro, N.C.
McAdoo, Orpheus	" "
McNeil, Alexander H.	Wilmington, "
Minnis, Jackson	Liberty, Va.
Moore, Alfred A.	Lexington, "
Powell, Ephraim	Murfreesboro, N.C.
Robinson, John	Hampton, Va.
Roulache, Lewis	Windsor, N.C.
Smith, Jesse D.	Hampton, Va.
Smoot, Robert	Aiken, S.C.
Thompson, Robert A.	Lynchburg, Va.
* Turner, Daniel F.	Elizabeth City, N.C.
Unthank, Walter	Greensboro, "
* Vanison, Charles	James City Co., Va.
Vaughn, Moses	Potecasi, N.C.
Weaver, William B.	Winton, "
Williams, Whit	Danville, Va.

JUNIOR CLASS

Blackburn, Bettie	Rock Island, Ill.
Brown, Olive	St. Augustine, Fla.

* Left before the close of term.

* Carney, Mary	Portsmouth, Va.
Chisman, Elva	Hampton, "
Christian, Mary B.	Petersburg, "
Davis, Sallie	Norfolk, "
Dickerson, Sophie	Aiken, S.C.
* Drew, Patience	Elizabeth City, N.C.
Harris, Sarah A.	Abingdon, Va.
Hubbard, Amanda	Hampton, "
Jarvis, Mary A.	" "
Johnson, Martha J.	Ruffner Station, N.C.
Keeling, Margaret	Norfolk, Va.
Leary, Lucy	Wilmington, N.C.
Leftridge, Laura A. B.	Salem, Va.
Mallette, Maria	Wilmington, N.C.
Madella, Mary C.	Alexandria, Va.
Madella, Augusta I.	" "
McAlpine, Charlotte	Mont Clair, N.J.
Mills, Laura	" " "
* Mitchell, Mary	Raleigh, N.C.
Overton, Margaret C.	Elizabeth City, "
Parker, Sarah J.	Drummondtown, Va.
Peterson, Sarah	Matthews Co., "
* Smith, Harriet	" " "
Stewart, Lucy	Oxford, N.C.
Stokes, Mary A.	Norfolk, Va.
Turner, Ella	Hampton, "
Walker, Ellen	Petersburg, "
Washington, Margaret	Yorktown, "
Webb, Rosa	Portsmouth, "
White, Ellen	Matthews Co., "
Bartlette, Miles	Elizabeth City, N.C.
Billups, John H.	Bonsack, Va.
Bivins, Severn	Pungoteague, "
Blackburn, George D.	Rock Island, Ill.
Bonaparte, Henry	Hampton, Va.
Bright, Armstead	Hampton, "
Brooks, James H.	Washington, D.C.
Brown, Jacob	Hilton Head, S.C.
Byrd, Edmund A.	Abingdon, Va.
Clark, Norris B.	Alexandria, "
Corbin, Charles	Hampton, "
Fantleroy, Joseph	Elizabeth City Co., "
" , Noah	" " " "

* Left before the close of term.

* Foster, Henry	High Point, N.C.
Gardner, Henry	Hampton, Va.
Garrison, William	Norfolk, "
Gerrideau, Lawrence	Darien, Ga.
Gregory, Marcus	Charlotte, N.C.
Gwaltney, George	Windsor Station, Va.
Hackley, Elias	Catawba, "
Holcombe, Charles	Farmville, "
Irving, David	Beaufort, N.C.
Jones, Richard P.	Salisbury, Md.
Jones, Albert P.	Harrisonburg, Va.
Johnson, Robert J.	Wytheville, "
Johnson, James	Norfolk, "
Johnson, Walter T.	" "
Lassiter, Lawrence	Northampton Co., N.C.
Lynch, Webster	Norfolk, Va.
McKinney, Alexander	St. Augustine, Fla.
Merchant, Thomas	Lynchburg, Va.
Mews, Richard	Wayland, Mass.
Moody, Moses	Hampton, Va.
Mosely, Montgomery	Pemberton, Va.
Oliver, Patrick	Big Lick, "
Parker, James H.	Hampton, "
Parker, William	Drummondtown, "
Perry, Royal J.	Lynchburg, "
Randall, Richard	Hampton, "
Randolph, Shirley J.	Rough Creek, "
Randolph, William F.	Scottsville, "
*Rayford, Josiah	Big Lick, "
Reid, William	Gatesville, N.C.
Rogerson, Jesse	Hertford, N.C.
Russel, James S.	Palmer's Springs, Va.
Scarbor, Cornelius B.	Elizabeth City Co., "
Scott, Sterling C.	Charlotte, "
*Smith, William T.	Mill Creek, "
Sparks, Horace F.	Stevensville, "
Spotswood, Samuel	Mill Creek, "
Taylor, Charles	Harrisonburg, "
Townes, Southall	Clarkesville, "
Walker, John P.	New Haven, Conn.
Washington, Bessick	Elizabeth City Co., Va.
Wharton, Littleton	Drummondtown, "
White, Boswell	Matthews Co., "
White, Braxton	Windsor Station, "

* Left before the close of term.

Williams, Abram C.	Hampton,	"
Wright, Major	Warwick Co.,	"

PREPARATORY CLASS

Bright, Eliza	Hampton, Va.
Broady, Alice	Abingdon, "
Coleman, Susan	Hampton, "
Collins, Mahala	" "
Essex, Cora A.	Charleston, W.Va.
Everson, Charlotte	Harrisonburg, Va.
Fields, Kate	Hampton, "
Fisher, Emma	Beaufort, N.C.
Green, Lavonia	Gatesville, "
Harrison, Francis A.	Richmond, Va.
Hays, Lucy A.	Matthews Co., Va.
Hilton, Pauline	Farmville, "
Johnson, Agnes	Hampton, "
Johnson, Rosa L.	Darien, Ga.
Moody, Maria	Hampton, Va.
Nichols, Clara S.	Abingdon, "
Pryor, Jane	Hampton, "
Rooks, Lucy E.	Gatesville, N.C.
Saunders, Joanna	New York City
Weaver, Lucy A.	Charleston, W.Va.

Artis, John	Southampton, "
Bolling, Thomas	Charles City Co., Va.
Cheeks, James	Speedville, Va.
Clark, Edward T.	Philadelphia, Penn.
Copeland, William	Portsmouth, Va.
Curtis, John H.	Hampton, "
Furguson, Charles F.	Lynn, Mass.
McDowell, John	Staunton, Va.
Pulley, Edwin W.	Boydton, "
*Strange, James	Richmond, "
Thomas, Henry	Wilmington, N.C.
*Turner, William	Eastville, Va.
Waters, John E.	Wilmington, N.C.
Williams, James	Norfolk, Va.

POST GRADUATES

Inge, Hutchins	Danville, Va.
Davis, George	" "

* Left before the close of term.

THE BUTLER SCHOOL

Is held in the large cruciform building erected by General Butler[32] during the war, and now belonging to the Normal School property. It is a county, and also preparatory school to the Institute, and contains a class of thirty-one who are on the Normal School rolls and most of whom are boarders, expecting to enter the Junior class of next term. The assistant teachers are in part supported by the Institute. One wing of the building has been fitted up as the residence of Mr. and Mrs. George Dixon, through whose efforts in England, the means of support for forty-five students of the Institute were secured. The Butler School is in charge of Eunice C. Dixon,[33] assisted by George Davis,[34] a graduate, and one undergraduate.

SUMMARY

Girls			Boys			Totals
Senior	Class	11	Senior	Class	40 =	51
Middle	"	26	Middle	"	40 =	66
Junior	"	32	Junior	"	58 =	90
Preparatory	"	20	Preparatory	"	14 =	34
			Post Graduates		2 =	2
		89			154	243

WORK DETAILS

Girls		Boys	
Industrial Room	72	Farm	90
House Work	6	Printing Office	3
No work has yet been found		Painters	3
for the day scholars	11	Carpenters	4
		Coopers	3
		Shoemakers	3
		Janitors	4
		Office Duty	2
		Mail Carriers	2
		Waiters	11
		Employed by Teachers	2
		Police and General Duty	6
		Day-Scholars on Orderly Duty	19
		Teaching	2
	89		154

MISCELLANEOUS

CALENDAR

Term commenced Thursday, October 1, 1874, and continued until June 10, 1875.

Vacation from June 10 to October 1, 1875.

National and special holidays are observed.

Students are expected to spend the vacation at home, and in order to lessen the burden of their school expenses, are encouraged to secure, during that time, profitable employment.

ADMISSION

Candidates for admission to the Junior class are expected to be able to *read* and *write,* and to pass a satisfactory examination in *Arithmetic* through *Long Division.*

Sound health, testimonials of good character, and intention to remain through the course, are required of all applicants.

Candidates for admission coming from common schools or from other institutions, must present letters of honorable dismission and recommendation. Preference will be given to those who expect to become teachers.

The stated time for examination is the first week in October of each year. Parents are desired to come with their children so far as practicable.

No one under fourteen, or over twenty-five years of age, will be admitted to the Junior class.

Every student is, by enrollment, committed to the discipline and regulations of the school.

The first year is probationary.

Admission at any other than the stated time is allowed only in special cases.

COURSES OF STUDY

COURSES OF STUDY EMBRACE THREE YEARS, AND INCLUDE —
NORMAL COURSE:

LANGUAGE	MATHEMATICS	HISTORY	NATURAL SCIENCE	MISCELLANEOUS
Spelling	Mental Arithmetic	History of United States	Geography — Map Drawing	Science of Civil Government
Reading	Written Arithmetic	History of England, — Reading from English Writers	Physical Geography	Outline Study of Man
Sentence Making	Algebra	Universal History	Natural History	Bible Lessons
English Grammar			Natural Philosophy	Drill in Teaching
Analysis			Physiology	Book-keeping
Rhetoric			Botany	Vocal Training
Composition				Instrumental Music
Elocution				

AGRICULTURAL COURSE

(Studies of the Normal Course at discretion).

Lectures on the following subjects:
Formation of Soils
Rotation of Crops
Management of Stock
Fruit Culture
Cultivation of Crops
Drainage
Market Gardening
Meteorology
Practical instruction in the routine of farming and market gardening

COMMERCIAL COURSE

(Studies of the Normal Course at discretion).

Instruction in Book-keeping — Single and Double Entry, — in Business Letters, Contracts, Account of Sales, and other Business and Legal Papers, and in Commercial Law.

Each student is required to keep his account current with the Institute in proper form.

MECHANICAL COURSE

(Studies of the Normal Course at discretion).

Practical instruction in the different varieties of Sewing Machines in use, and in household industries.
Penmanship
Printing

36

EXPENSES AND LABOR

Board, per month	$ 8 00
Washing and lights, per month	1 00
Fuel, " "	75
Use of furniture, " "	25
	$10 00

Clothing and Books extra, to be paid for in cash.

Able-bodied young men and women over eighteen years of age are expected to pay HALF IN CASH and HALF IN WORK; that is, five dollars per month in cash, and to work out the balance.

Boys and girls of eighteen years and less, are required to pay six dollars per month.

Should sufficient work not be supplied in term time to meet the obligations of the school, it will be provided during vacation either at the school or elsewhere.

Students' labor will not be accepted in lieu of cash payments unless it is satisfactory and of real value.

Students are held responsible for all balances against them that they may not have worked out.

The amount of profitable labor being limited, it is desired to extend its advantages as far as possible; hence, a very few, only, who are absolutely unable to pay anything in cash, are allowed to work out their whole expenses.

Young men and young women, whose parents desire that they shall not be taken out of school to work, may, upon payment of ten dollars per month, attend school without interruption, but will nevertheless be required to labor on Saturdays, and at such hours as may be assigned them.

Labor is required of all for purposes of discipline and instruction. To this end, day scholars are expected to labor at the rate of an hour per day, at such industries as may be assigned them.

Bills are made out and payable at the end of the month. The regular cash payment is to be MONTHLY, IN ADVANCE.

The regular annual tuition fee of the Institution is seventy dollars. It is remitted to all deserving students. As the amount has to be secured by the Trustees by solicitation among the friends of education, students are called upon annually to write letters of acknowledgement to their benefactors. These letters are regarded as among the tests of capacity and of merit.

In accordance with the law donating college land scrip to this Institution, one hundred students will be received from the public free schools of Virginia, free of charge for tuition and room rent, at the rate of two from each of the forty-three senatorial districts of the State, the other fourteen from the State at large. All application for State students should come through the County Superintendent of Schools, and should not be made later than ten days previous to the opening of the term, October 1st.

State students, having precedence over others, should secure their places promptly in order that others may not be kept waiting. State students are expected to pay ten dollars a month for board, etc.; but, if able-bodied, they can meet their personal expenses by paying five or six dollars per month, according to age, and working out the balance.

CLOTHING

The Girls' Industrial Department is open for the benefit of young women who are seeking an education in this Institution. They are furnished with work in proportion to their desire for employment and the demand for the articles manufactured. Those who buy garments of their manufacture may be sure of honest-well-made articles.

Students from abroad are recommended to purchase their outfit of clothing at the Industrial room, thus saving expense and aiding those who deserve aid.

DISCIPLINE

Courtesy and mutual forbearance are expected of both pupils and teachers, as indispensable to good discipline.

Every student is by enrollment committed to the discipline and regulations of the school.

Students are subject to suspension or discharge for an unsatisfactory course in respect to either study, conduct, or labor.

The use of ardent spirits and tobacco is prohibited.

Letter writing is subject to regulation.

The wardrobes of all students are subject to inspection and regulation by the proper officers.

Students are subject to drill and guard duty. Obedience to the commandant must be implicit. The rights of students are properly guarded.

PUBLIC WORSHIP

There are daily devotional exercises at which students are required to be present.

They are also required to attend Sunday morning services at the public chapel in the National Cemetery, Sabbath-school in the afternoon, and evening lecture.

LIBRARY AND APPARATUS

It is hoped that the friends of the school will interest themselves in furnishing it with what is wanted to make a good basis of instruction in Literature, in Physical Science, and in Natural History.

But little scientific apparatus has been provided, and there are no collections for illustrating Natural History.

The Library greatly needs standard works in all its departments. A Reading-room has been provided in connection with it, and is furnished with a variety of journals and periodicals. The Library committee of the Trustees is expecially charged with the duty of collecting history and incidents of the war, and full accounts of all national, State, and philanthropic efforts for education in the South. Co-operation is invited.

CABINET OF CURIOSITIES

Whatever is illustrative of manners, customs, character, and of interesting localities abroad, is useful as a means of more thorough instruction. Missionaries and others in foreign lands can do our cause good service by helping in this department. Those so disposed are invited to correspond with the Secretary of the Trustees, with the view of making the way clear for the procuring and transmission of materials for this department.

Copy in Huntington Memorial Library ViHaI. The illustration facing the title page is the same cut as that illustrating the certificate of achievement, June 10, 1875.

[1] The American Missionary Association (A.M.A.) was a Congregationalist organization founded in 1846 by antislavery members of four northern missionary groups. It sought to spread education and Christianity among both free and enslaved blacks in Africa and America. It also founded missions for American Indians. After the Civil War the A.M.A. gave priority to educating the freedmen. The association and its teachers faced hostility and occasionally physical violence from white southerners, but the A.M.A. regarded the freedmen's plight as a moral problem which churchmen could not in good conscience ignore. By 1870 the

A.M.A. was providing support for a number of black schools in the South, including Hampton Institute. In 1883 a bureau of women's work was founded to attract more northern women into southern missionary and educational work.

² George Whipple (1805-76), president of the Hampton board of trustees from the founding of the institute until his death, had deep roots in abolitionism, industrial education, and Congregational church work, all major forces behind Hampton's success. Born in Albany, N.Y., he was associated with Theodore Dwight Weld as an Oneida Institute student (1827-31) and as a faculty member at Lane Theological Seminary (1833-34). He was one of the Lane Rebels who left the seminary over the issue of abolitionism, following Weld to Oberlin, where he enrolled in the seminary and worked summers (1835-37) for the American Anti-Slavery Society as an agent in western New York and Ohio. Upon graduating from the seminary in 1836, he became principal of Oberlin's preparatory department and, two years later, professor of mathematics. An ordained Congregational minister, he taught at Oberlin for a decade until, with Lewis Tappan and Simeon S. Jocelyn, he helped found the American Missionary Association in 1846. He served as corresponding secretary of the association for the remaining thirty years of his life, and was senior man during the Reconstruction decade (1866-76), during which the A.M.A. did its most important work. A worker for the Freedmen's Aid Society of the Methodist Episcopal Church during the war, Whipple afterward became a close friend of Oliver O. Howard of the Freedmen's Bureau, sharing with him the view that the bureau and the A.M.A. were engaged in a common cooperative campaign. He personally inspected and approved the site of Hampton Institute in 1867, and served as president of its board beginning the following year. Whipple's contact with industrial education dated from as early as his Oneida Institute days, that institution being one of the first manual-labor schools in the country. Oberlin also had originally been founded as a manual-labor institute. (See Drake, "American Missionary Association and the Southern Negro.")

³ Robert William Hughes (1821-1901), a native Virginian of an old and respected family, was editor of the Richmond *Examiner* from 1852 to 1857 and from 1861 to 1865. He was an extreme secessionist, but after the war he became a moderate Republican and a favorite of President Grant, causing many of his old friends to consider him "worse than a carpetbagger" and a "Judas." Grant appointed him U.S. attorney for Virginia in 1871. He resigned in 1873 to run unsuccessfully for governor. Grant appointed him a U.S. district court judge in 1874, a position he held until 1898. He joined the Readjuster reform movement in the 1880s, but eventually opposed its leader, Governor William Mahone. (Moger, *Virginia: Bourbonism to Byrd, 1870-1925*, 23; Maddex, *Virginia Conservatives, 1867-1879*, 195.)

⁴ Alexander B. Hyde (1814-81) graduated from Williams College in 1834 and practiced scientific farming on his family's farm at Lee, Mass. He was a teacher, wrote articles on practical farm management, and in 1881 was a member of the Massachusetts state legislature.

⁵ Samuel Chapman Armstrong, principal of Hampton Normal and Agricultural Institute from its founding in 1868 until his death in 1893, had a deep and lifelong influence on the life and social philosophy of BTW. Born of missionary parents on Maui, Hawaii, Jan. 30, 1839, he was educated through the first two years of college at Punahou Royal School (Oahu College after 1855), where some manual labor was required of all pupils. His father served as minister of public instruction and Armstrong had an opportunity to observe the program of

the Hilo Manual Labor School, where Hawaiian boys boarded, paying expenses by working in carpentry, housework, gardening, and similar jobs. Though he preferred to finish college at Yale, his father wanted him to go to Williams College, where he could study with its president, Mark Hopkins. There for two years (1860-62) he lived at the president's home, rooming with Hopkins's son and establishing a permanent friendship with both.

Armstrong volunteered for the Army in 1862. He and his regiment were captured at Harpers Ferry and paroled in the West, where he made his first acquaintance with the condition of the Indians. His regiment was exchanged in time for him to play an important role in defense of Cemetery Hill at Gettysburg. Armstrong completed the war as colonel in command of Negro troops and then served briefly in Texas in support of republican insurgents challenging Emperor Maximilian. Breveted as brigadier general, he was quickly tapped by Oliver O. Howard to serve as Freedmen's Bureau agent and also as superintendent of schools of ten counties on the Virginia peninsula.

In the year after he assumed charge of the great camp of Negroes at Hampton, Va., Armstrong became bound to the idea of establishing a school on the Hilo model for the freedmen (later to include Indians as well). In 1867 he successfully appealed to the American Missionary Association to secure the estate on which he was living for his proposed school, which opened the following year. Committed to the institute and energetically raising funds for it in the North ($370,000 by 1875), he twice turned down the presidency of the new Howard University, Washington, D.C., proffered him by General O. O. Howard. Hampton was incorporated by the Virginia legislature on June 4, 1870. The school's characteristic industrial education and cadet training reflected Armstrong's Hawaiian missionary background, his army experience, his open and pronounced though benevolent racism, and the social-service influence of Mark Hopkins.

Armstrong married Emma Dean Walker (d. 1878) of Stockbridge, Mass., in October 1869 and named his first daughter Louise Hopkins Armstrong after the daughter of his mentor. He married Mary Alice Ford, a Hampton teacher from Lisbon, N.H., in 1890. His health was poor following a stroke in 1886 and deteriorated further after paralysis in November 1891. In his last decade an important adviser and supporter of Tuskegee Institute, Armstrong died May 11, 1893.

6 Thomas Kendall Fessenden (1813-94), a minister in Farmington, Conn., served in the Connecticut legislature (1867-69) where, as chairman of the Committee on Humane Institutions, he secured a charter for an industrial school for girls. He gave vital services to Hampton Institute as financial secretary (1871-77) and trustee (1870-82).

7 James Fowle Baldwin Marshall (1818-91) was born in Charlestown, Mass., the son of a prosperous banker. Entering Harvard in 1834, he was forced by eye trouble, a lifelong problem, to drop out in his sophomore year. In 1838 he moved to Honolulu, Hawaii, eventually becoming a partner in one of the largest of the islands' trading firms. During 1843 he played a major role in Hawaiian diplomacy, traveling to London to challenge successfully claims that Lord George Paulet had presented as grounds for provisionally annexing the islands to Britain. His mission to London aided the joint recognition of Hawaiian independence by Britain and France. Marshall was deeply involved in the islands' public affairs. He served in the Hawaiian legislature, urging abolition of feudal land tenure and advocating temperance, Native rights, and the adoption of agricultural improvements.

Marshall spent the Civil War years in Boston, serving as quartermaster general of the Massachusetts state militia and agent for the state's sanitary commission. Afterward he became interested in the Hampton venture of Samuel C. Armstrong, whom he had once taught in Sunday school in Hawaii. Accepting the position of treasurer of Hampton Institute in 1869, he was Armstrong's closest adviser during the next decade and a half. In 1884 he retired from Hampton because he was told he might be blind in two or three years. He returned to New England, where he led the missionary efforts of Boston Unitarians to build up the Crow Indian school in Montana and was also superintendent of the southern and Indian educational work of the American Unitarian Association in Boston. He resided on his estate at Weston, Mass., until his death.

[8] Oliver Otis Howard (1830-1909) was born in Leeds, Me., and attended Bowdoin College and the U.S. Military Academy. During the Civil War he saw action in many battles. At Fair Oaks during the peninsular campaign, two horses were shot from beneath him and his wounded right arm was amputated. He was back in action in less than three months, taking part in the battles of Fredericksburg and Gettysburg and Sherman's march through the South. In May 1865 he became head of the Bureau of Refugees, Freedmen and Abandoned Lands, later known as the Freedmen's Bureau. Though Howard spoke often of the active role the bureau should play in securing the complete freedom of the freedmen, including the necessity of granting them land, he was unable to translate his noble ideas into effective action. The most recent study of Howard and the Freedmen's Bureau concludes that his work "served to preclude rather than promote Negro freedom," that his was "a record of naivete and misunderstanding, timidity, misplaced faith, disloyalty to subordinates who were loyal to the freedmen, and an attempt to diminish the Negroes' aspirations." (McFeely, *Yankee Stepfather: General O. O. Howard and the Freedmen,* 5, 8.)

While head of the Freedmen's Bureau, Howard was instrumental in pressing Congress in 1867 to charter a school of higher education for freedmen in Washington, named Howard University after him. General Howard served as the school's president from 1869 to 1873. Then he returned to his army career, spent in the western Indian campaigns except for 1881-82, when he was commandant of West Point.

While head of the Freedmen's Bureau, Howard arranged for the barracks at Camp Hamilton to be turned over to Hampton Institute. In addition, $52,000 of the Freedmen's Bureau construction fund was appropriated to the school. Howard was a member of the original board of trustees of Hampton, serving until 1875.

[9] Michael E. Strieby (1815-99) was secretary of the American Missionary Association from 1864 to 1899. A graduate of Oberlin College and Seminary, he was a Hampton trustee from 1870 to his death, serving as president of the board from 1877 to 1884.

[10] James Abram Garfield (1831-81), a Union major general in the Civil War, congressman (1863-80), and President of the United States (1881). A graduate of Williams College in 1856, Garfield shared Armstrong's enthusiasm for the philosophy of Mark Hopkins. In 1869 Garfield served on a committee of inquiry of the American Missionary Association which journeyed to Hampton to decide whether the site was suitable for the proposed school. He joined the school's original board of trustees in 1870 and assisted and advised Armstrong particularly on legal matters. Garfield thoroughly believed in the kind of intellectual training he had received at Williams College, and he counseled Armstrong not to commit himself to "the policy of manual labor in schools as a principle of general appli-

cation." He added, however: "I fully and cordially support the labor feature of your school as the proper course at least for the present. I defend it on the ground of the peculiar and exceptional situation in which we now find the colored race at the South. The problem is, how best to lead them up from the plane of mere drudgery to one of some culture and finally of high culture." (Garfield to Armstrong, Sept. 27, 1870, Garfield Papers, DLC.) As Garfield's public duties caused him to be too busy to attend meetings of the Hampton trustees, he resigned in 1876, but continued a friendly interest. Hampton sent a contingent of cadets to march in his inaugural parade. On June 5, 1881, Garfield took time from his busy months as President to visit Hampton, where he spoke briefly after the baccalaureate sermon.

[11] Edward Parmelee Smith (1827-76), U.S. Commissioner of Indian Affairs (1873-76) and former field secretary of the American Missionary Association, died in Accra, Gold Coast, shortly after his appointment as president of Howard University.

[12] John Francis Lewis (1818-95), born in Lynnwood, Va., was a leading Republican in Virginia after the Civil War. A delegate to the Virginia secession convention of 1861, he refused to sign the secession ordinance. He won the lieutenant governorship on the Republican ticket in 1869, and was appointed to the U.S. Senate in 1870, holding the seat until 1875. In 1878 President Hayes appointed him a U.S. marshal for the western district of Virginia. He was again elected lieutenant governor in 1881 on the Readjuster ticket.

[13] Robert Curtis Ogden (1836-1913), born in Philadelphia, spent his early years learning the dry-goods business, becoming at sixteen an apprentice in his father's firm, Devlin and Company in New York. Later as junior partner and agent of this firm he made his first trip to the South just before the beginning of the Civil War. In 1879 he joined the firm of John Wanamaker in Philadelphia, becoming in 1896 the manager of the new Wanamaker branch in New York City and a partner. His first contact with Negro education came through his friend, Samuel C. Armstrong, shortly after the Civil War. He soon was an active champion of Negro schools. He was one of the first friends and trustees of Hampton Institute, and later served on the board of Tuskegee. He became increasingly interested in the education of southern whites, and in 1898 founded the Conference for Education in the South, patterned after the Mohonk Indian Conferences. In 1901 he established the Southern Education Board to campaign for increased school taxes and higher standards of supervision for both white and black schools in the South. In 1901 and annually thereafter for more than a decade he financed a trip in a special train of Pullman cars through the South to popularize public education of both races. While expressing continuing interest in Negro education, Ogden believed in granting money only for industrial education, a philosophy that allowed him to remain a constant ally of BTW. Retiring from active business in 1907 because of a heart condition, he remained active on the Hampton and Tuskegee boards until his death.

[14] Samuel Holmes (1824-97), a Montclair, N.J., manufacturer, was a member of the executive committee of the American Missionary Association. He was a Hampton trustee from 1870 to 1884, and also served on the Fisk University board of trustees.

[15] Anthony Morris Kimber (1824-1917), a merchant living in Philadelphia, was a Hampton trustee from 1870 to 1886.

[16] Edgar Ketchum (1811-82), a New York lawyer and member of the execu-

tive committee of the American Missionary Association (1865-79), served as a Hampton trustee from 1870 to 1881.

[17] Erastus Milo Cravath (1833-1900) was born in Homer, N.Y., the son of a prosperous farmer whose house in New York was a terminal for the Underground Railroad. The family later moved to Oberlin, Ohio, where Cravath received his education, graduating from Oberlin College in 1857 and from the theological department in 1860. After preaching for a brief time and serving as a chaplain in the Union Army during the Civil War, he became a field secretary for the American Missionary Association, raising funds in the North and supervising newly established schools in the South. Two of the schools he helped establish were Atlanta and Fisk universities. Cravath became the first president of Fisk in 1875, serving until his death. He was a trustee of Hampton Institute from 1870 to 1877.

[18] Edmund Hamilton Sears of Weston, Mass., was a Harvard graduate of 1874. After a year at Hampton he taught at the University of California and in 1885 established a school for girls in Boston. Later he was the head of the Mary Institute for Girls at Washington University in St. Louis. He died in 1942 at the age of ninety.

[19] Mary Fletcher Mackie, who administered BTW's "entrance exam" at Hampton Institute (BTW, *Up from Slavery,* chap. 3), was in charge of the academic department and served as assistant principal for twenty years. One of five sisters, she returned to Newburgh, N.Y., in 1891 to help her sisters operate the Mackie School, a preparatory school for girls. Mary Mackie died Dec. 30, 1917.

[20] Amelia Tyler, of Brattleboro, Vt., taught at Hampton from 1874 to 1877. She later was a contributor to the school and lived in Washington, D.C.

[21] Mary Swift Hungerford of Mt. Pleasant, Iowa, taught at Hampton Institute from 1872 to 1875, leaving to teach school in West Haven, Conn. She died in 1926.

[22] Helen Wilhelmina Ludlow (1840-1924) dedicated virtually her entire life to Hampton Institute. The daughter of a New England Presbyterian clergyman, she came to Hampton in 1872, answering S. C. Armstrong's plea to her: "Five millions of ex-slaves appeal to you. . . . There's work here and brave souls are needed. . . . We want you as a teacher." In the next thirty-eight years she taught English, edited the *Southern Workman,* aided in fund-raising activities, and accompanied the Hampton Student Singers on their numerous tours as special tutor. She prepared *Twenty-two Years of Work* (1891), a compilation of the lives and work of Hampton graduates, and *Ten Years Work for Indians at Hampton Institute* (1888); and with Mary Francis Armstrong wrote *Hampton and Its Students* (1874) and *Hampton Institute 1868 to 1885: Its Work for Two Races* (1885). She also wrote *Tuskegee Normal and Industrial School for Training Colored Teachers, at Tuskegee, Alabama, Its Story and Its Songs* (1884). Retiring from teaching in 1910, she remained on the editorial board of the *Southern Workman* until 1918. She died at Hampton at the age of eighty-four. (See obituary in *Southern Workman,* 53 [July 1924], 295.)

[23] Julia E. Remington of Manlius, N.Y., taught, served as a housekeeper, and cared for General Armstrong's children while at Hampton. She left in 1876 to work as an Episcopal missionary among the Onondaga Indians in New York. Ill health forced her retirement in 1903. She died at a Philadelphia home for the aged in 1922.

[24] Martha Mercelia Waldron (1850-1930) came to Hampton in 1872 after graduation from Vassar College. She left in 1875 to pursue a nurse-training course in New Haven, then returned to take charge of the training school for nurses.

She left again to attend Woman's Medical College in Philadelphia (1878-81). Receiving her M.D., she returned to Hampton as its first resident physician. She remained until retirement in 1910. She served several times as an adviser on Indian health problems to the federal government.

[25] Thomas P. Fenner (1829-1912), born in Providence, R.I., and trained as a singer and violinist, helped establish the New England Conservatory of Music in Providence after the Civil War. Armstrong brought him to Hampton in 1872 to organize the Hampton Student Singers, and for the next three years Fenner was in charge of this group as they toured the northern states giving concerts and raising funds for Hampton. The tours were so successful that it was said that they "sang up Virginia Hall." (*Southern Workman,* 41 [Nov. 1912], 599.) Fenner later published a collection of Hampton songs. After leaving Hampton in 1875 he taught at the Temple Grove Seminary in Saratoga, N.Y., and again at the New England Conservatory, by this time located in Boston. He retired in 1898 to Hampton.

[26] Sabra H. Fenner (d. 1898), wife of Thomas P. Fenner.

[27] Susan P. Harrold of Franklin, Mass., served on the Hampton faculty until 1879.

[28] Charlotte L. ("Lottie") Mackie (1842-1925), sister of Mary F. Mackie, worked for Hampton Institute from 1870 to 1887 as steward, matron, and house-keeper of the Teachers Home.

[29] Albert Howe (1836-1925), born in Dorchester, Mass., went to Hampton in 1863 to recover his health after serving as a volunteer in a Massachusetts infantry regiment and perhaps also as a teacher of freedmen. With three partners he opened a store at Old Point for freedmen and disabled soldiers in 1865. He roomed with General Samuel C. Armstrong, then a Freedmen's Bureau district superintendent. When Armstrong left the bureau to found Hampton Normal and Agricultural Institute, Howe became its farm manager, an important position in view of the manual-labor organization of the school. Howe later also oversaw Huntington Industrial Works and the blacksmith and wheelwright shops. He supervised the building of the first brick building, Academic Hall, and Virginia Hall, the first building paid for by the earnings of the Hampton Singers. He was responsible for construction of some twenty-three buildings on the campus.

[30] George Dixon, born in Yorkshire, England, owned a large farm near Hampton Institute. He regularly employed several Hampton students on his farm and at times taught courses in agriculture.

[31] W. J. Butterfield left the Hampton staff after the single school year 1874-75.

[32] Benjamin Franklin Butler (1818-93), the Union general and politician, commanded Fortress Monroe near Hampton for six months in 1861. While there he issued a military order declaring slaves crossing Union lines to be contraband property and therefore not to be returned to their owners. It was presumably for this reason that the Butler School was named for him. The building that later housed the Butler School was probably one of those constructed to accommodate the contrabands.

[33] Eunice J. Congdon Dixon, wife of George Dixon, was in charge of the Butler School until 1880. She died at Hampton in 1907 at the age of eighty-six.

[34] George Jordan Davis, born in Chatham, Va., graduated from Hampton Institute in 1874 and remained on the staff for the rest of his life. He taught in the Butler School until 1880, when he became instructor of Indian boys in farming. In 1914 he became farm demonstration agent for the state of Virginia, a position he held jointly with his Hampton post until retirement in 1923.

A Student Petition
to Samuel Chapman Armstrong

[Hampton, Va., 1874-75]

Sir. We as members of Senior Cottage[1] and its court, feeling that the case of D. F. Douglass[2] was not carried to you in its proper form and that it was not by the consent of the court, but rather by a great abridgement of our rights. We therefore petition for said case for a legal trial. We feel that our rights should be respected so long as we are recognized as a court but we can not think that our court has any authority where cases are wrested from us as [at] present.

E. A. White[3]	R. H. Matthews[14]
E. A. Bird[4]	Isaac E. Harrison[15]
Robt. Kelser[5]	Alfred Moore[16]
A. W. Calvin[6]	W. A. Forsyth[17]
R. B. Jackson[7]	Geo. B. Bradly[18]
W. T. Williams[8]	Robert Smoot[19]
C. Voorhees[9]	Frank D. Banks[20]
Warren Logan[10]	P. W. Oliver[21]
W. M. Ivy[11]	B. T. Washington
W. R. Unthank[12]	J. C. Robbins[22]
W. M. Reid[13]	T. Berger[23]

ADS Armstrong Letters Received President's Office Vault ViHaI. Because space on the front of the document was exhausted after the first eight signatures, the remaining signatures, including that of BTW, were placed on the back.

[1] The term "Senior Cottage" did not signify that all of its residents were of the class of 1875. Some graduated in 1875, others in 1876 and 1877.

[2] Dennis D. Douglass, as his name was recorded by Hampton Institute, born in Augusta, Ga., in 1858, graduated in 1876. Whatever his delinquency was, it did not result in his dismissal. He taught in five schools in South Carolina for six years and in three schools in Georgia the following six years.

[3] Ackrel E. White (1850-87), as his name was recorded by Hampton Institute, was born in Isle of Wight County, Va. After graduation in 1876, he taught for the American Missionary Association for four years at Sherbro Island off the African west coast. Two of his students returned with him to receive further training at Hampton. Following a brief tenure in the postal service, he took charge of a school at Portsmouth, Va., in October 1884, his wife (Sadie Mackie, class of 1881) serving as assistant.

[4] Edmond Anderson Bird, born in Abingdon, Va., in 1859, graduated from Hampton in 1879. After teaching in schools in Virginia and New Jersey, he at-

tended Phillips Academy, Andover, Mass. Following graduation in 1889, he resided in Boston.

[5] Robert Kelser (1857-1914) was born in Albemarle County, Va., and graduated from Hampton in 1876. He taught in Vicksville and Scottsville, Va., and then at Charlottesville, where he married in 1885. He gave up teaching in 1912 because of failing health; he died of tuberculosis.

[6] Amos W. Calvin, born in Salisbury, N.C., in 1853, taught briefly in Greensboro, N.C., following his graduation in 1876. He then pursued a successful career in the grocery business, and became a planter and politician in Charlotte, N.C.

[7] Robert B. Jackson of Winnsboro, S.C., graduated in 1876 and taught in Malden, W.Va., and Atlantic City, N.J., before becoming a sleeping-car porter. He later worked as a valet in Boston.

[8] Whit T. Williams, born in Danville, Va., in 1857, was one of the Hampton Singers. After graduation in 1876 he taught in Drummondtown and Washington County, Va., and, after 1882, in Norfolk, Va.

[9] Charles C. Voorhees (1855-88) of the class of 1876 was born in St. Louis, Mo. In the twelve years between graduation and his death he taught in five different towns in Virginia.

[10] Warren Logan (1859-1942), treasurer of Tuskegee for forty-two years, was born near Greensboro, N.C. He graduated from Hampton Institute in 1877, where he gained some special training in bookkeeping under General J. F. B. Marshall. After teaching in Maryland, he went to Tuskegee in 1882 as a teacher of book-keeping, choral singing, and band. He soon persuaded BTW to make him the watch-dog of the Tuskegee Institute treasury. He served as acting principal in BTW's absence. After his retirement in 1924 he remained a member of the board of trustees until his death.

[11] Walter M. Ivy followed two brothers to Hampton, where he graduated in 1876. Returning home to Danville, Va., he died of a sudden illness the same year.

[12] Walter R. Unthank, born in Greensboro, N.C., graduated in 1876 and taught for one year prior to his death in 1878.

[13] William M. Reid, born in Gatesville, N.C., in 1857, graduated from Hampton in 1877. Reid taught school in North Carolina for several years and then took a job as a clerk in General Samuel C. Armstrong's office at Hampton, where he was in charge of the school post office. In 1885 he married Alice Harris, also a Hampton graduate, and they settled in Portsmouth, Va., where Reid practiced law.

[14] Reuben Hearde Matthews taught for four years before coming to Hampton. Born in Columbus, Ga., in 1852, he returned there to teach following graduation in 1876. Failing in health after one year, he moved to Pensacola, Fla., where he became principal of the black public school. Going into the mercantile business in 1882 and afterward taking a post-office job, Matthews returned to the principalship in 1885.

[15] Isaac E. Harrison returned to his Danville, Va., home after graduation in 1876, where he worked in a tobacco factory to support his elderly parents.

[16] Alfred A. Moore, born in Rockbridge County, Va., in 1850, went north after graduation in 1876 to further his education. Unsuccessful in his efforts to earn enough money in Philadelphia to enter Oberlin College or Lincoln University, he moved to Boston to take advantage of the city's educational facilities, working in a hotel and going to an evening high school.

[17] William Alexander Forsythe of the class of 1876 married after graduation and taught in Columbus, Ga. He later went into the cotton business in Augusta, Ga.

[18] George B. Bradley, graduate of the class of 1876, was born in Edgecombe County, N.C., in 1854. He taught in Campbell County, Va. (1876-82) and in Charlotte County, Va. (1882-88), before going into the coal business in Naruna, Va.

[19] Robert Smoot, Jr., of Charleston, S.C., graduated in 1876. He taught in Aiken County, S.C., until rheumatism forced his retirement after seventeen months.

[20] Frank D. Banks (1855-1930), a Hampton graduate of the class of 1876, was born in Appomattox County, Va. He taught briefly in Southampton County, Va., before becoming a clerk in the Hampton treasurer's office in 1877. He rose to the position of head bookkeeper at Hampton and held that position until his retirement in 1923. During these years he was the treasurer and business manager of the Hampton Supply Company. He also helped found the People's Building and Loan Association, serving as a director, and founded and served as manager of the Bay Shore Hotel on Chesapeake Bay.

[21] Patrick W. Oliver of Big Lick, Va., graduated in 1877 and returned home to teach. In 1882 he purchased a lot and constructed a store and home, building a successful grocery business.

[22] J. C. Robbins worked in the principal's office at Hampton after graduation in 1876. He also worked with the Indian students and in 1880 went west to work with them in their homes and in a mission school. Robbins later studied medicine and then became a divinity student.

[23] Tapley S. D. Berger was born in Pittsylvania County, Va., in 1859. He graduated from Hampton in 1876, studied at Wayland Seminary, and graduated from Howard University in 1883. He attended Howard Law School briefly, supporting himself with a position in the Treasury Department, until stricken with malaria. After teaching at a private school in Washington, D.C., for two years, Berger took a position as teacher in Clarksville, Tex.

Three News Items on the 1875 Graduation Exercises at Hampton Institute

Fortress Monroe, Va., June 10th 1875

.　　.　　.　　.

THE SEVENTH ANNUAL COMMENCEMENT

To-day, Thursday, June 10th, the exercises of the seventh annual commencement have been held. Your correspondent has had some experience of college commencements in New England and elsewhere, but he has never witnessed or listened to exercises so completely satisfactory from beginning to end, nor which, taking into consideration the objects and aims of the course of instruction, gave such ample proof of a good work accomplished. The design of the school is to fit its graduates to do helpful work among the ignorant and degraded colored masses of the south. For such an object Latin, Greek, and the higher mathematics are useless, and they are wisely omitted from the course. A practical English education is given, sufficient to make good teachers, and with it there seems to have been imparted some comprehension of the needs of the race and a genuine missionary spirit.

There were present at the exercises a goodly number of distinguished friends of the school from the north and from Virginia. Among the former were the Revs. E. E. Hale[1] and Phillips Brooks[2] of Boston, the Rev. Dr. Taylor[3] and Dr. Whipple of New York, the Rev. Dr. Spear[4] of Pittsfield, the Rev. Messrs. Harding[5] of Springfield, Grout[6] of Concord, Fessenden of Connecticut, Charles L. Brace[7] of New York, W. E. McKee[8] of New Haven, Foster of Meriden, Edgar Ketchum and E. M. Cravath of New York, A. M. Kimber of Pennsylvania, representatives of *The Courant,* Springfield *Republican,* Richmond *Dispatch,* New York *Times* and *Tribune, Christian Union* and *Congregationalist.* Among the southern gentlemen present were Colonel B. S. Ewell,[9] president of William and Mary's college and formerly chief of General Joe. Johnston's staff, General Page,[10] of Fort Morgan and other fame, Judge R. W. Hughes of Richmond, Judge Dorman[11] of Norfolk, the Rev. Mr. Jones[12] of Richmond, formerly chaplain of General Lee. The morning was devoted to a survey of the farm, and to the closing term examinations. The graduating class were questioned in bookkeeping, history, physiology, Algebra, (the rudiments) and in primary lessons in metaphysics. They showed satisfactory progress, having evidently been taught to think for themselves, and to inquire into the reason of things.

At twelve o'clock the students and visitors assembled in Academic Hall, where several of the old songs were sung, after which the graduating class were escorted by the others to Virginia Hall, where a plain dinner was served. The invited guests inspected the admirable culinary arrangements of the building and then met at the president's house, upon the piazza of which they enjoyed a bountiful lunch. At half-past one the graduation exercises began in the beautiful chapel in Virginia Hall, which was crowded to overflowing. Many citizens were present, and a number of officers from the fort with their wives. Following is the

Order of Exercises

Music — "My Lord, What a morning"
Salutatory   Alice Ferribee[13]
Recitation — Horatius at the Bridge   William Henry[14]
Essay — Beauty   Sallie Gregory[15]
Music — "Nobody Knows the Trouble I've seen"
Essay — Compulsory Education   Charles Green[16]
                                                    Robert J. Whiting[17]
Debate on the Annexation of Cuba
                                                    Booker Washington
Music — Male Quartette. "Farewell my own true Love"
Reading — From Dickens' "Squeers' School"[18]   M. M. Mendenhall[19]
Recitation — High Tide on the Coast of
   Lincolnshire   Maria Ferribee[20]
Essay — Old Time Music   Joseph B. Towe[21]
Music — Old Plantation Melodies
Recitation — Sandalphon   Joseph C. Mebane[22]
Valedictory — The Black Man as a Voter and
   Citizen   John Collins[23]
Presentation of Diplomas
Music

The exercises were notable for the good taste of all who participated. The girls were dressed plainly and neatly with no attempt at display, and they, in common with the young men, conducted themselves with unassuming dignity. Alice and Maria Ferribee are two sisters of full African blood and features. The former delivered a well-expressed address of welcome, which would compare favorably with similar addresses at our northern high-schools, and the latter gave a recitation which indicated an appreciation of the beauty and pathos of the composition. The essay on "Beauty," dwelt especially on the methods available to all of beautifying their homes, and evidenced an aesthetic taste and the beginning of culture. The essay by Green in favor of "Compulsory Education," contained good ideas well put. The Cuban debate was above the average of such performances, the speaker on the negative making an excellent and logical argument, indicating a careful study of the question and a keen appreciation of its merits. But the great feature of the oratorical exercises was the address on "Old Time Music." I do not hesitate to say there will be nothing better, nothing half so effective, at any of the coming commencements. There will be more of the graces of oratory, doubtless, but in originality of conception, beauty of expression, earnestness, and power to sway the feelings of the listeners, there will be nothing to compare with it, and I venture to say there has been nothing to equal it at Yale or Harvard in a dozen years. The speaker, Joseph B. Towe, is a full blooded North Carolina negro, formerly a plantation hand. The musical talent has been especially developed in him, and he has been one of the leading jubilee singers of Hampton. His theme was the old plantation music, and he carried his audience with him in warm sympathy as he told of its origin, its varieties, plaintive, joyous, spiritual and festive, and of its wonderful power over the music-loving and superstitious negroes. After describing each different variety, he led the school in singing a specimen, producing an effect simply indescribable. When he concluded there was hardly a dry eye among the visitors. I am able to give but the faintest outline of the address, which is worth publishing in full, or, which would be better, the young man could make this one of the most attractive parts of the jubilee concerts by repeating it at the cities of the north.

The other rhetorical exercises are worthy of mention, but I will only specify the valedictory which showed a comprehension of the ignorance and superstition of the black race, and the necessity of virtue, intelligence, and harmony between the races. The native whites he said must convince the blacks that they are their best friends, and this can only be done by action, for the blacks have learned that words are cheap. It should be mentioned that all the essays and addresses were original productions, revised by the teachers only in cutting down. The singing furnished by the students added greatly to the attractions of the afternoon. The diplomas for the graduating class were presented with a few appropriate remarks by Dr. George Whipple of New York, president of the board of trustees.

General Armstrong then announced that a few remarks would be made by visitors, and introduced the Rev. E. E. Hale of Boston, who spoke to the students. He said he had been to many college commencements but this was the first where the scholars furnished their own music, and it had been better than any other. He had known students to hire a band for $1,000, but they had not been so much entertained and uplifted as we have to-day. There is a lesson in it for you. The future is in your own hands. If you will take care of that as you have of your music, that's all. In the good providence of God you happen to represent your race at this 1875. You were not wiser nor better than others, but you have been providentially chosen. You must not falter nor be discouraged until there is a similar institution in every southern state. Don't use the good you've got for yourselves but for your race. Don't be satisfied until there are 15,000 teachers in the field. You must hold together, not by grips, pins, secret organizations, but as children of the living God, followers of Jesus. Every day do His work as He tells you, and then you'll keep together. Follow your leader.

Colonel B. S. Ewell, President of William and Mary's college, said he felt it a great privilege to be present, and believed this institution was second to none of its kind in the country. It is the good fortune of the pupils to be taught that they are to be the architects of their own fortunes.

Other addresses were made by the Rev. Dr. Taylor of New York, Judge Hughes of Virginia, Dr. Gail of Massachusetts, Col. Crocker[24] of Portsmouth, Va., the Rev. Mr. Harding of Springfield, the Rev. Mr. Jones of Richmond, and the Rev. Dr. Adams[25] of Hampton. While it would be interesting to report all, for all were excellent, I can only speak of the admirable tone of the remarks from the southern gentlemen. Judge Hughes, who was once a rabid fire-eater, said it was gratifying to put to rest the old belief that one race was inferior in capacity to the other. Major Crocker, superintendent of the schools at Portsmouth, expressed himself as more than delighted. The thinking people of Virginia have determined, he said, that their best good is in a generous and liberal education of all her children. She knows no distinction. He wished to assure the northern gentlemen that this great institution is not regarded as an alien, but as the beginning and illustration of the great good which they hope to accomplish. "We don't mean that you shall consider this as your institution; we mean to be your co-workers." He had been impressed not only with the beauties of the thoughts expressed on the stage, but by the soundness of the principles. I see if all are like these we are all brothers. It will only be a question of time; prejudice and habit are only overcome gradually, but we mean that the school house shall solve the questions which puzzle the statesmen. Chaplain Jones expressed hearty sympathy with the work. It is a work in which men of different views can stand on common ground. The venerable Dr. Adams, of Hampton, expressed the sympathy and regard of the surrounding people in the institute, and thought it was especially fortunate in having such a principal as Dr. Armstrong.

The exercises concluded with a prayer by the Rev. Phillips Brooks. The party of northern friends of the school left New York Tuesday afternoon on the Norfolk steamer "Old Dominion," under the charge of Mr. W. N. Armstrong[26] of New York, and reached Fortress Monroe last night, where they were quartered at the Hygeia House, and were entertained in the evening by a concert by the jubilee singers. They leave for home to-night by the Baltimore steamer up the Chesapeake, having enjoyed a most delightful trip.

J C K[inney]

Hartford *Courant,* June 14, 1875, 1. The account of commencement was preceded by several paragraphs on the history and nature of Hampton Institute.

[1] Edward Everett Hale (1822-1909), for forty-three years minister of South Congregational Church, Boston. A Harvard graduate, Hale was ordained in 1842 and assumed his Boston pastorate in 1856. With the coming of the sectional crisis and war, he worked with the New England Emigrant Aid Company and the U.S. Sanitary Commission, and in 1863 wrote his famous short story, "The Man without a Country." It was in his church that the Hampton Singers made their first Boston appearance, and Hale believed their plantation songs to be the only true American music. A leader of the Lend-a-Hand movement, he promoted Hampton's Indian work in the organization's *Lend-a-Hand* magazine. He regularly visited Hampton Institute in the later years of his life.

[2] Phillips Brooks (1835-93), Boston Episcopal bishop with a long interest in the Negro, was born in Boston and attended Harvard and the seminary at Alexandria, Va. Ordained in 1859, he became pastor of the Church of the Advent, Philadelphia, and organized the Pennsylvania Freedmen's Relief Association. Made pastor of Holy Trinity Church, Alexandria, in 1862, he achieved a distinguished reputation as an inspiring minister and an important supporter of Lincoln. In 1869 he moved to Boston, where he headed Trinity Church and was elevated to bishop in 1891. Brooks was a member of the first board of trustees of the Slater Fund (1882-89) and a leader of the American Missionary Association.

[3] William M. Taylor (1829-95), born and educated in Scotland, was pastor of the Broadway Tabernacle Church in New York City from 1872 to 1892, editor of *Christian at Work* from 1876 to 1880, and a president of the American Missionary Association.

[4] Charles V. Spear (1825-91) was a minister and teacher at Maplewood Institute, Pittsfield, Mass., which he purchased in 1864.

[5] John Wheeler Harding was pastor of the First Congregational Church, Longmeadow, Mass., for forty-two years. He died in 1896, at the age of seventy-four.

[6] Lewis Grout (1815-1905) served as a Congregational missionary to the Zulus in South Africa from 1847 to 1862. Later he published several books on the Zulus and their language. In 1865 he became secretary of the American Missionary Association, a position he held until 1884, when he resigned to devote a full year to collecting funds for Atlanta University. He was minister of a church in Sudbury, Vt., from 1885 to his retirement in 1888.

[7] Charles Loring Brace (1825-90) studied at Yale Divinity School and Union Theological Seminary before traveling to Europe, where he made a special study of reformatory and philanthropic institutions. Returning to New York in 1852, he helped found the Children's Aid Society the following year, leading the organization's efforts on behalf of the slum community for the next thirty-eight years.

For many years prior to his death, he annually spent a week at Hampton for rest and relaxation.

⁸ William E. McKee.

⁹ Benjamin Stoddert Ewell (1810-94) was president of the College of William and Mary from 1854 to 1888.

¹⁰ Brigadier General Richard L. Page, C.S.A., commanded Fort Morgan, located at the entrance to Mobile Bay, during the Civil War. He became famous for holding the fort for almost three weeks under a heavy attack by Admiral Farragut's fleet before finally surrendering, on Aug. 23, 1864.

¹¹ Orland Dorman, a retired lawyer and judge living in Norfolk, listed in the 1870 census as sixty years old.

¹² John William Jones (1836-1909), born in Louisa, Va., graduated from the University of Virginia in 1859 and attended the Southern Baptist Theological Seminary before serving in the Confederate Army as a chaplain. He became known for his revival meetings, at which large numbers of soldiers were converted. After the war he served in a variety of capacities, including assistant secretary of the Home Mission Board of the Southern Baptist Convention, chaplain of the University of Virginia, agent for the Southern Baptist Theological Seminary, superintendent of the Virginia Baptist Sunday School Association, and chaplain general of the United Confederate Veterans.

¹³ Alice M. Ferribee Lewis was born in North Carolina in 1855 and graduated from Hampton in the class of 1875. After graduation she taught school in North Carolina and Virginia for two years before marrying another Hampton graduate, Peyton Lewis, a Methodist minister. The Lewises settled in Indiana.

¹⁴ William P. Henry was born in Philadelphia in 1857. He taught school in Virginia and then Maryland after his graduation from Hampton.

¹⁵ Sallie P. Gregory Johnson was born in Chatham, Va., in 1854. After graduating from Hampton she taught for more than eight years in Chatham and for three years at the Virginia Normal and Collegiate Institute in Petersburg. In 1893 she was residing in Lynchburg.

¹⁶ Charles W. Greene (1849-1926), born in North Carolina, later became an important member of the Tuskegee Institute staff. After graduation from Hampton he taught and farmed in Virginia and North Carolina. He came to Tuskegee Institute in 1888 to work under J. H. Washington as farm manager and was placed in charge of the brickyard. He remained farm manager until 1902, a period in which the size of the farm increased from 40 to over 2,000 acres. After 1902 he held a number of positions of steadily decreasing responsibility until his retirement in 1918.

¹⁷ Robert W. Whiting (1856-90), born in Campbell County, Va., taught in the public schools of Virginia until 1885, when he became secretary and later treasurer and business manager of Virginia Normal and Collegiate Institute in Petersburg.

¹⁸ Squeers was the schoolmaster of Dotheboys Hall, a Yorkshire academy in Charles Dickens's *Nicholas Nickleby.* The novel described the incompetence, closed-mindedness, and cruelty of education in a supposedly typical English academy of his day.

¹⁹ Madison M. Mendenhall was one of the few graduates who apparently was not greatly influenced by the Hampton philosophy. Reports to his alma mater at various times after his graduation indicated that he "went to sea," was "a rolling stone," and finally "was keeping a bar-room and passing off for a white man." (*Twenty-two Years Work,* 54.)

54

[20] Maria L. Ferribee Watkins, born in 1857 in Elizabeth City, N.C., was the sister of Alice M. Ferribee. She taught in North Carolina and Virginia for two years before moving to Brooklyn, N.Y., where she married.

[21] Joseph B. Towe, a Hampton Singer and member of the class of 1875, became the head of the largest black primary school in Norfolk, Va. He served as an agent of Hampton Institute, spending summer vacations in the North on the school's behalf until his death in 1880.

[22] Joseph C. Mebane, born in 1853 in Mebane, N.C., remained after his graduation to teach one year in Hampton's Butler School. Later he attended Oberlin College for a time and in 1882 joined a troupe of traveling singers. "When last heard of," *Twenty-two Years Work* noted, "he was keeping a 'Gentleman's Bar-Room' in Ohio" (p. 54).

[23] John W. Collins taught for two years after graduation and died in 1878.

[24] Colonel or Major Crocker was superintendent of schools at Portsmouth.

[25] Rev. Adams, a white Southern Baptist minister, took part in the installation of Richard Tolman as Hampton chaplain in 1871.

[26] William N. Armstrong, brother of Samuel C. Armstrong, was born and raised in Hawaii, where he was a schoolmate of David Kalakaua, who later became king of the islands (1874-91). Armstrong lived most of his adult life in New York City but maintained his connection with Hawaii and served in the cabinet of King Kauikeaouli (1825-54) and as attorney general and commissioner of emigration for his friend, King Kalakaua. Armstrong accompanied Kalakaua on his trip around the world in 1881 and resigned upon his return in opposition to the monarch's free-spending policies. Armstrong later wrote a book about the trip, *Around the World with a King* (1904).

Hampton, Va., Thursday, June 10, 1875

COMMENCEMENT DAY WITH THE COLORED STUDENTS

The morning previous to the trying ordeal of public speaking was spent by the students in examinations, at which great numbers of guests were present. I was struck with the fact that, though the rooms were crowded with strangers, and the students were naturally in a state of high excitement, the dress and manner of all were exceedingly quiet and modest. The girls looked like respectable working-girls, and the boys much as young country teachers would anywhere. All had remarkably good heads, and many showed large frontal development of the brain; some few were so white that at the North no one would have dreamed of their being of the negro race. The majority seemed, however, of the pure black stock. The first class I visited was in grammar, which was very ingeniously taught by a sentence written on the board in *echelon,* as it were and then copied by the students, and each phrase parsed by the means of a sort of grammatical notation, written opposite each word.

55

There was no copying from one another, and no help from the teacher, but each performed the work perfectly. Another class in algebra were almost equally successful. Geography was also well done, and map-drawing, though I missed here Guyot's[1] system. A spelling match called out much interest, but the crowning examination was to be one in a most difficult study, some metaphysical lectures on man, by President Hopkins.[2] Gen. Armstrong evidently felt nervous in conducting it. One can judge of its scope when it is remembered that within half an hour the students were compelled to give their ideas on such topics as the "Difference between the Animal and the Vegetable," the "Distinction between Animal and Man," the "Definition of Higher and Lower Orders of Life," the objections to the "Development Theory,"[3] and the "Analysis of the Nature of Man," besides numerous other points. On the whole, the young men did as well as could any college class of white students on such abstruse topics, the only deficiency observable being of vocabulary, owing probably to their less range of reading. The student who distinguished himself most, bore the name of "Washington." The thought, however, crossed one's mind, whether this tasting of science was in any way useful to such youth.

When we listened afterwards to the songs of these young men and maidens, all born in slavery, wherein there were tones which thrilled the very heartstrings, and which seemed to be vibrating with the incredible pain and longing of the years of bondage, and then heard those sweet and moving words which drew tears from every eye, picturing the heaven of peace and brotherhood they had never known on earth, and looked on the solemn, earnest, dusky faces, wherein the history of generations of white wrong-doing seemed written, and then thought of science sweeping away their only hope and consolation, we felt that of such Paul's words would be pre-eminently true, "They are of all men most miserable," and that a little learning would be a wretched compensation. For, after all, such armor as President Hopkins can furnish against modern skepticism is but weak, and it were a pity to disturb faith by raising objections.

In the afternoon we met in the grand new Memorial Hall, (just endowed by a bequest,) which I have before described. A large audience of blacks and whites, the colored visitors usually sitting (though not in all cases) on the side with the students, and many colored working people crowding at the doors, listening with intense interest to the words of their young orators.

56

No other Commencement that I ever attended had one tenth of the moving interest of this, for a deep tone of reality vibrated through it. All in sympathy with the college felt that this was a fore-post of civilization on the old ground of barbarism. All knew that cold and hostile eyes were on every act of the performance, and both whites and blacks were conscious that this was a portion of the great test which was to show the quality and destiny of a race.

One Southern gentleman afterward, in a most friendly and humane speech, alluding touchingly to this being "Decoration Day" at the South, spoke of the line of mighty events which lay between "those graves and this institution." One could not but think solemnly of how many brave men had died before this simple school for blacks could be, and what a serious thing the experiment was. Then each original speech bore on the great questions of the day, and as they were all evidently the composition of these youth, they seemed to throw light on some of the most important problems of State; that is, how this great colored population and their chosen young men regarded certain questions of vital interest. Never, therefore, was a college Commencement so listened to. The feature which struck me most in these speeches was the remarkable good sense and moderation of them, and their freedom from all tinge of bitterness. The speakers apparently felt the difficulties of the great problem as much as white speakers would. They even, in some cases, deprecated the giving of suffrage to either white or black without the "intelligence test." They apparently saw the danger in admitting a vast mass of ignorant persons at once to complete political control in their communities. They confessed the readiness by which their race were influenced by demagogues and sharpers, and while admitting the virtues and sacrifices of Northern men who had come South truly to befriend the blacks, they denounced the adventurers or "Carpet-baggers," who would merely make use of the negroes to secure money or office. One speaker advocated in the strongest terms compulsory education for both whites and blacks. An exceedingly interesting feature in the exercises was an animated debate on the "Annexation of Cuba," by two Virginia negroes, Whiting and Washington. The arguments for it, such as would naturally attract the colored race, such as the emancipation of the Cuban blacks, the doing away of the slave trade, the increase of the colored vote, and the new market for products, was presented with much skill by the former. But the second disputant, Washington, gave a most terse and vigorous argument against

annexation; urging that the difficulties before the country in the emancipation of 4,000,000 blacks were quite enough without adding that of
the Cubans; that annexation would flood the country with ignorance
and crime, and above all, would increase the power of the Roman
Catholic Church, which "was already so degrading to the great masses
of white voters." The speaker dwelt on the curses of the recent war,
under which the whole country was suffering, and called upon the
people not to plunge into another war for the sake of useless territory.
These and other points, presented with great vigor, evidently carried
the whole audience, both white and black, with the speaker, who was
enthusiastically applauded. Many of the students alluded to their former condition of slavery, but without any tone of reproach or of desire
for vengeance, and yet there was an expression on their faces which
showed that all had felt the "iron in the soul." One was pointed out
to me, nearly white, who, while a teacher, had been driven from his
school into the woods by the Kuklux — his two assistants being murdered, and he himself barely escaping with his life. It was said that
he was in the college nearly a year before he would describe these
circumstances. Another student, who read an extract from Dickens
very dramatically, was as white as the majority of men one meets at
the North, and yet it seemed to me that his expression was the saddest
to be seen on any face. He probably knew that his fortunes were inevitably intertwined with those of the inferior race.

Not an expression of hostility or ill-feeling appeared in any address.
Each speaker seemed to feel that the fortunes of his race depended
on the self-control, virtue, and intelligence of each individual, and that
their future was in their own hands. They all, apparently, deprecated
any intruding of themselves socially, or of pressing their social rights
beyond what was proper and convenient. Their advice to their com-
panions as to whom they should vote for and what share they should
take in political life was characterized by remarkable good sense and
sharpness of understanding. The valedictory address, by John Collins,
a Maryland negro, on "The Black Man as a Voter and Citizen," was
a striking instance of this wisdom and sound sense. The most interesting
speech of the occasion was made by Joseph Towe, a full-blooded negro
from North Carolina, on the "Old Time music of the Negroes." He
stated that the beautiful melodies which so much delighted every lover
of music when sung by the negroes were derived from native African
airs, and that an old negro still lived in North Carolina who spoke the

African languages, and knew more of these melodies than any other negro in the South. The speaker described with what eagerness the slaves would work to some of these cheerful melodies, and, suddenly stopping, said, "I will give you an instance," when immediately a chorus in the audience struck up a lively plantation song, which called out vociferous applause. The speaker then detailed the different melodies which were once in favor among the slaves, and stopped while describing each class for the chorus among the students to give an example. The effect was wonderfully lively and impressive. The student stated, what no doubt is true, that as the negroes are emancipated and become educated, they are dropping this old music which belongs to the days of slavery, and that, unless they are preserved in type, these sweet melodies are destined to entirely pass away. The speaker was greatly applauded when he closed, and the address hereafter will be published as a remarkable contribution to our knowledge of "negro music." One young girl, Sally Gregory, a Virginia negress, read a very pretty essay on "Beautifying the rooms of a house." All agree that these young women, as they go to households of their own, keep remarkably neat and tasteful rooms, and show the aesthetic ability of the race by creating beauty from very simple materials. A peculiar feature of all the addresses was that they closed with a fervent and sincere religious sentiment — for the college is peculiarly a religious seminary.

It was a cheering thought after these Commencement exercises that this band of modest, sensible, and intelligent men and women were going abroad through the South to be teachers and leaders of their race. This class of forty or fifty will, during the Summer months, earn money by waiting in hotels or by household service, and then in the Autumn they will take charge of schools for colored pupils, for which places there are vastly more teachers demanded than the institute can supply.

After the speeches, various Southern gentlemen were called out to give their views in regard to the college. They were evidently representative men, one having been a clergyman who was imprisoned by Gen. Butler in the Rip-Raps[4] for preaching violent secessionist views, another a friend of Gen. Lee, who had written his biography, another a Superintendent of Schools at Norfolk, and another a Superintendent at Richmond. They one and all, however, expressed the highest approval of the plan and working of this "Freedmen's College," and several stated that Virginia would only be too happy to take upon herself the expense of its support if she were not so impoverished by the war. This good feeling has been brought about mainly by the practical wisdom and thorough good sense of Gen. Armstrong who has shown in all his proceedings to the Virginians that he is seeking only the highest good to the State and through the most practical means.

[Charles L. Brace]

New York *Times,* June 15, 1875, 5.

[1] Arnold Henry Guyot (1807-84), a Swiss-born geographer, introduced scientific study of geography into American common schools. His textbook, *The Earth and Man* (1849), and other books gained wide acceptance in American public schools.

[2] Mark Hopkins (1802-87), long-time president of Williams College (1836-72), was born in Stockbridge, Mass., and educated at Williams and at Berkshire Medical College, where he received an M.D. degree in 1829. Appointed to the Williams faculty as a professor of moral philosophy in 1830, he quickly excelled as a teacher and at the age of thirty-four was named president. Hopkins was a vital force in molding the character of Williams graduates, including Samuel Chapman Armstrong, who often spoke of his influence. While president, he required all seniors to spend a good part of their final year with him engaged in a Socratic dialogue on the theme of the Christian conscience in a world of precipitate material progress. Hopkins considered it his prime duty to develop in each Williams student the confident use of the rational powers of his own mind, but he stressed character-building over intellectual training. Retiring from Williams in 1872, Hopkins served as president of the American Board of Commissioners for Foreign Missions until his death at the age of eighty-five. (See Rudolph, *Mark Hopkins and the Log.*)

[3] As a conservative Congregationalist minister, Hopkins struggled with evangelical fervor against theological liberalism. His writing and teaching were a reaffirmation of traditional Christian beliefs and values in the face of the growing secularism of his age. He opposed transcendentalism and unitarianism in antebellum New England and launched an attack on Charles Darwin as soon as *Origin of the Species* was published in 1859, and also opposed Thomas Henry Huxley's popularization of the Darwinian "development" theory.

[4] Rip Raps, Va., a small island near Hampton, off Old Point Comfort, used as a resort before the Civil War.

Hampton, Va., Thursday, June 10. [1875]

COLORED YOUTH ON THE COMMENCEMENT STAGE

THE TWO RACES AT AMITY IN VIRGINIA HALL —
A REMARKABLE PAPER ON PLANTATION MUSIC

From Our Special Correspondent.

Our visiting party is largely increased, this morning, by native Virginians of intelligence and distinction, who are here to participate in the annual examinations, and the rhetorical exercises of the graduating class. It is a most emphatic tribute to the intrinsic merit of the school, as well as to the wisdom of its management, that it is winning, from year to year, a more general and hearty approval from those who might naturally regard it with suspicion and distrust. Virginia hall, a beautiful audience-room, seating about 600, was crowded with a curiously assorted company of whites and blacks and intermediate complexions, representing pretty much all sections, conditions and professions, from the elite of Fortress Monroe and the F. F. V's. down to the Uncle Neds and the newspaper men. Col. Benjamin S. Ewell, president of William and Mary college, and brother of the famous confederate general,[1] in the course of the afternoon speeches, spoke in glowing terms of the eminent success of the institute, and congratulated Gen. Armstrong as a brother educator. Judge Hughes of Norfolk bore similar testimony, and remarked that, having been for six successive years a punctual and observant visitor of the university of Virginia, comparing its commencement exercises with these, he must allow that the comparison, considering the antecedents and circumstances of the two institutions, was exceedingly favorable to the Hampton students. He was sorry that one-half instead of one-third of the agricultural college land grant to Virginia had not been given by the state Legislature to Hampton. He acknowledged that the white citizens of Virginia were most of all persons indebted to the colored people. "Although," said he, "we are at present poor and unable to contribute in our proportion toward paying the debt, yet I hope that we shall, by and by, be able to vie with our northern friends in their noble liberality." Major Crocker of Portsmouth, superintendent of public schools, and Mr. Jones, formerly Gen. Lee's chaplain, now representing the Richmond *Dispatch,* and also for this occasion the New York *Tribune,* spoke eloquently to the same effect, and with cordial allusions to the growing sentiment of unity between North and South as evinced, among other things, by the recent decoration services.

To return to the stated school exercises, the morning examinations in the several class rooms in algebra, arithmetic, geography, grammar, history, physiology, reading, spelling, moral science, and Dr. Hopkins's "Outline of Man,"[2] were, as a whole, very creditable. A greater proportionate dependence on memory and less of mental self-reliance, perhaps, than pertains to white youth who have been intellectually trained from early childhood and under different moral surroundings,

— but, at the same time, abundant evidence of mental quickness and versatility. The most satisfactory tests, however, appeared upon the stage of the Virginia hall chapel, in the rhetorical exercises of the afternoon. The graduating class of 40, out of an average school attendance of 150, made a very manly and womanly appearance, and showed unmistakably the good results of their training. They were modest, self-possessed, simply dressed, and to a marked degree, in common with the whole school, correct and even refined in manners and deportment. The girls wore cambrics neatly fitted, and nothing in their ornaments or make-up suggested the "loudness" often supposed to belong to negro taste. The majority were black and comely, and it seemed to me that their mental ability was rather in the ratio of their depth of color. At least, the pure-blooded negro appeared to carry the palm in sturdy force of character. Such were Alice Ferribee, the salutatorian, and John Collins, the valedictorian, who both spoke their genuine sentiments with great propriety, modesty and good sense.

Mr. Collins spoke of "The Black Man, as a Voter and a Citizen." He was thoroughly "down" on the demagogue carpet-bagger, while neatly qualifying his denunciation with an eye to the "northern friends." There was great danger, he thought, of the blacks' blindly voting in a body, under the single aim of the average voter, to perpetuate his personal freedom, joined with the instinctive political fear of his former master. Yet the blacks have no hatred of the whites of the South, and nothing can be more absurd than the idea of a war of races. The future of his race he viewed as dark and dreary in the present outlook, but beyond this wilderness there appeared in hopeful vision a promised land. Education and time are the two great levers for the elevation of the colored people. They need more of self-respect and self-reliance, and to furnish themselves competent leaders of their own race; and for this such schools as Hampton are their hope.

Sallie Gregory, a quadroon with liquid voice and eyes, read an essay on "Beauty," — herself a good illustration. After descanting with charming sentiment on the beauty of nature, she turned the thought to beauty in household arrangements — "the pictures on the pure white wall, trailing vines, hanging baskets, pretty effects of color, light and shade, the center table with books and magazines and vase of fresh flowers, — the silent and powerful influence of beauty over the family, especially the little ones — the little things that make life attractive." It was a prophecy of her ideal home, evidently modeled after her pretty little white-walled dormitory and her teachers' parlors in Virginia hall. Our good friend and contributor, Mr. Alexander Hyde of Lee, was so charmed with it, that he interviewed the fair authoress in the interest of his "Lee Gleaner," in whose columns it will appear in full.

There was a debate on "The Annexation of Cuba," in which the negative man, Booker Washington, a mulatto, made a very terse, logical and lawyer-like argument, briefly, this; 1, Spain has a right to Cuba by discovery and colonization; 2, the United States have more than enough, let them take care of themselves; 3, the interests of peace forbid the risks of entanglement in bloody and costly war; 4, the situation of Cuba and character of her inhabitants would make her a burden. Wait till the Cubans are more capable of self-government. As to helping their ignorance, we have enough of that article already. A whole South is stricken with it. This country lately passed through an awful crisis, in which its very foundations were shaken. Wouldn't it be wise, before we risk a war for Cuba, to redeem ourselves from the meshes of the last war?

The most interesting of all the performances was "Old Time Music," by Joseph B. Towe, a pure black and once a plantation slave. The music interspersed throughout the exercises had been the best of its kind, and fairly electrified us again and again. But this capped the climax. It was a historical and illustrated analysis of the plantation music. The writer, himself brimful of song, a powerful soloist, with a voice of wonderful sweetness, took us back into the past of slavery, and even further back, into Africa itself, for the original sources of this strange music. It flowed straight from the invisible fountains of the heart, its joy or sorrow leaping forth into music. Mr. Towe divided the negro songs into three kinds — the spiritual, the work songs and the comic. In his plantation days there were soloists or leaders of high repute, both among the white and colored people, and especially famous was one John Jones, who could speak the African language. The planters would often pay a large price for one of these soloists, for it paid well in the increased amount of work when the air was alive with the work songs. "I knew a man," said the speaker, "who could travel half a day when the fields were full of music, and learn every new song that he heard on his journey and hold them, and there were many like him." The "long sliding movement" or peculiar chorus variations prolonged on a single word, came from Africa, and there was the origin also of many curious superstitions and allusions to witch-craft woven into their improvisations.

The spiritual songs raised their musical passion and skill to the highest pitch. Let one of the distinguished soloists strike up in the congregation, and supreme happiness began to reign. It took from one to three minutes for the assembly "to draw in their wandering thoughts and place their whole mind on the soloist," but, attention once fixed, they began to make motions with the whole body, up and down, right and left, — continuing this motion, and increasing the time, until the *spirit* came, as they phrased it. Then a sweet accompaniment began, a kind of humming or steady moaning, and, at suitable intervals, other soloists would interject words between the words of the original leader, or between the words of the chorus, so giving extra emphasis and liveliness to the general effect. "After the soloist had wrought the assembly into one beautiful movement, while sweet accompaniments all through the congregation were sprinkling and enlivening the music, and the people seemed to be almost mesmerized by it; then by the change of his voice, the expression of his face, or his gestures, he could make the people laugh, cry, slap their hands and shout." The same musical fascination pertained to preaching, exhorting and praying. In these exercises "they would begin slowly and increase in swiftness of speech, and gradually change from clear talking to a sort of chant, and from common gestures to a regular motion in time, and at length the people, in their musical sensitiveness, would give themselves up to the tune, and begin their rhythmic motions and responsive accompaniments, till roused to an almost delirious enthusiasm." If anybody attempted to preach, exhort or pray without breaking into the chant or tune, it had no spiritual effect. This musical passion had a powerful influence in training the memory. Almost all these religious ideas were learned, memoriter, from the white people, and in process of time incorporated into song. For example, —

> If in this road you wish to be —
> I am the bread of life,
> O come along and follow me —
> I am the bread of life,

— when the speaker came to such an illustration, he would sing it with his clarion voice and the whole school would send back the chorus. To show how this memoriter method sometimes failed to convey ideas, one of the refrains rendered into written words reads, —

"Jesus is King of Manual."

"Many of these songs," said the speaker, "oozed from the mind instantaneously in times of unspeakable distress. The words were earnest and solemn, full of patience and asking for help. The tunes were the deepest minor, and all we can say, is, they were the escape of sorrow after the heart was full." The major songs, on the other hand, were the pouring out of joy and gladness. We were so fairly enchanted by one of these major songs that the speaker could not go on, for the applause that encored it, till Gen. Armstrong gave him the signal for its repetition. Thus the song was born.

In Chowan county, N.C., there lived a hard master, who forbade his slaves to sing or pray. Shortly after his death, the tender-hearted old mistress, who had always favored religious meetings, called them all into the front yard and gave them liberty to sing or pray as much as they wished. It was a blessing great as it was unexpected. While some of them with tears of joy were bowing and giving thanks to their mistress, others began to slap their hands, shout and give God the praise. In the company was one man named Henry, who had been bought and sold several times from his family, and whose life had been full of sorrow. "But," said the speaker, "he trusted in his Lord. He had been the composer of several minor songs, but had never been in the required state, that overpowering of the mind and soul with joy, which made the heart send forth the thrilling and cheering major tunes until now." He rose, slapped his hands and said, "Let us give God the glory," and began this *then* new song: —

> O talk together, children,
> Don't you get weary.
> Cheerah!
> Oh, better day coming,
> Don't you get weary.
> Cheerah!

Stretching out *The Republican*'s hand for this admirable essay, I found it already preempted by Rev. Edward E. Hale for *Scribner's Monthly,* in which it will probably, by and by, appear with the music. Mr. Hale made it the text of his speech; comparing it with the hired, costly and perfunctory music of the white college commencements, he said, "If you will take care of your future as you do of your music, that's all." Alluding to the marvelous changes in their status since the "contraband" era of twelve years ago, and to the noble buildings and complete advantages they enjoyed, "among the best I have ever seen and that you will ever see," he asked: "Were you selected as any better or wiser than four millions more? No, you are representatives of your race. Go out, boys and girls! Bear aloft the banner of your institute. Don't be satisfied until in every one of these southern states there is a Hampton. Don't be so mean as to go out and use these advantages for yourselves: use them for your people. Hold together, not only you forty who graduate, to-day, but as allied in the brotherhood of your people, and not by grips, and breast-pins, not by any secret organizations, but by the common impulses and inspirations kindled here, as you go out the representatives of true learning, of a pure religion, as children of the living God and followers of Jesus Christ. If, on the other hand, you try to paddle each your own canoe into your own mud-hole, you will fail." Dr. Taylor of New York and others followed with stirring and encouraging words, and the exercises were concluded with prayer by Rev. Phillips Brooks of Boston.

The institute must be accepted as already a grand success and promising better things to come. Its 150 graduates stick to teaching, and are mostly employed in the Virginia public schools. Favorable accounts are given of them and there have been no complaints, while the demand for them far exceeds the supply. And it is by no means as teachers alone that they will make their mark. The civilizing, industrial, moral and religious influences of their Hampton training will tell to the best effects on the future homes, and churches, and farms, and all other worthy enterprises of the colored people, and, what is better still, upon their character. From such schools as Hampton must come those uplifting impulses and motives, without which the negro's vices and vicious antecedents, — ignorance, idleness, licentiousness, intemperance, — will only make his new condition of liberty a swifter impetus on the downward grade of social and civil ruin, — despite all that civil rights bills[3] and mere political changes can do with their utmost hindrances.

H.[4]

Springfield *Daily Republican,* June 26, 1875, 8.

[1] Richard Stoddert Ewell (1817-72), a West Point graduate and twenty-year

U.S. Army veteran, served as a Confederate lieutenant general under Stonewall Jackson. Late in the war he commanded the defense of Richmond.

[2] Hopkins's *Outline Study of Man* (1873) was a popularization of its author's conservative theological and metaphysical concepts, an answer to Darwinism.

[3] Probably a reference to the Civil Rights Act of Mar. 1, 1875.

[4] Almost certainly John Wheeler Harding, who regularly reported on Hampton and later Tuskegee for the Springfield *Republican*.

A Certificate of Achievement
from Hampton Institute

[Hampton, Va., June 10, 1875]

HAMPTON NORMAL AND AGRICULTURAL INSTITUTE

[*Picture*]

HAMPTON, VIRGINIA

The Trustees and Officers of the HAMPTON NORMAL AND AGRICULTURAL INSTITUTE hereby certify that *Booker T. Washington* has completed, with credit, a *3* years' course of instruction in this Institution, and they hereby recommend *him* as competent to teach a *Graded* school.

IN TESTIMONY WHEREOF, the undersigned have affixed our signatures, this *10th* day of *June* 1875.

Geo. Whipple PRESIDENT BOARD OF TRUSTEES
S. C. Armstrong PRINCIPAL

PDS "The Oaks" (former residence of BTW), Tuskegee Institute.

From Samuel Chapman Armstrong

[Hampton, Va.] Feb 12 [187]7

Dear Washington   Yours of the 6th is recd.

I have no agreement of any kind among my papers in regard to making John & Fannie Smith[1] exceptions to the School rule. I made the offer that you referred to but I had no means of knowing that

67

John & Fannie were covered by it — unless, indeed, at the time I made the offer you mentioned their names, or I might have then said it would be all right. I have no memory or record of any such compact and am not able to recall any such remote conversation. They entered school without any such special understanding & when I called them up they neither of them mentioned any agreement protecting them. I am willing to make such agreements with students but, in all such cases, I depend upon the student to remember the particulars of his case and I am ready to take his word for it. I answer over 200 applications a year and don't undertake [to keep][2] track of every statement I make in words especially.

Now if I made any such agreement with you in regard to these two people please tell me just what it was. John & Fannie came to me as full pay students, on the usual basis & never asked any special consideration. I will keep to anything I said to you & take your word for it just what is it[3] that I agreed to with respect to John & Fannie. Yours truly

S. C. Armstrong

ALpS   Armstrong Letterbooks   President's Office Vault   ViHaI.

[1] Fanny Norton Smith Washington (1858–May 4, 1884) was born in Malden, W.Va., daughter of Samuel Smith, who was part Shawnee, and Celia Smith. She knew BTW from childhood. His pupil in the Malden school, she gained admission to Hampton with his help. She soon fell behind in her school payments and left Hampton in 1878, spending two years teaching school near Malden in order to settle her account. She walked three miles to and from work each day to save on board, and struggled to support her mother as well as to pay her Hampton bill. At the time she sent her final payment of $48 to J. F. B. Marshall in January 1880, she indicated that she was earning $32.50 a month but using most of it to meet household expenses. Marshall then placed her on the roll of honor, "those graduates or students who, leaving the school in debt to it, have paid their debts in full from their earnings as teachers or otherwise." (*Southern Workman,* 9 [Mar. 1880], 26.) Fanny graduated from Hampton Institute in 1882 and married BTW that summer, joining the Tuskegee faculty immediately. The Tuskegee Institute teachers boarded with the Washingtons in their rented house, and Fanny carried the burdens of institute housekeeper. She was also responsible for broadening the curriculum for Tuskegee girls, developing a home-economics training program. She and BTW had one daughter, Portia Marshall. Fanny's first name, as it appeared on her tombstone at the Tuskegee Institute Cemetery, was "Fanny" rather than "Fannie," as she was sometimes known. (See inscription on tombstone of Fanny Smith, May 4, 1884.)

[2] Corner of letter torn.

[3] Probably intended "it is."

Six News Items on
the West Virginia Capital Campaign[1]

Charleston, [W.Va.] June 27, 1877

OUR COLORED CAPITAL MEETING

The meeting of the colored citizens of Kanawha, called for Wednesday, June 27th, was held pursuant to call.

The meeting was organized by appointing James H. Davis to the Chair, and W. P. Campbell,[2] Secretary.

The Speakers of the evening were Messrs. W. M. Davis,[3] Booker Washington, N. V. Bacchus and Stepto Tinsley,[4] who discussed, in turn, the great benefits to our section of the State, to be secured by the location of the Capital at Charleston.

The following resolution on motion of Fleet Porterfield,[5] was unanimously adopted:

Resolved, That we, the colored citizens of Kanawha, feeling keenly the wrong and injustice inflicted upon our section of the State, by the removal of the Capital, and claiming the right to a fair portion of the public institutions, will work diligently and constantly, that every colored voter of Kanawha shall be at the polls, on the 7th day of August, next, and vote for Charleston as the permanent Seat of Government, for the State of West Virginia.

On motion, the meeting adjourned, with three rousing cheers for Charleston.

James H. Davis, Chm'n.
W. P. Campbell, Sec'y.

NOTE. The speeches at the above meeting did great credit to the speakers, and demonstrated that our colored citizens are awake to the importance of the location of the Capital at Charleston.

Charleston *West Virginia Courier*, July 4, 1877, 2.

[1] When West Virginia became a state on Dec. 31, 1862, the seat of government was at Wheeling and remained there until 1870. In 1869 citizens of Charleston petitioned the state legislature promising that they would build a statehouse at their own expense and donate it to the state if the capital was moved to Charleston. The legislature passed a law removing the capital to Charleston after Apr. 1, 1870. Charleston received additional support in 1872, when the state constitution of that year declared Charleston to be the seat of government. Undaunted, the citi-

zens of Wheeling promised the legislature that if the capital was returned to Wheeling they would build a statehouse superior to the one at Charleston. On Feb. 20, 1875, the legislature made Wheeling the capital.

To put an end to the floating-capital question the legislature passed an act on Feb. 21, 1877, submitting the issue to a vote of the people. In the election held on Aug. 7, 1877, Charleston received a majority of the votes cast. The capital question, while of considerable local importance at the time, apparently passed quickly as a significant issue with most West Virginians. The capital remained at Wheeling until May 1, 1885, when it was moved permanently to Charleston.

BTW was one of a number of citizens from Kanawha County who desired to see their own region grow as a result of the capital's location at Charleston. BTW's role in promoting Charleston was in several ways characteristic of his later life. The capital question offered the opportunity for him to engage in a local community issue designed to aid and uplift the people of Kanawha County, white and black. Furthermore, the issue was not highly controversial in a partisan political sense. Citizens of Kanawha County were expected to support Charleston, the county seat. It was simply a question of getting the maximum voter turnout. BTW was a spokesman for the black citizens of Kanawha County in an issue on which the white citizens were in total agreement. Even when BTW spoke outside of Kanawha County he was still doing what was expected of a partisan of Charleston, and he apparently confined his tour to the surrounding counties, which also had an interest in having the capital nearby. Predictably, Kanawha and Greenbrier counties voted overwhelmingly for Charleston. Kanawha County gave 6,140 votes to Charleston, 42 to Clarksburg, and 2 to Martinsburg. Greenbrier gave 1,902 votes to Charleston and 5 to Clarksburg.

[2] William P. Campbell was reported in the 1880 census as a twenty-one-year-old black schoolteacher in Charleston, W.Va.

[3] Probably William Davis, BTW's former teacher, then in Charleston.

[4] Stepto Tinsley was reported in the 1870 census as a day laborer in Malden. In 1880 he was listed as a forty-eight-year-old black servant of Joel Ruffner in Charleston, W.Va.

[5] Fleet Porterfield was listed in the 1880 census as a mulatto laborer, thirty-four years old, living in Charleston. In 1870 he reported his occupation as cooper.

[Charleston, W.Va., July 18, 1877]

COLORED VOTERS, ATTENTION!

ELECTION, AUGUST 7TH:

B. T. Washington will address the colored people on the Capital question at the following times and places, viz: At Lewisburg, July 18th, at night; White Sulphur Springs, July 19th, at night. Let all attend.

Charleston *West Virginia Courier,* July 18, 1877, 4.

Hinton, W.Va., July 18, 1877

Editor Courier: The colored citizens of this place were interestingly and eloquently addressed by Mr. B. T. Washington, of your county, at the Court House. He aroused the people to a sense of their duty, and allow me, through your columns, to assure my brethren in your county that we will stand by them in August.

A Central Committee was appointed and resolutions adopted pledging ourselves to work and vote for Charleston.

T. J. Twinke

Charleston *West Virginia Courier,* July 25, 1877, 5.

[Lewisburg, W.Va., July 18, 1877]

Capital Meeting

At a meeting of the colored voters of Lewisburg, Greenbrier county, West Virginia, July 18th, 1877:

On motion, Mr. Edward Curry was appointed Chairman of the meeting, and H. B. Rice Secretary.

Mr. B. T. Washington, of Kanawha county, was introduced to the meeting, who delivered a very interesting speech in favor of Charleston.

The meeting was well attended, considering the inclemency of the weather. Good order prevailed, and strict attention was paid to the speaking. After the speaking the following resolution was adopted:

We, the colored voters of Lewisburg and vicinity, feeling ourselves deeply and seriously injured by the removal of the Capital from Charleston, and feeling the injustice done our end of the State in numerous other ways; and believing that its permanent location at Charleston will greatly benefit us as citizens; therefore, be it

Resolved, That we resolve ourselves into a committee of one to work for Charleston, and cast our votes solid for that place on the 7th day of August next.

On motion, the meeting adjourned.

Edward Curry, Chairman
H. B. Rice, Secretary

B. T. Washington, Esq., addressed quite a large audience at the Court-house on the night of the 18th inst., in the interest of Charleston as the permanent seat. The audience was composed of both white and black. Mr. Curry (colored,) was called to the chair, and introduced the speaker, (who is a colored man from Charleston,) with a few appropriate remarks, availing himself to the opportunity to urge upon his friends to turn out and vote on the 7th proximo. Mr. Washington made a very good speech indeed, giving the arguments in favor of Charleston in good style, and expressing his ideas in a clear manner and with appropriate words, interspersing his speech with apt anecdotes, illustrating his arguments. We would urge upon our colored friends to turn out and hear this champion of Charleston when the occasion presents itself, and by all means on the 7th of August, vote for Charleston.

Lewisburg *Greenbrier Independent,* July 21, 1877, 2.

[Charleston, W.Va., July 25, 1877]

Booker Washington has returned from Lewisburg. He reports good meetings wherever he spoke, and says the colored voters are a unit for Charleston every place he has been.

Charleston *West Virginia Courier,* July 25, 1877, 5.

[Lewisburg, W.Va., July 26, 1877]

A correspondent writing to us from Anthony's Creek, says that Booker Martin,[1] (colored.) addressed the colored people of Anthony's Creek on the 26th ult., on the Capital location question, and was listened to with marked attention, giving them many solid reasons why they should vote for Charleston as the permanent seat of Government. He also gave them much sound and sensible advice in regard to their general course in voting, calling their attention to the identity of interest between the races, &c., &c.

Lewisburg *Greenbrier Independent,* Aug. 4, 1877, 2.

[1] Almost certainly BTW.

To the Editor of the Charleston *West Virginia Journal*

[Malden, W.Va., August 1877]

Editors Journal: This question has presented itself to me, "can we not improve?" I mean the colored people, for I am a colored man myself, or rather a boy. When I look over the record of the colored people for the last ten years, I see many things for which they ought to be praised, but again when I look on the other side I see many things that we might improve ourselves in faster than we have done. First, let us take up the matter of education. Does each parent do all in his power to give his child an education? Does each parent consider the importance of educating his child? The time has come when we are expected to play our part in this republic as American citizens. Let every parent then see that his child is led to perform his duty as an American citizen. The time is fast coming when bondage can no longer be a plea for our ignorance. Our many friends who have stood by us in the past, and who are still willing to befriend us, want to see us accomplish something ourselves.

I know that there are many who will plead poverty as a reason for not educating themselves and their children, but let such look at Vice-president Henry Wilson,[1] who amid poverty and discouragements, rose from the shoemaker's bench to one of the Nation's highest officers. Let such, also, look at Abraham Lincoln who rose from the humble log cabin to the Presidency of the greatest republic on earth. Let them remember the old maxim, "where there is a will there is a way," and take courage and resolve never to give up in despair of getting an education till they have exhausted all the means in their power. I am afraid that there are too many of our people who do not improve the privileges they have within their reach. I am afraid that there are too many who spend too great a portion of their time in street walking or in vain or vile talk. I think there are many who, if they would count up the time spent by them in vain and idle street talk, would find it to amount to hours and days enough in which they might have obtained for themselves a valuable and respectable education. If we expect to make an intelligent nation we have no time to spend in idleness. It behooves us to properly employ every minute of our time. If the colored man will only improve his opportunities and persevere, I believe the time is not far distant when a great portion of them will be equal

in education, equal in wealth, equal in civilization, and equal in everything that tends toward human advancement, to any nation or people
on earth.

B. T. W.

Southern Workman, 6 (Aug. 1877), 62. The letter was titled "Can We Not
Improve?" and was prefaced by the editorial comment: "A Letter to the West
Va. Journal, from a Hampton Graduate."

¹ Henry Wilson (1812-75) was born in poverty in Farmington, N.H., as Jeremiah Jones Colbath. At the age of ten he was bound by an indenture and worked
for more than ten years as a farm laborer. Mostly self-educated, Wilson, at the
age of twenty-one, went to Natick, Mass., where he worked as a shoemaker for
several years and continued to read and take part in local political affairs. He
became an abolitionist, was active in local politics, and in 1855 was elected to
fill the Senate seat of Edward Everett. From the U.S. Senate he became an outspoken critic of slavery. During Reconstruction he supported measures to aid the
freedmen. In 1872 Wilson was elected as Vice-President in Grant's administration.
He died in office after a stroke suffered at the Capitol.

To a Hampton Teacher

[Malden] W.Va., March 26, '77 [1878]¹

Dear Teacher: I am very grateful to you for those books you sent me.
I would have sent you the enclosed fifty cents, but I thought probably
you might send me the other two in a day or two, so I waited for
them. My scholars think them splendid and are making fine progress
in them. I have a much larger school this year. I like teaching more
and more every day. I have over 60 scholars. I have been teaching
Algebra ever since my school began, but I must say I never understood
Algebra till I began to teach it this year. I have only one scholar studying it and I think he is excellent in it. I enjoy teaching now as I never
did before. My scholars all seem anxious to learn, and this gives me
pleasure and patience to labor with them. I require all to keep their
clothes neat and clean, and their hair combed every morning, and the
boys to keep their boots cleaned. To see that this is done I have a
morning inspection, as we did at Hampton. I have now a news table
where I keep all the fresh papers and magazines that I can get for
the children to read, so that they will know what is going on in the
outside world. They take great delight in this. If you could send me any

newspapers from there that are not used, and will let me know, I will send the money to pay the postage on them. I know you have heard very little of me at H. this year, but it is only because I have been so busy with my school. Yours faithfully,

W.

Southern Workman, 7 (July 1878), 52. The fact that the letter was written from West Virginia, where BTW was then conducting a school, and was signed "W" suggests that it was probably his letter, as does its general tone and style. The editors of the *Southern Workman* introduced the letter with these remarks: "From West Virginia comes a cheerful report. To introduce military inspection and a reading room to a public district school shows enterprise and progress, and an encouraging appreciation of some of the best lessons Hampton aims to give of the value of training outside of text-books."

[1] Because the letter was published in July 1878 it was probably written in 1878 and not in 1877 as printed.

From Samuel Chapman Armstrong

[Hampton, Va.] Feb 10. [187]9

Dear Washington: I write to invite you to make the *Post Graduate* Essay at the next Anniversary May 22nd.[1] I hope it will be convenient for you to accept.

The idea is to bring out the facts of actual experience, to show what clear heads & common sense colored graduates of this school have attained, and to win the respect of all by a generous noble manly spirit.

We would wish you to come here by May 1st to confer with you on your piece after it is written & give you time to learn it. You would not be charged for your board. Sincerely yours

S. C. Armstrong

ALpS Armstrong Letterbooks President's Office Vault ViHaI.

[1] BTW said of this speech in *Up from Slavery,* chap. 6: "This was an honour which I had not dreamed of receiving. With much care I prepared the best address that I was capable of. I chose for my subject 'The Force That Wins.'" The speech was refined and memorized under the supervision of his old teacher, Nathalie Lord, and pleased both students and teachers. A reporter for the *Congregationalist* of Boston said of the speech: "I must not forget to mention the post-graduate address. It is a pleasant custom of the Institute to recall each year one of its alumni to speak out of his new experience to the under-graduate members. It is a wise

thing to do, as done here. This year Mr. Booker Washington of Malden, W.Va., a graduate in the class of 1875, and a teacher of his own race since he left Hampton, was the speaker. His subject was, The Force that Wins, and his address was an earnest appeal to his colored hearers to believe in patient, unostentatious, consecrated labor in their efforts to help their race. Mr. Washington is a remarkable man. There are some graduates of Yale or Harvard, of four years' standing, who can write a better address than his, but they are not very many. Fewer yet are they who manifest such dignified ease upon a public platform, and hold so mixed an audience in such close attention. The Institute that can develop such a man, and send him out, may well take credit to itself for doing good work." (*Congregationalist*, 31 [May 28, 1879], 169.)

From Samuel Chapman Armstrong

[Hampton, Va.] July 1 [187]9

Dear Washington,   Yours of the 16th is received.

Your claim is fair. I will allow you $25.00 per month[1] for your services here as teacher and assistant in study hour & other duty that may be assigned you. Yours very truly.

S. C. Armstrong

If you know a very capable & deserving but poor student who wishes to come he can come.[2]

ALpS   Armstrong Letterbooks   President's Office Vault   ViHaI.

[1] BTW's financial account for his two years on Hampton's faculty is recorded in the Hampton Institute Ledger, 1879-80, and the Hampton Institute Journal C, 1879-81. Though many of the entries are cryptic, the records do indicate that his salary was paid quarterly, and that it was raised to $30 per month for his second year. From this he made regular board payments, amounting to some $13 a month in his second year. In addition he made substantial contributions to the student account of his adopted brother James during 1879-80, $24.65 in December and $33.48 in March, and a small contribution to the account of his future first wife, Fanny Smith. By his second year he was apparently able to build a savings account. Two large transfers from BTW's account to the Home Savings Bank are recorded for 1881, $129.44 in June and $200 in July. (See "Officers and Teachers" Ledger Book, 170-71, and Journal C, especially pp. 33, 139, 213, 244, 264, Business Office Vault, ViHaI.

[2] BTW induced several of his pupils to go to Hampton. In addition to James Washington and Fanny Smith, his brother John also attended. According to Dr. Samuel E. Courtney, a prominent Boston physician who grew up in Malden, six of BTW's Malden students attended Hampton. "We were known as Booker Washington's boys," he recalled. (Interview in Boston *Journal*, Mar. 29, 1896, clipping in Con. 6, BTW Papers, DLC.)

A Paper Read at a Memorial Service[1]
at Hampton Institute

[Hampton, Va., Aug. 1, 1880]

So far the death rate of the class of '75 has kept pace with the years. Five years have passed since the class graduated, and five of its members have passed away. First was John W. Collins, probably the most mature mind that ever left this Institution, then Mrs. Weaver[2] and D. Y. Turner,[3] and now J. B. Towe and Geo. M. Harrison.[4]

I best knew Mr. Harrison as a janitor here, he and I being janitors together for three years, working out our expenses in that way. As a scholar he was not bright in everything, but earnest in all his studies. In mathematics he was excellent. In some respects he was a model scholar. In all the records of the Institution I don't think there could be found any thing against the character of Geo. M. Harrison. No teacher I suppose, ever thought of marking him in deportment or promptness. He was not one of the shirky kind, wherever his duty called he was always to be found. He cared little for games and social entertainments and seldom attended them. I think no one ever saw him spend ten minutes in foolish or idle talk. He came here for an education, and he thoroughly devoted himself to his books. All his actions were characterized by a deep sense of honesty; he scorned all ideas of dishonesty in work or study. He had no taste for mere outward show. His highest ambition was to fit himself to do his people good; he often talked of the good that he hoped to do when he left here. The reports that we hear from his field of labor justify us in saying that he carried out his ambition so far as he was able.

From his short life we may all glean a lesson, always remembering that "We live in deeds not in years. . . ."[5] He most lives who thinks most, feels noblest, acts best." We all should so shape our lives that when we shall have passed away it can be said of us as we can truly say of him, "He hath done what he could."

B. T. W.

Southern Workman, 9 (Sept. 1880), 90.

[1] For Joseph B. Towe, George M. Harrison, and Maria Alvis Mallette, in the Virginia Hall chapel.

[2] Matilda Jane Brown Weaver, taken to the Pennsylvania State School of Soldiers' Orphans in Bridgewater, Pa., at the age of twelve, completed a four-

year course there and taught for one year before entering Hampton Institute in 1873. After graduation she married William B. Weaver of the same Hampton class and taught in North Carolina and Virginia before returning to Bridgewater in 1877.

[3] Daniel Y. Turner, born in King William County, Va., taught for four years at Big Island and Charlemont, Va.

[4] George M. Harrison taught at Enfield, N.C., after graduation and in 1878 entered Fisk University.

[5] Ellipsis in original.

An Article in the *Southern Workman*

[Hampton, Va., September 1880]

INCIDENTS OF INDIAN LIFE AT HAMPTON[1]

WORK, MUSIC, NEW ARRIVALS, CARE OF SICK

Ask the average American what he knows of the characteristics of the ancient Angles and Saxons, or the Romans, and he would not hesitate for an answer. Ask him what he knows of the real character of the American Indian, and he is confounded. To show the public that the Indian is a man, that he thinks, does wrong, does right, has a mind and body capable of improvement, is the object of these "incidents."

VACATION

Vacation to the Indians here does not mean a pleasant trip home, the meeting of parents and friends, or three or four months spent in idleness. To them it means work. No drones are allowed in this hive. The thirty boys who remain here are divided into three squads, who spend three weeks alternately in the country, in camp life, under the supervision of a teacher. This plan was tried last year and it works well. Two squads have already returned in an improved condition. The boys work eight hours a day, some working at their trades and the others on the farm. The wheelwrights, blacksmiths and carpenters are reported as doing exceedingly well. There is a general improvement in their work. It is seldom now that they have to be spoken to for any slackness. It is common to see five or six in a hoeing race, with the end of a beet or corn row for the goal.

SYMPATHIES

Has the Indian any of the tender feelings? One or two examples will answer this question. Among the Indian chiefs who visited the school month before last, was an uncle of Frank Yellowbird,[2] one of our students, whom he had not seen for two years. Their meeting was truly affecting. For five minutes they stood clasping each other's hands, unable to speak a word, and weeping as though their hearts would break, but with joy instead of sorrow.

The following notes written by some of the girls to Miss F.,[3] one of their teachers, just before they started North, show something of their feeling towards their teachers:

"Dear Miss F.:

"I never will forget you in my life. when I go home to Dakota I never will see you again, but if you are good and I am good we shall meet to gether in the heaven.

"Sarah Walker"[4]

"Dear Miss F.:

"I never forget you because you my good teacher. My dear teacher please you help me pray every night. I go way to far away. when I come back here I glad to see you. I am very sorry for you to day. I hope you will see me again. I will trying hard to do right. I will keep your card. Good bye.

"Josephine Molnoury"[5]

Many other such instances could be given to show that the Indian has all the feelings that any other race has. Cultivation is all that is needed.

CARE OF THE SICK

During the late sickness of Ecorruptahah,[6] White Breast[7] was detailed to assist a colored student in waiting on him. It is surprising how well he performed his duty. A trained nurse would not have done better. He was almost never away from his bedside, unless made to go. If I went into his room at midnight, or early in the morning, I found White Breast near the bedside. He was unwilling to trust anyone else with the care of his patient. He seemed to anticipate his smallest wants and was always ready to administer to them. Nothing has so strengthened my confidence in the civilization of the Indians as the actions of this boy around the bed of his sick friend.

Music

The following report on their progress in music is made by Mr. Hamilton,[8] who taught them vocal music last term:

"While much has been said, from time to time, concerning the progress of the Indian students at Hampton in their studies, but little or nothing has been said about their study of music. In this, as in other studies, some love it, and show much aptness; others care little for it, and were it not for the calling of the roll, would never be present when the time comes for singing: in this, they are like other people. Some of the boys and girls who have attended the agency and mission schools have learned to play quite creditably on the organ and piano by note. One of the young men plays the organ in their Sabbath-school, held every Sunday by Rev. Mr. Gravatt.[9]

"Let us now look in at the singing class and see what they are doing. The roll is called, and we begin by drawing five lines, and asking, 'What is that?' A few voices answer, 'Staff,' followed very quickly by many others giving the same answer. This being made clear to all, we continue the lesson. The *G* clef is next put on the blackboard — not on the staff, at first; when all have been made to understand the name of this character, it is then put on the staff, and they are taught the names of the lines and spaces as they are when this clef is used. It is somewhat amusing to hear them trying to say the word *clef*. Some, more persevering than others, continue to say it over until it is said correctly; while some, with a shake of the head, give it up. It is quite a study to observe the facial expressions of satisfaction or disappointment at their success or failure.

"Well, having found names for all the lines and spaces, together with the first added line below the staff, the scale of *C* is written upon the staff, ascending and descending. The syllabic names are said over and over, until all are able to repeat them quite readily; then the singing commences. Having sounded the *do* and sung the scale over several times, they are required to imitate. Imagine fifty or sixty musicians with as many instruments, including all kinds, taking them, without being tuned, and attempting to play, and you will have some idea of the effect produced by these untuned voices. Nor is there much improvement with the second and third trial. And for a considerable time some will sound the 3d and 5th of the scale instead of the 1st. 'Patience and perseverance conquer all things,' it is said. After resorting to the use of various syllables used in vocalization, such as *a, e, o* and *ah,* first spoken, then sung, I succeed in getting their ears trained and voices tuned, so that the scale is sung smoothly and correctly, ascending and descending. This course is repeated nearly every time they meet for a singing lesson. Whole notes are employed in writing the scale, without saying anything about their value or time name. For some time they are drilled on the scale in this simple form, then half-notes are introduced. A teacher is at no little disadvantage in that he can do but little explaining by words. The lesson must be put on the board and then sung, requiring them to watch carefully the manner in which it is done and then to imitate. Most of them seem to enjoy this to an unusual degree, counting and beating time. But if they get to a place in an exercise that is a little difficult, while they are trying to think it out their hands will pause, the time drag, and then, if you don't push them, they will drag to the end.

"During the term considerable advancement is made. Towards the latter part of the term just past many of them could tell the names of the various characters as fast as they could be put on the board, and sing the scale and other exercises readily and in tune. Taking advantage of times when the organ would not be locked, many of them have learned to play by ear such tunes as 'Martin,' 'Sweet by and by,' &c.

"They show no little fondness for the Plantation Melodies sung by the colored students, 'Hail! Hail! Hail!' 'I wonder where shall I go,' and 'Who'll join the Union?' being special favorites. And passing any of them, girls especially, a little before the hour for singing, I would be besieged on every side to sing one or all of the above pieces 'to-night at singing-school.' I taught them a verse of each piece, and they might be heard almost any time singing,

> " 'Roll up, Jordan, roll up high,
> Roll up, Jordan, let me by,
> To ease my trouble in mind.'

"Or,

> " 'Look up yonder what I see,
> Bright angels coming after me;
> I'm on my journey home.'

"Many of the Moody and Sankey songs were taught them by their teachers, and these we can hear ringing about the buildings, not in strict time, however. Those who were taught to read in the Dakota language before coming here are often heard singing hymns in that language to such familiar tunes as 'Arlington,' 'Autumn,' 'The Missionary Hymn,' &c.

"We sometimes get them to sing some of their war and love songs. These songs are very strange and almost indescribable, the attempt to write them being well nigh a hopeless one, though I have succeeded in taking down the words and notes of two 'love songs' and have a third nearly completed. As they become educated, they don't care to sing these songs, especially the war songs — which are accompanied by slapping the hands and stamping the feet, ending with a yell that is rather startling when heard for the first time.

"Educate the Indian and the Negro, and with the spirit shown by each at this Institution, I am willing to leave the question as to their future to them, without any fears as to the result.

"R. H. H."

New Arrivals

Since our last report we have had five new arrivals — three boys and two girls, from the Winnebago and Omaha Agencies. Neither of these tribes has been represented here before. Two of the boys go at the carpenter's trade, and the other one, by his own choice, is learning engineering. The average health of the boys is not very good, but all of them seem bright and earnest, and now that the first few days of homesickness are over, they take hold as if to make the best of their time while here.

Some of the actions of the new boys, before they get initiated into the habits of civilized life, are quite amusing to the old boys, who forget that it has been but a few months since they acted in the same way. Their fun began when one little fellow, who evidently meant to begin his life at Hampton by doing his work well at the table, for that purpose, left his coat in his room.

The little fellow was the object of much admiration from the other boys, and he unconsciously furnished them much amusement during the whole meal. The older boys were particularly interested in the inspection of rooms the first two or three mornings after the arrival of the new boys. When it came to inspection of the new boys' rooms the older boys would crowd around the door to see what strange sights could be seen — and they did not look in vain. For instance, one boy made up his bed and left both sheets and the pillow-case off; another insisted on covering his pillow with the blanket, and all would forget to sweep their floors. Things went on in this way for several mornings without improvement, and I had to turn the joke on the old boys by making them take the new boys for roommates and teach them to keep house. Now, the smoothness of their beds and the neatness of their rooms would teach a lesson to some lady housekeepers.

EVENINGS

After eight and a half months' hard study during school, the Indians are not pushed much in that line during vacation. Still, no time is left for weeds to grow. Many little things that tend to elevate them are artfully pushed in. Monday and Thursday evenings the boys and girls meet together in a large room for games. These meetings have a good effect upon their social natures, and help in a great degree to give the boys a more civilized opinion of the girls. Checkers, dominoes, and "words and sentences" are played with a good degree of skill; while "Clap in and clap out," "Go bang" and "Simon says thumbs up" are enjoyed to such an extent that they dislike bed time to come. But the bell rings and they must go. Before departing, all join merrily in a pleasant hymn, then come the "good nights," and all leave, benefited in more ways than one. Friday nights they have prayer-meeting, which is well attended and much interest is shown in it. Sunday nights they have a Bible story or a short talk on some other subject; this, mixed in with the singing, they like very much. At one of their meetings considerable anxiety was felt as to who should lead the singing, their teachers not being experts in that line; this anxiety was pleasantly removed when one of the boys boldly led off, followed in a good chorus by the others. The singing at most of their meetings is led by one of the boys or girls. The girls and the new boys have object lessons for an hour four days in the week.

WINS A PRIZE

The untutored Indian is anything but a graceful walker. Take off his moccasins and put shoes on him, and he does not know how to use his feet. When the boys and girls are first brought here it is curious to see in what a bungling way they go up and down stairs, throwing their feet in all sorts of directions as if they had no control over them. In marching out of the dining-room they excel in *not* keeping step to the music. They will either take two steps while the others take one, or *vice versa*. Yet after a few months' training quite an apparent change is made. They hold themselves more erect, step firmer and more surely.

One of the chief features of an entertainment given in Virginia Hall recently, was a jumping match and a promenade, with a prize for the six most graceful couples. The Indians did not succeed very well at raising themselves three or four feet from the ground. They entered the walking match, with twenty five or thirty other couples, with more determination. After all had gracefully moved around the room to the tune of "Grant's Grand March," came the decision of the judges, and all were surprised and gratified at the announcement that gave Mr. Alexander Peters[10] and Miss Mary Goulet,[11] both Indians, the fourth prize. They walked politely up to the stand and received their prize amid the cheers of the colored and Indian students.

B. T. W.

Southern Workman, 9 (Sept. 1880), 93.

[1] In September, 1880, BTW succeeded J. C. Robbins as dormitory supervisor of "The Wigwam," the Indian men's dormitory, and continued Robbins's monthly column on "Incidents of Indian Life at Hampton" in the *Southern Workman.* The column appeared throughout the 1880-81 academic year, with the exception of the November issue. BTW's duties at "The Wigwam" went far beyond the keeping of order. By precept, example, and daily inspections, he had the responsibility of inculcating in the Indian youths the "ways of civilization" and, more precisely, the mixture of Puritan ethic and social-service ideals that characterized all of the teaching at Hampton Institute.

[2] Frank Yellowbird, a Sioux from the Dakota Territory, was nineteen when he entered Hampton in 1878. He remained until 1881, learning the trades of wheelwright and blacksmith. He returned home to farm and was married in 1883, a year before his death of blood poisoning.

[3] Cora M. Folsom, Hampton teacher and nurse, coordinated the school's Indian work almost from the beginning. She handled all correspondence with the Indian graduates, visited most of them in their homes to report on their progress, and established an Indian museum. She retired in 1922 and died in 1943 at the age of eighty-eight.

[4] Sarah Walker, a Gros Ventre, first came to Hampton from the Dakota Territory at the age of twelve in 1878. She attended Hampton from 1878 to 1884 and from 1885 to 1887. She returned home to teach, initially in a school supported by Boston Unitarians.

[5] Josephine Malnourie, as her name was spelled in the Hampton school records, was a Gros Ventre from the Dakota Territory. She entered Hampton at the age

of eighteen in 1878 and left in 1881. After her husband died she devoted her time to educating her four children.

⁶ Ecorruptahah, a twenty-year-old Mandan from the Dakota Territory, died of tuberculosis at Hampton on June 28, 1880.

⁷ White Breast was a Mandan, probably from the same tribe as his sick friend Ecorruptahah. He returned home in 1880 and worked as a carpenter until his early death in 1888. White Breast's health was poor while at Hampton due, according to Hampton records, to the fact that he "had been through the ordeal of the sun-dance. . . ." (*Twenty-two Years Work*, 332.)

⁸ Robert H. Hamilton, held in slavery both in Louisiana and in Mississippi, fled to Philadelphia during the Civil War. Possessing an excellent voice, he earned enough from his singing to subsidize his education until he entered Hampton in 1872. There he was a member of the Hampton Singers. After graduating in 1877, he taught for a year and a half at Butler School and also learned the tailoring trade. Returning to Hampton, he headed the industrial department, led the choir, and taught vocal music. His primary interest centered in preserving plantation songs. Leaving Hampton in 1886, he taught briefly at Norfolk Mission College before taking charge of music instruction at Tuskegee in 1887. While in the North on business for Tuskegee, he died on Mar. 27, 1895, at Dobbs Ferry, N.Y.

⁹ John J. Gravatt served as rector of St. John's Episcopal Church in Hampton (1876-93) before accepting a parish in Richmond. As many of the Hampton Indian students were Episcopalian, Gravatt arranged special services for them at St. John's twice a week, as well as holding Bible classes for advanced students. He also made eight trips to the Dakota Territory, accompanying Indian graduates to their homes and returning to Hampton with new students from the reservations. For several summers Gravatt served as chaplain of Hampton. He died in Richmond on Mar. 14, 1925.

¹⁰ Alexander Peters, a Menominee from Wisconsin, was twenty years of age when he entered Hampton in 1879. He remained until 1883 and received further training as a blacksmith at Haskell Institute, Lawrence, Kan., before returning home to engage in farming.

¹¹ Mary Goulet was a Sioux from the Dakota Territory. Entering Hampton in 1879 at the age of fourteen, she remained until 1884, then returned home, married, and settled on a farm.

An Article in the *Southern Workman*

[Hampton, Va., October 1880]

INCIDENTS OF INDIAN LIFE AT HAMPTON

MAGNANIMITY OF THE NEGRO TOWARD THE INDIAN

The magnanimous spirit shown by the colored students toward the Indians at this Institution has been, to say the least, something worthy of praise.

The introduction of fifty or sixty Indians here from the woods, among two hundred and fifty colored students was an experiment to be carefully watched. The Negro has shown the same generous spirit toward the Indian as he has toward all races. I think the true test of civilization in any race, is shown by the desire of that race to assist those whose position is more unfortunate than theirs. I do not mean to say that the Negro is thoroughly civilized, but I do mean to say that it reflects much credit on his civilization to see him, while he himself is yet struggling for a place among civilized races, reaching out his hand to assist a less fortunate race. It shows that though he himself was oppressed, he has become enough enlightened to rise above mere race prejudices in doing his duty toward other men.

I think that the treatment the Indians have received at this Institution at the hands of the colored students is quite a rebuke to many white Institutions both North and South, especially such veneered institutions as West Point, where the sons of the so called civilized parents refuse to associate with a colored boy.[1]

It is not difficult to imagine the result had fifty or sixty Indian or *colored* students been ushered all at once into one of the average white institutions of this country.

Many instances could be given to show that the general feeling toward the Indian is of the best kind.

It was gratifying when visiting one of the debating clubs last winter to see that the colored students had elected an Indian as secretary. Many of the colored students have volunteered to take them as room mates that they might in that way teach them English. When an Indian girl leaves this school she receives as many warm hand shakes as any other student, and her departure is as much regretted by the colored girls as if she was one of their own color.

It seems a little strange, yet it is a fact, that it was only a few Sundays ago that an Indian and a colored student went calling together on lady friends in Hampton. The colored student told me that his manners were excellent and that he liked to call with him.

The introduction of the Indian here will at least show that the colored man has learned enough to know that it is his duty to help the unfortunate wherever he finds them, whether clothed in black, white, or red skins.

GENERAL IMPROVEMENT

As the Indians are watched from month to month a general improvement is apparent. They begin to take more interest in work as they see that it is only meant to benefit them.

There is an increasing desire to learn trades. Those who are learning are doing well, only a few have to be told to go to work in the morning. The teacher in charge of the squads at Shellbanks[2] reports that they do better work every day. They are growing more careful in their dress. There was never any great trouble in getting them to wear proper outside clothing. Many of them are a good while learning that their under garments must be kept clean and frequently changed. Some of them have made great improvement in this particular while others would rather go without under clothing and spend their money for trifles, if they are not watched. With their long hair once off no more trouble is experienced, they voluntarily keep their own hair cut nicely. One or two of them act as barbers to the others. I have noticed recently that some of them are beginning to shave — a strange thing for an Indian.

The majority of them take great pride in keeping neat rooms, floors are scrubbed every two weeks and in some cases every week; pictures and other ornaments are tastefully hung around the room. To enter some of their rooms one would not think he was in a student's room.

A higher sense of honesty is gradually being spread among them. Cases of dishonesty are gradually decreasing as they begin to understand what it is to be honest.

A general improvement in their manners is noticeable. A "good morning" and a "good evening" are taking the place of a low grunt. The broad, gruff "no" and "yes" are being exchanged for a polite "no sir" and "yes sir."

The following extracts are made from two boys' letters written to their friends telling them what they are doing here: "I am doing well here at this time and I am glad to tell you how I learn. When I came here I was very glad to go to school in morning and afternoon I work. Now I want to do this way alway and when I go back home I want to teach the other Indian People. That way I think and try hard and study English words but English word very hard words, but I try always and now I know some English word, and I want to know more English word, when first I came here I don't know any English word, but I try hard and study hard, and now I know some, and when I go back home I will tell the other Indian people because our Indians don't know how to live good."

Another writes:

"I thought I would write to tell you how I got along here. Indian boys and girls getting along very well and they learn English and great many other things since they came here, some work on the farm and some work in the shop and some work in the Sawmill. Before I came here I did not know nothing and I expect to go home in three years and if I can Teach the Indians at my home I will try. I will be very glad to teach them if I can, I can not say that I will teach them but I say I will try to and I expect to do some kind of Business when I get *home*."

GIRLS

One of the ladies who assists in taking care of the girls speaks of them as follows:

"When school was in session our Indian girls numbered twenty-one; but when the time came for all to put aside their books for a while, eight of them bade their friends good-by, not to return to their homes nor spend the summer with their friends as many of the teachers and colored students do: they left to spend their vacation North as helpers in strange families.

"Soon after the departure of the eight girls, three of the remaining ones were sent to their Western homes. Since then two bright girls, Julia St. Cyr[3] and Sophia Little Bear,[4] from the Industrial School in Nebraska, have been added. Both of them can speak the English language very readily. The older one, Julia St. Cyr, was organist in the Industrial School until she came here. No Indian girl has ever been able to enter the Preparatory class; but Julia, I think, can enter the Junior class.

"As soon as possible after the close of school the girls had their summer work assigned them. Two were made assistant cooks, one a waitress and the others helpers in the students' diningroom. They do their work comparatively well, and are learning rapidly the many little things necessary to good house keeping.

"Monday, Tuesday and Wednesday mornings all the girls and the last three boys that came have had object lessons given them from nine to ten o'clock. It was thought best that they should be kept in school only one hour as the weather was so very warm. Thursdays and Fridays are their washing and ironing days.

"Some of the girls show a good deal of taste in arranging things and are very particular how they carry themselves. Any allusion to their former condition throws a gloom over their feelings. They do not like to be questioned at all by strangers.

"There have been a great many excursionists here this summer and of course all of them had to see the Indians. At first the girls did not mind them very much; but they came in such bodies, crowded around them in such numbers and asked so many absurd questions that they soon got tired and would hide when they heard them coming. When these people succeeded in hemming in a poor girl they would begin to ask such questions as these: 'What is your name!' 'Are you wild?' 'Can you speak English?' 'Do you live in a house at home?'

"One day when a crowd got around one of the girls, she thought she would let them see how they would feel in her position. So when they began, Are you wild? she said, 'yes, very wild; are you wild?' Another time when she was asked if she could speak English, she replied, 'No I can not speak a word of English.' "

Our Indian girls are doing well in their Northern homes. In a few weeks they will return to resume their studies. There is no doubt but that, when they get back, those who have remained will feel their deficiencies and exert themselves to do as well as their friends.

The following is a letter written by little Sarah Walker in her summer home in Massachusetts.

"Pittsfield, Mass., August, 1880

"*Dear Mrs.* ——: I will answer your letter now I don't know why I didnt answer your letter before I want go back to Hampton and go to school. I am not home sick now I have very nice time over here. I want to see you all very much I am glad that the girls have been well. Are they any more Indian girls gone home? I hope my sister will come, pleas give my love to Annie Lyman[5] and Mary Hinman.[6] O Mrs —— I very nice time picnic all the boys and girls came there but Kawhat[7] and George Bush Otter[8] did not come. I was very glad to see all the boys and girls. I thank you very much for the stamps that you give me. Carrie[9] and I we go to church every sunday and also to sunday-school. I wash the dishes every day and sweep the kitchen and do my washing and ironing, Mrs. Foot, give me a nice dress. your friend,

"Sarah Walker"

Reading Room

A reading room has recently been opened in the boys' quarters. Most of the leading newspapers in English, and all the papers printed in their language are kept here for them. The papers are assorted and nicely arranged every morning by one of the boys. One seldom enters the room without finding some of the boys with a paper. As they get more enlightened their desire for general reading is increased. They have a special fondness for papers printed in their own language.

In School

The first of September brought the close of vacation for the Indians who spent their vacation here. There are few students who have done more faithful and willing work this summer than these Indians. It has fitted them for good study during the next term. They were anxious to get in school. They say that their three years here are shortening very fast and they want to get all they can while here.

For the month of September, they were all taught by one teacher, and it was quite a question how one could teach twenty-five or thirty Indians of different grades. On visiting the recitation room I saw that this problem had been pleasantly solved. When I first entered I heard such a buzz of voices that I thought there must be disorder in the room. Looking around I found that the teacher had divided them into four or five divisions with an Indian teacher for each division. I don't know when I have seen more lively work being done in a school room.

The teachers did not seem in the least embarrassed by being visited. One of the girls was going over the multiplication table with her class; while some of the other classes were going over the capitals of the middle states. The teachers seemed very proud of their positions and tried to assume the air of veterans. The scholars seemed equally proud and much interested in being taught by one of their own number. When they had gone over their lessons in this way several times their teacher had the teachers and all recite before him. He said their recitations generally showed that the work of his subordinates had been well done. They were much elated when their teacher told them that they were having a normal school.

My first impression of Indians as school teachers was a very pleasant one.

B. T. W.

Southern Workman, 9 (Oct. 1880), 103.

[1] Of the twelve black men appointed to West Point between 1870 and 1886, only three graduated. Henry O. Flipper, appointed in 1873 and the first black graduate, reported in his autobiography (1878) that he was avoided by virtually all white cadets at West Point.

[2] Shellbanks Industrial Home, located on Hampton Institute's Hemenway farm about five miles from campus.

[3] Julia St. Cyr, a fifteen-year-old half-blood Winnebago, attended Hampton from 1880 to 1885 and returned home to Nebraska to teach.

[4] Sophia Little Bear was a Nebraska Winnebago, age twelve, who attended Hampton from 1880 to 1885; she later married an Indian who had attended government school.

[5] Annie Lyman, a Sioux from the Dakota Territory and daughter of an army officer, entered Hampton in 1879 at the age of sixteen and remained until 1885. She returned home to marry a farmer.

[6] Mary Hinman, a Sioux from the Dakota Territory, was twelve when she entered Hampton in 1879. She left in 1885. After an unfortunate marriage, she died the following year.

[7] Kawhat, brother of White Breast, changed his name to Thomas Suckley. A Mandan from the Dakota Territory, he was twelve when he entered Hampton in 1878. He remained at Hampton until 1881 and continued his education at Ft. Stevenson, N.D., Genoa, Nebr., and Carlisle, Pa.

[8] George Bushotter (1860-92) made a substantial contribution to the ethnography of the Dakota Indians. Bushotter was a Dakota whose mother belonged to the Teton tribe and whose father belonged to the Yankton tribe. As a baby Bushotter narrowly escaped an accidental death, and in consequence of this his father named him Oteri, meaning "difficult," to characterize his life. Bushotter was sent to Hampton and there his name was recorded as George Bush, Oteri; afterward he became known as George Bushotter. He attended Hampton from 1878 to 1881 and from 1883 to 1885. He is also reported to have studied for a time at the Episcopal Theological Seminary in Alexandria, Va. In March 1887 he was employed by the Smithsonian Institution's Bureau of American Ethnology as an assistant to Rev. James Owen Dorsey (1848-95), an ethnologist studying the Siouan Indian language family, of which Dakota is a part. Under Dorsey's direction Bushotter wrote in Dakota some 287 texts (over 2,000 manuscript pages), consisting of folk tales, accounts of social life, customs, and games, and an autobiography describing his life prior to entering Hampton.

During the summers Dorsey worked in Hedgesville, W.Va., to avoid the humid Washington climate. There Bushotter met and married Elvina Hull. The couple traveled to Dakota for a brief period, during which Bushotter was employed as a teacher to Dakota Indian children. Forced to return to Hedgesville due to poor health, he practiced the wood carving he had learned at Hampton, carving the pews for a local church and doing much ornamental work. He was a popular local figure, known for his early-morning jogging around the township in Indian moccasins and for his ability with the bow and arrow. On his death of tuberculosis in 1892, an obituary in the Martinsburg *Independent* reported that during his five years' residence in Hedgesville, Bushotter "won many friends by his genial and social disposition." His wife lived on until 1946.

After Dorsey's death other scholars became interested in Bushotter's texts. John R. Swanton, of the Bureau of American Ethnology, attempted to prepare them for publication in 1909. He did not complete the work, and the texts were sent to the anthropologist Franz Boas, of Columbia University. Boas and various of his students worked with them. In the 1930s Ella Deloria, a Dakota, aunt of author Vine Deloria, Jr., revised the texts under Boas's direction, and rewrote them phonetically, with interlineal and free English translations. These revised texts were never published, and are deposited in the American Philosophical Society Library in Philadelphia. The original texts are in the National Anthropological Archives at the Smithsonian. (Interview with Raymond DeMallie, Jr., doctoral candidate in anthropology, University of Chicago, Mar. 14, 1971.)

9 Carrie Anderson, a Sioux from the Dakota Territory, was twelve when she entered Hampton in 1878. Remaining until 1881, she continued school at Genoa, Nebr. She then returned home, married, and with her husband ran a prosperous farm.

An Article in the *Southern Workman*

[Hampton, Va., November 1880]

"THE PLUCKY CLASS"

The school has been divided heretofore into four classes, known as the Preparatory, Junior, Middle, and Senior classes, but, last term another was added, known at first as the Night class, but which won from the Vice Principal[1] during the term, the title of "The Plucky Class."

To work from seven o'clock in the morning till six o'clock at night, and then study from seven o'clock till nine or half past nine, is an undertaking that few young men would be willing to stick to through all the seasons of the year. Yet this is just what thirty-five young men at Hampton have done for the past year. All of them came here with no capital but their determination to get an education, and hands that could work for it.

It was thought at first that it would be hard to keep them awake, but a few jokes, their own earnestness, and many interesting questions reduced this supposed obstacle to nothing. It was a rare thing to find one asleep. Their hard work in the day seemed to give them an appetite for study at night. They studied and recited the same night. They digested a good deal of what they studied at night, while at work in the day. Passing by them at work, one could almost always hear them discussing some point in grammar or some problem in arithmetic. They would generally have a number of questions to ask at night, which they had failed to agree upon or to understand during the day. One was noticed to carry a broken piece of slate about with him on which he could work examples while the wheel-barrow of dirt he had loaded, was being emptied. Their books were in their hands at every spare moment. No teacher ever had a more interesting class.

With all their zeal for study, they made excellent workers, and the superintendent of the Industrial works, by whom most of them were employed, showed his appreciation of their services by making each one a nice present at the end of the year.

For such study to amount to anything, it must, of course, be very systematic. The young men seemed to understand this, for their attendance was remarkably regular, some I think, not missing more than two nights in the year. They were willing to shut themselves out from the world awhile for an education. Whether the weather was good or bad, their attendance and earnestness were the same. They not only did well during the coldest winter months, but through the months of July and August, up to the middle of September, their zeal did not abate in the least.

The first week in October, they entered the day-school, seven passing an examination for the Middle class, the others for the Junior Class. It is doubtful if Hampton teachers ever received more glad and earnest faces into their classes.

These young men not only enter school with enough knowledge to pay them for this year's work, but they have saved an average of seventy dollars apiece, after buying their clothes. This amount, with their earnings during school and in vacation, will keep them in school two years. Thus, seven have saved enough in one year to graduate them at the institution, and the others enough to take them into their senior year.

What these have done, others can do. With such privileges offered to our young men, poverty can no longer be pleaded as an excuse for ignorance. There are thousands of young men all over this country who could, if they would sacrifice a few evenings' pleasure for a while, open the door to a respectable education. How much better this would be than to be compelled by ignorance to spend the remainder of their lives as the lowest kind of servants! They would not then go through the world as mere pretenders to an education, as so many do, nor would they then feel the necessity of spending all their money for fine clothes with which they vainly hope to hide the poverty of the inner man.

Give a man a chance to work out his own education, and, as a general thing, you do far more for him than you would by paying his way in school for three or four years. A man who is not willing to work for his education will do nothing with it after he gets it.

It is safe to predict for the members of the Night class as bright a future, and as good work after their graduation, as that of any graduates who have left this school, and if they continue in the future to show the same spirit and earnestness that they have here in their work and studies, they will continue to bear the title — "Members of the Plucky Class."

B. T. W.

Southern Workman, 9 (Nov. 1880), 112.

¹ James Fowle Baldwin Marshall.

An Article in the *Southern Workman*

[Hampton, Va., December 1880]

INCIDENTS OF INDIAN LIFE AT HAMPTON

All at home and at their studies. The fifteenth of October brought the Indian boys and girls back, who spent their vacation in Massachusetts,¹ and a happy set they were. Just the capers each one cut, or the many ways that they found to show their joy at being at home again would be hard to describe. They expressed it in Indian, in English and by signs. One little fellow spoke for all, when he said; "I glad to go and glad to come." It took them several days to get cooled down. The warmth with which they remember and greet their friends is one cheerful sign for the future.

Compare this arrival with their arrival here two years ago. How different their dress, their walk, their language, their thoughts, their actions, their intentions — how different their ideas of the white man; and how different also are the ideas of the white man, with whom they have come in contact, toward them. Will another two years produce as great a change in as many more Indians? We hope so. Will another two years cause as many whites to change their minds in regard to the Indian? (We believe the Indian will make still more change.) Surely if the *Indian* can be converted from his wrong ideas, the white man ought to be from his. If the white man changes his mind he can change the Indian. If the Indian continues to change his mind, he will change the white man's. The future will tell which will have the honor of changing the other.

Wherever the Indians went in the North, they made favorable impressions. Their employers say they gave satisfaction in their work. The Indians got many ideas of the white man's civilization, which they will never forget. Many warm friendships were formed between employer and employee, as the many letters since exchanged, testify. These youths will teach their people, on their return, that the white man is not their sworn enemy.

The improvement made in English was very marked. One had so improved, that when asked what language he spoke, replied, "I speak English."

A Day in the Country

After five days of study and work, it is thought a good plan for their health, to let them spend Saturdays in the country. The Indians, accustomed all their lives to the open air, the chase, the war dance, athletic sports and a free and easy life in general, can not be cut off from all this too abruptly, without serious injury to their health. The boys made their first excursion, for this term, a few Saturdays ago, about eleven o'clock, arriving at a suitable place for pitching tent — a long, beautiful beach on the Chesapeake Bay, — dinner was hastily cooked, the dinner call sounded, and, in a moment every man was at his post, ready for duty. Appetites were good, and they ate till — till there was no more. The boys make excellent cooks, and need little teaching in getting an out-door dinner. They engaged in all kinds of games: "prisoners' base," "leap frog," ball, jumping and racing, till all were tired and glad to start for home. Some of the older boys tried to start a war-dance but had some trouble in making it go, most of them being inclined to get above that sort of amusement now. Some, when asked to join, replied, "I no know how now, used to know, but forgot," others would say "war-dance no good." One was finally started, the boys were very shy about it, and it lacked much of the spirit and earnestness that usually characterize such performances. The boys have bought themselves a foot-ball, which will add much to the enjoyment of the next trip. The girls spent the next Saturday in the country, and enjoyed themselves as well as the boys.

Study Hour

To attend study hour like the colored students, and have a big pile of school books, has been one of the great desires of the Indians. This they have not been permitted to do heretofore, to any great extent, as most of their teaching has been by objects.

When the night for the first study hour came, it was quite amusing to see all crowding to the room with arms full of books, of all sizes and descriptions.

As their eyes begin to get opened they begin to realize that they are being treated as little children, both as to studies and discipline, and from this comes their desire to be placed on a footing with others as soon as possible.

It will take some time still to teach them how to use their text books to good advantage.

Trying to Improve Affairs at Their Homes

The following piece of sensible advice, written by a Shawnee boy twenty years of age, in the Middle Class here, to his tribe, is an indication of what some at least of the Indians will try to do for their people, when they return home. He was elected one of the chiefs of his tribe just before coming here.

It was by accident that I saw this letter before it was mailed, and it is fair to presume that others containing the same kind of advice have been sent. The following is an exact copy:

Normal School   Hampton Va. Oct 27, 1880
To the Chiefs, Headmen and others of Shawnee Nation, Shawnee Town I.T.

Sirs: I heard some way that stealing and introduction of liquor into the Territory are still going on more or less; and that you are trying to anticipate it by making laws and regulations as a protection for our good citizens at Shawnee Town.

If such is the case you are doing right.

I am going to say a few words to our fellow men, which I hope will encourage you also in that matter above named; but you must not expect to hear a good *square talk* from me for I am but a youth yet, and not able. I am going to say that we all know that stealing, drinking and gambling are wrong. When a man begins to practice in these things at the same time he begins to go down until he finds himself at the bottom of a pit-fall where no man is able to pull him out;

every one despises him; every one's eye is upon him; therefore in order
to avoid these mean low ways of life, we must encourage our fellowmen to labor. We know that it is the only way to get along, and that
the red men would have to do like white men; that is, to go to work
and raise such things we shall live upon, and raise our families; raise
corn, wheat and stock, &c. Give our children up to be educated in this
way, that when they should grow up to be men and women, they
would be respected by good white people, and become wise and good.
I myself saw the evils of gambling, stealing and drinking, and those
who have left off these bad ways, among our people, are now doing
well. They not only have plenty to do them now for the present, but
they look forward to be provided with plenty to sustain them in their
old age, when they are unable longer to labor, and therefore, they
work hard now. My dear friends, this is the course we had better all
pursue in future, and then the white people would look upon us as
they do on their own people, and respect us; but as it is, they do not,
for they look upon the thief and drunkard with a scornful eye, and
upon him who breaks his promise with contempt, and hate him.

My friends, it is now high time that we should try and do something
for ourselves. I mean in this, that we should frame such laws and
regulations as to protect our good citizens, and not allow those who
do not work to impose on us. When I use to go to school there in
Shawnee Mission, strangers often visited the Mission, and these people
would ask me what kind of laws the Shawnees had — the answer was,
none; they would ask if they had any chiefs, and who was their head
chief, the answer was, that they had, and that John Esparnia was
their head chief.

The reply generally was — "Well he is a good chief." Now you
may say you have chiefs, I ask you what we have chiefs for? I, for
my part, do not know. I will try and explain. We have chiefs to do
the nation's business. You have sent them to work for you, but you
never give them anything to work with. You might as well send them
to the field to hoe your corn without hoes. Suppose you were to do
that, how could you expect them to hoe your corn? But still you
would turn around and grumble at them for not doing your work.
Just so now, are our chiefs situated; we ask them to attend to our
business, and have given them no authority to do it, and we have
turned on them and complained because our business is not attended
to, and because we do not stop this bad way, we are not getting along.
If one man owes another anything and won't pay him, how is the
creditor to get his money? One may say to him, go to the chiefs and
they will assist you. Now let me ask you, what power have the chiefs

to do anything for him. I answer none at all. This is just like sending out to work and nothing to work with. Now, let us make laws and give our chiefs some authority to work, and they can work; they will make a good crop for the nation.

I hope they will all agree (if they [have] not agreed already) to go to work and make laws for our government, and authorize the chiefs to put these laws in force, so all of us may be protected in possession of our property and in our person. This is my wish, but of course, is nothing more in my part than a wish.

I am, sirs, yours respectfully,

Thomas J. Wildcat[2]

EDITING AND PRINTING

The readers of the "WORKMAN" will be interested to know that the matter contained in the Indian Column of the page called the Hampton Students' Own is gotten up exclusively by the Indians. Most of the writing is done by a Pawnee boy,[3] who also sets the type for their column. He takes a great deal of interest in it. He has a friend at Carlisle learning the same trade, both are trying to make all the progress they can, so that they can carry on the business together when they return home. At present, we have only two boys working in the printing office; there are others who want to learn the trade, but the confinement is not thought good for their health.

PREPARING FOR HOME

As the Indians begin to realize that their stay here is now very short, they take hold of their studies and work with more interest.

Once it was a task to get them to go to work promptly; now they give almost no trouble, many going to work before the time. Saturday is given to them as a holiday, but some prefer to spend a good part of it in improving themselves in their trades.

The following application will speak for itself:

Indian Cottage, Oct. 30, 1880

Gen. Armstrong: as I told James Murrie that I want to work all the time, that is to work every day except Sundays, and go to night-school as I am advanced in Primary books, I want to learn how to be a good farmer like Mr. Cock, so when I go home I can just go right ahead and work on a place which I will pick out for myself, and also teach my people how to be farmers, and besides, I want to be with the colored boys and talk with them in English, to go to school with them; this way I think I can learn fast, both in books and work.

Jonathan Heustice[4]

Another one, who returned to his Dakota home last summer, has the following account given of him, by a white lady, in a card to an officer of the school:

Fort Berthold, Oct. 29, 1880

Lieutenant R.,[5] I was lately enquireing about Mr. White Breast. He has arrived here and we are all delighted with his great improvement. He is working to day and seems to desire to be a *man.*

I have just heard of a resolution that the boys made while on their way from Massachusetts, to the effect that they were going to try to obey every school law this term, and make all the progress possible in every thing. So far they seem to be holding out well; for the transgressions have been few.

B. T. W.

Southern Workman, 9 (Dec. 1880), 125.

[1] In the summer of 1880, twenty-five of Hampton's Indian students were sent to farms in the Berkshire Mountains of Massachusetts to learn practical agriculture. The *Southern Workman* noted that "they will be scattered on neighboring farms, where they will share the home life and be kindly cared for, doing light work for their board, and under the general supervision of Mr. Alexander B. Hyde of Lee, one of the school's trustees. This was proved last summer to be a very valuable part of the year's experience, invigorating their health, improving their English, and broadening their outlook." (*Southern Workman,* 9 [July 1880], 77.)

[2] Thomas Wildcat Alford, a Shawnee, the great-grandson of Tecumseh, was born in the Indian Territory in 1860. Sent to a mission school at the age of twelve, he learned enough English to be employed as an interpreter at the Shawnee trading post. In 1879 he went to Hampton on a scholarship arranged by a local missionary and paid for by the Philadelphia Society of Friends. The Hampton philosophy greatly affected him and he spent the rest of his life attemping to change his fellow Shawnee to the white man's ways. He returned to his home in 1882 and and in 1883 became principal of the government boarding school for the Shawnee, which he organized along the Hampton lines. Later he served at various times as a land surveyor, interpreter, and clerk in the Indian bureau and as head of the Business Committee of the Shawnee. In effect, he became a kind of intermediary between the Shawnee and the white man. He sought to preserve Indian rights against the avaricious Oklahoma "sooners." At the same time he tried to modify Shawnee customs so that they could play a more positive role in American life. A sharp businessman, Alford took advantage of the Oklahoma land rush and his position as a land surveyor to acquire substantial landholdings. With the help of Florence Drake, Alford published an autobiography, *Civilization* (1936).

[3] James R. Murie (1862-1921). Murie, whose Indian name was Le-taw-cuts-

je-haw-le or Young Eagle, was perhaps Hampton's most distinguished Indian graduate. A full-blooded Pawnee born at the Pawnee agency, Indian Territory, Murie came to Hampton in 1878. He had previously attended school for one year and knew some English. While at Hampton he quickly showed his academic aptitude. He worked in the printing office and edited the column "From the Indians" for the *Southern Workman.* Graduating in the class of 1883, he returned to his home, where he taught for a year at the agency boarding school. In 1884 he took twenty-one of his students to the newly opened Haskell Institute in Kansas, where he remained for two years as assistant disciplinarian and drillmaster. Promised an appointment as a teacher in the Pawnee school by the U.S. Commissioner of Indian Affairs, he returned home, but the local Indian agent claimed that he had never received any instructions and refused to give Murie the job. Disappointed, he began a farm on a twelve-acre plot of land he had claimed near the Arkansas River. In the tradition of his alma mater, however, he continued to consider it his duty to help his people "in every way I can, whether it is an Indian man with his machine, or an Indian woman with her sewing machine, or telling my people the stories of Christ, for I want them to put their superstitious ideas aside, and believe in the white man's Great Spirit." (*Twenty-two Years Work,* 197-98.)

While pressing for such change, Murie apparently began to appreciate his own culture more fully and became interested in the ancient traditions, mythology, and songs of the Pawnee, a project that soon attracted the interest of several American ethnologists. In 1894 he collaborated with Alice C. Fletcher on a study called "The Hako: A Pawnee Ceremony," which was published in 1901 by the U.S. Bureau of American Ethnology. Fletcher's preface to the volume praised Murie's field work: "How difficult his undertaking has been, and still is, can only be appreciated by those who have attempted to accomplish a similar work. His patience, tact, and unfailing courtesy and kindness have soothed the prejudice and allayed the fears of the old men who hold fast to the faith of their fathers and are the repositories of all that remains of the ancient rites of the tribe" (p. 14). With George Amos Dorsey, Murie wrote *Traditions of the Skidi Pawnee* (1904) and *The Pawnee Mythology* (1906). He was at various times employed by the Field Museum of Natural History in Chicago and by the U.S. Bureau of American Ethnology to do research work on the Pawnee. In 1914 his study, "Pawnee Indian Societies," was published in the Anthropological Papers of the American Museum of Natural History. Murie also wrote a study of more than 2,000 pages, "Ceremonies of the Pawnee," that has never been published.

During his career as an ethnologist, Murie maintained his home in Pawnee, Okla., and worked as a cashier for a local bank. In 1915 he was elected president of the Indian Farmers' Institute in Pawnee.

[4] Jonathan Heustice, a Pawnee, attended Hampton from 1879 to 1881 and traveled for several years with "Texas Charlie's Indian Show" before settling down as a farmer.

[5] Henry Romeyn was a regular-army first lieutenant assigned to command of the cadets at Hampton Institute from 1878 to 1881. Listed as forty-seven years old in the 1880 census, Romeyn had joined the Army in 1862 as a corporal and risen to the rank of brevet major by the end of the Civil War. For a time he was an officer of the Fourteenth U.S. Colored Troops. After the war Romeyn took part in the Indian campaigns. His services against the Nez Percé in the battle of Bear Paw Mountain, Mont., in 1877, earned him a Medal of Honor, issued in 1894, and a severe wound, probably resulting in his temporary assignment to Hampton. He retired from the Army in 1897.

Edward Sugg to George Henry Corliss,[1]
with BTW's Endorsement

Hampton, Va., Jan. 12, 1881

Dear friend: This is the story of my life. My father and mother was slave. I was born Sept. 1852, and when I became two years of age, my mother was carred to Halifax N.C. and sold at auction. A man bought her by the mame of Geo. C. Sugg,[2] M.D. and he carred to his plantation, a bout telve miles from Tarboro, N.C. and I stade with her two or three years, and I was taking from her and carred to his resident to nurse, I stad there a year, and then I was carred back to his plantation; My father and mother are bouth dead! My father was a carpenter, he fell from the tope of a house, and his head fell in a stage pole hole and broke his neck. That happen June, or July the year, 1852. And after that my mother married again: And bout one or two years later, then the great strugel came on hand. My mother and her husbon was sold, from each-orther and she married a gain, and after Leee surrended my step-father would not send me to school; he had me at work all the time tell I be came at age. I went to school six months be fore I came to this Institution. A graduate from this Institution told me a bout this Institution and advised me to come to it. He told me that this Institution was the best Institution that he knew of, He told me that I could come here and pay one half in cash, and work the orther half-out. I came hear, Jan. 20, 1879. and entid the prepartory class. and during the vacation I remaine here and work in the Engineer the partment. and by sodoing I be came interrested in the work and wanted to learn the traed. and Gen. S. C. A.[3] and Mr. J. B. H. G.[4] The Chieftain-engineer give me a chan to learn it by staying out of school two years and work at the trade. I had a good-time here vacation and during the vacation. I had one week for holiday, and I went home to see my peoples and I found theme well; I must confest the truth. I did not knew that the African race was so low in civilization, untilt I came to this Institution and went back home, in the guards of education they are suffing for the need of edcation there want teachers very bade now. Teachers are very scace at my home, which is Rich Square N.C. North Hampton Co. The principal occupation is farming! Som of the colored peoples in my nabor-hood if you talk to them a bout sending their childrens to school the will tell you that they are going to send them to the cotton patch and corn-field school. The say that they are not got the money to send their childrens to school like the white peoples are. My occupation are engineer at the saw-mill of this Institution. I try to learn all I can a bout it. I am going to the night school now, and I truly hope that I will be success as som of the night class did least year, som of them by hard studing mad the middle class. I myself expect to study hard to learn my lessons. I have a good teacher, Mr. B. T. W. he labors hard with his class. Dear friend. I can't express my thinks to you for paying my scholarshipe I intend to make good youth of my time with the helpe of god. My god blest you through all the jouney of your life, and the end of your last houre God will say com my good and faithful servant where was prepare for you from the foundation of the world. Yours Respectfully

Edward Sugg

[*Endorsement*]

Edward Sugg, the writer of this letter, is one of the students who works in the day and goes to night school in order that he may earn money to pay his board bills in day school next year. This is the second year that this young man has been working out earning money and at the same time learning the engineer's trade. He has learned very fast and is now in charge of the "Corliss Engine" here. His opportunities for schooling have been few. He is one of the most faithful and earnest in the night school. He will enter the day school next year with mon[e]y enough to pay his board bills for two or three years.[5] He is about twenty eight years of age.

B. T. Washington, teacher

ALS and AES   George H. Corliss Papers   RPB.

[1] George Henry Corliss (1816-81) launched his manufacturing career with the development of an improved machine for sewing boots. In 1848 he and two partners formed the corporation Corliss, Nightingale and Company to manufacture a steam engine incorporating a valve system that was revolutionary in its conservation of steam and fuel. As president of the firm, incorporated as the Corliss Engine Company in 1856, Corliss directed all business activity, including legal defense of patent rights. He served in the Rhode Island General Assembly (1868-70) and was a Republican presidential elector in 1876. In 1879 Corliss helped move Hampton's program beyond farming by donating a sixty-horsepower engine and boiler, a gift valued at $4,000. On BTW's first fund-raising tour in the Northeast for Tuskegee, following the 1881-82 school term, Corliss donated $10. He later became one of the school's most important contributors.

[2] George C. Sugg was listed in the census of 1860 for Edgecombe County, N.C.,

as a thirty-one-year-old white farmer, married with five children. Sugg owned real estate valued at $56,000 and personal property worth $36,000.

[3] Samuel Chapman Armstrong.

[4] John B. H. Goff, reported in the census of 1880 as a forty-year-old white man born in Massachusetts, married with one child.

[5] There is no record that Edward Sugg graduated.

An Article in the *Southern Workman*

[Hampton, Va., January 1881]

INCIDENTS OF INDIAN LIFE AT HAMPTON

A letter received recently from the U.S. commissioner of Indian affairs,[1] informs us that a gentleman[2] is now in the West, looking up more Indians to be educated at Hampton and Carlisle. These are to come from Arizona and New Mexico, and will probably reach here some time in January. As yet we have had no Indians from either of these territories, at this school. If a few representatives can be secured from these two territories, they will no doubt in a few months, cause a general interest in the matter of education to be awakened in those parts.

"Strike while the iron is hot," is an old adage that will apply very properly to the Indian question now. The Indians, throughout the greater part of the Western plain, are now beginning to see the importance of education. While a part of them have begun to make efforts in the right direction, is it not the most auspicious time to move the whole Indian race at once? With the boat once started from the sand bar, no force must be relaxed until she sails in the broad deep sea.

THE HEALTH QUESTION

A little experience with Indians will teach one that the trouble with their health comes not so much from a change of climate as from carelessness on their part. The Indians are slow to learn that when they adopt the white man's dress, they must also adopt his health laws. They must be taught that they can not wear two coats to-day, and to-morrow none, a dry shirt to-day, and to-morrow a wet one.

They appear to have an idea that their bodies are weather proof. Some will seemingly take as much delight in playing out of doors when the rain pours as when the sun shines. To get their feet wet and keep them so all day is a small matter. Few think of changing clothes after getting wet. They do not mind going all over the building and even out of doors in their naked feet. But a few minutes ago, I found a boy, already affected with a fearful cough, in the absence of a chair, sitting squarely down on a floor that had been scrubbed only about five minutes before. In summer it was their great delight to sleep in the open air with no covering but a *bare* skin.

A few nights ago, I made an inspection of the whole of the boys' building, about midnight, to see how far they observed the laws of health and neatness in their sleep. I found about half the forty-six boys fast asleep with their heads buried beneath two or three blankets. In many cases all ventilation was excluded from the room, making the air anything but healthy. It is a habit with them to cover up their heads when they sleep, if no other part of the body. Ask them about these practices and they will freely acknowledge that they are unwholesome. They do these things not because they do not care, but because the habit of carelessness about their bodies has grown upon them so that it is a hard task for them to reform. For a long time they will have to be carefully instructed, watched, and helped in regard to their health.

From the Girl's Quarters

"Since the return of the twenty-five Indians who went to Massachusetts, last summer, there has been a marked improvement in those who remained at Hampton. The former, being taken altogether from those who could not speak the English language to any extent, and scattered among people who spoke nothing else, made rapid improvement in the expression of their thoughts. Learning to speak the English language more correctly was not the only thing accomplished by these Indian girls. They have fallen out with their old ways of doing things. The hair must now be arranged becomingly, the colors that adorn their persons must correspond, there is a certain dignity exhibited in their carriage which rather encourages one. There is nothing that tends more to excite the ambition and draw out the best qualities of a race than the example of those who stand high in that race. The Massachusetts girls' ideas are the leading ideas among the girls. There is not one of them who would not gladly be a 'Massachusetts girl.'

"The afternoon sewing school is quite an interesting branch of the girls department. Every afternoon, at half past one o'clock, they must learn to make their own clothes, and other articles. Every evening but

Wednesday, the girls who have not entered the Preparatory Class meet to study their lessons for the next day.

"This is quite new to them now, but it is hoped that after a while it will prove a success. The latter part of Tuesday and Friday evenings is given to Bible studies."

THE TRAINING SHOP

The following report made by Mr. J. H. McDowell,[3] a thorough mechanic, in charge of the Indian Training shop, speaks well for the Indians:

"In complying with the request to furnish these columns with a brief statement of the progress of the Indian boys as mechanics, I wish to say before doing so that I came to the superintendency of the Indian work shop with no little prejudice against the race; a prejudice (as I believe is mostly the case) the out growth of ignorance of the Indian character, and which unfortunately has been and is too often entertained and acted upon almost to the extermination of the race.

"My views have been radically changed in my brief intercourse with the Hampton Indian students, for instead of finding them indolent, indifferent, intractable and without interest in acquiring mechanical knowledge, as I was led to believe would be the case, I find the reverse to be the fact. In my experience of more than twenty years as a practical mechanic, most of which has been spent either as foreman, superintendent, or master mechanic, and consequently with much to do with the instruction of boys, I have not found any, who, as a class, have learned more rapidly, been more eager to learn or more obedient to rules and regulations of the shops, than those at present under my charge. Carpenter work, tinsmithing, shoemaking and locksmithing are being done by them, that would be highly creditable to any race, even with more experience in these branches; while a knowledge of painting, glazing, blacksmithing and wheel-wrighting is being rapidly acquired by them.

"Taking into consideration their former mode of life, devoid as it has been of any system of labor, together with the fact of their limited knowledge of the English language in which their instructions are given, this progress is truly remarkable. I would not have it understood that there are no exceptions as to interest and industry in their respective branches, but will say that the exceptions are as few as will be found in the same number taken from any class. This, to me, seems an opening for an early solution of the vexed 'Indian Question' for if interest in and application to educational, agricultural, and mechanical pursuits can be created and fostered in the race, they then have taken the first step in 'White man's ways' which should and must inevitably lead to the rights and privileges of white men, thus placing them in a position to settle their difficulties without recourse to retaliation by force of arms which has been the case in the history of the past."

FARMING

What ever else the Indians may not know, they ought to know something of practical farming. A few days ago, one of the boys here told me of two Indians at his home who accumulated quite a sum of money, left the reservation, bought themselves nice farms and supplied them well. This new movement was closely watched by their fellow Indians. At the end of four years, their farms were total wrecks; and they returned discouraged to the government reservation, laughed at by the other Indians. The cause and effect of this failure are apparent.

Mere book learning without some knowledge of farming and trade will benefit the Indians little on their return to the West.

It is to meet this difficulty that Hampton's efforts are mainly directed. The rule here is that no matter what other business a boy learns, he must know something of farming. At present, the boys here are taught farming in classes of two or three and are kept under the eye of a teacher and made to understand each step as they go.

The following programme, kindly furnished by their farm teacher, Mr. Geo. J. Davis, will give an idea of what a class is taken through in a day:

"They begin with currying the horses, then watering, then cleaning stable, feeding for dinner. Then to the cow stable; cows are cleaned, and watered, cow stable cleaned, cow-feed prepared for dinner. They are then taken through the school room and taught the names and uses of the different kinds of tools. For instance a rake is taken and kept before them and they are questioned about it, till they understand that all tools made like it are called rakes and used for certain purposes. Wagons are greased, and they are taught the different kinds and parts of wagons. The carriage house is next taken and they are made to understand all about the different kinds of carriages. In the harness room next they are taught the names and uses of the different parts of the harness, beginning with the bridle, each part taken separately, the bit, throat latch, head band, reins &c., they are made to understand. They are told that the whole building is called a barn, then which the stable, stalls &c., are. They are shown how to cut and mix different kinds of food, and how to make beds for horses and cows. Harnessing and unharnessing horses is gone through with. At the proper season they will be taught about the cultivation of the ground. They are of course ignorant at first of the names and uses of tools &c."

Their teacher reports them as doing well and willing to learn.

B. T. W.

Southern Workman, 10 (Jan. 1881), 7.

[1] Rowland Ebenezer Trowbridge (1821-81), U.S. Commissioner of Indian Affairs from February 1880 until his death. He previously served in the U.S. House of Representatives from Michigan (1861-63, 1865-69).

[2] Sheldon Jackson (1834-1909), a Presbyterian minister and missionary, brought fourteen Indians from Arizona Territory to Hampton Institute in February 1881. A graduate of Union College and Princeton Theological Seminary, Jackson served for many years as a missionary to the western Indians from Minnesota and Iowa to Alaska. As a special U.S. agent he gathered and brought to Hampton and Carlisle young Indians of the Pueblo, Pima, Papago, and Apache tribes in New Mexico and Arizona. Spending most of his later years in Alaska, he organized there the first canoe mail service in 1883 and reindeer mail service in 1898. He introduced public schools to Alaska in 1885. His numerous books and official reports on Alaska form a valuable commentary on the region's social and ethnic history.

[3] J. H. McDowell served from 1880 to 1890 as head of the Indian training shops and technical school at Hampton Institute. In 1890 he moved to Tennessee to pursue a career in the building industry.

The Alabama Statute
Establishing Tuskegee Normal School[1]

[Montgomery, Ala., Feb. 10, 1881]

An Act to establish a Normal School for colored teachers at Tuskegee.

Section 1. *Be it enacted by the General Assembly of Alabama,* There shall be established, at Tuskegee, in this State, a normal school for the education of colored teachers. Pupils shall be admitted free of charge for tuition in the school, on giving an obligation in writing to teach in the free public schools in this State for two years after they become qualified. The school shall not be begun or continued with a

107

less number than twenty-five pupils, nor shall the school be taught for a less period than nine months in each year.

Sec. 2. *Be it further enacted,* There is appropriated out of the general school revenue, set apart to the colored children, the sum of two thousand dollars, annually, for the maintenance and support of the school; and the apportionment of the general fund for the colored race shall be made to the different counties of this State, after the deduction of the sum of two thousand dollars herein appropriated for the school at Tuskegee.

Sec. 3. *Be it further enacted,* The school shall be under the direction, control and supervision of a board of three commissioners, who shall consist of the following persons, to-wit: Thos. B. Dryer,[2] M. B. Swanson,[3] and Lewis Adams,[4] who may fill any vacancy that may occur in the board of commissioners. The commissioners shall elect one of their number chairman, and they shall report quarterly to the Superintendent of Education, how many pupils have been in attendance, what branches have been taught, and other facts of interest and importance appertaining to the school.

Sec. 4. *Be it further enacted,* The chairman of the board of commissioners shall give bond in double the amount of the appropriation of the school, for the legal and faithful application of the sum appropriated, the bond to be approved by the judge of probate of Macon county, and a certified copy thereof sent to the Superintendent of Education to be filed in his office.

Sec. 5. *Be it further enacted,* The chairman of the board of commissioners, after having given bond as hereinbefore provided, and the bond shall have been approved as herein provided, and a certified copy thereof filed in the office of Superintendent of Education, shall present to the Superintendent of Education a requisition for the amount herein appropriated; and the Superintendent of Education shall thereupon certify the amount of two thousand dollars to the State Auditor, who shall draw his warrant for the sum on the State Treasurer, payable to the chairman of the board of commissioners, for the maintenance and support of the normal school.

Approved February 10, 1881.

Acts of the General Assembly of Alabama Passed at the Session of 1880-81 (Montgomery, 1881), 395-96.

[1] Representative Arthur L. Brooks of Macon County, a member of the House Committee on Education, introduced House Bill 165 to appropriate state funds to

a colored state normal school at Tuskegee. The bill was strongly supported in the Alabama Senate by Wilbur F. Foster of Macon County. Foster had agreed in his campaign for the Senate in 1880 to sponsor a bill for a colored normal school in Tuskegee in return for black support in the election. The bill apparently elicited no challenge or even discussion in either house or in the press. Perhaps the bargain that had given birth to the bill was privately understood, at least by the Black Belt legislators. There was not even much sectional opposition from the northern Alabama hill counties, where representatives of the poorer white farmers resented the cooperation between conservative whites and blacks which allowed the Black Belt to dominate the politics of the state. The Tuskegee normal-school bill passed by 48 to 20 in the House and 21 to 7 in the Senate. While Black Belt legislators voted 33 to 11 for it in the House and 16 to 4 for it in the Senate, northern Alabama legislators also supported it, 15 to 9 in the House and 5 to 3 in the Senate. The act was signed by Governor Rufus W. Cobb on Feb. 10, 1881. (Dryer, *Origin of Tuskegee Normal and Industrial Institute,* 5-9.)

[2] Thomas B. Dryer was a prominent dry-goods merchant in Tuskegee. He was about fifty years old in 1881. He favored education of blacks, but scorned the white teachers who taught the freedmen. Soon after getting the momentum for a black normal school started, he became ill and died on June 18, 1881.

[3] M. B. Swanson was one of Tuskegee's leading merchants. At the time of the founding of Tuskegee Institute, Swanson was about forty-five years old. He continued to be one of Tuskegee's warmest supporters.

[4] Lewis Adams was born a slave on a Macon County plantation within a few miles of Tuskegee in 1843. As a youth he worked in a livery stable owned by his white father and master in the town of Tuskegee. At first he carried meals to the other workmen but was soon apprenticed as a blacksmith. During the Civil War the shop in which he worked manufactured "shoes for the Government," which may have been either horseshoes or footwear since Adams had training as both a shoemaker and a blacksmith. Immediately after the war Adams was able to rent the shop from his father and former owner, and he eventually acquired ownership of the business, which was expanded into a tin, harness, and blacksmith shop. In the 1880 census Adams appeared as a leading black citizen of Tuskegee. He owned a hardware store on the courthouse square and was responsible for roofing many of Tuskegee's buildings. According to local tradition, it was Adams who engineered the bargain with Wilbur F. Foster in the election of 1880 that brought about the creation of the normal school. One of the original trustees, he joined the faculty in 1890 and was placed in charge of the tin and harness shop. He also helped in the construction of several buildings on campus. He died on April 30, 1905, of a stroke while singing in the A.M.E. Zion Church in Tuskegee, where he was superintendent of the Sunday school. (M. T. Driver to Emmett J. Scott, May 15, 1905, Con. 300, BTW Papers, DLC.)

An Article in the *Southern Workman*

[Hampton, Va., February 1881]

INCIDENTS OF INDIAN LIFE AT HAMPTON

Two years schooling makes the Indians so much like other people that it is hard to find anything interesting to write. Here the writer has been patiently waiting for the last three weeks for some genuine Indian incident to turn up, but in spite of all, the Indians seem determined to leave off their peculiarities and give the anxious scribe nothing to write. They dress as fine as any one else, if they can get the clothes, speak some of Webster's and Clay's English, eat like other people, only a little more, and most of them study without compulsion.

A CHRISTMAS DINNER

It is the custom of the students here to form themselves into clubs for Christmas dinners. This Christmas, the Indian boys came to the conclusion that they had been behind in this matter long enough! Several weeks before Christmas, they began to talk about a Christmas dinner. When the time came, a meeting was held and each one agreed to furnish his proportion of the money required. Just how to begin and make proper arrangements for the party was quite embarrassing to them, and some assistance was required. The first perplexing question was whether or not they should invite the girls. Some readily saw the propriety of this, but others resisted it with all their might; they could not see why they should spend their money for food that the girls would eat.

After the matter had been discussed by them, it was decided by the teachers that the girls should pay their proportion of the money.

The next question that troubled the brains of the gallant braves was how to arrange matters so that each boy could accompany his particular lady friend. It was a question of etiquette with them whether the boy should ask the girl or the girl the boy, for this privilege. To decide matters some-what, word came from the authorities at the girls' quarters that the girls would not be permitted to sit at the boys' table unless by invitation from the boys. The boys now saw their position. How to comply with this condition did not reach their brains till late in the night before the party was to come off. They called a hasty meeting and each boy's name was set opposite the girl's he wished to accompany. In this way all the girls were chosen except those that were pronounced too small or too something else. The small proportion of girls to boys left a good many poor fellows to plod their way alone.

The next day, the boys chosen to attend the table were on hand and did their parts well. With some assistance their table was made to compare favorably with the more expensive ones. They took great pride in decorating and trimming their table. *"Dakota Club"* in large evergreen letters, made by two of the boys, marked it. Every thing being ready, the bell gave the signal for the different clubs to march into the dining room. Although some pains had been taken to couple the ladies and gentlemen so that they would march in and sit together, success did not attend this part of the programme. For when they saw the good things on the table, there was a general haste to find seats, and in many instances, the gentleman found himself seated at one end of the table and the lady at the other, or her on one side and himself on the other. One or two gentlemen got seats for themselves and left their ladies running around the table in search of a vacant chair.

Notwithstanding these little mistakes, they did full justice to what was on the table when they got at it. It was a very pleasant occasion to them, and when next Christmas finds most of them in their western homes they will pleasantly turn their thoughts to their "Dakota club" at Hampton.

B. T. W.

Southern Workman, 10 (Feb. 1881), 19.

An Article in the *Southern Workman*

[Hampton, Va., March 1881]

INCIDENTS OF INDIAN LIFE AT HAMPTON

CLOTHES

The Indians that have been here between two and three years, are now beginning to learn the value and use of clothes. They see that it is a little more trouble to get a suit of clothes than a blanket, which they could make answer for hat, coat, vest and pants. The girls who are accustomed to keep both body and head buried beneath heavy shawls on all occasions and in all places, are beginning to leave them off more frequently. A few mornings ago, a girl came in the class with her shawl all drawn up round her head. One or two of the girls began at once to motion and pull at her. She soon dropped it from her head. One of the girls seeing that I had been noticing what was going on, said, "Indian girls at Mr. H's school wear shawls on their heads, but Hampton girls not do it." Suspecting that they had been recently lectured on the subject, I replied, "I am glad they know better." Several times in the same class a girl would unconsciously gather her shawl about her head, but a mere nod or look from the others was enough to make it drop. I think a reform in this matter has begun.

One unaccustomed to deal with the Indians would be surprised at the large amount of clothes required for them the first one or two years after taking off the blanket. To say that the boys are hard on clothes is to put it too mildly. The first two years they found many strange uses for their bed clothing. Blankets would be cut up and decorated for fancy pants, sheets would be turned into strings to serve their many purposes and even now if a boy is in need of them he will not hesitate to use his coat linings. Whatever is new must be worn in preference to any thing else. If a boy has a new summer suit, it is hard to make him understand why he should not wear it in February. They think they ought to be permitted to wear a new pair of cotton overalls to the exclusion of the woollen pants, for a few days, till the novelty of them is gone.

The following is about the average of the principal garments needed for a boy for the first two years: 8 outside coats, 9 prs. pants, 2 over-coats, 10 prs. shoes, 11 outside shirts, 14 prs. socks, 9 neckties, 6 prs. suspenders, 8 hats or caps.

Wise Doings of the Boys

The quietness of the girls' sewing school was somewhat disturbed a few days ago by the appearance of little Kawhat at the door. When asked what he wanted, the reply was, "I want sew." As much as the girls laughed, they could not shame him out of his object. The teacher gave a needle and thread and a garment to him. He sat down and worked on it the remainder of the afternoon. When he was done, the girls themselves could but pronounce it well done.

While discussing the Atlantic and Pacific oceans in the geography class, they were told that the Atlantic was noisy and stormy, while the Pacific was calm and smooth. As soon as the explanation was understood, the boys began, "Girls, Atlantic Ocean. Boys Pacific Ocean." The girls attempted in vain to turn the joke.

Shutashnay[1] left an order at the tailor's shop a few days ago, for some standing collars to be made with his shirt. When they were finished, he came to me very much discontented, with the collars limber and wrinkled, just as they came from the tailor, and said "I want standing collars, these collars no good, they no stand." When told that they would be washed and starched, he replied "they clean now." After some more explanation, he reluctantly agreed to send them into the wash.

WHAT THEY ARE LEARNING

A FARMER

Geo. Bushotter tells what he learns on the farm.

"I am here two years now; since I came here I always work on the farm. I want to learn more about planting. I want learn plant corn, potatoes and everything. Next summer I think I learn more about planting, that is the reason I want to go on farm. I will tell you something that I learn since I come. When I first come here I do not know anything about the work, but now I learn this first, how to drive horses with wagons, and how to brush the horses off, and feed the horses, and how to clean out the stable, how to feed the cows, and how to brush the cows off, and how to clean the cow stable, and how to milk. I learn this in barn, but besides this I learn how to make hay, and how to load hay, and how to mow hay with hand, and to take care of the cows and the sheep."

A SHOE MAKER

What Samuel Brown[2] knows about shoemaking.

"I have been working in shoe making now five months and I want to learn the trade so when I go home I can teach others, and I can make my living in that way. There are no shoemakers out where I live. I have learned to patch and stitch shoes already, and I can make a good looking shoe if I take time to do so. I hope by the time I get ready to go home I shall be able to do anything in the line of shoemaking. So I have not much to say this time but I will next time, that is all."

A BLACKSMITH

Alexander Peters tells how he is mastering his trade. "I am going to tell you what I have learned at Hampton School. Why I have been learn how to be blacksmith, and now I can do most every thing in my trade. Certainly I can mend those springs on the carriage's body, or I can shoe horses, and I mend chains, also I can iron it the cart. And those things which I have not quite learned yet I will try to complete before I go home, and I will do the best I can in my work. I know it is only way to do to make useful man, so I can help my people when I get home.

A WHEELWRIGHT

Ahuka[3] writes about making carts and wagons. "When I came to Hampton I thought I would like make carts and wagons, so I work in work shop and make carts. I make some carts and some wagons. I like Mr. Williams[4] very much, he show me how to work, and tell me how to make carts and wagons. I think when I go home I will make carts for my people, and many other things. I think I will go with that man work in the shop; I mean in my home, one man works in the shop making carts. I am getting all right in my work. This is all I have to say."

WASHING DISHES

Julia St. Cyr tells how she makes clean dishes and sets a nice table. "All of us, Colored and Indian girls, wash the dishes every time, after every meal and I wash dishes with two Colored girls. We have a table which some of Middle class boys and girls eat at, and so we always try to make every thing look nice, and when we all get through washing dishes we report our tables to Miss D.,[5] and when she says it is all right, then we empty our dish pans and put all our cups and saucers away. One Indian girl has the care to put all the cups in order, and another girl has the care to keep the saucers, plates, and gravy dishes, and soup dishes, in order, and two Colored girls give the dish towels out. And sometimes just the Indian girls wash dishes so the Colored girls can have prayer meetings, and when they come down Miss D. says all the girls that are glad say I, all of them shout I at once, and always want to do any work well whatever it may be, and all of us enjoy ourselves washing dishes, and it is funny to see all of the girls washing dishes, and one girl cleans the sink where we all pour our water, and two or three girls wash dishes in a room which we call the dish room, and I think I have told you enough about washing dishes."

A PRINTER

Jas. Murie writes what he knows about printing, and then to prove it, sets up the type for it himself.

"Since October I went in the printing office, as I was working on the farm last term. I thought that I would try and learn the printers' trade, as I saw that one of the Pawnee boys at Carlisle was learning the trade. I thought that I would learn it so that both of us would have the same trade, so we may be able to start the same trade out in the Territory. And I went in the printing office with a Shawnee boy. The first thing we were to learn was looking over the cases and learn where each of the alphabets belong to. I learn that; and I got so I could distribute some type that had been set. I work two days every week. And now I can set types for the Southern Workman. I like this trade very well, but then I will not say that I will start this trade out in the Territory; I don't know whether circumstances will permit or not, for my tribe need education, and I expect to be a teacher among them. I like this trade very well, and wish to learn as much as I can while here."

DRILLING

Sergeant Frank Yellow Bird describes a dress-parade.

"I want to tell you about the school Battalion. First thing the bugle blows, then we fall in. The battalion is made of four companies, A, B, C and D. Each company is formed, then we march up in front of Virginia Hall where the battalion is formed. Then the Adjutant and Captain give command. The first thing is, Adjutant says to all the companies, right dress, and after then says to all the companies, guides post, and after then says, first Sergeants to the front and center march. First Sergeants report, Sergeants to your posts, march. Adjutant faces the Captain and says, Battalion formed with some men absent. The Adjutant goes on the right of the battalion, and then we have open order. After that the Captain inspects. Then sometimes he gives these commands; Break from the left and march to the right. The Captains of each company give commands, right forward, fours right. Then we go to wigwam for prayers; after prayers we go to school."

A CARPENTER

Zedo Rencontre[6] does a great deal better with his tools than with his pen. The foreman of the shop, says that Zedo is one of the brightest boys that he has ever had under his charge, and that there is no doubt about his making a first class carpenter.

"I want to tell you something about my work; first thing I make table. I learn about carpenter just as well as workman. I wish I know to write so I could tell you what I learn. I learn how to fix windows, and door lock, I can work myself about carpenter. I guess I can teach my people when I go back to my own home. Teach about carpenter, perhaps, and some book too. I think this will be good for me. I know my people don't know anything about carpenter or arithmetic. When first I came here I don't know anything about the carpenter. Now I learn some. I want learn some more carpenter and arithmetic. I want learn to teach carpenter work. Some more things I want write, but too hard for me to write in your language."

THE SCHOOL-ROOM

David Simmons[7] speaks about his books.

"I want write a few lines to day, and to tell what I have learned since I came here to this school. When I first came here to this school I don't know how to work examples in division, but I could read a little in third reader.

When I was at home in Dakota Territory. Now I want to tell what I did and learn at this school.

First, I was in Preparatory class: third reader, table book, spelling, brief course in geography; but now I am in B. Section, Junior Class; these are the books I studying now: fourth reader, grammar, arithmetic, spelling, writing, geography, then go to study hour in the morning and evenings. That is all I got to say now."

AN ENGINEER

Thomas Smith[8] has only been a short time with the engineer, but he says that Thomas can already be entrusted with many important duties. This is what Thomas says,

"I am going write this letter and tell what I learning in Engine-room now. These things that I had learned in there, and I only been in there five months now, so I don't learn much yet, and I can running the engine, and I can pump water from the well to the tank, and I can pump water into the boiler when no water in boiler, and clean engine sometimes too, and I can grease the engine, and I learn to make fire. I learn how to cut the pipes. I can run the engine and stop it again, and I like to work in there very much, and learn something. And also I like to be a good engineer, and go back to my own home. That is all I have to say."

A TINNER

We have two Indian boys who are going ahead making nearly all the tin-ware needed for the school, and Winnebago[9] is one of them.

"When I first came here I don't know anything about how to work and how to talk English, but now I learn good deal something about tin-shop. So make me happy all the time, and when I go back home I will try to teach my people.

Every afternoon I go to work in the shop, and when Mr. McDowell got something to work he come to me ask me, he say "Winnebago do this," then, I say yes sir, I will.

Then he show me picture, then I try one of them. When I try first time, little good, and next time I make all right.

I tell you this thing I made: pails, jars, oil cans, molasses cans, pitchers, bread pans, cake pans, dish pans, stew pans, sauce pans, dust pans, wash basins, coffee boiler, tin cups, dippers, iron bake pans. Those things I made myself. When some things I can't make then man show me once, then I make myself. So when I go home to Dakota I shall teach my friends. That is all I have to say, because I don't know how to write English."

SEWING

Little Carrie Anderson tells us about sewing.

"I always go to the sewing school, and other girls too. And the girls sew the clothes for themselves. I like to sew, but then sometimes I don't feel like to sew very much, but I have to though. Annie, Mary, Sophia Little Bear make the doll's clothes, and they don't have to sew their own clothes, but the other girls sew their own clothes. Sometime ago we make some bags for the boys to put their clothes in, and Mrs. Seymour[10] said we made them nice. Miss E.[11] said if some of the girls sew very fine and look so neat, then she will pick out some of every kind and keep it, and see what the Indian girls can do."

Edward Ashley[12] tells how he keeps the neatest room in the building.

"I have been here about two years, now. I always wish to do well, but I don't want what is wrong, because when I go to Dakota Territory I wish to teach my relations, and also something else about dirty and not cleanly. This time I want always cleanly everything. But I don't want dirty. And then all the time I take care of my room; every morning I make cleanly my room. This is my trade in the morning. Then I go to school, and in the afternoon I work on farm. But always before breakfast, first I work in my room. I sweep floor, and then I make clean table, and chair, and looking-glass, window, or anything in my room. I wish everything very clean in my room. I know how to keep room clean now, because I am learning every morning. I have two trades always, one early morning, one afternoon, it is these, keeping room and work on farm. I like both very much. All the time every Saturday I wash my floor, and door, and window, and chair, and table, because I don't want look ugly my room. I study hard, too."

Josephine is a faithful worker and does a good part of the cooking for the Indians, who have special diet when sick.

"I thought I would write to you a few lines to let you know about Indian boys and girls who are sick. I cook for them, every morning, beef, oat meal, coffee, tea, eggs, light bread. I think this is a very large breakfast. Some of the Indian boys come over to breakfast, and sick boys I send their breakfast over to them. I cook for them until 9 o'clock, then I go to school. Sometimes 10 o'clock I go to school. I not cook for supper and dinner.

I was very glad to cook for the sick boys and girls who are sick. One morning I was setting the table, and I forgot my meat, so it burned up. I was very sorry, indeed; I cook some more meat. I like to cook, but sometimes very hard work."

Chief-elect Wildcat, a Shawnee boy, in the Middle Class, is improving his spare time by compiling a small English Indian dictionary. He says that his tribe has no such book, and one is greatly needed. They had one a good while ago, but it has gone out of print. He has not gotten through with the A's yet, but it shows great care and patience, and will, no doubt, prove a great benefit. The following is his description of it:

"I have been translating a few English words into the Indian language since last summer, and I expect to continue in my work, if nothing prevents, little by little each day, until I shall accomplish my little book. I take only five or ten common and most simple words in the English language, and of course only those that I know how to use. I study and compare them carefully. Sometimes it takes a long time to find a suitable word which has the same meaning as the other.

It is strange to say that I have found some of the most common words in English language that have no words in Indian to take their places. But many others do have, but still would have a little different shades of meaning either in English or in Indian. Take the word *mata*, (mahtah) for instance, which means *no,* and also it can be used in place of the word *not,* which would mean almost the same, and it is nearest word I could get. It depends greatly where the emphasis is placed, and the use of it. My object in this little work, though very slow, is to get all the most common and familiar words in the English language translated, if I can, so that when I go home to teach, it may be an advantage, and useful to me in explaining and teaching others, because I shall know just what English word to use in place of Indian word."

B. T. W.

Southern Workman, 10 (Mar. 1881), 31-32.

[1] Leroy Shutashnay, a Two-Kettle Sioux from the Dakota Territory, was fifteen when he came to Hampton in 1878. He remained until 1881 and afterward became a farmer.

[2] Samuel Brown was a Sioux from the Dakota Territory. He was seventeen when he entered Hampton in 1879, remaining until 1883. Subsequently he became a farmer.

[3] Ahuka, an Arikara from the Dakota Territory, entered Hampton in 1878 at the age of twenty and remained until 1881. He died several years later.

[4] No Mr. Williams appeared on the list of Hampton faculty in 1880-81. He may have been a local resident who employed Hampton students.

[5] Probably Phebe C. Davenport, a housekeeper on the Hampton staff.

[6] Lezedo Rencontre, a Sioux from the Dakota Territory, sixteen years old when he entered Hampton in 1878. After leaving Hampton in 1881, he taught for several years before beginning a prosperous career as a farmer.

⁷ David Simmons was a Sioux from the Dakota Territory who entered Hampton at thirteen in 1878 and left in 1881. He subsequently had a varied career as a teacher, interpreter, clerk, and farmer.

⁸ Thomas Smith, a Gros Ventre from the Dakota Territory, was fifteen when he came to Hampton in 1878. After leaving in 1881 he became a farmer.

⁹ Joseph Winnebago, who later changed his name to Joseph W. Thompson, was a Sioux from the Dakota Territory. He entered Hampton at seventeen in 1878 and left in 1881. He later worked as a carpenter.

¹⁰ Mrs. Lucy A. Seymour, matron for Indian girls.

¹¹ Probably Isabel B. Eustis, a teacher of Indians at Hampton.

¹² Edward P. H. Ashley, a Sioux from the Dakota Territory, was eighteen years old when he entered Hampton in 1878. He remained until 1881 and returned for the years 1883-85. He later served as financial and property manager of Miss Howard's industrial home.

An Article in the *Southern Workman*

[Hampton, Va., April 1881]

INCIDENTS OF INDIAN LIFE AT HAMPTON

THE ARIZONAS

With the representatives of five Arizona tribes, we have Indian children here from 16 different tribes, viz., 37 Sioux, 1 Cheyenne, 2 Pawnees, 4 Menominees, 5 Gros Ventres, 3 Arickarees, 1 Mandan, 3 Winnebagos, 2 Omahas, 4 Shawnees, 1 Cherokee, 3 Apaches, 1 Yuma, 3 Mohaves, 6 Pimas, 3 Papagos. Total number of students 79.

Almost without exception, these tribes mingle together as pleasantly as so many white young people from as many states. The children of the sly and quarrelsome Sioux, live peaceably in the same room with the children of the fierce and war like Apache. As we see them here, there are few of those characteristics which are so vividly pictured out to us in story and picture books.

On first seeing an Arizona, perhaps the only thing that would indicate his being an Indian would be his hair. They have a brownish color, resembling very much the colored people. On the morning of the arrival of the sixteen Arizonas, the Sioux gave them a very warm welcome, though neither understood the others' language. It was a great pleasure for little Anna and Carrie¹ to have the honor of waiting on them at their first breakfast here. The Sioux boys made excellent aids in giving them their first lessons in civilization. Having themselves been taken through the same cleansing process two years ago, they knew exactly what to do. The first thing was to bathe and relieve them of a portion of their hair. This was nicely done by three of the Sioux boys, who have made themselves experts in hair cutting. They were shown how to bathe and dress by a Sioux boy, who took great pride in his work. Each boy had to be shown how to sleep in a bed, some having never slept in a bed before in their lives. One of the Sioux boys was detailed to teach them how to take care of their rooms. When told that he was to be their teacher for a while, he went about his work with as much earnestness and delight as any teacher ever went into a class-room.

First, he showed them how to air their rooms; then, taking them one by one, he showed them how to make up their beds; then, how to sweep and dust, and put everything in proper order; then, how to black their shoes. In fact, the Sioux boys taught them those lessons so well, that they had many of the newcomers blacking their shoes three times a day. Their Indian teacher went through these exercises with them for four or five mornings, and now they can make their beds look quite neat, and are beginning to take pride in their rooms.

One of them, who is trying to keep himself very tidy, even sent his black necktie in to be washed after wearing it one week. To teach them the lesson of the tooth-brush, I formed them into a line, and gave them an object lesson in the art, until they understood what it meant. They were very much amused at my performances.

It is pleasant to say that they did their first hour's work here, under the superintendence of a Sioux, who, a few months ago, was in their condition, but has so improved, that he can be trusted with many responsible duties. As far as possible, the new boys are put in rooms with the old boys for a while, that by mingling together, they may the sooner learn decency and order. To-day is Saturday, the day on which they scrub their rooms. George Bushotter, a Sioux boy, volunteered to show the new boys how to do their first scrubbing. When he had showed them how to move all the furniture and give the floor a good cleaning, everything was tastefully replaced and the room presented an appearance that would have made any one proud. Bushotter came to me and said, "I show new boys how to clean room, they got nice room now, and now I take walk with them and show them saw mill and everything. I like to teach them all what I know." Taking two of the little fellows by the hand, he showed them all over the school grounds as lovingly as if they had been his brothers.

The old boys watched the strange actions of the new comers with as much curiosity as any one, forgetting probably that some one had watched them the same way a few months ago. When they saw one of the Arizonas take his blankets and make his bed in the front yard, or go to bed at night on the top of all his blankets and sheets, they were filled with wonder. One of the new boys being called early in the morning to go to breakfast, jumped instantly out of his bed and started off at a quick pace in his night dress. This made quite a joke for the Sioux.

The Arizonas' first war dance was watched with as much curiosity by the old boys as if they had never seen or heard of one before, it being a quieter and more civilized war dance than the Sioux's. The principal feature of it is a vigorous patting of the feet to music without tune; while the Sioux skip, hop, jump, squat down, kneel down, and twist their bodies into all conceivable positions, keeping time to some kind of a drum, aided by voices that have a few musical notes to them now and then.

Antonito,[2] the son of the chief of the Pimas is a kind of father to the whole party, giving the young ones rebuke whenever they need it, teaching them what and how to do, as he himself is taught. He uses common sense about everything, and is willing to learn anything that will benefit himself, or his people.

He is very anxious to learn farming: he says that he and his people try to farm, but don't know how. For instance, they have no fruit trees, and know nothing of the care of them. They know that there are such things as onions, peas, beans, potatoes, cabbages and tomatoes, but do not know when, or how to plant them. When planted, they know nothing at all about taking care of them. They only know how to raise barley and wheat. He says that he wants to take a mowing machine with him when he returns home. In giving advice as to what trades would be best for his boys to learn, Antonito has been of great service. That this man at thirty years of age should leave his family and come hundreds of miles to be taught in the school-room and on the farm, by the side of his little nine year old boy, means something.

FIRST PAIR OF SHOES

Paul Rios[3] and Stago,[4] two of the Arizonas, have made their first pair of shoes. Paul completed his in three days after going into the shop, and Stago, a boy of thirteen, in six days. Of course they were under the direction of a teacher, but did the entire work themselves. The shoes are not finished in the best style, but will last longer than many store shoes. Neither of them ever worked at the trade before. Their progress is truly marvelous. It is fair to presume that within a few months they will be able to make a valuable and respectable shoe.

Every Day Life

A glance at the daily life of the seventy-nine Indians here, will probably be interesting to some of our readers who have never visited here.

The rising bell, at quarter past five, is the signal for all to prepare for breakfast. Toilets being arranged, at six o'clock the bell sounds for breakfast. Five minutes more and the dining room doors close, leaving those who have lingered too long in their beds to pay the cost by the loss of their breakfast. Breakfast over, the boys spend the time till after seven, in cleaning their rooms. It is particularly encouraging to see how much pride and taste the boys show in their rooms, decorating them with pictures and many of their own drawings. Many of them, not satisfied with the bare table and blanket-spread furnished by the school, have bought themselves fancy table spreads. Their smooth beds with square edges, show a skill in bed-making that is not often seen. When the rooms are cleaned, the boys spend their time in some sort of outdoor exercise, generally in jumping, till fifteen minutes after eight, when the bell rings for inspection. A few minutes pass, and every man is expected to appear in his company, to answer the roll call. The bugle sounds, and the companies march on the line of dress parade, while the school band furnishes excellent music. The battalion formed, the band again plays, and every man is inspected, to see that his shoes are properly cleaned, that no buttons are off, that the necktie and collar are on, and in order, and that his whole person is in proper condition to begin the duties of the day. The inspection over, the Colored and Indian students repair to their respective assembly rooms for devotional exercises. The Indian school is opened by singing, the school recites together some familiar verses of scripture, then follows a short prayer. Ten or fifteen minutes are spent in Bible instruction, or drill in singing. They sing very nicely, such hymns as "Yield not to temptation," "Jesus keep me near the cross," "Jesus lover of my soul," "My faith looks up to thee," &c. Like many other people, they sometimes make the wrong use of scripture; for instance, when one boy was afraid he would have to work one rainy afternoon, he printed this sentence, in large letters, in a conspicuous place: "verily verily I say unto you, thou shalt not work to-day because too much rain."

Class Rooms

We find them at work there in about the same way as in other schools, making mistakes and correcting them, retaining a part that they are taught and forgetting a part. We find some very smart ones, and some very dull ones; some paying attention to the lesson, and some doing everything else but that. In the spelling class, the teacher writes the words on the board one day, to be copied and studied by the student for the next day's lesson. Having studied these words, the next day they are again required to write the words. It is very seldom that you see an Indian make a misspelling; first, because, as he learns an English word, he is required to write it so many times that he cannot forget it; second, because, knowing little of English, he has never had the disadvantage of seeing words spelled wrongly. The boy by the side of whom I happened to sit, on a visit to a class, wrote these words without a mistake: proud, beef, draw, mean, bottom, rein, rain, twenty, wren, company, seldom, squirrel, swallow, touch.

In the reading class, a dialogue was nicely read by two little girls, the others criticizing them when they were through. The copy books in the writing class, presented an appearance of which any school might feel proud, with few blots and good penmanship — the Indians seem to be by nature good penmen.

I found the class in English conversation, conversing on a very delicate subject, not the subject of truth, but lying, about which, so many untruths are often told. Just when to say, he lied on the grass and he lay on the grass, is often a puzzle to many better acquainted with English than the Indians. Yet, in thirty minutes they were nearly masters of this verb. The teacher put the verb on the board something like this, substituting the word chief, (it having a significant meaning to them) for what we call the principal parts:

1st chief,	*2nd chief,*	*3rd chief,*	*4th chief.*
Lie,	Lying,	Lay,	Lain.

When they had been drilled a short time on the use of these chiefs, the following sentences were put on the board, having a blank for the verb, which was correctly filled in a minute:

"Do not lie down on the grass." "Have you lain down to-day?" "Did you lie down on the boat?" "Yes I lay down on the boat."

What, an Indian class in Natural Philosophy! Yes, like other ignorant people, they need to be taught to understand and appreciate nature, which is near to them, instead of something far off. A few minutes spent in this class will convince any one that this study is causing them to think about the world, and investigate nature. I heard these questions asked: How do we get a knowledge of the outside world? The answer came, "By our five senses, seeing, hearing, feeling, tasting, and smelling." "What is matter?" "Matter is anything that we can see or feel." "How many properties has matter?" "Two, general and specific." Then they took up some object and readily gave its general and specific properties. Under the head of divisibility, the question was put, "What is an atom?" The answer at once came, "Something so small that it cannot be divided." They had quite a talk on this question, and several questions were asked by them, which showed that they understood what they were talking about.

In the arithmetic class, I found them studying so much like other students, that no account of it is needed. They are quick to arrive at a fact, but their limited knowledge of the language prevents them from giving the reason with accuracy. The following are specimens of the examples worked out correctly, in a recent written examination: "A man having 500 cows, bought 47 more from A, 275 from B, and 12 from C; 376 died and 28 were stolen, how many has he left?"

2. "Sarah Walker had 498 chickens, 99 died, she then sold the others at 19 cents each, how much money does she get?"

3. "Yellowbird sold 14 oxen at $15 each and bought calves with the money at $5 how many calves can he buy?"

In geography they have thoroughly mastered the general outline of the political and natural divisions of the earth. In naming the five races, I have heard them murmur to each other, "who is red man?" "I am not red."

While reciting the four conditions of men, as to their mode of life, when one would be describing the savage life, many subdued whispers could be heard. "We savages, we savages."

The Arizonas work in the forenoon and attend school in the afternoon. In school they are just making a beginning. They are now learning to count as far as twenty, and to pronounce such sentences as "I write." "I want to write."

In the Indians' study hour, from seven till eight, P.M. they do real earnest work. Two nights in the week they have a prayer meeting from eight to nine. Wednesday evening they have a prayer meeting of their own, which is pretty well attended. Besides these meetings, they attend church, Sunday School, and a Sunday evening lecture.

Recently a morning inspection has been instituted for the Indian girls. With their dish washing, cooking, washing and ironing, and sewing school, in the afternoon, the girls are kept almost as busy as the boys.

It is pleasant to make a visit in the afternoon to the different work departments. In the training shop, we find one boy fitting a pair of shoes on the last, one patching a pair; over there, another making a lamp, and another a dish-pan; here, another boy making a table, and another one repairing a bench.

On the farm, they are more scattered. Here we find two boys preparing a hot bed, yonder a squad cleaning off some ground, two or three repairing a fence, one boy plowing with a two horse plow. At the barn, one boy is preparing cow feed, while another is milking.

At the wheel-wright shop one boy is making spokes, and another is painting a cart just finished. In the blacksmith's shop, one boy is blowing the bellows, while another is making a horse shoe, or shoeing a mule. At the engine room, we find the two engineers either firing up the engine or cutting pipe, while, at the printing office, we see a Shawnee and Pawnee hard at work setting up "Incidents of Indian Life."

Our only Indian tailor, we find hemming a towel or repairing a pair of pants.

Take it all in all, from morning till night, we have a pretty busy set, and the progress in study and work is steady and encouraging.

B. T. W.

Southern Workman, 10 (Apr. 1881), 43.

[1] Probably Annie Lyman and Carrie Anderson, both Sioux.

[2] Antonito Azul was thirty years old and remained slightly over a year at Hampton (1881-82), studying the adaptability of Hampton-type industry to the circumstances of his tribe.

[3] Pablo or Paul Rios, a seventeen-year-old Papago, proved too violent-natured for Hampton. He was returned home in 1883 and died the following year.

[4] Benjamin Stago, an Apache, age thirteen, attended Hampton from 1881 to 1884. His record following his return home was erratic. He served as teacher and interpreter but also spent time in jail and was reputedly a drunkard.

Samuel Chapman Armstrong
to George Washington Campbell[1]
and Other Trustees of Tuskegee Normal School

[Hampton, Va.] May 31 81

Gentlemen   Yours of the 24th is recd.

The only man I can suggest is one Mr. Booker Washington a graduate of this institution, a very competent capable mulatto, clear headed, modest, sensible, polite and a thorough teacher and superior man. The best man we ever had here.

I am satisfied he would not disappoint you.

He cannot well be spared till Oct. 1st.

Could you give him time and how much?

Are the buildings all ready?

Is the appropriation one to be depended on from year to year?

Is his being colored an objection?[2]

He can find first[3] colored assistants.

I am confident he would not disappoint you.

I know of no white man who would do better.

He has been teaching in this institution the past year & I am ready to promote him because he so richly deserves it.

I go to Europe on the 10th June.

Please answer by night telegram[4] at my expense if satisfactory; also by letter promptly. Yours respectfully

S C Armstrong

ALpS   Armstrong Letterbooks   President's Office Vault   ViHaI.

[1] George Washington Campbell, an ex-slaveowner and leading citizen of Tuskegee, joined the board of trustees following Thomas B. Dryer's retirement due to illness in the spring of 1881. A fifty-two-year-old merchant and banker, Campbell remained a trustee throughout his life, serving Alabama as one of three commis-

sioners representing the state's interests on the board. BTW wrote that Campbell "was never appealed to when he was not willing to extend all the aid in his power." (*Up from Slavery,* chap. 7.) At crucial times in BTW's career, Campbell gave the black educator fatherly, conservative advice. Later members of Campbell's family continued to aid the institution. Campbell died in 1905.

2 BTW remembered that the commissioners, apparently unable to believe that a black man was capable of such a responsibility, asked Armstrong to recommend one of his white teachers. George W. Campbell wrote first to J. T. Murfee of the Marion Military Institute, where Campbell had sent two of his sons to be educated. Campbell asked Murfee to recommend one of his graduates. ". . . I thanked him for the compliment," Murfee said many years later, "but told him that I [had] not prepared any man for that work, and I did not approve of the methods of any negro schools in the States, excepting the one at Hampton, Va., under Gen. Armstrong. . . ." As Murfee recalled, he advised Campbell to ask the general for his best graduate. (Letter of J. T. Murfee to Charles W. Thompson, May 20, 1902, in Washington *Post,* June 2, 1902, and in Montgomery *Advertiser,* June 5, 1902. See also BTW's account of the correspondence in *Up from Slavery,* chap. 7.)

3 Armstrong probably intended "first-rate," or possibly "fine."

4 According to BTW, *Up from Slavery,* chap. 7, they replied in substantially these words: "Booker T. Washington will suit us. Send him at once."

An Article in the *Southern Workman*

[Hampton, Va., May 1881]

INCIDENTS OF INDIAN LIFE AT HAMPTON[1]

BEARS HEART[2] RETURNS TO THE WEST

Six years ago, Bears Heart left the Indian Territory, a United States army prisoner, clad in a blanket and moccasins, with his long hair flowing down his back, his ears jingling with ear rings, and his tomahawk and bow and arrows swinging from his side. In this condition he was torn from his friends and sent to Florida where he remained three years a prisoner of war, and the other three years he has been a student at the Hampton Institute.

A few days ago he left for his home. But what a change! Instead of his blanket he wears back a neat suit of the school gray uniform decorated with a sergeant's and colorbearer's stripes which he has well earned.

Instead of the tomahawk, he takes back a chest of carpenter's tools; instead of his bow and arrows, he takes the bible and many other good volumes.

His long hair and moccasins he has long since forgotten, and instead of the weak, dirty, ignorant piece of humanity that he was, with no correct ideas of this life or the next — his only ambition being to fight the white man — he goes back a strong, decent, Christian *man,* with the rudiments of an English education, and hands trained to earn himself a living at the carpenter's bench or on the farm. I can almost see him as he arrives home. He is surrounded by a crowd. See how they gaze and wonder at his changed appearance. What has he done to himself? Is he the same man that left us a few years ago? Ah! his aged mother hears the news and runs out to meet her captive son; the sight is almost too much for her. Overcome with joy they sink down in each others embrace: But now comes his trying time. He enters his mother's house. It is not his clean airy room that he left at Hampton — no pictures are on the walls, no clean smooth beds, but the house is dark and gloomy, dirt here and dirt there, and no signs of order and comfort. Bears Heart thinks of Hampton, he wishes himself there. He takes courage. He lies down and rests his body on a bed of rags, as best he can. He gets up in the morning resolved to make a change in the appearance of things, and he quietly and resolutely goes about his work of reform. In a few weeks I can imagine the appearance of his mother's house entirely changed, and Bears Heart going about trying to help his neighbors.

Who knows but that the capturing of Bears Heart and his associates marked the beginning of the solution of the Indian question? Brave Bears Heart! Noble Little Chief! Praised be all that band of prisoners, for the transformation begun in your Florida prison has roused the nation to think that it is its duty to educate all your brethren.

Bears Heart was one of the most obedient and kind hearted students that ever entered this school. He was always ready to inconvenience himself to please others.

On the day of his departure, he said that he would like to speak to the Indian boys and girls before leaving. They gladly assembled to hear his parting words. He was a great favorite among the students, although not one of them belonged to his tribe. When they had finished singing a hymn, Bears Heart rose and said: "Dear Scholars; I am pleased to give you a few remarks in regard to my departing from you all. I am glad that I have been friends to you all and I am sorry that I have to leave Hampton. But boys and girls remember that it is better to obey your teachers and all the others. You must all study hard and try to see what boys or girls will go ahead of all the others and also you must all attend prayer meeting and Sunday school just as well as going to school through the week. You must all try for yourselves and learn how to read and write: that is what you all left your homes for; to learn to read and education. For some people think that Indians can not learn, so I will say once more try hard in your study. I bid farewell to you all. Boys and Girls good bye." When he had finished, "I am sorry" "I am sorry" echoed from all parts of the room. After singing another hymn, Bears Heart withdrew to pack his trunk for the far West.

Order in His Room

One of the boys who had been troubled by other boys playing too much in his room, put the following notice up behind his door:

"March 28, 1881

H. N. and A. Institute

Dear friend Boys? Please, you must not play in here. If you want play go outside play, and don't foolish in here dear friend? That is way to do good way. This all I have to say, my dear friends   Gentleman, his wrote,

Mr. Laughing Face"[3]

Ziewie[4] and Her Father

The following story is told about Unspesni the father of Ziewie, by Mrs. D. wife of the Indian agent[5] at Crowcreek, D.T. When Ziewie left home in 1878 to come to the Hampton Institute she left her father in his blanket and long hair, living in a tipi and in all things leading a regular Indian life. Ziewie's going away to school made such an impression on him that he resolved to change his mode of life. When he began to reform Mrs. D. was not at home. When she returned after some weeks' absence she saw a gentleman sitting up in the house talking to Mr. D. She did not recognize him. Mr. D. asked her if she was not going to speak to *Unspesni*. She could hardly believe her own eyes when her husband told her that it was Unspesni. How different he appeared to her with his hair cut and citizen's dress on. Unspesni sat smiling all the time receiving the greatest enjoyment from the joke. He has built himself a nice house and has it well furnished. A short time after he began to wear citizen's clothes he got Mr. D. to purchase a small stock of goods for him in order that he might start a store. Mr. D.

purchased the goods for him. *Unspesni* started his store with a small capital. Since that time by patient industry his business has increased and he is now worth three thousand dollars. While making other reforms, he reformed his name. *Unspesni* in English means Don't know how, but he thought that it would not do to have all that painted on his sign so he abbreviated it and hung out his sign marked D. K. Howe. At his present rate of improvement I think he can safely change his name to Do Know How in a few years. How pleasant it will be for his daughter Ziewie to go back and find her father so far on the road to civilization.

B. T. W.

Southern Workman, 10 (May 1881), 55.

[1] This was BTW's last report on his Indian work at Hampton. There appeared subsequently in the *Southern Workman,* in June 1881, an article by a Hampton Indian student, J. M. (probably James Murie). According to this account: "Every Saturday we have a meeting with Mr. B. T. Washington, to talk to us what he thinks we ought to do and what we ought not to do. When his meeting is over, then he lets the Indian boys have their meeting. . . . I know one Indian boy who wanted to go home, but Mr. Washington talked to him, which made him feel strong, and have never complain about it anymore, and is now here with us, cheerful as he can be." (*Southern Workman,* 10 [June 1881], 71.) At the Hampton anniversary on May 19, 1881, BTW gave an address on "The Negro and the Indian." Rev. Henry C. Potter of New York City said of it: "Never have I heard a definition of civilization such as Mr. Washington gave us today — 'the true test of civilization in any people is the desire shown by that people to lift up those who have been less fortunate than themselves.' " (*Ibid.,* 70.) The definition was almost identical to the one BTW offered in the October 1880 "Incidents of Indian Life at Hampton" column.

[2] James Bear's Heart, a Cheyenne, was thirty years old when he came to Hampton in 1878. He returned home after three years and died in 1882.

[3] Laughing Face was an Arikara, seventeen years old when he entered Hampton in 1878. He left the school in 1881 and died three years later.

[4] Ziewie Davis, a Sioux from Dakota Territory, came to Hampton when she was seventeen. She attended Hampton from 1878 to 1881 and afterward worked as cashier and bookkeeper in her father's store until her health failed. She died in 1882.

[5] William Edgeworth Dougherty (1841-1915), a captain in the U.S. Army, was acting Indian agent at Crow Creek Agency, Dakota Territory, in 1881.

An Article in the *Southern Workman*

[Hampton, Va., May 1881]

SEVEN MONTHS WELL SPENT

MORE ABOUT THE "PLUCKY CLASS"

Seven months ago, two young men, Julius Murray and Joseph Haws, came here without money enough to pay their way in the day school, so they have been attending night school and working in the day that they might earn money with which to pay their board in school next year. Murray began to work at the blacksmith's trade and Haws at the wheelwright's trade. They have so far mastered their trade that, a few weeks ago, with a little aid, they made a first class cart, Murray doing the iron work and Haws the wood work. Neither of them ever worked at their trades before coming here. They have not only done well in mastering trades that will be worth every thing to them in the future, but both have been earnest and faithful in the night school and are doing well in their studies. Why could not the thousands of young men who hang around the streets of our cities imitate Murray's and Haw's example?

B. T. W.

Southern Workman, 10 (May 1881), 57.

To James Fowle Baldwin Marshall

Tuskegee Normal School, Tuskegee Ala. July [June]¹ 25 [1881]

Dear friend: Arrived here yesterday. The place has a healthy and pleasant location — high and hilly — think I shall like it. Will open school 1st Monday in July.² Please send me the addresses of some publishing houses where I can get my books at reduced rates. I will use about the same kind of text books as you use there. Will thank you for any help you can give me in the way of getting any kind of books. Yours

B. T. Washington

ACS   BTW Folder   President's Office Vault   ViHaI.

[1] Both the internal evidence and the docketing, "R&A June 29," indicate that the card was written on June 25.

[2] On May 23, 1881, the state commissioners for the Tuskegee Normal School placed in the Tuskegee *Macon Mail* a notice: "If a competent teacher, and the requisite number of pupils can be had by the 1st Monday in July next, we propose to open the Tuskegee Normal School." The notice appeared again on May 25 and June 1, 1881. On June 29, 1881, the *Macon Mail* commented editorially: "We will celebrate the 4th of July by opening the Colored Normal School for the education of teachers, under the Superintendence of B. T. Washington, from Virginia. What will Bob Toombs and Bill Arp say to that?" Robert Augustus Toombs, a former U.S. senator and governor of Georgia, was an "unreconstructed" southerner, as was Major Charles Henry Smith, who wrote a rustic humor column in the Atlanta *Constitution* under the pseudonym Bill Arp.

During the week before the opening of the school, BTW interviewed applicants for admission, enrolled about thirty persons, and turned others away. Most of the applicants were from Macon County, some of them accompanied by their parents. He accepted none under sixteen, but some were nearly forty. The older pupils were often already teachers in the public schools. The teachers often were accompanied by their former pupils, and in several cases the pupil entered a higher class than his former teacher.

To Francis Chickering Briggs[1]

Tuskegee, Ala., June 28 1881

My dear friend Mr. Briggs: I will open school the 1st Monday in July. Judging from present prospects I shall have about thirty students the first day and a steady increase. This a pleasant town — a high and hilly location, good water, and a pleasant breeze most always. I think that it is about as pleasant here as at Hampton in the summer.

My first great need is apparatus, such as maps writing-charts, globes, &c &c. I thought by writing to you I might get a great many of these kind of thing which you would not miss there, I especi[a]lly need a Spencerian writing chart. I think that there is an old one there. I think Miss Lothrop[2] has a great many library books which she does not use or care for these would make an excellent beginni[n]g for my library. You know what I need and *any thing* that you can send me I will be thankful for. You can send by freight. The businessmen here say that it is perfectly safe. We will be able to pay the freight on anything sent.

I write to you about these things because I know that you will attend to it. I hope to give you all an extended account of my work here as soon as I get time. Yours truly

B. T. Washington

133

ALS BTW Folder President's Office Vault ViHaI. This is the first appearance of the letterhead: "Tuskegee Normal School for the Education of Colored Teachers. B. T. Washington, Principal."

[1] Francis Chickering Briggs (1833-1908), born in Norward, Mass., served as business manager of Hampton for twenty-nine years. A descendant of founders of Plymouth colony, he attended Phillips Academy, Andover, Mass., and received business training in Newburyport, Mass. After operating a Boston china-importing firm for many years with his brother Richard, he retired because of ill health. On a recuperative trip to Hampton in 1878, he became interested in Hampton Institute. He joined the staff in 1879 and became a close friend of Samuel C. Armstrong. His sister, Mary B. Briggs, also joined the faculty, coming from Wheaton Seminary, Newton, Mass.

[2] Emma H. Lothrop served Hampton as teacher and librarian until 1883.

To James Fowle Baldwin Marshall

Tuskegee, Ala., June 29 1881

Dear Genl: You have probably heard of my safe arrival here. I found things as represented. This is a beautiful, quiet, little town, with a high and healthy location — excellent water. Both the whites and colored seem to be very kind and pleasant. I expect to open school next Mon. and shall have not less than thirty students the first day. Nothing could be more beneficial to the teachers and people of this section than a good Normal School.

Genl, I want your advice at once on this point. The state pays for tuition $2000 annually. The trustees hope to save enough out of this am't to put up a cheap building. They have not selected a site for the building yet. As soon as I got here I went to work looking for a suitable place for the building while doing so I came to this conclusion: that the people in this part of the South are not able to send their children to school and pay $9 or $10 per m. for their board, so I have decided that the only way to make this a *permenant* and successful school is to get it on the labor system as soon as possible. I have walked all around town and examined the land, finally I have found a farm about half a mile from town which I think will suit above all others. My self and one of the trustees, an intelligent and well-to-do colored man,[1] have just seen the owner of the farm. He says that it contains one hundred acres, that he will sell it to us for $500 — $200 when he gives possession and the remainder to run at 8% till paid.[2] The land has several old buildings on it which we could make answer for school purposes for the present, besides this there is a young orchard on the place which is worth at least $75 itself. The owner is a very nice, wealthy man, probably the most wealthy here. Every one says there is no question about his not having a good title. In case we get it, we expect to have it deeded so that the state will have no control over the land, then in case the state with drew its appropriation at any time the school could still live. The colored people here are very anxious that the school shall be a success and are willing to do what little they are able to do for it. The plan I have stated will, I think, ensure the complete success of the school. Shall not do any more towards it till I get your advice. At present we are renting a building. Love to all my friends. Please let Mr. Banks[3] read this letter. Yours truly

B. T. Washington

Later, Since the other part of my letter was written I have stated my plans to the other trustees — two intelligent and wealthy southern gentlemen and they agree with me in every particular.

B. T. W.

P.S. Could you not telegraph your approval or disapproval?

ALS   BTW Folder   President's Office Vault   ViHaI.

[1] Lewis Adams.

[2] With a loan from J. F. B. Marshall, BTW did arrange for purchase of the land early in July and, upon payment of the full $500 plus interest, received clear title to the property Apr. 10, 1882. He purchased the property from William Banks Bowen, a fifty-five-year-old white man who had operated a plantation there prior to the Civil War. During the war the residence burned, and Bowen abandoned the plantation, which became locally known as "the Old Burnt Place." Bowen served as postmaster of Tuskegee from 1871 to 1875. (Deed, Apr. 10, 1882, Deed Book 7, p. 661, Macon County Probate Court, Tuskegee, Ala.)

[3] Frank D. Banks.

To James Fowle Baldwin Marshall

Tuskegee, Ala., July 5th 1881

My dear friend: Your telegram was rec'd this A.M. worded as follows: "I advise the purchase of your representation of the farm." I thank you for the advice.

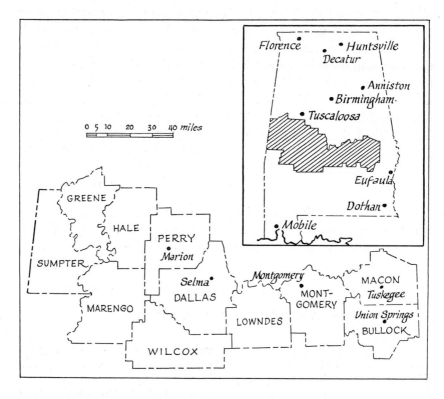

Map 2. The Black Belt counties of Alabama.

That we may move our school on the farm at once I want to ask a loan of $200 from the school till Oct. 1st 1881 and I will pledge my salary for its payment at that time.

By moving there at once the school will gain in influence, the buildings there will be more convenient and useful, and we will be enabled to save a large amount of temporary work as all the work we do on the new place will be permanent. Have no fear about not raising the money by the time named. I can get a good part of it from the white and colored people in this town. Yours truly

B. T. Washington

ALS BTW Folder President's Office Vault ViHaI.

To James Fowle Baldwin Marshall

Tuskegee, Ala., July 7 1881

Dear friend: I opened school Monday, have had an average attendanc[e] of 37 students for this week. I write to ask you to try to persuade Miss Davidson[1] to come here at once. My school will grow larger soon. It is impossible to get an assistant any where here who is worth anything. I know that you will see the importance of her coming at once. Have just written her. Yours truly

B. T. Washington

ALS BTW Folder President's Office Vault ViHaI.

[1] Olivia A. Davidson Washington, second wife of BTW, was born in Tazewell County, Va., June 11, 1854. She was possibly the mulatto child of four listed in 1860 among the slaves of James C. Davidson. Her mother Eliza Davidson and other members of her family made their way to Ohio. The family settled in Albany, Ohio, to take advantage of the opportunities at the black-owned, black-operated Albany Enterprise Academy. Albany contained many escaped and manumitted slaves, who in 1863 bought and sold stock at $25 per share to raise a fund sufficient to establish an academy. The Albany Enterprise Academy received a donation of $3,000 from a white philanthropist, Isaac Carleton of Syracuse, N.Y., and a loan of $2,000 from the Freedmen's Bureau. The supporters erected a three-story farm building known as the Ladies Dormitory and a two-story brick chapel and classroom building. Rev. Thomas J. Ferguson, an able and well-educated Negro, was the principal teacher. For two decades it was well patronized by blacks from several surrounding states, until the burning of the dormitory in 1885 ended its existence. After education at the academy, Olivia accompanied one of her brothers, Joseph, to Hernando, Miss., where they taught the freedmen during Reconstruction.

After the brother's death, reportedly murdered by the Ku Klux Klan, she moved to a school in Memphis. In 1878 a yellow fever epidemic broke up her school, so she twice volunteered to serve as a nurse. This was refused because she was not acclimated. In an effort to improve her ability to teach, she enrolled at Hampton Institute because of its reputation of offering opportunities for self-help. She entered the senior class in 1878 and graduated in 1879. A gift of Mrs. Rutherford B. Hayes paid her tuition. She was disappointed to find that the instruction at Hampton was not more advanced, but one of the teachers, Tileston T. Bryce, introduced her to his aunt, Mrs. Mary Hemenway, on the latter's visit to the school. Mrs. Hemenway was so impressed by Olivia Davidson's charm and talent that she offered to pay her way through Framingham State Normal School in Massachusetts. Graduating from Framingham in 1881 after two years, she came to Tuskegee following a summer's rest. Never physically strong, she had nearly collapsed at the end of her schooling, and her health remained precarious for the rest of her life. She threw herself into the work of the school, and deserved equally with BTW the credit for its rapid growth. Her superior education improved the quality of instruction at the school, and her feminine charm was an important element in the early fund raising in the North. On Aug. 11, 1886, at the home of her sister Mary, wife of Dr. Noah Elliott, in Athens, Ohio, she married BTW. She took good care of her three-year-old stepchild Portia and had two sons of her own, Booker T. Washington, Jr., and Ernest Davidson Washington. In January 1889, soon after the birth of her second child, her home burned in the middle of the night and the exposure reactivated an old respiratory disease. After some care by Dr. C. N. Dorsette of Montgomery, and a trained nurse sent by a friend in Boston, she was taken as a last hope to Massachusetts General Hospital in Boston. There she died on May 9, 1889. Her life was characterized by her genteel manner, religious devoutness, and determination, despite her frailty, to render social service.

From James Fowle Baldwin Marshall

[Hampton, Va.] July 7 [188]1

Dear Booker, I recd yours of 29th ult. & telegraphed my approval of your proposed purchase of the farm for the use of the School. At the price named you cannot run much risk of loss & the experiment is well worth trying, tho' at this distance with no knowledge of the market & the capabilities of the farm any opinion could not be of much value, except as to the general plan which I think is a good one. Besides what you can raise for your Boarding Dept, can you find a market for all else — or can you raise cotton at a profit to help pay your expenses. You will have to purchase or hire implements & horses or mules to carry on your work. Is the place in good condition or is it worn out, as this school farm was when Mr Howe[1] took it in hand — and needing to be brought into good harvest with fertilizers & careful tillage. If the farm is in good condition with buildings that can be utilized for school purposes, it seems to me a very cheap purchase. You could not put up even a cheap building for much less than the cost of the whole farm & buildings. I shall feel greatly interested to know how you are getting along, and shall be glad to aid you in any way in my power. How far are you from Talladega? If within easy reach you could get valuable advice from Mr Chase or whoever is the farmer at the colored A M Assn College there.[2] Miss O Davidson is here. I hope you will have her aid. Yours faithfully

J. F. B. Marshall

ALpS   Business Office   ViHaI.

[1] Albert Howe.

[2] Talladega College in Talladega, Ala., supported by the American Missionary Association. The superintendent of the agricultural department of Talladega during the 1881-82 academic year was André A. Southwick. No Mr. Chase was listed in either the faculty or student body of the college. Perhaps Marshall had in mind the Rev. F. A. Chase, a member of the faculty of Fisk University, Nashville, Tenn.

From James Fowle Baldwin Marshall

[Hampton, Va.] July 9 [188]1

Friend Booker, Yours of 5th inst is received. The proposition that the H. N. S.[1] should advance Capital for the State Normal School of Alabama is rather startling. I have no authority without a vote of the trustees to do any such thing. But as your demand seems to be urgent, I should be very sorry to have you hindered. I take the personal responsibility of loaning you till Oct 1st the needed sum, and herewith enclose my check No 435 on Home Savings Bank of Norfolk (payable in New York) for Two hundred dollars, for which please send me your receipt according to the terms of your letter. This is an unusual transaction & I depend on your fulfilling your pledge. Yours faithfully,

J. F. B. Marshall

ALpS   Business Office   ViHaI.

[1] Hampton Normal School.

To the Editor of the *Southern Workman*

Tuskegee, Ala., July 14, 1881

Dear friends: I arrived here four weeks ago. Instead of finding my work in a low marshy country as I expected, I find Tuskegee a beautiful little town, with a high and healthy location. It is a town such as one rarely sees in the South. Its quiet, shady streets and tasteful and rich dwellings remind one of a New England village. After my arrival I had one week in which to prepare for the opening of the Normal School. I utilized this time in seeing the teachers and others who wished to enter the school, and in getting a general idea of my work and the people. Sunday I spoke in both churches to the people about the school, and told all who wished to enter to come and see me at my boarding place during the week. About thirty persons called and had their names enrolled, others called whose names, for various reasons, I could not enroll. With the young people many of their parents came. I was particularly impressed with the desire of the parents to educate their children, whatever might be the sacrifice.

On Friday I rode about fourteen miles into the country to visit the closing exercises of one of the teachers. From this trip I got some idea of the people in the country. Never was I more surprised and moved than when I saw at one house, two boys thirteen or fourteen years old, perfectly *nude*. They seemed not to mind their condition in the least. Passing on from house to house I saw many other children five and six years old in the same condition. It was very seldom that I saw children anything like decently dressed. If they wore clothing it was only one garment, and this so black and greasy that it did not resemble cloth. As a rule, the colored people all through this section are very poor and ignorant, but the one encouraging thing about it is that they see their weakness and are desirous of improving. The teachers in this part of Alabama have had few advantages, many of them having never attended school themselves. They know nothing of the improved methods of teaching. They hail with gladness, the Normal School, and most of them will be among its students. If there is any place in the world where a good Normal School is needed, it is right here. What an influence for good, first on the teachers, and from them on the children and parents.

I opened school last week. At present I have over forty students —

anxious and earnest young men and women. I expect quite an increase in September and October. The school is taught, at present, in one of the colored churches, which they kindly let us have for that purpose. This building is not very well suited to school purposes, and we hope to be able to move to a more commodious place in a short time. The place referred to is on a beautiful and conveniently located farm of one hundred acres, which we have contracted to buy for $500. The state pays for tuition. The farm I hope to pay for by my own exertions and the help of others here. As a rule, the colored people in the South are not and will not be able for years to board their children in school at ten or twelve dollars per month, hence my object is, as soon as possible, to get the school on a labor basis, so that earnest students can help themselves and at the same time learn the true dignity of labor. An institution for the education of colored youths can be but a *partial* success without a boarding department. In it they can be taught those correct habits which they fail to get at home. Without this part of the training they go out into the world with untrained intellects and their morals and bodies neglected. After the land is paid for, we hope to get a boarding department on foot as soon as possible.

The good-will manifested towards the school by both white and colored is a great encouragement to me to push the work forward. I have had many kind words of encouragement from the whites, and have been well treated by them in every way. The trustees seem to be exceptional men. Whether I have met the colored people in their churches, societies or homes, I have received their hearty co-operation and a "God bless you." Even the colored preachers seem to be highly in favor of the work, and one of the pastors here, fifty years old, is one of my students. I fear I am making my letter too long, I will write again soon. Yours sincerely,

B. T. Washington

Southern Workman, 10 (Sept. 1881), 94.

To James Fowle Baldwin Marshall

Tuskegee, Ala., July 16 1881

Dear Genl: Both your letters dated the 7th and 9th inst. respectfully have been rec'd, the latter containing your check for Two hundred dollars. I felt, very sensitively, when I made the request for the loan that it was an unusual transaction, but I sincerely hope and believe that the good that will result from it will fully warrant the departure from business rules. With all my heart, Genl, I thank you for this kindness. I have delayed this letter and the receipt longer than I should because I found myself so used up after teaching all day and doing other work that I had to delay writing till Saturday.

I thank you for your advice in the letter of the 7th. We now have the farm under control. About 25 acres are cleared, the other under wood. This I think is an advantage. I think the cleared land is in a better condition than the farm there was, though it is more hilly. This is a hilly country and it is hard to find a level place in a tract.

The land is deeded to the trustees not to be held as state property, hence the state has no control over the land. We expect to pay for that out side of state money.

Out side of what is raised for the school we hope to raise cotton as that seems to pay well.

Talladega is about one hundred and twenty five miles from here.

I am very sorry that I urged on Miss Davidson so hard to come here, since I have heard her condition. I now see that it is best for her to rest till Sept and come in a good condition. I am going to try to make other arrangements till then.

I hope that the Institute[1] was a success. Sincerely yours

B. T. Washington

[*Enclosure*]   Tuskegee Normal School, Tuskegee Ala.

Received, July 13th, 1881, from Gen. J. F. B. Marshall treasurer of the H. N. & A. Institute, ($200) Two hundred dollars to be used in the purchase of a farm for the Tuskegee Normal School, said Two hundred dollars to be returned Oct. 1st 1881.

B. T. Washington, Prin.

ALS and ADS   BTW Folder   President's Office Vault   ViHaI.

[1] This was a three-week teachers' institute conducted at Hampton Institute in the summer of 1881 with the aid of a $1,000 grant from the Peabody Education Fund.

To Francis Chickering Briggs

Tuskegee, Ala., July 16 1881

Dear, friend Mr. Briggs: I have been very glad to get the papers which you have been so kind as to send. I thank you for seeing about the maps &c.

I opened school two weeks ago with thirty students, now I have over forty. Many of them are school teachers and never have attended school themselves before. You can judge of their teaching.

The state only gives two thousand dollars annually to the school and this is to pay for tuition, though the trustees hope to save enought out of this amount to assist in building. Take away from Hampton every thing but the $10,000 which Va. gives and you about have our condition, only ours is $2000 for tuition.

The farm of 100 acres which we have just bought is deeded to the trustees not to be held as state property, but in the same way that the Hampton trustees hold that property, then in case the state at any time withdraws its aid we can go on with the school.

I borrowed $200 from Gen. M.[1] to be returned the first of Oct. next, with which to make the first payment on the land so that we could get immediate possession. The whole cost is $500. For the payment of the $200 at the time named I have pledged my salary. I hope to pay for the farm by the aid of friends here and elsewhere. Any thing you can do for us North in this direction or in any other way for the school will be very acceptable.

Very hot here now. Sincerely yours

B. T. Washington

ALS   BTW Folder   President's Office Vault   ViHaI.

[1] James Fowle Baldwin Marshall.

To James Fowle Baldwin Marshall

Tuskegee, Ala., July 18 1881

Dear friend: Yours of the 15th inst. is recd. and I confess that your remarks concerning my request to Mr. Hamilton[1] to come here have both surprised and hurt me very much. If there is any thing that I abhor in others, it is ingratitude to friends and to be accused of it myself strikes me pretty deeply.

Gen, I simply asked Mr. Hamilton to come here and stay till the first of Sept. I thought that there was no impropriety in doing so for these reasons: I knew he was employed there during Institute, I thought by the time my letter reached him that it would be closed and he would be with out employment by the school as he was last summer. I knew he spoke of going to the hotel last summer for work. I saw no more impropriety in asking him to spend a part of his vacation with me, than in asking Mr. Boswell White,[2] Miss Eliza Davis[3] or any one else who is not employed by the school during vacation. Mr. Hamilton told me before I left that he thought of spending part of his vacation North. He also told me that if it were possible he should like very much to come down here and help me make a start. I had no *idea* of inconveniencing you all in the least; for I did not think of his being employed any further than the Institute. Considering these facts I can not see where in I have acted improperly.

Though, granting all I have said to be so I may still be in the wrong, if so I can honestly say that it was an error of the head and not of the heart.

I think Gen, that you misconceived my intention. I wish you would ask Mr. H. to let you read my letter to him. I hope I may never live to be the student to show ingratitude to, or in any way hinder the progress of the institution whose officers and teachers I love so dearly and to whose parental care I owe all that I am. I hope that your reply will relieve me of a burden.

Please thank Miss Ludlow for her kindness and tell her that if she has found no one I will try to make out till Miss Davidson comes as the time is so short.

Am glad that the Institute was a success. Sincerely yours

B. T. Washington

ALS   BTW Folder   President's Office Vault   ViHaI.

[1] Robert H. Hamilton.

[2] Boswell S. White, born in Matthews County, Va., in 1856, attended Hampton, where he was a member of the Hampton Singers. After graduating in 1877 he taught school in Matthews County before leaving for Boston in 1884.

[3] Ann Eliza Davis, born in Whitewell, Va., in 1854, graduated from Hampton in 1878 and served as assistant in the sewing department there until her death in 1881.

To James Fowle Baldwin Marshall

Tuskegee, Ala., July 23 1881

Dear Genl: I telegraphed you yesterday that I would not need Miss Snodgrass,[1] but think that it was kind in her to volunteer to come. Accidently I found out that John W. Cardwell,[2] a graduate of Hampton in the class of 75 and who has also graduated at Lincoln University, was very near here and could come at very small expense and stay till Miss Davidson. You will remember him as a "singer." He begins with me Monday. Just what the traveling expenses are from there here, I could not find out here, and I thought this would be the safe plan as it is questionable whether one would be made whole or not coming from there, for so short a time.

The school does not board Miss Davidson or pay traveling expenses. Her salary will be $45 per m. for this term. Board about $12 per m. Yours truly

B. T. Washington

ALS   BTW Folder   President's Office Vault   ViHaI.

[1] Margaret E. Snodgrass was born in Bellefont, Ala., in 1854, and received her education in the public schools of Battle Creek, Mich., where her parents had fled from slavery. She attended Hampton during the school year 1878-79 and taught school in several Virginia towns before going to Tuskegee in 1881. For three years she taught the Negro public school of Tuskegee as a demonstration school for Tuskegee's normal program. In 1884 Miss Snodgrass taught in an Alabama school that had once housed the shop where her father had worked as a slave.

[2] John W. Cardwell (1856-86), born in Rockingham County, N.C., attended Hampton Institute as one of the Hampton Singers and graduated in 1875. He taught school in his home county before joining the Tuskegee faculty for the 1881-82 school year. He left Tuskegee to go to Clark University in Atlanta.

To the Editor of the *Southern Workman*

Tuskegee, Ala., Sept. 10th. 1881

Editor Southern Workman: Please allow me through your paper to express my heart felt thanks to the "vacation" students of Hampton for their noble efforts in behalf of the Tuskegee Normal School.

We were all no little surprised and gratified when we received a letter a few days ago, from Mr. M. M. Snowden,[1] stating that the students had raised, through an entertainment $60 or $75 to help us in the purchase of our farm.

To all who in any way aided in raising the money, the teachers at this school join me in words of praise and thankfulness.

With this generous gift and the aid of other friends, we are already nearly able to return the $200 borrowed to make our first payment. We have directed nearly all our efforts towards paying for the land, because this will give us a sure foundation on which to work.

That the colored people begin to help each other, is the best evidence of their progress. I was about to say that every dollar that we can get out of the colored people themselves, for educational purposes is worth two coming from elsewhere.

There is hope for an individual or a race when they begin to look outside of themselves.

In my last letter I reported that the school opened with thirty students. Now we have an enrollment of sixty.

We have made some efforts to interest the people in the different counties, in education. Many of the teachers and others begin to see their deficiencies and new students come in every week.

The people in this state have suffered not so much from the failure of the state to support the free schools, but from incompetent teachers. We hope within a few months to make our humble efforts here felt in the surrounding counties. Of course we have to labor under many disadvantages, not having apparatus, school furniture and suitable buildings. This ought not to be so, for when teachers come here thirsty for knowledge and with only money enough to remain in school a few months, we ought to be able to give them the best advantages at once. Some of these wants are being supplied by friends and we hope in a few months to double the advantages of the school. There is much that is encouraging in the work. The students are anxious to improve and they pin themselves down to study without coercion.

B. T. Washington

Southern Workman, 10 (Oct. 1881), 101.

[1] Morgan M. Snowden was born in Leesburg, Va., in 1854. He was a member of the Hampton class of 1881 and taught school in several Virginia localities. Later he became a railroad porter. In 1888 he married Ellen L. Walker of the Hampton class of 1877 and settled in New York as a janitor.

Olivia A. Davidson to Mary Berry[1]

Tuskegee, Ala., Sept. 12, 1881

My dear Mary; (May I call you so?) Miss Trask[2] wrote me that you had succeeded in getting a position in your town as teacher and I am so glad for you. I suppose you have already begun your work. May you be successful in it and find it pleasant in every way. Dont you feel sad when you think that now the girls are back again at work at F[3] and we are not to return? The thought really makes me homesick at times, but I try to keep it from effecting my work. I reached here Aug. 25, and found plenty of work to do I assure you. Ah, Mary dear, I feel very very weak when I look about me at the work there is to be done. Our school is fast growing. Already there are nearly seventy in attendance and although they are mostly young men and women in age, in their mental acquirements they are far below your average grammar school pupil of the first year. And besides, having come from the most ignorant families most of them are entirely uncultivated in manners and habits and need so much training, and with all this to contend with we must go on and do our school work with nothing outside of ourselves with which to do it — not a reference book of *any* kind belonging to the school! Think of it — a Normal school without even a Dictionary or map of the U.S.!!

But I am not going to fill my letter with complaints. I shall try to be grateful that I have so soon found work to do in such great abundance. This reminds me of Emma Coolidge.[4] I do hope she will be able to get work this year. Write to her. I know it would be such a pleasure for her to get a letter from you for she was very much attached to you

— poor dear child. How patient and good she is! Miss Daniels[5] I learn has obtained the Fram. School (Primary Dep't).

I went thirteen miles in the country Saturday evening to a camp meeting, and had a most novel and interesting time. There were a great many people there and these with their strange costumes, customs wild religious services, songs and shoutings, together with the mules oxen and strange vehicles of every description, made up a scene which, having once seen one can never forget but which is utterly indescribable. I wish you could have seen it all. I "camped out" in one of the "tents," a low log hut, of which there were many built for the purpose on the ground. Returned Sunday night by moonlight — enjoyed it all very much.

The first vol. of the "Round Robin" is finished and starts in the morning to Miss Emerson.[6] I have put your name in Miss Daniel's place, so Emma Coolidge will write to you, as I did not wish to have Miss Baker[7] & Daniels, both in Fram., so near together. You will write to Mattie Davis.[8]

Please write to me telling me how you have spent the summer and all about yourself — you dont know how lonely I get here sometimes.

Remember me kindly to your mother and sisters. With much love, I am   Very sincerely your friend

Olivia A. Davidson

ALS   File XT5   Framingham State Normal School Manuscripts   MH.

[1] The Boston *Transcript,* June 29, 1881, listed the members of Olivia Davidson's class of 1881. Mary Berry was not listed.

[2] Mary E. Trask of South Jefferson, Me.

[3] State Normal School, Framingham, Mass.

[4] Emma A. Coolidge of Hancock, N.H.

[5] Jennie M. Daniels of Newton, Mass.

[6] Bertha L. Emerson of Milford, Mass.

[7] Edith B. Baker of Lunenburg, Mass.

[8] Martha J. Davis of Dunstable, Mass.

To James Fowle Baldwin Marshall

Tuskegee, Ala., Sept 28 1881

Dear Genl: Please find enclosed post office orders for $95 and letters from Miss Longstreth[1] and Gen. Armstrong assuming $125.00 of the debt.

I will not need, however, to accept all of Gen. A's loan as I shall be able next week to send you at least $25 more in cash.

If these letters do not give satisfaction please let me know and I will forward the cash next week.

We are all under many obligations to you for your kindness. We now begin to see our way to the light. Our work is growing rapidly. Faithfully yours

B. T. Washington

P.S. Please return letters.

ALS   BTW Folder   President's Office Vault   ViHaI.

[1] Mary Anna Longstreth (1811-84) conducted a small school in Philadelphia with her sister for fifty years after 1829. In 1872, becoming interested in Hampton Institute, she raised funds and collected materials in the Philadephia area. In 1898 the Mary Anna Longstreth Alumnae Association was formed to carry on charitable work in her memory.

To James Fowle Baldwin Marshall

Tuskegee, Ala., Oct. 7 1881

Dear Genl: You will find enclosed post office orders for $61 to be credited on your loan.

I feel much encour[a]ged by the generous response of friends. In a few more weeks I think that I shall be able to send you the bal. due.

I have just rec'd a letter from the Smith Organ Company[1] of Boston saying that they have made us a donation of one of their organs. Mrs. Hemingway[2] and Prof. Warren[3] are doing much for us.

We have about seventy students now and new ones come in every week.

I met the state supt. a few days ago in Montgomery and he seems to be much pleased with our work.

Miss Davidson's services are inestimable. She wishes to be remembered to you.

I hope that Hampton may have a prosperous year.

I have just received an invitation to lecture before an audience in Montgomery. Faithfully yours

B. T. Washington

ALS BTW Folder President's Office Vault ViHaI.

¹ The president of the Smith Organ Company was Samuel D. Smith, one of the vice-presidents of the American Missionary Association.

² Mary Tileston Hemenway (1793-1894) was the daughter of Thomas Tileston of Boston, who had made a fortune in Latin-American shipping. Married to another prominent shipper, Augustus Hemenway, she became a prominent philanthropist, supporting archaeological and ethnological research, maintenance of the Old South Meeting House of Boston, preservation of Pueblo Indian culture, and many educational enterprises. She founded Tileston Normal School, Wilmington, N.C., for the education of poor whites, as well as the Boston Normal School of Gymnastics and the Boston Normal School of Cookery. Her contributions to Hampton totaled over $35,000.

³ Henry Pitt Warren (1846-1919), born in Windham, Me., attended Phillips Academy, Amherst, and Yale University. In 1879, after serving as principal and teacher at lower grades, he became principal of the New Hampshire State Normal School at Plymouth. During the summer of 1881 he conducted a three-week teacher's institute at Hampton Institute.

To James Fowle Baldwin Marshall

Tuskegee, Ala., [Nov.?] 3 1881¹

Dear Genl: Yours is rec'd. It is very encouraging to us to know that you are so deeply interested in our work.

In regard to reading matter, we have been pretty well supplied with papers since you have been sending the "Ledger"² and "Christian at Work,"³ but I rec'd a card today from the publishers stating that the subscription to the "Chris. at Work" had expired. We have no monthlies at all and such magazines would be of great value to us.

We have a photographer and he says that he thinks he can do the work next week, though he is somewhat on the Larribee style.⁴ We thank you very much for your kindness in the matter.

As you say there is a great work before us, but by hard work and a trust in God we b[e]lieve we can accomplish some of it. One can not understand how much is needed to be done here till he dwells in the midst of the people for a while.

Our first object is to pay for the land. To aid in this we have started a subscription paper round among the white and colored citizens of this town. Don't know yet what the result will be. We are also getting up an entertainment for the same object. In these two ways we hope to raise a good part of the $3.19[5] still due.

You will see by the photograph that we must have more suitable buildings. The attendance of students this year has been greater than was expected, but we hope to make the present buildings do for this year. I have no idea that the state will do more than pay for tuition, that seems to be their general policy in all the schools. I met the State Supt[6] a few days ago, in Montgomery, who seems pleased with our work and promises to try to secure Peabody[7] aid for us next year.

We hope to pay for the land before our school term ends. After this Miss Davidson and I have been planning to spend a good part of our vacation in trying to get up a building. We *must* have a building by next term or we will have no where to accommodate the students.

One great difficulty under which we have to labor now, is the irregular attendance of our students; most of them are so poor that they are not able to stay here and pay board for more than three or four months at the time before they have to go to teaching again. Some remain in school a few days or weeks, and have to go out and work on their farms a while and return. Most of the former teachers are married wh[i]ch makes it an exceedingly hard struggle for them. The sacrifices that many of the students are making for the purpose of remaining in school are most praise worthy. Of course the irregular attendance detracts much from the value of our work. While some have to go others come and our present attendance is about eighty and will probably remain about that this term. Now as soon as we are able to put our land under cultivation we will be able to remedy this difficulty to a certain extent. With the coming spring we ought to be able to make at least a start so that the farm will be of some value to us the next year, but we are without implements, stock, vehicles or capital, yet we may see our way to the light by the time spring approaches. We must have at least a small amount of the things I have mentioned before we can do anything.

Our land is not the regular cotton land though it will grow cotton, but I am satisfied that that will not be the most profitable thing to cultivate. The regular cotton land is low and swampy. Our land will produce all the common vegetables and especially sweet potatoes. Such things will pay us well, we can sell what we do not consume.

We hope to unite the common school here, with our school as a model school.[8] In this Miss Snodgrass will be very valuable to us.

The students seem to appreciate our work for them, and it is quite encouraging to see the great improvement which they are making in every way.

Mr. Fessenden[9] has been very kind to us in several ways. Through him we have secured the gift of an excellent organ from the Smith organ company.

Miss Davidson's services are inestimable. She throws her whole self into the work.

I shall try to remember your advice and make haste slowly. Shall be glad of any suggestions from you in regard to our future plans.

Please remember me kindly to Mrs. Marshall.[10]

Miss Davidson sends her regards to you.

If there is any other point on which you want information about the school I shall be glad to write you. Faithfully yours

B. T. Washington

ALS   BTW Folder   President's Office Vault   ViHaI.

[1] The month seems to be November, since BTW thanked Marshall for the Philadelphia *Ledger* in late October and in late November a large donation enabled Tuskegee to pay for the land. (See BTW to Marshall, Oct. 24 and Nov. 28, 1881, BTW Folder, President's Office Vault, ViHaI.)

[2] The New York *Ledger,* a weekly magazine published in New York City "devoted to choice literature, romance, the news, and commerce," was first published in 1856 and terminated in 1899.

[3] *Christian at Work,* a religious weekly published in New York City under varying titles — *The Christian Work, Christian Work and the Evangelist, Christian at Work.* The magazine was first published in 1874 and was merged into *Christian Century* in 1926. It was edited from 1880 to 1913 by Joseph Newton Hallock (1834-1913), a Congregational minister and temperance worker who also wrote a biography of Dwight L. Moody (1900).

[4] William F. Larrabee was a white photographer in the vicinity of Hampton Institute.

[5] Actually $319.

[6] Henry Clay Armstrong (1840-1900). Armstrong was born in Georgia and after serving in the Civil War moved to Tuskegee, Ala. There he practiced law and in 1874 was elected to the legislature. He was superintendent of education in Alabama from 1880 to 1884. Later Armstrong again served in the legislature and from 1885 to 1889 was consul general at Rio de Janeiro.

[7] The Peabody Education Fund for southerners of both races was established by George Peabody in 1867 with an initial gift of one million dollars. A native of Massachusetts, Peabody began the accumulation of his fortune in Baltimore but for thirty years was a resident of London. Barnas Sears, former president of Brown College, became the fund's first director, and he channeled the money toward the training of teachers who would carry education into the poorer and more depressed sections of the South. Part of the task of the fund was to stimulate interest in education, and some of the money was given directly to individuals as scholarships for prospective teachers, usually for about $50, sometimes less for black students. Sears served as agent from 1867 to 1880, and he was especially generous to Fisk University, Atlanta University, Hampton Institute, Richmond Normal School, and schools in Louisiana and West Virginia. In 1881 Jabez Lamar Monroe Curry was agent of the fund, and BTW's program at Tuskegee especially appealed to him. From the beginning the Peabody Fund supported normal and industrial training and school segregation.

[8] The model school which Tuskegee succeeded in opening the following academic year replaced two existing black schools, one Baptist and one Methodist. Olivia Davidson reported the event as a milestone in overcoming traditional denominational prejudice in the black community: "To day, for the first time here in many years, I suppose, the children of the two denominations met in school together. We hope for much good in the way of influence upon both parents and children as a result of this union." The model school began with about 300 students, three times the attendance of the normal school itself. (Olivia A. Davidson to editor, Oct. 15, 1882, in *Southern Workman*, 11 [Nov. 1882], 109.)

[9] Thomas Kendall Fessenden.

[10] Martha A. Twicross Johnson Marshall (1824-91).

From James Fowle Baldwin Marshall

[Hampton, Va.] Nov 12 [188]1

Dear Booker, I enclose Cashiers check Bank of Norwich No. 24 340 for $200. This is a donation in and of your enterprise from Moses Pierce Esq[1] of that place. Mr. P. is a friend of the Mackies[2] and of the School. Miss Ludlow through whom he sent the check, will write you of its object. I congratulate you both upon this liberal gift & hope it is but the preview of many others to help on the good work. Let me here impress upon you the importance of keeping a careful record of all receipts and expenditures. The detailed reports annually rendered from this office, as we have often been assured by our friends, have given confidence to donors & unstinted liberality, because they knew that every dollar would be accounted for.

I was very glad to receive your letter & shall try to make good use of the information it contains. How do you propose to hold the property, land, buildings implements &c that you may acquire for the School use. It should be made secure against all risk of misappropriation so as to inspire confidence. What is the State doing for education generally? Can you send me the last Report of the Supt of Public Instruction? or give me any information about it. Yours faithfully,

J. F. B. Marshall

ALpS Business Office ViHaI.

¹ Moses Pierce (1808-1900) was a strong advocate of industrial education for southern blacks and one of the earliest northern friends of Tuskegee Institute. He made his fortune in textiles, owning major interests in the companies in Norwich and Jewett City, Conn. He was a close friend of John Fox Slater, a Norwich neighbor, whose cotton mills were located in Jewett City. In the early 1880s Pierce was instrumental in convincing Slater to channel a million dollars into a special fund for the education of Negroes, the future Slater Fund. Pierce gave Hampton Institute a two-story brick shop for its iron work in the 1880s.

² Charlotte L. and Mary Fletcher Mackie.

To James Fowle Baldwin Marshall

Tuskegee, Ala., Nov. 18, 1881

Dear Gen: Your letter containing a check for $200 from Mr. Pierce, is received. We had scarcely dared to hope for such a surprise. Our thanks are more than I can express. You should have been in our school room the morning that I announced the news to the students. They made the room ring with cheers and sent a hearty vote of thanks to the donor. We have every thing to encourage us. Our indebtedness is now only a little more than $100 and we are making strong efforts to raise a large portion of it here and think that we shall be successful.

If possible we want to begin the cultivation of the farm in the spring or probably before.

I thank you for your advice in regard to keeping a strict record of every thing and I shall follow it closely.

I propose to have the land &c. deeded to the state trustees but it is not to be held by them as *state* property. Our trustees so understand it. I would be glad of your advice on this point.

The State has not failed to appropriate money for education, but it has been expended in a way to do the people but little good. They have employed teachers with no regard to their competency. They build no school houses nor do they supply teachers with any other conveniencies. In short they simply pay the teachers.

I met the State Supt, Mr. H. C. Armstrong, a few days ago in Montgomery. He seemed pleased with our work here. He is a fine man and I think that if he remains in office he will make quite an improvement in the school system in a few years. I send you one of the last reports. New ones will be out soon. Will send one.

Express charges from here to N.Y. are $1.00 for 10 lbs, and $4.50 per hundred, 5 lbs, .75 cts, & so on.

The charges on freight from N.Y here are .90 cts to $1.50 (according to the class) per hundred. We receive and send mail twice every day in the week.

We have had to change somewhat from our original plan. It was our intention to have moved on the farm by this time. We have not done so for this reason: when I spoke of moving there I did not think that we would have more than sixty students this year, but now we have eighty and new ones come in every week. We have four good recitations rooms on the farm, but no *one* of them will do for an assembly room as the school stands now. The church which we occupy now makes a pretty good assembly room and we have taken the public school house, (which would have been Miss Snodgrass') and made two rooms of it. So Miss Snodgrass is going to open her school on the farm and the other rooms not occupied by her, our students will use for dormitories. Under the circumstances this is the preferable plan. By next term we will either have up a new building or so enlarge one of [the] present rooms as to make it fit for an assembly room.

We expect to have a man trim our fruit trees next week. With care I think that they will bear well next year.

Miss Davidson and Mr. Cardwell desire to be remembered to you. They both join me in thanks to you and other Hampton teachers for your many kindnesses. Sincerely yours

B. T. Washington

ALS BTW Folder President's Office Vault ViHaI. Docketed "R&A Nov. 23" in Marshall's hand.

From James Fowle Baldwin Marshall

[Hampton, Va.] Nov 23 [188]1

Dear Booker, I recd today your note of acknowledgment of Mr Pierces Donation. I now have the additional pleasure of sending you my check for one hundred Dollars, a gift from Mrs [Hemenway] who says "This is my tribute to Olivia, & shows the entire faith I have in her capacity & willingness to do a good work for her people." She is hoping to get off a box for her next week. Mrs H. had promised to send the [$100] whenever Mr Pierce sent his $200. I hope these gifts will only stimulate your people and friends there to do even more than they expected. God helps those who help themselves. I hope you will raise the money for a proper School building & for your needed apparatus & implements. If you have full confidence in your trustees, they may be the best ones to hold the School property &c in time, but you had better advise with Genl Armstrong as to your whole plan. With best wishes to yourself & your colaborers. Yours faithfully,

J. F. B. Marshall

ALpS   Business Office   ViHaI.

To Samuel Chapman Armstrong

Tuskegee, Ala., Nov. 27 1881

Dear Gen. I am glad to say to you that we have in hands all the money needed to complete the payment on the land.

I want your advice as to how the land and other property should be deeded. I had thought of having it deed[ed] to the present state trustees to be held by them in trust for the education of colored people, but they are not to hold it as *state* property. I suggested this to them and they agreed to it. But I should rather have your advice on the subject before the deed is made out. Miss Davidson and Mr. Cardwell desire to be remembered to you. Faithfully yours

B. T. Washington

ALS   BTW Folder   President's Office Vault   ViHaI.

To James Fowle Baldwin Marshall

Tuskegee, Ala., Nov. 28, 1881

Dear Gen: Your letter of the 23rd inst. containing your check for $100.00 coming from Mrs. Hemenway, is received.

Tuskegee Normal School can never forget its Northern friends.

Miss Davidson has written Mrs. Hemenway a letter of thanks.

With this generous gift we are able to complete our payment on the land, however this will not cause us to slacken our efforts in doing all we can for ourselves.

Miss Davidson deserves all the good things which Mrs. Hemenway says of her.

Please find enclosed my check for $19.00 which I believe is the bal. due on your loan. Sincerely yours

B. T. Washington

ALS   BTW Folder   President's Office Vault   ViHaI.

To James Fowle Baldwin Marshall

Tuskegee, Ala., Nov. 29, 1881

Dear Gen: Enclosed you will find a letter which I have just received from Mr. Pierce. If hard work and perseverance will do it we will try to come up to his proposition.[1] It is very encouraging to know that our friends are so interested in us.

Thanks for your direction about the paper. Shall send to Mr. Betts[2] for it. Please return letter. Sincerely yours

B. T. Washington

I send you today a copy of State Supt's last report.

ALS   BTW Folder   President's Office Vault   ViHaI.   The acknowledgment by BTW here of "your direction about the paper" establishes the correspondent as Marshall. BTW had written Marshall eight days earlier requesting information on paper supplies. (BTW to Marshall, Nov. 21, 1881, *ibid.*)

[1] The proposition is further explained in BTW to *Southern Workman*, Dec. 18, 1881.

[2] Charles W. Betts, of Wilmington, Del., became manager of the Normal School Press at Hampton in October 1881.

From James Fowle Baldwin Marshall

[Hampton, Va.] Dec 3rd [188]1

My dear Washington I have your letter with check for $19. balance of your loan account, for which I hand you my receipt herewith. Gen Armstrong wishes me to say that he received your letter of 27th asking his advice as to the trust matter, and that we have consulted together about it. We think that as these donations are given, through our faith in you that it would give more confidence to the friends who are likely to aid your enterprise to have you, one of the Trustees, in charge of the School property. You certainly ought to have a voice in its management. We think also that there should be a declaration, by the Trustees, of the objects for which they hold the Trust, a copy of which declaration could if necessary at any time be printed and sent to friends, to inspire confidence that the money will be well applied. I congratulate you on having paid for your farm, and on your good prospects generally. With kind regards to the Hamptonians with you, I am yours truly

J. F. B. Marshall

HLpS Business Office ViHaI.

To James Fowle Baldwin Marshall

Tuskegee Ala, Dec. 4, 1881

I addressed the report to you. If it has not reached you when you receive this card I will send another one. Pronounce Tuskegee with g hard, accent on "ke." Yours

B. T. Washington

ACS BTW Folder President's Office Vault ViHaI.

To Hampton Institute

Tuskegee Ala   4 Dec 188[1][1]

How is Fannie answer quick by telegraph

B T Washington

WSr   BTW Folder   President's Office Vault   ViHaI.

[1] The year is presumably 1881, when Fanny Smith was completing her last year at Hampton. By December 1882 she was married to BTW and residing at Tuskegee.

To the Editor of the *Southern Workman*

Tuskegee, Ala., Dec. 18, 1881

Dear Friend: Four months and a half ago, without a dollar of our own, we contracted to buy a farm of one hundred acres, at a cost of $500, on which to permanently locate our school. To-day the last dollar has been paid. While most of the money to pay for the farm has come from the North, the people here have not failed to help themselves. Almost one month ago, when we wanted but one hundred dollars more to complete the payment on the land, we resolved to raise that amount here in Alabama. To do this, three plans were put on foot. First, the students were to give a literary entertainment; second, a supper or festival was to come the next week after the entertainment; third, two of the leading citizens were appointed to solicit subscriptions among the whites and colored.

The students were made to understand that others were willing to help them provided they did something for themselves. With this in view they went to work, taking as little time for preparation from their regular studies as possible. In a few weeks all had their parts well learned. On the night of the exhibition, each student seemed to feel a personal responsibility. There was an air of earnestness and order in everything they did. The entertainment was attended by a good house of colored citizens and some whites. One of the latter[1] who had already subscribed five dollars towards paying for the land, was so well pleased with the entertainment that he sent up word at the close that he would give five dollars more. Another one said that it was the best exhibition of the kind he had ever attended. From this entertainment we netted over $20.00. Directly afterwards we began preparations for the supper, Miss Davidson taking the lead. That we might incur as little expense as possible, each student having parents or friends living in town was asked to get them to give something towards the supper. Five ladies here in town kindly volunteered to assist Miss Davidson in carrying out the supper. An hour was appointed for contributions to be brought to the hall. It was a real pleasure and encouragement to see how generously the people responded. A long table was soon laden with cakes, turkeys, chickens, &c., &c. At night the people turned out *en masse.* In this also the students did not fail to do their part. The girls in our junior or highest class, originated the idea of their having a table of fancy candies, &c. They begged the money with which to carry out their plan, and from that table we realized a handsome sum. Some of the girls attended the table, while others would drum up customers. One girl played the "peanut woman" well through the crowd, while one little fellow peddled apples for his share of the work, and another one candy. To make sure of a good attendance at the hall, fifteen young men formed themselves into a committee to canvass different parts of the town. From the supper we cleared $50.00.

Through the subscription papers we received aid from both white and colored. Almost every prominent citizen of both races, either has given something or has promised to do so soon. As a result of the exhibition, supper and subscription papers, we now have in hands $94.00, and, before this letter is read, we expect to receive enough from unpaid subscriptions to make the sum more than one hundred dollars.

While we were in the midst of carrying out the above named plans, we were very pleasantly surprised by receiving a donation of $100.00 from a lady in Boston,[2] who has never failed to help the Negro to help himself; and in a few days more a letter came from a generous friend in Connecticut,[3] who had already given us $200.00 towards paying for the land, saying that if we would raise $115.00 (the amount then due on the land) in Alabama by the first of next January, he would donate to us $100.00 more with which to buy tools, seeds, &c., for the equipment of the farm. We only want twenty-six dollars more to comply with his proposition. We will get it.

Now that the farm is paid for, it should not be permitted to remain idle. Our students are too badly in need of the aid which can come from it. We want to put in a crop as soon as the weather permits. To do this we need stock, vehicles, tools, a stable, cash to pay for first year's labor, &c. What a lift up it would be to our students could we get the three or four hundred dollars needed to make this start.

One thing that probably retards the progress of education in the Normal and other high schools in the South more than anything else, is the "in and out" system. Few students are able to remain in school an entire term because they are *not able to pay board*. More than once this term when students have stayed here till their last dollar was spent, have they come to me with tears in their eyes to say, "I must go." Several are cooking for themselves, that they may squeeze through the term. We do not want our students to become objects of charity. We only want to make the school able to give them a *chance to help themselves*. Our plan will have two advantages: first, it will permit the students to remain in school; secondly, it will teach them how to labor.

In the South, education of the head and hand must go together. While the girl learns arithmetic she must learn to set a table, or she will never learn it. Trained farmers are as much needed as trained teachers.

As soon as the farm is equipped, we expect to direct our energies towards getting up a school building by next term. The present buildings on the farm will be entirely insufficient to accommodate the school next term. We may seem to be planning much, but remembering that God helps those who help themselves, we will go forward. Yours faithfully,

B. T. Washington

Southern Workman, 11 (Jan. 1882), 9.

[1] J. A. Grimmett, a Republican, later postmaster of Tuskegee.
[2] Mary Tileston Hemenway.
[3] Moses Pierce.

To Oliver Otis Howard

Tuskegee, Ala., Jan. 10 1882

Dear Sir: You will doubtless be surprised on receiving this letter. I am a graduate of Hampton Inst. of which you were one of the founders. Was appointed Prin. of this school about seven months ago. We want to establish our school on the Hampton plan. We have already bought and paid for a farm of 100 acres. We have done this independent of state aid. The students begin the cultivation of the farm this season. Within the last few weeks I have rec'd enough money from the North with which to make the start on the farm. We expect to have up new buildings by the next school year.

Knowing that you have always been an active friend to the colored people I write to ask you if you will not become one of the trustees of this school. We expect to have in all 9 trustees including the 3 State Commissioners who control the state appropriations. Most of the other trustees are to be selected from the North.

Our school has the confidence of Gen. Armstrong and you can refer to him for any fact concerning it.

The only excuse I have to offer for my boldness in writing you, is that I believe that you are the one to do us good and have written you accordingly. Yours Sincerely

B. T. Washington

ALS   Oliver Otis Howard Papers   MeB.

From [Moses Pierce]

[Norwich, Conn., January 1882]

While it is very important to learn to read, write and cipher, it is equally important to learn to work, and to form the *habit* of industry. At great cost of life and treasure, your race have obtained freedom and the right of suffrage. Now what you need is knowledge and independence, which can only be obtained, each one for him or herself, by hard study and diligent labor. Never spend a penny for anything without full consideration of the necessity of doing it. Industry and economy lead to independence. Wealth does not always secure independence. The man with a saw-buck, who saws wood for a living, who owes no man anything, except love and good will, who lives and provides for those dependent on him with his daily earnings, is often more independent than many men with more money.

Self reliance and self-respect are important for every man and woman to have — not pride, but consciousness of the will and ability

Map 3. Macon and surrounding Alabama counties.

to make a place for themselves in the world. Spend no time in making a reputation; they are often made and destroyed in an hour; but look well to the character you are making; this is the work of a lifetime. A good character for honesty, industry — for good will to all men, with a will and desire to do right to all, with that love to God and man, which is our reasonable service; forms a character like the marble column; pure and white, and is only stained or marred by our own wrong-doing. The color of a man or woman will not blemish the white column; bad conduct, unkind feelings towards others will, whether they have a black or white skin.

The true glory of a man or woman is goodness; not wealth or learning, both of which it is important to have if we make good use of them in doing good to others.

For more than fifty years I have taken a deep interest in your race, and labored for their freedom until it was obtained, and since they have been made free, I have a strong desire that by their sobriety, their industry, their diligence in well-doing, they may prove to the world that they are worthy, and that they will make a good return for all that has been done for them.

With my best wishes for your success in your efforts to raise up teachers and to do good to your race and to all men, with kind regard to all your teachers, and scholars, as well as yourself, I am yours truly,

[Moses Pierce]

P.S. I like the pleasure of giving, but not the notoriety; therefore do not wish my name published in connection with any thing I do.

Southern Workman, 11 (Jan. 1882), 10. The editors of *Southern Workman* considered this letter, accompanied by a gift, "so full of kindly and valuable counsel that we fully agree with Mr. Washington's wish to give it a wider audience; only regretting that we may not add to it the force of the writer's name." Correspondence of the previous two months suggests that the writer was Moses Pierce.

CATALOGUE

OF THE

AT

TUSKEGEE, ALABAMA,

FOR THE ACADEMICAL YEAR,

1881--82.

HAMPTON, VA:
Normal School Steam Press,
1882.

STATE COMMISSIONERS

Mr. GEO. W. CAMPBELL, Tuskegee, Ala.
Mr. M. B. SWANSON,   "   "
Mr. LEWIS ADAMS,   "   "

TRUSTEES

Mr. G. W. CAMPBELL, Tuskegee
Hon. HENRY D. SMITH,[2] Plantsville, Conn.
Hon. H. CLAY ARMSTRONG, Montgomery, Ala.
Mr. LEWIS ADAMS, Tuskegee
Miss ABBY W. MAY,[3] Boston, Mass.
Mr. M. B. SWANSON, Tuskegee, Ala.
Mr. B. T. WASHINGTON, Tuskegee, Ala.

INSTRUCTORS

BOOKER T. WASHINGTON, Principal
Miss OLIVIA A. DAVIDSON
JOHN W. CARDWELL

STUDENTS

JUNIOR CLASS

Adams, Virginia L.	Tuskegee
Allen, Ella	Gueryton, Bullock Co.
Bowen, Kaziah	Tuskegee
Bowen, Berry	"
Bowen, Neelie	"
Calhoun, Josie. A.	Opelika, Lee Co.
Floyd, Laura B.	" " "
Greenwood, Amelia	" " "
Lyman, Louisa	" " "
McCullough, Ella	Tuskegee
Torbert, Alice A.	" 10[4]
Anthony, Wm. J.	"
Allen, Alexander G. W.	Enon, Bullock Co.
Campbell, Meridith C.	Union Springs, Bullock Co.
Dawkins, John H.	Salem, Lee Co.
Greenwood, Peter W.	Opelika, Lee Co.
Gomez, Reuben L.	Tuskegee
Gassaway, Brantt	"
Gregory, Wm.	Dick's Creek, Macon Co.
Hollis, John T.	Cotton Valley, " "

Harvey, B. Town   Gueryton, Bullock Co.
Harvey, Austin H.   "   "   "
McCullough, Lewis D.   Ft. Mitchell, Russell "
Reese, Howard J.   Tuskegee
Stevens, Bell C.   "
Stakely, John W.   Cotton Valley, Macon Co.
Thweatt, Hiram   Tuskegee
Todd, Franklin L.   Union Springs, Bullock Co.
Thomas, John C.   Troy, Pike Co.   18
     —
     28

PREPARATORY CLASS

A SECTION

Alexander, Amy E.   Montgomery
Bunkley, Francis [Frances?]   Tuskegee
Bunkley, Alice   "
Chapell, Roxy   "
Cropper, Lulu M.   "
Hendree, Mary   "
James, Leanna   "
Ligon, Eliza   "
Pollard, Mattie   "
Smith, Caroline   "
Stevens, Emma   "
Thomas, Ella   "
Thomas, Cornelia   "
Varner, Clara   "   14

Adams, Wm. T.   Tuskegee
Cropper, Wm. A.   "
Edwards, Floyd   Salem, Lee Co.
Evans, Thomas   Tuskegee
Hoffman, Robert L.   "
Harris, Washington   "
Harris, Rigdon   Cotton Valley, Macon Co.
Haynes, Elijah G.   "   "   "   "
Ivory, Lewis   Glenville, Russell Co.
Irving, Charles   Tuskegee
Motley, John B.   "
McMorris, Thomas S.   Tallassee, Elmore Co.
McLemore, John F.   Cusseta, Chambers Co.
Mackey, J. Robert   Lafayette, "   "
Mennifield, Wm. Butler   Montgomery
Pew, Wiley   Tuskegee
Phillips, Randall R.   Gueryton, Bullock Co.

Peterson, Lewis	Tuskegee
Pace, George W.	Creek Stand, Macon Co.
Thomas, Cary	Farrowville, Bullock　"
Thweatt, Raymond S.	Tuskegee
Vaughn, Major B.	Crawford, Russell Co.
Woodall, Nelson	Society Hill, Macon Co.
Wilson, Alexander	Troy, Pike　"
Welborn, Russel[l?] T.	Hurtville, Russell　"
Young, Lewis	Tuskegee　　26

$$\frac{}{40}$$

B SECTION

Adams, Mary A.	Tuskegee
Bradley, Sallie	"
Daniels, Catherine	Tallassee, Elmore Co.
Foster, Lucy	Tuskegee
Foster, Minerva	"
Gilbert, Annie	Three Knott, Bullock Co.
Hughly, Isore	Opelika, Lee Co.
Harrison, Amarinthea	Tuskegee
Holland, Ella	"
Ligon, Eugenia	Cotton Valley, Macon Co.
McCollough [McCullough?], Mary	Ft. Mitchell, Russell　"
Neal, Sarah A.	Union Springs, Bullock "
Rogers, Ella	Tuskegee
Ross, Katie	Tallassee, Elmore Co.
Rushing, Julia	"　　　"　　　"
Smith, Rowena	Tuskegee
Smith, Mary E.	Shorter's Station
Smith, Fanny	East Tallassee, Tallapoosa Co.
Strong, Missouri	Tuskegee
Towns, Alice	"
Torbert, Martha	Hurtsville, Russell Co.
Williams, Sallie	Ft. Hull, Macon　"
Williams, Callie	Tallassee, Elmore　"
Wilborn, Rowena	Tuskegee
Wright, Minnie	Union Springs, Bullock Co.　25

Chapell, Robert C.	Tuskegee
Colquitt, Lewis	Opelika, Lee Co.
Dawkins, James W.	Gueryton, Bullock Co.
Freeman, Henry	Lafayette, Chambers Co.
Harris, Edmond	Cotton Valley, Macon Co.
Huffman, Hiram	Ft. Hull,　　　"　　"
Jenkins, Cullen	Hurtsville, Russell　"

Johnson, Seymour	Warrior Stand, Macon Co.
Key, Daniel	Creek Stand, " "
Ligon, Charles	Tuskegee, " "
Moore, Edward	Warrior Stand, " "
McClarren, Wm.	Clough's Station, " "
Payne, Woodly	Farrowville, Bullock "
Reid, Wm.	Warrior Stand, Macon "
Torbert, Luke	Tuskegee, " "
Thompson, Edmond	Cusseta, Chambers "
Trammel, Andrew	Milltown, Chambers "
Wright, Henry	Union Springs, Bullock Co.
Wilkinson, John H.	Tuskegee 19

44

SUMMARY

Junior Class	
Girls	10
Boys	18
Preparatory Class	
A. Section	
Girls	14
Boys	26
B. Section	
Girls	25
Boys	19
Total	112

COURSE OF STUDY

The course of instruction continues through a period of four years, beginning with the Junior year.

JUNIOR YEAR

LANGUAGE

Elocution and Reading — Physical and vocal drill.

Orthography — Spelling and dictation exercises, (both written,) and punctuation.

Composition — Original composition, oral and written, including sentence-making, letter-writing, (business and friendly,) and composition on general topics; abstracts.

Grammar — Analysis of sentences; parsing.

MATHEMATICS

Mental and Written Arithmetic — Completing factoring, decimal and common fractions, U.S. money and denominate numbers, and begin percentage.

GEOMETRY

Study of lines and angles and common forms of surfaces and solids.

GEOGRAPHY

Study of natural and political divisions of land and water, commercial geography, special study of the geography and history of Alabama, and map drawing.

HISTORY

History of the United States and outlines of form of government of. Lives and characters of prominent men connected with each period.

WRITING

Elements of letters and Spencerian copy-book.

GYMNASTICS

VOCAL MUSIC

B Middle Year

LANGUAGE

Reading and Elocution — Physical and vocal drill; definitions of terms used and principles.

Orthography — Spelling and dictation exercises (written,) and punctuation.

Composition — Original, oral and written, including simple stories, letter-writing (business and friendly,) and compositions on general topics; abstracts.

Grammar — Analysis and parsing; simple figures of speech.

MATHEMATICS

Mental arithmetic completed; written arithmetic and elementary algebra.

GEOMETRY

Geometrical drawing.

GEOGRAPHY

Mathematical and physical geography, first half of year.

ASTRONOMY

Simple lessons in, during last half of year.

HISTORY

Outline of universal history.

PHYSIOLOGY AND HYGIENE

VOCAL MUSIC

WRITING

Elements of letters and Spencerian copy-books.

GYMNASTICS

A Middle Year

LANGUAGE

Elocution
Orthography
Composition — Oral and written.
Rhetoric

LITERATURE

Study of lives and principal works of American authors.

MATHEMATICS

Written Arithmetic and Elementary Algebra, completed.

GEOMETRY

Geometrical drawing.

NATURAL PHILOSOPHY

HISTORY

English history and review of American history in connection with.

ZOOLOGY AND BOTANY

Elementary lessons in.

VOCAL MUSIC

GYMNASTICS

SENIOR YEAR

LITERATURE

Study of lives and principal works of English authors.

MATHEMATICS

Review of Arithmetic; book-keeping.

GEOMETRY

Elementary Geometry.

CIVIL GOVERNMENT

Special study of Constitution of the United States and school laws of Alabama.

ZOOLOGY AND BOTANY

CHEMISTRY AND MINERALOGY

MENTAL PHILOSOPHY

GYMNASTICS

VOCAL MUSIC

We expect in future to have a training school in which students of the Normal School may receive practical training as teachers. Lectures on practical subjects are given throughout the course.

GENERAL INFORMATION

CALENDAR

The school began its first session July 4, 1881, and continues till March 30, 1882 — nine months. Hereafter, the school will open the first

Monday in September and continue in session nine months, closing the last Thursday in May. Vacation from the last of May till the first of September. Students are expected to enter promptly at the beginning of the term. Applicants for admission must be present for examination the first Monday.

By communicating with the Principal, those unable to be present at the opening examination may have special arrangements made for their entrance.

CONDITIONS OF ADMISSION

For entrance to the Junior Class, students must be able to pass a satisfactory examination in reading, and in arithmetic through long division.

Students able to read and write and having some knowledge of arithmetic, but who are not able to pass the examination for the Junior Class will be admitted to a Preparatory Class.

All applicants before admission must be fourteen years of age and must pledge themselves to teach two years in the public schools of this State after they have become qualified, but they are not expected to teach without compensation; they must also furnish satisfactory proof of good moral character.

EXPENSES

Board can be obtained at from six to eight dollars per month. Those desiring to board themselves can obtain furnished rooms and have their cooking done at from two to three dollars.

Students will have no other expenses except for books, as the State pays for teaching.

ADVANTAGES

The school has the advantage of being situated near the centre of the State, in one of the most healthy and cultivated towns of the State, and can be easily reached by rail road. It is undenominational, but students are expected to attend church and Sabbath school. They are at liberty to choose their own place of worship.

Through the generosity of friends, the Trustees have been fortunate in securing a farm of one hundred acres on the suburbs of the town, on which to locate the school. This farm will be cultivated so as to supply labor, as far as possible, to those students unable to meet their boarding expenses.

Means for purchasing tools, stock, &c., for beginning the cultivation of the farm have already been secured.

The prospects now are that suitable buildings for school purposes will be erected on the farm by the beginning of another school year.

An effort will be made to obtain schools, as far as possible, for those students who are competent and who wish to teach during the summer vacation.

Library and Reading-Room

Since the beginning of the school nearly three hundred volumes have been donated to the library and additions are still being made.

A reading-room to which the students have access, is constantly well supplied with the best periodicals and papers.

The Literary Society

The young men hold weekly a Literary Society, in which they have an opportunity for extemporaneous speaking and to acquaint themselves with parliamentary usages.

Regulations

The rules governing the school are those which best promote the welfare and happiness of all.

The use of intoxicating drinks or tobacco is not tolerated.

Regular habits, as to study, rest and recreation, are required.

Students are not permitted to be absent from their homes at night except on Wednesday and Sunday nights.

Students are liable to have their names dropped for inability to master their studies, irregular attendance and for failure to comply with the regulations of the school.

History

The school was established by an act passed by the Legislature of the State of Alabama, in 1880,[5] and was opened July 4, 1881. An annual appropriation of two thousand dollars, for the payment of teachers' salaries, was made at the time. In addition to this over eight hundred dollars have been raised, a part of which was given by friends of the school, and the remainder raised by efforts of the students. Five hundred dollars of this sum has gone towards the purchase of the farm.

For further information, address

B. T. Washington, *Principal,*
Tuskegee, Alabama

DONATIONS

Cash received from			Miss M. A. Longstreth, Philadelphia, on account of farm,	$25.00
"	"	"	Miss Abby E. Cleaveland,[6] Poughkeepsie, N.Y., on account of farm,	20.00
"	"	"	African Zion Sunday School,[7] Malden, W. Va., on account of farm,	2.13

174

"   "   "   Miss E. Thurston,[8] Brooklyn, N.Y., on account of farm,   25.00

"   "   "   Vacation students. Hampton, Va., on account of farm,   84.00

"   "   through Miss L. D. Gillett,[9] Westfield, Mass., on account of farm,   70.00

"   "   from Rev. H. B. Frissell,[10] Hampton, Va., on account of farm,   5.00

"   "   "   Miss S. P. Harold,[11] South Framingham, Mass., to purchase books, &c.,   12.00

"   "   through Rev. T. K. Fessenden, Farmington, Conn., for purchasing hymn books,   6.00

"   "   from a friend in Connecticut,[12] on account of farm,   300.00

"   "   through a friend, Framingham, Mass., on account of farm,   10.00

"   "   from a friend, North Adams, Mass., on account of farm,   1.00

"   "   "   Mrs. A. Hemenway, Boston, Mass., on account of library,   25.00

"   "   "   Col. Wm. B. Bowen, Tuskegee, on account of farm,   5.00

"   "   "   Mrs. A. Hemenway, Boston, Mass., on account of farm,   100.00

"   "   "   Exhibition by students,   20.85

"   "   "   Supper,   50.20

"   "   "   Mr. J. A. Grimmett, Tuskegee, on account of farm,   10.00

"   "   "   Mr. Henry Bowen,[13] Tuskegee, on account of farm,   5.00

Cash received from Subscriptions, Tuskegee, on account of farm,   25.65

"   "   "   Mr. G. E. Brown,[14] Boston, Mass., on account of freight,   11.00

"   "   through Miss Abby E. Cleaveland, Poughkeepsie, N.Y., on account of beneficiary fund,   15.00

"   "   from Miss Esther C. Mack, Salem, Mass., on account of general expenses,   28.00

Total, $855.83

Received from Smith American Organ Co., Boston, Mass., one Cabinet Organ.

175

"   "   a friend, Framingham, Mass., two barrels books and clothing.

"   "   Century Publishing Company, two dozen "Songs for the Sanctuary."

"   "   Normal School, Framingham, Mass., two barrels books and clothing.

"   "   Framingham Unitarian Sewing Circle, one barrel of clothing, &c.

"   "   Mr. G. E. Brown, Boston, Mass., one set of maps, charts and primers, one box of blankets, four boxes of clothing, &c., and two and one-half barrels of fancy crackers.

"   "   Rev. E. E. Hale's church, Boston, Mass., one lot books and clothing.

"   "   "Boston Sewing Circle," through Mrs. A. Hemenway, one lot of clothing.

Copy in DLC.

[1] The catalog apparently went to press prior to O. O. Howard's acceptance of a position on the school's board of trustees, Feb. 21, 1882. The catalog also makes no mention of the building-fund drive which the circular of Feb. 13, 1882, helped launch.

[2] Henry D. Smith (1820-99), born in Hartford, Conn., graduated from Yale University in 1844. After teaching in Southington and North Haven, Conn., he founded Meriden Institute in West Meriden, Conn., in 1847. In 1850 he left the institute and entered business, founding a firm in Southington which revolutionized the manufacture of carriage hardware through the introduction of new machinery. Smith was an abolitionist, temperance advocate, and supporter of education. Beginning in 1873, and for several elections thereafter, he was the state's Prohibitionist candidate for governor. He was a member of the original board of trustees of Tuskegee Institute, serving until 1892, was one of the trustees of the Connecticut Industrial School for Girls, Middletown, Conn., and was an active member of the American Missionary Association.

[3] Abigail ("Abby") Williams May (1829-88) was one of the earliest donors to Hampton Institute and a trustee (1881-88). She rose to prominence as a wartime leader of the New England Women's Auxiliary Association of the U.S. Sanitary Commission, and as head of the Finance Committee of the New England Freedmen's Aid Society. Born into a Brookline, Mass., family and educated at her wealthy uncle's Boston home, she played a leading role in education and women's rights following the war. Appointed to the Massachusetts School Board in 1879, she took a special interest in the state normal school at Framingham, and may have come to know Olivia Davidson either at Hampton or at Framingham. The Rev. Samuel May of Leicester, Mass. (1810-99), her older brother, was a long-time secretary of the Massachusetts Anti-Slavery Society and for two decades aided Hampton Institute with his money and influence. He made annual contributions to the Abby May Home for teachers at Hampton.

[4] An error in tallying. This should have been 11, changing the junior class total to 29 and the school enrollment in the summary to 113.

[5] Actually became law Feb. 10, 1881.

[6] Abby E. Cleaveland, a native of Poughkeepsie, N.Y., served as a volunteer teacher at Hampton from 1879 to 1881. After returning home she continued her interest in Hampton by handling the Hampton graduates' correspondence for thirteen years. She visited Hampton annually and initiated a program of soliciting Christmas boxes and contributions from her northern friends for rural schools taught by Hampton graduates. She died in 1908.

[7] Probably the Sunday school of the African Zion Baptist Church which BTW attended as a boy and young man. When he taught school in Malden between 1875 and 1879, he was clerk of the church.

[8] Ellen Thurston, who, with her sister, Miss C. Thurston, was a contributor to both Hampton and Tuskegee.

[9] Lucy Douglas Gillett of Westfield, Mass., served on the Hampton faculty from 1879 to 1881. Her brother, the Springfield lawyer Frederick Huntington Gillett, served thirty-two years in the U.S. House of Representatives.

[10] Hollis Burke Frissell (1851-1917), chaplain and later president of Hampton Institute, became a close co-worker with BTW in Negro and southern educational matters. He was born in South Amenia, N.Y. His father, Amasa C. Frissell, had been a Lane Seminary rebel, and for twenty-five years was secretary of the American Tract Society. Hollis Frissell attended Phillips Academy, Andover, and Yale University, graduating in 1874. He taught for two years at DeGarmo Institute, Rhinebeck-on-Hudson, N.Y., then read for the ministry under an Episcopalian from North Carolina who exposed him to a sympathetic view of southern problems. During his study at Union Theological Seminary, where he graduated in 1879, Frissell spent the summer of 1878 doing home mission work in New Brunswick, N.J. He found mission work congenial, but became assistant pastor of a fashionable New York church, the Madison Avenue Presbyterian Church. He then worked for the American Missionary Association for a time, and on an observation visit to Hampton Institute in 1880 he accepted General Armstrong's invitation to be the school chaplain.

Frissell had influential family connections that were useful to Hampton Institute. His brother Algernon Sydney Frissell was president of the Fifth Avenue Bank. In 1883 he married Julia, daughter of Amzi Dodd, a prominent New Jersey judge. Leading a more worldly life than the typical missionary clergyman, Frissell was a member of the Century, City, and Yale clubs in New York and of the Cosmos Club in Washington, where he found some of the donors to his school. He became vice-principal and ran the school during Armstrong's frequent and protracted illnesses after 1886. When Armstrong died in 1893, Frissell succeeded him.

Very different in temperament from the founder, Frissell continued Hampton Institute much as Armstrong had originally conceived it. Whatever creativeness this gentle man had went into efforts to establish interracial dialogue in the South. He was one of the more active participants in the Mohonk Conferences of the 1880s and 1890s, and with Robert C. Ogden, a Hampton trustee, helped found the Conference for Education in the South and the Southern Education Board. He worked closely with BTW in founding the Anna T. Jeanes Foundation for Negro education in 1907. He continued Armstrong's conservatism both in education and in relations with southern whites. He could quietly rebuke bigotry, but was not a forceful speaker or actor.

[11] Susan P. Harrold.

[12] Moses Pierce.

[13] Possibly Henry Bowen, listed in the 1870 census as a thirty-five-year-old mulatto, married with five children, working as a hostler.

[14] George Edward Brown of Boston was for twenty years a donor to Hampton Institute. He died early in 1894.

A Circular Appealing for Donations

Tuskegee Normal School, Tuskegee, Ala. Feb. 13, '82

Dear Friend: The farm of one hundred acres which we contracted to buy for the School a few months ago, has been paid for, deeded to a Board of Trustees, and its cultivation begun. On the place are four small buildings which we thought at the time of purchase could be used to answer for school purposes for at least the first year, but the attendance being so much larger than we expected, we have been unable to use them in that way. For the present session we are kindly permitted by one of the church congregations in town, to use its house of worship and public school building. These buildings do not answer the purpose; besides we cannot trespass on their kindness another session. The attendance has averaged about eighty this session, and will doubtless be much larger next session. There is no alternative. *We must have a building.* We have plans for a building containing one large assembly room, six recitation rooms, library and reading room, office, boarding-hall in basement, and sleeping quarters for girls on attic floor. The cost of this building will be about $3,000.

We want to lay the corner-stone of this building on the day of closing exercises of the present session (Thursday, March 30th). To get the foundation work in proper condition for laying the corner-stone will cost about $300, which we are now making an effort to raise, and it is earnestly hoped that all friends who receive this circular will give us *something* towards laying the foundation of our first building.

B. T. Washington,
Olivia A. Davidson,
Jno. W. Cardwell

PDSr BTW Folder President's Office Vault ViHaI, titled "Circular." Also printed in *Southern Workman*, 11 (Mar. 1882), 29. In response to this, twenty-three teachers of Hampton Institute contributed a total of $70, of which Samuel C. Armstrong gave $12 and J. F. B. Marshall $11. Forwarding the money to BTW, Marshall advised that future appeals carry a certificate of endorsement from well-known northerners in order to distinguish Tuskegee from the many poorly run and untrustworthy institutions in the South. (J. F. B. Marshall to BTW, Apr. 14, 1882, Business Office, ViHaI.)

From Oliver Otis Howard

[West Point, N.Y.] Feb. 21 82

Dear Sir: If it will be any gratification to you and if you think it will be any benefit to the interests of your institution you may put my name on as a Trustee, as General Armstrong advises it, but you must not expect much of my time, on account of my continued occupation.[1] Very truly yours

O. O. Howard
Bvt. Major General, U.S.A.

HLpS   Oliver Otis Howard Papers   MeB.

[1] Howard served as a trustee from 1882 to 1895. He was never active in that capacity, though he remained a friend of the school. An entry in a small notebook kept by BTW recorded a $50 contribution by the general in May 1889. (Con. 978, BTW Papers, DLC.) Howard apparently never attended a meeting of the board of trustees.

A News Item from the Philadelphia *Inquirer*

[Philadelphia, Pa., Mar. 24, 1882]

THE NATION'S WARDS

Two circles and the parquet at Association Hall were crowded last evening on the occasion of the introduction to the Philadelphia public of some Hampton students. There was "a reception in the interest of education for freedmen and Indians," under the auspices of the Society of Friends and the patrons of Carlisle School.

Hon. E. A. Rollins[1] was introduced by Mr. Samuel R. Shipley[2] as chairman, and said that Columbus thought he had discovered China, and if he had really done so the question would have been, not shall the Chinese go, but shall the Anglo-Saxon come? The aboriginal right of occupation was generally conceded by the law of nations. The right of discovery covered rights as between the Christian nations, not as related to the Indians.

The theory of the law was hard; its practice monstrous. Penn's treaty, never sworn to and never broken, was a notable and noble exception. Government treaties had been made with the Indian under duress, pushing him further and still further back toward the West, till now the Indian, in his own continent, was a stranger in a strange land. The government had been faulty; individuals and agents criminal. The red man might be worse than the white, but was not to be judged by the same standard — especially not to be robbed of his land and his home and then punished because not up to the Christian standard of the thieves. What the Indian was now he owed to the white, and the white man owed it to him to give him all the civilization he was capable of receiving.

In the year the first cargo of slaves was brought to Virginia the Pilgrims landed in the Mayflower, and for two hundred years the battle raged between these elements till slavery went down in blood. For years it was an offense against the State to teach a slave to read his Bible. Now it is an offense against Heaven not to teach the freedman to read his Bible.

To-day the nation is demanding the abolition of the tribal system and asking the tenure of Indian lands in severalty.

Senator Rollins then referred to the Hampton School, and introduced an undergraduate of that institution, Mr. Benjamin F. Jones,[3] who delivered an extract from the late President Garfield's inaugural, on the subject of general education. Mr. Jones is a very dark-skinned African, with all the characteristics of his race strongly marked in his face and figure. He "spoke his piece" with vastly superior elocution and refined intonation.

Chief of the Shawnee Tribe, Thomas Wildcat, made the next address. He said: Dear friends, I am now a Hampton student, and have been steadily promoted till now I am to go forward among my people to act among them as a beacon light; to uplift them from the darkness of barbarism. The Shawnees are willing to embrace whatever may be for their advantage. They see that civilization is sweeping towards them like fire over the prairie. My father was a soldier of the Federal army, in which he served for three years. (Applause.)

The Shawnees speak English; but, I am sorry to say, the first thing they learn in English is to swear, a natural consequence of their association with the worst class of white men. When I leave Hampton no doubt many more of my people will come to it. The only source of universal peace in this land is universal education. I will do my best in the work before me. Others will take it up and do better.

Mr. Rollins next, with a reference to the Pawnees, introduced James Murie, two years a member of the Hampton School, who explained the names of the four sub-divisions of his tribe, and breathed the same aspirations for the elevation of his people; gave a humorous account of a visit to New England and told how time was employed at Hampton. He expressed the thought that the money given to the Indians should be employed in supplying them with agricultural implements to enable them to support themselves.

Mr. G. Booker Washington,[4] of Alabama, was the next speaker. I was born, said he, in Virginia, a slave. Till fifteen I worked in a coal mine. I heard of the Hampton Institute. For two years I saved my money till I thought I had enough to take me to Hampton. When I arrived there I had five cents left. I tried for the janitorship, to which was attached a small salary. I had a chance of getting it and improved it. I had a room to sweep, and I swept it five times, and was elected. Once I was set to teaching Indians. I supposed they could not learn, but I found that they were very much like other people.

Mr. Washington spoke with excellent effect and genuine eloquence of the desire of the freedmen for education, and was followed by Senator Hawley,[5] of Connecticut, who urged self help as the great means of benefiting the Indians, and in the course of his remarks asked this question: Can the vast power of civilization overcome the Indian? How we brag of it! There are fifty-one or fifty-two millions of us, and we have the outcome and flower of Christian civilization, and shall we acknowledge that such civilization cannot civilize 261,000 people? In New York and North Carolina are some very respectable Indians. Indeed, 100,000 of the whole number are self-sustaining to-day.

Continuing, Senator Hawley spoke of one difficulty in the work of civilizing the Indians, arising from the necessity of sending the students back among their people, when yielding to the influences around them, they often relapsed into Indian customs and habits. "Sometimes," said he, "on the plains you meet people that you suppose to be savages, and are surprised to find them address you in elegant English. I had a singular instance of the kind under my own observation recently. A friend of mine, who thought his time had come when an Indian looked over the bluff at him, was agreeably surprised when the supposed savage hailed him by name, and reminded him of their meeting at some educational institute in the Eastern States." Senator Hawley also read the Cherokee chief's thanksgiving proclamation, pronouncing it the best of the year.

General Armstrong, the founder, and, after fourteen years, still the head of Hampton, as the chairman said on introducing him, made a noble and justly-deserved appeal for a cordial support of Captain Pratt,[6] whom he pronounced one of the greatest educators of America. What he has done, said he, no one knows. Disregarding the advice of his brother officers he went right in among the despairing savage prisoners, without a guard; met them when they were desperate enough to be contemplating suicide, fixed them with the power of his eye, and faced them down. He has, under God, said General Armstrong, made humble Christians, consistent Christians, of men red-handed and marked on the government records as guilty of murder. That work is the inspiration of Hampton and Carlisle.

The general then cautioned his hearers against a probable movement to send Captain Pratt back to his company on the plains. "At Carlisle," said he, "Captain Pratt is doing more for the pacification of the Indian tribes than a hundred captains can do on the plains. I know that the whole power of the War Department will be leveled at Captain Pratt to drive him back to his company. See that you, people of Philadelphia, do not suffer it to be done."

The general described the Hampton system, the essence of which is, said he, not what can the students do for the farm, but what can the farm and school do for the students, and concluded with an enthusiastic defense of Indian theology and character — denying that the race was dying out, and showing that bringing the Indians East was reducing the death rate.

An interesting feature of the occasion was the appearance of the Indian students in the really tasteful and beautiful dress of their respective tribes.

On the platform were ex-Mayor Fox,[7] ex-Governors Hartranft[8] and Pollock,[9] Judge Tourgee,[10] Rev. Dr. Syle, Rev. Dr. Dana,[11] Messrs.

J. L. Baily,[12] George H. Stuart[13] and others whose names have long been associated with this good work.

Philadelphia *Inquirer*, Mar. 24, 1882, 3. BTW's speech was also reported briefly in the Tuskegee *Macon Mail*, Mar. 29, 1882, 3.

[1] Edward Ashton Rollins (1826-85). During the Civil War Lincoln appointed him cashier of the Bureau of Internal Revenue. Andrew Johnson's efforts to dislodge him from this position led to a violation of the Tenure of Office Act, for which the President was impeached. Rollins spent his later years in the life-insurance business and in banking.

[2] Samuel R. Shipley (1828-1908), a Philadelphia importer and financier, associated with many charitable causes in Philadelphia.

[3] Benjamin F. Jones, a Hampton graduate in 1882, was born in Virginia in 1859. After graduation he taught for three years at Butler School in Hampton and for two years in New Jersey. He later graduated from Howard University's medical department, and practiced medicine in Washington, D.C.

[4] BTW.

[5] Joseph Roswell Hawley (1826-1905). He was a Free Soil supporter in the 1850s and for a while editor of the Hartford *Evening Press*. After fighting in the Civil War Hawley became a prominent Republican and served as governor of Connecticut, congressman, and U.S. senator from 1881 to 1905.

[6] Richard Henry Pratt (1840-1924), a captain in the U.S. Army, brought the first Indians to Hampton in 1878 and founded the Industrial School for Indians at Carlisle, Pa., a year later. He headed the Carlisle school until he retired in 1904. Born in Rushford, N.Y., Pratt grew up in Indiana. He joined an Indiana regiment in 1861 as a corporal and rose during the war to the rank of captain. After two years in civilian life running a hardware store, Pratt returned to the Army as a lieutenant and was stationed in the West. In 1875 he was in charge of transferring seventy-two Indian prisoners from Fort Sill, Okla., to Fort Marion in St. Augustine, Fla. Believing the Indians could be "civilized," Pratt used the St. Augustine experiment to prove his theory to the Army. Instead of keeping the prisoners locked up, Pratt put them to work in the St. Augustine community and enlisted local help in educating and Christianizing them. After three years, when the Army was unwilling to continue the experiment, Pratt raised money from St. Augustine residents to pay the expenses of twenty-two Indians who stayed in the East for further education. In 1878 he brought fifteen of these to Hampton, staying himself to help begin Hampton's program for the Indians. Later in 1878 he brought forty-nine more Sioux from Dakota to Hampton. In 1879, becoming dissatisfied at the prospect of educating Negroes and Indians together, he asked the Army to let him use the deserted barracks at Carlisle for a separate school for Indians. Authority over the property was transferred to the U.S. Department of the Interior, then under the direction of Carl Schurz, who also believed strongly in the necessity of educating the Indians. Pratt brought 129 Indians to Carlisle to begin the school. By 1904 more than 1,200 students were attending Carlisle and Pratt was credited with changing the prevailing feeling among Americans that the Indian could not be educated or civilized. At the time of his retirement, Pratt had reached the rank of brigadier general.

[7] Daniel Miller Fox, a lawyer and a Democrat, was mayor of Philadelphia from

1869 to 1872. He also served as superintendent of the U.S. Mint in Philadelphia and as a member of the U.S. Postal Commission.

[8] John Frederick Hartranft (1830-89), Republican governor of Pennsylvania from 1872 to 1874. He was also a Union brigadier general, auditor general of the state, commander of the national guard, postmaster of Philadelphia, and collector of the port of Philadephia.

[9] James Pollock (1810-90), congressman from 1844 to 1849 and governor of Pennsylvania from 1855 to 1859. He served as director of the U.S. Mint in Philadelphia from 1861 to 1866 and from 1869 to 1873, and originated the use of the phrase "In God We Trust" on U.S. coins.

[10] Albion Winegar Tourgée (1838-1905) was born in Ohio and attended the University of Rochester. He lost an eye as a Union soldier at the first battle of Bull Run. After the Civil War he began a law practice in Greensboro, N.C., published a Radical Republican paper, *The Union Register* (1867), and became a member of the North Carolina Superior Court (1868). Tourgée was the stereotype of a carpetbagger in the minds of many southerners. He championed education for blacks and later wrote an exposé of the Ku Klux Klan. As a Reconstruction judge and prolific writer Tourgée was well known in both North and South. In 1879 he moved to New York and continued to publish books, poetry, and a magazine (*The Continent,* 1882-84). His most popular book was *A Fools Errand, by One of the Fools* (1879). Others were *Bricks without Straw* (1880), *Appeal to Caesar* (1884), and *Black Ice* (1888). In 1892 Tourgée became one of the defenders of Homer Adolph Plessy in the landmark *Plessy* v. *Ferguson* case (1896) that established, much to Tourgée's chagrin, the doctrine of separate but equal that was soon applied to school systems as well as public transportation. The newly formed Niagara Movement, led by W. E. B. Du Bois, met several months after Tourgée's death in 1905. It honored three "Friends of Freedom," William Lloyd Garrison, Albion Tourgée, and Frederick Douglass. BTW was cool toward Tourgée in his later years and did not attend his funeral, but wired: "My race owes much to the courage, and helpful work of Judge Tourgée, which we shall not forget." (Olsen, *Carpetbagger's Crusade,* 350.)

[11] Stephen Winchester Dana (1840-1910), pastor of the Walnut Street Presbyterian Church in Philadelphia and a trustee of Lincoln University in Pennsylvania.

[12] Joshua Longstreth Baily (1826-1916), Quaker philanthropist and senior partner of Joshua L. Baily and Co., a Philadelphia and New York dry-goods firm. Baily was president of the Philadelphia Society for Employment and Instruction of the Poor, a generous contributor to Negro education, and a noted temperance worker and peace advocate.

[13] George H. Stuart, a Philadelphia merchant. Stuart served as head of the Christian Commission, a charitable organization which did evangelical work among the soldiers and freedmen, and aided returning war veterans. He was a close friend of President U. S. Grant, and it was rumored that he turned down a position in Grant's cabinet in 1869 offered him in return for his support in the election of 1868. (Collins, *Philadelphia,* 312.)

BTW and Olivia A. Davidson
to the Editor of the *Southern Workman*

[Tuskegee, Ala., ca. Mar. 30, 1882]

This institution closed its first session March 30th, 1882, with appropriate exercises.

The last day dawned bright and beautiful, and long before the hour for beginning the exercises, a large crowd of people had gathered in the town, many of them having walked or ridden long distances that they might be present, for the first time at the closing of such a school.

The exercises began at 10 A.M. with class recitations, which lasted till 11:30. At this hour the school and friends formed a procession and marched to the farm lately purchased, where the corner stone of the new school building[1] was laid by Hon. W. Thompson,[2] county Superintendent of Education. Hon. H. Clay Armstrong had expected to perform the ceremony, but being unavoidably called to Washington, he deputed Mr. Thompson.

Throughout the day the interest shown by the people present was very marked but it was particularly noticeable at this time.

The day had by this hour grown exceedingly warm, and the sun beamed with full force upon those who stood about the building, but in spite of this, the majority stood, quiet and attentive, throughout the ceremony, which lasted some time. After the stone was in place, Mr. Thompson ascended the stand and delivered an address which was listened to with deep interest, and seemed to inspire every one present with new hopes for the future. Parts of it are given below, for, coming as it does from a representative Southern white man, it will perhaps be of interest to the friends of the colored man.

Besides the colored citizens of Tuskegee and adjacent counties, there were present many prominent resident white citizens, among whom were the mayor of Tuskegee and pastors of the churches.

After the ceremony of laying the stone was concluded, the people were dismissed for dinner, which was served in true picnic style, on the ground under the trees, from bountifully filled baskets.

At 2 P.M. all returned to the church for the rhetorical exercises, consisting of singing, speaking, &c. The preceding evening the students had brought armfuls of roses, and with these the church had been beautifully decorated. Raised seats had been placed at one end of the church facing the audience, and on these the scholars were seated. Just above them was a beautiful arch of roses and evergreens, while in almost every spot where space could be found, bouquets and wreaths of roses were placed, filling the room with fragrance and beauty.

The church floor and gallery were filled with an attentive audience, in which both races were represented.

The following was the programme.

PROGRAMME

SINGING

ESSAY. "Normal Schools." *Wm. Anthony,*[3] *Tuskegee.*
RECITATION. "The Drunkard's Daughter." *Alice Torbert,*[4] *Tuskegee.*

SINGING

RECITATION. "The Charcoal Man." *Louise Lyman,*[5] *Opelika.*
ESSAY. "Work." *Jno. T. Hollis,*[6] *Cotton Valley.*

SINGING

ESSAY. "Habits." *Ellen McCullough,*[7] *Tuskegee.*
RECITATION. "Independence Bell." *Hiram Thweatt,*[8] *Tuskegee.*

SINGING

ESSAY. "The Teacher's Work." *Josie A. Calhoun,*[9] *Opelika.*
RECITATION. "Waiting." *Virginia Adams,*[10] *Tuskegee.*

SINGING

RECITATION. "Go to Work." *B. Town Harvey,*[11] *Gueryton.*
ESSAY. "Home." *Nellie Bowen,*[12] *Tuskegee.*

SINGING

RECITATION. "Curfew must not ring to-night." *Ella Allen,*[13] *Gueryton.*
ESSAY. "The Colored Citizens of Alabama."
Lewis D. McCullough,[14] *Ft. Mitchell.*

At the conclusion of these exercises, Rev. C. C. Petty,[15] pastor of the largest colored church in Montgomery, delivered an interesting and eloquent address. In conclusion he said with much feeling, "I thank God for what I have witnessed to-day — something I never saw before, nor did I ever expect to see it. I have seen one who but yesterday was

one of our owners, to-day lay the corner stone of a building devoted
to the education of my race. For such a change let us all thank God."

Mr. Petty was followed by Rev. Mr. Oliver, pastor of one of the
white churches in Tuskegee, who was earnest in his words of thankfulness for the changes that have come about, and the progress being
made by all races.

The principal of the school then, in a few words, thanked the people
of Tuskegee for their kind interest and help in the work since its beginning, after which the exercises closed with the Doxology, in which
the whole audience joined, and benediction.

As the friends dispersed, many of them came to the teachers and gave
them a hearty grasp of the hand and fervent "God bless you for the
work you are doing."

It is with much satisfaction and some degree of pride that the friends
and teachers of the school review the work of the year which has just
closed.

The school was first opened nine months ago with thirty pupils, and
with no means except the $2,000 appropriated annually by the state
for the payment of teachers. During the year one hundred and twelve
students from various parts of the state have attended the school, and
now, during vacation, many of them are doing good work as teachers
by which to earn money to return next year.

No provision being made by the state for a school building, we were
compelled to begin and continue the school in a church, with two small
shanties for recitation rooms.

Seeing the necessity of a permanent location and the manual labor
system as carried on at Hampton as a means of helping the students
to help themselves, we contracted to buy a beautiful and conveniently
located piece of land of one hundred acres on which to permanently
locate the school.

By the aid of the colored and white friends in and around Tuskegee,
and friends in the North, $500, the price of the land, was paid in six
months. This farm has been deeded to a board of trustees, some of
whom reside in the North and some in the South, who hold it in trust
for the school. A generous friend in Conn.[16] provided means to purchase seeds, tools &c., and one-third of the land is now being cultivated
with prospects for a fair crop.

The building whose corner stone has just been laid being necessarily
larger than was at first contemplated, is estimated to cost when finished,

$4,200. The number of students for next year will undoubtedly be much larger than it has been this, and even could we get the use of the church and shanties that were used this year, they would not contain the school another year.

By the aid of the people in Tuskegee, in labor and money, and help from Northern friends, the lumber is now on the ground, and the building is being framed and we are making every effort to have it completed by the beginning of the next session, September 1st, 1882. Should we succeed in this, the advantages to the students, heretofore necessarily limited, will be largely increased, and the influence for good upon them be greatly strengthened.

ADDRESS BY HON. WADDY THOMPSON

"The State Superintendent of Education, Hon. H. Clay Armstrong, expected to be present here to-day, and perform the work which I have attempted; but I received a note from him a few days ago requesting me to represent him on this occasion as he thought it important that he should attend a meeting of State Superintendents which convened at Washington about this time.**[17] No State is great until its educational facilities are great, and placed at the door of the poor boy in the cabin, as well as in the reach of the child of wealth and fortune. No defense is cheaper to a community or commonwealth than education; it is a stronger bulwark, more unfailing and vigilant than the most powerful armies, or splendid navies, for it makes its recipients, the boldest defenders of the right and the most uncompromising enemies of the wrong. When you scatter the darkness of the mind by the light of knowledge, you make better citizens, better workmen in shops, better farmers in the field, better merchants, and mechanics, and associates co-operating in all the circles of business. It is for this reason that good men every where feel a deep interest in the cause of education, and are ever ready to bid God-speed to any honest effort made in its behalf. This is perhaps an occasion of greater interest to the colored people than to the rest of us, because it marks the beginning of a new era in their history. We have to-day for the first time witnessed the laying of the foundation of a building to be erected and used solely for their education. Perhaps there are some here to-day whose minds are shrouded by the night of ignorance, and they cannot now fully understand or appreciate the importance of this event, but in years to come, when they see the grand results that are to be reached, and are now hoped for, they will look back to this time as eventful in their history, when they witnessed the laying of the corner stone of a building to be used for the purpose of training teachers to educate their children.

*   *   *   *   *[18]

"You cannot hope to gain anything from false, indifferent or mean teachers, but if you have teachers trained to their work, who are true to you, true to themselves, and true to God, you may expect your children to grow in the knowledge of all that is good, and become truly elevated. This is the object for which this building is to be erected. It is the object which the legislature had in view when it appropriated a sum of money to pay the teachers of this institution. It is the object which the trustees had in view when they selected the present able and efficient Principal to take charge of the school, and it is the object which he has in view, manifested by the deep interest he takes in the cause, and the efforts he has made to advance it. We bid him God-speed, and trust that this building and his labors may indeed prove a blessing to his race.

"You have recently been invested with the privilege and burdens of citizenship. This boon was conferred on you by the State of Alabama, and she has extended a liberal hand to aid you to become good, useful and happy citizens. I do not mean to say that the appropriation for schools is adequate, or sufficient; but I do mean to say that Alabama in her poverty has done all that she can, and has given to your race, the same that she has to the white children of the state. This liberality on the part of the state was prompted by a desire to make all her citizens good and useful.

"We believe the time is near at hand when public education will be recognized as a measure of public economy, for as intelligence is the best antidote for vice and crime, the expenditures for education will lessen the demands for charity and correction, or as Governor Critten-den of Missouri[19] strongly puts it, 'parsimony towards education is liberality towards crime.' When public education is regarded as a measure of public economy, public sentiment will demand a sufficient appropriation for public schools, and Alabama will give us a system of free schools sufficient to educate all her people as they should be, making all her citizens useful, contented and happy, and those who have contributed to bring about the results will receive the lasting gratitude of posterity. I have thus presented a few thoughts that have suggested themselves to my mind without attempting to elaborate or develop the ideas. If I have said anything that may create in your minds a more favorable sentiment for public schools, or increase your faith therein, I have not spoken in vain, and I sincerely hope that the laying of the foundation of this building may be the broadening of the firm foundation on which our public school system rests."

B. T. Washington

O. A. Davidson

Southern Workman, 11 (May 1882), 56.

¹ Later named Porter Hall after Alfred Haynes Porter.

² Waddy Thompson, a forty-year-old Tuskegee lawyer, was Macon County superintendent of education.

³ William J. Anthony, a thirty-year-old native of Tuskegee, had taught school before enrolling at Tuskegee. He evidently did not graduate.

⁴ Alice A. Torbert was a fifteen-year-old student from Tuskegee and a member of the junior class. She graduated in 1885 and later was a clerk in the treasurer's office at Tuskegee.

⁵ Louisa Lyman, as her name was listed in the Tuskegee school records, was a member of the junior class but apparently did not graduate.

⁶ John Taylor Hollis worked his way through Tuskegee by teaching during the summers and cooking during the school year. After graduation Hollis taught in Richland, Ga., from 1885 to 1892 and later farmed and taught at Armstrong Station, Ala.

⁷ Ellen or Ella McCullough, a native of Tuskegee, graduated in 1885 and later taught in Brundidge, Ala.

⁸ Hiram H. Thweatt, age eighteen, a resident of Tuskegee, was listed in the census of 1880 as a carpenter. After graduating from Tuskegee in 1885 he began a newspaper, *The Black Belt,* in Tuskegee. He published what was considered an incendiary article about whites, and BTW convinced him to stop publication of the paper. He later taught carpentry at Christiansburg Normal and Industrial Institute in Cambria, Va., and served as principal of a school in Thomasville, Ga.

⁹ Josie A. Calhoun Tyson graduated from Tuskegee in 1885. Before her graduation, in the summers, she taught school at Society Hill, Ala., and after graduation she developed a full-time school there based on the Tuskegee model. She wrote to Olivia Davidson: "I found them [the people near Society Hill] very ignorant. . . . Some of them had never left the plantation since their birth." (Ludlow, ed., *Tuskegee: Its Story and Its Songs,* 23-24.)

¹⁰ Virginia L. Adams was the sixteen-year-old daughter of Lewis Adams, one of the founders of Tuskegee, and was a member of the class of 1885. In 1887-88 she taught at East Tallassee, Ala., a school aided by the Woman's Home Missionary Association of Boston, of which BTW's former teacher Nathalie Lord was home secretary. The county school fund paid for only three months, but the association paid an additional sum through BTW to keep the school open for nine months.

[11] B. Town Harvey, of the class of 1885, taught in the Tuskegee training school and later moved to Columbus, Ga., where on June 20, 1887, he began publishing a weekly newspaper, *The Columbus Messenger*. Within a year and a half the paper became a successful daily, but Harvey ceased his newspaper work to take a job in the Railway Mail Service. He was living in Peru, Ind., in 1902-3, working as a public school teacher and preacher.

[12] Cornelia Bowen was born in 1858 in Tuskegee, and her mother was a slave of Colonel William Bowen, the man who sold Tuskegee Normal School much of his land. The house in which Cornelia Bowen was born later became an industrial building at the school. She graduated from Tuskegee in 1885 and became principal of the "Children's House," the institute training school. In 1888 she began a school at nearby Mt. Meigs, similar to BTW's school but smaller.

[13] Ella Allen was a member of the junior class.

[14] Lewis D. McCullough worked his way through school and graduated in 1885. He believed in the BTW formula of hard work, writing: "I am not ashamed to put my hand to any kind of honest labor. I see a blessing and beauty in it." (Ludlow, ed., *Tuskegee: Its Story and Its Songs,* 22-23.) A native of Fort Mitchell, McCullough returned there. The Tuskegee catalog of 1894 listed him as deceased.

[15] Charles Calvin Petty (1849-1900) was pastor of the African Methodist Episcopal Zion Church in Montgomery. Born in Wilkesboro, N.C., Petty attended Biddle (later Johnson C. Smith) University in Charlotte, N.C. After leaving college he taught for a time and began preaching. In 1879 he founded a high school for black youth in Lancaster, S.C., sponsored by the A.M.E. Zion Church. In 1884, while still pastor at Montgomery, he was chosen general secretary of the A.M.E. Zion Church and in 1888 was elected a bishop.

[16] Moses Pierce.

[17] Probably indicates a break in thought and not an omission.

[18] Probably indicates the omission of a paragraph or more in the original text.

[19] Thomas Theodore Crittenden (1832-1909) was governor of Missouri from 1881 to 1885. A Union lieutenant colonel in the Seventh Missouri Cavalry, he was attorney general of Missouri and a congressman before being elected governor.

A Speech before the Alabama State Teachers' Association

[Selma, Ala., Apr. 7, 1882]

INDUSTRIAL EDUCATION

I shall speak, for a few minutes, of Industrial Education, mainly as it relates to the colored people at the present time. I think that three distinct advantages may be claimed for such an education. First — Under wise management it aids the student in securing mental training; secondly, it teaches him how to earn a living; and, thirdly, it teaches him the dignity of labor.

Take the colored people in their present condition and we find very few students who are able to enter a boarding school and remain through one year, without a break, and the number able to finish a course of study without interruption is still smaller. There are thousands of poor but ambitious young people, far out on the back plantations, and in the woods and hollows, who, if given the chance, would gladly enter school and work their way through. The cost of board in most schools ranges from $8.00 to $12.00 per month. By a wisely organized labor system this price can be reduced one-third or one-half. Suppose there were a farm, carpenters' shop, tin shop, shoemakers' shop, or other branches of industry connected with the school, and each department so organized that students could have four days of mental training, and Saturday and one school day for manual labor; or Saturday and the spare hours before and after school. Let the arrangements be so that the girls can do the making, mending, and washing of the clothes, and all the other domestic duties; and at the same time let them be taught flower gardening and other decorative arts. And here I would add, that the condition of the average colored girl is such that if she does not learn how to properly keep house while at school she will never learn it.

If this, or some similar plan, were carried out, the time usually spent by students in lounging about would not only be utilized in a way to bring pecuniary aid to themselves, but work would create an appetite for study, and *vice versa,* and thus many of our schools that are too apt to represent the stagnant pond would be transformed into sweet flowing streams hastening slowly on to pour their contents into the great ocean of usefulness.

It may be suggested that a market cannot always be found for the articles produced, but when we consider that in a large school a great deal that would be produced would, necessarily, be consumed in the school, and by producing such articles as can be sold in a convenient market, we have the obstacle almost overcome.

The idea of combining mental and manual training is not a new one. Napoleon Bonaparte was among the first to put it into practice, and it is now being carried on, successfully, in England and some parts of America. I believe that it presents to the majority of young colored men and women, in the South, the only alternative between remaining ignorant and receiving, at least, a common, practical education. I am aware that such a course of training has its disadvantages as well as advantages, but it is immeasurably better than no training. It is far better to have a student feel that he has, by perserverance, with his own hands *worked* his way through school, than have him feel that he has been dependent on the charity of some friend; for to have a student's entire expenses paid for him is too often to make a "hot-house plant" of him.

But, doubtless, the hardest problem that the colored man has to solve, from year to year, is, how to make a living? View, for a moment, four millions of people plodding on, from year to year, without homes, and with no plan or system for work, but merely dragging out an existence. Their sons are growing up without trades, and their daughters with no idea of household economy. Such a glance must give one an idea of the importance of industrial education.

It is said that thirty counties in the State of Mississippi, if properly cultivated, would yield the last year's crop of six million, five hundred thousand bales of cotton. This is doubtless a fair example of the kind of agriculture carried on in the South. What a change could be made in a few years if the students who go out from our schools every year, could go with a practical knowledge of the most thorough methods of tillage, the best stock, and how to take care of them, the most improved instruments, and an intelligent plan for work. Before such a class of young men the mortgage system, with all its kindred evils would soon be swept where they would torment us no more. With the young man there would go a young lady, skilled in all that makes a home inviting.

An eminent educator recently said that the superior culture of the New England States was not so much due to the influence of their schools as to the influence of their perfect homes, and, reversing the same idea, I would say that a great deal of the degradation in the South comes not so much from inferior schools as from the degrading surroundings of the home life. Place one couple, trained as I have mentioned, in every community — a couple in whom the people can see exemplified all that is comprehended in the word civilization, and let them be teachers, not only in the school-house, but on the farm, in the flower-garden, and in the house, and we have a central light whose rays will soon penetrate the house of every family in the community.

Just the position that the Negro laborer will occupy among the skilled laborers in this country, fifty or a hundred years hence, must present a serious question to every thinking mind. The first-class carpenters, tinsmiths, blacksmiths, wheelwrights, brickmasons and other skilled workmen, made so by slavery, are disappearing and few of their places are being filled. Northern competition has completely shut the skilled Negro workman out from that section, and the continual stream of well-trained European laborers that is continually flowing into the West leaves him no foothold there. We are compelled to admit that he holds his place in the South to-day, not so much by an over superiority of workmanship as from lack of competition. When the day comes, as it evidently will, when that great train of sturdy Englishmen and Germans begins to fill up the South, unless the Negro prepares himself thoroughly for the conflict, during the interim, his only resort will be in the cotton field.

Again, industrial education, combined with mental, tends to make men practical. Many students, with fine mental training, find themselves completely swamped when they are launched out into the real business of life. My experience, of recent years, has been that it is easier to find men with uncommon sense than with common sense.

Two hundred years of forced labor taught the colored man that there was no dignity in labor but rather a disgrace. Acting on this principle the majority labor, not because they see God's blessing and beauty in it, but from a physical necessity. The child of the ex-slave, naturally influenced by his parents' example, grows up believing that he sees what he thinks is a curse in work. To remove this idea is one of the great missions of the industrial school. The school teacher must be taught that it will not disgrace him to work with his hands when he cannot get a school. The incompetent preacher must be taught that the Bible, which he attempts to explain, teaches him that work is preferable to idleness. The scores of strong and promising young men who are whiling away their lives on the street corners must be taught that if they would but apply themselves to some branch of industry that in a few years they could become independent citizens. Mark the contrast between James A. Garfield during a recess of Congress, with his coat off, driving an ox team, and our citizens standing on the streets whittling sticks.

Let us learn a lesson from the founders of New England. They first made themselves masters of the soil, their sons were schooled and taught trades, then came the small factories and trading houses, then they began to multiply their colleges and professional schools, then followed those learned in the professions and fine arts. Thus following the great law of the condition and the conditioned they have built up a civilization which is a beacon light to the world.

We have a striking example of industrial education in the later Jews, who required that every father, however wealthy, should teach his son a trade, so as to provide against misfortune and prevent his son from becoming a pauper or a thief.

While I would not discourage our young men's entering the learned professions, yet I do say that until more brain is put into agriculture and the industrial arts the young doctor and lawyer will enter their professions, in many cases, only to become discouraged and make second-rate school teachers.

It is true that we need lawyers and doctors, and at the same time we need inventors, machinists, builders of steamboats and successful planters and merchants. Such persons will do more to banish prejudice than all the laws Congress can pass. It is plain that the branches of industry mentioned are the foundations on which all other occupations rest, and if the foundation of the building be weak it matters little how much we paint and decorate the walls, the weakness still remains. When the builders of our national capitol began their work they put the foundation stones down deep and solid, then upon them they reared a structure which will stand, unimpaired, through ages to come. So may we, in laying the foundation for a race, lay it so well that the race can stand securely thereon till it has served the great ends of our Creator.

Minutes of the First Annual Session, Alabama State Teachers' Association, April 6-7, 1882 (Selma, 1882), 22-24, A-Ar.

A Recommendation from Henry Clay Armstrong, with the Endorsement of Rufus Wills Cobb[1]

Montgomery, April 11th 1882

To whom it may concern: It affords me pleasure to commend to the public Mr. B. T. Washington, Principal of the "Colored Normal School," located at Tuskegee, Ala. as being entirely reliable and trustworthy.

Any contributions intrusted to his care, in aid of the institution over

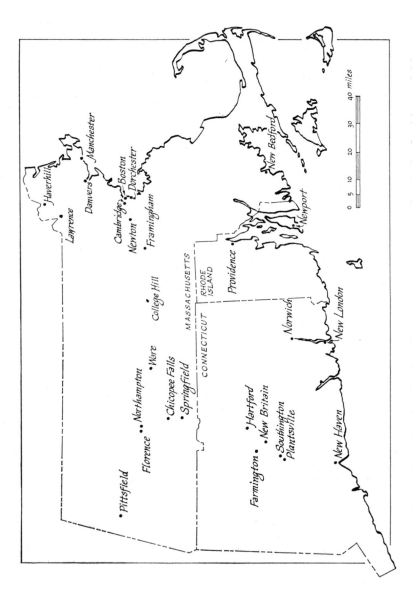

Map 4. Connecticut, Rhode Island, and Massachusetts: scene of early fund-raising activities.

which he presides, will be faithfully applied to the purposes for which it is given. Very respectfully

H. Clay Armstrong
Supt. of Education
State of Alabama

The above named B. T. Washington comes to me very highly recommended by gentlemen in whom I have much confidence & therefore think him worthy of the above recommendation.

R. W. Cobb
Governor

ALS and AES Con. 16 BTW Papers DLC.

[1] Rufus Wills Cobb (1829-1923), born in Ashville, Ala., practiced law there before the Civil War. After service in the Confederate Army, he resumed his law practice in Helena, Ala. From 1873 to 1891 he was president of the Central Iron Works in Helena, and was an attorney of the Louisville and Nashville Railway. He was governor of Alabama from 1878 to 1882.

Three Items from a Notebook

[Apr. 15–July 14, 1882]

Expenses, April 15–May 9, 1882

EXPENSES

		Apr. 15 Telegram	.60
	Trav.		Hamp to Farmington	11.00
		Board N.Y.	2.50
May	1	Farm. to Plantsville	.30
		Plantsville to Florence	.50
May	2	Florence to Northampton	.20
May	3	Northampton to Springfield	.50
"	"	Telegram to Boston	.25
"	"	Lodging & Board	1.00
"	4	" "	1.00
	6	Draft	.15
	"	Lodging and meals	1.50
	7	" " "	1.00
	8	" " "	1.25
	9	Expenses from Springfield to Chicopee	

MONEY SENT, APRIL 20–JULY 14, 1882

MONEY SENT

Apr. 20	From	Hampton		$95.00
May 6	"	Springfield		40.00
7	"	"		30.00
15	"	Hartford		35.00
15	"	"		10.00
16	"	"		100.00
20	"	"		20.00
24	"	"		23.00
31	"	Prov[idence]		50.00
31	"	"	Miss Snod[1]	5.00
June 2	"	"	Prov.	15.00
" 4	"	New Bed. for Miss S.[2]		5.00
" 5	"	" "		75.00
" 13	"	Hartford		40.00
July 14	"	Malden		110.00
				653.00
				110.00
				$543.00

DIARY, MAY 1–MAY 8, 1882

MONDAY 1ST 1882

Started from N.Y.[3] at 8 A.M. and arrived at Farmington at noon. Called on Mr. Fessenden[4] who rec'd me kindly and gave me valuable advice, also a general letter and a number of letters of introduction. I left Farmington about eight for Plantsville. At 8½ P.M. I called on Mr. H. D. Smith who rec'd me more kindly than I had ever been by any white man.

I remained with all night. We talked over together the general interests of the school. His wife, son,[5] and daughter are an excellent set. He promised to give something and said that he thought that he could get one or two other gentlemen to give $100 each.

He took me to call on his fatherinlaw Dea. Higgins[6] the next morning. He is a very cheerful old man. Gives all his income for charitable objects. Said that he would think of us. Saw one other gentleman who promised to get something from his Sunday School.

MAY 2ND

Left Plantsville about 10 A.M. for Florence, Mass. Before I left Dea

Higgins and Mr. Chas. Smith very kindly showed me over the different factories. The latter accompanied me to the depot and gave me $5.00.

When I got to Florence I found out that Mr. A. L. Williston[7] the gentleman whom I went to see, had moved to Northampton Mass. Took horse cars for Northampton. I called on Mr. Williston at 7½ P.M. He has a large mansion finely furnished. He said that he would give something but could not give much as he has so many calls. He promised to forward his am't to Gen. Marshall. Mr. Mead (A.M.A.)[8] came in and I left.

MAY 3

Took 10.15 AM from Northampton to Springfield, Mass. arrived at S. about 11.30 A.M. Called on Mr. Homer Merriam[9] Pub. Webster's Dictionary. He rec'd me kindly, but did not care to give any money for reel estate. He said that he would help one or two needy students when school began. Called on Mr. Chas Merriam. He said that he was out of business and was too [old?] to make money — was supporting a S. School Mis. in Ala. which was all he was able to do now. He rec'd me kindly.

MAY 4

Went back to Northampton to get Miss Davidson's letter but found none. Called on Rev Dr Eustis[10] who gave me a letter of introduction. Did not collect any money. Things looked rather gloomy.

MAY 5

Returned to Springfield from Northampton. Started out with a new will to succeed. Called on Drs Gladden[11] & Buckingham.[12] The latter gave me encouragement and several good names. Collected from individuals $40. Called on Mrs Geo. E. Howard[13] who gave me several good names and treated me kindly.

MAY 6

Was not so successful as on the preceeding day. Collected from individuals and got more promised $13.00. Dr. Eustis invited me to speak in his church Sunday evening.

MAY 7

Spent most of the day at hotel. Spoke in the evening at Dr. Eustis' church to an appreciative audience. Rec'd several small gifts.

MAY 8

Accepted an invitation from Mr. A. H. Tolman[14] to visit Chicopee Falls. Collected one small sum and got the promise of more.[15]

AD Con. 949 BTW Papers DLC. BTW entered these items in a small (6¼" x 3½") leather-bound notebook, his name and address entered on an end page. The items occupied only 11 of the notebook's 130 pages. BTW filled many of the other pages with notes on expenses, payments, receipts, and other school business. Some 22 pages listed subscribers, contributors, and contacts in the Northeast.

[1] Margaret E. Snodgrass.

[2] Also Miss Snodgrass?

[3] Before leaving the New York area BTW solicited a number of large gifts for the school, of which the first and largest was $500 from Alfred Haynes Porter toward the building which later bore his name.

[4] Thomas Kendall Fessenden.

[5] Charles Dwight Smith, twenty-seven-year-old son of Henry D. Smith, who worked as a mechanical engineer.

[6] Timothy Higgins of Southington, Conn., presumably a deacon of a local church.

[7] A. Lyman Williston (1834-1915) of Northampton, Mass., headed the Greenville Manufacturing Co., makers of cotton goods, for thirty-one years and was a director and president of the First National Bank of Northampton. A graduate of Williston Seminary in 1852, a school founded by his uncle Samuel Williston, he later served as a trustee and from 1885 to 1895 as president. He was also deeply involved in the financial direction of Mount Holyoke, Amherst, and Smith.

[8] Charles L. Mead (1834-99) was chairman of the executive committee of the American Missionary Association from 1875 to 1898 and president of the Stanley Rule and Level Co., New Britain, Conn.

[9] Charles and Homer Merriam were two of five surviving sons of a West Brookfield, Mass., printer, all of whom began to learn the trade in their father's firm when they reached the age of twelve and subsequently followed business careers in printing. Charles (1806-87) helped found the Springfield firm G. & C. Merriam in 1832 which, after the death of Noah Webster in 1843, published the Webster dictionary. He was a staunch Congregationalist and a liberal contributor to church missionary activities. His younger brother, Homer Merriam (1813-1908), moved to Springfield and joined G. & C. Merriam in 1855, becoming a full partner in 1876 and serving as president (1892-1904) after the firm was incorporated. Like Charles, he was active in a variety of philanthropic causes. BTW recorded a $10 gift from Homer Merriam on this trip.

[10] William Tappan Eustis (1821-88), of Congregationalist background, was pastor of the (Independent) Memorial Church, Springfield, Mass., from 1869 until his death. Eustis gave BTW $2 on this trip.

[11] Washington Gladden (1836-1918), of New England ancestry, graduated from Williams College in 1859 and became a Congregational minister, first in Brooklyn, N.Y. (1860-66), and then in North Adams (1866-71) and Springfield, Mass. (1875-82). A college reporter for the Springfield *Republican,* he later worked on the editorial staff of the New York *Independent* (1871-75), and edited

Sunday Afternoon, a Magazine for the Household, renamed *Good Company,* from 1878 to 1880. Gladden was a prolific writer, popularizing the results of the new biblical criticism, advocating interdenominational cooperation, and preaching the social gospel of religious concern with the social relations of the industrial age. In 1882 he became minister of the First Congregational Church of Columbus, Ohio, where he remained to his death. From 1894 to 1901 he was vice-president of the American Missionary Association, and from 1901 to 1904 its president. After a trip to Atlanta University in 1903 and a meeting with W. E. B. Du Bois, Gladden expressed shock at the condition of blacks in the South and began to voice criticism of industrial education. He resigned as president of the American Missionary Association to become moderator of the National Council of Congregational Churches.

[12] Samuel Giles Buckingham (1812-98) was pastor of the South Congregational Church of Springfield, Mass., from 1847 to 1894. He was a descendant of one of the founders of Yale and graduated from Yale's divinity school. His older brother, of whom he wrote a biography (1894), was William A. Buckingham, Connecticut governor and U.S. senator.

[13] Mrs. George E. Howard was the wife of one of the directors of the First National Bank of Springfield, Mass.

[14] Albert Harris Tolman (1856-1928), principal of Chicopee Falls, Mass., High School from 1878 to 1882, became a widely published Shakespearean authority and professor of English at the University of Chicago. He was educated at Williams College, Johns Hopkins University, and the University of Strassburg. His uncle, Richard Tolman (1817-94), was chaplain of Hampton Institute from 1871 to 1878. Albert Tolman donated $2 to Tuskegee on this occasion.

[15] The Congregational Church and Sunday School at Chicopee Falls donated $73.

A Recommendation from
George Washington Campbell and Waddy Thompson

Tuskegee Ala   April 22 1882

To whom it may concern. The bearer of this Mr. B. T. Washington is Principal of the Tuskegee Cold. Normal School, and is now making a tour of the Northern States, soliciting pecuniary aid for the purpose of completing a building now being erected as a school house for the use of said School. We can with confidence recommend Mr. Washington as a *gentleman,* and hope he may meet with success in this enterprise.

This School was established by an act of the Legislature of this State during a session of 1880, and an annual appropriation of Two thousand dollars was made for the support and maintenance of said school. The building we now use is not sufficient to meet the growing require-

ments of the school, and we have determined to erect a suitable building for the purpose, and we hope Mr Washington may meet with
success.

G. W. Campbell
Prest. Board Trustees

Waddy Thompson
Co. Supt. of Ed.

ALS   Con. 16   BTW Papers   DLC.

To [James Fowle Baldwin Marshall]

Northampton Mass. May 2n 1882

Dear Genl: I saw several gentlemen yesterday in Plantsville and one
here to day who signified their intention of doing something for us;
and said that they would send their amts to you.

As we want to have the building ready to use by Sept 1st it is important that no time be lost. For this reason I want to ask you to forward
what ever amt you receive to Mr. G. W. Campbell, Tuskegee. He
understands the whole arrangemts at Tuskegee and will see that the
money [is] correctly applied. He and I had an understanding before
I left. Mr. Campbell is to keep the accounts and one of the other commissioners is to superintend the work.

Please get his receipt. Mr. Fessenden[1] & Mr Smith[2] have been very
kind to me. I have met with encouragement so far. Yours faithfully

B. T. Washington

P.S. Any mail sent to Norwich Ct before the 8th inst will reach me.

B. T. W.

ALS   BTW Folder   President's Office Vault   ViHaI. BTW's instructions to
forward contributions to Campbell establishes the correspondent as J. F. B.
Marshall. A letter the following month acknowledged receipt of funds from
Marshall. (George W. Campbell to Marshall, June 26, 1882, *ibid.*)

[1] Thomas Kendall Fessenden.
[2] Henry D. Smith.

Two News Items from
the Springfield *Daily Republican*

[Springfield, Mass., May 8, 1882]

A Colored Man's Experience among His Own People

B. T. Washington, principal of the Alabama colored normal school, talked instructively at the Memorial church last night and answered a number of questions about his work. The school began with a small number of pupils last July and over 100 had been gathered in when the session closed in March. The state appropriated $2000 for the payment of teachers' salaries, as an experiment, but made no provisions for buildings or apparatus. During the year the principal has paid for a farm, and is now at work securing $4200 for a substantial school building, a part of this sum having been pledged at the North and South. He and his three assistants, who are also Hampton graduates, have been kindly received by their white neighbors, and there is a good prospect that the appropriation for the school will be increased by the Legislature this year. It is located in the heart of the state, and there is an ignorant colored population within a radius of 15 miles. The colored people of Alabama have very little to do with politics, not more than half of them voting. Most of them are kept poor by the mortgage system, which uses up a good part of the crop before it is harvested, because of the local merchants' lien on it for provisions advanced. The majority of colored teachers now in service are very ignorant, as are the poor-whites who also teach in the colored schools, and they get their certificates through the county superintendents, who are usually merchants, by promising to trade at their stores. One of the points made by the speaker was that the northern people who help the cause of negro education at the South are sure to benefit the white population of that section. In the county where he lives the people secured local option by petitioning the Legislature for a special act for their benefit, and as a consequence no liquor has been legally sold there this year.[1] In general the country colored people are not nearly as intemperate as those who dwell in cities. Mr. Washington is confident that the colored people have a better chance for advancement at the South than at the North, because the competition in all occupations is not so close. He finds that those who live in Alabama are lacking in ambition as compared with those of Virginia, where he was reared and educated. The great need of the negroes of the Gulf states is the presence among them of intelligent men of their own color who shall stir them up to good works.

Springfield *Daily Republican,* May 8, 1882, 5.

¹ An Alabama statute "To prohibit the manufacture or sale of spirituous, vinous and malt liquors within the limits of Macon County, Ala.," approved Feb. 26, 1881, went into effect on the last day of that year. It may have been inspired by the prospect of a black normal school, authorized a few weeks earlier. The cycle of local opinion soon swung the other way, however, perhaps because of a consequent decline of Tuskegee as a rural market town when farmers found they could not buy liquor there. The prohibition act was repealed two years after enactment, "so far as the same relates to beat No. 3, known as Society Hill Beat, and to the town of Tuskegee." The Alabama statutes included many other similar local statutes prohibiting liquor sales around schools and churches. (*Acts of the General Assembly of Alabama, Passed at the Session of 1880-81* (Montgomery, 1881), 45-46; *ibid., 1882-83,* 353.)

[Springfield, Mass., May 9, 1882]

B. T. Washington, the colored man who is working in the interest of the Tuskegee (Ala.) normal school, says that northern people can have very little idea how degrading labor is regarded by many people at the South. He says he met one old negro with his ax over his shoulder, the other day, and asked him how he was getting along. The reply was that he was able to get a living, but that in so doing he was committing sin all the time, because it is a sin to work. This proposition was contested, but the old man told his visitor that if he would take the trouble to walk over to his cabin he would prove it from his Bible. The offer was declined, and the veteran was asked why, if labor be such a sin, he went forth every morning to toil with his ax? He answered that he did it because he must, or else starve, and then added, "But I expect to be beaten with many stripes for it, by and by."

Ibid., May 9, 1882, 6. This anecdote was probably a part of BTW's speech of May 7, reported above.

To [James Fowle Baldwin Marshall]

Springfield, Mass. May 9 1882

Dear General: I came here a few days ago intending to stay only a day, but meeting with more opportunities than I expected I have just gotten ready for a new field.

Mrs. Howard[1] and Drs. Eustis[2] and Buckingham[3] have been very kind to me. I spoke in Dr. Eustis' church Sunday evening.

The "Springfield Republican" has favored me. I guess you have seen an account it gave of the meeting in Dr. Eustis' church. I notice that the last four issues[4] have referred to my being here in one way or another. Mr. Tolman[5] came over from Chicopee Falls to invite me there. I speak there next Sunday evening. I go to Ware and Enfield tomorrow.

Most every one on whom I have called has helped me some, but it comes in small sums which will necessarily require a good deal of time to be spent in the collection. I feel much encouraged so far. Have not heard from Miss Davidson yet. I saw Miss Gillett[6] a few days ago who has also helped me.

I think I told you that I called on Mr. H. D. Smith of Plantsville. He is a capital man.

Any communication sent to Hartford Ct. before the 15 inst will reach me. Yours faithfully

Booker T. Washington

ALS BTW Folder President's Office Vault ViHaI. Clipping of May 7, 1882 (Springfield *Republican*) attached. BTW's reference to his previous mention of his visit to Smith establishes the recipient as Marshall. BTW had mentioned this visit a week earlier. (See BTW to Marshall, May 2, 1882.)

[1] Mrs. George E. Howard.
[2] William Tappan Eustis.
[3] Samuel Giles Buckingham.
[4] Springfield *Daily Republican,* May 6, 1882, 6; May 7, 1882, 6; May 8, 1882, 5; May 9, 1882, 6.
[5] Albert Harris Tolman.
[6] Lucy Douglas Gillett.

To [James Fowle Baldwin Marshall]

Hartford Ct. June 22/82

Dear Gen'l: I was in Norwich a few days ago. Mr. Pierce[1] took me to see Mr. Slater[2] who knew about our work at Tuskegee and was very much interested in it. He kept me at his house about half an hour, explained all about his fund, and showed me a few of the hundreds of letters which he is receiving from all over the world. He says that he thinks Tuskegee stands a fair chance for some of his fund, though none of it will be paid out for a year.

Have seen Phelps, Dodge and Co.[3] of N.Y. and they are going to ship the tin roof at once.

I feel confident that they are going to donate it. They would not let me pay for it, but said if there was anything to pay on it they would let us know in the future.

I took them a letter from Mr. Monroe[4] of Southport.

Every thing is quite encouraging and we feel confident that all the money for the building is now sure except a few hundred which we will probably get soon.

Will be by Hampton next week. Yours faithfully

Booker T. Washington

ALS BTW Folder President's Office Vault ViHaI. Docketed "R&A June 25" in Marshall's hand.

[1] Moses Pierce.

[2] John Fox Slater (1815-82) was the son of John Slater, who had brought the secrets of British textile machinery to the United States around 1804. Slater successfully invested his inheritance, amassed a fortune, and two years before his death created the John F. Slater Fund for Negro Education.

[3] The founding of Phelps, Dodge and Company in 1832 climaxed the business career of Anson Greene Phelps (1781-1853), a merchandizer and importer of tin plate and other metals. Under the leadership of Phelps and his son-in-law William Earl Dodge (1805-83), the firm diversified into manufacturing, mining, and railroad enterprises. A devout Presbyterian and a philanthropist, Phelps supported missionary work and Negro colonization efforts. Dodge, a former congressman, was well known for philanthropic work associated with religion and temperance. He also served on the board of trustees of the John F. Slater Fund.

[4] Probably Elbert B. Monroe, who was a Hampton trustee. Serving on the boards of trustees for some thirty organizations, including the American Missionary Association, Monroe donated liberally to the building program at Hampton Institute. On this trip he donated $25 to Tuskegee, and his wife donated $10.

To James Fowle Baldwin Marshall

Malden W.Va. July 19, 1882

Dear General: I suppose by this time that you are at Hampton again. Your letter containing the check for $215.50 has been forwarded to me from Tuskegee.

I am here resting for a few weeks and do not go to Tuskegee till after the first of August. I hear from there that things are going on nicely.

I thank you for your advice in regard to keeping our accounts straight. We are making a special effort to keep every thing straight so that we can have a detailed acct of our rec[e]ipts and expenditures printed and sent to each donor directly after the work is done. Directly after I go to Tuskegee I will try to write you just how every thing stands.

Miss Davidson is at her home in Ohio resting.

I was sorry not to see you and Mrs. Marshall at Hampton. Yours faithfully

Booker T. Washington

ALS   BTW Folder   President's Office Vault   ViHaI.

The Register of Marriage
of BTW and Fanny Norton Smith

[Charleston, W.Va., Aug. 2, 1882]

DATE AND PLACE OF MARRIAGE		FULL NAME OF THE PARTIES	
DATE	TOWN OR		
1882	COUNTY	HUSBAND	WIFE
Aug. 2		Booker T. Washington	Fanny N. Smith
AGE BEFORE MARRIAGE		PLACES OF THEIR BIRTH	
HUSBAND	WIFE	HUSBAND	WIFE
26	24	Kana Co. Va.[1]	Kana Co. Va.

Places of Their Residence		Name of Person Performing
Husband	Wife	Marriage Ceremony
Kana. Co. Va.[2]	Kana. Co. Va.	I. C. Taylor

Remarks
John F. Hubbard[3]

Marriage Book 1, 192, Kanawha County Courthouse, Charleston, W.Va.

[1] Should have been recorded as Hale's Ford, Va.

[2] Should have been recorded as Tuskegee, Ala.

[3] John F. Hubbard, born in 1831, moved to Malden at age twenty and worked in the general store of Colonel William Dickinson. He then went into the mercantile business for himself and in 1881 moved to Charleston. In Malden he was active in the Presbyterian Church. He once served as Kanawha County sheriff. The purpose of the "Remarks" column of this document is unclear, but presumably Hubbard was the person who reported the wedding to the county officials.

To James Fowle Baldwin Marshall

Malden W.Va. Aug. 2, 1882

Dear Gen'l: Your letter containing the two checks rec'd. Have just sent Miss Davidson's to her at *Lee P.O. Athens Co. Ohio.*

Fanny and I both are very grateful for your kind remembrance. Yours &c

Booker T. Washington

ACS BTW Folder President's Office Vault ViHaI.

To James Fowle Baldwin Marshall

Tuskegee, Ala. Oct. 18/82

Dear Genl: I write to know if you and Gen Armstrong think it best for us to make any formal application for help from the Sclater — fund?[1] I should be glad of any advice about it.

Our school has been open about six weeks and we have almost one hundred students and they still come. This is double the number we had the same time in the term last year. I fear we shall have to stop admitting them directly.

The new building was not ready for us to open in, but we expect to be able to move into it next month. It is very beautiful and the whites seem about as proud of it as the colored. The whole cost without furniture is $4550.00 and I am glad to tell you that it is now all provided for. Mr. Bicknell[2] of Boston wrote me a very nice letter in answer to your visit. I have just finished a letter to the "New England Journal of Education."[3]

We have the Meth. & Bap. town schools united now and they are both being taught on our place. Miss Snodgrass[4] is assisted by Lucy Smith.[5] They will have 300 students making in all on the farm over 400.

Mrs. Washington is well. All send love. Yours faithfully

Booker T. Washington

ALS   BTW Folder   President's Office Vault   ViHaI.

[1] The John F. Slater Fund.

[2] Thomas Williams Bicknell (1834-1925) was editor of the *New England Journal of Education* from 1875 to 1886. He was Rhode Island Commissioner of Education in 1869. He published and edited several other educational journals and helped to found the National Council on Education in 1880, serving as its first president. He lectured widely on education, temperance, woman suffrage, and municipal reform.

[3] See BTW to editor, *New England Journal of Education,* 16 (Nov. 9, 1882), 299. The letter summarized the history of Tuskegee Normal School.

[4] Margaret E. Snodgrass.

[5] Lucy E. Smith was born in Williamsburg, Va., in 1860. She graduated from Hampton in 1879 and taught at several schools before joining the Tuskegee faculty for a year in October 1882. From 1883 to 1885 she was a student teacher at St. Augustine's College, Raleigh, N.C. She married William E. McKenzie, a schoolteacher and farmer, in 1886 and settled in Ettrick, Va.

From James Fowle Baldwin Marshall

[Hampton, Va., Oct.] 23 [1882][1]

Dear Booker, Yours of 18th is recd. Gen A. says you should write to Moses Pierce Esq Norwich for advice as he is a friend of Mr Sclater & of Tuskegee. There will be no appro. paid this year, but your application should be made as soon as Mr P. thinks the time has come. Your accommodations are likely to be as severely taxed as ours. We are not only refusing applications but sending many away that have come — having no room or work for them. Yours faithfully,

J. F. B. Marshall

I congratulate you heartily on the completion of your building without incurring a debt.

ALpS   Business Office   ViHaI.

¹ The date is suggested by BTW to Marshall, Oct. 18, 1882, also misspelling Slater as Sclater. Also, the letter appears in the letterbook in a sequence suggesting that date.

The Annual Report of Tuskegee Normal School

Tuskegee, Ala., November 8, 1882

MR. G. W. CAMPBELL,
   President Board of Commissioners:

Dear Sir: The Normal School, established by the last Legislature, at this place, was opened July 4, 1881, with 30 students and the session closed with 112. The second or present session opened with 66, and the present attendance is 98, and is likely to reach 140 before the session closes. The total number in attendance since the school began has been 142.

STUDIES

Branches taught thus far: Orthography, reading, mental and written arithmetic, descriptive and physical geography, language lessons, grammar and composition, United States and ancient history, physiology, geometrical drawing, vocal music, and gymnastics.

The town public school is taught on the Normal School grounds, and is used as a model school for the Normal students.

The course of study extends through a period of four years and includes, besides others, all the branches laid down in the State school law.

GENERAL INFORMATION

Instructors employed	3
Average age of students	18½

Counties represented	9
Non-residents	81
Residents	61
Number who have taught	46

LAND

In order to give the students a chance to pay a part of their expenses in work, to teach the dignity of labor, and to furnish agricultural training, the friends of the school have bought a farm of one hundred acres, on which the school is located.

BUILDINGS

The building erected during the summer, by contributions from friends in Tuskegee and in the North, is 67 x 58, and is three stories high, without the basement. It contains six recitation rooms, one large chapel, reading room and library, office, dormitories for girls in third story, and is to have a boarding hall in the basement.

Besides the large building, there are three smaller buildings on the place, containing in all five rooms, also devoted to the use of the school.

FINANCE

The officers of the school have collected, and expended for the objects named, the following amounts, outside of the State appropriation:

New building	$4,450.00
Cost of farm and improvements	707.00
General expenses	131.59
Beneficiary fund	115.00
Books for library	48.35
Furniture for dormitories	70.00
Total, outside of State appropriation	$5,521.94
State appropriation	2,000.00
Total, with State appropriation	$7,521.94

DONATIONS OF MATERIALS

Volumes for library, 600; 1 cabinet organ, and many other valuable articles.

The school owes much of its present prosperity to the hearty co-operation of both the white and colored citizens of Tuskegee, and in the future, with the continued outside help and State aid, it will move on to greater usefulness. Respectfully submitted,

B. T. Washington, *Principal*

ANNUAL REPORT OF GEORGE W. CAMPBELL,
CHAIRMAN OF THE BOARD OF COMMISSIONERS OF THE
TUSKEGEE COLORED NORMAL SCHOOL,
FOR THE YEAR ENDING AUGUST 31, 1882

DR.

1881		
Oct. 4	To amount received from State	$2,000.00
1882		
Sept. 1	To balance on hand	$ 226.71

CR.

1881				
July 1	By am't paid for nails and screws for building			.94
Oct. 5	" " B. T. Washington, Principal, as per voucher			300.00
	" " J. W. Cardwell, Assistant, " "			56.25
	" " Olivia Davidson " " "			45.00
8	" " J. M. Dill, for desks, as per voucher			20.80
29	" " freight on chairs and books, as per voucher			.85
	" " Raymon Thweat,[1] for work, " "			12.00
	" " "Macon Mail," printing indentures, as per voucher			7.50
Dec. 31	" " Ramon Thweat, for work, as per voucher			5.00
1882				
Jan. 6	" " B. T. Washington, Principal, as per voucher			300.00
	" " J. W. Cardwell, Assistant, " "			135.00
	" " Olivia Davidson " " "			135.00
	" " freight, as per voucher			14.50
8	" " Lewis Adams, for wood, stove, brooms &c., as per voucher			23.60
March 3	" " J. C. McLaren,[2] for lumber for building, as per voucher			100.00
31	" " J. W. Cardwell, Assistant, as per voucher			135.00
April 1	" " Olivia Davidson " " "			135.00
10	" " catalogues, as per voucher			11.50

I I	"	"	B. T. Washington, Principal, as per voucher	300.00
I5	"	"	for lumber	31.85
Aug. 30	"	"	"Macon Mail," for indentures	3.50
			Balance on hand	226.71
				$2,000.00

Report of H. Clay Armstrong, Superintendent of Education of the State of Alabama, for the Scholastic Year Ending September 30, 1882 (Montgomery, 1883), 23-25.

[1] Ramon [Raymond?] Thweatt, a black carpenter living in Tuskegee, was reported as forty-six years old in the census of 1880. He helped construct the first buildings at Tuskegee Institute. Thweatt's two older sons, Hiram and Raymond, were Tuskegee Institute students.

[2] J. C. McLaren, born in Vermont about 1841, operated a sawmill in Tuskegee.

Olivia A. Davidson
to James Fowle Baldwin Marshall

Tuskegee, Ala. Dec. 8, 1882

Dear friend: I fear you have felt that I have not been as prompt in the payment of my debt[1] to you as I might, or should have been, but we have only just received the payment of our first quarter's salary — or rather, it is the second quarter's, but you know I did not come till the first quarter was almost ended.

I am very, very grateful to you for lending me the money and waiting so patiently for its repayment.

Our school is getting on nicely. As I look back upon what has been accomplished since I came to you to know about the school, it all seems like a story, and not a transaction in real life with which I have been intimately connected.

We are all very busy (we Hamptonians I mean), and have already begun to look forward with pleasant anticipations to the rest and pleasant meetings with friends which the summer will bring us. I look forward to meeting with few with more pleasure than I do with the good friends of H.

Within the last few weeks we have received quite a number of boxes and barrels from friends at the North which contained books and clothing — and one barrel from Mr. Brown[2] containing *cakes* and *choice crackers.* There are two more on the way containing *choice bread.* I suppose he is under the impression that we have a boarding hall, as he sent us a large box of blankets, counterpanes and towels. The blankets &c will do good service in future, I hope, but I must admit that I am puzzled as to what I shall do with the barrels of bread. The other three have quite a joke of it on me — "Three barrels of choice bread for Miss Davidson" is the story told by the bills of lading. The girls at Fram. N. School sent us an excellent box of clothing, as did also the ladies of the Unitarian Church, Fram., and of Rev. E. E. Hale's Church, Boston — the latter came through Mrs. Hemenway. We are becoming somewhat proud of our little library — at present, we have nearly three hundred vols. Will you give me Prof. Warren's[3] address. I fear I have forgotten it, as two letters written him have remained unanswered when he asked for information as to how he should send some promised books which we are very much in need of.

Please remember me most kindly to Mrs. Marshall. I trust her health is entirely restored & that she is able to be at H. With Miss Mackie[4] absent and Mrs. Gen. Marshall also, I am sure Hampton would not be Hampton to me. Again with thanks for your kindness, I remain, Yours truly

Olivia A. Davidson

ALS   BTW Folder   President's Office Vault   ViHaI.

[1] Returning from her northern fund-raising trip, Olivia Davidson found herself short by $175 of the amount that her books indicated she had collected for the school. Though she was certain she had not spent the amount, she was unable to find either the money or the error in her bookkeeping. She personally accepted full responsibility and, with her first quarterly paycheck not due for several weeks, borrowed the money from Marshall to avoid delaying the work of the school. Marshall, distraught over her predicament but recognizing her personal responsibility and the object lesson it provided in Hampton's teachings, tried unsuccessfully to help her find the mistake in her figures. (Davidson to Marshall, Aug. 26, Sept. 5, 1882, BTW Folder, President's Office Vault, ViHaI; Marshall to Davidson, Sept. 13, 1882, Con. 88, BTW Papers, DLC.)

[2] George Edward Brown.
[3] Henry Pitt Warren.
[4] Either Charlotte L. or Mary Fletcher Mackie.

An Amendment to the Act
Establishing Tuskegee Normal School

[Montgomery, Ala.] February 16, 1883

To amend "An act to establish a Normal School for Colored Teachers, at Tuskegee."

SECTION 1. *Be it enacted by the General Assembly of Alabama,* That "An act to establish a normal school for colored teachers at Tuskegee," approved February 10th, 1881, be amended so as to read as follows:

SEC. 1. There shall be established at Tuskegee, in this State, a normal school for the education of colored teachers. Pupils shall be admitted free of charge for tuition in said school, on giving an obligation in writing to teach in the public schools in this State for two years after they become qualified. The school shall not be begun or continued with a less number than twenty-five pupils, nor shall the school be taught for a less period than nine months in each year.

SEC. 2. There is hereby appropriated out of the general school revenue set apart for the education of colored children, the sum of three thousand dollars annually, for the maintenance and support of said school; and the apportionment of the general fund for colored children shall be made to the several counties of this State after the deduction of the sum herein appropriated. The said appropriation shall be under the control of the commissioners hereinafter provided for, and shall be applied in such manner as they may deem best, to carry out the purposes of this act.

SEC. 3. The school shall be under the direction and control of a board of three commissioners, which shall consist of the following persons, to-wit: George W. Campbell, M. B. Swanson, and Lewis Adams, who shall select one of their number as chairman of the board, and shall have power to fill any vacancy that may occur in the board. In case a majority of the commissioners cannot agree upon a person to be chairman, or a person to fill a vacancy, in the board, then such disagreement shall be certified to the Superintendent of Education for the State, and that office shall forthwith appoint a member of the board to be chairman, or a person to fill the vacancy, as the case may be and the member of the board so appointed as chairman and the person so appointed to the vacancy, shall have the same power and authority as if he had been selected by the board. The commissioners shall, at the end of each quarter, make a written report to the State Superintendent of Education of the condition and progress of the school, the teachers that have been employed, the number of pupils that have been in attendance, the manner in which the appropriation has been expended, the branches that have been taught, and such other facts relating to the school as may be of public interest and importance.

SEC. 4. The chairman of the board of commissioners shall give bond in double the amount of the appropriation for the safe keeping and faithful application of the sum appropriated; the bond to be approved by the judge of the probate of Macon county, and filed in his office, a certified copy of which shall also be forwarded to the State Superintendent of Education, and placed on file in his office.

SEC. 5. The chairman of the board of commissioners shall, after the execution, approval and filing of the bond, and the certified copy of the same as provided hereinbefore, present to the State Superintendent of Education a requisition for the amount herein appropriated, and the Superintendent of Education shall thereupon certify the amount to the State Auditor, who shall draw his warrant for the sum on the State Treasurer, payable to the chairman of the board of commissioners, for the maintenance and support of the said normal school as hereinbefore provided; and a like requisition shall be presented and the sum herein appropriated so drawn each year, as the same shall accrue.

Acts of the General Assembly of Alabama, Passed at the Session of 1882-83 (Montgomery, 1883), 392-93.

To the Editor of the *Southern Workman*

Tuskegee, Feb. 19, 1883

Editor Southern Workman: When you heard from us last, I think we had just moved into our new building. Everything now is beginning to appear quite home-like in our new hall.

So far in the term about 130 students have entered. Some of our classes have, of necessity, been too large. We have students from almost every part of the State, and even Georgia is represented.

Just now we are all feeling unusually lifted up, notwithstanding the *absence* of the State Treasurer.[1] The Legislature has just passed a bill giving us $1,000 more annually. The bill came up in the House the next day after the defalcation was reported, and passed by a large majority. I was invited to make a statement of our work before the committee of the Senate, on education, and it seemed especially interested in the industrial feature.

The State Supt. of Education, Hon. H. Clay Armstrong, has notified us that Dr. J. L. M. Curry,[2] by his advice, has decided to give us $500 from the Peabody fund.

It is certainly a cheering sign to see how interested some of the leading Southern whites are becoming in the education of the Negro. It is said that when the bill to increase our appropriation for tuition was before the House, that the Speaker,[3] a staunch democrat, made one of the most stirring and eloquent speeches of the session in favor of Negro education.

We had a very pleasant two-days visit last month from the Rev. R. C. Bedford,[4] pastor of the Congregational church of Montgomery. He spoke one evening to the students and citizens in the chapel. The chapel was crowded, and he seemed to impart new life to every one.

I think we have not told you about Thanksgiving Day. In the day we had exercises in the chapel, and addresses were delivered to the students and visitors by the pastors of the white Baptist and Presbyterian churches and by one of the colored pastors. During Thursday and Friday evenings, and Saturday in the day, Miss Davidson, assisted by other teachers, held a Fair to raise means for the school. All thought at the Fair the people showed in a practical way that they were willing to help *themselves* all they could.

We netted from the Fair $145.00. $45.00 of this amount came from a "jug breaking" Friday evening. The jugs had been given out a month previous to twelve students, who left few persons unbegged for a nickel.

Our students are not ashamed to work. Soon after we moved into the building, the young men were called together and told that a large amount of earth would have to be removed from the basement before it would be completed, and if we had to hire it done the cost would be $30 or $35. One young man suggested to the others that, since friends had been kind enough to pay the greater part needed to put up the building, students ought to be willing to give in work whatever they could. A proposal was made that they be divided into squads, and each squad work every day in turn for an hour after school. This was done. The basement is now cleared out. Not one young man showed the least unwillingness to do his part.

Within a few days, a kind friend from Connecticut[5] has sent us means to purchase an additional forty acres to our farm, making in all 140 acres.

We have not been able yet to take out any insurance on our building. This is the most pressing matter before us now.

By invitation of Capt. Wilson,[6] Supt. of Education of Bullock county, I go to-morrow to hold a two-days' Institute with the teachers of his county. I will try to send you an account of my trip for the next month.

Booker T. Washington

Southern Workman, 12 (Apr. 1883), 38.

[1] Isaac H. Vincent, the state treasurer, fled to Mexico in 1883 after embezzling a quarter of a million dollars. He was later recaptured, convicted, and sent to prison.

[2] Incorrectly printed as J. T. M. Carey. Jabez Lamar Monroe Curry (1825-1903), born in Lincoln County, Ga., received his education at Waddell Academy in South Carolina, Franklin College (later the University of Georgia), and Harvard Law School. After service with the Texas Rangers in the Mexican War, he pursued a political career that included the Alabama legislature and the U.S. and Confederate congresses. He fought in the Confederate Army. In the postwar years he became an early southern promoter of public education for both races, served as a Baptist minister, and was president of Howard College in Alabama from 1865 to 1868. He was professor of English in Richmond College from 1868 to 1881. In 1881 he became general agent of the Peabody Education Fund, a position he held until his death except for a brief sojourn as minister to Spain in the 1890s. After 1890 Curry also served as agent of the John F. Slater Fund for Negro Education. He guided the Ogden Movement for southern public education during its early years, and was the first supervising director of the Southern Education Board from 1901 until his death. His principal work of educational leadership was the promotion of city high schools in the South for whites and of industrial education for blacks. He ardently admired BTW, sought subtly to guide him, and promoted the interests of his institution. He was best known throughout the South for his oratory in behalf of education at meetings of state legislatures and other public occasions. His approach was essentially conservative. He warned of the threat of barbarism and violence from an uneducated population.

[3] Wilbur F. Foster of Tuskegee. He was reported in the 1870 census as a thirty-year-old grocer, born in North Carolina. Called Colonel Foster, presumably from Confederate service, he played a prominent part in local Democratic politics and aided Tuskegee Institute. He was elected to the Alabama House in 1881. On Nov. 15, 1882, he became speaker of the House, and fourteen days later he introduced a bill to appropriate to Tuskegee Normal School an additional $1,000 per year.

⁴ Robert Charles Bedford (1849-1912), a white minister, was founder of a black Congregational church in Montgomery, Ala. He served as pastor from 1882 to 1890. Born in Sutton, Cambridgeshire, England, and educated at Beloit College, Andover Theological Seminary, and Chicago Seminary, he was ordained in 1875. Before coming to Alabama he served churches in several small midwestern towns. An early champion of Tuskegee, he became a trustee in 1883. When he lost his church at Montgomery because the congregation demanded a black pastor, Bedford wished to continue his connection with Tuskegee. He persuaded BTW to employ him as the school's financial agent in the Midwest. In 1893 he became secretary of the board of trustees, a position he held until his death. One of the few white employees of Tuskegee, Bedford was not permitted to spend more than a few months each year on the campus, so that it could not be said even incorrectly that the school was actually being conducted by white men. He assumed the pastorate of a Rockton, Ill., church in 1890, moving to Beloit, Wis., in 1898. His part-time work for Tuskegee continued to grow. As BTW extended his speaking tours after 1895, Bedford was his advance agent and arranger of his itinerary. A man of remarkable memory, personally acquainted with nearly all of Tuskegee's graduates, Bedford also served the school as a roving visitor to graduates and particularly the schools founded by graduates. A rather garrulous correspondent, Bedford wrote BTW almost daily for twenty-five years, giving him not only detailed information but endless advice on the school and on BTW's career. There is reason to believe that BTW valued Bedford's services more highly than his advice, but he had a warm affection for the white man who had befriended him at the beginning of his work. Bedford died on New Year's Day 1912, far from home in Los Angeles, Calif., in the service of the school. One of the graduates asked: "Who will be our 'Father' now?" BTW devoted his next Sunday-evening talk in the chapel to Rev. Bedford, and among his notes were these words of appraisal: "Little thought of self. Simple. Could not be insulted." (J. H. Ward to Emmett J. Scott, Jan. 22, 1912, Con. 489; BTW notes, Jan. 7, 1912, Con. 619, BTW Papers, DLC.)

⁵ Moses Pierce.

⁶ W. C. Wilson.

To Cornelius Nathaniel Dorsette[1]

Tuskegee, Ala., Feb 28, 1883

D. sir: Yours of 21 inst rec'd. In reply I would say that I suggested to Miss Mackie[2] that Montgomery would be a good place for you. In all the South I know of no place that would afford a better opening for you than Montgomery which is only two hours' ride from us — 40 miles. I think it has a population of about $30,000 inhabitants — more than half colored.[3] Some are quite wealthy. There is no colored M.D. there. Most of the large southern cities have one or two.

The white congregational minister[4] is *very* anxious for you to locate there.

I am well acquainted with the leading ministers there and through them and their churches I could give you an introduction that would go a good ways.

One col. M.D. in Atlanta is making $2000 a year. Don't see why one can't do as well in Montgomery. There are some good progressive col. people in Montgomery whom I know you could depend on.

Any thing in the way of information or otherwise that I can do I shall gladly do.

April or May will be good months in which to come. If you are here in May I should much like to have you at our Commencement (May 31). It would be a good opportunity to get advertised.

I shall hope to hear from you soon. Hastily yours

B. T. Washington

ALS in possession of Editors. Donated by Dorsette's daughter, Emma D. (Mrs. Vernon F.) Bunce of Orange, N.J.

[1] Cornelius Nathaniel Dorsette (1859-97) was born in slavery in Davidson County, N.C. Separated from his mother when he was two months old, he lived with his grandmother until after emancipation. Receiving only an irregular education until he enrolled in Hampton Institute, he graduated in 1878 and went to New York, where he studied Latin in preparation for medical school. He overworked himself at the Medical College of Syracuse and was unable to continue because of bad health and lack of money. Applying to the University Medical College of New York City when he regained his health, he was rejected because of his color. Finally Dorsette graduated from the University of Buffalo Medical Department, borrowing money from a former employer to pay his way. After graduating in 1882 he accepted a position as assistant physician at the Wayne County alms house and insane asylum and paid off his debts before moving in 1884 to Montgomery, Ala. He was the first Negro to pass the Alabama medical examination. Dorsette built a sound medical practice in Montgomery. Later he also entered the drug business there. He helped organize the National Medical Association, for Negro doctors, and served as its president. Dorsette fully endorsed BTW's program at Tuskegee and was a trustee of the institute before his death. He was Tuskegee's unofficial representative and BTW's personal contact in Montgomery.

[2] Probably Mary Fletcher Mackie.

[3] Montgomery's population in 1880 was actually 16,713, of which 9,931, or 59 percent, were black.

[4] Robert Charles Bedford.

To James Fowle Baldwin Marshall

Tuskegee, Ala., March 4 1883

Dear Gen'l: I hope you received the copy of the state Supt's report which I sent you some days ago.

I think our work this year has been as encouraging as it was last. In my letter to Miss Ludlow[1] I spoke of the additional appropriation of $1000 annually by the legislature. I almost gave up hope after our treasurer[2] "skipped." But it happened that the speaker of the House[3] was a resident of our town and he made a clear and forcible representation of our work. Heretofore the other two colored schools in the state have each received $500 annually from the Peabody Fund. This year by advice of the State Supt. Dr Curry takes $500 from one of the other schools and gives it to us. So I think in the future we will have to spend for tuition $3500.00.

Mr. Pierce has paid for an additional 40 acres of land for us.

I have just received a letter from Dr. Calloway[4] accepting an invitation to speak for us Commencement. I guess you have heard of him recently as the one who has been associated with Dr. Haygood[5] as Vice Pres. of Emory College Ga. He resigned his position there this year to accept the Presidency of a colored institution to be supported by the southern white methodists. He is widely known and respected in the South and I think he will do us much good. We doubtless would have gotten Dr. Haygood but for the miscarriage of one of my letters.

We expected to have the new building dedicated at our close, probably by the State Supt.

I spent two days of last week holding a teachers' institute with the teachers of Bullock Co. Both they and the Co. supt. seemed to enjoy it. I had planned on my programme for a discussion of the "Word Method," but found the leap from Webster's "Blue Back" to the "W. Method" too much.

All of us are blessed with good health. Mrs. Washington has not been sick abed a day since we have been here. I should like to write oftener but all this term I have been so *very* busy that I could not. Hereafter I hope to be somewhat relieved as we add another teacher[6] tomorrow. He is a fine young man — graduate of the Worcester Academy Mass.

I am sorry that we are not able just now to insure our building. We have some incidental expenses that we must provide for next. We are now preparing for a consert.

I suppose that you all will see Miss Davidson soon. Mrs. Washington and all the teachers desire to be remembered to you and Mrs. M. Yours faithfully

B. T. Washington

P.S. I enclose a piece concerning Dr. Calloway which I hope you will return when you have read it.

ALS   BTW Folder   President's Office Vault   ViHaI.

[1] Helen Wilhelmina Ludlow.

[2] Isaac H. Vincent, Alabama state treasurer.

[3] Wilbur F. Foster.

[4] Morgan Callaway (1831-99), as correctly spelled. Born into a slaveholding family of Wilkes County, Ga., Callaway graduated from the University of Georgia in 1849 and attended a law school in Augusta. He practiced law and taught at Andrew Female College in Cuthbert, Ga. He served as a colonel of Confederate artillery. After the Civil War he became a Methodist minister for three years in Washington, Ga., and for two years was president of La Grange Female College. In 1870 he joined the faculty of Emory College, Oxford, Ga., as professor of Latin, later changing to professor of English. The historian of Emory called Callaway "one of the truly great teachers of all her years." He became vice-president of the college and was strongly influenced by the moderate racial liberalism of President Atticus G. Haygood. When the General Conference of the Southern Methodist Church voted in 1883 to establish Paine Institute in Augusta, Ga., for the higher education of black Southern Methodists, the reformist faction of the denomination considered it a substantial victory. Callaway left Emory College to become president of the new school, but when it failed to secure what he considered adequate financial support, he returned to Emory and resumed his professorship. (See Bullock, *History of Emory University,* 160.)

[5] Atticus Greene Haygood (1839-96) graduated from Emory College in 1859 and during the Civil War served as a Confederate chaplain. After the war he was active in the Southern Methodist Church, serving as editor of the *Wesleyan Christian Advocate* from 1878 to 1882, and in 1890 he became a bishop of the church. From 1875 to 1884 he served as president of Emory College. He attracted wide attention in 1881 with the publication of *Our Brother in Black,* a collection of his writings calling for the training of blacks as vital to the uplift of the South. Haygood argued that there was an "essential unity" among the races of men, challenging the racist doctrines of the time, but he accepted racial segregation and manual training for blacks. His mild racial liberalism, as reflected in *Our Brother in Black,* led the Slater Fund trustees to choose him as agent in 1883, and between 1884 and 1890 he devoted his full energy to disbursing funds. He did not give away the Slater money in a systematic manner, and, to the chagrin of the board members, often let personal preferences sway him. BTW's ideas attracted him, and he was generous to Tuskegee Institute with Slater money. He left the Slater Fund in 1890, accepting the position of bishop in the church.

[6] M. J. Maddox. He taught history and elocution at Tuskegee in the 1883-84 school year.

To [James Fowle Baldwin Marshall]

Tuskegee, Ala., Mar. 20 1883

Dear General: Your card found every thing going nicely with us. I hope before this time that you have arrived safe at Hampton. Almost nothing in the history of our school has so encouraged us as your visit. The students often speak of you.

It is now time that we were looking out for teachers for next term. We are not yet sure whether or not Miss Snodgrass will return. Whether she does or not we shall need some one to take Lucy Smith's place. I write to know if the Gen. would consent to let Lucy Boulding[1] come here next term, and if he would consent do you think the objection you mentioned to me, so serious as to make it unwise for us to secure her. Her energy, and training under Miss Hyde[2] are strong points in her favor, but if you and the others there think she would not do well on account of the objection you mentioned we shall try to get some one else. In that case I shall let Miss Davidson attend to it when she comes there in May.

I shall try to send you another letter tomorrow concerning the matters we talked about.

All are well and send love. Yours faithfully

B. T. Washington

ALS BTW Folder President's Office Vault ViHaI. Marshall's answer of Apr. 5, 1883, establishes him as the correspondent addressed here.

[1] Lucy J. Boulding, born in 1858 in Burkeville, Va., graduated from Hampton in 1881 and taught there for a while. Like BTW and other Hampton graduates, she preached temperance and morality. She married George H. Stephens of the Hampton class of 1874, and lived in Lynchburg, Va.

[2] Elizabeth Hyde, a graduate of Framingham State Normal School in Massachusetts, became principal of the Butler School at Hampton in 1881. This was a training school for Hampton students preparing for teaching careers, and she supervised their practice teaching. Later, she succeeded Mary Mackie as lady principal of Hampton Institute. She retired in 1923 and died in 1928.

To James Fowle Baldwin Marshall

Tuskegee, Ala., Mar. 26, 1883

Dear General: Our building is now receiving the second coat of paint, and the trimmings. It looks beautiful.

I have seen Mr. Varner[1] about selling us the property in front of the school and he says that he does not care to sell it. I have an idea that he will sell it some time in the future as he is quite changeable.

The brick yard is the matter that I want to get started at once, if possible, for several reasons.

The young men are willing to go to work any time. Out side of making brick for the boys' building I feel sure that the yard will pay for itself within a few months.

There is a company organized here to build a cotton seed oil factory, and I feel almost sure that we can get their order for brick if we can get started soon.

The work that we can give the students in the yard will go a great way towards destroying the idea that to educate a colored man will make him stop work. Mr. Campbell and the other commissioners are very anxious for us to start the yard.

Mr. C. also suggested to me yesterday the idea of getting a printing press and I told him what you had said.

About the brick yard I want to ask you if you know of any one who would lend us $200. for 8 or 10 months at a reasonable rate of interest. We might be able to return it sooner. This I think would get the yard on foot.

In regard to keeping the boys on the place next year, my idea now is, since we were disappointed in securing the houses in front of us, to use all our out buildings for that purpose. In addition to this I am thinking of trying to build some cheap barracks that can be used for something else when we get the boys' building up. If we can not do this we may be able to rent several houses from Mr. Varner. I should very much like your advice on this point.

The students have sold nearly all the concert tickets. As soon as the concert is over we want to turn our attention towards getting the building insured.

I have written Mr Chaney.[2]

All send love to you and Mrs. Marshall. Yours faithfully

B. T. Washington

ALS   BTW Folder   President's Office Vault   ViHaI.

[1] Probably R. R. Varner, a white contractor in Tuskegee, twenty-six in 1880. The Varner family owned a large tract of land including a beautiful plantation house, "The Grey Columns," on the old Montgomery road out of Tuskegee. During the Civil War, General James Wilson's Union raiders marched through the town with orders to burn Tuskegee to the ground. An officer in Wilson's command discovered, however, that Ed Varner, who had been his fraternity brother at Yale, lay wounded at "The Grey Columns." The officer interceded to save the town. The Varner mansion became a monument of the Old South far more appropriate than the stereotyped Confederate soldier, facing north, who later appeared in the courthouse square. R. R. Varner was apparently the member of the family with whom BTW negotiated in the school's first years concerning use and purchase of Varner land, the fitting up of a school brickyard, and the sale of bricks. (See BTW to R. R. Varner, Jan. 6, 1886.)

[2] George Leonard Chaney (1836-1922), a Unitarian minister in Atlanta. After graduation from Harvard and Meadville Theological Seminary, Chaney served in the U.S. Sanitary Commission during the Civil War and then was minister of the Hollis Street Unitarian Church in Boston until 1877. He went to Atlanta to establish the Church of Our Father in 1881, formed a southern conference of the church in 1883, and became southern superintendent of the American Unitarian Association. He edited the *Southern Unitarian*. From 1883 to 1904 he was a Tuskegee trustee. After 1898 he lived in retirement in Leominster, Mass.

To Cora M. Folsom

Tuskegee, Ala., Mar. 31 1883

Dear Miss Folsom: About all I hear of the Indian Department is through the "Workman" and then I can not make out who writes the "Incidents."

I have thought of you many times, but my spare moments are *few*. The school is full. I have a little more time for writing now since we have added another teacher.

I do wish you could see our new building. It is beautiful.

We expect to start a brick yard soon. Gen Marshall says he is going to send us a printing press, so look out for a young "Workman."[1]

Gen. Marshall's visit was a *real* treat.

We are busy now preparing for a concert next week and Commencement in May.

Don't think I shall be at H. again before the Alumni meeting in '84. Mrs. W. has not been sick a day since being here. She wishes to be remembered to you. Hastily yours

B. T. Washington

ALS   BTW Folder   President's Office Vault   ViHaI.

[1] In January 1884 Tuskegee began publication of the *Southern Letter*, a monthly newsletter which was sent to graduates and friends of the school. When the *Tuskegee Student* was established in 1889 as the alumni newsletter, the *Southern Letter* was written more exclusively for northern white readers. Tuskegee Institute often sent the *Southern Letter* free to donors and potential contributors. In addition, in 1894 BTW claimed the publication had 2,500 paying subscribers.

From James Fowle Baldwin Marshall

Hampton, Va. April 5 1883

Dear Booker, I am & have been too busy to write you at length since my return. I have your letters. I will advance you $200. for your Brick Works — tho' I shall have to borrow it. You can return it within a year at 6% per annum interest, which is what I pay. Send me your note for the amount. You must be careful to keep all your different accounts separate and full & clear. I feel some anxiety on this point, as you have not the time to master the practical details of your Book-keeping, & I saw that your Books were not correctly kept, tho' I have no doubt that you understand the exact position of your affairs. But they will grow yearly more intricate, & it is very important that a correct system be established at the outset. Send me the enclosed with your signature & I will send check for the $200, or if you prefer it in two instalments, for half now & the balance when you want it, of course being charged interest only as the amount is paid. I hope you will get a competent man to manage the kiln. Be sure to charge the Brick Works with all it costs whether in cash, labor, or wood from the farm, so you can see just how much the Bricks cost, & then credit them with all Bricks sold or used for your own buildings at market rates and then you can tell how far the industry is profitable or otherwise. We credit the Farm with the clay, & use of ground — as both prevent that portion of the land from being made profitable in other ways, and also with use of teams for hauling. *You* will also have to credit it with the wood taken for the B. K.[1]

Ask Miss D. if she got a little book of poetry I sent her for Missouri Strong,[2] from Thomasville. I will have Registers with my letter sent you. Have told the story of my visit to the Teachers graduates & seniors.[3]

I find the Little Printing Press has been disposed of, for which I am very sorry. Will try to get one contributed for the school.

I shall send a box of sundries for the school as soon as I can find time to git them together.

I am anxious about your fire risk. Get insured at once, & have your glass lamps exchanged for Houses Patent — or some other safe kind — as soon as possible.

I am confirmed by our teachers in the opinion I expressed to you about a choice of assistant teacher. You had better take no action till Miss Davidson has been here & conferred with us on the subject. Yours faithfully

J F B Marshall

April 4[4] 1883

P.S. If you can rent the houses from Mr Varner at any fair rate, you would accomplish two purposes, viz: quarters for your boys & a riddance of undesirable neighbors. You must watch Mr V's moods, & when he is in the mood of selling secure the refusal of the land, if you have not the means to buy, till you can hear from friends on the subject. I hope to see Mr Pierce[5] here soon, and talk with him about the matter. How would you like to have me write to Mr Varner about the land, & ask his cooperation in your work, by preventing undesirable tenants whose influence would be a hindrance to your efforts to elevate the character of your students. Give my best regards to all your fellow workers — especially to Mrs W. & Miss Davidson. Yrs faithfully

J F B Marshall

ALS Copy BTW Folder President's Office Vault ViHaI.

[1] Brick kiln.

[2] Missouri C. Strong Blanks graduated from Tuskegee in 1887 and taught school in East Tallassee, Ala.

[3] See J. F. B. Marshall, "Tuskegee: A Hamptonian's Visit to the Young Hampton," in *Christian Register*, 62 (Apr. 5, 1883), 214. In it he told the story of

Tuskegee's beginnings and of the rapid expansion of the school. He emphasized the "esteem and confidence" BTW had earned from "the leading white citizens of the place," and concluded with a plea for contributions needed for new buildings. He said: "I know of no more worthy object or one conducive to more important results than this school enterprise, and I trust the friends of negro advancement and education will not suffer it to languish or be hampered for want of funds. They may rest assured that these will be wisely expended and most worthily bestowed."

4 Since Marshall docketed BTW's letter of Mar. 26, 1883, "R&A Ap 5," the date of the postscript seems to be in error.

5 Moses Pierce.

To James Fowle Baldwin Marshall

Tuskegee, Ala., April 22 1883

Dear Gen'l: I sent you a card recently acknowledging the receipt of the two checks. We are very thankful to you for your kindness and will make every effort to return the $200. soon. The brick yard is already being cleared off by the students and we expect to begin moulding by the latter part of next week. Shall let you hear often of its progress. We have been fortunate in securing a good part of the out fit for the yard. We went to Mr. Varner who operated a yard some years ago to b[u]y his moulds, brick barrows &c. and he very kindly *gave* them to us. There are 14 prs. of moulds and several barrows. The city marshall has also very kindly given us the free use of the town scraper with which to clean the yard off.

My conscience is not at all at ease about our accounts, though I am more careful now than ever. I want to ask what you would think of Mr. Parrott,[1] our music teacher, spending apart of his vacation in your office doing whatever work that would aid him most in getting hold of your methods? He is careful with figures and a good penman. If you could give him enough useful work to pay his board it would aid us much. However we can probably manage to pay his board for a short time if it can not be arranged for him to work it out. I shall follow st[r]ictly your advice with regard to the accounts of the Brick Works.

I suppose you have rec'd Miss D's note telling you that she received the book of poetry for M. Strong. We have recei[v]ed the Registers. Dr. Mayo[2] whom I met in Montgomery also gave me a number of copies. We all like your acct of Tuskegee very much and are sure that it will do much good.

Ever since you left I have been casting about to see how we could get insured. I asked the State Commissioners to do it with some money that was left over from last year, and they very readily consented. So I think that I shall be able to get the policy made out tomorrow. The more I have to do with Mr. Campbell, the more I am sure that his heart is set on doing our people good.

We shall let the matter of securing a teacher go till Miss D. comes there.

When I have seen Mr. Varner further I shall write about securing control of that property.

Mrs. Washington and all the teachers send love to you and Mrs. M. Yours faithfully

B. T. Washington

ALS   BTW Folder   President's Office Vault   ViHaI.

[1] R. S. Parrott taught music at Tuskegee from the fall of 1882 until November 1883.

[2] Amory Dwight Mayo (1823-1907), born in Warwick, Mass., graduated from Deerfield Academy and Amherst College. Before the 1880s he was a Unitarian preacher and professor of church polity in Meadville Theological Seminary. Then, as chief editorial writer for the *New England Journal of Education* and the *National Journal of Education,* and as a private citizen, he traveled some 200,000 miles in the South studying educational conditions, advising on educational matters, and composing voluminous histories of education in the various southern states for the annual reports of the U.S. Commissioner of Education. Formerly of Radical Republican sympathies, he lauded and encouraged the educational efforts in the New South, urged the uplifting of the "brothers in black," and expressed sympathy with the New South creed of industrialization and intersectional reconciliation. (See Gaston, *New South Creed,* 101-2.)

To James Fowle Baldwin Marshall

Tuskegee, Ala. April 28, 1883

Dear Gen'l: I rec'd the policy from the insurance agent yesterday. The building is insured for $3000. for one year.

Have just returned the brick yard — every thing is now in working order and we moulded 50 for a start this P.M. Expect to begin moulding 5000 per day Monday.

B. T. W.

ACI   BTW Folder   President's Office Vault   ViHaI.

To Olivia A. Davidson

Tuskegee, Ala., May 17 1883

Dear Miss Davidson: Enclosed you will find a letter just rec'd from Pres. Ware[1] in regard to Miss Hunt.[2] It may help you in deciding about others.

I think highly of the recommendation but very much fear that she will not leave her present position for the model school. She closes her present school soon so I shall write and mention the matter to her now.

Things are going well. Algebra glass [class] doing nicely. Hope you and the girls had a pleasant trip. Sincerely yours

B. T. Washington

ALS Con. 84 BTW Papers DLC.

[1] Edmund Asa Ware (1837-85), president of Atlanta University. Graduating from Yale in 1863, he became an agent of the American Missionary Association in Nashville and Atlanta. In 1867 he became a Freedman's Bureau superintendent of education. He helped to establish Atlanta University and became its first president (1869-85). He sought to pattern the school's curriculum after the best white colleges, but the poor preparation of many pupils made necessary a preparatory department that was larger than the collegiate department.

[2] Adella Hunt Logan (1863-1915) graduated from Atlanta University in 1881 and taught for two years in rural areas of the South before joining the Tuskegee faculty in 1883. President Ware recommended her highly to BTW: "We felt that she gave promise of making an excellent teacher; were so sure of it, that we offered her a position as teacher here in our own school. She felt, however, that she was needed where she was, and so did not come." (E. A. Ware to BTW, May 1, 1883, Con. 84, BTW Papers, DLC.) Adella Hunt married Tuskegee's treasurer, Warren Logan, in 1888. She later taught only part time, devoting her time to caring for their six children, most of whom died before reaching adulthood.

Olivia A. Davidson to the Editor of the *Southern Workman*

Tuskegee, Ala., June 11, 1883

My Dear *Southern Workman:* A Hampton Correspondent of the Boston Journal recently spoke of a belief in "Hampton weather." If we dared to generalize from so few special cases we at Tuskegee might begin to believe in "Tuskegee weather," but perhaps it is better for us to wait till we have left our baby-hood before we speak from *experience*. 'Tis an old saying that nature never repeats herself, but I am inclined to believe she preserved the pattern of your "Hampton day" for our "Tuskegee day" a week later, using an artificer's privilege of improving upon her pattern. We know she has an eye to the fitness of things, and what more fitting than that Hampton and Tuskegee should be dealt with alike by the old lady, with a slight partiality for the *baby?*

Thursday, May 31, our closing day, was a perfect day. Wednesday it rained quite hard from morning till night, and many a time during the day the anxious question, "Do you think it will rain to-morrow?" was asked. When the morning came, every body was made glad — glad of the rain that had fallen, giving such a beautiful freshness to every thing — glad of the lovely day promised by the morning. Even the birds seemed to share in the general gladness. They gave us a perfect Hallelujah Chorus from the trees about us.

We had the good fortune to secure for our main speakers Rev. Geo. L. Chaney of Boston, whose work is now in Atlanta, and Rev. Dr. M. Calloway,[1] formerly of Emory College. Both arrived on Wednesday. The latter was the guest of the white Methodist minister of the town, Rev. Mr. Holcomb. The first part of the morning was occupied with opening exercises, including a military drill with the young men, and class recitations which lasted till 11 o'clock. At this hour all assembled in the chapel to listen to the dedication of our new building by Rev. G. L. Chaney.

His subject was one befitting the occasion, and I am sure few of the large audience went away no better men or women than they were when they came. If I could I would give you a review of his excellent and helpful address, perhaps I may be able to furnish you with it entire later, and from it you can give your readers such portions as you may have room for. Mr. Chaney has very kindly consented to have it printed in pamphlet form for distribution among our students.

At 12.30 the "flow of soul" ended for a season, and our "feast of reason" began. We owe many thanks to Rev. Mr. Holcomb for the thoughtful kindness manifested by him. The speakers and a few of the guests were cordially invited to dinner at his house. As most of the students and friends brought baskets, dinner was partaken of in picnic style and was made quite a pleasant social event.

At 2 o'clock we reassembled for the rhetoricals and the other of the two main events of the day — Dr. Calloway's address. It was with a feeling akin to reverence somewhat mingled with awe that I listened to him. I think the latter feeling was awakened by the expression of his face. No one can look into it without the feeling that there is a powerful mind under the most complete subjection to the *will* of the man behind it. As I thought of what his resignation of an honored position among his own race, his acceptance of a work among us, his being here on such an occasion, meant for him — as I thought these things in connection with what he is — a man of southern birth, training and sympathies, a feeling of deepest respect for the one who for the sake of a conviction, could forego so much that was brightest, and in many respects, pleasantest, and assume so much that is hard and unpleasant, arose within me. Carlyle says, truly, I think, that we are all, more or less hero-worshipers. As I listened to his strong, earnest plea for the elevation of the Negro on the basis of his *humanity,* I felt that Georgia had given us another hero. Rev. Mr. Owen,[2] pastor of a large colored Baptist Congregation in Mobile, followed Dr. Calloway. His earnest entreaty to those present to make the aspiration of the Greek Slave, quoted by Mr. Chaney in the morning, "Not, Oh, that I *had* this or that, but, Oh, that I *were* this or that," theirs, was most forcible.

The students who took part in the rhetorical exercises of the afternoon — three young women and three young men — acquitted themselves well. They were of the Junior and Middle classes. We shall have no graduating class till year after next. The singing throughout the day was good. Mr. Parrott's[3] success in his department deserves special mention. The result of his work was praised by all present. By-the-way, I presume he is now making his first acquaintance with Hampton's — industrial — shades. He expected to go to H. very soon after leaving here.

In the evening all the students and many of their friends came together in the chapel for an informal social entertainment. The evening was spent pleasantly with a few well-rendered duets and solos, recitations, conversation, music, and marches. Towards the close of the evening "Judgment Day" they used to call it at Hampton, arrived. Amid the most profound stillness the names of the students constituting the different classes for next year were read. There were many happy faces and a few sorrowful ones among the students when this was over.

Soon after, students and friends turned their faces homeward, and the newly christened "Porter Hall" was shortly wrapped in darkness, and its tired inmates in welcome slumber.

The year just closed has been an encouraging one in many respects to us and at present our prospects for the future, though somewhat clouded by the *fear* of financial embarrassment, are hopeful. We *hope* by the close of another year to have a brick building for the boys well on towards completion.

The bricks are being made on the farm now. We have a promising crop of cotton, cane, corn, sweet potatoes and fruit. Our "Uncle Harry"[4] is not Mr. Howe,[5] but he has learned his *three* C's. Few, under like circumstances, can show a better crop of cotton, corn and cane than can "Uncle Harry."

A number of our students hastened away Friday and Saturday after the close of the school to be on hand in as many districts to begin schools the following Monday morning.

This they do to earn money with which to meet their expenses next year.

Some months ago, the colored teachers of Bullock, an adjoining county to this (Macon), expressed a desire to have a summer institute held in the county. To this their Supt., a white man,[6] gave a ready consent, and at his request Mr. Washington is now there in the work.

A few of the teachers of this county and of Montgomery, and of Lowndes County are here for the summer in a similar work with myself.

The weather, which through April and May was remarkably cool for this climate, is now quite warm. Old heads say we are "in" for a long hot summer. Already I begin to wish for some of Hampton's cool breezes.

Wishing you and all your readers a pleasant and *breezy* summer's vacation, I am   Yours truly,

D.

Southern Workman, 12 (Aug. 1883), 89-90.

[1] Morgan Callaway.

[2] A. F. Owen[s?] was a black minister and school principal in Mobile, Ala. He played a leading role in the formation of the National Baptist Convention in 1880.

[3] R. S. Parrott.

[4] Henry Clay Ferguson. Ferguson was born in 1859 in Franklin County, Va. He was probably the slave of Josiah Ferguson, who lived across the road from

BTW's birthplace near Hale's Ford, Va. In 1880 Henry Clay Ferguson lived in Charleston, W.Va., with his mother, Mary Ferguson, and five brothers and sisters. He graduated from Hampton Institute in 1883, and for five years was farm manager at Tuskegee Institute. In 1888 he moved to Texas, where he became a landowner and taught agriculture at Prairie View State Normal and Industrial College.

[5] Albert Howe.

[6] W. C. Wilson.

To James Fowle Baldwin Marshall

Tuskegee, Ala. July 1 1883

Dear Gen'l: I want to speak about the $100.00 due you. When we rec'd the $200.00 from the Marquand Estate[1] I was not sure whether you would think us right in keeping any part of your loan any longer. My only excuse for doing so is this: I thought when I wrote you that I would be able to rent enough rooms for the boys next term. I now see that I can not do it and have decided to put a long common frame building near the woods. Mr McLeran[2] has let us have most of the lumber at less than half price so by using the $100 I see my way clear to take care of the boys on the place next term. If we can use the money in this way I feel safe in promising its return by the middle of September.

I shall not invest it in the way mentioned until I hear from you. Sincerely yours

B. T. Washington

ALS   BTW Folder   President's Office Vault   ViHaI.

[1] The estate was that of Frederick Marquand (1799-1882), a Connecticut-born New York jeweler and merchant who retired at age forty to devote his life to philanthropy. His niece was the wife of Elbert B. Monroe, trustee of Hampton Institute. When BTW visited Southport, Conn., on his fund-raising trip following the 1881-82 school term, Marquand donated $25; Monroe, $25; and Mrs. Monroe, $10. Marquand died July 14, 1882, leaving a large sum to education including a donation to Hampton. The $200 to Tuskegee was among many small bequests.

[2] J. C. McLaren.

To James Fowle Baldwin Marshall

Tuskegee, Ala., July 23 1883

Dear Gen'l: We thank you for extending the time on remainder due you on note.

I acknowledged the receipt of Mr. Carrington's[1] money.

The basement is now being bricked up with brick from our first kiln. We were successful with the kiln though the work, by my absence, was not pushed as it should have been. It is hard to get a good foreman, one who will push hands and who also has a practical idea of all the details of the business. Shall try another man next time. The kiln contained about 70,000 brick and we have been lucky enough to sell them all except what we are using for the basement. Mr. Varner buys most of them. He will take now more than we have. Another kiln will be begun next week and I expect to see that the work is pushed. One of the merchants puts up a brick store soon as a result of the brick enterprise. It has done much good in many ways. I want to get hold of some letter files and a copying press. Will you be kind enough to advise as to the kind and where to get them.

I hope that Mr. Parrott is doing well. I sent you some papers containing accts of our close. You will see that the South deals in high-sounding titles.

Yes, we have a sweet little girl which adds much to our happiness. With your permission Mrs. W. and I desire to call her "Portia Marshall Washington."[2] Sincerely yours

B. T. Washington

We have the receipt book.

ALS   BTW Folder   President's Office Vault   ViHaI.

[1] Probably George M. Carrington of West Winsted, Conn., who contributed regularly to Hampton Institute in the early 1880s.

[2] Portia Marshall Washington Pittman (b. June 6, 1883), BTW's only child by his first wife Fanny, was named Portia after the character in *The Merchant of Venice*, and Marshall in honor of J. F. B. Marshall. She lost her mother at the age of two and was cared for by nurses until BTW's second marriage to Olivia A. Davidson. Portia was fond of her first stepmother, but at first violently objected to BTW's third marriage to Margaret James Murray, whom she regarded as a rival for the affection of her father. In time, however, she came to respect and admire her second stepmother. Her early adolescence was spent largely away from home. In September 1895 she entered the practice school of Framingham State Normal

School in Massachusetts, where she studied music and Latin. She was under the watchful eye of Mary C. Moore, an English teacher at Framingham, and Ellen Hyde, the principal, both friends of Olivia Davidson Washington. She lived in the dormitory there for four academic years, 1895-99. The summers she usually spent at Hopedale, Mass., the home of Miss Moore's sister, near enough to her father's summer headquarters in Boston to see him frequently. While at Framingham, attracted by the ritual and music of the local Protestant Episcopal church and influenced by Miss Moore, Portia left her father's Baptist faith and was confirmed as an Episcopalian. She returned to Tuskegee for the 1899-1900 school year and graduated. She was required at Tuskegee to learn dressmaking, which she hated, but her father wisely insisted that she take chemistry from the school's most distinguished faculty member, George Washington Carver. Another Tuskegee instructor tutored her in German, for she had ambition for further education.

In the fall of 1901 Portia Washington entered Wellesley College as a special student. She studied German, music theory, and piano. Ostensibly because she was not a full-time student but also because of pressure from southern students in the college, Portia Washington was denied accommodations in the college yard. She found quarters in a nearby boarding house, but life there surrounded by older people was dull and lonely for one of her lively temperament. Besides, musical training was not emphasized at Wellesley, and she realized she was not prepared for college work. At the end of a year she withdrew. Enrolling in Bradford Academy (later Bradford Junior College) in Bradford, Mass., she received kind and helpful attention from Miss Laura A. Knott and the other teachers. Her grades had been poor at Wellesley, but at Bradford she made As and Bs. She received a scholarship in piano, studying under Samuel Downes. She graduated in 1905, being the first Negro to graduate from Bradford.

Portia Washington sailed for Europe in the summer of 1905, accompanied by Tuskegee's lady principal, Miss Jane E. Clark. They spent much of the summer in London and Paris. She went on to Berlin for two years of piano study under Professor Martin Krause, who had been a pupil of Franz Liszt. She considered herself fortunate to win admission to his classes, and he gave close attention to his first Negro pupil and the Negro music that she introduced him to, arranged by Samuel Coleridge-Taylor, the Afro-British composer. In the summer of 1907 her stepmother and brother, E. Davidson Washington, came over to meet her; they traveled to Rome, Venice, and elsewhere in Europe.

Soon after her return home, Portia Washington married William Sidney Pittman, a Washington, D.C., architect, on Oct. 31, 1907. Pittman, who was born in Montgomery, was one of Tuskegee's brightest graduates and, with a loan from BTW, spent three years, 1897-1900, studying architecture at Drexel Institute of Art, Science and Industry in Philadelphia. He returned to Tuskegee to teach drafting and to supply drawings for the mechanical shops. Quarreling with the school's chief architect, Robert R. Taylor, and complaining that he was underpaid, Pittman left in 1904 to establish his own architectural office. He lived in and promoted the development of Fairmount Heights, a black suburb of Washington. He designed the 12th Street YMCA in Washington. Portia Pittman moved into the home her husband had designed. That winter BTW bought her a piano as a wedding present, and on May 31, 1908, she gave a concert in Washington to raise money to send Clarence Cameron White, a black violinist, to Europe. She played Chopin and Liszt, but one of her numbers was "Sometimes I Feel Like a Motherless Child," by Coleridge-Taylor. As a child she had been fondest of Chopin, but in her mature years she seldom played without including one of Coleridge-Taylor's works.

In Washington were born Portia Pittman's three children, William Sidney, Jr., Booker T., and Fannie Virginia. Her husband found the opportunities for a black architect too limited, however, in a time and place where most of the housing was built and owned by whites. He won the competition for the design of the Negro Building at the Jamestown Exposition in 1907 and he secured contracts for occasional black churches, schools, and lodge halls, but this was not enough to support his growing family. In 1913 the Pittmans moved to Dallas, Tex., where Portia had a piano recital at an A.M.E. church on Apr. 25, 1913. For fifteen years she taught music at Booker T. Washington High School in Dallas.

Portia Pittman returned to Tuskegee in 1928 to teach music, at the request of Principal Robert R. Moton. She directed the Tuskegee Institute choir, taught piano, and devoted much attention to the spirituals and other black folk music her father had sought to preserve and promote. She organized her own music school in Greenwood, a housing development adjacent to the institute. Retiring in 1955, she lived in Washington, D.C., with her eldest son Sidney, a graduate of Howard University and for many years a post office employee. After his death in 1967, she lived for two years in Kansas City with her daughter Fannie and her husband, Alphonso Marcelle Kennedy, a physician. After her son-in-law's death in 1969, she and her daughter returned to Washington. Her second son, Booker, became an accomplished jazz clarinetist, playing in the 1920s and 1930s in America and Europe with such leading jazz musicians as Louis Armstrong and Count Basie. He moved permanently to Brazil in 1937 and continued his musical career there until his death in 1969.

To James Fowle Baldwin Marshall

Tuskegee, Ala., Aug. 7, 1883

Dear General: I am very sorry to hear of Mr. Parrott's non success. I think your suggestion good, but it is impossible for us to carry it out this summer. Logan[1] is engaged for the summer and we will be compelled to have him here Sept 1st.

I thought of Logan before Mr. P. went but I was under the impression that [I] heard either you or Mr. Banks[2] say that he was inclined to be careless with accts.

Miss Davidson suggests the idea of letting Mr. Parrott and Logan *together* take the books for next term — making each responsible for certain work. I think that will be an improvement but not what we want. I shall not rest till our books are in the hands of a responsible person — and I shall be glad of any suggestion from you looking towards that end. Yours faithfully

B. T. Washington

ALS BTW Folder President's Office Vault ViHaI.

¹ Warren Logan.
² Frank D. Banks.

To James Fowle Baldwin Marshall

Tuskegee, Ala., Sept 26 1883

Dear Gen'l: Yours containing money for freight is received and I enclose receipt for same.

I am quite busy now making out a report of our receipts and disbursements since the organization of the school. We hope to have it out within a few days now.

School opened on the 4 with the largest number we ever had at the beginning. They are still coming in very fast.

Our boarding department is on foot and going nicely. In getting it started we have been compelled to make a furniture debt which we are going to try to pay off next month or the month after.

We received some weeks ago a letter from Miss May[1] telling us about the press and asking for shipping directions. Her letter was answered, but we have not heard from the press since. We are under many obligations to both you and her for the kindness.

I think we have the most satisfactory set of teachers we have ever had. In the Normal School there are Miss D. Mr. Parrott, Mr. Maddox, Mr Logan, Miss Rosa Mason,[2] (teacher & matron) and myself. In Training School, Miss Adella Hunt (Atlanta University) and Adie J. Wallace.[3]

Portia and her mother are well and send love. Sincerely yours

B. T. Washington

ALS BTW Folder President's Office Vault ViHaI.

¹ Abigail (Abby) Williams May.

² Rosa Mason, who in her early years was called Rosetta, was born in Norfolk, Va., in 1861, and graduated from Hampton Institute in 1880. She taught in Virginia schools for two years before coming to Tuskegee in 1883, where she served

at various times as matron, housekeeper, head of the night school, and, from 1888 to 1890, acting lady principal. She resigned from the Tuskegee faculty in 1890, returning to teach in Virginia, but taught again at Tuskegee from 1897 to 1899.

[3] Addie J. Wallace was born in Milledgeville, Ga., in 1862 and graduated from Hampton in 1882. She taught at Tuskegee for the three years 1883-86. She resigned to marry William C. Brown, settling in Macon, Ga.

To [Samuel Chapman Armstrong]

Tuskegee, Ala., Oct 11, 1883

Dear Gen'l: Yours of the 8 inst in regard to the series of meetings North[1] is rec'd.

We are heartily thankful for the opportunity and I shall be ready to comply with the request.

The arrangement for Dec. 4 will suit me.

Shall go to Montgomery tomorrow night to see Mr. Armstrong.[2] Shall do my best to get him to attend. Will write again after I have seen him.

The Alabama legislature does not assemble this year.

Our boarding dept is going nicely. School has never been so full as now. We have in all 8 teachers this year. All send love. Sincerely & gratefully yours

B. T. Washington

ALS BTW Folder President's Office Vault ViHaI. Armstrong is established as the correspondent by BTW's promise to write again on his return from Montgomery, which he did three days later. (See BTW to Armstrong, Oct. 14, 1883.)

[1] Armstrong arranged to take BTW and a quartet of Hampton singers on a tour of important northern cities to raise funds for Tuskegee Institute.

[2] Henry Clay Armstrong.

To Samuel Chapman Armstrong

Tuskegee, Ala., Oct. 14 1883

Dear Gen'l: I have just returned from seeing Colonel H. C. Armstrong. He says that he will go, though he may have to ask that the dates of the meetings be changed to a week earlier or a week later.

When I saw him he had not received your letter and said that he would let you know definitely about the date aftering receiving your letter. He seemed much pleased with the idea. I am sure that he will make a fine impression. He is a man of fine physique and an excellent speaker.

By all means I wish that you would arrange it so that he can visit Hampton. That within itself will make him 25 per cent a more valuable man.

Dr. Haygood has given us a wind-mill. All are well. School is very full. Faithfully yours

B. T. Washington

ALS   BTW Folder   President's Office Vault   ViHaI.

To the Editor of the *Southern Workman*

Tuskegee, Ala. October 18, 1883

Editor Southern Workman: Our third session began September 1st. The attendance is larger than ever. The students represent a much larger area of the State, and are of a much better quality than at any time since the organization of the School.

For the first time, the students now board on the School grounds. The girls are reasonably well cared for in Porter Hall; the boys are in temporary quarters. To start a Boarding Department, with almost no money, has been indeed "making bricks without straw"; and, had not some of us been at Hampton in its childhood, and experienced eating with no table-cloth, drinking corn coffee from yellow bowls, seeing wheat bread but once a week, and sleeping in tents, we doubt if our faith would have brought us through thus far. Our students are manly, and endure privations and inconveniences in a good spirit. The girls have made the sheets and the bed-ticks, and the boys some of the furniture. We hope that most of the days that "try men's souls," and women's, too, are over; yet we do have much anxiety about the boys standing the winter in their present poor quarters with the few blankets we are able to give them. However, the advantage of having the students together counteracts, in a great measure, the disadvantages under which we labor.

The spirit of labor is growing, and there is not a student on the place who does not work out some part of his expenses. A few work out all, and others as much as half of their expenses. The girls do the washing, ironing and mending for the boys.

The increased appropriation from the State has enabled us to increase our teaching force. The following compose the Faculty, and it is the most satisfactory we have had:

B. T. Washington, Principal and teacher; Hampton Institute.

Miss O. A. Davidson, Assistant Principal and teacher; Hampton Institute and Framingham.

Mr. R. S. Parrott, Music teacher; Washington High School.

M. J. Maddox, teacher; Worcester Academy.

Warren Logan, teacher; Hampton Inst.

Miss Rosa Mason, Matron and teacher; Hampton Institute.

Miss Adella Hunt, teacher of Normal Classes and Principal of Model School; Atlanta, Ga.

Miss Addie Wallace, teacher in Model School; Hampton Institute.

Mr. H. Clay Ferguson, Farm Manager; Hampton Institute.

Mrs. Fanny N. Washington, Housekeeper; Hampton Institute.

The farm has been held back somewhat by the drouth and other causes. Now that we have been able to add a farm manager, this industry will be made still more valuable.

Through Dr. A. G. Haygood, Gen. Agent of the "John F. Slater Fund," we have a wind-mill which will supply all the buildings with water.

We are indebted to the thoughtfulness of General Marshall, and the kind interest of Miss Abby W. May of Boston, for a printing press and outfit which is now on its way. Several of the boys are anxiously awaiting its arrival in order to try their hands at printing.

We have burned one kiln of bricks, and another will be ready to burn next week. The students do all the work at the yard except what is done by two outside hands.

We need very much the necessary tools to begin a carpenter's shop. Much money is paid to outsiders for carpentering that should go to the students. Several of the students are anxious to learn the trade. Our plan is to produce on the place, as nearly as possible, everything consumed.

We have now in press a Report showing the receipts and disbursements of the School since its organization July 4, 1881, to September

30th. Hereafter, this Report will appear annually. By this Report it will be seen that the receipts from all sources, for the two sessions, have been $11,659.69. The greater part of this amount was given for the erection of Porter Hall which, we are glad to say to our friends, is completed without a debt.

Our great and pressing need is another large and substantial building. The quarters occupied by the boys are crowded, and the young men are so exposed to the weather that it is impossible for them to keep comfortable enough to study to advantage; besides, the students need to be taught as much as other things, habits of order, cleanliness, and neatness; and this it is hard to do the way they are now situated. The young men say that they will make the bricks, and what they want is the money with which to put the building up. The faithfulness with which they now work in the yard testifies that they will keep their promise. A building such as we need will cost $10,000. A part of this amount has been secured.

Miss Davidson is going to spend November in Boston and vicinity, soliciting donations for the building, and if our friends aid us in the future, as they have in the past, we feel sure that we shall not be long in proving that their gifts have been well bestowed.

B. T. Washington

Southern Workman, 12 (Nov. 1883), 115.

To James Fowle Baldwin Marshall

Tuskegee, Ala., Nov. 4 1883

Dear Gen'l: I thank you for your letter in regard to organizing a Band of Mercy. I have recd a letter and badges from Mr. Angell.[1] Shall try to look after the matter soon. A large band was organized a few days ago in Montgomery.

I have just performed the sad[d]est duty that has come upon me since my connection with the school. I have just asked Mr. Parrott to give up his position. Letters came into my possession showing that a vulgar correspondence was going on between him and one of the students (a married woman) and that an opportunity was only wanting for them to have criminal intercourse. It was a shock to all of us, but

I felt that for the sake of the example and the purity of the school it was best to get rid of them both. (Later) Both have now gone. It is unfortunate, but I feel that it can but little retard the progress of the work which under God we mean to accomplish. I scarcely know where to look for a music teacher. We need some one like Hamilton.[2] In the class room Mr. Parrott was a success and the students will lose.

I am glad to hear that Miss Davidson is making such a good start.

We have received $100. from Slater Fund to help purchase a windmill. At my request Mr. Bedford[3] of Montgomery goes Tuesday to see Dr. Haygood in the interest of the school. I wrote the Gen'l some days ago telling him that since Mr. H. C. Armstrong promised me that he would speak at the meetings, I have received a card from him stating that it will be impossible for him to leave the state during Dec. I have not heard from the Genl since I wrote. I am very anxious to know what to do. Mr. Foster[4] thinks that Congressman Herbert[5] from Montgomery will go, and that he will produce about as good an eff[e]ct as Mr. Armstrong. Not hearing from the Genl I do not know whether to see Col. Herbert or not. I have written Mr. Bedford to learn Mr. Armstrong's final decision, but Mr. Bedford says that Mr. A. has not been in Montgomery for a week. Please write any information.

We all feel much anxiety about Mrs. Marshall and Miss Kimball[6] and hope that they may soon be well. Sincerely yours

B. T. Washington

ALS   BTW Folder   President's Office Vault   ViHaI.

[1] George T. Angell, president of the Massachusetts Society for the Prevention of Cruelty to Animals, established Bands of Mercy in the South. In 1883 a Band of Mercy was formed at Hampton Institute, and the parent society supplied star badges inscribed with the pledge of the society to all the members.

[2] Robert H. Hamilton.

[3] Robert Charles Bedford.

[4] Wilbur F. Foster.

[5] Hilary Abner Herbert (1834-1919), a former Confederate colonel and a Democrat, represented Alabama in Congress for eight terms following Reconstruction (1877-93) before serving as Secretary of the Navy under Grover Cleveland (1893-97). A spokesman for southern conservatives, he edited a collection of essays supporting sectional recalcitrance (*Why the Solid South* [1890]). In 1900 he addressed the Montgomery Race Conference in favor of disfranchisement of Negroes and of poor and uneducated whites.

[6] Emily Kimball, Mrs. Marshall's niece, was born in Massachusetts. Her age was recorded as twenty-seven in the census of 1880. She taught at Hampton Institute from 1877 to 1880. She died in Boston in 1885.

From Atticus Greene Haygood

Oxford, Ga. Nov. 7. 1883

Mr. B. T. Washington   I will appropriate one thousand Dollars to your school — to be used in equipping your industrial departments & in paying the salary of your farm Superintendent — not more than Fifteen Dollars per month being used for the Superintendent.

A. G. Haygood

Send voucher when signed to Mr. M. K. Jesup.[1] 52 Williams St. New York.

ALS   Con. 88   BTW Papers   DLC.

[1] Morris Ketchum Jesup (1830-1908), treasurer of the John F. Slater Fund. A self-made New York businessman, Jesup began work at a locomotive factory at the age of twelve. He became a supplier of railroad equipment and an investment banker. After retiring from business in 1884 he continued to give his energy and talent to philanthropic work. As a trustee of the Slater and Peabody funds and the General Education Board, the three leading foundations involved in Negro and southern education, Jesup exerted a powerful influence for industrial education, for which he had an almost religious devotion. He substantially aided Hampton and Tuskegee and enhanced their influence as models for other schools aided by the philanthropic boards. A gift to Tuskegee made it possible for the school to operate the "Jesup Wagon," a mule-drawn agricultural classroom on wheels which carried the message of scientific agriculture to black farmers of Macon County.

From Atticus Greene Haygood

Oxford, Ga. Nov. 7, 1883

Dear Sir: I suggest & desire that the $1,000 be used approximately as follows:

1. Tools	$ 200.00.
2. Horse, wagon, harness etc	225.00.
3. Finishing wind mill	150.00.
4. Carpenters Shop (pay)	200.00.

5. Girls' Industrial Department	90.00.
6. Farm Superintendent	135.00.
Total —	$1000.00.

Yrs

A. G. Haygood
Gen'l Agent[1]

ALS   Con. 88   BTW Papers   DLC.

[1] General agent of the John F. Slater Fund.

To James Fowle Baldwin Marshall

Tuskegee, Ala., Nov. 9 1883

Dear Genl: I sent you a telegram to day informing you that $1000.00 has been donated to us from the Slater Fund. We are all feeling quite jubilant over it.

At my request Mr. Bedford went to see Dr. Haygood Wed. for us. Mr. Bedford says that he found him very much interested in us and that he made the appropriation with almost no solicitation. He says that the Dr. spent most of the day with him making and suggesting plans for the use of the money. That you may see what he says I enclose two of his notes to me.[1]

He sends us word to get two good horses and a wagon at once. $250.00 has been paid and the remainder is to be paid quarterly — quarterly payments being the rule of the board. He was so anxious that we should secure the whole am't at once in order to improve the farm &c. that he wrote a note to Mr. Campbell which he said would be to me good collateral.[2] So I think we shall secure the whole am't in cash within a few days.

The Dr. expects to visit us within a few weeks.

These letters I hope you will return when you have read them.

All are well and send love.

We hope that Mrs. Marshall is much better now. Faithfully yours

B. T. Washington

ALS   BTW Folder   President's Office Vault   ViHaI.

[1] Atticus Greene Haygood's two letters to BTW, Nov. 7, 1883.

[2] Atticus Greene Haygood to George Washington Campbell, Nov. 7, 1883, Con. 88, BTW Papers, DLC.

To James Fowle Baldwin Marshall

Tuskegee, Ala., Dec. 27, 1883

Dear Genl: Yours informing us of the kindness of Mr. Corliss[1] is rec'd.

We owe you $50. on the loan of $200, $30. for cash advanced for my traveling expenses while North, and something for my board at Porter's Mansion while in N.Y. Mr. Hamilton[2] will probably know the am't of it if the bill has not been sent in. We want you to take out the interest due on the loan @6%. The loan was made April 9/83.

May 10/83 paid $100.
Nov. 12 " 50.

It was my intention to have remained North till all the money for the building was collected but Miss Davidson grew so feeble that I thought best to return. She is now taking complete rest for a while and I think she will soon be strong. We are going to still try to keep the building before the people in all the ways possible till we get the money. I think that we did reasonably well North. It was a noble act in Gen A.[3] All send love. Yours

B. T. Washington

ALS BTW Folder   President's Office Vault   ViHaI.

[1] A memorandum by James Fowle Baldwin Marshall, Jan. 2, 1884, indicates that George Henry Corliss donated $200 to Tuskegee Institute. (BTW Folder, President's Office Vault, ViHaI.)

[2] Robert H. Hamilton.

[3] Armstrong's invitation to tour the North with him and the Hampton Singers. (See BTW to Samuel Chapman Armstrong, Oct. 11, 1883.)

To [Samuel Chapman Armstrong]

Tuskegee, Ala., Feb. 4 1884

Dear General: Miss Davidson has not been able to do any work since my return and she is now in Montgomery taking complete rest for a few weeks. Her condition has prevented my carrying out exactly the plan that we spoke of when I saw you. She is now getting better and hopes to take hold by the 20 inst.

I now plan to spend the whole of March North if possible, and attend the meeting in Washington on the 18 of March. On my return April first Miss Davidson will probably go North if able and spend April & May. In addition I expect to make a summer campaign among the smaller towns. What do you think of the plan? Should like your advice as to the best way and place of spending my time during March.

The meetings are still bearing fruit. We shall be glad to see Miss Mackie.[1]

Things are going well. Please have speech sent at once. Yours

B. T. Washington

ALS BTW Folder President's Office Vault ViHaI. Presumably one of the sequence of letters to Armstrong discussing arrangements for fund raising in the North. (See BTW to Armstrong, Oct. 11, 14, 1883, Feb. 18, Apr. 29, 1884.)

[1] Mary F. Mackie visited Tuskegee in the spring of 1884 and wrote back that the school reminded her of Hampton twelve years earlier: "The teachers here laugh themselves over their exact imitation of the *alma mater.* . . ." In some respects, however, she thought Tuskegee had "improved upon us." She was particularly struck by the plantation melodies which BTW called for after evening prayers: "Their rendering makes ours seem artificial; there is more of the real wail in their music than I ever heard." (*Southern Workman,* 13 [Apr. 1884], 43.)

To the Editor of the *Southern Workman*

Tuskegee, Ala., Feb. 15th, 1884

Dear *Workman:* No less than ten hands went up in the chapel a few nights ago, in answer to the inquiry among the young men as to how many had been frost-bitten during the cold weather. At this showing, the teachers were not surprised, for on more than one night when some teacher was making a tour of the rooms at a late hour, to give a comforting word when there were no more blankets to give, have the young men been found hovering around the fire while the cold wind poured in from the roof, sides and floor of the room. Sitting up with overcoats around them was preferable to going to bed. While there has been this suffering, yes, I say *suffering,* so anxious have the students been to remain in school, that there has been almost not a murmur of complaint, but on the other hand they have shown cheerfulness throughout.

The school does not own the shanties in which the young men stay, consequently, in our present condition, we can't lay out money to repair another's property when we are only using it temporarily. The severe winter finds us wholly unprepared. The worst having, we trust, passed, the young men will be content with their condition for the remainder of the winter. But must they be asked to endure the same thing another winter? We have faith to believe not. They want nothing done for them which they can do for themselves. The new building which has now been begun will cost $10,000.00, and over $5,000 of this amount has been raised. The young men are now digging out the basement for the building, and preparing the clay for bricks in order to begin moulding brick for the building as soon as the weather will permit. In order that the students' work may be utilized to the highest extent, we need a horse-power brick machine very much; the regular price of a good one is $300, but the manufacturers agree to let us have one for $200. I write this believing that God will put it into the heart of some kind friend or friends to give the needed amount for the machine, in order that the students may have a chance to help themselves.

B. T. Washington

Southern Workman, 13 (Mar. 1884), 29.

To Samuel Chapman Armstrong

Tuskegee, Ala., Feb. 18 1884

Dear General: Mr. M. Pierce has very kindly decided to add about 440 acres more of land to our farm. This will be a great help.

I write to know if it is possible for you to do any thing that will help us towards getting a good strong printing press. The one we have is only fit for small job work. We want to begin publishing a small paper about 2/3 of the size of the "Alumni Journal."[1] Such a paper *well* gotten up as to workmanship and matter, can be made to arouse the people — both white and black, on matters of education and industry. There is no such paper in the State. The people must be waked up. Thro the paper our friends North would be constantly informed of what we are doing.

Damon & Peets[2] of N.Y. offer us a very good press that will answer the purpose for $150., but we have no money for any such purpose. Can you suggest anything?

Have broken ground for the building and expect to begin work soon. A carpenters' shop is going up. Faithfully yours,

B. T. Washington

ALS   BTW Folder   President's Office Vault   ViHaI.

[1] Presumably the journal of this name published by the Alumni Association of Hampton Institute.

[2] George Damon and Elias S. Peets, manufacturers of printers' materials.

To Fanny Norton Smith Washington

604 Pine St   Philadelphia   Mar. 22 1884

Dear F. I send you a telegram today so you may know where to write. Write me at once. I shall probably stay here till April 1, when I shall come home. Had a fine a[nd] *very* large meeting here last night. Love to all. Kiss Portia for me. Yours

B.

ACI   Con. 86   BTW Papers   DLC.

To the Editor of the Tuskegee *Macon Mail*

[Tuskegee, Ala., Apr. 16, 1884]

Editor Mail: I take this method of expressing the thanks of the Tuskegee State Normal School to the Magnolia Hook and Ladder Fire Company, colored, of Tuskegee, for their very generous donation of $25 towards the proposed new building. The race will grow in proportion as we learn to help ourselves in matters of education.

B. T. Washington

Tuskegee *Macon Mail,* Apr. 16, 1884, 3.

To Samuel Chapman Armstrong

Tuskegee, Ala., April 29 1884

Dear General: Matters are going reasonably well with us. The foundation for the new building has been dug out and the lumber has been contracted for and is being put on the ground. The carpenter is getting out the window casings and we are making brick by machine at the rate of about 6000 per day. As soon as we get a kiln burned the brick work on the building will begin.

The sickness of my wife caused me to have to leave Philadelphia when in the midst of success.

My point in writing this letter is to get your advice about holding a series of concerts during the summer at different watering places, in the North. Say let Mr. Hamilton lead a quartet or quintet of singers. To make it pay, the ground would have to be well mapped out.

I have spoken with Mr. Hamilton more fully on the subject and he has my ideas.

With the work once started on the building we don't want it to stop and I fear a crisis during the summer if something is not done. Faithfully yours

B. T. Washington

ALS   BTW Folder   President's Office Vault   ViHaI.

The Inscription on the Tombstone of Fanny Norton Smith Washington[1]

[Tuskegee, Ala., May 4, 1884]

Fanny Norton Washington
d. May 4, 1884   Aged 26 years
Our Lord is risen
from the dead
Our Jesus is gone
up on high.

Tombstone in Tuskegee Institute Cemetery, Tuskegee, Ala.

[1] Fanny Washington's death, like her life, was obscure. She was said to have fallen from a farm wagon and suffered injuries, but other accounts attributed her death to "consumption of the bowels." Writing of her in the early 1890s, BTW concluded: "Perhaps the way in which Fanny was able to impress her life upon others most was in her extreme neatness in her housekeeping and general work. Nothing was done loosely or carelessly. In this respect, she taught our students many valuable lessons. Her heart was set on making her home an object lesson for those about her, who were so much in need of such help." (*Twenty-two Years Work,* 177.)

A Report of the Triennial Meeting of the Hampton Institute Alumni Association

[Hampton, Va., May 23, 1884]

The third triennial meeting of the Alumni Association of Hampton Institute, organized in 1878, was held this year, and made a very pleasant addition to the Anniversary exercises. Ninety-seven were present: fifty-four alumni and forty-three alumnae; representing ten States, seventy-nine from Virginia, the rest from N.C., D.C., Penn., Mass., N.Y., Ala., Md., S.C., and Tenn.; and eleven of the 13 classes which, besides the present one, have been graduated from the Institution. All arrived in time to attend the anniversary exercises, in which five of their number had part as speakers. They lunched together in Virginia Hall as guests of the school, and were received in the evening by the Principal, meeting also their friends among the officers and teachers, but saddened by the fact, which some learned for the first time, that it would be their last greeting in his official capacity from the friend who had given his Godspeed to every class, the honored Treasurer of the school, Gen. J. F. B. Marshall.

The morning of the 23d was occupied by the business meeting of the Association. In the afternoon, a public meeting was held in Whitin chapel, Virginia Hall, and largely attended by the officers and teachers, the class just graduated, and others. The President of the Association, Mr. B. T. Washington, made a feeling and eloquent speech. "What does this coming together every three years of Hampton's sons and daughters mean? That we love our mother; that we want to bear our share of her burdens, drink fresh of her spirit, keep pace with her progress, keep up our friendship with each other, and accomplish better and better work. From whatever distant post we come, from success or disappointment, joy or sorrow — to some the sound of marriage bells, to some the funeral knell since we last met — we know that the arms of our Alma Mater are ever ready to give cheer and comfort to us; as when we first came to her, some with no capital but stout hearts and brawny muscles and untutored brains, she gave us a chance. As we see how building after building has gone up here, what does it all mean? That Hampton's work has just begun. I know I express the feeling of every graduate when I say to our Principal — in the arduous work of battling with ignorance, you have our honor and our love.

"And I cannot close without saying to him whom, as we learn with sorrow, we meet here for the last time as our honored Treasurer; if in your retirement it will be in any degree a comfort and satisfaction, remember that you have a place down deep in the hearts of every graduate of Hampton.

"And now I know every one of us will leave here to go to our places of work, determined to work harder to carry out the Hampton idea, which is education of hand, head and heart."

The orator of the day, Mr. B. T. McNeil,[1] class of '80, repeated the expression of the feeling that binds all Hampton graduates together as children of one family, and the sympathy for those bereaved by the angel of death; and welcomed the new recruits.

"Class of '84, we welcome you into our lines — to win your spurs. It is our purpose to join forces against the enemies, immorality, prejudice, ignorance and oppression, and fight till the warfare is ended. It is our purpose to avoid writing Strut and Pretension over our doors; we recognize the fact that respectability and common sense better become our sign-boards. Sympathizing friends cannot lift us by force to our feet and match us against more powerful foes; we must gain our own footing by those powerful levers, intelligence and wealth, or we shall fall back to the mortification of our friends who have given, and are giving, us the best possible aid. They have shoved us the *cane*, Education, and by its help we are fast getting the *crutch*, Wealth, and with their united aid and our own energy we propose to rise to fall no more. Wealth and intelligence are better guarantees to Civil Rights than any legislation state or national; and, since Civil Rights are to be thus obtained, in the course of time they will be ours. The hatchet of race discord must be buried, and it is our purpose, with the spade of intelligence and moral and social advancement, to bury it so deep and securely, that it shall never be disinterred. The sons and daughters of Hampton, with few exceptions, are exponents of the fact that we are rising. Yes, we are rising, and as fast as we rise in the social, moral, and intellectual scale, just so fast rises the sun whose rays are laden with healing and hope, and soon will be seen coming arkward over the fast subsiding waters of prejudice and ignorance, the dove bearing the olive-branch of peace, prosperity and happiness."

Rev. T. M. Stewart,[2] professor of history and belles lettres in the College of Liberia, visiting the school to study its industrial system for the benefit of that college, delivered, by invitation, an address before the Alumni. Its subject was The Condition, the Measure of Success. It was full of good sense and eloquence, and we would regret that we have room for but two or three of its striking passages, were it not that it will be published by the Association in pamphlet form, and can be obtained on application to Mr. Wm. M. Reid, editor of *Alumni Journal,* Hampton Institute.

Mr. Stewart held that it is not color that embarrasses the race, but condition. Other races have been enslaved and oppressed: the Helots in Sparta, the serfs in Russia, the Britons in Rome, the Chinese here, the Irish, the Jews in England, till the wealth of Rothschild and the intellect of Disraeli threw around the latter the marks of respectability.

That is the secret; "to receive recognition, we must represent something. Get something that men want, and you break down all barriers. When our representatives stand as members in the stock and produce exchanges, the clouds of prejudice will flee away. In the effort to change our condition, we should first of all strive for good and upright character, and recognize with all our heart, mind and strength the dignity of labor. Some of our young people complain, 'We are crowded out — are pushed and jostled.' True, the white race push; and they succeed because they push. They push under mountains with their wonderful tunnels, and span rivers with their marvelous bridges; they make hills to fall and valleys to rise. They see the lightning flash along the vaulted sky, and they catch it and make it speak their words and do their bidding. They see the steam in the tea-kettle, and they bid it go and it goeth, come and it cometh; all this they do and more, because they push. They seem to be inspired with the sentiment of the un-lettered farmer who turned his pigs into a field of frozen turnips, with the remark, 'Root hogs, or die.' They seem to echo and re-echo the strong declaration of Napoleon Bonaparte, '*Impossible,* is the language of fools.' Let us catch this spirit of *push*."

The speaker closed with an earnest appeal for Africa.

The Principal and Treasurer were called on for speeches, but preferred not to divert the thoughts of the audience from the good words already spoken, by more than a brief tribute to the interest of the occasion. An unexpected addition to its interest was then made by the presentation of a beautiful ebony gold-headed cane from graduates to General Marshall, with a few graceful words from the president of the Alumni, Mr. B. T. Washington: "General Marshall, that the graduates of this Institution love you, you are perfectly aware; that we shall never forget you, we need not say, but we wish to do our part as graduates, to express the esteem in which you are held, and our recognition of your long and valuable services to our Alma Mater, and your kindness to all her sons and daughters, by presenting you with this token, hoping that it may be, with our love, some support in your future years." On the head of the cane was the inscription:

> Presented to Gen. J. F. B. Marshall by the Alumni of the Hampton Normal and Agricultural Institute, as a token of their appreciation of his valuable services as Treasurer of said Institute, May 23, 1884.

The Treasurer, taken quite by surprise, found few words most expressive: "That I appreciate this gift, you know, and if before receiving it I was unable to express adequately my feelings on this occasion, you must know that words fail me now. I can but thank you, and assure you that I shall cherish your beautiful gift and the feelings which prompted it, and always in the future, as in the past, feel constant and affectionate interest in Hampton and its graduates."

The pleasant re-union was agreeably closed that evening by the Alumni dinner, at which the Association and their invited guests, their old friends among the officers and teachers, and some others sat down to one long table, stretching the length of the large dining-room in Virginia Hall, and spread with a bountiful feast, ending in the orthodox way, with appropriate sentiments and speeches.

The next day they began to scatter again to their various fields of labor, carrying with them Hampton's Godspeed. We hope it may always be true, as their president, Mr. Washington says, that Hampton graduates are distinguished for their love for each other and their Alma

Mater. The results of her work make its inspiration and cheer; her sons and daughters growing in true manliness and womanliness, fulfilling the trust here committed to their hands, are her "glory and crown of rejoicing."

Southern Workman, 13 (June 1884), 75.

[1] No person named B. T. McNeil was reported in the class of 1880. The only McNeil who graduated from Hampton between 1871 and 1890 was Alexander H. McNeil, class of 1877, born in Oakley, N.C., in 1858, a teacher in Maryland and Virginia after his graduation.

[2] Thomas McCants Stewart in 1884 was teaching history and literature at Liberia College in Africa. Born in 1852 of free parents in Charleston, S.C., Stewart attended Howard University and the University of South Carolina, where he received both a B.A. and a law degree in 1875. He then attended Princeton Theological Seminary and was ordained after two years there. In 1879 he became pastor of the Bethel A.M.E. Church in New York City, remaining there until attracted to Liberia in 1883. Returning after two years, he established himself as a lawyer and leading black Democrat in New York City. He actively supported Grover Cleveland in the elections of 1888 and 1892 and helped organize black Democratic political clubs. He was appointed to the Brooklyn Board of Education in 1891, a position he held until complaining Democrats dislodged him in 1895, causing him to switch angrily to the Republican party. A close friend of BTW, Stewart supported industrial education and racial business cooperation. After his return from Africa in 1885 he spoke mildly against colonization though supporting the idea of aid to and commercial relations with Africa, but he returned to Liberia in 1906, convinced that the struggle for equality of opportunity in the United States was hopeless. He was later named an associate justice of the Liberian Supreme Court. He published several books, including *Liberia — The Americo-African Republic* (1886) and *The Afro-American in Politics* (1891), as well as numerous articles for black newspapers and journals.

A Speech before the National Educational Association[1]

Madison, Wisconsin, July 16, 1884

THE EDUCATIONAL OUTLOOK IN THE SOUTH

Mr. President, Ladies and Gentlemen:

Fourteen years ago it is said that Northern teachers, in the South for the purpose of teaching in colored schools, were frightened away by the whites from the town of Tuskegee, Alabama. Four years ago the Democratic members of the Alabama legislature from Tuskegee voluntarily offered and had passed by the General Assembly a bill, appropriating $2,000 annually to pay the salaries of teachers in a colored normal school to be located at Tuskegee. At the end of the first session of the school the legislature almost unanimously passed a second bill appropriating an additional $1,000 annually, for the same purpose. About one month ago one of the white citizens of Tuskegee who had at first looked on the school in a cold, distant kind of a way said to me, "I have just been telling the white people that the Negroes are more interested in education than we, and are making more sacrifices to educate themselves." At the end of our first year's work, some of the whites said, "We are glad that the Normal School is here because it draws people and makes labor plentiful." At the close of the second year, several said that the Normal School was beneficial because it increased trade, and at the close of the last session more than one said that the Normal School is a good institution, it is making the colored people in this state better citizens. From the opening of the school to the present, the white citizens of Tuskegee have been among its warmest friends. They have not only given of their money but they are ever ready to suggest and devise plans to build up the institution. When the school was making an effort to start a brick yard, but was without means, one of the merchants[2] donated an outfit of tools. Every white minister in the town has visited the school and given encouraging remarks. When the school was raising money to build our present hall, it occurred to one of the teachers that it would be a good idea to call on the white ladies for contributions in the way of cakes, etc., toward a fair. The result was that almost every lady, called on, gave something and the fair was made up almost entirely of articles given by these friends. A former slaveholder working on a Negro normal school building under a Negro master carpenter is a picture that the last few years have made possible.

Any movement for the elevation of the Southern Negro, in order to be successful, must have to a certain extent the cooperation of the Southern whites. They control government and own the property — whatever benefits the black man benefits the white man. The proper education of all the whites will benefit the Negro as much as the education of the Negro will benefit the whites. The Governor of Alabama would probably count it no disgrace to ride in the same railroad coach with a colored man, but the ignorant white man who curries the Governor's horse would turn up his nose in disgust. The president of a white college in Tuskegee[3] makes a special effort to furnish our young men work that they may be able to remain in school, while the miserable unlettered "brother in white" would say, "You can't learn a nigger anything." Brains, property, and character for the Negro will settle the question of civil rights. The best course to pursue in regard to the civil rights bill in the South is to let it alone; let it alone and it will settle itself. Good school teachers and plenty of money to pay them will be more potent in settling the race question than many civil rights bills and investigating committees. A young colored physician[4] went into the city of Montgomery, Alabama, a few months ago to practise his profession — he was the first to professionally enter the ex-Confederate capital. When his white brother physicians found out by a six days' examination that he had brains enough to pass a better examination, as one of them said, than many of the whites had passed, they gave him a hearty welcome and offered their services to aid him in consultation or in any other way possible — and they are standing manfully up to their promise. Let there be in a community a Negro who by virtue of his superior knowledge of the chemistry of the soil, his acquaintance with the most improved tools and best breeds of stock, can raise fifty bushels of corn to the acre while his white neighbor only raises thirty; and the white man will come to the black man to learn. Further, they will sit down on the same train, in the same coach and on the same seat, to talk about it. Harmony will come in proportion as the black man gets something that the white man wants, whether it be of brains or of material. Some of the county whites looked at first with disfavor on the establishing of a normal school in Tuskegee. It turned out that there was no brick yard in the county; merchants and farmers wanted to build, but bricks must be brought from a distance or they must wait for one house to burn down before building another. The Normal School with student labor started a brick yard. Several kilns of bricks were burned; the whites came from miles around for bricks. From examining bricks they were led to examine the workings of the school. From the discussion of the brick yard came the discussion of Negro education — and thus many of the "old masters" have been led to see and become interested in Negro education. In Tuskegee a Negro mechanic[5] manufactures the best tinware, the best harness, the best boots and shoes, and it is common to see his store crowded with white customers from all over the county. His word or note goes as far as that of the whitest man.

I repeat for emphasis that any work looking towards the permanent improvement of the Negro South must have for one of its aims the fitting of him to live friendly and peaceably with his white neighbors both socially and politically. In spite of all talks of exodus, the Negro's home is permanently in the South: for coming to the bread-and-meat side of the question, the white man needs the Negro, and the Negro needs the white man. His home being permanently in the South, it is our duty to help him prepare himself to live there an independent, educated citizen.

In order that there may be the broadest development of the colored man and that he may have an unbounded field in which to labor, the two races must be brought to have faith in each other. The teachings of the Negro in various ways for the last twenty years have been rather too much to array him against his white brother than to put the two races in cooperation with each other. Thus Massachusetts supports the Republican party, because the Republican party supports Massachusetts with a protective tariff, but the Negro supports the Republican party simply because Massachusetts does. When the colored man is educated up to the point of reasoning that Massachusetts and Alabama are a long way apart and the conditions of life are very different, and if free trade enables my white neighbor across the street to buy his plows at a cheaper rate it will enable me to do the same thing, then will he be consulted in governmental questions. More than once have I noticed that when the whites were in favor of prohibition the blacks, led even by sober upright ministers, voted against it simply because the whites were in favor of it, and for that reason the blacks said that they knew it was a "Democratic trick." If the whites vote to levy a tax to build a schoolhouse, it is a signal for the blacks to oppose the measure, simply because the whites favor it. I venture the assertion that the sooner the colored man South learns that one political party is not composed of all angels and the other of all devils, and that all his enemies do not live in his own town or neighborhood, and all his friends in some distant section of the country, the sooner will his educational advantages be enhanced many fold. But matters are gradually changing in this respect. The black man is beginning to find out that there are those even among the Southern whites who desire his elevation. The Negro's new faith in the white man is being reciprocated in proportion as the Negro is rightly educated. The white brother is beginning to learn by degrees that all Negroes are not liars and chicken thieves. A former owner of seventy-five or one hundred slaves and now a large planter and merchant said to me a few days ago, "I can see every day the change that is coming about. I have on one of my plantations a colored man who can read and write and he is the most valuable man on the farm. In the first place I can trust him to keep the time of the others or with anything else. If a new style of plow or cotton planter is taken on the place, he can understand its construction in half the time that any of the others can."

My faith is that reforms in the South are to come from within. Southern people have a good deal of human nature. They like to receive the praise of doing good deeds, and they don't like to obey orders that come from Washington telling them that they must lay aside at once customs that they have followed for centuries, and henceforth there must be but one railroad coach, one hotel, and one schoolhouse for ex-master and ex-slave. In proof of my first assertion, the railroads in Alabama required colored passengers to pay the same fare as the whites, and then compelled the colored to ride in the smoking car. A committee of leading colored people laid the injustice of the matter before the railroad commissioners of Alabama, who at once ordered that within thirty days every railroad in the State should provide equal but separate accommodations for both races. Every prominent newspaper in the State pronounced it a just decision. Alabama gives $9,000 annually towards the support of colored normal schools. The last legislature increased the annual appropriation for free schools by $100,000, making the total annual appropriation over $500,000, and nearly half of this amount goes to colored schools, and I have for the first time to hear of any distinction being made between the races by any state officer in the distribution of this fund. Why, my friends, more pippins are growing in the South than crab apples, more roses than thorns.

Now, in regard to what I have said about the relations of the two races, there should be no unmanly cowering or stooping to satisfy unreasonable whims of Southern white men, but it is charity and wisdom to keep in mind the two hundred years' schooling in prejudice against the Negro which the ex-slaveholders are called upon to conquer. A certain class of whites South object to the general education of the colored man on the ground that when he is educated he ceases to do manual labor, and there is no evading the fact that much aid is withheld from Negro education in the South by the states on these grounds. Just here the great mission of

INDUSTRIAL EDUCATION

coupled with the mental comes in. It "kills two birds with one stone," viz.: secures the cooperation of the whites, and does the best possible thing for the black man. An old colored man in a cotton field in the middle of July lifted his eyes toward heaven and said, "De cotton is so grassy, de work is so hard, and de sun am so hot, I believe this darkey am called to preach." This old man, no doubt, stated the true reason why not a few enter school. Educate the black man, mentally and industrially, and there will be no doubt of his prosperity; for a race who has lived at all, and paid, for the last twenty years, twenty-five and thirty per cent interest on the dollar advanced for food, with almost no education, can certainly take care of itself when educated mentally and industrially.

The Tuskegee Normal School, located in the black belt of Alabama, with an ignorant, degraded Negro population of twenty-five thousand within a radius of twenty miles, has a good chance to see the direct needs of the people; and to get a correct idea of their condition one must leave the towns and go far out into the country, miles from any railroad, where the majority of the people live. They need teachers with not only trained heads and hearts, but with trained hands. School-houses are needed in every township and county. The present wrecks of log cabins and brush arbors, where many of the schools are now taught, must be replaced by comfortable, decent houses. In many schoolhouses rails are used for seats, and often the fire is on the outside of the house, while teacher and scholars are on the inside. Add to this a teacher who can scarcely write his name, and who is as weak mentally as morally, and you then have but a faint idea of the educational condition of many parts of the South. It is the work of Tuskegee, not to send into these places teachers who will stand off and tell the people what to do, or what ought to be done, but to send those who can take hold and show the people *how* to do. The blacksmiths, carpenters, brickmasons, and tinners, who learned their trades in slavery, are dying out, and slavery having taught the colored boy that labor is a disgrace, few of their places are being filled. The Negro now has a monopoly of the trades in the South, but he can't hold it unless the young men are taught trades while in school. The large number of educated loafers to be seen around the streets of our large cities furnishes another reason in favor of industrial education. Then the proud fop with his beaver hat, kid gloves, and walking cane, who has done no little to injure the cause of education South, by industrial training, would be brought down to something practical and useful. The Tuskegee Normal School, with a farm of five hundred acres, carpenter's shop, printing office, blacksmith's shop, and brick yard for boys, and a sewing department, laundry, flower gardening, and practical housekeeping for girls, is trying to do its part towards furnishing industrial training. We ask help for nothing that we can do for ourselves; nothing is bought that the students can produce. The boys raise the vegetables, have done the painting, made the brick, the chairs, the tables, the desks; have built a stable, a carpenter's shop, and a blacksmith's shop. The girls do the entire housekeeping, including the mending, ironing, and washing of the boys' clothes; besides they make many garments to sell.

The majority of the students are poor and able to pay but little cash for board; consequently the school keeps three points before it: first, to give the student the best mental training; secondly, to furnish him with labor that will be valuable to the school, and that will enable the student to learn something from the labor *per se;* thirdly, to teach the dignity of labor. A *chance* to help himself is what we want to give to every student; this is the chance that was given me ten years ago when I entered the Hampton Institute with but fifty cents in my pocket, and it is my only ambition in life to do my part in giving it to every other poor but worthy young man and woman.

As to morals, the Negro is slowly but surely improving. In this he has had no standard by which to shape his character. The masses in too many cases have been judged by their so-called leaders, who are as a rule ignorant, immoral preachers or selfish politicians. The number of these preachers is legion. One church near Tuskegee has a total membership of two hundred, and nineteen of these are preachers.

Poverty and ignorance have affected the black man just as they affect the white man. They have made him untruthful, intemperate, selfish, caused him to steal, to be cheated, and made the outcast of society, and he has aspired to positions which he was not mentally and morally capable of filling. But the day is breaking, and education will bring the complete light. The scales of prejudice are beginning to drop from the eyes of the dominant classes South, and through their clearer and more intelligent vision they are beginning to see and recognize the mighty truth that wealth, happiness, and permanent prosperity will only come in proportion as the hand, head, and heart of both races are educated and Christianized.

E. Davidson Washington, ed., *Selected Speeches of Booker T. Washington* (Garden City, 1932), 1-11. The speech was also published in the *Journal of Proceedings and Addresses of the National Educational Association, Session of the Year 1884, at Madison, Wis.* (Boston, 1885), pt. 2, pp. 125-30. That version differed in wording and punctuation from the E. Davidson Washington text used here. It did not capitalize "Negro" as BTW made a point of doing, and omitted the salutation.

[1] At this gathering of more than 10,000 educators there were many Alabamians, even some from Tuskegee itself. An ugly racial situation almost developed after the president, Thomas W. Bicknell, made Negro and Indian education a prominent feature of the program and invited BTW and several other black speakers. Many black teachers came, and some were denied the rooms they had reserved in the headquarters hotel weeks earlier. When the N.E.A. threatened to sue the hotel, however, the Negroes secured their promised rooms. In the tense atmosphere that followed such a confrontation, the situation demanded the instinctive tact for which BTW later became famous. In the audience of some 4,000 who heard him, there were several from Tuskegee who expected him to criticize the white South and even their home town. The speech, however, contained not a word of abuse, and BTW even strained to find grounds for praising the South. A teacher at the Alabama Conference Female College in Tuskegee wrote back to her girls: "He spoke well. I have heard nothing better as to manner, matter and spirit. He represented things as they are at the South, and said some nice things of the Tuskegee citizens." (Interview of Thomas W. Bicknell, in Boston *Advertiser,* July 7, 1903, clipping, Con. 1036, BTW Papers, DLC; letter of M. A. O. in Tuskegee *Macon Mail,* July 23, 1884.)

[2] R. R. Varner.

[3] John Massey (1834-1911), born in Choctaw County, Ala., was president of the Alabama Conference Female College in Tuskegee (which later moved to Montgomery as Judson College) from 1876 to 1909. He graduated from the University of Alabama in 1862 and served as an officer in the Confederate Army until a wound forced his resignation in 1864. After briefly teaching military tactics at the University of Alabama, he was principal of a boys' school in Summerfield, Ala., from 1866 to 1874. Massey was a Democrat. He held important lay positions in the Methodist Episcopal Church, South, was a member of the Southern Education Association, the National Educational Association, and the Alabama Education Association, of which he was president in 1894-95. He and BTW cooperated closely to preserve good will between the schools, though the black school quickly eclipsed the girls' school. BTW persuaded some of the philanthropists who aided Tuskegee to make small gifts to Massey's college.

[4] Cornelius Nathaniel Dorsette.

[5] Lewis Adams.

Olivia A. Davidson to
Eleanor Jameson Williams Baker[1]

Spruce Cottage   Jackson, N.H. Sept. 6 [1884][2]

Dear Mrs. Baker, I wish I could express to you my deep sense of all your kindness to me. I almost feel that it is an imposition, this having such long helpful letters from you in addition to all the arrangements and inquiries you are making for me.

Your letter came yesterday, and I did not reply in this morning's mail because I wished to take a night to think of it, and then it was too late to send to the mail. This is my reply to your proposition. I am willing to do anything that promises to restore me to health. If it were not for the uncertainty about what is the real state of my health, I should perhaps hesitate about going again to a hospital, but since the opportunity offers to assure myself whether or not there is internal trouble, I think it would not be wisdom to fail to benefit by it. My friends at Framingham are anxious to have me come there, and if it were not that I do not know what is the matter with me, and the fear that I might be losing time in trying to get well by resting only, I think I would prefer going there to going any place else as one, at least, of my best earthly friends is there (the one with whom I have been this summer, and who has made me strong so often when I have grown discouraged). I was not surprised to learn that Mrs. Hemenway offers me a home at Readville for the present, as this is only in keeping with her great kindness throughout. When I was at the hospital she came in person to tell me that I need have no hesitancy in applying to her for whatever I needed. If I were very, very rich in money, I could not repay Mrs. Hemenway all I owe her, for whatever my life has been worth to me and to others in the past few years is due to her. Through her the whole tenor of my life has been changed. Thinking of all her kindness to me and all I owe to her I have been unwilling to burden her so soon with my helplessness. Three years was not long for one to work in a new field before completely breaking down was it? But since before I was well grown I have had a life, *always* full of work, and often full to overflowing of trouble and suffering, so that when I went into the work at Tuskegee, though fresh from school I was not fresh in bodily and mental strength.

It was a great surprise as well as pleasure to meet Gen. Armstrong. He was not mistaken. I am trying to get the best out of my stay here, and as far as possible, I refrain from thinking or worrying about things, feeling willing to fold my hands and wait, if only in the end I can be myself again and go back to work. It is pretty hard at times to keep still and be patient and I could not do it alone, but I feel that my Father is helping me, by surrounding me with as much that is beautiful and lovely — Jackson grows more lovely every day — I think I would never grow tired and sick if I could, when at work, drop all now and then and go out and look at my beautiful mountains — "lift up mine eyes to the hills whence cometh my strength." I must not write more. If Miss Jones has not gone please give her my best wishes for her success in her new work. With best wishes for yourself and a deep sense of all you have done and are doing for me, I am, Very truly yours

Olivia A. Davidson

ALS Con. 949 BTW Papers DLC.

¹ Eleanor Jameson Williams Baker (1806-91) was born in Boston. In 1840 she married Walter Baker of Dorchester, a manufacturer of chocolate and cocoa, who left her a considerable fortune on his death in 1852. All of their four children died in infancy. As a widow, Mrs. Baker devoted her considerable energies to a variety of charitable and intellectual pursuits, and established a salon for Boston intellectuals. During the Civil War her house was a center for making uniforms for the Massachusetts volunteer troops. She was also active in hospital work for the wounded soldiers, and made several tours of inspection of army hospitals. Among her efforts for the education of the blacks during Reconstruction and afterward was her provision of three annual scholarships at Hampton Institute after 1871. She also aided many individual blacks including Olivia A. Davidson, who named her first child Baker T. Washington (later changed to Booker T. Washington, Jr.).

² That the letter was written in 1884 is shown by references in BTW to Samuel Chapman Armstrong, Sept. 11, 1884.

To [Samuel Chapman Armstrong]

Tuskegee, Ala., Sept. 11 1884

Dear General: Your letter is rec'd. Our campaign will end on the 26th inst. as Hamilton says he can not be out longer than that now. He is willing to go on in the late fall, or winter. Receipts in towns will be slim till the people settle down for the winter, therefore under the circumstances I think it will pay us best to lay by for a while and make a vigorous campaign during the latter part of Nov. and the month of Dec. In that case I think of letting our boys go in school at Hampton till needed if you are willing. I am compelled to remain here for at least a month longer to get every thing going smoothly. Miss Davidson's not being able to return made it impossible for me to remain away at the opening.

I did want to begin the campaign again about Nov. 1st but it will probably be as well for me to go alone during some part of that month and depend on getting Hamilton to lead the singers when your campaign is over. We can do nothing in the singing line with out him as Mr. Logan and I both can not be away at the same time. Logan is the only one that I know who can lead the singers.

My having to leave the singers has, I think, been some what of a misfortune, though they have done reasonably well and have given the school a good advertisement, besides clearing some money.

We can't afford to lose any valuable time in pushing the subscriptions for the building. The work is going on nicely on the building and it is going to keep us stirring to not let it stop.

Shall be glad to follow any suggestions from you in regard to any matters I have mentioned.

Am very sorry about Miss Davidson. It is going to be hard to fill her place. Will write Miss Mackie.[1]

We have a large school and matters are going well, but teachers are too hard worked on acct of two being away.

Have just rec'd a letter from Woman's Home Mis. Soc.[2] agreeing to pay the Sal. of an additional teacher. This helps us much.

Please let me hear from you soon. Sincerely yours

B. T. Washington

ALS BTW Folder President's Office Vault ViHaI. Because James Fowle Baldwin Marshall left Hampton Institute at the end of the 1883-84 school year, and the letter is in the Hampton Institute files, the recipient is assumed to be Armstrong.

[1] Mary Fletcher Mackie.

[2] Woman's Home Missionary Association (Congregational), of which Nathalie Lord was secretary, had its headquarters in Boston.

To Samuel Chapman Armstrong

Tuskegee, Ala., Oct. 16 1884

Dear Gen'l: Your letter concerning singers is rec'd. You will see by the letter that you rec'd from me a few days after yours was written that I had come to the same conclusion. I was led to it by the reasons which you express. I have never been satisfied with the singing, and then while Mr. Hamilton means well, he lacks the power of control[l]ing men and centering their interest.

The building is going on nicely. Sincerely yours

B. T. Washington

ALS   BTW Folder   President's Office Vault   ViHaI.

To Samuel Chapman Armstrong

Tuskegee, Ala., Jan. 19 1885

Dear Gen'l: About the last of Feb. or first of March I think of going on a money trip to Phila, New York, an[d] Brooklyn. What do you think of it? You remember that I was in Phila last March directly after our meeting there in Horticultural Hall and collected a good amount. I think of calling on the same ones who gave last year and others. In Brooklyn am thinking of asking Mr. Porter[1] to help me and Dr. Robinson[2] in New York. I know very few persons in the two latter cities of whom I can ask aid.

The work on the building is still going on. The brick work of the 3rd story is now being done.

My object in making the trip at the time named is to avoid being so closly pushed for funds during the spring and summer months as we usually are. We have purchased and paid for most of the material for the building, but there will be a constant drain on our fund till the building is completed and I want to guard against any possibility of shortage.

What do you think of our getting a small saw mill? We spend a large amount every year for lumber. We would be at no expense for logs as we have them on our land. My brother John agrees to come and take charge of it. It seems to me that if we can get the machinery that the mill will prove a great saving. An outfit to answer the purpose will probably cost $1000. Have thought of writing to Mr. Corliss[3] about an engine.

Our quarters are running over with students. All well. Yours Sincerely

Booker T. Washington

ALS BTW Folder President's Office Vault ViHaI.

[1] Alfred Haynes Porter, an important early contributor to Tuskegee, was a Wall Street broker who lived in Brooklyn, N.Y.

[2] Probably Charles Seymour Robinson (1829-99), who was pastor of the Presbyterian Memorial Church in New York City from 1871 to 1887 and a director of Union Theological Seminary. A prolific writer, Robinson compiled numerous collections of hymns and spirituals as well as several volumes of his own sermons and biblical studies. He was also, with Lyman Abbott, an editor of *The Illustrated Christian Weekly,* published by the American Tract Society from 1871 to 1887.

[3] George Henry Corliss.

To the Editor of the *Southern Workman*

Tuskegee Alabama, February 10th, '85

Editor Southern Workman: I know that you will be glad to know what a practical friend Dr. C. N. Dorsett,[1] of Montgomery, is to the Tuskegee Normal School. Last Christmas he surprised the students with a large quantity of oysters for their Christmas dinner, and last week came another surprise from him in the shape of a large school bell, a long needed article. Dr. Dorsett deserves the wonderful success that he is having in Montgomery.

B. T. Washington

Southern Workman, 14 (Apr. 1885), 41.

[1] Cornelius Nathaniel Dorsette.

A Recommendation from Robert Curtis Ogden

Philadelphia, March 19th 1885

It is with much pleasure that I commend Mr. Booker T. Washington, Principal of the State Normal School at Tuskeegee Ala., to the confidence of any disposed to aid the Educational work for the colored people of the South. Mr. Washington possesses a sincere missionary spirit, his work has been prosecuted with singular energy modesty and discretion, the results attained fully justify all the aid thus far extended and give a proper basis for larger claims. The work of the Tuskeegee School is founded upon a manual labor system and aims to create character while it provides education. It has the unanimous endorsement of the Faculty and Board of Trustees at Hampton.

Robert C. Ogden
Hampton Trustee in Philadelphia

ALS   Con. 16   BTW Papers   DLC.

A Recommendation from Samuel Chapman Armstrong[1]

Hampton, Va., March 28 1885

This is to express my entire confidence in the bearer Mr. Booker T. Washington, Principal Tuskeegee Normal School Alabama.

I have known him since he came as a student here in 1872 and regard his career as a most remarkable one, having arisen to a leading position today among the best men of his race.

I commend him heartily to the kindness and confidence of all and regard his school as second to none among those for the colored people.

S. C. Armstrong

ALS   Con. 16   BTW Papers   DLC.

[1] Armstrong recommended BTW about once a year. On July 16, 1884, Armstrong called BTW "the leading colored man today in the state of Alabama." On Mar. 1, 1886, Armstrong wrote to the oil millionaire Charles Pratt that BTW was "a noble, able, level headed colored man. He has 'sanctified common sense'

in a rare degree & has a way [of] succeeding in what he undertakes. Not a bit of vanity or nonsense about him." On Nov. 12, 1886, Armstrong wrote that "implicit reliance can be placed in his statements and in his Christian character" and that "he is doing I believe the best work done by colored people in this country, and one worthy to be compared with any for that race." On Feb. 18, 1887, he said: "He has proved himself, and what he says may be depended on." On June 8, 1887, Armstrong said: "Tuskegee is the only colored institution in the South wholly under the management and control of colored people themselves, and I regard it as useful and valuable to the cause as any school devoted to the Negro race." On Apr. 16, 1889, he wrote: "I have known from the first Mr. Washington and his work and believe that there is no work being done for his people better or more worthy of help than his." (Con. 16, BTW Papers, DLC.)

To the Editor of the *Southern Workman*

[Tuskegee, Ala., March 1885]

Self-Help

At the suggestion of citizens in Montgomery, a meeting was held in that city in February last, in the interest of education. The special object of the meeting was to secure aid towards furnishing rooms in the new building, "Alabama Hall," at the Tuskegee Normal and Industrial School.

The meeting was very largely attended by the best citizens. Addresses were made by the State Superintendent of Education, Maj. Solomon Palmer,[1] Dr. Hecht,[2] the Jewish Rabbi, the leading colored ministers and the Principal of the Normal School. The speaking was interspersed with singing by the Tuskegee choir.

The State Superintendent was very enthusiastic in his praise of the work of the Tuskegee Institute and exhorted the colored people to aid it by practising economy and self denial, and he himself set the example by giving $2.50 which he said was one-tenth of what he had saved in the last year by abstaining from the use of tobacco.

The meeting was in every respect satisfactory and $65 in cash were voluntarily given by the audience to aid in furnishing the rooms. We think this creditable considering that this was the first meeting of the kind ever held in the city or probably in the State. The poorest seemed anxious to give something.

The people showed their interest in the cause of education by asking that another meeting of the same kind be held in Montgomery next year, when they promise to do more.

The meeting doubtless had its greatest value in teaching the people self-help.

B. T. Washington

Southern Workman, 14 (Apr. 1885), 39.

¹ Solomon Palmer (1839-96) was born in Blount County, Ala., graduated from the University of Alabama in 1861, and fought in the Civil War. He then taught school in Blount County for several years and entered the Alabama House of Representatives. He was admitted to the bar in 1870. Elected state superintendent of education in 1884, he held the position until 1890.

² Sigmund Hecht was born in Hungary in 1849 and educated at the University of Vienna. He was a rabbi at Montgomery, Ala., from 1876 to 1888. Later he served as rabbi in Milwaukee and Los Angeles.

To the Editor of the Montgomery *Advertiser*

Tuskegee, Ala., April 24, 1885

Editor *Advertiser:* Judging from some of your past utterances that you are in favor of justice being shown the colored man on railroads, I am encouraged to write the following for insertion in your paper.¹ Having to some extent noticed the position of many of the county papers relative to the subject, I am glad to know that they, too, are outspoken in condemnation of the wrong which colored railroad passengers are made to suffer. In fact, I have not conversed with a single intelligent, progressive white man who has not shown the right spirit in the matter.

I wish to say a few words from a purely business standpoint. It is not a subject with which to mix social equality or anything bordering on it. To the negro it is a matter of dollars and cents. I claim that the railroads in Alabama do not provide as good accommodations for the colored passengers as those furnished white passengers for the same money and that the fare is not first class as claimed on the face of the ticket.

My reasons for the above assertions are (a) that in most cases the smoking car and that in which colored people are put are the same; (b) when not put directly into the smoking car they are crammed into one end of a smoking car with a door between that is as much open as closed, making little difference between this and the smoking car; (c) on some of the roads the colored passengers are carried in one end of the baggage car, there being a partition between them and the baggage or express; (d) only a half coach is given to the colored people and this one is almost invariably an old one with low ceiling and it soon becomes crowded almost to suffocation and is misery to one knowing the effects of impure air. The seats in the coach given to colored people are always greatly inferior to those given the whites. The car is usually very filthy. There is no carpet as in the first class coach. White men are permitted in the car for colored people. Whenever a poorly dressed, slovenly white man boards the train he is shown into the colored half coach. When a white man gets drunk or wants to lounge around in an indecent position he finds his way into the colored department.

Plainly this treatment is not an equivalent for value received. Why should the railroads be allowed to make a discrimination that no other business man or business corporation makes? I enter a dry goods store in Tuskegee, buy a yard of calico, I am shown to just as good a counter, am treated just as politely by the clerk and for the same money receive just as good (though a separate) piece of calico as the white man. I subscribe for the *Advertiser*. For the same money you send me a paper printed just as nicely, done up as well and that costs you just as much in every way as the one sent a white subscriber. A lawyer is engaged to take a case for me. For the same money he seats me in his office, talks to me just as pleasantly and works for me just as hard before the courts as for a white client. Why should the railroads be an exception to these rules.

This unjust practice toward the negro cuts off thousands of dollars worth of negro travel every year, while just treatment of the negro would stop no white travel. There are ten times when I would take my wife or a lady friend on the railroad that I only do so once, and then am compelled to, because I shudder at the mere thought of the accommodations. Numbers of other colored men have expressed the same feeling. The mere thought of a trip on a railroad brings to me a feeling of intense dread and I never enter a railroad coach unless compelled to do so. On account of these discriminations the New Orleans Exposition has lost many dollars. Since the Exposition opened I have asked many colored people in Northern States if they were going to attend, but in almost every case the answer came that they would like to do so, but feared the railroads.

If the railroad officials do not want to let us enter the first-class car occupied by white passengers, let them give us a separate one just as good in every particular and just as exclusive, and there will be no complaint. We have no desire to mix. Even in Philadelphia and other Northern cities where there are no social barriers, the colored people have their own churches, schools, hotels, &c., showing that there is no disposition on the part of the colored to obtrude themselves on the whites when they can receive equal, separate accommodations. I have in mind the railroad running between Selma & Marion,[2] which furnishes a coach of the same length and height and just as good in every detail as that furnished the whites. Running in one direction the whites use one of the coaches and running in the opposite direction the colored passengers use the one previously used by the whites. There is never any discrimination on this road. A party of colored people recently travelling over it were so well pleased with this feature, and the gentlemanly bearing of the conductor, that they passed a resolution of thanks to be sent to the controllers of the road. There are a few other roads in the South whose treatment of colored passengers can be commended.

If the railroads will not give us first class accommodations, let them sell us tickets at reduced rates. This will be somewhat in keeping with the laws of honest trade.

The railroad officers make the mistake of supposing because many of the colored people are untidy, careless of their habits and contented to ride in a car with chain gang convicts that all are to be thus classed.

The writer is in favor of assortment and discrimination, for there are many colored people with whom he does not care to ride, but let assortment be made on the ground of dress and behavior.

In Virginia, where colored people are not prohibited from riding in a first-class car, I have always noticed that colored passengers when not well dressed, voluntarily take the second class car.

I have written thus plainly because I love the South, had rather live here than in the North, and expect to remain here. My faith is that the influences which are going to permanently right such wrongs are going to come from within the South and from the Southern people. National legislation and other outside attempts fail.

I appreciate the fact that customs that were years in forming cannot be blotted out in a day, and I am willing to exercise a wise patience, but on this subject I believe that Southern public opinion is ripe for the righting of this wrong.

Regardless of the opinions of wild theorists, the negro and the white man are to remain in the South side by side. Under God I believe we can do so without these jars in our business relations. We can be as separate as the fingers, yet one as the hand for maintaining the right.

B. T. Washington

Montgomery *Advertiser,* Apr. 30, 1885, 2.

¹ On the same page was an editorial on "The Negro and the Railroads," referring to BTW's letter and saying: "It is proper to say that he is a man who stands well in the community where he lives and is highly spoken of by all his white acquaintances. The letter deals with the subject of accommodations on the railroads for white and colored passengers, and is not only conservative in tone, but has justice on its side in what it asks." The *Advertiser* added further: "Prof. Washington expresses his entire willingness to be patient in reaching the end desired, but at the same time the railroads need not compel the colored passenger to wait forever for an exclusive first-class apartment for first-class pay. We commend the letter to railroad officials."

The incident that spurred this letter probably occurred when a party of Tuskegee teachers went on a train ride. One of the party, Samuel E. Courtney, later gave a vivid description of the incident:

"I was mobbed once during my travels in the South. Some of the Tuskegees were traveling with me from Montgomery to another town, some distance away. Two in the party were going to get married. We were about half way to Macon, when the train stopped at a way station about 20 minutes for refreshments.

"We teachers happened to be riding on the first car of the train. All of us were mulattoes, and would pass for white people on a pinch. Down there it is a criminal offence for a negro to ride on the same train with a white man, however.

"The 'crackers' (poor white people in that section) all began to flock about the train.

" 'There are three coons on that first class car,' one of them sung out.

" 'Put 'em off,' said someone else.

"Before that we had left the car for lunch. I was talking to an old man, and asking him something about the camp meeting that was going on in the place, when 12 white men stepped up to us, each one with a revolver in his right hand. One of them said to me:

" 'Say, you look like an intelligent nigger. Don't you know better than to ride in a first-class car? Before we'll let you ride any further in that car we'll take you out there in the field and fill you with bullets.'

"We were obliged to ride the remainder of the way in the Jim Crow car, so called.

"When we got to Macon we brought the matter to the attention of the Superintendent of the road, who said he was sorry, but could do nothing. He very kindly furnished us with a private car for the remainder of the distance from Macon to Opelika, Ala. We were satisfied.

"Later in the journey the bridegroom was arrested and fined $25 on some trumped up charge. We paid the fine, with costs, and then he was immediately rearrested by the County officers and fined $35 on another trumped up charge. After paying this we decided to go the remainder of the distance on horse back, and that night we drove 35 miles through the woods." (Boston *Journal,* Mar. 29, 1896, clipping in Con. 6, BTW Papers, DLC.)

2 The Cincinnati, Selma, and Mobile Railroad. The railroad's name reflected the dreams of its owners more than the reality of its operations. It ran only 61 miles from Elizabeth, Ala., near Selma, to Akron, Ala., north of Marion.

To Samuel Chapman Armstrong

Tuskegee, Ala., April 29 1885

Dear Gen'l: Mr. Howe[1] stayed with us 4 days and no one's visit has done us the real good that his has. His suggestions were valuable and criticisms frank. He has been especially helpful in his suggestions regarding our land and brick works. He seems to have greatly enjoyed his stay here. Yours &c

B. T. Washington

ALS BTW Folder President's Office Vault ViHaI.

1 Albert Howe.

From George M. Elliott[1]

Selma Ala. 4-30-85

Dear Prof. Washington: Your kind letter was found on my table on returning from New Orleans: This accounts for the delay in answering.

I went yesterday to see the Editor[2] of The "Dallas Post" about extra copies of the issue to which you refer. I did not get to see him, but I think they can be secured. If you can send me names of R.R. officials, I think I can send them out. I am not through writing on the subject however, and what I have yet to say I will send abroad also.

Unavoidable duties, and an absence to the Exposition have Interferred with my regular work. I agree with you that we should act at once; and not only at once, but continuously. I intend to continue to agitate the matter till my object is reached. Let us labor unitedly, and success will be ours.

Please keep me informed as to Mr. Logan's case, and about other matters germane to the question. Yours in haste

G. M. Elliott

ALS   Con. 84   BTW Papers   DLC.

[1] George M. Elliott, born in Virginia in 1849, was a preacher and principal of Knox Academy, a normal school in Selma, Ala. Later he moved to Beaufort, S.C., where he was pastor of the Berean Presbyterian Church and one of the founders of an industrial school.

[2] Probably W. H. Mixon (b. 1859), of Selma and Montgomery, an A.M.E. clergyman.

From George M. Elliott

Selma Ala. 5-4-85

Dear Sir: Yours of the 30th ult. is received. I inquired at both of our book stores for a copy of the *Advertiser,* of which you speak, and I could not get one. They do not keep it on their stands. Will you therefore be so kind as to send me a copy containing your letter. I am anxious to see it.

As chairman of the committee it devolves upon you to fix the time when we shall appear before the commissioners.[1] I can attend whenever called on. I also think we must continue active in the matter. I have matters to keep my pen going a long time. I cannot however do much till after the school closes as there is so much to occupy my mind till the close of this month. Respectfully Yours

G M Elliott

ALS   Con. 84   BTW Papers   DLC.

[1] There is no evidence that BTW or Elliott appeared before the state railroad commission.

To Joshua Longstreth Baily

Tuskegee, Alabama, May 15 85

Dear Mr. Bailey: By this mail I send you a marked copy of the "Montgomery Daily Advertiser"[1] containing marked articles on a subject about which we talked when I was there.

The "Advertiser" is one of the bitterest democratic papers in the South. Yours Sincerely

B. T. Washington

Thanks for your temperance speech.

ALS   Quaker Collection   PHC.

[1] Probably the issue containing BTW's letter to the editor on April 24, 1885.

From George M. Elliott

Selma Ala. 5-18. 1885

Dear Sir. Yours of the 15th inst. was duly received. I am glad that so much is being done in the matter of the Railroads. I have believed all the time that our object would be reached. I went to work with that in view. I do not intend to discontinue the matter till I see all that is desired on the roads of the South.

I have been delayed in publishing the matter that I have. My trip to New Orleans, school & church duties all combined have given me no time to write. Then the resolutions were in Marion for a long time & I was unable to get them that I might prepare my matter. I can now devote some time to writing. I hope I shall be able to accomplish all that I have before me. I intend to give the *Times* an opportunity to say something on the subject.

Have you seen my last article in the *Post*[1] on that subject.

I am glad that you have broken the ice on the W.R.R.[2] I hope I shall find things all right, when I pass over it. It is the only R.R. that I have not been brought in contact with. I believe I have been successful on all the other roads leading into Selma.

Nothing providentially preventing I shall be on hands to meet the

Commissioners. You say Monday June the 1st is the time. You did not mention the place, I presume it is Montgomery.

Please let me know if you got all the *resolutions*. With kindest regards, I remain, Yours sincerly

G. M. Elliott

ALS Con. 84 BTW Papers DLC.

¹ The Selma *Dallas Post*.

² The Western Railway of Alabama in 1885 ran the 132 miles from Selma, Ala., through Montgomery, to West Point, Ga., where it connected with the Atlanta and West Point. First chartered in 1834, in 1875 it became part of the Central of Georgia Railroad, and in 1888 part of the Richmond Terminal system. To reach the Western station at Chehaw, 5½ miles from Tuskegee, residents of that town used the Tuskegee Railroad, of narrow three-foot gauge.

A News Item from the New York *Evening Post*

[June 9, 1885]

SELF-EDUCATION OF THE NEGROES

A SUCCESSFUL ALABAMA SCHOOL

I came to Tuskegee, a characteristic Southern village of about 3,000 inhabitants, for the sake of seeing the most successful effort of the negro at self-education in this country. Candor compels the admission that when left to his own resource the negro is apt to do slack work. This is the natural result of his residence in this country during the last two unhappy centuries. But there is one large school which has been under negro control from its inception, at which everything is done neatly, thoroughly, and with intelligent despatch. That school is the Tuskegee Normal Colored School. Here you have a small Hampton which was founded and has always been manned by the colored race. This baby Hampton has come into existence mysteriously and almost as suddenly as did Aladdin's palace.

In the winter of 1880¹ the Legislature of Alabama passed an act setting aside an annual appropriation of $2,000 for the establishment and maintenance of a colored normal school at Tuskegee, with the condition that the money should be used in paying teachers' salaries. In order that advantage might be taken of this offer, somebody had got to be found to establish the school who had the pluck to bestir himself and secure funds for buildings and the necessary equipment. The State Superintendent of Instruction wrote to General Armstrong, of Hampton fame, asking him to find a principal. General Armstrong named Mr. Barker T. Washington, one of his numerous protégés, who had come to Hampton with only 50 cents in his pocket.

Mr. Washington opened his school in a dilapidated country church on the 4th of July, in 1881, after only one week's preparation, with a membership of thirty students.

If any one is in doubt as to whether Mr. Washington was the right man for the place, let him know that in less than four short years the school has attained a membership of nearly 200 students, each one of whom signs a contract when he comes here that he will teach at least two years in the public schools of Alabama, and has twelve teachers, for whose service the State now pays $3,000 a year. That the institution owns 580 acres of land, free of debt; a brickyard from which 10,000 bricks are daily turned out by the students, and a wind-mill and tank sixty-five feet in the air, with pipes and attachments for carrying water to any part of the premises; that there is one college building which cost $6,500, and another to cost over $10,000 in process of erection — being built by students — besides a large number of cottages for boys, poultry-houses, sheds, etc.; that there is a printing office, a carpenter shop, a laundry, a sewing school, forty acres of growing crops, with live stock and tools; and that preparations are now being made with the limited funds that are at the command of this most deserving school to add to the industrial department black-smithing, tinsmithing, shoemaking, fruit-canning, broom-making, and a saw-mill!

There is also a night school for the very poorest scholars (to whom the institute furnishes employment by the day) and a public colored school to give normal practice to those prospective teachers, after the analogy of the Butler School at Hampton.

As I came up from the narrow-gauge depot I was at once forcibly impressed with the beauty of the site of Tuskegee and the typical Southern dilapidation of the town itself. I wended my way along tor-tuous but broad streets, shaded by glorious old oaks, to the pleasant site of the school. It was the hour of the regular morning inspection and the boys were drawn up in two companies facing each other, with the brass band of the institute at an intermediate point. I noticed with mortification that when the boots were inspected according to custom mine were about the least shiny in the lot. It might have been worse, however, as a guest of the school I might have been asked to conduct the inspection! I thanked my stars that I had been spared this humiliation.

After some simple evolutions the boys filed into Porter Hall and ascended to the chapel, where they were joined by the girls, whose rooms had been inspected at the same time. Where are habits of neatness and cleanliness needed more than in the Southland?

At the service of prayers I noticed another Hampton feature reproduced with but slight modifications. The names of a dozen students were called at random from the class-cards, and each person called upon had to rise and repeat some item of news gleaned from the last daily newspaper in the reading-room. After this exercise other students were called upon and cross-examined upon the same news. Alaska had been mentioned incidentally, and some one was responsible to tell the history of Alaska's purchase from Russia. The news of John A. Logan's[2] election to the Senate had been chronicled, and now a sketch of Logan's life was required. The English Lord Chancellor had been referred to, and now the term Chancellor had to be defined.

After chapel prayers public recitations were conducted for three hours in the various classrooms. This gave me an opportunity not only to study the excellent class-room methods employed, but also to see what a clever, clear-headed, wide-awake set of young men and young women has been secured by Professor Washington to assist him in his work.

Then I went on a tour of inspection of the premises in company with Professor Washington, the State Superintendent of Education, and some other prominent white citizens. The splendid work of the young principal has won the sympathy and cooperation of even the Southern white people. We saw mammoth potatoes, turnips, cabbages, peas, and various other vegetables.

"Our land is poor," said Professor Washington, "but I wouldn't have it otherwise. I got it with that fact in view. I want the students to learn how to make good land out of poor land. It is a small achievement to grow good crops on rich land. We are trying to raise an intelligent class of farmers." In the carpenter-shop were exhibits of furniture made by the students, beds, washstands, tables, etc. In the girls' industrial department were shawls, aprons, shirts, hats, tidies, and other articles of apparel or household use.

New York *Evening Post,* June 9, 1885, 3. Reprinted from the Chicago *Inter Ocean.* The correspondent was a Mr. Shumway. (See BTW to Samuel Chapman Armstrong, June 15, 1885.)

[1] Actually February 1881.

[2] John Alexander Logan (1826-86). A Democratic congressman from southern Illinois, Logan resigned his seat in 1862 to join the Union Army. An excellent soldier, he rose to the rank of major general. The war also changed his politics, and he returned to Congress in the Reconstruction period as a radical "Black Republican." He was a leader in the impeachment of President Johnson, and served as U.S. senator from 1871 to 1877 and from 1879 to 1886.

To Samuel Chapman Armstrong

102 W 37. St   N.Y., June 15–85

I send by this mail a marked copy of the "Evening Post" containing an article, on our work which you may have seen.[1] I send it thinking that you might be able to get some of the Boston papers to copy.

There are some inaccuracies in the article, but on the whole will do good. It is by a Mr. Shumway. Yours &c.

B. T. Washington

I go to Hartford tomorrow.

ACS   BTW Folder   President's Office Vault   ViHaI.

[1] See A News Item from the New York *Evening Post,* June 9, 1885.

To the Editor of the *Southern Workman*

[Tuskegee, Ala., July 1885]

Editor of *"Southern Workman."* Our Anniversary exercises which occurred on the 28th of May, were by far the most interesting and encouraging in the history of our institute. The day was beautiful, not too hot nor too cool. The rain the day before cooled the air and laid the dust. Several days before Commencement, friends of the school began

1. James Burroughs, ca. 1860 (*left*), and Elizabeth W. Burroughs, ca. 1880.
Booker T. Washington National Monument

2. Booker T. Washington's childhood home (not his birthplace), ca. 1900.
Story of My Life and Work (1900)

3. Booker T. Washington as a Hampton student, ca. 1873.
Southern Workman, 31 (May 1902)

4. Samuel Chapman Armstrong.
frontispiece, Edith Armstrong Talbot,
Samuel Chapman Armstrong (1904)

5. Graduating class of Hampton Institute, June 10, 1875. Booker T. Washington is second from the left in the first row; Mary F. Mackie is first on the left in the second row; J. F. B. Marshall and S. C. Armstrong are standing at the extreme left.

6. The house in Malden, W.Va., in which Booker T. Washington lived
when he began teaching.
World's Work, 20 (Oct. 1910)

7. The Wigwam, Indian dormitory at Hampton.
Hampton Institute Archives

8. James Murie (The Coming Sun), Pawnee student at Hampton, 1900.
Smithsonian Institution, National Anthropological Archives

9. Lewis Adams, 1902.
Frances Benjamin Johnston Collection,
Library of Congress

10. Fanny Norton Smith Washington, ca. 1882.
Tuskegee Institute Archives

11. Olivia A. Davidson Washington, ca. 1887
Outlook, 67 (Jan. 5, 1901)

12. Margaret James Murray Washington, ca. 1890.
Booker T. Washington Papers, Library of Congress

13. Tuskegee Institute campus when it was first bought, 1881.
My Larger Education (1911)

14. Booker T. Washington,
1881 (*top left*).
Christian Endeavor World,
13 (Apr. 21, 1899)

15. Booker T. Washington,
1880s (*top right*).
Booker T. Washington Papers,
Library of Congress

16. Booker T. Washington,
1888 (*bottom right*).
World's Work, 20 (Oct. 1910)

17. George W. Campbell, n.d.
Booker T. Washington Papers, Library of Congress

18. John Henry Washington, 1905.
Frances Benjamin Johnston Collection, Library of Congress

19. Warren Logan, 1905.
Frances Benjamin Johnston Collection, Library of Congress

to arrive. On Thursday, long before the hour for beginning the class work, wagons, buggies, &c. filled with friends and parents, began to arrive in large numbers.

Later came the excursionists from Opelika and Montgomery. By noon the grounds and buildings swarmed with people and by two o'clock, when the rhetorical exercises were to begin, it was quite a question what to do with the people. In a few minutes after the Chapel doors were opened it was filled to overflowing and a large number were left on the outside. At 2 o'clock, the following Programme was presented:

MUSIC — Normal School Brass Band

Salutatory: *"How can we improve our Homes?"*
Ella McCullough, *Ft. Mitchell, Ala.*

MUSIC

Recitation: *"How he saved St Michaels"*
Hiram H. Thweatt, *Tuskegee, Ala.*

"Needed Improvement in Agriculture"
Lewis D. McCullough, *Ft. Mitchell, Ala.*

MUSIC

Recitation: *"Rock of Ages"*
Neelie Bowen,[1] *Tuskegee, Ala.*

Valedictory, *"Poverty No Hindrance to Success"*
B. Town Harvey, *Gueryton, Ala.*

MUSIC

Annual Address
Prof. J. C. Price,[2] *Salisbury, N.C.*

MUSIC

Presentation of Diplomas
By Hon Solomon Palmer State Sup't of Education.

MUSIC

In his address, before presenting the Diplomas to the graduates, the State Superintendent of Education was most feeling and appropriate in his remarks, and every one in the audience was impressed that he meant and felt all that he said. He began by remarking: "I can not express the pleasure it affords me to be present on this occasion. The fame of this school has spread throughout the State and even throughout the South; consequently I had expected much, but the progress manifested to-day has surpassed all hope and my most sanguine expectations. Free from unnecessary display, every thing has been practical, sensible and thorough. These evidences are seen in the essays, class work, on the farm, brick yard, in the carpenters 'shop,' printing office, girls sewing room &c."

He said that he felt honored in being allowed to present the diplomas to the first graduating class of the Tuskegee Normal School; that he thought the State had been paid high interest on its appropriation to help support this school and that the State in view of such marked success as this institution has achieved, would be inclined to increase its appropriation.

After the presentation of the diplomas, the audience joined the students in the doxology, and the benediction was pronounced by Rev. Allen Hannon[3] of Montgomery.

All of the 10 graduates go out professing Christians, and the progress in real manly and womanly growth among the graduates during this term has been the most satisfactory part of the year's work. Each one goes out with a strong heart, determined to carry the light to some dark corner.

B. T. Washington

Southern Workman, 14 (July 1885), 83.

[1] Cornelia Bowen.

[2] Joseph Charles Price (1854-93) was born in Elizabeth City, N.C., of a free mother and slave father. Price received his early training in the schools provided by the occupying army during the Civil War. In 1871 he began teaching in Wilson, N.C., but decided that he needed more education and attended Shaw College. There he received a call to preach and continued his education at Lincoln University, graduating from the theological department in 1881. He made a trip to Britain in 1881 to raise money for an A.M.E. Zion college, which he shrewdly proposed to name for the Scottish explorer, David Livingstone. On his return, he founded Livingstone College in Salisbury, N.C. During the 1880s Price gained a national reputation as an orator and toured throughout the country. He outshone BTW as a rising young race leader of a somewhat more militant persuasion. Price's constructive achievements, moderation, and abstention from politics gave him a following among both whites and blacks. His untimely death of Bright's disease in 1893 stopped a career in many ways parallel to that of BTW.

[3] Allen Hannon, the first black pastor of the Old Ship A.M.E. Zion Church of Montgomery.

To Samuel Chapman Armstrong

Tuskegee, Ala. Oct. 31 1885

Dear Gen'l: We will pay the note Nov. 15.

I have just returned from a ten day's treatment under Dr. Dorsette and think I am now in a good condition for the year's work. I have been down again since I wrote you.

Matters are going well. Hastily yours

B. T. Washington

Many thanks for the extension.

ALS   BTW Folder   President's Office Vault   ViHaI.

To Samuel Chapman Armstrong

102 W. 37 St   N.Y. Nov. 26 85

Dear Gen'l: Soon after our conversation in Phila. I arrived here and found a letter announcing that the Misses Mason[1] had given us $7000. *Faith* and *hard work* I find will accomplish anything. Yours &c

B. T. Washington

ACS   BTW Folder   President's Office Vault   ViHaI.

[1] Ellen Frances and Ida Means Mason were two unmarried sisters who were among the earliest, most regular, and largest contributors to both Hampton and Tuskegee institutes. Born in the 1850s into a wealthy Brookline, Mass., family that dated its interest in Negro welfare to the girls' grandfather, Jeremiah Mason, the two sisters were left with a large inheritance at an early age. While still adolescents, they began aiding Hampton in 1869 after meeting General Armstrong, and continued to contribute regularly for more than sixty years. In the 1890s they each made semi-annual contributions of $3,000 to Tuskegee. They owned large homes on Beacon Hill in Boston and in Newport and often opened them for fund-raising activities for Hampton as well as entertaining many Hampton students there. The Mason sisters also supported other cultural and charitable organizations and helped many individual students. Learned in Greek and widely traveled, they compiled together a volume on ancient Athens, and Ellen translated some of Plato's essays. Ida died in 1928 and Ellen in 1930.

To John Elbert McConnell[1]

Tuskegee, Ala. Dec. 17th 1885

Dear Sir: After unavoidable delay I now attempt to give you my opinion on the questions submitted by you, though I fear the answer will reach you too late to be of value.

In my opinion nothing would be more conducive of general prosperity and general intelligence than an educational qualification. Reasons — Political parties needing the votes of the ignorant ones would seek to have them educated just as in some states they see that the poor man's tax is paid in order that he may vote. (The number of illiterate whites as well as Negroes is alarmingly great in the South.) It will tend to lessen the political animosity between the black and white races since the leading whites now claim that the Negro is thwarted in his political rights by them because of his ignorance. Time for preparation should be given before such a law is put in operation. The fact of those with a certain amount of education being allowed to vote would create an ambition in the minds of the ignorant Negroes that would soon lead them to seek education. The non-voters would soon be considered to belong to an inferior class.

The reconstruction acts would have been carried out with much less bitterness and blood shed, in consequence of more moderation on the part of the Negroes in the exercise of their newly acquired political rights. For instance, the legislatures of S.C., La. and other Southern States would not have been filled all at once with ignorant and unscrupulous legislators.

The passage of the Blair Educational Bill[2] will bring about the most speedy remedy for illiteracy. In my mind, the political condition will be most speedily remedied by a division of the present political parties. At present, the Democratic party is composed almost entirely of whites and the Republican party almost entirely of blacks — it is one race against the other. When both races are largely represented in both parties, there will be fair and peaceable elections. The beginning of this change I think is not far distant.

I have attempted to speak of these matters as they bear on the condition of things in the South. Yours truly

B. T. Washington

HLS   John E. McConnell Papers   WHi.

[1] John Elbert McConnell (1863-1928) was born in Farmington, Wis., and graduated from the University of Wisconsin in 1887. He was admitted to the bar in 1889. He was a Republican and had a deep interest in the Reconstruction period and racial aspects of American political history.

[2] The Blair bill was the creation of New Hampshire Republican Senator Henry W. Blair (1834-1920), chairman of the Senate Committee on Education and Labor from 1881 to 1891. Originally conceived in 1881, the year that BTW began his work at Tuskegee, the bill provided large sums of federal money ($77 million in total) for public schools over an eight-year period in decreasing amounts. A common complaint was that it was designed to expend the surplus created by the protective tariff. The criterion for distribution of the fund was to be the amount of illiteracy in a state. Thus, about 75 percent of the Blair bill appropriation would have gone to southern states. The first appropriation was to be $15 million, which would provide more than $1 million to Alabama alone. Alabama's entire state school expenditure in 1881 was less than the proposed Blair appropriation.

The Blair bill passed the Senate three times during the 1880s before it was finally defeated in 1890, leaving its sponsor embittered and frustrated. The bill was never considered in the House due to strong Democratic opposition from Speaker John G. Carlisle. The bill allowed for segregated schools, but it upheld the doctrine of separate but equal. Federal and state funds, according to the bill, should be expended "equally for the education of all the children, without distinction of race or color." Southern white sentiment was divided, but generally in favor of the bill. Most blacks also supported the bill since, even if the funds were unequally distributed, it would have meant a substantial increase in the otherwise paltry aid to black education. (See Crofts, "The Blair Bill and the Elections Bill.")

To Frederick C. Jones[1]

Tuskegee, Ala. Dec. 21 1885

My dear Sir: Yours of Dec. 17 containing your check for $25. is received. We are very grateful to you for the help and shall try by hard work to prove ourselves worthy of your confidence.

It's very encouraging to know that such friends as Mr. Cable[2] and others are so interested in the Southern work. Mr. Cable has certainly proven his friendship for us in a manly way. If a few more Southern people would come out boldly as Mr. Cable has it would help matters much. There are many in the South who *think* as Mr. Cable does but have not the moral courage to express their sentiments.

We are going to send you the "Southern Letter," a little paper published by us, that you may see what we are doing. Sincerely yours

Booker T. Washington

ALS   George W. Cable Collection   LNHT.

¹ Frederick C. Jones was a resident of Farmington, Conn.

² George Washington Cable (1844-1925), a distinguished southern novelist and liberal critic of the South's racial practices, was born in New Orleans and fought in the Confederate Army. For a time he worked as a clerk before securing a position as a reporter on a New Orleans newspaper. Writing during the vogue of local-color fiction, Cable moved from romantic evocation of New Orleans life in *Old Creole Days* (1879) to a deeper probing into southern social problems. He wrote *The Grandissimes* (1884), probably his best work. Thereafter, Cable spoke so frankly on the issue most southerners wanted to ignore that he was increasingly uncomfortable in the South. Only a Confederate veteran like Cable could safely confront lynching and other racial matters when he spoke at southern universities. After the publication of *The Silent South* in 1885, Cable made Northampton, Mass., his home for the next forty years. Seeking more material on southern racial affairs, he asked BTW about Negro emigration from the South and rural debt systems. Though BTW's private responses to Cable were frank and revealing, the black educator undoubtedly drew a lesson from Cable's exile that blunt speech on racial questions was dangerous and would only alienate white southerners. The two men shared some beliefs and attitudes, but BTW's public stance of accommodation was in marked contrast to that of the militant agitator Cable. On one of his northern fund-raising trips, BTW dined with the Cables in Northampton, but apparently the friendship soon cooled. (Butcher, "George W. Cable and Booker T. Washington," 462-68.)

To James Fowle Baldwin Marshall

[Tuskegee, Ala.] Dec. 22 [188]5

Dear Gen'l: Your letter came while I was North and since returning I have been so very busy that I am just answering your letter. We all deeply appreciate your suggestions and your kindly interest in us.

We are having the book containing specimens of printing prepared and expect to send it within a few days. There is no book bindery in Tuskegee and we may be able in the future to make this a paying industry.

The school property is not subject to taxation. In the act of the legislature there is no limit put to the amount of property we can hold. Enclosed I send a copy of the Act of the legislature establishing the school. Further than this we have no charter. The Commissioners mentioned have control of the money given by the State only. I have been thinking for some time that the *Trustees* who hold and control the property should have a charter distinct from this. It has been my intention to consult our friend Mr. W. F. Foster about the matter and your letter shows me the necessity of it I think more clearly than ever. However I shall do nothing about the matter till I hear from you again. I also enclose the list of trustees to whom the property is deeded. You will notice that the 3 State Commissioners are included. There has always existed the most perfect harmony between them and the Trustees.

All our buildings of any size are insured except the Carpenters Shop. The rate insurance on Porter Hall is 2% and on Alabama Hall 1¼%. Porter Hall for $5000 — Alabama Hall for $9000.

At present we are free from debt and are, I think, in a better condition than we have been for some time. One of our greatest needs is a convenient and substantial stable. We are compelled to keep considerable stock on hand and are not able to give them the care that they should have with our present conveniencies. Much valuable manure is also lost for want of the proper means to take care of it. We do not think it wise to lay out any more money on our present stable because we do not think it can ever be made to answer the purpose. About $1000 will put up one such as we need. We already need a cottage f[or] young men. The 3rd story of Porter Hall will not begin to hold them all. We still occupy the shanties and every room is crowded to its greatest extent. We plan to get up a 3 story brick cottage to cost about $4000 or $5000 to contain mainly sleeping rooms.

Mr. Logan I consider gets on well with the accounts. This is the first year I have ever felt in any degree satisfied about the accts. It is now so arranged that Mr. Logan gives almost all of his time to them and I am beginning to feel proud of the degree accuracy that we have reached.

The school is now stronger in its relations to both white and colored citizens than it has ever been. During the summer there was some bad feeling shown against the school by a few of the whites on acct of a speech made by one [of] our graduates and misunderstood by the whites who heard it. But this feeling has disappeared. During the last two months we have had more hearty recognition and encouragement from the leading whites than ever before. They seem to feel now as never before that the school is a real benefit to the whole community. They seemed as much rejoiced over the Misses Mason's gift as we. Two cases were especially noticeable. One Col. Abecrombie,[1] the leading democratic politician came to me after he had heard of the Mason gift and warmly congratulated the school and offered his good wishes. Col. A. had before this scarcely spoken to me or taken any notice of the school. Another one, a Mr. Felts,[2] who at first acted in about the same [way] as Mr. A. has come around in a wonderful way. He has visited the school recently and takes every opportunity to speak in the highest terms of the work of the school. Mr. Campbell and Col. Foster are still our firm friends. We can always rely on them. There has never been other than a friendly spirit shown by all classes of colored people. This term we have students from all parts of the state and they represent a better class of families than we have had represented before. Among the students is a son of excongressman Haraldson.[3]

At present I think we are in a better position to secure more aid from the State than ever before. The legislature meets again next winter when we shall see what can be done.

We do not mind your speaking to us often about the importance of accurate accts because we know it comes only from your deep interest in us.

As yet the cases where we have had special funds that could not be used for other purposes have been few and there has been no particular method of securing them from being drawn on by other needs, except in case of the State Fund which is kept deposited with Mr. Campbell, our banker, and we draw from it quarterly. We should like information on this point.

It is our purpose to see what can be done towards making the knitting of socks &c. a paying industry and shall prob[ab]ly through you want to get information from Mr. Thompson.

By this mail we send one of our reports which is just out. It is our own printing. We shall be glad of your criticism.

We are all very glad to hear that you have been placed at the head of the Unitarian Bureau for work in the South and shall endeavor to keep you well supplied with information relative to our work. The South is certainly greatly indebted to Unitarians for what they have done and it is but just that the world should know just how generous they are. Then I am sorry to say that I *know* of colored men who make their living by making collections in the North for objects that have no existence and never will have.

I showed your letter to Mr. Courtney.[4] Little Portia sends love to you and Mrs. Marshall. She is well and always happy as a lark.

All of us send Christmas greeting to you and Mrs. Marshall. Faithfully yours

Booker T. Washington

ALpS   Con. 91   BTW Papers   DLC.

[1] Robert Haden Abercrombie (1837-91), born in Macon County, Ala., attended law school in Tennessee and graduated in 1859. He went to Tuskegee and began practicing law in the firm of Williams, Graham, and Mayes. In 1862 he entered the Confederate Army and was elevated to colonel after the battle of Atlanta. Returning to Tuskegee after the war, he continued to practice law in the firm of Graham and Abercrombie (later Abercrombie and Bilbro). He moved to Gadsden, Ala., in 1888.

[2] This could have been Willie Felts, a thirty-year-old white barkeeper in Tuskegee, but more probably was Charlie Felts, a twenty-nine-year-old white grocer.

[3] Jeremiah Haralson of Selma was born a slave in Georgia in 1846. Self-educated, Haralson moved to Alabama, where he became a preacher. He was elected to the Alabama legislature in 1870 and the Alabama Senate in 1872. He served one term as U.S. congressman (1875-77), and later filled a number of federal appointments. Haralson roamed over much of the southern and western United States engaging in farming, coal mining, and other enterprises. He was killed by wild beasts near Denver, Colo., about 1916. His son Henry attended Tuskegee for one year, 1885-86, as a member of the junior class.

[4] Samuel E. Courtney (b. 1861), teacher of mathematics and drawing at Tuskegee from 1885 to 1888, became a prominent Boston physician and valuable ally of BTW a decade later. He was born in Malden, W.Va., the son of a wealthy white planter and his mulatto slave. He attended the school taught by BTW and through his teacher's arrangements went to Hampton Institute. Courtney's father, trained as a physician, paid for part of his son's education at Hampton and interested him in studying medicine. After graduating in 1879, Courtney worked in Massachusetts to pay his school debts. He taught briefly in Virginia and then attended the state normal school at Westfield, Mass. He joined the Tuskegee faculty immediately after graduation and also worked as a northern agent of the school.

Courtney left Tuskegee in 1888 to attend Harvard Medical School, where he graduated in 1893. In a few years he had a flourishing Boston medical practice in which most of his patients were white. He was a Unitarian and a Republican, and served on the Boston public school board. In 1896 he represented Massachusetts at the Republican national convention, where he backed Thomas B. Reed for the presidential nomination.

He was BTW's loyal lieutenant in Boston, active in the local business league. The National Negro Business League was founded at his home in 1900. He opposed the activities of William Monroe Trotter and other anti-Bookerites. At the Boston Riot, at the height of the excitement, Courtney shouted, "Throw Trotter out the window." He attended to the medical needs of BTW and various members of his family when they were in the Boston area.

To R. R. Varner

[Tuskegee, Ala.] Jan. 6 [188]6

Dear Sir: I meant to have seen you before you left but failed to do so.

My object in writing is to know if you are willing to sell all or apart of the lots in front of the Normal School. We shall not need to use the rooms much longer and when we give them up I should rather buy the houses and land than to have them occupied by a mean class of people. If you are willing to sell please state your lowest price and best terms. Yours &c.

B. T. Washington

ALpS Con. 91 BTW Papers DLC.

To John Mercer Langston[1]

[Tuskegee, Ala.] Jan. 14 [188]6

My dear Sir: Some days ago I sent a letter to you, directed to Washington concerning the subject about which I now write.

We are very anxious to have you deliver the annual address at our next Commencement (Thurs. May 28).

Some weeks ago I wrote Prof. Greener[2] to write or speak to you concerning the matter and he wrote that he had done so or would do so.

Prof. Greener delivered the address for us year before last and is well acquainted with the character and work of our institution. Prof. J. C. Price of N.C. spoke for us at our last Commencement. If necessary you can refer to either him or Prof. Greener.

This is the State Normal School and we have made it a point every Commencement to have a large representation of both races from all parts of the state. With the leading whites and colored people present much has been done on these occasions towards shaping public sentiment.

Both races in this part of the South want to see and hear you and I am sure that by coming here you can accomplish much good.

Your traveling expenses charges &c we are willing to meet.

We should like to know as soon as possible whether or not you can come and on what conditions. Yours Sincerely

B. T. Washington

P.S. Prof. James Storum[3] has visited our institution and has lectured here.

ALpS Con. 91 BTW Papers DLC.

[1] John Mercer Langston (1829-97), next to Frederick Douglass probably the most well-known race leader of the nineteenth century. He was the son of a Virginia planter and a slave mother. After the death of his parents, Langston was sent to Ohio in 1834 for an education. In 1849 he graduated from Oberlin College and became a lawyer in the town of Oberlin. He was an abolitionist orator and president of the National Equal Rights League in 1864. During the Civil War he recruited black soldiers for the Union Army and later served as inspector general of schools for the Freedmen's Bureau. During Reconstruction he held several appointive offices, including two terms as consul general in Haiti. He was twice a delegate to the Republican national convention. He became dean of the law school and vice-president of Howard University. In 1885 he became president of Virginia Normal and Collegiate Institute in Petersburg. He won election in 1888 to the U.S. House of Representatives in a close race in which Langston appealed directly to black Virginians to elect him because of his race. Much of his two-year term was taken up with feuds regarding his seating. His election disturbed not only Democrats but white members of his own party, and he lost the next election. Langston's political beliefs changed sharply from time to time. In the late 1870s he encouraged blacks to leave the South to escape oppression. A decade later he was optimistic about black-white relations in the South and concluded that blacks themselves would solve the "Negro problem" through intelligence and acquisition of wealth. In 1894 Langston wrote an autobiography, *From the Virginia Plantation to the National Capital.*

[2] Richard Theodore Greener was born in Philadelphia and educated in Massachusetts. In 1870, at the age of twenty-six, he became the first black graduate of Harvard University. Greener was principal of a black school in Philadelphia (1870-72), and then worked variously as teacher, lecturer, and editor. He also worked in the office of the U.S. attorney in the District of Columbia. From 1873 to 1877 he was the only black faculty member at the University of South Carolina, where he taught metaphysics and logic. In 1876 he received an LL.B. degree from the University of South Carolina and was admitted to the District of Columbia bar the next year. The hard-working, ambitious lawyer became a professor of law and later dean of the law school at Howard University. In 1882 he began a vigorous private practice in Washington, D.C. Greener received numerous political appointments under McKinley and Roosevelt. He spent more than seven years as U.S. consul at Vladivostok. He was a U.S. representative during the Boxer Rebellion and represented British and Japanese interests in the Russo-Japanese War. In 1906 his political fortunes ran out and he was unable to find another appointment. Still seeking an active political life, Greener turned to BTW for help and worked for BTW as a spy at the Harpers Ferry meeting of the Niagara Movement. BTW, however, was unable to find an appointment for Greener, who then retired to live in Chicago.

[3] James Storum taught at Wayland Seminary in Washington, D.C., from 1870 to 1882. He was active in the Bethel Literary and Historical Association of Washington, D.C., from its founding in 1881 and served three terms as the association's president (1888-91). During this time he arranged for many outstanding blacks to speak to the association including Frederick Douglass, Robert H. Terrell, Mary Church Terrell, Kelly Miller, and Archibald H. Grimké. The association frequently held meetings that dealt with the black man's role in America and stressed economic solidarity and cooperation among blacks.

To Clara Hobson

[Tuskegee, Ala.] Jan. 14 [188]6

Dear Madam: Your letter came some days ago. In reply I would say that your son[1] will start home just as soon as he gets the money from you.

I must say that you have done your son an injustice. The very fact of his knowing that he could do wrong and then be upheld in it to the extent of being permitted to come home because he did not feel like obeying the rules of the school. If you had made him feel that he was in our hands and must obey there would have been nothing of this.

It would not be the thing for us to take him in school again another term for we would have no control over him since he would know that you would take him home the first time he did not want to obey. Yours truly

B. T. Washington

ALpS Con. 91 BTW Papers DLC.

[1] Eugene W. Hobson of Meridian, Miss., entered Tuskegee in 1884 and was a junior in 1885-86.

To Atticus Greene Haygood

Tuskegee, Ala. Jan. 16 1886

Dear Sir & Friend: On or about the 11 of Feb. we are going to have a large educational mass meeting in Montgomery for the purpose of giving the colored people a chance to contribute something toward industrial education in the same way that Northern people do. The special object of the meeting will be to get the colored people to contribute enough to fit up a *good* blacksmith's shop here. Last year we held a meeting of the kind and had about 700 present. The State Supt and several prominent whites were present and spoke. At the meeting this year we expect to have the Gov. present. The people contributed quite liberally at the other meeting.

My object in writing is to ask if it will be possible for you to be present and speak at the next meeting. You would have a *very large* audience and I know great good would be done in the way of stirring our people up to the importance of trying to help *themselves*. Shall be glad to hear early as we want to print the programmes &c. Yours &c.

B. T. Washington

ALS OFH. This letter was enclosed with a note from Atticus Greene Haygood to Rutherford B. Hayes, dated Jan. 18, 1886. Haygood wrote: "Dear Mr. Hayes: There is promise of fruit. Read the inclosed. You need not return it. The writer is a colored man — doing admirably at Tuskegee. I accept of course." (Both letters are in Rubin, *Teach the Freeman*, 1:169-70.)

To Solomon Palmer

[Tuskegee, Ala.] Feb 2 [188]6

Private

Dear Sir: Please do not think me bold in what I am about to write. I simply mean to try to do good.

I am sure that I represent the feelings of the colored teachers in the county when I say that we hope you can see your way clear to the appointment of Col. Pinkard[1] as Co. Supt. of Education for Macon Co. He has fitness for the office and we all feel that in his hands the free schools will prosper.

Whatever is done we certainly hope and pray that no such misfortune shall befall our county as to have a merchant made Co. Supt. No one knows better than you that there is only one in a hundred that has any training or qualifications for such an office.

I think I understand pretty well the feelings of the leading whites in the county in regard to the matter and feel sure in saying that the solid men of the county want Col. Pinkard. Yours &c.

B. T. Washington

ALpS Con. 91 BTW Papers DLC.

¹ Lucius Pinckard interrupted his education at the University of Alabama to fight in the Civil War and earned the rank of colonel in the battle of Sharpsburg. A planter, Pinckard was elected sheriff of Macon County in 1884 and held the position for four years. He did not secure the appointment as county superintendent of education. Later he moved to Atlanta and entered the life-insurance business. Charles Winston Thompson, a Tuskegee merchant, was appointed county superintendent in 1886.

To the Editor of the *Southern Workman*

Tuskegee, Ala., Feb. 18, 1886

SELF-HELP AMONG THE COLORED PEOPLE IN ALABAMA

Editor of the Southern Workman. On Sunday Jan. 31st, the ministers of the colored churches in Tuskegee suspended their services in order that themselves and their congregations might be present at an educational mass meeting called to meet in the Normal School chapel.

When the hour arrived for beginning the exercises, every part of the room was closely packed with people.

A short educational sermon was preached by Rev. P. J. McIntosh,¹ a graduate of Talladega College and present pastor of the Tuskegee Methodist Church, and several short addresses were made. A collection in which all joined heartily was taken up for the general support of the institution. The collection and the meeting throughout was a credit to the people of Tuskegee.

At the suggestion of citizens of Montgomery, a very large and successful educational meeting was held in Montgomery a year ago for the purpose of giving the people a chance to show their interest in the work of this institution in a practical way.

That meeting was very large and the best class of citizens were present, and nearly $100. was given towards furnishing rooms in Alabama Hall.

On last Thursday night, Feb. 11th, a similar meeting was held, the object being to keep the people alive to the importance of education and self-help. Between one thousand and twelve hundred people were present. Governor O'Neal,[2] State Superintendent, Maj. Palmer, Col. H. R. Shorter,[3] President State R.R. Comm., were present and made stirring and encouraging addresses. Dr. A. G. Haygood had promised to be present and was on his way but his train was unavoidably delayed. Besides these mentioned, many more of Montgomery's best white citizens were present and showed as much interest as the colored.

To add to the interests of the meeting a double quartette of singers from the Tuskegee Normal School was present and interspersed the exercises with singing that was highly enjoyed by the immense audience.

To give point to the meeting a collection was taken up to be equally divided between the Swayne Public School in Montgomery and the Tuskegee Normal School. That for the Swayne School is to be used in putting a fence around Swayne School and that for the Tuskegee Normal School to be used in purchasing a set of blacksmith's tools for the new shop at Tuskegee. While the collection on account of very dull times in the South was not as large as it was last year, the crowd was larger and the interest in the meeting seemed greater. The most encouraging interest was shown from beginning to end and lasting good was done.

Booker T. Washington

Southern Workman, 15 (Mar. 1886), 35.

[1] Peter J. McEntosh, as his name was reported in the Talladega College catalog, graduated from Talladega's theological department in 1880. He was pastor of a Tuskegee Methodist church from 1883 to 1887. Later he headed an A.M.E. Zion church in York, Pa. McEntosh died in 1905.

[2] Edward Asbury O'Neal (1818-90), governor of Alabama from 1882 to 1886, was born in Madison County. He graduated from LaGrange College in 1836 and was admitted to the bar in 1840. Before the Civil War he served for four years in the state legislature and lost a bid for the U.S. Congress. After compiling an exceptional record in the Confederate Army, he entered Alabama politics as a Democrat during Reconstruction. He played a prominent role in the Alabama constitutional convention of 1875. As governor, O'Neal was notable for establishing several normal schools for whites, founding the state agricultural department, acquiring land for state schools, and securing better treatment for convicts.

[3] Henry Russell Shorter (1833-98) grew up in Eufaula, Ala., graduated from the University of North Carolina in 1853, and was admitted to the bar in 1854. He served in the Civil War and later resumed his law practice. A staunch Democrat, Shorter was wounded during a street scuffle with Radical Republicans in 1874. In 1885 Governor Edward A. O'Neal appointed him president of the Alabama Railroad Commission, a position he held until 1897.

To the Editor of the *Southern Workman*

Tuskegee, Ala., Feb. 18, '86

SOUTHERN PRISONS

EDITOR SOUTHERN WORKMAN. For one who wants to do the work of a Howard or a Wilberforce surely there is no greater opportunity presented anywhere than is found in the prisons of the Southern states. With few exceptions all the Southern states let their convicts, both state and county out to private contractors for so much a month. These contractors work their prisoners on farms or in coal mines. During the prisoner's entire confinement there are no forces at work that tend to make him a better man when released, but rather a worse one. This fact alone, to say nothing of the terrible suffering endured, ought to influence some Christian reformer to give his life to the work.

But let a few examples which I have gotten within the last few days illustrate what I mean. When reading this it should be remembered that the thermometer in most parts of the South has stood below zero many times this winter.

"The feet of a colored boy rotted off a few days ago. This was caused by his being worked in the county chain-gang all the winter without shoes." *Atlanta Defiance*.

Now let the coroner's jury tell the story of Alex. Crews who was unlawfully forced into prison in the first place and while there was so inhumanly treated that he dropped dead before he could reach his home after being released.

The Negro, Alex. Crews, whose pitiful story of distress and suffering was so graphically described in the *Dispatch* of yesterday, died as he was entering a hack to be taken to the depot on his way home.

The coroner was notified, and summoned a jury of inquest. After examining the witness, the jury rendered this verdict: "We, the jury impaneled to investigate the cause which led to the death of Alex Crews, a colored man, now lying dead in this office, are unanimous in the opinion that the deceased came to his death by cruel and inhuman treatment at the hands of those who had him in charge on the convict farm, and we recommend that proper means be taken to bring the guilty party into court to answer the charge."

The Montgomery *Daily Dispatch* further says: "After his conviction and sentence to the chain-gang he laid in the jail for a considerable while and his attorney applied for a release on a writ of *habeas corpus* which was denied by the lower court. The application on writ was then taken to the supreme court which body decided that he was entitled to release. While the matter was pending in the supreme court, Crews was unlawfully sent to the Smith convict farm." Hear what the State penitentiary physician, who visited the Smith convict farm recently, has to say: "I was at Smith's farm in Tallapoosa County, Jan. 30th. I found the clothing of the convicts very defective, being thin and worthless, insufficient for protection during the cold weather. Many of them had no shoes beyond a sole tied to their feet, there being no uppers, and some with no protection for the feet except rags tied around them. I told Mr. Smith that the clothing and sanitary condition of the men were miserable and outrageous." Still another newspaper report says: "Capt. Irwin who works convicts at his mill on the other side of the river states that he had received during the coldest portion of the late cold spell, five convicts who came from the Smith farm in Tallapoosa Co., Ala., and that their condition when they arrived at his mill was most miserable. They were poorly clad, having on only shirts and pants and those garments were made of very light material. Personally the prisoners were in a very bad condition, being covered with dirt and vermin."[1]

This statement of Capt. Irwin, who is known to be a just man, bears out the assertion of the poor unfortunate who laid down his life in this city (Montgomery, Ala.) a victim to the inhumanity of man.

The above are examples of what goes on in a greater or less degree in almost every Southern prison. Be it said in justice to the Southern press that every prominent paper is beginning to condemn this horrible mode of treating prisoners.

B. T. Washington

Southern Workman, 15 (Apr. 1886), 47.

[1] The Montgomery *Daily Dispatch* noted on Feb. 18, 1886, that Colonel R. H. Dawson, president of the board of convict inspectors, notified Governor O'Neal in the midst of an inspection of the Smith farm that he found "seven convicts more or less frost bitten, and that one of them, William Smith, of Russell, will probably die." The *Dispatch* commented: "This is a horrible state of facts. It establishes the truth of almost the very last words that the dying convict Alex. Crews said to a *Dispatch* man: 'Are there other convicts as bad off as you are?' 'Oh, yes, boss; some of them are a heap worse.' "

To Cecil Gabbett[1]

[Tuskegee, Ala.] Mar 10th [188]6

Dear Sir: Within the last twelve months there have been not less than 500 trips made over your R.R., including long and short distances, by our students and teachers.

We have paid out for freight brought partly or wholly over your road within the last 12 months $540.00. A part of this was paid by merchants in the town on goods ordered expressly for us. With these facts before you I apply for a pass over your road and not only on the ground stated, but because if the pass is granted, that, during the next twelve months, I can increase the number of passages over your road at least ⅓ and in two years double the number.

I have succeeded in making the school as large as it is by traveling among the people, but am not able to pay out the amount in R.R. fares [in] the future that I have [in] the past. Am sure that you will be repaid many times for granting the pass.

The freights would also be increased. The facts given above I can get reliable citizens of Tuskegee to certify to if necessary. Yours truly

B. T. Washington

HLpS Con. 91 BTW Papers DLC.

[1] General manager of the Western Railway of Alabama.

A Speech by Olivia A. Davidson before the Alabama State Teachers' Association

[Selma, Ala., Apr. 21, 1886]

HOW SHALL WE MAKE
THE WOMEN OF OUR RACE STRONGER?

I feel the honor as well as the responsibility of this opportunity of appearing before this audience to-day. Public speaking is not to my taste. For years past my life has been full of work, but generally in a different direction — at least by different methods, and if I consulted my inclinations I would not be before you to-day, but in view of the vast amount that may be said and done in the direction of the subject, I have chosen, to a convention of teachers who are inquiring for ideas from any source, I may be able to say something at least suggestive.

How shall we make the women of our race stronger physically, morally and intellectually? Many of the ideas that I shall bring before you in my endeavor to find a few answers to this question are not really new, but as far as their application to every day life among our people goes, they are new, in the main. Several years of work in positions that have brought me in close contact with many of the women and girls of the race have brought a deep conviction of the need for them of physical, mental and moral development.

It is true there is no people or class of people whose development in all these directions is perfectly symmetrical, or what it should be in any one of them, but among all people except uncivilized ones, more prominence is given all these phases of development than we are giving them.

First, let us consider how the physical development of one woman can be accomplished: James Freeman Clarke,[1] in his inimitable essay on the training and care of the body,[2] says, "Good health is the basis of all physical, intellectual and moral development. We glorify God with our bodies by keeping them in good health." Mainly because I believe this is true, I have put this part of my subject first.

I think most people would be surprised at the result if a test were in some way given with a view to finding a few perfectly healthy women in any of our communities. Diogenes' search after an honest man was more fruitful of results than this one would be. Why is this? Why are there so many of us miserable invalids either utterly incapable of rendering service in any station or to whom life is a burden, because of the effort of will necessary to be put forth constantly if any thing is accomplished? Nervous and organic diseases have laid tyrannous hands upon us and are leading us helpless captives away from the highest avenues of usefulness into the darker ways of suffering and too often of selfish narrowness, for though a strong, earnest spirit may rise above, and inspire a weak body, generally the weakness of the body will crop the wings and keep the soul from soaring. To answer specifically why this is true is, of course, impossible, but when great and universal evils exist there are usually general causes that can be formulated. First in the list of causes of our physical weakness, I would put the use of stimulants and of tobacco. A large part of the suffering from diseases of various kinds among us comes directly from the use of alcoholic drinks, and all our united influence should be given to deliver ourselves and our afflicted sisters from this frightful wellspring of suffering. The evils that come to us from the use of these drinks are of two kinds — those inherited from intemperate parents and those brought upon ourselves by our own intemperance.

I do not mean to speak here in general of the evils of intemperance, but only of its evil results upon our bodies.

First let us speak of inherited evils. That the sins of the fathers are visited upon the children is no more true anywhere than it is here. The drunken parent destroys or weakens not alone the body God gave him for the temple of his own soul, but transmits to the child a heritage of suffering, perhaps observable in general organic weakness or in fearful deformities or painful diseases. Perhaps the commonest form the inherited evils take is the first — inherited weakness. This is especially true of women whose more delicate organizations are more easily affected. As the child grows to womanhood the weaknesses are developed into diseases by the hardships and exposures incident to such a life as is an outgrowth of the intemperance of the father or the mother.

Teachers, especially you who are in the country, can do much towards mitigating this evil by exerting a strong and aggressive influence against the use of whiskey. By precept and example help the people to the conviction that its use is sapping away their own and their children's strength. Take no part in, and frown upon, the tendency to enter into shameful excesses at the holidays when the farmers have "settled" their accounts, which is often but another way of saying they have gone more deeply in debt for a jug of whiskey.

I have put the use of whiskey first in my list of causes, but now that I begin to think and write of another fruitful source of suffering, I am almost persuaded that it should come first. I refer to the use of tobacco. How sad that any one, least of all, a woman, should defile the beautiful temple, all clean and pure and undefiled when received from God's hands by making it reek with the foul fumes of tobacco! "My Father's house is a house of prayer, but ye have made it a den of thieves." Your soul's house is the rightful temple of God, but ye have made it a den of filth. I can not speak too strongly against one of the commonest forms of the use of tobacco among Southern colored women, and indeed among all classes of Southern women — the use of snuff. Aside from the fact that the habit is a disgusting one, its influence upon the health is most pernicious. No human body can be vigorous and healthy when part of its daily food is tobacco.

Another source of suffering less serious only because less universal, is the use of morphine and similar drugs. This is a surer destroyer of every power of body, mind and soul than any mentioned, and though its victims are now fewer, it is to be feared their number is on the increase. One way of working against this evil is by resisting the administration of morphine in any form by physicians except in cases of extremest suffering, for more harm than good is done the entire system, especially the nervous system, by giving it. The taste formed this way often becomes a confirmed habit impossible to be gotten rid of.

Aside from these particulars, the general manner of living in the homes where most of the colored girls' and women's lives are spent is productive of disease. Go into the miserable shanties and hovels in town or country in which the majority of them live and you have all about you germinators of disease. Insufficiency, if not actual want, is plainly written every where on fire, food and raiment, while the cracks in floor and walls tell their own tale of suffering and exposure. Here mothers and daughters toil from Monday morning till Sunday morning over the wash tub or ironing table or at the sewing machine, as often as necessary benumbing the brain and straining the back by carrying huge baskets of clothes on their heads longer or shorter distances. Added to all this is their general carelessness in the care of themselves arising from their complete ignorance of the laws of health. Some one has said, "Cleanliness is next to Godliness," but I would say that cleanliness is godliness. No soul can be a godly one that willingly inhabits an unclean body or submits to unclean outer surroundings. We can help here by using every opportunity for inspiring in those with whom we come in contact, an ambition to have better homes, and by teaching them in every way possible how to care for their bodies. Here, my sister teachers, is a wide and special field for you. By your own example in dress and daily habits as well as by precepts show them how to clothe and care for themselves according to hygienic laws. In the schoolroom teach physiology and hygiene by general lessons if you don't have the regular text-book work in them.

It is safe to say that three-fourths of the colored women are overworked and under-fed, and are suffering to a greater or less degree from sheer physical exhaustion. The overworking is generally a result of underfeeding, and this is a result of their ignorance of the art of cooking. If ever in their possession, good cooking is a lost art now among the colored women in general of the South. The rations of sodden, unappetizing food that are served three times a day in most families are so many outrages upon those faithful but much abused servants, the digestive organs.

Any school that succeeds in arousing in one of our young women an ambition to become a good cook does God and humanity a noble service.

Seeds of disease and suffering are sown in infancy, childhood and girlhood by mothers, at first, through ignorance of proper methods of caring for their little ones from the time of their birth, and later through carelessness and ignorance in allowing them to go blindly on, ignorant of the laws of life, leaving them to come unshielded by any word of advice or caution to the possession of knowledge, whose possession is vicious in its influence upon health and character only, because its acquirement is made a thing of chance, or which the child feels she must obtain surreptitiously.

I beg the women of this convention to be earnest in their endeavors to shield the young girls in their districts from the fearful sins of ignorance in this direction. Try to make the mothers feel the serious responsibility that rests upon them. Show them in every way you can how to shield their girls from wrong and suffering brought on by pernicious habits.

Let us now turn to the consideration of that part of the question which asks how can we make the women of our race stronger intellectually. I would not have you think, especially you my brother teachers, that we are seeking to find out how we can produce more "strong minded" women as that term is used in its most objectionable sense. Indeed it would require stronger evolutionary force than even Prof. Huxley would dare to advocate to evolve strong-minded women out of [the] mass of intellectually deformed beings who compose the female portion of our race.

Slavery with its offsprings of misery in the form of physical, mental and moral deformity has left its impress upon us, and its influence will be seen in us, for generations to come. It must be [the] work of the earnest reformers among us in each generation to make this influence weaker and to hasten the day when slavery with all its entail will be a thing of the past indeed.

The school room must mainly be the place in which, and the teacher's hand the one by which, the intellectual emancipation of the women of our race is accomplished. It is our privilege to have in hand a large part of the mental development of the colored women of the generations to come directly after us.

Let us see to it that nothing on our part is left undone toward bringing them back to the estate of mental vigor in which God placed them.

We cannot indeed expect them to spring Minerva-like into this estate, from the very grasp of the monster, slavery, but by careful and patient training, they can be brought to it.

In the school room the teacher should aim to make the work such as will best train the girls' mental powers in their fourfold nature. In order to do this, he must himself know what these powers are, and be able to inquire wisely in his study of his pupil what they are capable of, in each individual. In case his previous preparation for his work has not given him this knowledge his first endeavor should be, to fit himself for it by study. John Locke, Froebel, Pestalozzi and many others have in their writings made the way so plain that no earnest seeker can greatly err in finding it.

And here, though it is not exactly within the province of my paper, I want to urge upon the younger teachers in this association the importance of fitting themselves by constant study and reading for their work.

We now come to the part of the subject that is of most vital importance to us as a race or as individuals.

We glorify God with our bodies, by keeping them in good health. We glorify Him in a higher degree by so training and strengthening our mental powers that they will be capable of clear and protracted thought and the direction of wise actions; but above all this we can glorify God by permitting our moral natures to attain their full growth. This is true of all humanity, and it is equally true that all humanity fail to reach full moral growth, but it is especially true of our race, and most especially true of the women among us.

Two hundred years of such training as was given in the school of slavery, was calculated to dwarf the moral nature of its pupils. The disregard of family relations, of personal rights, of the property of others, and hundreds of other outrages upon human rights, from which the slaves were sufferers, or in which they were participants, or of which they were daily witnesses, were not without their influence upon character, and that influence is still strong upon us. This influence is seen in the looseness with which our family relations are regarded to-day, in the weak cry, if any, of the outraged virtue and purity that goes up from among us, when immorality in the form of sins against social or moral laws is found in our midst, in the number of our women who are daily brought before the police courts in our large cities, and [in the] low moral tone that is almost a second nature in the majority of us and gives color to the commonest transactions of our every day life.

Much that has been suggested in this paper as a means to bring about physical and mental health will also obtain here. You cannot succeed in getting a woman to see that she is injuring her health by the use of tobacco or whiskey, or by keeping herself and surroundings in filth, and to be willing to reform in these matters without raising the tone of that woman's moral nature. There are action and reaction here that are equal; and in the case of many doubtless the desire for physical good is the only motive of action you can appeal to successfully. Though something can be done by us by patient and wise effort for the moral uplifting of the more mature women, the young women and girls are the hope of the race, and fortunately it is over them that with wise and Christian effort we can gain our strongest influence. The forces we have to work against are inherent tendencies, home influences, evil associations and in some cases the tendency to devour low literature. Here again their lives are against them. Take the life of the average country girls, in their homes they huddle at night in sleeping rooms with fathers, brothers and often the hired hands; day by day they work beside men in the fields, often untidily and often indecently dressed. All this through the week. Saturday, they come streaming into town to stand about on the streets or in stores and saloons, dip snuff, beg for treats, gossip and listen to, and pass jokes that ought to be insults to any girl or woman in whom there is a spark of womanly modesty. Over all this is thrown an atmosphere of looseness in thought, language and action. Little here to cultivate moral sentiment, but much to blunt it. That we should make any thing but comparatively rapid progress against all this is not to be expected under any circumstances, and if we go into a community and be mere school teachers in the narrowest use of that term, we shall not make any headway against it. It is in this respect — the routine work of the schoolroom forms so small a part of the work of the earnest teacher — that the colored school teachers' lives are peculiar.

We must work outside the school-room, we must see the girls in their homes, make friends with them, be interested in them if we would help them. I have in mind a teacher who went into one of the worst communities. The very atmosphere of the place was immoral. The result of two years' earnest, patient work there on her part was, that in every home in the community, the spirit of improvement was noticeable; and she did it mainly through the girls. She made friends of them, she visited their homes, she organized them into self and home improvement clubs, got them to give up taking snuff, to lay aside the old white cotton wraps and arrange their hair neatly, to wear collars, cuffs and aprons to school, encouraged them to plant flowers in their yards, gave them pictures and papers (supplied by friends whom she had interested in them) for their walls, and so appealed to their pride, and modesty, and self-respect that there was no longer the Saturday Hegira to town, and in [the] majority of the families, separate sleeping apartments were provided. Among the more thoughtful and intelligent she formed a reading club, and read to them or told them about the lives of noble women and other things that would still further arouse their ambition to become good women. What this teacher did we can do and perhaps some of us are doing.

We cannot too seriously consider this question of the moral uplifting of our women for it is of national importance to us. It is with our women that the purity and safety of our families rest, and what our families are the race will be.

Fifth Annual Session of the Alabama State Teachers' Association Held at Selma, Alabama, April 21-24, 1886 (Tuskegee, 1887), 3-8. Copy in A-Ar.

[1] James Freeman Clarke (1810-88) was a New England Unitarian clergyman active in the antislavery, temperance, and woman suffrage movements. He authored several books on religious topics.

[2] *Self-Culture: Physical, Intellectual, Moral and Spiritual, a Course of Lectures* (Boston, 1880). The passages Olivia Davidson presented were paraphrased from p. 54 of this work.

A Recommendation from S. Griffitts Morgan[1]

New Bedford   July 7th 1886

The Bearer of this Mr. Booker T. Washington, Principal of the Tuskegee (Alabama) Normal School again visits New Bedford to call upon those interested in the education of the Colored people of the South. I have known Mr. Washington for a number of years, first as a student under Genl Armstrong at Hampton Va & since as the founder & successful chief manager of the Tuskegee Normal School.

I gladly vouch for Mr. Washington, as a gentleman of high respectability, integrity & intelligence & would kindly solicit sympathy for his cause.

S. Griffitts Morgan

ALS   Con. 16   BTW Papers   DLC.

[1] S. Griffitts Morgan, listed in the 1880 census as sixty-three years old, was a New Bedford merchant and philanthropist. He gave scholarships to both Hampton and Tuskegee. His contributions to Hampton in 1872-75 paid for BTW's tuition. BTW visited him in 1882 and several times later in the interest of Tuskegee.

The Announcement of the Wedding of BTW and Olivia A. Davidson

[Athens, Ohio, Aug. 11, 1886]

Marriage Ceremony
at
Residence of Bride's sister,
Mrs Dr Noah Elliott[1]
Athens, Ohio,
Wednesday afternoon, Aug. eleventh
at four o'clock.
Booker T. Washington   Olivia A. Davidson.
1886.

PD   File XT5   Framingham State Normal School Manuscripts   MH.

[1] Mary A. (Mrs. Noah) Elliott was the sister of Olivia A. Davidson Washington.

In the 1880 census she was reported as a mulatto thirty-eight years old. Her husband, a black man aged forty-eight, was a physician born in Kentucky. In 1880 they lived in Albany, Ohio, but later moved to Athens and then to Columbus, where she established a millinery store. Very fond of her sister, she continued to take an interest in all of the Washington children.

To William Hooper Councill[1]

[Tuskegee, Ala.] Sept 9 [188]6

Dear Prof. Councill: I write to say that Robert Langston[2] of Montgom[er]y was expelled from this institution for being guilty of very bad acts. He also owes our school a bill of $19. which has run for more than a year. It is needless for me to say what I think your duty is in the matter for the precedents for action in such cases are too well established in all institutions of standing. Viewing Langston as an individual I would not seek to deprive him of any opportunity for improvement, but we as a race *can not* afford to be slack in such matters. This you have often emphasized. I write of course supposing that you are ignorant of the fact that he has ever attended this school. This is the first time that I have had occasion to correspond with you regarding such a matter but it has always been a custom between Talladega, Marion and other institutions and Tuskegee, to take in no student suspended or expelled from the other institution and I suppose you have the same understanding.

I am glad to see that you have had a prosperous beginning. The "Index"[3] I am always glad to see and always read it through.

Should be glad to be remembered to your teachers. Yours sincerely

B. T. Washington

ALpS Con. 91 BTW Papers DLC.

[1] William Hooper Councill (1848-1909) was born a slave in Fayetteville, N.C., and taken to Alabama by slave traders in 1857. He attended a school opened by northerners at Stevenson, Ala., in 1865, remaining there until 1867, when he began teaching. During Reconstruction he held minor political positions in Alabama, taught for a time at Morris Brown College in Atlanta, and edited a newspaper in Huntsville, Ala. He served as secretary of the 1873 National Equal Rights convention. In 1876 he was appointed to head the new Alabama Agricultural and Mechanical College in Huntsville after he had thrown his political support to conservatives. As president of Alabama A & M, Councill often came into con-

tact with BTW, a relationship that became more of a rivalry as they competed for favors and funds from the Alabama legislature and northern philanthropists. In 1887 Councill attracted wide attention when he complained to the Interstate Commerce Commission of harsh treatment on an Alabama railroad, an action that prompted his superiors to relieve him of his duties as president of Alabama A & M for one year. The experience may have helped alter his position on the proper role for a black man to play in the South, for after that he advocated accommodation and acceptance of second-class citizenship to the point that one historian has spoken of his "unctuous sycophancy," and that prompted BTW to characterize him as "simply toadying to white people." (Meier, *Negro Thought in America, 1880-1915*, 77, 110.) Under his leadership the school at Huntsville became second only to Tuskegee in size among Alabama Negro industrial schools. According to Horace Mann Bond, Councill "was plainly an adroit and shrewd student of the foibles and prejudices of his white contemporaries, and bent his educational and public career to take best advantage of the susceptibilities of his masters." (Bond, *Negro Education in Alabama*, 204.) Councill combined his accommodationist position with an advocacy of racial solidarity and self-help and support for the redemption of Africa, even aiding Bishop Turner's emigrationist movement. An A.M.E. minister and learned enough in the law to be admitted to practice before the Alabama Supreme Court, Councill published widely in newspapers and journals and wrote an early history of Negroes, *Lamp of Wisdom, or Race History Illuminated* (1898).

² Robert L. Langston entered the preparatory class in 1883 and returned for the 1884-85 school year.

³ Presumably a newsletter published by the Alabama Agricultural and Mechanical College.

A Speech before the Unitarian National Conference[1]

Saratoga, New York, Sept. 21 1886

OUR OPPORTUNITY THROUGH THE SOUTH

The opportunities in the South are so many and varied that it is difficult to attempt to point out the direction in which most good can be done. But on one point all will readily agree: there is no lack of opportunities to give and all will agree too that there is help that *helps* and help that does *not help*. When our good Unitarian friends take it for granted that every one hailing from the South clothed in a black skin or in a white skin claiming Northern charity by virtue of his being a Negro or being connected with some Negro educational or religious enterprise, presents an opportunity through which to aid the South they help in a way that *does not help*. Now I claim that we are entitled to nothing either good or bad because we are black men. We deserve and claim help because we have been unfortunate just as the Irishman or Italian ask help when unfortunate.

American Unitarians whose good seed for the last twenty years have been scattered far and wide through the South, not a little we fear by the wayside, some upon stony places, some among thorns, have made the supply so constant and generous that much has fallen on good ground and brought forth "some an hundred fold." This body to my mind is to be congratulated especially on the fact that within the last year it has organized the department of "Southern and Indian Education work" headed

.   .   .   .[2]

something the white man wants whether this something be of brains or of material. Let there be in a community a Negro farmer who by virtue of superior knowledge of the chemistry of the soil, his acquaintance with the most improved tools and best breeds of stock, can raise fifty bushels of corn to the acre while his white neighbor only raises thirty and the white man will come to the black man to learn — furthermore they will sit down in the same rail road coach and on the same seat to talk about it.

When the Tuskegee Normal School was first opened some of the county whites were opposed to the establishment of a Negro Normal School in their Midst. It happened that there was no brick yard in [the] community. Merchants and farmers wanted to build but bricks must be brought from a distance or they must wait for one house to burn down before building another. The Normal School with student labor started a brick yard. The whites came from miles around to buy bricks. From examining bricks they were led to examine the working of the school. From the discussion of the brick yard came the discussion of Negro Education and thus many of the "old masters" have been led to see and become interested in Negro Education. We must hasten the time when it will not surprise one to meet successful colored architects, master builders, owners of printing establishments, brick makers, mechanics, planters and manufacturers of all kinds. I am praying and working very hard for the time to come when a colored man enters the office of a Boston Manufacturer he, the manufacturer, will have to debate the question in his mind for at least a moment whether his visitor comes as a solicitor of charity or to buy a thousand dollars worth of goods.

My people at the South want to be taught every day practical religion rather than religious dogmas and abstruse doctrine — that it is better to be a Christian man a Methodist or Baptist to save a soul than subscribe to a creed. While I have great faith in mental and religious training yet I confess I have learned by experience to have but little faith in the religious honesty of a man who goes to bed night after night hungry.

At the Tuskegee Normal School, and here I wish it understood that I speak of the T.N.S. only as representing the kind of work done by members of other Southern institutions,[3] in Alabama we have this year an attendance of 260 young men and women from various parts of the south and while we do all in our power to give them the best mental and moral training at the same time we give special attention to industrial training for we believe that this is the best moral training. On our large farm, in the blacksmith shop, at the brick yard and saw mill, in the printing office, in the girls sewing room, laundry and cooking class, we seek to furnish the student with paying labor to enable him to partly work his way through school, to teach the dignity of labor and self-help, then to teach trades and furnish him with practi[ca]ble business-like ideas of how to make a living, so that after their graduation they can go as teachers in the [. . .[4]] & onto the large plantations — and I would here remark that one, to get a true idea of the poverty, ignorance and superstition — the terrible crime of slavery, the enormity of the work yet to be done for the Negro before he will cease to be a dangerous factor in our republic, should leave the towns and rail roads and go miles out into the country on the large plantations where the majority of the colored people are to be found. It is to this class that the Tuskegee Normal School seeks to send teachers, educated mechanics and farmers. The whites as a rule have left these plantations, leaving the masses of ignorant blacks with neither guides nor examples except those furnished by the preachers (Story) and incompetent teachers. In Alabama the schools on these plantations are in session on an average 67 days in the year and the teachers receive an average salary of $22. per month while a comfortable school house is a curiosity. The people are in this miserable condition not beca[u]se they do not work. As a rule the race works. We know we often hear the opposite stated but usually by some white man lounging around under a shade tree whittling sticks and we know too that like all races we have some black sheep in ours, but [it] is unfair to judge us by our worst. The trouble is the Negroes do not know what to do with the results of their labor. The cursed mortgage and rent systems rob them of nearly half their earnings.

What is the remedy and where does the best opportunity for aid present itself? I have in mind a young lady who graduated from our school a year ago. She went into a community to teach where everything was just as dark and discouraging as anything I have mentioned. She began her work by calling weekly meetings of the parents. In these meetings she told them how to stop mortgaging their crops, how to buy land and how to put their money into the education of their children instead of spending it for whiskey and snuff. The result of that teacher's years work is that those people built and paid for a neat comfortable school house and instead of letting the school stop when the usual public term of three months expired, they came together and paid enough themselves to extend the term to four months and this year they will have five months. Not till every community gets a teacher like this one can there be rest or letting up in this work. The Tuskegee school could be educating fifty or a hundred more such teachers to day if it were sure that a $50. scholarship to pay for the education of each one would be forthcoming. During the five years existance of the school it has sent out fifteen graduates besides nearly ~~a hundred~~ fifty[5] undergraduates with willing heads, hands and hearts who are doing the same kind of work that the young lady referred to is doing. To my mind the sending out of such workers as these through the south is the only solution of the "Negro Problem." To aid in sending them out not only from Tuskegee but from other worthy institutions in the south in my mind presents the great opportunity for work to this Christian body.

Few will deny that the opportunity for the wisest and most effective work is presented where the work can be done in cooperation with the state Public School authorities when this can be done without sacrifice of manhood or principle. We have a striking example of this in the grand and effective work of Dr. A. D. Mayo in his "Ministry of Education." One of the most encouraging signs in the southern field lies in the fact that the Southern whites are beginning more and more every year to feel their responsibility in the matter of helping up the Negro. Alabama appropriates cheerfully, every year $3000 to aid in s[u]pporting the Tuskegee Normal School. This term there are three students in our school whose personal expenses are being paid by southern white men. After attending our Commencement exercises last May, a wealthy southern planter came to me and said that if he could secure one of the graduates to open a school on his plantation, he would build him a comfortable school house and pay a part of his salary and the promise has been kept. The fact is for a number of years after freedom the southern whites thought that as soon as the Negro was educated he would become too proud to work. Now that they are seeing that when the Negro is properly educated, the reverse of this is true they are beginning to help more cheerfully. Then the great business success of individual colored men is teaching them that if the Negro is turned loose in the race of life with an even start with the representatives of other members of the human family and the devil is told to catch the hindmost he will not catch a Negro every time.

(Douglas Story)

In conclusion I can not refrain from adding that there is opportunity by forethought and generosity to save from worry, over-work, anxiety and untimely death and to save to the southern work such wise, whole-souled, and self-sacrificing workers as Gen. S. C. Armstrong.

Through all these avenues we have an opportunity of doing a work that will *"pay"* now in this life a hundred fold and in the world to come "eternal life"!

HDf   Edith Washington Shehee Collection   ATT.

[1] Reports in *The Unitarian* of the Unitarian National Conference, held Sept. 20-25, indicated that more than 2,000 persons were in attendance.

[2] Pages 3-7 of the original manuscript are missing. A condensation of this speech appeared in the *Official Report of the Proceedings of the Twelfth Meeting of the National Conference of Unitarian and Other Christian Churches* (New York, 1886), 224-26. The pages missing here were condensed as follows:

"The most striking need of the negro in the South will suggest the opportunities for help. The negro needs help in making the white people in the South know and respect him as a man.

"The same mistake is made in regard to the negro that is made in regard to other unfortunate races. It has been clearly demonstrated that those living nearest the Indian, with opportunities for knowing the most about him, really know the least about him. For years, the frontiersmen said that the Indian had only a wild side. They put him down as an untamable savage. The trouble is that the white people do not come in contact with the black man in the way of knowing him in the highest sense. The white people know the colored people as servants, cooks, waiters, or they are known as loafers and chicken thieves. An eminent Southern senator said in the United States Senate, some time ago, that, although in the last twenty years private and public aid had been lavished upon the negro, yet during that period he made no perceptible progress. If an investigation were made, it would be found that that man had never spent an hour in a colored school-house and had never entered the home of an educated negro. If a colored man gets into a fight, or steals a chicken, or does anything of that kind, it appears in the papers in glaring head-lines. If he buys a hundred acres of land or builds a home, or his son graduates from a school, it is not mentioned.

"Against these comments of the senator, I put the remarks of Dr. [Atticus Greene] Haygood, who knows more about the negro than any other man in this country. He says that the progress of the negro in the United States during the last twenty years is one of the marvels of history.

"My point is this: that negroes will never be known and respected as men until their business side, as well as the mental and religious side, is developed. The best thing to do in regard to civil rights bills, and bills of like intent, in the South, is to let them alone, and throw our force to making a business man of the negro. I find that our Southern people are much like people elsewhere. Harmony between the two races will come in proportion as the black man gets something that the white man wants."

[3] The clause set off by commas was inserted in BTW's hand.

[4] The phrase beginning "in the . . . " was inserted in BTW's hand and is not completely decipherable.

[5] BTW deleted "a hundred" and inserted "fifty."

To Anderson Bryant[1]

[Tuskegee, Ala.] Nov. 4 [188]6

Dear Sir: In regard to the two boys who came this week I would say that I understood from your letter and from Mr. Lewis that it was your object to have them enter the regular day school — not night school. Now they both say that you desire them to work in the day and attend school at night.

It is against our rule to take students in as work students unless they are 18 years old and against our rule to take them in school at all unless they are at least 14, the small is only 13 he says.

This is the best I can do, I will take the older one in as a work student and allow him to learn the carpenter's trade. The younger one will have to attend day school. This will cost you about $6 per month.

This arrangement I hope will suit you since it is the best we can do and we have broken our rules in both cases in order to let them remain. Yours &c.

B. T. Washington

ALpS Con. 91 BTW Papers DLC.

[1] Anderson Bryant was a black man living in Union and later in Lumpkin, Ga. The elder of the two boys he sent to Tuskegee in 1886 was Shepherd L. Harris, his

nephew. Harris remained at Tuskegee for three years but did not graduate. He died in Togo, West Africa, in 1902, as a member of the Tuskegee expedition to raise cotton there. It is probable that Aaron Harris and Daniel A. Harris, who entered Tuskegee's night school in 1884 and remained for four and three years respectively, were Shepherd Harris's brothers. The thirteen-year-old boy mentioned by Bryant was probably Henry P. Clayton, who entered the day school in 1886 but did not return in 1887. (See J. T. Harrison for Anderson Bryant to BTW, June 4, 1903, Con. 264, BTW Papers, DLC.)

From Hiram R. Davidson[1]

Idiotic Asylum   Columbus Ohio   Nov 4th 1886

Dear Brother. I received your letter some days ago, but did not get time to ancer it. Mother[2] got a letter from Mary[3] last week stating that Emma[4] had got her boxes. her PO address is Cincinnati Ohio. I was not aware that Ollie[5] was in B.[6] have not had a letter from her since you left W.va. you said in your letter that you contemplated puting in watter works. I send you with this mail some papers treating on sanitary water suply, which may be of use to you. Mother and Matt[7] bouth send their love. hoping that you are all well, I am yours very truly

H. R. Davidson

ALS   Con. 84   BTW Papers   DLC.

[1] Hiram R. Davidson, Olivia Davidson Washington's brother. It is not clear whether he was an inmate or an employee of the asylum in Columbus. According to a letter from his sister, Mary A. Elliott, to BTW on Dec. 9, 1892: "Is it possible that Hiram written to you. I am glad poor Hiram he is to be pitied, more than censured poor brother." (Con. 17, BTW Papers, DLC.)

[2] Eliza Davidson, the mother of Olivia Davidson Washington, was a slave in Tazewell County, Va., probably born in the early 1820s. Escaping with several children during the Civil War, she became the cook of the Union general George A. Custer and remained for a time after the war as a Custer family servant before moving to Ashtabula and later to Albany, Ohio.

[3] Mary A. Davidson Elliott.

[4] Presumably not a member of the Davidson family. The 1870 census listed no person named Emma in the household.

[5] Olivia A. Davidson Washington.

[6] Boston.

[7] Probably Martha L. Davidson, sister of Hiram and Olivia, born in 1856 or 1857.

To [Abby E. Cleaveland]

Tuskegee, Ala. Nov. 5th 1886

Dear Miss ———— Your annual letter came to-day. I have only time for a very short letter. November seems the busiest month in the year. We are always glad to hear from you in this way, and I have said to outsiders more than once that I think much of Hampton's value and popularity is in the fact that it follows its graduates with so much interest.

Your allusion to General Armstrong is touching and inspiring; touching because he seems like a father to us — in fact is one; inspiring because no one can even think of what he has done for the race without feeling that we ought to renew our efforts to help ourselves.

At present our attendance is 256 and there is scarcely a day that new students do not come. This number does not include those in our "Butler" school.

Mrs. W. is now in Boston in the interest of the school for a few weeks. There are 14 Hamptonians here now — 20 teachers in all.

Would love to write more if I had time.

All send love. Yours sincerely

B. T. Washington

Southern Workman, 15 (Dec. 1886), 125. The presumption that the recipient was Abby E. Cleaveland rests on the fact that she handled the Hampton Institute's correspondence with graduates from 1881 to 1894.

To James Fowle Baldwin Marshall

[Tuskegee, Ala.] Nov. 9 [188]6

Dear Gen'l Marshall: At the time we made the agreement with Mr. Liddell[1] of Montgomery to purchase the engine & boiler we were not sure what the cost of the other part of the out fit would be nor how our money would hold out so we arranged to pay him $500 cash and the remainder $647, Jan. 1st 87. In fitting up the saw-mill the following amt's have been paid out:

Saw Mill and Log wagons $320.00

Labor — (out side)   53.70

Freight   61.90

Lumber, board of engineer,

     etc.   65.34

Fixtures   148.10

We deferred the payment till Jan 1st because we did not want to be cramped for cash with which to get the proper out-fit to start the mill. We shall be able to meet the terms of the agreement although you see we only have a little over $400 left with which to do it, but we are realizing something now regularly from the sale of lumber &c. We have just taken a contract to furnish the lumber and build a two room house for a gentleman for $300. At the soonest time practicable we shall add the planer &c.

The above items only include cash out lays and do not include student work &c. nor oxen &c. purchased to draw logs, these being charged to farm. The saw-mill is proving a satisfactory addition to our industries and as we gain more experience in the matter it is going to be still more so. Already the out side demand for lumber is so great that we find it hard to keep enough on hand for our own use.

I am very glad to hear that Mrs. Marshall is better and hope you are well. We are running over with students. Second handed clothing are in great demand with us this term.

All send love. Yours faithfully

Booker T. Washington

ALpS Con. 91 BTW Papers DLC.

[1] Forbes Liddell, founder and president of Forbes Liddell Company in Montgomery, Ala., did business with Tuskegee Institute, selling sawmill machinery, engines, and taking special orders.

From William Edward Vasser[1]

Athens Ala. Dec 19th 1886

My dear Sirs — Please write me at your earliest convenience answers to the following questions. When was the Tuskegee Normal established. How many graduates has it turned out? How many of them teach in the state and how many have failed to teach the required terms of years? What is the school property worth, and what is the estimated cost of running the school including salaries, repairs, insurance, &c, &c? I need this information to enable me properly to meet the attack which is now being made on the schools, both by a portion of the press and a dangerous minority in the Legislature. I have, sir, the honor to be   Your obedient servant,

Wm E. Vasser

ALS Con. 84 BTW Papers DLC.

¹ William Edward Vasser, a farmer near Athens, Ala., served one term in the Alabama House of Representatives in 1886-87. He was chairman of the House Committee on Education.

To William Edward Vasser

[Tuskegee, Ala.] Dec. 22 [188]6

Dear Sir: Replying to yours of the 18th inst asking information about our State Normal School, I would say that the school is now in the 6th year of its existence being established by act of the legislature passed in 1880 and the school was opened July 4th 1881. Our course of study embraces 4 years consequently we have graduated but two classes. The first class was composed of 10 members and the 2nd of 5 — 15 in all and I am glad to say to you that every one is now teaching in the public schools of the State and have been teaching ever since they graduated. Our present senior class which graduates next May is composed of 20 members and each one expects to teach in the State.

Besides the graduates I am pleased to say to you that 64 of our under graduates have taught or are now teaching in the State. While these have not completed the course of study they have been enough benefitted by their attendance here, to make a marked improvement in the work they do as teachers.

I feel that I am safe in saying that 90% of our students expect to make teaching a profession — their life work.

At present we have 271[?] students in school. We admit none till they are 15 years old. In our training school where the Normal School students receive practical lessons in teaching we have 125 pupils. The school property is estimated to be worth $60,000.

The cost of running the school including salaries, repairs, insurance &c. is $15,000 (about) a year.

By this mail I send you our last year's catalogue which will give you some more information.

It is my intention to be in the vicinity of Athens within a few days and I shall call to see you and speak about some other matters not mentioned in this letter. Very Sincerely & Gratefully yours

B. T. Washington

ALpS   Con. 91   BTW Papers   DLC.

From John W. Stakely[1]

Inverness, Ala., Jan. 3, 1887

Dear Principal: I cannot hear anything from you. What can be the matter? I wrote you, as I thought, a very important letter, desiring to hear from you, but cannot hear a thing from you. I am getting along very nicely with my work, considering the very hard times and scarcity of money. Think I have succeeded in getting the Public to run my school 5 months. I have beaten two white men out, who have been robbing the township for at least six years, claiming to have had so many transfers when they did not. You ought to have seen how I had them trembling. Prof. I mean to have what I work for. The eyes of the colored teachers of Bullock County have been open by the operation. I can ruin the Trustees and County Superintendent If I would. Think I shall do it. The colored teachers of the State shall always be chiseled if there is not a stop put to just such actions. Miss Mary Hendor has almost been cheated out of $60. Prof. owing to so much sickness in our family, I cannot possibly settle Elnora's[2] board bill. My little brother has been under Medical treatment for at least 3 months; and I am responsible for its payment. Though I shall settle for half of it next month; and the remainder at the expiration of this quarter. The people all seem to be very much pleased at the progress of their children and the manner which I conduct the school. Shall feel very grateful to you for all of the reading-matter which you may send. Remember me kindly to all of the teachers. Truly Yours,

J. W. Stakely

ALS Con. 86 BTW Papers DLC.

¹ John W. Stakely, a native of Cotton Valley in Macon County, graduated from Tuskegee in 1885 and after teaching at Union Springs moved to Mitchell's Station near Inverness. Stakely often wrote BTW boasting of his ability, achievements, and hopes; but his career never matched his expectations.

² Elnora Stakely, listed in the Tuskegee catalog of 1885-86 as a resident of Montgomery, was in the preparatory class. She perhaps dropped out of Tuskegee after 1886 because of financial reasons, and John W. Stakely, presumably her brother, was attempting to pay her board bill.

From William B. Paterson[1]

Marion, Ala., Jan 5, 1887

Dear Friend Washington, I have been so busy and also sick that I do not know whether I answered your kind letter or not.

The real facts are that twenty to thirty of the Howard Cadets[2] surrounded *one* of our students, because he would not get off the sidewalk to let them pass. They clubbed him and would have killed him but for his agility and bravery. He defended himself heroically and no one knowing the truth can blame him.

A petition is now being circulated by the trustees of Howard College to abolish or remove our School. We are neither scared nor hurt yet, and will hold the fort.

There was great excitement for a few days, and we were prepared to repel an attack by Howard boys.

Our people are talking very independently, and I am sure that good will come out of it. This question of self-defence must be settled and the sooner the better. An educated man will not and can not take the abuse that an ignorant one will. We are all in good health and spirits. It reminds me of fifteen years ago, and stirs up my desire to do more for your people.

Remember me kindly to all. Yours sincerely

Wm B Paterson

I had a letter from Gen Marshall relating to Council.[3] I told the *truth* as far as I knew.

ALS   Con. 86   BTW Papers   DLC.

[1] William B. Paterson, president of the Alabama State University for Colored Students at Marion, Ala., also called the Lincoln Normal University (est. 1872?). In the summer of 1887 the Colored University (as it was popularly called) was moved to Montgomery, where its name was eventually changed to Alabama State College. As a white man, a racial moderate, and an advocate of industrial education, Paterson had both advantages and disadvantages in dealing with state officials, the black community, and the philanthropists of the Peabody and Slater funds. BTW felt a keen rivalry with Paterson and sought to protect Tuskegee's constituency from the challenge of another Negro school only 40 miles away. His name was frequently misspelled with a double *t*. This error will not be corrected or noted further.

[2] Howard College, founded in 1841 at Marion, Ala., was a white Baptist school. Tradition has it that the school was named for an Englishman, John Howard, who died in 1790 after an active career as a prison reformer. With only 108 students, the college was suffering by 1885 from lack of endowment and from competition for students with other schools in the area. The trustees, meeting at the Baptist convention of 1886 in Birmingham, proposed that the school be removed to Birmingham, where it stood a better chance in the booming economy of the "Pittsburgh of the South." A controversy raged for more than a year between advocates of removal and those who wanted the school to remain at Marion. The feud almost caused a factional split in the Baptist churches of the state. Howard College was finally removed to Birmingham in 1887, the same year that Paterson's school was removed to Montgomery. Col. J. T. Murfee, long-time president of Howard, remained at Marion and established the Marion Military Institute in 1888. In 1965 Howard College became Samford University. (Garrett, *Sixty Years of Howard College, 1842-1902*.)

[3] William Hooper Councill.

From Henry Woodfin Grady[1]

Atlanta Ga. Jany 10th 1887

Dear sir; What I said about the colored race in my speech at New York[2] was said in sincerity, and from the depths of a heart grateful to them for their honorable conduct during the war. There need be no hostility either of action or sentiment between the white and colored people in the south. Their interests are identical, and they should be friends in the best sense of the word. I am sure that when there is a

full understanding betwe[e]n them, there can be nothing but friendship. Yours very truly,

H. W. Grady

TLS   Con. 86   BTW Papers   DLC. Also in Montgomery *Advertiser,* Jan. 15,
1887, 5.

[1] Henry Woodfin Grady (1850-89), the leading spokesman of the New South,
was the son of a prominent Athens, Ga., merchant. After graduation from the
University of Georgia in 1868 and a year studying law at the University of Virginia, he turned to a journalistic career. All through the 1870s he worked for
several Georgia newspapers and as Georgia correspondent for several northern
papers. In 1876 he joined the staff of the Atlanta *Constitution;* four years later he
bought a quarter-share of the paper and became its editor. Through editorials and
frequent public speeches he came to symbolize the spirit of the New South. Grady
died suddenly of pneumonia at the age of thirty-nine. BTW's public professions of
optimism about the progress and racial justice of the South made him in many
respects a black counterpart of Grady. BTW later paid warm tribute to "our
beloved Grady" as a spiritual father of the Atlanta Compromise address. (BTW
letter to the editor, New York *World,* Sept. 20, 1895, 2).

[2] Grady said in his speech: "The relations of the southern people with the
negro are close and cordial. We remember with what fidelity for four years he
guarded our defenseless women and children, whose husbands and fathers were
fighting against his freedom. To his eternal credit be it said that whenever he struck
a blow for his own liberty he fought in open battle, and when at last he raised his
black and humble hands that the shackles might be struck off, those hands were
innocent of wrong against his helpless charges, and worthy to be taken in loving
grasp by every man who honors loyalty and devotion. Ruffians have maltreated
him, rascals have misled him, philanthropists established a bank for him, but the
South, with the North, protests against injustice to this simple and sincere people.
To liberty and enfranchisement is as far as law can carry the negro. The rest must
be left to conscience and common sense." (Nixon, *Henry W. Grady: Spokesman of
the New South,* 346-47.)

From Cornelius Nathaniel Dorsette

Montgomery, Ala. 1/11 1886 [1887][1]

Dear Prof. I happened by accident to have an interview with one of
Marion School Prof of Col. who was here yesterday trying to work up
the interest of the school. He gave me in detail how the troubles occurred (while riding with me) and says the school is compelled to be
removed and their intention is to locate it in Montg. I of course took
side with him & got what little he knew regarding it. He wants Montg

321

Col. people to offer some induc[e]ment in money to get it saying that Birmingham wants it also & will make a good offer for it. He knew nothing definite & seemed to be over merely on a feeling visit to see what sentiment existed. Now you may hear of my support &c but please understand me it's simply to be able to keep you posted as to their movements &c. You know I am with & for Tuskegee first second & last, and always shall be.

If I learn anything definite as to their action I will write you. He has promised to keep me posted in the matter. Very truly yours

C. N. D.

ALI Con. 99 BTW Papers DLC.

[1] Dorsette wrote 1886, but internal evidence concerning the Marion school dates the letter as of 1887.

From Mary Clarke Shannon[1]

Newton [Mass.] Jany. 11th 1887

Mr. & Mrs. Washington, Enclosed please find our little donation of Ten dollars each to your valuable Institution, also One dollar for The Southern Letter, making Twenty One dollars in all, from Mary C. and Mary Shannon, Newton, Mass.

It was with great pleasure we read your marriage in the paper. The union of two such noble souls engaged in the *same glorious cause,* cannot but be a *mutual* help, and kindle afresh your inspiration in your arduous duties. We are glad we have looked into *both* your *faces,* Mr. Washington, at our cottage at Bar Harbor, and Mrs. Washington at our Newton Home. You have our best wishes for your *happiness,* and *prosperity* in all your undertakings.

We are pleased that you have Miss Mayo[2] in your Institution, for her *influence* over the pupils, must be of the *highest* type. We have known Miss Mayo for many years, and truly appreciate her fine character, and lofty aims to elevate her race.

We were delighted to read that Genl. Armstrong is to visit you at Tuskegee; he cannot but be proud of his *offspring* of Hampton, Va. His presence in the midst of your pupils will be perfectly electrifying, something that I should enjoy witnessing. Do make the Genl. careful of his health, for we need his *power,* and influence for many years. Please remember us kindly to Miss Mayo, and believe us, Your True friends,

Mary C. Shannon

Please acknowledge receipt of check by postal. M. S.

ALS Con. 88 BTW Papers DLC.

[1] Mary Clarke Shannon, a friend of Negro education, was for forty years, prior to her death in 1887, a resident of Newton, Mass. She lived on an estate with her niece, Mary Shannon.

[2] Lovey A. Mayo, born in Raleigh, N.C., in 1860 and a graduate of Hampton Institute in 1880, taught for five years in the Indian department at Hampton before joining the Tuskegee staff in 1886 as matron. She also took charge of Tuskegee's missionary work. She left Tuskegee in 1888 because of ill health and returned to Raleigh, where she taught and did temperance and church work.

From John C. Leftwich[1]

Selma Ala. Jan 17th 1887

Dear Sir. I am desiring to attend your School at once. I want to come at once. I have been going to School here at Selma, but it dont agree with me here, and I want to come to Tuskeegee at once, my home is at Forkland ala, and if I come I can get great many to attend from Forkland. But Sir I am a poor student no one to help me, but I am willing to work, and help or pay my board. I hope sir you will take pity on me and see if you can find a place where I can work every evening and stay in School. I am willing to work and I am not a shame to work and also let me know what time can I graduate I am now finishing up higher Algebra geometry Xenophon Caesar & geology. I have finish Chemistry and Ancient History.

Please let me know at once. I want to come at once. Yours

J. C. Leftwich

ALS Con. 89 BTW Papers DLC.

[1] John C. Leftwich did not attend Tuskegee Institute. In 1899 he founded an all-black town, Klondike, Ala., eight miles southwest of Montgomery. An advocate of black self-help and economic uplift, he spoke at the National Negro Business League in Boston in 1900. He described in glowing terms the future of the black man in the South: "When colored merchants will be doing a prosperous business

in every city and every town; when colored banks shall groan with Negro deposits; when colored men and women shall astonish the world with law, logic, and ability; when we shall have thousands of colored doctors who can cure and kill as quick as any doctors of other races; come and see seven millions of colored people rise up every day and slay the forests like a mighty army; come and see them around the whirring spindles, see them with the ploughs and hoes in the tranquil valleys of white and golden harvests; come and see their thousands of cattle on hundreds of hills; come and see their happy homes, their water still and pastures green, with wealth in their hands and their poorhouses empty. . . ." (National Negro Business League, *Proceedings, 1900,* 119.) In 1903 he lived in Oklahoma City. Like many southern blacks, he hoped that new opportunities for blacks would be possible in Oklahoma Territory. This hope was blasted in the decade that followed.

From George Mellen Prentiss King[1]

Washington, D.C., Jan 18. 1887

Dear Bro. Washington: "The Southern Letter" tells me a little about you, but not as much as I wish to know. This is my excuse for writing: I hope to provoke a good long letter from you. Your progress in the great work which you are doing seems wonderful: it is no more than might have been expected from your practical good sense and natural push. Accept congratulations, and tell me all about yourself.

You will be glad to know that we are full and enjoying the year's work very much. We have 150 students thus far this year. Now and then I grow impatient with our slow progress and want to invent some way to go faster. Do your students ever trouble you with their slowness? Some of our students are *the do tomorrow* sort of mortals.

I hear from Deans and Berger occasionally. The former married an uneducated country young lady who took him to her home. The latter is in Texas.

You are happy in having a wife to help you in the work of the year. Please to introduce me to Mrs. Washington. Best wishes. Yours Truly

G. M. P. King

ALS Con. 118 BTW Papers DLC.

[1] George Mellen Prentiss King (1833-1917), a white Baptist minister and president of Wayland Seminary and College in Washington, D.C., influenced BTW in his youth. BTW, who spent between six months and a year at Wayland after graduation from Hampton, attributed his later ability in public speaking to the

training in English and elocution he received from G. M. P. King. During the Civil War King worked for the U.S. Christian Commission. In 1867 he became principal of the National Theological Institute in Washington, and when the institute became part of Wayland Seminary in 1869, King was appointed Wayland's president. King retired in 1897, but he had no pension and was forced to return to teaching in 1899 at Virginia Union University in Richmond, a school formed that year by a combination of Wayland and Richmond Theological Seminary. He continued as a professor of English language and literature at Virginia Union until his death.

From Jesse C. Duke[1]

Montgomery, Ala. Jan 20th 1887

Yours Recd. I have had quite a hard time since you was here, about this thing. Paterson has gone around here among his friends, and set up a clamor for the school. The report has also been circulated that Dr Dorsette and Mr Bedford told Mr Paterson that the congregation church[2] reflected colored sentiment here I dont believe they said so, because I believe both are to sensable to have told Paterson that knowing that he is a Baptist. Wm Watkins,[3] Sam Phillips;[4] The Jenken family the Loveless[5] and many others of lesser influence are very much worked up on the matter, Phillips and Watkins particularly, they have been to see me and has demanded that I take up the subject and discuss it. I absolutely refuse to do so, I spent all day Sunday trying to convince them that the school would not be move here, and that it was foolishness to try to get it, but that it was probable for us to get our own school and that it was our duty to get that here &c. Mr McEwen,[6] wanted to take up the fight for the Marion School and said that I was being accused of being bought off by you &c. Yours

J. C. Duke

ALS Con. 85 BTW Papers DLC.

[1] Jesse C. Duke was reported in the 1880 census as a twenty-seven-year-old grocer in Selma, Ala. In 1887, as editor of the Montgomery *Herald,* a black newspaper, he represented BTW's interests in discouraging the removal of William B. Paterson's Marion school to Montgomery. In mid-course Duke shifted his position and became active in a committee of black citizens favoring removal to Montgomery.

During the summer of 1887 a keen rivalry developed between Montgomery and Birmingham over where the black school should be located. In July, Montgomery made the best offer, including a $5,000 subscription to be raised by black citizens, and it was agreed that the school would be moved to a predominantly black suburban area of Montgomery. In early August, at the height of the interest in the Colored University, Duke wrote an editorial in his paper attacking lynching. He suggested that some so-called rapes of white women were not rape at all. "We greatly suspect," wrote Duke, "it is the growing appreciation of the white Juliet for the colored Romeo as he becomes more intelligent and refined." (Montgomery *Advertiser,* Aug. 18, 1887, 1.)

Duke's editorial caused a furor among white citizens. The Montgomery *Advertiser,* which had strongly supported the black school's coming to Montgomery, linked the Duke incident with the Colored University. White Montgomery citizens wondered whether educating blacks would perhaps lead to more men like Duke. The *Advertiser* hinted that a few of "the boys" should give Duke "whatever warning might be necessary" for his affront to southern womanhood. (Montgomery *Advertiser,* Aug. 16, 1887, 4.) A citizens' committee of ten was chosen to force Duke to leave town. The committee was in effect a lynch mob, and Duke fled to Memphis, Tenn. White Montgomery was so outraged that a minor witch hunt occurred that threatened a black lawyer, A. A. Garner, who had spoken in Duke's defense, and Dr. C. N. Dorsette, BTW's closest ally in Montgomery, who was accused of having a "big head" for speaking out on behalf of his race. Some whites also turned their wrath on the new black school, but Governor Seay and Paterson convinced the citizens that no action against the school was possible without legislative approval. Duke wrote to the *Advertiser* from Memphis admonishing his black critics and exonerating Garner and Dorsette of any complicity in his editorial. He asked to be allowed to return to Montgomery and offered to give up his journalistic career, but white Montgomery remained hostile. (Montgomery *Advertiser,* Aug. 21, 1887, 2.)

Duke later settled with his family in Pine Bluff, Ark., where he was a leading opponent of the work of Tuskegee Institute. He led the town's black community in seeking the removal of Tuskegee graduate Isaac Fisher from his position as principal of the Branch Normal College in Pine Bluff. When Duke's son graduated from Harvard, however, Duke sought BTW's aid in finding employment for him.

[2] The Congregational church headed by Robert C. Bedford.

[3] William Watkins, a member of the committee of black citizens favoring removal of the Marion school to Montgomery. He was listed in the 1880 census as a thirty-four-year-old carpenter, married, with four children.

[4] Samuel Phillips, a member of the black citizens' committee, appeared in the 1880 census as a forty-five-year-old carpenter, married, with two children.

[5] Probably Henry A. Loveless and Anderson S. Loveless, black butchers in Montgomery, both twenty-five years old in 1880 and members of the black citizens' committee. Henry was later noted in BTW's *The Negro in Business,* 96, as a "successful undertaker of Montgomery."

[6] A. N. McEwen, pastor of the Dexter Avenue Baptist Church in Montgomery and a member of the black citizens' committee. Born in Mississippi in 1849, McEwen was converted at a revival in Tennessee after the Civil War. After Jesse Duke's hasty departure from Montgomery, McEwen edited the Montgomery *Herald.* Later he became a trustee of Selma University and a member of the state executive committee of the Republican party.

From Timothy Thomas Fortune[1]

New York, Jan 21 1887

My Dear Mr Washington: Your letter of the 18th has just been received; together with a copy of Mr. Grady's letter to you. I am sure I thank you very much for sending me the letter. I shall make it the basis of an editorial review of the Southern problem, and Mr. Grady in particular. Yes, it commits him, and you are correct in saying we should clinch the matter.

Shall be pleased to see you and talk over the magazine matter.[2] Yours truly

T. Thos. Fortune

ALS Con. 85 BTW Papers DLC.

[1] Timothy Thomas Fortune was the leading black American journalist of the late nineteenth and early twentieth centuries. He was born in 1856 in Marianna, Fla., notorious for Ku Klux Klan outrages. His father, Emmanuel Fortune, was a free tanner and shoe merchant who was harassed by the Klan during Reconstruction because of his political activities and close relations with many whites. The family felt compelled to move to Jacksonville, Fla., in 1866, where Emmanuel Fortune continued his political career, serving as marshal and acting mayor of the city, as member of the Florida constitutional convention, and as a five-term state legislator.

T. Thomas Fortune received no formal education while growing up in Florida. He was tutored by his mother and later worked as a printer's devil for the Marianna *Courier* and in the composing room of the Jacksonville *Courier*. He also served as a page in the Alabama Senate and as a post-office employee before traveling to Washington, D.C., in 1875. There he attended Howard University for a time while working in the Customs House and the Treasury Department, and as a printer for the Washington *People's Advocate* until that newspaper failed. He returned to Florida, married, and taught briefly in the public schools.

In 1879 Fortune moved to New York, where he worked on the editorial staffs of the *Sun* and the *Daily Witness*, and at night developed his own paper, *Rumor*. The latter evolved into the *Globe* (1882-84). He began publishing the New York *Freeman* in 1884, soon afterward renamed the *Age*. Fortune gained national recognition through the forum provided by the editorial pages of the New York *Age*, reputed to be the best of the black newspapers, and through his book, *Black and White: Land, Labor and Politics in the South* (1884). His book took up the cause of black and white laborers combating industrial slavery.

By the late 1880s Fortune was moving away from an earlier enthusiasm for cooperation between Negroes and reform and labor movements. He placed greater stress upon middle-class black self-help and industrial education. In 1887 he called for the formation of a black protective association, the Afro-American League, to fight for black civil rights through the courts and to publicize racial injustice. At least twenty-three states had chapters of the league by 1890 when

Fortune united them as the National Afro-American League (later the Afro-American Council).

Fortune developed a rather mysterious dependency on BTW, possibly because the latter extricated him from the consequences of frequent bouts of alcoholism. A close if unstable alliance grew up between the two men. Fortune defended BTW as having done more for the race than was generally acknowledged, and BTW made large financial contributions to the New York *Age* and frequently influenced Fortune's editorial policy, not only on Tuskegee but on general racial matters. The *Age* was a publicity vehicle for the National Negro Business League and other BTW interests. Fortune wrote much of BTW's *The Negro in Business,* copyedited *The Story of My Life and Work,* and edited some of BTW's speeches. BTW supported Fortune for the presidency of the Afro-American Council (1903-4) in opposition to the anti-Bookerite nominees. BTW's influence was also behind Fortune's appointment by Theodore Roosevelt in 1902 as special labor commissioner for the War Department to study the possibilities of Negro migration to the Philippine Islands.

Fortune often strongly disagreed with BTW, however, for he was more militant and flamboyant than the Tuskegean. Fortune was often sharply critical of the Republican party, as when he allied with the Prohibitionist party in the election of 1880. Later he was openly critical of President McKinley; and he broke with President Roosevelt after the latter's summary dismissal of black troops involved in the Brownsville incident, whereas BTW urged reconciliation. Fortune believed, unlike BTW, that the right to vote was fundamental, regardless of literacy or property considerations. These contradictions between Fortune's militancy and the conservative positions forced by his alliance with BTW create a paradox only partly explained by his economic dependence on BTW. He had been a major black leader before BTW's arrival on the national scene, but in the end BTW was the dominant partner.

In September 1907 Fortune suffered a mental and physical breakdown. The following month he sold his interest in the *Age* to Fred R. Moore, who was secretly financed by BTW. From then until 1923 he worked either as a short-term employee or a free-lance writer for the New York *Age,* New York *Amsterdam News,* Rochester *Herald,* Norfolk *Journal and Guide,* and New York *Tatler.* He also purchased shares in the Washington *Sun,* in September 1914, serving briefly as editor. Finally, in 1923, he became editor of the *Negro World,* organ of Marcus Garvey's movement. For three decades plagued by illness and poverty, he died at Philadelphia in June 1928.

² For many years Fortune and BTW discussed the possibility of Fortune editing, probably at Tuskegee, a magazine that would be a major voice of the intellectuals of the race. This dream was never fulfilled.

From Cornelius Nathaniel Dorsette

Montgomery, Ala. 1/22 1887

Dear Prof: I recd yours this a.m and ans at once, regarding my position relative to the school you know too well just where I stand in that matter, and I have said nothing to any one about this matter one way or the other, the thing has not been talked up by any one that I know of & if Duke has heard any thing its more than any one else has. The only remark I have heard was from one of our citizens saying that I opposed the matter, but farther than that I have not heard of the matter, really I dont think Patterson wants to move the school or will have to, when ever it come to the time to take a stand against it and a definite blow struck I shall be at my post but until this then I dont think it neccesserry for any clamoring over the matter. If you learn of anything definite thats being done in the matter let me know.   Yours truly

C. N. D.

ALI   Con. 85   BTW Papers   DLC.

From Samuel Chapman Armstrong

Jacksonville, Fla., Jan 22 1887

Dear Mr Washington   I expect to leave Florida in from 7 to 12 days — go to Atlanta for a couple of days & thence to Tuskegee to see your work.

Some letters will be sent me in your care: please look out for them. Cant tell just when I will reach you.

Please send me word care Atlanta University Atlanta Georgia whether you'll be at home & the best place to stop at in town.

I hope all is well with you. Sincerely yours

S. C. Armstrong

ALS   Con. 85   BTW Papers   DLC.

From Cornelius Nathaniel Dorsette

Montgomery, Ala. 1/28 1887

Dear Prof   I was very glad to rec. your last letter for (to be frank) I feeling hurt & vexed at its tone, my fidelity to your school and its

advancement has never grown less & I have continued to use the mite
of influence I have for its good first & 2ndly for the good to Negro race
for which *It* is doing such grand work and until *It* ceases to do for my
race what its now doing I shall ever be the same, no matter what
momentary & *spasmodic* & *self advantage* friend like J. C. Duke may
write or say to you. I can see through his game very clearly & know
just why he claims such interest &c. But however time will show you
who in case of emmergency will stand firm when there is nothing personal to be gained.

I shall be glad to welcome Gen. Armstrong & would like to come up
but really cant afford it, cant you come down & we will show him the
city?

The printed matter arrived thanks, what the bill? Ask Logan to arrange that note according to our agreement. yours truly

C. N. Dorsette

ALS   Con. 85   BTW Papers   DLC.

James Fowle Baldwin Marshall
to Samuel Chapman Armstrong

Boston, Mass. Jan 31 1887

Dear Genl Armstrong, I hope you will visit the Colored Normal School
at Huntsville Ala, or at least get an authentic account of it and of the
character of its Principal Prof W. H. Councill. He came here this
winter with most complete endorsements of the State Authorities of
Alabama, and of leading men in Phila including Dr Furness,[1] & R. C.
Ogden &c &c and brought me a letter from Dr Hale[2] asking me to
do all I could for him. I was unwise enough to add mine to the many
endorsements. Now he is reported to me, by competent persons whose
names I cannot use as a man without moral principle as a political
leader and demagogue, who sold out his party to the Democrats and
was rewarded by being given the charge of this Colored Normal School
which was established for the purpose. That since he has been in this
position his moral character has been bad, that he shot a man whose
family he had broken up, and had committed rape on one of his pupils

for both which offences he was indicted, but through some favo[ri]tism escaped punishment. That he is not trusted by his own people, and that a white democratic politician when asked why he was tolerated and supported in the face of such outrageous conduct replied "that we may say to the colored people thus we stand by those who vote with us." A public exposure of such infamy at the North would Save much money from being worse than wasted. He has a good presence and makes a good impression at first sight. I have tried to undo any mischief my name may have made, but wish very much to get the facts in a way that they can be used. I shall endorse no more Professors from the South without personal knowledge, even if the Angel Gabriel himself urges it.

I trust your trip is one of both pleasure and profit.

Mrs Ms only remaining sister Mrs Lydia Oliver died last week after three days of suffering. Yours faithfully

J F B Marshall

ALS Con. 88 BTW Papers DLC. Enclosed in Armstrong to BTW, Feb. 11, 1887.

[1] William Henry Furness (1802-96), born in Boston, attended Harvard College and Harvard Theological Seminary. For a half-century after 1825 Furness was pastor of the First Unitarian Society of Philadelphia. A prolific author of theological essays, he produced also several translations of German works. He was called the dean of Philadelphia's clergy.

[2] Presumably Edward Everett Hale.

To Warren Logan

Montgomery, Ala. Feb. 2 1887

Dear Mr. Logan: Mrs. Mead[1] and the ladies will be there Friday. Have some good singing prepared. I may be there tomorrow. Look closely after the sick. A personal talk or visit does great good. Tell Ada Scott[2] that I will arrange about her going home on my return. Think there is no chance for our getting an increased appropriation. Marion in my opinion will be abolished or removed. The tide is heavily against them. My object is to prevent the Marion school from being located here.[3]

Our land bill[4] I think will go through. Hastily yours

B. T. Washington

ALS Con. 86 BTW Papers DLC. Written on stationery bearing C. N. Dorsette's letterhead.

1 Presumably Mrs. Charles L. Mead, wife of a New York businessman and officer of the American Missionary Association.

2 Ada Scott, a student at Tuskegee from Lowndesboro, Ala., from 1886 to 1890, never graduated.

3 The Alabama legislature passed and the governor signed on Feb. 25, 1887, House Bill 902, which provided for the creation of the "Alabama Colored People's University." Eight trustees appointed by the governor were to select the new site and sell the property of the Marion school. The trustees were free to pick any site except that "no place shall be selected against the wishes of the people of said place," and "the commissioners shall have regard to the proper distribution of schools for the colored people." The school was to receive $10,000 for land and buildings and $7,500 a year for expenses. (*Acts of the General Assembly of Alabama, 1886-87,* 198-201.)

4 Also approved on Feb. 25, 1887, was Senate Bill 299, authorizing "conveyances and devises of lands to trustees for the use of the Tuskegee Normal School. . . ." The act gave the trustees as a group the power to buy, hold, and protect the title to land used for the purposes of the school, and, therefore, apparently extracted some power from the three-man board of commissioners, which was responsible solely to the state superintendent of education. Though the three commissioners served on the board of trustees, there were at this time six other trustees. The act was careful to limit to landholding the grant of power, stipulating that the "trustees shall have no authority to control the operation of said school, or in any manner to interfere with the management thereof." (*Ibid.,* 940-41.)

From Benjamin Winston Walker[1]

Montgomery, Feby 4th 1887

Dear Sir One of the most important bills for the colored people passed with favorable report from our Committee on public buildings this A.M. & will be up for passage at once.

A bill to erect suitable buildings at Tuskaloosa for the Colored insane of this state.[2] The committee appropriated $20,000 for the buildings.

I will nurse the normal school bill which you are interested in and shall urge its being removed to Green County.[3]

I want you to think of the propriety of going up North & seeing if you cant get up a land co. Yours Truly

B W Walker

ALS Con. 88 BTW Papers DLC.

1 Benjamin Winston Walker (1848-1907) represented Macon County in the

state legislature in 1886, and was the first Republican elected to the legislature from the county in twelve years. Later he served as U.S. marshal for the southern and middle districts of Alabama.

[2] House Bill 705, "Providing additional Accommodations for the colored insane of Alabama." The bill was approved on Feb. 25, 1887. (Alabama *House Journal, 1886-87*, 1326.)

[3] On Feb. 28, 1887, the governor signed Senate Bill 271 to establish a colored normal school in Greene County in the western part of Alabama, and appropriate $2,000 per year for its maintenance.

From Samuel Chapman Armstrong

Atlanta, Ga. Feb 11 1887

Dear Mr Washington: Please look up all you can about the man & school[1] mentioned in the enclosed letter from Genl Marshall which please read & let me know what you can find out.

Expect me next Monday by 1 PM. train from here instead of next Saturday as I telegraphed. Yours sincerely

S. C. Armstrong

ALS Con. 85 BTW Papers DLC. Enclosed James Fowle Baldwin Marshall to Samuel Chapman Armstrong, Jan. 31, 1887.

[1] William Hooper Councill, president of Alabama A & M College at Huntsville.

From Cornelius Nathaniel Dorsette

Montgomery, Ala. 2/17 1887

Dear friend   yours rec'd this A.M. Was sorry I did not see you as I had had a long talk with Prof Patterson on my way from Selma, and if his plans mature as maped out I think it will all result for the best of both schools, however I will see you when you come down.

We want to make it as plesant as posible for Gen. Armstrong. I told Mr Bedford that I thought the Gen. would not care to speak & so we have not arranged for any public talk yet if he decids to tellegraph tomorrow by 1 P.M & we can work up a very intelligent audience if not large one. Let me know. Yours truly

C N Dorsette

ALS Con. 85 BTW Papers DLC.

From Benjamin Winston Walker

Montgomery, Feby 24th 1887

Dr Sir   I arranged as I told you to have your bill[1] called up when my name was reached.

This was done & the bill has passed and is now a law fixing titles of your property. Respfy

B. W. Walker

ALS   Con. 88   BTW Papers   DLC.

[1] Senate Bill 299.

An Announcement to Students

[Tuskegee, Ala.] Feb. 26 [188]7

In answer to the request made to me by the students, I would say that a "Students' Court" may be established and may have power to decide upon offenses and inflict punishments there for except in cases where the principal reserves the right to try those offenses himself and the Principal reserves the right to change or modify any punishment inflicted by said court. (Signed)

B. T. Washington

ALpS   Con. 91   BTW Papers   DLC.

From William B. Paterson

Marion, Ala., March 7. 1887

Dear Friend Washington, I do not know that I can say anything regarding Program. You have seen from the Herald[1] what we are doing. Our white friends are jubilant with us, the others hardly know what to think, and they say but little. I will run up to Montgomery tomorrow to see the Gov.² and keep him quiet till summer. We are all in good spirits, and hope to see everything come out all right. Yours sincerely

Wm B. Paterson

ALS   Con. 86   BTW Papers   DLC.

¹ Probably the *Baptist Herald,* a black weekly published in Montgomery.

² Thomas Seay (1846-96), born in Hale County, Ala., studied at Southern University until he volunteered for the Confederate Army at the age of seventeen. After the war he returned to Southern University and graduated in 1867. Admitted to the bar in 1869, he was elected to the Alabama Senate in 1876. He quickly rose to a position of leadership among conservative Democrats and was chosen president of the Senate in 1884. Elected governor of Alabama in 1886 and 1888, Seay continued the policy of his predecessors in reducing taxes, but warned in 1890 of further reductions, stressing the need for more expenditures for education. BTW considered Seay a "friend and champion of the Negro's rights" and "the best friend the Negro race ever had" (quoted in Bond, *Negro Education in Alabama,* 209), and Tuskegee continued to receive state aid and kind words from the state-house. In 1890 Seay was one of the first prominent Alabamians to propose a disfranchising convention in the face of the rising Populist movement in Alabama. Like many white conservatives, he favored restricting suffrage not on the basis of race but upon educational and property qualifications. Seay ran for the U.S. Senate in 1890 but was defeated by James M. Pugh. He retired to his farm in Greensboro and died six years later.

From Samuel Chapman Armstrong

Hampton, Va., March 9 1887

Dear Mr Washington: I returned last Sunday safely. My return home from New Orleans was quick & rather tiresome but I saw a great deal.

I cannot but send you a word of thanks for & appreciation of your & your wifes kindness to me in Tuskegee. You gave up your sitting room for me & did everything to make it pleasant for me. Your work is on a good solid foundation and I believe it will stand. You are working out this problem of self help thoroughly and I think it will be a success.

Your problem is to make not only men but nature bloom out & the whole region around you will yet be changed as new ideas are taken up. Please remember me to all the teachers & believe me   Yours very truly

S. C. Armstrong

ALS   Con. 85   BTW Papers   DLC.

To Nathalie Lord

[Tuskegee, Ala.] Mar. 31 [188]7

Dear Miss Lord, The last tract of land that Miss Davis[1] purchased contains 34 acres and she is to pay $325 for it. She has paid $50 in cash and is to pay the other some time this year. The house in which she lives has been paid for. The school house is on a separate tract of land from the one mentioned above.

I can not close this letter without mentioning the wonderful religious interest existing in our school. Within the last week 106 students have become Christians. There are only a very few left now and the interest still continues. There is almost none of the usual excitement connected with such meetings. Much of this blessing is due to Miss Mayo's[2] faithful work. Yours sincerely

Booker T. Washington

ALpS Con. 91 BTW Papers DLC.

[1] Lilla V. Davis was a black teacher in Cotton Valley, Ala., aided by the Woman's Home Missionary Association and watched over by BTW.

[2] Lovey A. Mayo.

To William Jenkins[1]

[Tuskegee, Ala.] April 6 [188]7

Dear Mr. Jenkins: Yours of the 3rd inst. is rec'd. In reply I would say that the letter relates to a subject that Mr. Adams[2] and I have been considering and arranging for. You perhaps know that the school has bought the Corliss place — that is the part of it on this side of the road and Mr. Adams has bought the land on the opposite side with a view of putting on it some neat comfortable cottages for persons who may desire to settle around the school. Mr. Adams will agree to put a 3 roomed cottage on the place above referred to by fall if that would suit your friend. The rent of this would be about $5 or $6 per month. Or if he would like one nearer the center of town Mr. Adams will put him up a four roomed cottage the rent of which would be $7 or $8 per month. As Mr. Adams is just preparing to build it would be well if your friend decides to come, for your friend to write just the size house he wants and whether he would like it located on the edge of town and near the school or near the center of town.

We shall all be glad to do what ever we can to encourage him to locate his family here and should they come shall do our best to make them happy here. Yours Hastily

B. T. Washington

106 students have become Christians within the last few weeks.

ALpS Con. 91 BTW Papers DLC.

¹ William Jenkins, born in Pickens, S.C., in 1860, spent three years at Fisk University and one at Hampton, where he graduated in 1882. He taught for one year in Jordan, S.C., before coming to Tuskegee Institute in 1883 to teach mathematics and direct the band. He left Tuskegee in 1885 to teach in Tennessee and Arkansas, returned in 1887, but left again in 1888 to work at Fisk. Later he was a clerk in the Surgeon General's office in Washington and then became a registrar and receiver's clerk in the U.S. Land Office in Montgomery. He died in Montgomery in 1902.

² Lewis Adams.

From Samuel Chapman Armstrong

Hampton, Va., April 9 1887

My dear Washington   I am very glad to hear of the good work at Tuskegee. It is wonderful, & I hope the roots of correction will strike deep into the hearts of all in the school, and an abiding permanent good be wrought.

Please tell the students that we at Hampton are deeply interested in the revival at Tuskegee & feel that God has favored them with a blessed visitation of His Spirit.

I am constantly glad I have seen your work & hope that it will in every way prosper.

With kindest regards to your wife believe me   Yours sincerely

S. C. Armstrong

ALS Con. 85 BTW Papers DLC.

Olivia A. Davidson Washington
to Mary Elizabeth Preston Stearns[1]

Tuskegee, Ala., April 11, 1887

Dear Mrs. Stearns, I sincerely trust you are stronger than you were when I last saw you. So often I have thought of your feebleness then — resulting from your fall.

I hope too the winter has not been too severe for you. It has seemed an unusually long & severe one to us.

Just now I am writing you about a matter over which I have spent much thought. Perhaps you know of the summer training course (physical) for teachers to be had at Harvard this year under the direct supervision of Dr. Sargent.[2]

For some time past I have felt that Mr. Washington's present mode of life is unfavorable to his health.

He is not as strong, physically, as he was two years ago, and I am sure it is due to his close application to his work. I fear his nervous system will begin to show marks of overwork if he does not have some relaxation. All his summers heretofore since the school was organized have been given almost entirely to the school work. This five weeks of physical training under such wise auspices it seems to me is the thing he needs. I want to provide it for him myself, and this brings me to the point of which I would speak to you. Some months ago that excellent man, Dr. Wm. Curtis[3] of Westboro' died leaving among other bequests $500 each to this school and myself personally. This money will be paid I presume sometime this year. The estate is in the hands now of the executors. But it may be some months before it is settled and in the mean time I am sure there will never come a time when there will be just such a need of it as this. Does it seem indelicate or not in good taste for me to be planning in this way to spend the money before I receive it. I am sure you will understand my feeling about it. I shall be so happy to have it to spend in this way — in saving my husband perhaps from Gen. A's[4] condition — or at least from getting to the point where his work for the school will be much less efficient than it now is. I expect you have already concluded that all this is but a prelude to a request, as it is. Mrs. Stearns I want to ask you to let me have the money necessary if this bequest is not paid in time. The 5 weeks' term begins July 6. I think $100. will cover all expenses. The tuition is $50. Will you on the certainty that I shall be able in a few months to return it advance the money?

I have now something that I wish to tell you which I am sure will call out your sympathy with us. We expect to welcome to our home next month a little stranger. Owing to the fact that there is no physician here in whom we place confidence it has been decided that it is best for me to go away from home till after my confinement. I am to come to Boston to the New England hospital. I leave here about the 20th inst. and shall drop you a card as soon as possible after my arrival. In the meantime you can write here as mail will be forwarded if it does not come before I leave. I bring our little girl, Portia, to remain with friends in B. till I am well again. The expense of all this — though much smaller than I dared hope, the entire charge at the hospital being only $20. — will make such inroads upon our small savings that this other must be given up but for this help from an unexpected quarter.

The school prospers in all its departments. We enjoyed Gen Armstrong's visit so much. I fear from what I hear of his work in Boston, that he is doing too much — in the present condition of his health.

The season is very beautiful here now. With all good wishes, I am Yours Very Sincerely

Olivia D. Washington

ALS Con. 17 BTW Papers DLC.

[1]Mary Elizabeth Preston Stearns, born in Norridgewock, Me., in 1821, was the niece of abolitionist author Lydia Maria Francis Child (1802-80) and frequented transcendentalist circles in the 1830s and 1840s. In 1843 she married George Luther Stearns (1809-67), a wealthy Boston businessman and abolitionist who financially aided John Brown in Kansas and was one of the "secret six" who backed Brown's raid on Harpers Ferry. He was an active supporter of Radical Republican causes during and after the Civil War. After his death Mrs. Stearns continued her husband's interest in aiding blacks, though with none of his flair for action, probably due in part to her ill health and her reliance on homeopathy as a cure. She contributed financially to institutions devoted to educating freedmen, including Hampton and Tuskegee, and aided Negroes individually, including Olivia Davidson. She died on Nov. 28, 1901, leaving a bequest to Tuskegee. Mrs. Stearns, who had known John Brown well, was by her deathbed request "buried on December 2, day of execution of John Brown, to whose memory the day had been kept sacred for many years in her household." (DeLong, Wright, and Clark, "Mrs. George Luther Stearns," 21-22.)

[2] Dudley Allen Sargent (1849-1924) was assistant professor of physical training at Harvard University. A graduate of Bowdoin College and Yale Medical School,

he was appointed to the Harvard faculty in 1879. He resigned in 1889 to devote full time to his work as director of the Hemenway Gymnasium and president of the Normal School of Physical Training, both in Cambridge. Sargent wrote several books on physical education and invented gymnasium apparatus.

3 William Curtis (1816-87), a physician of Westboro, Mass., held many town offices and was prominent in the Unitarian Church.

4 Samuel C. Armstrong suffered a heart attack in the summer of 1886. He seemed to recover, but had a stroke in 1891 with substantial paralysis and died in 1893.

From James Fowle Baldwin Marshall

Boston, Mass., Apr 21, 1887

Dear Booker, I have yours of 16th. I will do what I can about the report of your commencement. When is it to be.

Ask Mrs Ws pardon in my behalf for my neglect to answer her question about Mrs Curtis.[1] I was told that she died before her husband, but dont remember who told me. Am quite sure that she is not living.

I had a letter some ten days ago from Prof Councill dated at Philadelphia, saying that he was on his way north to solicit aid for his School, and had called on Dr Furness who told him that I had branded him as an imposter. He wished to hear from me before coming further North. I answered him that I did not say that he was an imposter but that I had written to all who I thought [would] be influenced by my signature on his testimonials, that enquiry of competent parties as to his record and standing among his own people, had satisfied me that he had no claim for aid from the benevolent people of the North, and I wished my name erased from his book & advised him not to attempt to raise money on the strength of endorsements given in ignorance of the facts. He wrote Dr Hale & Mr Garrison[2] that he should come at once to Boston & vindicate himself from these unfounded charges, but as yet, I have not seen him. Mr Ogden gave him a plain talk. Yours faithfully

J F B Marshall

ALS Con. 88 BTW Papers DLC.

1 Mrs. William Curtis.
2 Francis Jackson Garrison (1848-1916), youngest son of William Lloyd Gar-

rison, was born in Boston and named after the wealthy Boston abolitionist, Francis Jackson (1789-1861). Graduating from Boston Latin School in 1859, Francis Garrison assisted his father in the publication of *The Liberator* and traveled abroad with him in 1865 and 1867 before joining Houghton Mifflin Company of Boston in 1871. Regarded as one of the best-informed authorities on the abolition movement, Garrison accumulated one of the most complete collections of anti-slavery literature in the country and co-authored with his brother, Wendell Phillips Garrison, a biography of William Lloyd Garrison (1889). In 1899 he raised money for BTW's trip to Europe and planned the trip, supplying letters of introduction. He defended BTW's policies and actions against the criticisms of William Monroe Trotter and other militant blacks in Boston.

From James Fowle Baldwin Marshall

Boston, Mass., April 22 1887

PRIVATE

My dear Washington, Prof Councill called on me today. I had some time ago, written to Dr Furness, Mr R C Ogden & others of Phila and to friends in this vicinity, who might have been influenced by my endorsement of him, withdrawing my confidence and giving the information I had received concerning him. He admits having had trouble in his school & having, in a frenzy of rage at being falsely accused of a heinous crime, shot at a man who as he says announced his intention of killing him. This denial of guilt was to be expected, but he brings an array of names in support of his claims, from such men as Bishop Payne,[1] Bishop Turner,[2] the Comr of Education of Washington,[3] and the leading Bankers & business men & clergy of Huntsville.

He said also that he had a letter of commendation from you, etc etc. I write to ask you in confidence, whether this is so, and whether you believe him worthy of support. I know how easy it is to get letters of recommendation, especially from the citizens of a place that is to be benefited by the money those letters may bring to it. But I cannot understand why a man of Councills record should find it so easy to get such strong and unreserved letters as those of Bishops Payne & Turner & the U.S. Comr of Education. Yours faithfully

J F B Marshall

Have just rec'd your letter, also the circulars which I will circulate. Hope Mrs. W. has no special reason to anticipate unusual risk in her coming trial.

Our treasurer AUA[4] will send you $100. 2 sch[5] today Lexington & Portsmouth.

ALS Con. 88 BTW Papers DLC. On stationery of the American Unitarian Association, of which Marshall was reported as in charge of "Southern and Indian Educational Work."

[1]Daniel A. Payne (1811-93) was the leading bishop of the African Methodist Episcopal Church. Born of free parents in Charleston, S.C., he was orphaned at age seven. He lived with his aunt and was educated in Philadelphia. From 1829 to 1835 he conducted a black school in South Carolina, which was eventually closed by state authorities. Ordained in 1838, he served as minister of churches in Washington, D.C., and Baltimore before being named bishop in 1852. He was a leading advocate of an educated ministry and was responsible in 1856 for the church's acquisition of Wilberforce College. He traveled in England to raise funds for the school, and served as its president from 1863 to 1876, and then retired to devote full time to speaking and writing.

[2] Henry McNeal Turner (1834-1915), born free in Newberry, S.C., advocated black nationalism and emigration to Africa. He believed that only when Negroes possessed their own nation could they live in dignity as free men. Not always consistently militant, he was always a spokesman of Negro self-defense. He opposed the accommodationism of BTW as well as optimistic black intellectuals who sought racial justice through protest.

At the age of twenty Turner won a large interracial audience while serving as an itinerant evangelist for the Methodist Episcopal Church, South. Convinced of the need for an all-black religious organization, he joined the A.M.E. Church in 1858 and became the minister of a Washington, D.C., congregation. He argued the right of blacks to fight in the Union Army, and became a chaplain.

During Reconstruction Turner acted as a Freedmen's Bureau chaplain, but he chafed at the racial discrimination he encountered. Later he established the first A.M.E. church in Georgia. He was active in the Republican party in Georgia and in 1868 and 1870 won election to the state legislature. The legislature, however, declined to seat him. Subsequently, Turner became disillusioned with the Republican party and supported the Democrats. He applied unsuccessfully for the position of U.S. minister to Haiti in 1869. He was appointed as postmaster of Macon, Ga., about 1869, but was dismissed after two weeks on charges of corruption that were never substantiated. A persistent charge of self-serving opportunism followed him throughout life.

Meanwhile, Turner rose in the A.M.E. Church, serving as chancellor of Morris Brown College and manager of church publications. In 1880 he became a bishop of the A.M.E. Church. A fiercely independent maverick in politics and religion, he continued to enrage both southern white men and black intellectuals with his exhortations to emigration and sermons preaching that "God is not white." He was hostile to the Atlanta Compromise in 1895 and accused BTW of doing irreparable harm to the Negro race. In 1905 he wrote: "Washington's policy is not worth a cent. It accomplishes no racial good except as it helps a thousand students at Tuskegee." (Quoted in Redkey, *Black Exodus,* 277.)

[3] Nathaniel Henry Rhodes Dawson (1829-95), a lawyer, Confederate Army veteran, and former speaker of the Alabama House (1880-81) from Selma, was

appointed U.S. Commissioner of Education in 1886 by President Cleveland. He resigned in 1889 upon the election of President Harrison.

⁴ C. H. Burrage of Boston, treasurer of the American Unitarian Association.

⁵ Scholarships.

From J. L. H. Watkins[1]

B'ham, April 24th 1887

Dear Sir. I received your letter, and intended to answer before this. I have made three efforts to see Mayor Lane.[2] Each one was unsuccessful. I intended to get him to refer me to some of the prominent citizens. I will call on him again to-morrow. I will immediately write you the results. Excuse a more lengthy letter. Write more to-morrow or day after. With regards, I am your friend,

J. L. H. Watkins

I think the citizens here will favor having the school established here.

ALS Con. 86 BTW Papers DLC.

[1] J. L. H. Watkins, a black man living in Birmingham, worked for BTW's interests in attempting to bring the colored university to Birmingham. He tried unsuccessfully to obtain a public-school teaching position in Birmingham.

[2] Alexander Oscar Lane, mayor of Birmingham from 1882 to 1892, was born in 1848 in Macon County. He moved to Birmingham in 1873 to practice law and rose quickly to political prominence. In 1880 be became editor of *Iron Age*. He served five successive two-year terms as Birmingham's mayor. In 1907 he was appointed associate judge of the Alabama tenth judicial circuit, and in 1911 was named one of the three commissioners of Birmingham under a new municipal charter.

From Arthur L. Brooks[1]

Tuskegee, Ala. 5/2 1887

Dear Sir. Whilst in Montgomery I saw Patterson. He came over to see Seay,[2] but as the Governor was out of town I don't know whether he got to see him or not. He seems anxious to have Commissioners[3] appointed *at once* in order that he may proceed against them by injunctions.

He is confident of success, but says he will try & get an opinion from the Attorney General to the effect that the bill is unconstitutional; in that event, he thinks the Governor will not appoint at all, but let the School remain in *statu quo*. I think now I will run down to Montgomy this week and view the situation. If any thing is likely to occur will wire you.

A L Brooks

ALS   Con. 85   BTW Papers   DLC.   Addressed to BTW in New York.

¹ Arthur L. Brooks, a forty-one-year-old native of Tuskegee, was an attorney, the publisher of the *Macon Mail,* and had been county superintendent of schools. He was elected to the Alabama House in 1880 and introduced the bill that established Tuskegee Normal School. In 1883 he won a seat in the Alabama Senate, and he continued to use his influence for Tuskegee Institute.

² Thomas Seay, governor of Alabama.

³ Presumably the eight trustees of the newly created Alabama Colored People's University, who, according to House Bill 902, were to be appointed by the governor. Paterson apparently felt threatened by the bill, which abolished his school and created the new university.

From Arthur L. Brooks

Montgomery, [ca. May 3, 1887]¹

Dear sir. I came down last night and saw Governor Seay only a few minutes. He was just in the act of leaving for Mobile on a fishing frolic — hence I had only a short conversation with him, but he told me that he would defer appointing commissioners two weeks or till your return. He returns to-night at which time I'll see him again.

If any thing should occur, will wire you. Yours Truly

A L Brooks

P. S. *Sub rosa,* since writing the above, I have had a conversation with Palmer.² He says that Seay told him that he (Seay) was in favor of Birmingham — that he had heard about our school, and that it would never do to locate the University here. P thinks we can carry our point.

A L B.

ALS   Con. 85   BTW Papers   DLC.   Addressed to BTW at 102 W. 37th St., New York.

[1] It is clear from internal evidence and the fact that BTW was away from Tuskegee on May 2 and 3 that the letter was sent about that time.
[2] Solomon Palmer.

From Warren Logan

Tuskegee, Ala., May 3d 1887

Mr. Washington. Lawyer Brooks was in to see me just now about the two articles which I send herewith. He thinks the longer of the two articles was either written or inspired by Patterson who I know has been in Montg'y for several days past. At Brooks' suggestion I sent Col. Foster who is in Montg'y today — a telegram asking him to call on Gov. Seay and urge him to defer the appointment of the Com. to locate the Univ. — until after next Tuesday. This is to give time to have the Birmingham City Council to pass a resolution favoring the establishment of the school in that city. Brooks thinks he can have the B'ham Age antagonize the Advertiser articles — and get the Council to adopt the resolution referred to. I heard from Mr Bedford on Sat. that Patterson had got a brief from Ex Judge Craig[1] of Selma — a fine lawyer — setting forth the unconstitutionality of the act of the recent leg. Brooks wants you to meet him in B'ham on Tuesday 10th inst.

Would have telegraphed but did not think it necessary. Yours Sincerely.

Warren Logan

ALS Con. 86 BTW Papers DLC.

[1] George Henry Craig (1845-1923), born in Cahaba, Ala., attended the University of Alabama, fought in the Confederate Army, studied law, and entered politics as a Republican during Reconstruction. He served as sheriff of Dallas County for a year. In 1869 he became judge of the criminal court of Dallas County and was appointed as a circuit judge in 1874. From 1880 to 1883 he served on the Selma Board of Education. He won a seat to the U.S. Congress in 1882 in a disputed election and lost the seat in another disputed election in 1884. Later he was U.S. attorney and member of the board of visitors to West Point.

From Warren Logan

Tuskegee, Ala., May 3d 1887

Dear Mr Washington. Your letter with cks. for $100.00 enclosed to hand.

I realize that it is doing our commercial reputation no good to have that planer remain in Montg'y — but then there are other matters just as pressing as that. The town merchants are importunate and must be paid — at least a part of what we owe them and then there are parties away in Montg'y & other places who have been dunning us right along for some time. It is my opinion that we get into these pinches much oftener than we should & much oftener than we would if we were a little more economical.

Matters are going reasonably smoothly at the school. There are some things that should be attended to — as soon as possible — as the summer work — announcement of names of those who are to take part in com. exercises — this latter I will make this week. When do you return? Yours Sincerely

Warren Logan

ALS   Con. 86   BTW Papers   DLC.

From William B. Paterson

Marion, Ala., May 3, 1887

Dear Sir: The present status of the School matter is: We have the written opinion of a good lawyer that the Bill[1] is unconstitutional in several particulars. The Governor still treats it as all right, and has requested me to get up facts to guide him in the choice of a location. It seems to be between Bgham and Montgomery. The whites of Bgham are at work to get a Baptist College there and will probably oppose the Colored.

There was a meeting here last night, and it was decided to still contest against removal.

The end will be reached soon I hope, as I am tired of it. I am, Yours Very Truly

Wm. B. Paterson

ALS   Con. 86   BTW Papers   DLC.

¹ House Bill 902.

From Samuel Chapman Armstrong

Hampton, Va. May 5 1887

Dear Mr. Washington: Your wife writes me that you think of taking gymnastic drill at Hemenway Museum[1] this summer — a very good plan.

You are in some risk of a break down — if your health fails your position will be bad: my own break down came after 18 years hard steady work & I could stand it better. Should you give way too soon people will say "folly." You may rest a while after 12 or 15 years work.

Meanwhile rest as you go; there is no other way. You lack strong supporting help especially on the woman side. Dont risk your help.[2] Dr Sargent[3] will hear of you. I enclose a note. Sincerely yours

S. C. Armstrong

ALS   Con. 1   BTW Papers   ATT.

¹ Hemenway Gymnasium.
² Presumably he intended to write "health."
³ Dudley Allen Sargent.

Samuel Chapman Armstrong to Dudley Allen Sargent

Hampton, Va. May 5 1887

Dear Dr Sargent   This will introduce Mr B. T. Washington Principal of the leading negro institution in Alabama who is doing a great work for his people & state. I beg your interest in him. He is no common "darkey." Very truly yours

S. C. Armstrong

ALS   Con. 16   BTW Papers   DLC.

Items from a Notebook

[Tuskegee, Ala., May 6-26, 1887][1]

Blooded chickens

Browning[2] gone home.

Wagon bodies &c at stable.

Committee on decoration for Com.[3]

Guard to eat at night.

Don't "Know Negro."
Military drill.

Sarah Lucus[4] to write mother.
Browning's suspension.

State Fair

Exp.[5] of May Party

Time spent in patching.

Miss M. R. Jackson[6]
Box 725
Birmingham, Ala.

Womens meeting.

Meeting in Montgomy.

No teacher with girls. Disorderly
coming over.

Medical Care.

See Prof. Wilson.[7]

Buying for cash, in town.

Teacher not exaggerate — their word
taken.

Laying corner stone of church.

Strictness in every thing.

Milk in Teachers' dining room.

See special diet students.

Write Maj. Palmer.[8]

those who stay during Summer.

N.Y. addresses.

Keep Treadwell[9] at work.

B. T. W.
Southern Letter written
Looking closely after girls when
at entertainment.

Write to Jones and Wheeler[10]
— Chicgo.

Teachers & students going together.

Model kitchen put in order.
Rains in it.

Total Height of ind.
the mean height in inches by ÷
mean lbs. in weight will give the
inches per lb. x total weight x
total height gives total weight.

Mean girth divided by mean
heights gives total. the m.g. ÷
m.w. = inches in girth
Waist measurement.

more stress upon depth than width.

Hip measurement in strong men
hips are & comparatively narrow.

Thigh measurement indicates general strength.

Heart weakness appears in those
who have large lower extremities.

Knee msmnt R.

Calf.

upper Arm R.M.
    "   L

Elbow, R.

Fore arm.

Wrist = Ankle.
the size of wrist & ankle indicate
temperment.

Depth of Chest — lasting power, vitality, strength.

Breadth of Head.
Family marks.
Breadth of Neck.
   "   Shoulder.
Broad S — gen. strength.

School Matters
Careless Driving.
Brooms ruining.
Obey orders,
Greatest freedom.
Waste in teachers boarding dep't.
Buying by one person.

Disturbing office work.
Hall windows not washed.
Bed ticks
Mil. suits.
Work.

How long students are to work in
   Night class.
Where to keep money.
Th[or]ough examinations.
Girls & Boys separate.
Work students report tomorrow.

Barrels in dining Room.
No light in dining Room.
Fire.
More lights.

Quiet in chapel

Books — to work.
Band
Programme.
Change time of bell.
More Rooms for girls.
Get a cook.
Mrs. Alexander.[11]

AD Con. 949 BTW Papers DLC. This notebook is one of many in which BTW jotted down aids to memory as he toured the Tuskegee campus or traveled. Some of the references are too cryptic to understand. Others, however, provide insight into the character of BTW's mind, his grasp of infinitesimal detail, and his watchful concern about all that happened on his campus.

[1] The notebook was begun on BTW's fund-raising trip to the north in March, April, and May 1887. The entries made on the trip which were mainly names and amounts contributed are omitted here. BTW returned home sometime after May 6, 1887, and apparently used the remainder of the notebook while at Tuskegee prior to the school's commencement exercises on May 26, 1887.

[2] John W. Browning, a Tuskegee Institute night-school student from Montgomery, entered in 1885. He apparently was suspended in 1887 and did not return.

[3] Commencement.

[4] Sarah Lucas, of Montgomery, Ala., entered the preparatory class at Tuskegee in 1886, but stayed only one year.

[5] Expenses?

[6] Miss M. R. Jackson, a black teacher living in Birmingham, was asked by BTW to join the Tuskegee faculty for the 1887-88 term to teach mathematics, but she declined the offer.

[7] William D. Wilson taught natural sciences, music, and rhetoric at Tuskegee from 1884 to 1889.

[8] Solomon Palmer, state superintendent of education.

[9] James R. Treadwell of Opelika, Ala., entered Tuskegee in 1885 and left without graduating in 1888.

[10] Lloyd G. Wheeler (1848-1909) was a prominent Chicago black businessman and friend of BTW born in Mansfield, Ohio. His father was active in the Underground Railroad until forced by Ohio law to suspend his activities. The family

then moved to Chatham, Canada. After the Civil War Lloyd Wheeler moved to Chicago, where he worked his way through law school. He married the step-daughter of John Jones, owner of a very successful cleaning and tailoring establishment in downtown Chicago that catered to upper-class whites. Upon Jones's death in 1879, Wheeler became manager of the business. He was one of the original founders of the Chicago branch of the National Negro Business League in 1901. Soon after this, however, he fell victim to business misfortunes partly connected with the increased discrimination against blacks in Chicago after a rise in black migration to the city. For a business like Wheeler's, which depended almost entirely on white patronage, such discrimination spelled virtual economic doom. In 1903 he left Chicago to become business agent of Tuskegee Institute.

[11] Probably the wife of John H. Alexander, a white resident of Tuskegee.

From William J. Stevens[1]

Selma, Ala., May 14, 1887

Dear Sir: Yours to hand and contents noted with care.

I think Duke[2] droved the nail in Montgomery's Coffin at the Press Convention, in a fool hardy effort for the School he over reached himself and thereby aroused a feeling that was a sleep so far as Selma was concerned. But to say the least he quicken the impulses of Birmingham and Selma. Nevertheless to keep the matter as quite as possible I succeeded in having Selma and Birmingham striken out of his resolution.

I will write the Gov a strong letter urging Birmingham or Selma as the place. Citing such reasons as will favor Birmingham more strongly than Selma. I think such a letter would do more good than a direct appeal, because it is now commonly understood by the Efforts of Prof Patterson that the three cities Montgomery, Birmingham, and Selma are applicants.

I cannot possibly come up for the reason that my wife will be from home. She has had the good fortune to get a free ticket to the "National [pride?]" Washington D.C. So I am forced to remain at home to care for the babies in her absent.

Love to the girls. Get one or both of them summer school if possible. Command me in any way that I can serve you. Respectfully

Wm J. Stevens

P.S. Excuse my pencil.

I have just concluded a three page letter to Gov Seay — would be glad if you or some of your friends could see it.

ALS Con. 86 BTW Papers DLC.

¹ William J. Stevens of Selma, born in 1845, was a leading Alabama black politician and editor of the Selma *Cyclone*. In the 1880 census he was reported as a saloon owner in Selma. Stevens represented Dallas County in the Alabama legislature from 1876 to 1877. Politically he was the leader of the "black-and-tan" faction of the Republican party and condemned the lily-white faction which attempted to exclude blacks from political offices. This factional dispute led him, in 1888, to praise the election of Grover Cleveland and, in 1894, to support Democratic gubernatorial candidate William C. Oates. In 1892 he helped incorporate the Afro-American Cotton Mill Company and shared membership on the board of directors with, among others, William H. Councill. Two of Stevens's daughters, Mary V. and Julia A., attended Tuskegee. Mary entered in 1884 and dropped out in 1887 because of illness. Julia entered in 1885 and did not return for the 1887-88 school term, apparently because the family had moved from Selma to the much more distant Anniston, Ala.
² Jesse C. Duke.

From J. L. H. Watkins

B'ham. Ala. May 14th/87

Dear Sir. I have not been able to accomplish anything in connection with the matter concerning which you wrote me. You must remember you enjoined secrecy. I did see the Mayor[1] however, who said that he thought that the citizens would favor the establishment of the school here. He said however that the City Council was not prepared to give any financial aid. I think however if the proper steps were taken an appropriation could be obtained. Prof. Patterson is in town working up an interest in the school. There will be a mass-meeting here Monday night to consider the matter. If anything important is done I shall write you. Prof. Patterson claims to have everything as he wants them. He says that the Gov. will appoint the trustees that he suggests. Now I would like at least half of these trustees to be colored men. Again I would like the majority if not all of the teachers to be colored. Can you arrange this? In fact I do not think that this Institution should be controlled by white men. If however Prof. P. is to be the controlling element, can you not arrange it so as to get a friend of mine, Dr. S. S. H. Washington[2] by name, on the Board of Trustees? If you can do this, myself and some friends will be under many obligations to you. Dr. Washington has just come to the state, and passed a very creditable examination before the Board of Medical Examiners. I can assure you that he is a man in every way competent to fill the positions. This is sub rosa. Please answer at your earliest convenience. With regards, I remain your friend,

J. L. H. Watkins

ALS Con. 86 BTW Papers DLC.

[1] Alexander Oscar Lane.

[2] Samuel Somerville Hawkins Washington, born in Charleston, Nevis, British West Indies, in 1858, received his M.D. degree from Howard University in 1886. He passed his examination and was certified to practice medicine in Jefferson County, Ala., in 1887, residing in Birmingham. From 1895 to 1897 Washington served as resident physician at Tuskegee Institute. He married the Tuskegee teacher and black newspaper writer Josephine Turpin. They later lived in Jacksonville, Ill.

From William J. Stevens

Selma, Ala., May 18th 1887

Dear Sir: Yours of the 17th inst to hand. Am pleased with the opportunity to be able to pay some thing on my acct by advertising.

You will greatly favor me with as liberal "ad" as possible and any other matter you may desire in our column, all of which will be deducted from my acct. Inclosed find Gov Seay's letter in recognition of the one written him.[1] Respectfully

Wm. J. Stevens

ALS Con. 86 BTW Papers DLC.

[1] Stevens enclosed a letter from James Kirkman Jackson, Governor Seay's private secretary, dated May 16, 1887. Jackson indicated that the governor intended to appoint the new board of trustees of the colored normal school very soon, and that they would decide upon the location of the new university. Jackson continued: "The Governor recognizes the importance of the exercise of great care in locating this Institution, and he will endeavor so to construct the Board that the very greatest good shall come to the cause of educating the colored youth of the State." (Jackson to Stevens, Con. 1, BTW Papers, ATT.)

To the Editor of the Tuskegee *Weekly News*

[Tuskegee, Ala., May 19, 1887]

The Sixth Commencement of the State Normal School occurs Thursday, May 26th. There will be class exercise and industrial work from 8.30 a.m. to 12 m. The graduating exercises take place at 2 o'clock p.m. Seventeen students graduate.

The annual address will be delivered by Hon. S. A. McElwee[1] of Tenn. Mr. McElwee is among the ablest of the colored men, and as an orator he has few equals. A short time ago the democratic and republican members of the Tennessee legislature united in making him a present of a gold watch for a speech delivered in the legislature.

The citizens of Tuskegee and vicinity are invited to attend any or all of these exercises. A large pavilion has been erected for the occasion and there will be plenty of room for all who attend.

B. T. Washington

Tuskegee *Weekly News,* May 19, 1887, 3.

[1] S. A. McElwee practiced law and operated a real-estate agency in Brownsville, Tenn. William Jenkins, a former Tuskegee faculty member who in 1887 was working at Fisk University, arranged for McElwee to speak at Tuskegee. He told BTW that McElwee was "much younger than anyone that you have heretofore had. And yet, I have no doubt but that he will make you a good speech. He represents the young men of today. And has had much experience for one of his age." (Jenkins to BTW, Apr. 25, 1887, Con. 85, BTW Papers, DLC.)

To Thomas Seay

Tuskegee, Ala., May 21 1887

Dear Sir: Enclosed I send you an invitation to be present at our Commencement which occurs Thursday May 26. Your presence would be a great encouragement to the people of my race and would do good in directions that would be of lasting benefit to both races.

The whites in this vicinity who always attend our Commencements will give you a hearty welcome.

We most earnestly hope that if your duties will allow you to, that you will recognize our work in this official way. Yours truly

B. T. Washington

ALS   Letters, Mar.-June 1887   Governor's Correspondence   A-Ar.

From Mary Elizabeth Preston Stearns

College Hill P.O. Masstts. May 23d 1887

Dear Friend. I have this day received yours of the 19th inst, requesting me to forward the sum of $25.00/Twenty Five Dollars/to Mr Allan Danforth,[1] Bursar Masstts. for the purchase of books relating to the physical training at Harvard. This I have done: and the check will go to him in the next mail.

I am pained to know of your overworked condition, tho' not surprised, and hope this timely aid at Harvard will be the means of complete restoration.

Had I not been so prostrated myself, I sh'ld have at least, *written* to Mrs Washington — and I will endeavor to do so immediately. More especially, as your anxiety about her strengthens my own. She has a vigerous constitution, and tho' it has been impaired, by devotion to her chosen work, still the original *stuff* is there, and I cannot but believe in the experience before her, it will stand by her to succour and save.

Be assured of my unfailing sympathy and believe me   Very Truly Yr's

Mary E. Stearns

ALS   Con. 700   BTW Papers   DLC.

[1] Allen Danforth, comptroller of Harvard University.

From William J. Stevens

Selma, Ala., May 24 1887

Dear Sir: I have put Mr S. W. John[1] and others to work, but am afraid we waited too long.

I see Montgomery is aroused and at work in earnest, I also learn from the Editor of the Selma Times that Birmingham have raised $35,000 in Cash, and that the Governor & Supt of Education both favor Birmingham, however, Selma will do her duty without making any fuss, with the hope of capturing the trustees, when appointed. I will keep you posted at this end and will leave no stone unturned. Respectfully

Wm. J. Stevens

ALS Con. 86 BTW Papers DLC.

[1] Samuel Williamson John (1845-1921) was born in Uniontown, Ala. He fought with the Confederate Army in the Civil War, graduated from the University of Alabama in 1865, and was admitted to the bar in 1866. He served several terms in the state legislature and was there when the Marion school dispute began. Later he moved to Birmingham and represented Jefferson County in the legislature. He served on the board of trustees for numerous schools as well as the Alabama Insane Hospital and the Alabama State Department of Archives and History.

To Moses Pierce

[Tuskegee, Ala.] May 31 [188]7

Dear Sir: Some months ago I wrote you the condition of our trade with Col Simms.[1] There has been no change since then. I saw him a few months ago about the matter when he was here. He said at that time that he was going home and send the deed, but has not done so. He has promised repeatedly to do the same thing. Lawyer Foster[2] of Tuskegee suggests that he give us a quit claim[3] if he can make the deed. This morning I wrote asking him to send the deed to his agent here if not to let us have a quit claim. Shall let you know what his reply is.

There is no question but what Mr. Simms means well and I think he means to give us the land but he is careless about having titles made. We have been using the land all the time just as if it were ours. When he was here he said that if he did not send the deed that he wanted us to keep the land, but this would not stand in law I guess. He understands that we hold the money to pay for the land when ever the deeds are made. Yours Sincerely

Booker T. Washington

ALpS Con. 91 BTW Papers DLC.

¹ W. E. Simms of Paris, Ky., sold 417 acres of land to Tuskegee Institute for the remarkably low price of $312 in 1898. (Deed, Feb. 7, 1898, Deed Book 5, pp. 329-30, Macon County Probate Court, Tuskegee, Ala.)

² Wilbur F. Foster.

³ BTW to Simms, May 31, 1887, Con. 91, BTW Papers, DLC, asked for a quit-claim.

From David Lee Johnston¹

Pratt Mines Ala.,² May 31-'87

Dear principal — While thinking of my may [many?] friends I thought I would write to you. Myself and several other of the boys from School arived here yesterday, we find plenty of work to do. We will all start to work tomorrow and will have an income of about $30. per month. We are very anxious to here from home and know how every thing is getting along. Mr. Washington, please send me a catalogue I want to write to some of the students and I dont know where their postoffices are. Much love to all the dear Teachers and Students that are at the building now. I am going to try and put in good time this summer and return to school the last of Sept. with a determination to do better than I have here before. I think I can gain some students to come to school nex term, any way I am going to do all I can toward the matter. Some have promised me already that they are coming.

I shall look for the catalogue. I am Mr Washington, Your obediant student

David L. Johnston

ALS Con. 85 BTW Papers DLC.

¹ David Lee Johnston, born near Tuskegee, spent much of his childhood farming there and in Dallas County. His parents' indigence forced him to work for their support. He entered Tuskegee Institute in 1885 and worked each summer in the mines, furnaces, or railroads in Pratt City, Ala., "enduring hardships which language can not describe." He graduated in 1889 and served as principal of a Negro school in Pratt City until his health temporarily failed. After working for several corporations, he studied pharmacy at Meharry Medical College in Nashville, Tenn., and upon graduation in 1896 operated a Birmingham pharmacy as a partner of George H. Wilkerson, a physician. (David L. Johnston, "A Druggist's Story," in BTW, ed., *Tuskegee and Its People*, 285-98.)

² The Pratt Mines were in Jefferson County, Ala., near Birmingham. The Tennessee Coal, Iron and Railroad Company bought the mines in 1886, and its Pratt

division eventually included ten mines. By 1889, 46 percent of the company's laborers were black, many of them first being hired as strike breakers. In 1888 the company began to use convict labor, and six years later more than a thousand convicts were working in the Pratt mines. In April 1894 the area exploded into labor violence after a strike called by the United Mine Workers.

To the Editor of the New York *Freeman*

Tuskegee, Ala., June 7 [1887]

To the Editor of THE NEW YORK FREEMAN: I must take just a moment to give you my hearty and thorough endorsement of your plans and suggestions for the formation of a Colored League.[1] Such an organization conducted on strong, intelligent and honest principles cannot fail to accomplish good. There are thousands of colored men and women in the South who are ready to support you in this matter. We shall wait to hear from you regarding a plan of procedure. Let us have something definite as soon as possible.

Booker T. Washington

New York *Freeman,* June 18, 1887, 2.

[1] The Afro-American League was the creation of T. Thomas Fortune, editor of the New York *Freeman* (later *Age*), who wanted an organization that would fight for black civil rights through the courts and publicize such issues as black voting rights in the South, the horrors of lynching, the convict-lease system, and discrimination in public accommodations. The league had chapters in twenty-three states by 1890.

In January 1890 league delegates mostly from the Midwest met in Chicago to form the National Afro-American League. The organization floundered within a few years, and in 1893 Fortune announced its demise due to lack of funds and failure to gain the support of black leaders and citizens. Five years later, as racial conditions continued to deteriorate, Fortune revived the league under the name of the National Afro-American Council. It received the support of black leaders but failed to gain mass support. The council was dominated by Fortune and the A.M.E. Zion bishop, Alexander Walters. Although BTW seldom attended its meetings, he had a powerful influence on the council through his long friendship with Fortune. The Afro-American Council gradually became identified with BTW's conciliatory approach to race relations and became a battleground of racial ideology. Race leaders who approved of BTW's conservatism were in a majority, but other members wanted the council to be more aggressive and militant in its approach to race problems. Floundering and strife-torn, the council was at a low ebb in 1905 when W. E. B. Du Bois called for a new, more militant organization, the Niagara Movement. Spurred by this competition, the council held its largest meeting in New York in 1906, when for the first time a few white men sat on the platform, including Oswald Garrison Villard, the grandson of William Lloyd Garrison. The general tone of the council was more militant than in the past, but its organization was weak and continued in name only until 1908. In 1909 leaders of the council and the short-lived Niagara Movement joined in the formation of the National Association for the Advancement of Colored People. (Thornbrough, "The National Afro-American League," 494-512.)

From Nellie A. Plummer[1]

Col'd Orphans Home, Washington D.C. June 11th. '87

Mr. Washington. How very, very busy those girls there (and boys) keep you. You never have time to write a line to an old friend. This is, you do not.

How have you been since I heard from you? Please do not be so selfish and write once a year at least. *You* a son of Wayland! Who ever heard of a sun keeping all of its rays to itself leaving the poor little sister planets in utter darkness.

It is very likely Miss Bartlett will not be here another year. Do not know whether I'll be changed or not.

I saw Prof. Storum today. He spoke of you.

How is Portia?

Two weeks from today I will be home with father.[2] Should you find time to write a line it will be gladly received. My address will be, Hyattsville, Pr. Geo. Co. Md.

Hoping I have not made too great an interruption by writing and that you will write *soon,* I am   As ever,

Nellie A. Plummer

Our schools close on the 22nd. Has yours closed yet?

ALS   Con. 86   BTW Papers   DLC.

[1] Nellie A. Plummer worked for the Colored Orphans Home, Washington, D.C.
[2] Presumably Henry V. Plummer, listed in the 1880 census as thirty-six years old, a government employee living in Hyattsville, Prince Georges County, Md.

To Warren Logan

4 Stevens st. Boston, Mass. June 14 1887

Dear Mr. Logan: I sent check for $25. this A.M. Hope to send more tomorrow. Send a receipt to Miss Eliza Brewer[1] for $50. Send it to 27 Kilby St. c/o Mr E. M. Brewer[2] also have "S. L."[3] sent to the latter. I forgot to give you an itemized acct of that $5.00. $4.00 were given Stevens[4] in connection with his seeing the Gov. about the University &c. and the $1.00 is to be charged to me.

The enclosed letter[5] I rec'd from Mr. Brooks yesterday it seems from it that matters are going well. If I can so arrange it I want to return to Ala. soon after the 20 — for a few days. Have no letters come about institutes? See that all my letters whether answered or not are kept where I can see them on my return. Say nothing about the contents of Brook's letter. If not too lat[e] you might mention in the "S. L." the photographs taken by Dortson — the average age of the class &c. See that good generous and encouraging letters are written the students in answer to theirs. The other cut to be used in running off the circulars will leave here next Saturday or Monday.

AL Con. 1 BTW Papers ATT.

[1] Eliza Brewer (d. 1926), of Milton, Mass., was the philanthropist daughter of the merchant Charles Brewer, who amassed a sizable fortune plying the trade between New England and Hawaii.

[2] Edward May Brewer (1842-1929), brother of Eliza Brewer, active in the family shipping firm.

[3] *Southern Letter.*

[4] William J. Stevens.

[5] Possibly the letter reproduced above, dated June 14, 1887.

From Arthur L. Brooks

Birmingham, Ala. 6/14 1887

Dear Sir. I came up last Friday. Every thing moving along as well as could be expected. There will be a meeting at Elder Petiford[1] Church to-night. Will write you full particulars. I went down Sunday morning to Montgomery. Seay will be pretty sure to make appointment next week. I talked to several prominent men in Montgomery — they all are opposed to the location of the school there.

I thought it best to have no more news paper controversy, as every thing is in as good position as I could ask. There was a communication in the Age[2] this morning from a col man in Selma, so I was told, giving his reasons why the school shold be located here — which was very good, but I told Watkins[3] it was best to have as little to say as possible. Will write you tomorrow. Resp

A. L. Brooks

ALS Con. 85 BTW Papers DLC. Addressed to BTW at 4 Stevens St., Boston.

[1] William Reuben Pettiford, Birmingham banker and Baptist minister, was born of free parents in North Carolina in 1847. Moving to Alabama in 1869, he studied at the state normal school at Marion and at Selma University. He became a Baptist minister in 1879, holding pastorates briefly in Marion and Union Springs. In 1883 he moved to a church in Birmingham. He established the Alabama Penny Savings and Loan Company in 1890 partially to help his parishioners to save in the small amounts scorned by the white banks. It became the second largest black-owned bank in the country, with some 10,000 depositors. BTW praised the enterprise as an illustration of "how closely the moral and spiritual interests of our people are interwoven with their material and economical welfare." (BTW, *Negro in Business,* 136.) The failure of Pettiford's bank during the cotton crisis of 1915, following the outbreak of World War I, had a traumatic effect on Tuskegee's dream of black capitalism and self-help.

[2] Birmingham *Age.*

[3] J. L. H. Watkins.

To Warren Logan

4 Stevens st. Boston, Mass. June 15 1887

Dear Mr. Logan: Your letter referring to enclosing one from Mr. Courtney &c. rec'd, but you did not enclose any.

Am doing all I can to hurry matters at this end. I certainly hope you have the Peabody money[1] ere this. Am expecting to hear from Westboro in the morning. Shall keep sending in something till we get straight.

In regard to Stevens I did ask him to use his influence against Montgomery, and told him that we would see that his expenses were paid when he went to Auburn to see the Gov. Some time before this I had heard rumors regarding his character but did not notice them much. The last time I was in Montgomery Duke told me about him more fully than I had ever known. But at this time I had spoken to him about seeing the Gov about Selma and as he was going to Birmingham I asked him to use his influence there. Since hearing what I have of him I have come to the conclusion that we had better have nothing more to do with him in this matter. I have just written him a letter asking him to do no more in our interest. Whether the school goes to Montgomery or elsewhere I intend to do nothing that I would be ashamed to have the public know about if necessary and this should be our rule in all actions.

Mrs. Washington, Portia and the baby[2] are doing well and send regards. Have no letters regarding institutes &c. come yet?

Shall write that music teacher at once. Yours Sincerely

B. T. Washington

ALS Con. 1 BTW Papers ATT.

[1] The annual report of Tuskegee Institute to the state superintendent of education, Oct. 1, 1887, reported a $500 contribution from the Peabody Education Fund.

[2] Booker Taliaferro Washington, Jr. (May 29, 1887–Feb. 5, 1945), originally given the name Baker in honor of his parents' benefactor, Eleanor Jameson Williams Baker. After the death of his mother, Olivia Davidson Washington, BTW Jr. was placed under the care of Mrs. Dora S. King and other nurses at Tuskegee and in New England until BTW's marriage to Margaret James Murray provided a more settled family life. BTW Jr. attended the Tuskegee Institute practice school. In 1902 he entered Wellesley School for Boys in Wellesley, Mass. Edward Augustine Benner, its principal, was an admirer of BTW, but he was one of a series of headmasters who were sorely tried by the son's schoolboy pranks, truancy, and fast motorcycle. Leaving Wellesley School in 1904, BTW Jr. spent a year in school at Tuskegee and graduated. He then entered Dummer Academy in South Byfield, Mass. He dropped out briefly in 1905 to build up his physical health, but returned to Dummer until the spring of 1907.

During his last year at Dummer Academy, BTW Jr.'s roommate was an old friend who had attended Tuskegee, Juan E. Gomez. BTW arranged this in the hope that Gomez, who was a good student, would have a good influence on his son, and BTW Jr. did well at Dummer. In 1907 both of them transferred to Phillips Exeter Academy, where Harlan P. Amen, the principal, was another admirer of BTW. In the fall of 1908, however, BTW Jr. suddenly left Exeter after refusing to be bound by its strict rules. The Exeter experience, however, shocked him into greater sobriety of behavior, and BTW later wrote a letter to Amen thanking him for bringing his son's life to a necessary crisis. Entering Fisk University, BTW Jr. showed a new maturity of outlook, made good grades, edited the *Fisk Herald,* and graduated in 1913. Searching for a career, he vowed he would establish the largest Negro drugstore in the United States. In the fall of 1913 he enrolled in the Northwestern University School of Pharmacy. On New Year's Eve 1913 he married Nettie Hancock, daughter of a teacher at Prairie View State College, herself a faculty member of the Colored Deaf, Dumb and Blind Institute in Austin, Tex. His wife accompanied him to Chicago for the rest of the school year, but in the summer of 1914 BTW built the couple a house in Greenwood, the residential area for the Tuskegee faculty. For the next four years BTW Jr. worked for the Julius Rosenwald Foundation in its work of constructing rural black schoolhouses in the South. In 1918 he was appointed claims adjustor for the 9,000 black employees of the Muscle Shoals nitrate plant in northern Alabama. Lacking his father's tact, he made a speech that infuriated the local white people, who forced him to leave town. He moved to Los Angeles, Calif., where he was a successful real-estate broker. His son BTW III is an architect in New York City. His daughter Nettie married the grandson of Frederick Douglass.

To Warren Logan

4 Stevens St. Boston   June 16 1887

Dear Mr. Logan: Enclosed I send checks for $1000 being from the Curtis Estate.[1] $500 of this amount as you know was left by Dr. Curtis to the school and $500 to Mrs. Washington.

Mrs. W. asks me to lend the $500 to the school for the present.

This is a great relief to me as I know it is to you. The money I collect in the next few days I shall have to give to Mrs. W. I send you a telegram to night which I thought you would understand.

I hope this am't will help you put matters in good shape. Am glad to know that Mrs. W. still improves. Hastily yours

B. T. Washington

Please send a statement showing how our acct will stand with the school.

ALS   Con. 1   BTW Papers   ATT.

[1] Estate of Dr. William Curtis.

From Warren Logan

Tuskegee, Ala., June 21st 1887

Dear Mr. Washington, Yours containing cks. for $1000 to hand one or two days ago. It was a great relief to me to get them. I sent $200. to Dr. Dorsette at once. I think with the $1000 and what you and Mr. C.[1] will be able to send in, we can tide the summer over with comparative ease. I hope we will not get into another pinch. I shall use my utmost endeavor to prevent it. I shall pay a number of our creditors in Tuskegee and away, something to keep them in good spirits.

Your telegrams were rec'd. Telegraphing is a rather expensive mode of communication. Our telegraph bill for May amounted to $10.95 — considerably more than they pay at Hampton for telegrams in one mo.

I enclose notes from Henderson.[2]

The Advertiser this morning brings news of the appointment of the trustees of the Col'd. Univ. I don't know whether the appointment of two B'gham men[3] on the Board has any special significance or not.

I send several letters.

I sent the only letters I have rec'd. in regard to the proposed institutes — one from Turpin[4] — and one from Patterson.

Kind regards to all. Yours Sincerely

Warren Logan

ALS Con. 86 BTW Papers DLC.

[1] Samuel E. Courtney.

[2] George W. Henderson of Troy, Ala., was a student from 1884 to 1889 but did not graduate. George Washington Henderson of Montgomery, who entered Tuskegee's A middle class in 1897 and graduated in 1899, was possibly the same man. After graduation, he was a coal and wood dealer in Warrior Stand, Ala.

[3] Henry Martin Caldwell (b. 1836) and Charles Whelan (1841-97), Birmingham physicians, were appointed to the board of trustees by Governor Seay in 1887. Caldwell owned a real-estate company and a hotel and was a director of the First National Bank of Birmingham, the Williamson Iron Company, and the Birmingham Iron Works.

[4] A. J. Turpin, a black teacher in Union Springs, Ala., headed a summer institute for black teachers of Bullock and Barbour counties in 1887.

From James Monroe Trotter[1]

Washington, D.C., June 21, 1887

Dear Sir: I have your favor of the 18th, inst., asking me to name a gentleman for music teacher at "Tuskegee." I take pleasure in suggesting the name of Prof. Fred'k E. Lewis,[2] Boston. I do not know that he would go, but he is well acquainted in his profession and would point out to you some competent person.

Thanking you for your kind wishes, wishing you continued and abundant success with your excellent school and hoping that you may succeed in securing the teacher needed I am cordially yrs.,

Jas. M. Trotter

P.S. In case you cannot succeed with Mr Lewis please consult, in same way, Mr. Henry F. Grant,[3] Music Teacher, 2034 17th st., N.W., Washington, D.C.

Also Fred'k White, Charles st., near A.M.E. Church, Boston. These people are all directly in the profession and ought to be able to serve you.[4]

ALS Con. 1 BTW Papers ATT.

[1] James Monroe Trotter (1844-1912) studied music in Hamilton, Ohio, and later contributed a biographical and critical study of Negroes in the field of music, *Music and Some Highly Musical People* (1878). He rose from private to lieutenant in Massachusetts' Fifty-fourth Regiment during the Civil War. Following the war he served eighteen years in the Boston Post Office. He resigned in 1883, dissatisfied with discrimination in the Republican party, and supported Grover Cleveland's election in 1884. He was recorder of deeds for Washington, D.C., from 1885 to 1887. His son, William Monroe Trotter, became after 1900 a leading critic of BTW's racial leadership.

[2] Frederick Elliott Lewis, born in Boston in 1846, was an accomplished black musician who played more than fifteen instruments including the piano, organ, violin, and flute. He taught privately in Boston, performed as a member of several Boston musical clubs, and composed and arranged music. Trotter thought enough of Lewis's talent to devote an entire chapter to him in his book. (Trotter, *Music and Some Highly Musical People,* 180-91.)

[3] Henry F. Grant sang tenor for the Colored American Opera Company of Washington, D.C., and won critical acclaim for performances in Washington and Philadelphia in 1873. (*Ibid.,* 245-50.)

[4] Apparently BTW was unsuccessful in attracting Lewis, Grant, or White to Tuskegee, for he later hired Robert H. Hamilton, Hampton's choir leader, as Tuskegee's music teacher.

To Warren Logan

Boston Mass   6/24/1887

If he needs it let Mr Brooks have money to see Trustees.

B T W

WIr   Con. 86   BTW Papers   DLC.

From Jeremiah Barnes

Tuscaloosa, Ala. June. 29, 1887

Dear Sir and Bro. Your favor of a late date is at hand and the contents duly noted. I have just returned from Montgomery and will say they have give up the idea of getting the State University. It is pretty well understood there, that they will not get it. So I think you will be alright. Please send me a Catalogue of your School, and your best terms for two Students[1] from the same family and oblige, Yours Very truly

Jeremiah Barnes

ALS   Con. 85   BTW Papers   DLC.

[1] Probably Cassie E. and Benjamin H. Barnes, of the junior class in 1887-88.

From S. Alexander Christian[1]

Greensboro, Ala., July 1st/'87

Prof. B. T. Washington: Your letter received. I have called to see Rev. F. M. Peterson,[2] and impressed him with *one* thought if no more. He says he thinks the two schools being state schools would be too close together, should Marion school be established at Montgomery — says he had never thought of the nearness of the schools before. But he has, or will not come to any conclusion until he meets the committee, and everything concerning the school is brought out. He hopes to meet you there — says he think[s] you should be there, to reason with the committee.

365

Rev. F. M. Peterson is one of Greensboro's *best* white men. A very conscientious man, and will do just what *he* thinks is right, regardless of others. He is a Methodist minister, and one of the faculty of The Southern University, at this place. If you can convince him that this school will benefit the *race* more at Birmingham, he will be on your side. He thinks it should go where it will do the *most good*. I think I succeeded in making a favorable impression on him for Tuskegee.

All well — would be glad to hear from you at any time. Your Friend,

S. A. Christian

ALS Con. 1 BTW Papers ATT.

[1] S. Alexander Christian, a white merchant of Greensboro, Ala., reported in the 1880 census as thirty years old.

[2] Francis Marion Peterson, Jr. (1854-1908), professor of ancient languages at Southern University and a member of the newly appointed board of trustees for the colored normal school. The son of a prominent Greensboro physician and Southern University trustee, Peterson graduated from Southern with a B.D. degree in 1874 and became a Methodist minister. He traveled the Alabama circuit for four years, then served on the Southern University faculty from 1877 to 1899 and as president of the Alabama Girls Industrial School from 1899 until 1907.

From E. J. Carter

Talladega, Ala., July 3, '87

Dear Friend   I received your letter a few days ago, and noted the contents. Dr. Otts[1] was away when I received yours but returned day before yesterday evening. I went to see him yesterday morning and had a long talk with him about the location of the university. I have done what I could againts Montgomery for your sake, and for the sake of the race. Do you know that the white people are thinking about uniting your school with the other university? If you don't know it, I will tell you they are and they intend to make Mr. Patterson the Principal. The governor is not allowing the Negro the chance of a dog in this matter, but let us work and wait. I hope you will be as unmovable as the everlasting mountain. Both Republican and democrat are trying to keep the Negro behind them, but God is leading on the army and if we will be led by him he will "carry us through." You have done a good work since you have come to Ala., and have thus planted yourself imperishably in the hearts of your people. You have my prayers, and my influence for the success of your good work. I believe you will succeed, for I know God is on your side. Your Friend,

E. J. Carter

ALS Con. 1 BTW Papers ATT.

[1] John Martin Phillips Otts (1837-1901), a white clergyman, was appointed president of the board of trustees of the Alabama Colored People's University by Governor Seay in 1887. Born in South Carolina, he received his education at Davidson College and Presbyterian Theological Seminary in Columbia, S.C. After joining the Confederate Army for one year, Otts was given a medical discharge. He served as a Presbyterian minister in Greensboro, Ala., Columbia, Tenn., Wilmington, Del., and Philadelphia before moving to Talladega in 1885. He retired from the ministry in 1888 to manage his father-in-law's estate in Greensboro.

From George W. Lovejoy[1]

Indian Branch Pike Co. Ala. July 4th, 1887

Mr. Washington: Your letter concerning the Institution was duly received. I attended to the matter at once. I put the argument on the ground you mentioned.

It was not merely from your request, but from an honest conviction. Your oppisition was mine precisely mine. I found there was a great deal of effort being put fourt, to secure the Institution at Montgomery, as I was on my way home from school.

I openly opposed the measure, while I was in Montgomery. I think you have a good deal of bad feeling to wards you in this matter.

A young lady told me she thought you took very unmanly steps in your opposition.

I tride to meet her with as good argument as she sent.

I am in hopes Montgomery's effort will be lost.

I am infavor of the South or western part of the state.

I wish the opposite party a defiet. Your friend and pupil,

G. W. Lovejoy

ALS Con. 86 BTW Papers DLC.

[1] George W. Lovejoy was born about 1859 in Coosa County, Ala. He picked up bits of an education before he met Robert C. Bedford in Montgomery, and Bed-

ford directed him to Tuskegee Normal School in 1884. After his graduation in
1888, Lovejoy, while employed by the school, wrote to a Mississippi newspaper con-
demning white lynch mobs. He was denounced in the local press as a liar and was
forced to flee from the school. BTW on his return to the campus denied that
Lovejoy's remarks reflected the views of the school. After teaching briefly in
Alabama, Lovejoy studied law under William M. Reid at Portsmouth, Va. According to his own account, which bears a notable similarity to BTW's *Up from
Slavery* on this point, he arrived in Portsmouth with only $1.25 in his pocket and
worked in the navy yard to earn expenses. He read law for three years and in
1892 returned to Alabama, where he won a license to practice law and settled in
Mobile. In the autobiographical account of his life, Lovejoy praised BTW but
chose not to relate the story of his forced exile from Tuskegee. (See Lovejoy, "A
Lawyer's Story," in BTW, ed., *Tuskegee and Its People,* 141-51.)

To Warren Logan

4 Stevens St. Boston, Mass, July 12-87

Dear Mr. Logan: You will have to depend largely on Mr. Courtney
for money. I must take some rest and my work at Harvard demand
some of my time. Mrs. Washington is much better and is getting strong.

Fill out "S L."[1] with whatever you can. Shall send some matter soon.

I want to see MSS. of financial report before it is printed. I hope
you will arrange to take a vacation in Aug.

Am keeping the saw-mill pay't before me and think we can be ready
for it.

Let me know what is being done and said about the university. Be
sure to watch matters carefully. We can gain nothing now by giving
way in the least. Is Prof. Wilson[2] still aggitating that matter? Yours
Sincerely

B. T. Washington

ALS Con. 1 BTW Papers ATT.

[1] *Southern Letter.*
[2] Presumably William D. Wilson of the Tuskegee faculty.

To Warren Logan

4 Stevens St   Boston, Mass, July 15-87

Dear Mr. Logan: I very much fear that the Col'd Baptist State Convention will make some effort to influence the Governor in the matter of locating State University. If you can, it will be well for you to be in Montgomery during its session. It meets on the 20th inst. Would not hint the matter to any one first as it may set them to thinking about it.

But in case you see the matter is going to be brought up, you could get Pettiford,[1] Rev. A. F. Owen and Hawthorne[2] to oppose the State Convention's meddling with the matter. Fill up "S. Letter" with what ever you think best.

Mrs. Washington is much better now. Yours sincer[e]ly

B. T. Washington

Has the Advertiser or any paper had more than that one article in it? You have sent only one paper, that contained Pattersons letter.

Write Mr. Bartol[?] a good letter in acknowledgement of scholarship.

ALS   Con. 86   BTW Papers   DLC.

[1] William Reuben Pettiford.
[2] Probably Rev. Keidor Hawthorne, pastor of the Anthony Street Baptist Church in Mobile, Ala.

To Warren Logan

47 Buckingham St. Boston, Mass. July 17-87

Dear Mr. Logan: I wrote you some three weeks ago that Norma Walker[1] paid me the $5.00 and how to charge it. I hope you got the letter.

Try to let Miss Jones[2] have all the stamps she wants for sending off those circulars. It is very important that they be sent out now as the next term is approaching.

I hope you have received money enough to meet the notes on the 15. I shall do my best for Aug. 1st. Mr. Courtney is here today and he and I are forming some plans.

Since my return I have been able to do but little my self as my wife's sickness and Harvard work have kept me close. Mrs. Washington is now I am glad to say, in pretty good condition, and I hope to be able to do more. If you can, let Mr. Brooks have money to go to Birmingham and Montgomery next week. It is important that he go to Birmingham. After that trip I think we shall have no more expenses of the kind. I am tired of the matter, but it will not [do] to let up now when we are so near victory. I have written Mr. Brooks what to do. Arrange to be in Montgomery on the 25 at the meeting of the board and watch matters. Some thing might come up that you could help in, though I think you will have no occassion to say anything.

Some of our opposers have tried to make the point that ours is not a State School and therefore should not be regarded in the location of university. When I was before the board I told them that Tuskegee was started by the State and is almost entirely under control of State Commissioners. Parties had also told them that we were under the control of some religious denomination and that our property was in the hands of Northern people. You will note that of the 12 trustees on our board, 8 live in the South. As they did not ask me I did not tell them who owned the property at Tuskegee, and this you need not speak of unless they ask about it.

The gift of the $3000 by the State makes ours a State institution and entitles it to the protection of the State that far.

But I think you will have no occassion to go before them. But you better be on hand.

If necessary Mr. Brooks will go before them, perhaps.

I hope you will do all you can in the matter.

It is my impression that I asked you in a previous letter to let me see the MSS. of financial report before it goes to the press.

Mrs. Washington sends regards to all. Yours Sincerely

B. T. Washington

If you say any thing before the trustees, it is best to speak only of the State Commissioners and not the trustees.

ALS   Con. 86   BTW Papers   DLC.

[1] Norma E. Walker Carter, of LaPlace, Ala., graduated from Tuskegee in 1889 and ran the school's industrial room for girls until 1893. After marrying John W. Carter, an instructor in carpentry, she was a dressmaker and taught in the night school. She moved to Richmond, Va., in 1901.

[2] Alice E. Jones Bailey, born in Spraguetown, N.Y., in 1863, graduated from Hampton Institute in 1885. She came to Tuskegee in 1886 and for two years was in charge of the girls' laundry. From 1888 to 1890 she was principal of the night school and librarian, and taught spelling and grammar. In 1890 she married and moved to Boston, Mass.

From Arthur L. Brooks

Tuskegee, Ala., July 19 1887

Dear Sir. On my return from Union Spring to-day I found your letter. The convention[1] decided to move the Howard College and appointed a Committee to confer with the citizens of Birmingham & Anniston and see how much each place will give. Birmingham has already proposed to give in money and land one hundred & seventy thousand dollars and say they will give that much more if necessary. The Committee will go up there this week, and I think it is best for me to keep on their track. So I will go up to-morrow or next day — from there will go to Greensboro. My great fear is that Caldwell[2] & the other trustee[3] from there will become weak-kneed. That point *must* be guarded. Will write you the day after I get there. Yours truly

A L Brooks

ALS Con. 1 BTW Papers ATT. Addressed to BTW at 4 Stevens Street, Boston, Mass.

[1] Baptist state convention.
[2] Henry Martin Caldwell.
[3] Charles Whelan.

From David Lee Johnston

Pratt Mines Ala. July 19-'87

Dear Principal: I guess as there are a good number of the boys from school here with me you would like at any time almost to hear from us. There are thirteen of the boys up here at Pratt Mines, and we are all getting along very nicely togather. When we all come togather sometimes it looks almost like the batalion every morning on the school grounds.

Mr. Washington, I have come to the conclusion that I will board at the building the remains of my time in school. I have consulted my people, and they leave the matter altagather with myself. Now I ask your views on the matter. Don't you think it would be best for me? I am sure I do. Heretofore I have been missing all of the important lectures given at night, all debating societies and all Wednesday night exercises, and I don't think from now on I can affoard to loose them. If you will give me some work to do so as to pay a part of my board, I will come in on the 28th of September. I cannt posibully come in before then. I am doing all I can to inlargen our school and I have succeeded in getting several young men to say posatively that they are coming in school with us. The weather is very warm up here. But by some means we all manage to stand it very well.

We all are having very good health, and on the whole we are doing nicely. The names of the boys up here with me are as follows. Marshall,[1] R. E. Anderson,[2] Torbert,[3] Henderson,[4] McClarren,[5] Gaserway,[6] Canty,[7] M. C. Williams,[8] Chambliss,[9] Watkins,[10] James Johnston[11] (my brother), Hubbard[12] and my self. They all like here very well but R. E. Anderson he is speaking of going home Sunday. Please let me hear from you soon and then I will know how to arange my business. I am, Prof., Your obediant student

David L. Johnston

ALS Con. 85 BTW Papers DLC.

[1] Shadrack Richard Marshall of Paschal, Ga., entered Tuskegee in 1884 and graduated in 1888. After graduation he taught in the public schools in Marshall and Columbus, Ga.

[2] Robert Edward Anderson from Montgomery, Ala., entered Tuskegee in 1883 and graduated in 1889. After graduation he taught first in Cotton Valley, Ala., and then in various other Alabama public schools. He also worked as a bookkeeper.

[3] Luke Torbert of Tuskegee first enrolled in Tuskegee in 1881 and was in 1887 a member of the senior class. He left school before the end of the 1887-88 academic year and did not return.

[4] George Washington Henderson.

[5] William Milton McClarren of Tuskegee entered the institute in 1887 and graduated in 1891. Later he taught in Alabama before moving to Washington, D.C., where he graduated from the Spencerian Business College and worked as a copyist with the U.S. Navy Department.

[6] Alfred Phileman Gazaway of Tuskegee entered the school in 1886 and graduated in 1891. Later he taught in Macon County and Birmingham public schools.

[7] James Monroe Canty, born in Marietta, Ga., in 1863, came to Tuskegee in

the spring of 1886 and graduated in 1890. He served as principal of the night school and commandant at Tuskegee during the 1890-91 school year, resigning to work as a blacksmith in Tuskegee. After 1893 he became superintendent of industries and commandant at West Virginia Colored Institute, Institute, W.Va.

[8] Major C. Williams of Greensboro, Ala., was a Tuskegee student from 1885 to 1887. He did not graduate.

[9] William V. Chambliss of Tuskegee entered Tuskegee Institute in 1886 and graduated in 1890. He taught for two years in the Tuskegee public schools before joining BTW's staff in 1893 to be an assistant in the agriculture department in charge of the dairy herd. He left the institute in 1900 to become manager of the Southern Improvement Company in Tuskegee.

[10] George J. Watkins of Courtland, Ala., attended Tuskegee from 1885 to 1887. He did not graduate.

[11] James Johnston of Tuskegee entered the school in 1886 and left in 1888. He did not graduate.

[12] Creed H. Hubbard of Montgomery, Ala., attended Tuskegee from 1884 to 1888. He did not graduate.

From Warren Logan

Tuskegee, Ala. July 20 1887

Dear Mr. Washington   I have just seen Brooks. He goes up to Birmingham this evening. Now that the Baptists have decided to remove Howard College from Marion, Brooks professes to be more solicitous than ever, about the location of the Negro Univ. He thinks that Howard will be carried to B'gham and then the same objection to placing the Negro School there can be advanced as is made against its remaining at Marion. Race antipathy will be as strong in B'gham as it is in Marion.

On reaching B'gham, if he thinks the exigencies of the case demand it he will employ a lawyer to present B'gham's claims for the Univ. The lawyer's fee, he thinks and I do too, should be paid by the B'gham people.

The Col. Baptist State Convention meets in Montgy today. I would have gone down but was sick. I shall go down tomorrow if I get better.

I send you a copy of the catalogue which we are now sending out. The col'd people of Montgy are keeping quiet about the school. I don't know whether they are on a still hunt or not.

Tommy[1] sent the letter and manuscript of the speech.

373

I don't think I can get the financial report ready for printing for some time yet. It seems hard for me to get to work upon it.

It is intensely hot here but the general health of the school keeps good. Yours sincerely,

Warren Logan

ALS Con. 86 BTW Papers DLC.

¹ Thomas M. Ferguson, a clerk in the principal's office. He later was employed by the General Land Office of the Department of Interior in Washington, D.C.

From Adella Hunt

Montgomery Ala. 7-20 '87

Dear Mr. Washington: Has the exact time for the first Teachers' Institute been given to the public? If so it has escaped me. I refer to the one to be held at Union Springs. I believe these Institutes are to last one week each. I think it well to begin the first one on the 8th of August and the second one week later. If this has been settled please let me know at once and infor[m] Mr. C.¹ of the same.

I had a talk with Maj. Palmer yesterday relative to holding one of our Institutes at Selma. I object to that on the ground that there are no schools being taught now in all Dallas Co. Not one. So of course it would be a failure in point of attendance. Also the teachers of Dallas have the benefit of those schools in Selma and I think do not need the help which the Inst. is designed to give so much as some back Co. teachers need it. Supt. P.² quite agreed with me and added that it would be more expensive for the teachers and less appreciated by the people in a city than in some smaller place.

He now says place it any where in either Hale, Dallas, Wilcox or Lowdnes³ Co. What place would you suggest? I think favorably of Greensboro. Prof. Patterson will not do any such work in just that district and is that not the best place for us?

Please advise concerning these matters at once as Supt. Palmer is to be here only a few days.

The Supt. is loud in his commendation of our work at Tuskegee and in his praise of our Prin.

It is a little cooler now than for several days passed. I hope to make a dozen or twenty calls to day. The mothers and friends of our students seem especially pleased with our teaching the young folks to work.

I trust that you will be benefitted by your physical training but you must not join the base ballists.

Love to your family. Yours truly,

Adella Hunt

ALS   Con. 85   BTW Papers   DLC.

[1] Samuel E. Courtney.
[2] Solomon Palmer.
[3] Lowndes.

To Adella Hunt

47 Buckingham St. Boston, Mass. July 22–87

Dear Miss Hunt: Your letter has just come, the institute for Union Springs is fixed for Aug. 15 and the other one is to be Aug. 22. Of all the places mentioned I think Camden Wilcox Co. the best one, but my impression is that it has no rail road accommodations and if this is true would be a bad place to hold it. Greensboro I think is the next best place.

Enclosed I send the ms. for a circular which I am going to have printed.

If Camden Wilcox County can be reached by R.R. you can change Greensboro to Camden.

Send the circular to Tuskegee at once and tell them to print 600 copies of it and send them to the teachers in the section of the State where institute is to be held. Tell them to print them and send them out right away. Sending those for Union Springs first.

Write me at once whether it is to be at Camden or Greensboro.

It is very important that these institutes be made a great success.

I am enjoying my work at Harvard though it is some what difficult, Dr. Dorsett I think would enjoy it as much if it is in his line. There are a good many physicians taking the course.

My family are all well and send love. Hope you will work up a large attendance of students from Montgomery. Yours Sincerely

B. T. Washington

ALS   Con. 86   BTW Papers   DLC.

To Warren Logan

47 Buckingham St. Boston, Mass. July 22-87

Dear Mr. Logan: In case you see that Birmingham has no chance in consequence of the removal of Howard College there, it will be best I think to help Patterson retain the school at Marion. Now I think the whites in Marion will want to keep the colored school. Speak to Mr. Brooks about this at once. Yours sincerely

B. T. W.

Patterson I think would help in this.

ALI   Con. 86   BTW Papers   DLC.

To Warren Logan

Boston Mass [July] 23 [1887]

Throw influence for school remaining at Marion if Birmingham fails.

B T W

WIr   Con. 86   BTW Papers   DLC.   Sent "c/o Dr Dorsette."

From T. W. Coffee[1]

B'ham Ala   July 27th 87

Dear Prof. Washington   I write to inform you that we lost the school after all our efforts. It could not be helped under the circumstances. The white Baptists got a petition signed against its location here & send a man to present it & make a speech against it. If that had not been done B'ham would have got it.

McAlpine[2] did us wrong in a speech before the Board. It was located at Montgomery. I am sorry it was located there. Hope it will not affect your school as much as we think it will. Mc told the Board he did not think it would hurt your school at all.

Pettiford did not meet the Board for some cause not known to us.

Clinton & myself did all could & but for the action of white Baptists it would have been located at B'ham. There was no money raised except what I had, of which I paid the expences of Clinton & self.

I have a balance of $3.00 subject to your order.

Dont forget the girl I wrote you about. She is an orphan girl & perhaps some one can be found who would give her a scholarship in your school.

Hope you much success. Yours Truly

T. W. Coffee

ALS   Con. 1   BTW Papers   ATT.

[1] T. W. Coffee was pastor of the A.M.E. Church in Birmingham from 1884 to 1887. Born a slave in 1854, he ran away from his master twice during the Civil War. The first time he was returned by a Union captain. On the second occasion, in 1864, he succeeded in escaping. His formal education was limited. He attended LeMoyne Institute briefly after the Civil War. Two years after his religious conversion, in 1876, he was licensed to "exhort," a position somewhat lower than preaching, by the A.M.E. Church. He was assigned to a mission in Decatur, Ala. A rapid succession of posts with the A.M.E. Church in Alabama followed, including positions in Selma, Mobile, Eufaula, and Birmingham. He impressed his superiors in Birmingham by erecting a church costing $8,000 and increasing the size of the congregation by more than a hundred. In 1896 he became presiding elder of the Birmingham district, and later held similar positions in the Montgomery and Greensboro districts. Coffee received his formal license to preach in 1898.

[2] Probably W. H. McAlpine (1847-1905), a black Baptist minister in Montgomery. Born in Buckingham County, Va., McAlpine was elected in 1880 the first president of the National Baptist Convention. He headed the Baptist Foreign Missionary Convention, 1880-83, and later was president of Selma University.

To Warren Logan

47 Buckingham St. [Boston, Mass.] July 28 1887

Dear Mr. Logan: What you say about the Adams[1] debt gives me more trouble than all our other debts and responsibilities. Out side of meeting Liddell's[2] note I would rather every thing else should be put aside if possible till Adams is paid a good proportion of what we owe him. He has I know done no end of talking and will do us more harm than we can recover from in a long time. It is *very* unfortunate that we should have gone on till he refused to sell us more goods. In a former letter (before the $200 from Mrs. Hem.[3] was sent) you spoke of being able to meet the Liddell note. Is it possible now to apply all the $200 to local debts? We must keep them down. What are the other two debts? Of cours[e] this is only a suggestion, you being on the ground know what to do better than I do, but I do hope you will find some way to let Adams have something and close his mouth. Shall try to write about other things tomorrow. Hastily yours

B. T. Washington

ALS   Con. 86   BTW Papers   DLC.

[1] Possibly Jesse L. Adams, partner in the Tuskegee butcher shop, Adams and Rains; the hardware merchant Lewis Adams; or the black dry-goods merchant J. W. Adams of Montgomery.

[2] Forbes Liddell & Co.

[3] Mary Tileston Hemenway.

To Warren Logan

47 Buckingham St. Boston, Mass. July 31–87

Dear Mr. Logan: Your telegram and letter regarding the action of the trustees have been rec'd. My faith is that Tuskegee will not suffer greatly for want of students even if the U. goes to Montgomery, but it is *very* unjust to put it there. We will waste no time worrying over it but throw our energy toward making Tuskegee all the better institution.

I realize forcibly what you say regarding keeping so many "heads" there during the summer. The truth is I did not have time to arrange the summer work as it should have been. Next term I shall take hold of it in time.

In some way I do hope you can start the work on the new building right away. Might get a small lot of lime from Montgomery.

I think it will be well for you to put another advertisement, using the other cut, in one of the Selma papers — the "Cyclone" or "Social Circle." I am very anxious to get more students from the counties in the "black belt" — and these papers circulate there. Then you see there are many students who have been attending Marion that will be influenced by our "ad." in one of these papers. Use the words found on back of last Teachers Association Minutes.

Pay Fortune's bill for advertising if he sends it there, Hastily yours

B. T. Washington

ALS   Con. 86   BTW Papers   DLC.

To Warren Logan

47 Buckingham St. Boston, Mass. Aug. 3–87

Dear Mr. Logan: I am very glad to hear about the "H. P. Haven" donation.[1] This is very encouraging. Some three years ago I called on Mr. Bond[2] regarding this, Mr. Courtney I guess saw him also. If you can possibly see your way clear to do so I wish you would get the plans it is very important that the ceiling flooring &c. be gotten ready now so that every thing will be well seasoned. There is much of the window and door facing that it will take a long time to get out if we do not have the plans.

I rec'd all the information you sent regarding the University.

As matters turned out I hardly see how the result could have been much different. It will surprise me if the Montgomery people raise a $1000 in cash. But perhaps the best thing has been done and it may prove a blessing in disguise to us.

We expect to start home about Aug. 10-87.

Send $1.50 to Menard[3] & Son Jacksonville Fla. to pay for and "ad" in their paper — the "Leader."

Mrs. W. and all send regards. Yours Sincerely

B. T. Washington

ALS   Con. 86   BTW Papers   DLC.

[1] A donation from the estate of Henry P. Haven, who died in 1876 at the age of sixty-one. Haven was the senior member of Haven, Williams & Company of New London, Conn., a firm that had extensive whaling operations. Active in state politics, Haven served in the Connecticut General Assembly and ran for governor on the Republican ticket in 1873. A Congregationalist, he was highly active in philanthropic, benevolent, and religious organizations and achieved a national reputation as a Sunday-school promoter.

[2] Henry Richardson Bond (1832-1909), president of the Bank of Commerce and

the Marine Savings Bank in New London, Conn., was trustee of the estate left for philanthropic purposes by Henry P. Haven.

3 J. Willis Menard, editor of the Jacksonville *Leader,* was the first black man elected to the U.S. House of Representatives. In December 1868, Governor Henry Clay Warmoth of Louisiana certified that Menard had been elected to fill a vacancy from the second district of Louisiana for the second session of the Fortieth Congress. A white man, Caleb S. Hunt, contested the election and the House settled the matter by rejecting both claims and leaving the seat vacant. Before Menard's claim was rejected, however, he was allowed to plead his case and thus earned the distinction of being the first Negro to speak on the floor of the House of Representatives. Only thirty at the time, Menard later settled in Florida, first editing the *Florida News* and later the Jacksonville *Leader.* Menard supported the Tuskegee idea of education and protested against the almost exclusive use of white teachers in most black colleges. "We demand educated colored teachers for colored schools," wrote Menard in 1885, "because their color identity makes them more interested in the advancement of colored children than white teachers, and because colored pupils need the social *contact* of colored teachers." (Quoted in McPherson, "White Liberals and Black Power," 1362.)

From Samuel Chapman Armstrong

Manchester Mass   Aug 5 [1887?]

Dear Mr Washington   Glad to hear from you & that you are improving. Please write me at once when & where I can see Dr Sargent as I wish to put myself under his care but I cannot go into town till next Wed. the 10th. Then I go to Mrs. Walter Bakers[1] at Dorchester with my girls. I wish to get all possible benefit from Dr Sargent's care. How long do the lessons last? Does the school soon stop?

What are the hours of each days lessons?

I think a set of gymnastic habits for daily life are very important. I will try to see you.

I am glad your wife is so well.

Please remember me kindly to her. Sincerely yours

S. C. Armstrong

ALS   Con. 1   BTW Papers   ATT.

1 Eleanor Jameson Williams Baker.

From J. F. Jackson

Birmingham, Ala. Aug 11 [1887]

Dear Sir   Yours received yesterday. I had thought before writing you, that my proposed suit against the railroad, following so close upon the case of Prof Councill and that other Huntsville incident, would probably stand in the way of my entering your school as a teacher. I am willing to make any personal sacrifice, but would not think for a moment of doing anything that would impair the usefulness of such an institution as yours or that would tend to create a feeling against it.

I am resolved, come what may, to bring the suit, if I can raise the $100.00, the attorney's fee. I haven't the money myself. My friends here said they would raise it for me, but I fear from the little interest taken in the case, they will not succeed. I can tell next week what can be done.[1]

Meanwhile I would not have you hold the position open, if you can fill it. Miss Shoecraft[2] is still without a position. Her address is Muncie Indiana. There is a young lady in Ann Arbor Mich whom I think you could employ. She took the degree of A.B. from Michigan University at the recent commencement, and has had several years experience in teaching. She is one of the brainiest colored women in the country and belongs to a family famous throughout the West for scholarship, culture and refinement. I know of no other lady whom I can so freely recommend to you. She desires to come South, and made application for a position in the new *university*. If you desire to correspond with her, address Miss Sophie Jones Box 1763 Ann Arbor, Mich.

Desiring for Tuskegee that the present may be her most successful year, and thanking you for the high (in my opinion too high) estimate you put upon my ability, I remain, sir, Very truly Yours,

J. F. Jackson

ALS   Con. 1   BTW Papers   ATT.

[1] No record was found of any suit brought by Jackson against an Alabama railroad.

[2] Miss Shoecraft later accepted a position at Alabama A & M College in Huntsville.

From William Hooper Councill

Huntsville Ala   Sept. 3rd 1887

My dear sir & brother: Please accept my sincere thanks for your kind
and sympathetic letter of 31st ult. I have received such from many
other prominent and patriotic friends. I had not planned an early visit
to Montgomery, but if it would be to my interest I can meet you there
at any time. I suppose that you know that I foolishly put *all* of my
money in the work here. Now, I have not ten dollars, hence you see
how necessary it is for me to go very slowly. As to my "plans & prospects": My troubles and the result, alone, have had my attention. I
have formed no plans & have no prospects — it is very dark indeed. I
do not know which way to turn. I suppose I will gather my wits soon.
Cant you kindly suggest something?[1] I am proud of the manner in
which the colored here & elsewhere have expressed their sympathies.
But our people are poor and can go little further than "feel sorry"
for ones troubles and misfortunes.

I am expecting every day a decision in my case before the Interstate
Commission.[2] That suit cost me $976.70. I have received about $75.
aid. Selma sent $30, Judge Gibbs[3] $25. Hunts Lodge $8.00, I.O.I.[4] so
far $13. The Commission will not award damages, but I am sure that
Southern Railroads will be forced to treat Colored passengers as they
do white ones.

Miss Wise,[5] although re-elected, refused to come. Miss Shoecraft
was also re-elected. She is expected. I cant see how Mr. Clark[6] got the
consent of his manhood to accept the place. When you thoroughly
understand this affair of June 4 & the subsequent persecution, you will
be utterly astounded at his coming here.

Several of our students will attend Tuskegee this year, I think.

My kindest regards & best wishes. Yours truly

W H Councill

ALS   Con. 85   BTW Papers   DLC.

[1] The letterhead of his stationery four months later (Councill to BTW, Jan.
11, 1888) indicates that Councill supported himself during his year's absence from
the presidency of Alabama A & M College by lecturing, practicing law, and
operating a teachers' employment bureau.

[2] In May 1887, Councill asked the Interstate Commerce Commission to award
him $25,000 damages "and such other relief as it may deem proper" from the

Western and Atlantic Railroad Company. He charged that on April 7 he was forcibly evicted from the first-class compartment of the railroad's Chattanooga-to-Atlanta run, though he possessed a first-class ticket. The railroad argued that such a damage suit was beyond the I.C.C. jurisdiction, but the commission insisted on confronting the broader question of racial discrimination. On Dec. 3, 1887, though declining to proceed on the damages claim, the I.C.C. ruled that the railroad be notified "to cease and desist from subjecting colored persons to undue and unreasonable prejudice and disadvantage. . . ." The I.C.C. based its ruling on the principle that "There is *no undue prejudice or* unjust *preference* shown by railroad companies *in separating* their *white and colored passengers* by providing cars for each, if the *cars* so provided are *equally safe and comfortable.*" In Alabama the state legislature reacted to the controversy by threatening to abolish Councill's school, Alabama A & M College at Huntsville, forcing Councill to resign from the presidency for a year. (U.S. Interstate Commerce Commission, *Reports, May 1887 to June 1888*, 1:292, 355, 638-41.)

3 Mifflin Wistar Gibbs, the first black city judge in Little Rock, Ark., was born in 1823. He led a varied and colorful career that included several business enterprises as well as being active in the antislavery movement and the Underground Railroad. In 1849, while on a lecture tour with Frederick Douglass, Gibbs decided to go west in search of gold in California. Later, still following the gold rush, he moved to British Columbia. Returning to the United States, Gibbs graduated from Oberlin in 1869 at the age of forty-six, and was admitted to the Arkansas bar. He was elected city judge in Little Rock in 1873. Later he was U.S. consul in Tamatave, Madagascar (1897-1901). His autobiography, *Shadow and Light,* with an introduction by BTW, was published in 1902.

4 Probably a lodge of the International Order of Twelve Knights and Daughters of Tabor, or I.O.T., founded in Illinois in 1855.

5 Presumably Miss Wise was appointed by the board of trustees to the Alabama A & M College faculty.

6 Peter Humphries Clark, who replaced Councill as president of Alabama A & M College during 1887, was born in Cincinnati in 1829. He led a varied life that reflected the black man's dilemma in America. The son of a barber, Clark attended the private high school of Rev. Hiram S. Gilmore in Cincinnati from 1844 to 1848, and then was apprenticed to a liberal white artisan, Thomas Varney, to learn the stereotyping trade. In 1849, when an Ohio law allowed blacks to organize their own schools, he became a teacher, working in a barbershop between sessions. After an altercation with a white racist in his barbershop, Clark swore he would never shave another white man, or if he did, he would cut his throat. In a mood of deep discouragement in 1850 he decided to emigrate to Africa, but got only as far as New Orleans. By 1852 he was an outspoken opponent of emigration. Throwing his energies into the Negro convention movement, he attended several national conventions before the Civil War and again during Reconstruction. In 1853 he lost his teaching position because the school board said he "commented on scriptures contrary to law." He was a Unitarian, and the objection was that he quoted passages other than those officially prescribed. For a while he worked as a grocery clerk, but he soon regained his teaching position. In 1855 he edited an abolitionist paper, the *Herald of Freedom.* For many years after 1857 he was principal of Gaines High School, the segregated public secondary school of Cincinnati. Clark was a Republican until 1872, when he joined the Liberal Republican movement. In the 1880s he was a Cleveland Democrat, a "Negrowump" who sup-

ported Democrats in protest against the collapse of Reconstruction and the Republican retreat from civil rights. He believed, however, that black men should seek their goals through economic power and the labor movement rather than through politics. He took a prominent part in the railroad strike of 1877 in Cincinnati. In 1878 he was a candidate for state school commissioner on the Workingman's party ticket, receiving 15,000 votes. He opposed desegregation of the Cincinnati public schools on the ground that this would turn over control of schools and teaching positions to whites. When the city desegregated its public schools in 1886, Clark lost his job as principal of Gaines High School. When Councill was forced to resign the presidency of the school at Huntsville because he insisted on pursuing his case before the Interstate Commerce Commission, Clark replaced him for the academic year 1887-88. Councill skillfully maneuvered to regain control of the school, however, and Clark moved on to St. Louis, Mo., where he was a high school principal and advocate of school segregation.

From J. L. H. Watkins

Birmingham, Ala., Sept. 7th 1887

Dear Friend. I wrote you a letter more than a week ago. I have looked anxiously for a letter. Well! the election of teachers took place last night. I was not elected, as I had anticipated. Can you yet see your way clear to give me something to do. If so, you will surely help a needy fellow. Professor, if you can let me have that money I let Mr. Brooks have, I would be very glad. It was $22.50. I would not ask for it; but to tell the truth I am completely out of money. To tell the truth I have not a dollar in cash. Hoping to hear from you immediately I remain Yr's. truly,

J. L. H. Watkins

ALS   Con. 86   BTW Papers   DLC.

From Mansfield Edward Bryant[1]

Selma, Ala. Sept. 8th 1887

My Dear Sir, I suppose you have heard of the terrible fight we have made for colored enterprises. I am more and more convinced that the Negro must make herculean efforts to rise up and walk himself. Every tree must absorb its own elements and grow from its own roots. We are doing a grand work here. We have two physicians, a drug store, cooperative store and one of the finest printing offices and Job offices in the State. Our power news-paper press will be here next week. We will then print both sides of our paper.

The colored people are standing by our enterprises. They are all doing grandly.

I am deeply interested in your school. It reflects credit on the Negro.

I want to make this proposition with you, viz.

We will run your advertisement one year for $20.00. We will in addition refer to you and your school in our locals. When Dr. Haygood, Langston or any other important man visits your school and speaks or whenever you have interesting exercises of any kind which would interest the public or when any of your students or teachers write essays or deliver orations such as would interest and instruct the public we will gladly publish free of cost which will keep your work before the public. You to appoint a reporter & send matter to us. This is more than we have ever promised any school. We do not make this offer purely as a business transaction but because we are interested in your work.

We would also give your students good commissions to work for our paper.

We are determined to do what we can to elavate our race but we must all be ase wise as serpents and as harmless as do[v]es.

I am giving my personal attention to my paper now. We hope to visit you soon. Yours for the Race

M. Ed. Bryant

ALS Con. 85 BTW Papers DLC.

[1] Mansfield Edward Bryant, A.M.E. preacher and editor of the *Southern Independent,* a newspaper published in Selma, was born in Seales, Ala., in 1853 and educated at Atlanta University. Leaving Atlanta only three months before he was to graduate, Bryant was converted to African Methodism and became a preacher serving churches in Selma, Mobile, and Florence from 1876 to 1883, returning to Selma in 1883 to be presiding elder of the district. In 1888 Bryant moved to Nashville, Tenn., to become the first editor of the *Southern Christian Recorder,* a newspaper published by the A.M.E. Church. Tuskegee Institute advertised in both newspapers edited by Bryant.

From Cornelius Nathaniel Dorsette

Montgomery, Ala. 9/10 1887

Dear friend   In conversation with A. S. Loveless[1] yesterday he informed me that he had at your request secured you a butcher for the school & also told me who it was, (viz Willie Green) a young man who use to work for me and is a most worthless low character, given to all the bad habits belonging to the human family — and would soon disgrace the school — unless you can get a good boy wanting to get & education that can do the business, you had better get along without any of the average butcher for they are a class of hard cases.

9/12 87

I saw mrs Stewart[2] and talked with her & think is Straight now — but they are a very peculiar set & the mother very foolishly simple over her children, she gave Duncan[3] trouble about them.

Please try and look out for Martha Mastin[4] as she is a widows daughter & a "Bro Mason."

I shall be glad to attend to any thing for the school and save you all the Traveling Expense I can.

Write me often. Remember my advice to you the night you met me a Chehaw & keep & eye single to the inter mingling of sex — whether Teacher or pupil. Truly your for the good of the Negro.

C. N. Dorsette

ALS   Con. 85   BTW Papers   DLC.

[1] Anderson S. Loveless.

[2] Presumably Lucinda Steward, the mother of Thomas W. Steward and Samuel Steward, Tuskegee students from Montgomery. Samuel entered in 1887 and left in 1889, Thomas entered in 1886 and graduated in 1890. A third boy, Georgie, attended Tuskegee for one year, 1889-90. The Tuskegee catalogs variantly spelled the last name Steward and Stewart.

[3] C. H. Duncan was partner in Dorsette's drugstore.

[4] Martha Mastin from Montgomery entered Tuskegee's junior class in 1887. She did not return for the next academic year.

From Cornelius Nathaniel Dorsette

Montgomery, Ala. 9/12 1887

Dear friend   I will doubtless worry you with many letters for some time but its all for the good of the School & the Negro race. I have really been on the "Still Hunt" for the past 3 months to see the exact position of Tuskegee & the people & the effect of the Marion School, & really I believe if any thing it will benifit rather than injure you. I may some times seem to be with Patterson but never fear its only to keep posted and to be prepared to work for Tuskegee and unless I loose my grasp on this people, you shall always have the major part of its pupils. Say but little yourself but let your *friends* (true ones) work for you, be slow & not commit your self again to any such men & Stephens[1] & Duke for they are momentary friends and for a dol they are to the extremes the other way. I see so much daily of the description of our so called friends that really I hardly know who in Montg. I could trust with anything of vital importance.

I realize somewhat the trying ordeal through which you pass daily with heart and hand to benifit all of our race and so few on whom you can rely for or go to for Council if needed. And too that man may Err, under all circumstances. But in the near future I think you will be able to show to Ala. that you are for the good of all directly the col People and indirectly the white. Hastily yours

Dorsette

ALS   Con. 85   BTW Papers   DLC.

[1] William J. Stevens.

From Collis Potter Huntington[1]

New York, Sept. 13th, 1887

Dear Sir. Your letter of 10th is at hand and in reply I would say that, while I would like very much to assist you in your good work, particularly as it is one that has always enlisted my warmest sympathy, yet my contributions this year have already gone past the limit that I had fixed and I don't feel that I can do anything more now. Regretting that I cannot give you a more satisfactory response, Yours very sincerely,

C P Huntington

ALS Con. 85 BTW Papers DLC.

¹ Collis Potter Huntington (1821-1900), a peddler and store owner by background, built a fortune through a merchandising business in Sacramento, Calif., and his participation with Leland Stanford in the Central Pacific transcontinental venture. From 1870 to 1890 he was the eastern agent of the vast railroad system controlled by the Southern Pacific and in 1890 became its president, breaking with Stanford over his preoccupation with politics rather than business. In 1869 Huntington acquired the C & O Railroad and, while extending it down the Virginia peninsula, became interested in Hampton Institute. He contributed over $31,000 in several gifts to Hampton for its industrial works and bequeathed another $100,000 endowment to the school in his will. At Newport News, where he controlled the shipyard and hired without distinction to race, he met hostility to his racially liberal hiring practices with threats to close the yards rather than exclude blacks. He opposed unionization. He aided education for both whites and blacks in the town. Near Richmond he built a reform school to teach farming and industrial skills to young Negroes. Samuel C. Armstrong believed Huntington had done more than any other one man to benefit the black race. Huntington's wife donated $50,000 to Tuskegee Institute in 1899.

From Cornelius Nathaniel Dorsette

Montgomery Ala. 9/13 1887

Dear Prof. I will see that woman about the matter, and I think you have acted wisely in the matter. Our people are so notion-fied[?] that you must be very firm & steady or they will impose on your kindness.

I shall be glad to do any thing for the good of the school in making purchases, and as you said it will give me a firm hand upon this merchantial world here — & I think I can buy to the advantage of the market.

I was thinking that it might save you a great deal of annoyance to send a circular letter to all the parent of the students saying for them to see me in matters as to childrens before worrying you over these small matters, and usually I can quiet them and doubtless save you much trouble. You may think over the suggestion & make such announcemen as seems best to you.

I am happy to know of Mrs Washington improvement and want

her to continue her medicine for some time until she feels perfectly strong.

Write urgent letters to Friends North of the schools needs & have Courtney to *Exert himself* as I think just now an important year for us & from the Southern deviltry I hope some Northern heart will open & soften for our good. This great weight of oppression must be lifted and Education is the lever & man the fulcrum. Truly yours

Dorsette

ALS Con. 85 BTW Papers DLC.

From Cornelius Nathaniel Dorsette

Montgomery, Ala., 9/26th 1887

Dear Prof. I have just arrived and met Mason Smith[1] at Depot, and listened for some time to his very unkind remarks regarding Tuskegee, and I see the whole trouble comes as I feared, & stated to you or Bedford, Viz, that he would mistake his position of student, & think himself a Prof. and demand more than the average student expects, and doubtless will attempt to tell some full grown lies against the school but I am here and shall be able to kill all he can say. I feared this knowing his disposition so well and that he was passed the age of reformation mentally, and if he does as he says — e.i. leaves the school it will be a good thing so dont make any efforts to retain him.

One thing more I hear considerable talk of the food and how its cooked. Now I think it would be well for you to call attention to it through the house keeper to see that every thing is cooked done it seems more as to manner of cooking than quality of food and it might be well to have a good bill of Fare as posible during the beginning weeks as many might get discourage then when they would not later in the term. These are mere suggestions & if practicle put them into us[e]. truly yours

Dorsette

ALS Con. 85 BTW Papers DLC.

[1] Apparently Mason Smith left Tuskegee before the 1887-88 catalog was written, for he was not listed there.

To Nathalie Lord

[Tuskegee, Ala.] Sept. 30 [188]7

Dear Madam: Yours of the 27th inst. asking my opinion regarding the advisibility of the Association[1] aiding Miss Calhoun's[2] School at Society Hill is received. In reply I would say that from my present impression of Miss Calhoun and the general surrounding of the community in which she teaches, I would say that it is a very good thing to do, but before advising it absolutely I should rather go to Society Hill. This I will do next Sunday — Oct. 2 — and shall try to write you Monday. Yours truly

Booker T. Washington

ALS Con. 91 BTW Papers DLC.

[1] Woman's Home Missionary Association.
[2] Josie A. Calhoun Tyson.

From Lucinda Steward

Montgomery, Ala. Oct 2nd 1887

Prof. Washington: I want you to take Tom[1] from carrying Brick right-away I dont want him to carry another brick and moreover that aint what you promise Tom in his letter you promised to put him in the carpenter Shop and that is where I want you to put him. if you cannot let Tom Serve the carpenter trade and cannot give him No other work he must not carry another brick. Very respectable

Lucinda Steward

ALS Con. 86 BTW Papers DLC.

[1] Thomas W. Steward.

To Richard Coulter Drum[1]

Tuskegee, Ala., Oct. 8 1887

Dear Sir: This [is] a state institution and is for the benefit of the colored people.

I write to know if it would be possible for us to secure the services of Lieut. Alexander[2] the colored man who recently graduated at West Point as professor of military tactics? Yours

B. T. Washington

ALS   Service Record of John H. Alexander, 3279 Appt. Commission and Personal Branch — 1887, Adjutant General's Office, RG94   DNA.

[1] Richard Coulter Drum (1825-1909), born in Pennsylvania, enlisted in the Army in 1846 as a private. Promoted to first lieutenant during the Mexican War, Drum remained in the Army and became assistant adjutant general during the Civil War. He was made adjutant general in 1880. He retired from active service in 1889 with the rank of brigadier general.

[2] John Hanks Alexander entered the U.S. Military Academy at West Point in 1883. Surviving the discrimination of cadets and faculty, he graduated in 1887, thirty-second in a class of sixty-four. Commissioned a second lieutenant, he was one of three black officers of the Buffalo Soldiers, four black regiments assigned to the West. He served in Nebraska, Wyoming, and Utah before coming to Wilberforce University as professor of military science and tactics. He died in service in 1894.

From Nathalie Lord

Boston, October 10 1887

Dear Sir: It gives me great pleasure to inform you that our Executive Committee empowered by the Board of Directors passed the following vote today.

"That this Association furnish the support of Miss Josie Calhoun, in Society Hill, Alabama, for 3 months at a salary of $39. a month.[1]

We shall be glad to have you hold the same relation to this school as to those in Cotton Valley and East Tallassee. Very truly,

(Miss) Nathalie Lord
Home Sec. C[olored?] M[issions?][2]

ALS   Con. 86   BTW Papers   DLC.

[1] Note on letter in hand other than BTW's: "Wrote to Miss Calhoun."
[2] Woman's Home Missionary Association.

From Richard Coulter Drum

[Washington, D.C.] October 11 [188]7

Sir: Referring to your letter of the 8th instant, inquiring whether it would be possible to secure the detail of 2d Lieut. John H. Alexander, 9th Cavalry, as professor of military science and tactics at the Tuskegee Normal School, I have the honor to inform you that the Army regulations forbid the detail of an officer for duty of this character until he shall have served three years with his regiment.

I enclose a copy of an order publishing the laws and regulations governing details of this character. You will observe that section 1225 Revised Statutes, as amended by act of July 5, 1884, permits the detail of forty officers, but requires that they be distributed throughout the United States according to population. In the apportionment made under this requirement, the states of Alabama and Florida are, jointly, entitled to one officer, and the one to which the two states are entitled is now serving at the Agricultural and Mechanical College of Alabama. It would therefore be impracticable, even if Lieut. Alexander were eligible, to make the detail desired. Very respectfully, Your obedient servant.

R. C. Drum

HLpS Service Record of John H. Alexander, 3279 Appt. Commission and Personal Branch — 1887, Adjutant General's Office, RG94 DNA.

To Samuel Chapman Armstrong

Tuskegee, Ala., Oct. 12 1887

Dear Gen. Armstrong: I go North about the 22nd to speak at the W.H.M.A.[1] annual meeting and to do my usual work in Boston.

Will you be at Hampton about the 23 inst.? There are some matters that I want to talk with you about. Then the new ideas that I get always pay me to stop at Hampton.

We have 306 students in school leaving out those in the training school. This is about 120 more than we had at the same time last year.

I have given Mr. Hamilton a position here and I hope he will do well. He will be here this week.

My wife is pretty well now. Yours faithfully

B. T. Washington

ALS   BTW Folder   President's Office Vault   ViHaI.

[1] Woman's Home Missionary Association.

From Missouri C. Strong

Felmington,[1] Ala., Dec. 1, 1887

My dear teacher: It is with the greatest of pleasure I write, anxious to tell you of my success in work. I am teaching at the same place I first taught.

My school opened on the seventh of Nov. with ten pupils, now I have forty on roll.

Daily attendance is about thirty six.

I am getting along very nicely at present.

The people seem to like my way of teaching very much.

My school will run for five months. Two of which will be independent.

There are only seventy six dollars of public money. The sum is quite small, but the people were so anxious to have me teach for them, I agreed to do so.

Since I have been here, I have gotten them to build a nice school house. It is very comfortable indeed. We also have it furnished nicely with stove, blackboards, globe, and desks.

I have a nice Sabbath School too; something that never has been allowed to have here before. From twenty to twenty five attend nearly every Sunday.

The scholars pay for their quarterlys every quarter.

I would be ever so glad to have you send us any kind of reading matter that you have to spare. The people seem to be very interested in the school work, and they try to do everything I ask of them towards building up the school.

I am trying all I can to break up some of the bad habits that so many of these people are guilty, such as using so much whiskey and tobacco especially.

There are very few own land, because these two things take all the cash they make.

Mr. Washington, I would like to take the Southern Letter. Please send it, and I will send the money at any time. Write soon. Yours truly,

Missouri C. Strong

ALS Con. 90 BTW Papers DLC.

¹ Probably Flemington, Ala., in Pike County about 50 miles south of Tuskegee.

From Charlotte L. Forten Grimké[1]

Jacksonville, Fla. Dec. 2 '87

Dear Sir, The near approach of the 80th birthday of the poet Whittier suggests to my mind a plan in which I would be very glad to have your co-operation. My suggestion is that the pupils of each of the leading colored schools of the South should contribute something towards a birthday present for the venerable poet, as a token of their admiration & esteem, and their gratitude for his earnest, untiring labors in behalf of our race. I presume all the older pupils in the schools know some thing of his life and his writings, and each action might therefore be confined only to them. I know the pupils in our schools are poor, but I suppose there are few who could not contribute the sum of ten cents, and in a large school, this would amount to a sufficient sum, for it would not be necessary to buy a valuable present. The simplest thing, as a token of their appreciation, would be sufficient. I know Mr. Whittier very well personally, and I know that such an offering would be most pleasing & gratifying to him. If you think favorably of it, will you propose the plan to your pupils? I am suggesting it to two other important colored schools, also.

Mr. Whittier's birthday will be on the 17th of this month. His address is Oak Knoll, Danvers, Mass. Anything sent by express would be sure to reach him there. If something characteristically Southern, or *Alabamian,* could be sent him, I think it would be peculiarly fitting. If your scholars should send him a present, will you have the kindness to let me know what it is, as I feel greatly interested in the matter.

Mr. Grimké[2] is well & joins me in kindest regards to you & Mrs. Washington & the dear little girl whose picture I prize very highly. Believe me, Very truly yours

Charlotte F. Grimké

ALS Con. 88 BTW Papers DLC.

[1] Charlotte L. Forten Grimké (1837-1914), granddaughter of the wealthy black Philadelphia sailmaker and abolitionist James Forten, married Francis J. Grimké in 1878. Born in Philadelphia, she was educated by tutors in her grandfather's home and in the home of her uncle, Robert Purvis. Sent to Salem, Mass., in 1854 to live with the black Salem abolitionist Charles Lenox Remond and to attend the Salem public schools, she graduated from Salem Normal School in 1856 and began teaching in the Epes Grammar School in Salem. During the Civil War she worked as a teacher among the freed slaves in Port Royal, S.C. Her journal of the Port Royal years is one of the most vivid documents of social history of the Civil War era.

[2] Francis J. Grimké was born in Charleston, S.C., Nov. 4, 1850. He and his brother Archibald were children of a slave mother and a wealthy planter father, Henry Grimké, whose sisters, Sarah and Angelina, were prominent abolitionists. Freed upon his father's death in 1852 and put under the guardianship of his white half-brother, Francis Grimké escaped at the age of ten when his half-brother threatened to reenslave him. He served as a Confederate officer's valet for two years, returned in illness to his mother's home, and was sold to an officer for the remainder of the war. After attending school briefly in Charleston, Grimké went north with his brother Archibald, eventually gaining entry to Lincoln University in Pennsylvania. While he was at Lincoln his Aunt Angelina, now the wife of Theodore Dwight Weld, discovered his identity and publicly proclaimed her relationship. Graduating as valedictorian in 1870, Francis Grimké studied law at Lincoln and Howard until 1875 and then attended Princeton Theological Seminary, where he graduated in 1878. A few months before his graduation from Princeton he married Charlotte Forten. He served as pastor of the Fifteenth Street Presbyterian Church in Washington until ill health drove him to assume the pastorate of the Laurel Street Presbyterian Church in Jacksonville, Fla., in 1885. He returned to his Washington church in 1889 and remained at its head until his death in 1937. In the 1880s and 1890s Grimké supported BTW enthusiastically, working to counteract criticism of the Tuskegean among his friends. Grimké wrote to *The Christian Register* in 1886: "The school speaks for itself. It has demonstrated its right to the respect, confidence, and generous support of the friends of education everywhere, especially of the education and elevation of the emancipated millions of the South. In this respect, it is doing a work whose importance cannot be overestimated." (*Christian Register,* 65 [Mar. 25, 1886], 182.) After 1900, however, BTW's accommodating stand on disfranchisement and other racial issues turned Grimké away from Tuskegee and toward BTW's opponents. He signed the call for the National Negro Conference in 1909 that led to the founding of the NAACP and later served as president of its Washington branch.

From John W. Whittaker[1]

Nashville, Tenn., Dec. 12, 1887

Dear Sir: Your letter came duly to hand. Contents noted.

I can only say that I have been studying with a view to preparing myself for just such a position as you say may likely open up in your school. I have always had a special fondness for teaching the youth and preaching the Word of God. And if there should be a call for me to come to your school to fill such a place, and duty seems to lay in that direction, I do not feel that I ought to refuse to accept, provided anythink like a decent living was offered me.

I am engaged here for one year, which ends the first of next Oct.

I shall be glad to hear from you again in regard to the matter. Give me all the particulars you can in regard to salary, parsonage, and so on.

Hoping to hear from you soon, I am   Very truly yours,

Rev. John W. Whittaker

ALS   Con. 91   BTW Papers   DLC.

[1] John W. Whittaker (1860-1936), a graduate of Atlanta University and Livingstone College Divinity School, an A.M.E. Zion school, came to Tuskegee Institute in 1888 as chaplain. In the summer of 1889 he toured the Black Belt, preaching to rural blacks, and wrote an article in the *Southern Workman* commenting on their immorality, poverty, and lack of education. Whittaker left the Tuskegee faculty in 1891. In 1901 he accepted a position as a financial secretary, one of several traveling fund raisers of Tuskegee Institute. He became acting dean of the Phelps Hall Bible Training School in 1906, and later became chaplain again until his retirement.

From Erastus Milo Cravath

Nashville, Tenn., Dec. 21st 1887

Dear Sir: We have no uniform method of designating scholarship by figures. In the monthly examinations, which are written, the papers are marked on the scale of 100. Some teachers mark daily recitations. The aim in marking is 1st to stimulate the student & 2d to help the teacher to judge justly of standing in promoting students. In most studies there seems to be no way of attaining a reasonable degree of fairness in promoting students except by some system of marking by daily recitations or by very frequent examinations.

It must however be admitted that the test is far from absolutely reliable. Very truly yours.

E. M. Cravath

ALS   Con. 94   BTW Papers   DLC.

A Speech before the Literary Society of Tuskegee

[Tuskegee, Ala.] 1887

Some Lessons from Socrates[1]

While Socrates had his short comings and peculiarities it is helpful to look above and beyond them to the great moral and religious truths which he taught and practiced.

Socrates like many other valuable men grew up in poverty, and as in many other cases his poverty enabled him to get near the heart of the common people, while his great wisdom enabled him to be associated with the opulent. It was his desire to *know* the people, to know wherein they were strong and wherein weak, in order that he might know how to benefit them.

His was the philosophy of every day life; and it was all the more interesting and valuable because it bristled with the living thoughts of the people.

He gave his whole life to one object even to the neglect of his personal comfort and the proper provision for his family. His entire energy was given to an effort to right the wrongs in morals, religion and politics in Athens.

What were his methods in teaching? In the first place we find him gifted with an extraordinary amount of common sense — a quality much lacking in these days. He knew how to talk to the most ignorant in a way to interest them and make them understand.

He disclaimed any pretentions to possessing wisdom or being classed among the philosophers of his day, but maintained under all circumstances that he was only a seeker after knowledge.

This position gave him an immense advantage over his contemporaries.

Coming more directly to his method of teaching we find it largely based on questioning. His questions were put in such a manner that an adversary was gradually and unconsciously convinced of his error.

Knowing that the most effectual way to bring about a reform was to begin with the young we find him spending much of his time moving about in an easy and unostentatious manner in their company.

He was continually before the people. His method was not to teach by set or formal lectures. Much of his work was with individuals — now spending an hour in conversation with an eminent artist, now with a common mechanic.

His reasoning was that the state was made up of individuals hence to inspire right principles in the hearts and minds of the individuals of the various crafts and professions was to reform the state.

One writer Says: "His usual method was to apply to the person whom he wished to bring over his own opinion with a pretended ignorance as one who wanted to obtain information and without asserting anything himself he would put to him in succession a series of questions which admitted but one answer, and so by degrees bring him to acknowledge the truth which Socrates wished to establish.

He used to make his appearance as it were by accident amidst the various tribes of Athenians who were listening to some famous Sophist and professing his admiration for such talents and eloquence and the straitness of his means which debarred him from the advantage of becoming a scholar of so able a master, he would propose some simple question to the Sophist to which an eloquent but diffuse reply would be given upon which Socrates would request him to so far honor his infirmities and slowness of comprehension as to proceed step by step. When this was done he soon made manifest the clearness and justice of his own opinions, and the confused and inconsistent notions of the Sophist, reducing him by a series of simple but closely connected questions to admit the truth which Socrates desired to prove. In vain did the Sophist treat with contempt the maxims of common sense and plain downright morality which were at variance with his own notions as to the best methods of prospering in life. Socrates returned with coolness of temper to the charge and by a series of such attacks exposed the inconsistency the shallowness of those "pretenders to wisdom."

Socrates was perhaps the purest and strongest character of antiquity and certainly we must admit him a most remarkable man when we consider that he was without those aids to right living which we of this age possess.

To find a man in that dark age devoting his entire life to helping others was something that the world was not then ready for.

He was a man of one idea and that was to do right as his conscience enabled him to discern the right.

During the trying ordeal of his trial before the Athens Court we find him exhibiting almost super-human moral qualities.

His knowledge that the charges against him had been concocted by his fellow philosophers who were jealous of his wisdom served more perhaps than anything else to bring out prominently his high moral qualities.

When brought before the court his most intimate friends could not persuade him to say any thing in the way of supplication.

After being condemned he concluded his address to the court in these words:

"But it is time that we should depart, I to die, you to live — but which for the greater good God only knows."

But Socrates reveals himself to us more clearly in his Apology or speech before the Athenian Court and his conversation with Crito. In his Apology when his enemies suggested that he should be ashamed to follow a calling for which his country men would condemn him to death, we hear him reply as follows: "You say not well my friend, if you think a man who is good for any thing ought to take into account the chances for living or dying, and not rather when undertaking any thing, to consider only whether it be right or wrong, and whether the work of a good or bad man."

When it was suggested that a promise from him to the effect that he would cease to teach the people, might secure his release and save his life he sets forth his position in these words: "Athenians I love and cherish you, but I shall obey the God rather than you; and as long as I draw breath and have the strength, I shall never cease to follow philosophy, and to exhort and persuade any one of you whom I happen to meet as is my wont: How is it friend, that you an Athenian of the city greatest and of most repute for wisdom and power are not ashamed to be taking thought for glory and honor and for your possessions that they may become as great as possible, while you take neither thought

399

nor heed for wisdom and truth and for your soul that it may become as good as possible?"

Again he says: "Listen then to what has happened in my life that you may know that to no man would I ever yield, through fear of death even though by not yielding I might instantly perish."

To the suggestion that he might stand a better chance for acquittal before the court if he would by shedding tears and by other outward demonstrations try to work on the sympathies of his judges he answers: "You probably think O citizens, that I have been convicted for the lack of such arguments as might have persuaded you, if I had thought it right to do or say everything in order to escape this sentence. Far from it, I have been convicted by a lack not of arguments, but of audacity and shamelessness, and of willingness to say such things as you would like to hear; because I would not weep and lament and do and say many other things to which indeed you are accustomed in others, but which, as [I] have told you would be unworthy of me. But I did not then think that on account of danger, I ought to do anything unmanly, nor do I now repent the manner of my defense. I would much rather die having thus defended myself, than live on such terms as these.["]

In his closing argument he thus addresses the judges: "But you too, O Judges, it behooves to be in good hope about death and to believe that this at least is true — there can no evil befall a good man whether he be alive or dead, nor are his affairs uncared for by God."

When urged by his friend Crito to escape from prison after his condemnation his high moral sense is brought out in this answer: "Then starting from these admissions we must consider whether I should be acting Justly or not in trying to escape when the Athenians refuse to release me, and if it appears that I shall be acting justly I shall make the attempt. . . . Then indeed my friend we ought not to heed what the multitude say about us but only what the one man who understands about the just and the unjust & what truth herself will say."

With one more lesson from him I close.

When still further urged by Crito to escape from prison he gives him to understand that he cannot commit such a wrong against the state, and adds: ["]Consider well, there fore whether you agree with me and are of my mind; and then let us start with this conclusion that it can never be right to commit injustice or to retaliate or defend ourselves by rendering evil for evil."

HD Con. 955 BTW Papers DLC.

¹ BTW probably used the *Translation of the Apology, Crito, and Parts of the Phaedo of Plato* (New York, 1878) by William Watson Goodwin of Howard University. The influence of the better-educated Olivia Davidson Washington on his speaking and writing style is strongly suggested by his frequent classical and literary allusions during his marriage, in contrast to the more plain and direct style both earlier and later.

From Cornelius Nathaniel Dorsette

Montgomery, Ala., 1/3rd 1888

Dear Prof Washington   There is a young man about 15 who lives near the city (in country) who wants to enter Tuskegee. I think his people are able to meet exp. and keep him up, he is of the crude country material & in time can be developed into a good young man if you can admit him ans by return mail as he will be in Thurs. for a reply. Yours truly

Dr Dorsette

ALS Con. 88 BTW Papers DLC.

From Henry B. Rice

Winifrede, W.Va. Jan. 7th, '88

Dear Friend, The Executive Board of the West, Va. Baptist State Convention, in its meeting at Charleston on the 3, inst. — appointed me to assist Elder C. H. Payne¹ to raise the "Shelton College" Fund; I therefore beg to draw upon you for some information on conducting a work of this kind.

We began this work in Aug. '86, and now after more than a year and a quarter have elapsed, we can point to the grand total of $173.13 as the result of our arduous efforts! Of course at this rate it is going to require more than fourteen years for us to raise the ($2800.00) amt. necessary to purchase. Is not this a sufficient apology for my asking advice from an honored, respected and successful solicitor of funds for educational purposes?

Will be thankful for any suggestion you may be pleased to make. Very faithfully and Truly yours,

Henry B. Rice

ALS Con. 90 BTW Papers DLC.

[1] Christopher H. Payne (b. 1848), a black minister, editor, and politician. Payne attended school in Charleston, W.Va. He taught in several public schools before attending Richmond Theological Seminary, where he graduated in 1883. He served as pastor of a church in Coal Valley, W.Va., and in 1885 established a weekly paper, *The Enterprise*, which advocated self-help, the purchase of land, and the building of homes. He was one of the most effective black Republicans in the state. In 1884 he was an alternate delegate to the Republican national convention and four years later served as a convention delegate. In 1890 he was appointed deputy collector of internal revenue at Charleston. He served as U.S. consul in St. Thomas, West Indies, under Presidents Taft and Wilson. After the United States purchased the islands from Denmark in 1917, Payne served as a judge in the new Virgin Islands territory.

From Robert Charles Bedford

Montgomery Ala   Jan 10 1888

Dear Prof   Yours of the 7th did not reach me till this morning. We are all rejoiced that the Dr[1] is much better. I agree with you that the matter of the church[2] is one of great importance and I am not sure in my own mind that I am satisfied as to what is the best solution of it. There will be no harm I am sure in delaying as long as necessary a final reply to Dr Ryder.[3] I am glad to hear of the good condition of the school and of the additional facilities for work. I am resolved to keep an eye on Lovejoy.[4] He will yet if he lives reflect credit on the school and honor the profession of the Law. Keep him largely on his own resources. I hope you will not do too much for Anderson.[5]

I am more and more convinced that the only way to teach the girls for their own good and the discipline of the school is to put at once before them what they must do within a certain time or suffer the extreme penalty for such cases as theirs. They have held so much to their statement that they did not know they could not come without permission till they were all ready to come that I have thought possibly there might be some misunderstanding in the excitement of the occasion which might serve to lessen their wrong a little. Prof Logan could not give details as to your directions but of the standing rule of the school with reference to withdrawals from its care.

It is supremely important that discipline be maintained even if every scholar is lost. I predict an enrollment of at least 500 before the close of the year. Hard, quiet, patient, sympathetic work for any thing is bound to tell. A great many are praying for Tuskegee and will continue to carry its interests as they have long done in their hearts. I will try and name a day before you go North. Let me know just when that will be. I may have to speak on "Some of the Steps that lead up to the Emancipation Proclamation." Preparation of this and much other extra work have taken time from my other subject and I shall not be able to get it ready till into Feb'y. I think the subject mentioned will interest the students and I hope profit them. It really involves Henry Wilson's great theme "The Rise and Fall of the Slave Power."[6] Will it do?

I saw Prof Paterson this morning. He has been greatly troubled as you will see when you come. Says he has written only what he was absolutely obliged. He has recd your letters and will reply to all to day.

I think more of him on acquaintance and if he can be trusted as I believe he can his heart is with us all and with every good work. I will try to have Mrs Bedford come with me.

She joins me in love to Mrs Washington the children and yourself. Your bro

R C Bedford

ALS Con. 87 BTW Papers DLC.

[1] Presumably Cornelius Nathaniel Dorsette.

[2] Refers to a proposed church or chapel at Tuskegee Institute.

[3] Charles Jackson Ryder (1848-1917), a Congregational minister, was born in Oberlin, Ohio, and graduated from Oberlin College and its seminary. He became corresponding secretary of the American Missionary Association and was a trustee of Oberlin, Fisk, and Tougaloo universities.

[4] George W. Lovejoy.

[5] Robert Edward Anderson.

[6] *History of the Rise and Fall of the Slave Power in America* (3 vols., Boston, 1872-77), a polemical work on the slavery struggle stressing the guilt of the southern "slavocracy" and the heroism of abolitionists and Radical Republicans.

From William B. Paterson

Montgomery, Ala., Jan. 11. 1888

Dear Friend Washington, Our whole work has been in a state of suspense for some time and while I have been busy, yet I have been afraid to anticipate anything as to the future.

Of course I would be pleased to talk to your students but if my reply comes too late, let it go.

I think the matter is settled so far as our school individually is concerned, but the Supreme Court may be called in to decide as to the Constitutionality of all the Normal Schools.[1] This I judge from editorials in the Dispatch.

———————

Noble Tarrant[2] was in good standing when he left our School.

———————

I will make a note of H. W. Cobb's[3] Expulsion.

———————

If desired, I can prepare a paper in any one of the following subjects or any other you may suggest:

"Character, the end of Education"
"The Ability and Responsibility of The Teacher."
"Language in our Common Schools."

———————

The Progress Printing Co transferred to me a claim of $34.00 against the Association.[4] How can I get it? I have written to Hazel[5] to Cheeks[6] and to Echols,[7] and have heard nothing from them. Regards to all   yrs truly

W. B. Paterson

ALS   Con. 90   BTW Papers   DLC.

[1] No record has been found of an Alabama Supreme Court decision on the constitutionality of normal schools.

[2] Presumably a student at the Alabama Colored People's University. Paterson and BTW cooperated in denying admission to students suspended or expelled from each other's school.

[3] Henry W. Cobb of Black Water, Fla., entered Tuskegee as a member of the preparatory class in 1887.

4 Alabama State Teachers' Association.

5 F. S. Hazel of Birmingham was treasurer of the Alabama State Teachers' Association in 1887.

6 Rev. R. M. Cheeks of Selma was a member and chairman of several committees of the Alabama State Teachers' Association.

7 J. H. Echols of Selma was a member and former treasurer (1886) of the Alabama State Teachers' Association.

From Celia Smith[1]

Malden, W.Va. Jan. 11th, 1888

Dear Sir. I rec'd your letter today, and was so glad to hear from Portia and hear she was well. I will give Mr. Parrish[2] the Receipt for my box, and he will see about it. I am tolerable well. Tell Portia I want to see her very much. I was glad to hear Portia could read. Portia you must learn to write, and write to Grandma. Give my love to your little brother[3] and Mama. to little John Washington[4] and Aunt Susie.[5] Tell me what your little brother is named. Any assistance you can give me will be thankfully received. My wrist has not gotten well yet. No more at present only write often to me about Portia. Yours truly

Celia Smith

P.S. I hope to get my box in a few days. I need it so much.

C. Smith

ALS Con. 90 BTW Papers DLC.

1 Celia Smith was the mother of Fanny Norton Smith Washington, BTW's first wife.

2 John W. Parrish, a white resident of Malden, was reported in the 1880 census as "Receiver of Court."

3 BTW Jr.

4 John Henry Washington, Jr., born about 1887.

5 Susie Miller Washington, wife of John Henry Washington. Formerly of Charleston, W.Va., she married Washington in 1886. The couple had eight children. She died in Tuskegee in 1932.

From William Hooper Councill

Huntsville, Ala., Jany 11th 1888

My dear sir: Please accept my thanks for your kind favor of the 11th inst. You may place me on your programme, and I shall observe your requests concerning "practical and definite subject," time &c. I would like for you to suggest a subject. However, if you are not inclined to do so, I shall take some branch of industrial training, say: *The Need of Educated Labor in the South.*

I hope that your work is as prosperous as you desire it to be, and that the dear good Lord is blessing you in all things according to your highest wishes. I am, with great respect,

W. H. Councill

ALS   Con. 87   BTW Papers   DLC.

From Cornelius Nathaniel Dorsette

Montgomery, Ala., 1/12th 1888

Dear Prof   I had a long talk with Mr Loveless[1] and also read him your letter and while he is much depresse and grieved over the matter yet he take a most rational view of it and attaches no blame to you or your care & vigilence in it. I also drew a diagram showing him the exact location of buildings, pump, & Girls dormitory, under which Miss Hunt tell my wife the act was committed. So I think he has the proper idea & will act accordingly upon my suggestion of quietude.

I am anxious to come up just as soon as I can and talk to the students for a few minutes of the care of their morals, & how careful they should live, and too while this matter is in their minds also regarding those that are put back & the feeling they should have in such cases.

All is going quite smooth here now. Saw the matter that will soon go to the Supreme Court of Ala. as to the legality of all Normal Schools, white and col. The auditor wishes to test the Constitutionality in as much as this Univ matter is to be dropped where it is & not carried up, will write you when I am more informed in the matter. Truly yours

Dorsette

ALS   Con. 88   BTW Papers   DLC.

¹ Presumably Henry A. or Anderson S. Loveless.

From Robert Charles Bedford

Montgomery Ala   Jan 12 1888

Dear Prof. Yours of the 11th Jan just recd. I saw the Dr¹ yesterday and we talked fully of the matter. We regret it exceedingly and yet feel that it is by no means an unheard of thing or at all peculiar to colored people. Nor do we regard it as in any way a source of discouragement or a thing that will injure the school. We appreciate your prompt and decisive action. It will put a premium on the school as a safe place for our sons and daughters. I feel very sorry for all concerned especially for the parents. I hope the 2 guilty ones may yet be saved. Shall try to see them. Let all your promptness and decisiveness of action be tempered with a most kind and sympathetic feeling.

I feel sure that both the Dr and myself rest fully in your good judgment and deep interest in all the scholars and yet with the great and ever increasing responsibilities laid upon you our sympathy and desire to be of service to you continually moves us. The thought of a church and some truly good and wise man over it is continually in my mind I feel sure that in answer to many prayers the Lord is going to help us unfold this new feature of the schools great work. Love to you and Mrs W   Your bro

R. C. Bedford

ALS   Con. 87   BTW Papers   DLC.

¹ Cornelius Nathaniel Dorsette.

From Peter Humphries Clark

Huntsville, Ala., Jan. 16th 1888

Sir: Your favor of 9th inst. is before me. Being so recent a comer into the ranks of the teachers of this state, I expected, for some time to come, to play the part of a listener, not a talker.

But accepting your kind invitation in the spirit in which it was undoubtedly given, I will prepare a discourse on this theme: The Moral training of Youth — the teacher's part in it.

The theme is of course not new, but newness in themes for a teacher's meeting is hardly to be expected at this late day.

I hear wonders related of Tuskegee. Wish I could spend a week with you and have the opportunity to study your work and perhaps adapt some of it to our work here.

As was expected I had some trouble in getting full hold here; but early obstacles are mainly overcome, and we have entered on our second term, with full classes and a good spirit for study. I am Sir, With respect, Yours &c

Peter H. Clark

ALS   Con. 87   BTW Papers   DLC.

From Cornelius Nathaniel Dorsette

Montgomery, Ala., 1/18 1888

Dear Prof Washington   I enjoyed my visit more than ever before since my long connection with the school, and while there was a most sincere feeling almost verging sadness that I could not account for, that frequently cause tears to fill my eyes, yet I enjoyed it and felt that I must do and say then as I knew not when I would pass that way again. I cannot express my admiration for the noble & unselfish work you are doing, and truly only Heaven can reward you   dolls[1] are inadequate to compensate you, for when I look over those 325 faces & think of the number of families they represent and over what a vast Territory you are sending those golden thought & principals of character to the up building of our race I feel more and more what I said to your Teachers that each one should feel that it was his or her duty to do *all* in his or her power to assist to the fullest extent of their mental & physical ability, never letting the thought of dolls entre into it at all. But how peculiar & Stern is human nature, Blind to its faults, impregnated with conceits, and un-tiring in relentless demands, and its to be regretted that the larger portion of our race is not wanting in any of the above. And when we find one without such its like the *Oasis* of the *Desert* to a weary traveler, glad to be found and sad to be parted with. And in conclusion I can only say as before I am with you at heart and shall ever pray that I may be of service to you in your work — with Love I am most sincerely yours

Dr Dorsette

ALS   Con. 88   BTW Papers   DLC.

¹ Dollars.

To Abby E. Cleaveland

Tuskegee, Ala., Jan. 19, 1888

Dear Miss C.: Your welcome and interesting annual letter has been on my desk for several months, and an answer has been put off, not because of any lack of interest in the subject, but from the fact, as you know, that the fall months are the most busy ones.

There is a colony of fourteen Hampton graduates here, besides one undergraduate. In all we have 24 officers and teachers. Our enrollment of students is now more than 400. This leaves out the number in the Training School. You can judge by these figures that we have grown a little even since I wrote you last year. In all I think there are 16 or 17 Hampton graduates in Alabama.

It is hard for one to realize how much good Dr. Dorsette is doing in Montgomery. I do not know of a single colored man in the South who is meeting with the same success in his profession, and who is, at the same time, doing so much good. I have never seen a man grow as he has. His heart and hand are ready for every good work. He comes to Tuskegee very often, and is as much interested in the work here as one of our own teachers.

At Pensacola, Florida, we have another Hampton graduate, Mr. Matthews.[1] He is also greatly interested in Tuskegee, and sends us a number of good students.

It is my intention soon to attempt to form a Southern Branch of the Hampton Alumni Association.

Whenever you have an opportunity I hope you will come to see us. Mrs. W., my little Portia, and my little boy Booker T., join me in love to you.

I should not forget to say that the Misses T.[2] still remain firm friends to us. Yours faithfully,

B. T. W.

Southern Workman, 17 (Mar. 1888), 29.

[1] Reuben Hearde Matthews.
[2] Probably Misses Ellen and C. Thurston.

From Samuel E. Courtney

Hartford, Conn., Jan. 28th 1888

Dear Mr. Washington, I enclose you Mr. Page's[1] letter which I found waiting my arrival here.[2] You know more about your plans for a knitting department and what kind of a machine you will want than I, so I will state to Mr. Page that you will write him at once as to your plans &c. I will tell him nothing about your plan, so write him as though I knew nothing about it.

He will want to know at once. We are having the coldest weather I ever felt. Rail road trafic is nearly stopped. Citizens say it is the coldest in 30 years.

I am quite well and stand it with no trouble. Love to all. Respectfully yours,

S. E. Courtney

ALS   Con. 87   BTW Papers   DLC.

[1] Thomas C. Page, treasurer of the Confectioners' Machinery and Manufacturing Company in Chicopee Falls, Mass.
[2] Page wrote to Samuel E. Courtney, Jan. 25, 1888 (Con. 89, BTW Papers, DLC) that General Armstrong "says the Tuskegee Normal School is all right." He offered the school a knitting machine.

From Blanche Kelso Bruce[1]

Moline, Ill. Jany 29 188[8]

Dear Sir: Yr valued favor 11th inst. inviting me to deliver the annual address at your next commencement was received at Indianapolis sometime since and forwarded, but through an error in the address only reached me yesterday. I sincerely regret that engagements long since made prevent my accepting your courteous invitation. Very truly yours

B. K. Bruce

ALS Con. 87 BTW Papers DLC.

[1] Blanche Kelso Bruce (1841-97) was born a slave in Prince Edward County, Va., the son of his master and a slave woman. Educated with his master's white son, he became the white half-brother's body servant until his escape early in the Civil War. He went to Hannibal, Mo., and began a school for Negroes. After the war he attended Oberlin College for two years. He then moved to Mississippi and established himself as a planter, accumulating a sizable fortune. He held several political offices in Mississippi during Reconstruction, including county assessor, tax collector, sheriff, and superintendent of schools. His political career culminated in election to the U.S. Senate in 1875. Bruce was the only black man to serve a full term in the Senate during Reconstruction.

In 1885 Bruce returned to private life after several political appointments following his Senate position. He spent much of his time lecturing around the country on the race problem and Republican factional politics. He was one of the most popular black speakers in American history. Bruce served the Harrison administration as recorder of deeds for the District of Columbia until 1893. As such, he was the dean of Negro federal officeholders. He continued his interest in education during his last years as a trustee of the Washington, D.C., public schools. After his death, Bruce's widow, Josephine B. Bruce, became the lady principal of Tuskegee. His son, Roscoe Conkling Bruce, was director of Tuskegee's academic department immediately after graduation from Howard in 1900, and later, with help from BTW, became assistant superintendent of schools for Washington, D.C., in 1907. R. C. Bruce had a stormy career as a well-trained but unrepresentatively conservative leader of education in Washington's black community.

From Mary A. Robinson[1]

Benton, Ala., 1) 29th) 1888

Dear Principal. Don't think hard of me for not writing to you in the way I requested to do. My misfortune is the cause of it I were married in last July the 10 my house was burnt down on the 29 of Nov. 1887. all we had were lost, my husband cotton, 5, bedstead one feather bed, $50.00, 4 pillars, father in law, mother in law, six children in family, we have not got up a house yet but soon will have one up the roads are so bad untill we can not traveble over them.

But with the aid of the people they have hlep us with some bed clothes & we also lost 3 hogs one beef flour sugar molasses it were for Xmas day but unfortionly lost them all.

But my father live over in Lowndes Co. he hope me to a load of coin & the day I went over there he told me to write to you to ask you to write to him for to let him know if there are any room for sister Maria[2] he want to send her to the Normal school now since I have got away from him. I have also lost every book, I that I had in the house wish that your could help me to some think.

The lord says blest it is those that lenthis to the poor he shall not loose it. I also had a bro. in law to get shoot axidently on the 16th, of Dec. 1887 age 14 Remember my love to all of my teachers.

I have had, hard times doing the past year.

I am not teaching School this Sesson. I am unable to do much yet any way I am sorrow that I can not come in the Normal School any moore for I am too poor now. I have all most lost all I have ever had from true student of youse all ways studing a bout your all but fail to write

M. A. Robinson

ALS Con. 90 BTW Papers DLC.

[1] Probably Mary A. Robinson, who attended Tuskegee Institute from 1882 to 1884 but did not graduate.

[2] Possibly Maria L. Robinson, who entered the junior class at Tuskegee in 1888. She did not graduate.

To Thomas C. Page

[Tuskegee, Ala.] Jan. 31 [188]8

Dear Sir: Mr. Courtney has forwarded me your letter written to him at Hartford and we are very glad that Gen. Armstrong wrote favorably of our work.

It is our desire to knit gloves and hosiery — you of course know the best machine for this purpose.

We have already a sewing department and want to start the knitting in connection with this.

There will be no trouble in finding a market for what we make, as many articles can be disposed of to our students and the out side community. Starting on a small scale we think we can make it grow into a valuable industry.

Some of our teachers were knitters at Hampton and understand how to operate the Lamb[1] machine. We shall not need a stand. Yours truly

Booker T. Washington

ALpS Con. 91 BTW Papers DLC.

[1] Perhaps a machine developed or improved by Joseph Lamb, a Manchester, England, inventor of textile machinery.

From Sarah Newlin[1]

Philadelphia, Feb. 6th [1888]

Mr. B. T. Washington, My sister and I send each fifteen dollars for the "matcher" hoping you will be able to get the balance needed. When you do will you devote the difference between the cost of buying windows and doors and that of making them at the school towards paying your debts for machinery, until they are extinguished? I sympathize with your strong wish to get the machines that save ultimate expense, but am always sorry to hear of debt, unless it can be cleared off at once.

I do not understand your commendation of Thweat[2] in your paper. He left teaching to publish the very poorest paper I ever saw — "The Black Belt" — of which he sent two copies to me. There were all kinds of mistakes all over it — misuse of big words ("chimerical" for chemical in almost the first line!) and an ignorant pretence that was pitiful to see. I hope there are but few of your graduates who undertake what they are so incompetent to do. Teaching the rudiments of an English education is so honourable and useful that it might well satisfy the ambition of any one who has had few advantages, and it is so very much better to do a little thing well, than to do a big thing badly!

413

A little paper "Journal of Woman's Work"[3] has just been started here. It interested me, and in subscribing for myself I thought your girls would be interested in it, so I had a copy sent to your school, subscribing for it for you for this year.

Enclosed cheque for $30. From Miss Katherine Newlin $15. myself $15. Your friend

S Newlin

ALS   Con. 90   BTW Papers   DLC.

[1] Sarah Newlin and her sister Katherine regularly contributed to both Hampton and Tuskegee for many years.

[2] Hiram H. Thweatt.

[3] Perhaps *Woman's Work for Women,* a monthly journal begun in 1886 by the Women's Foreign Missionary Society of the Presbyterian Church.

From Cornelius Nathaniel Dorsette

Montgomery, Ala., 2/9 1888

Dear Prof   I saw Dr Hill[1] & he will come up *Sunday* & see & attend to all the eyes that need attention, as to chg's he says he does [not] care much, just what ever you can do will be satisfactory to him. Make it as plesant as posible for him by showing him if he wishes any of your improvments & asking his opinion of Sanitary arrangements. That will please him as I know he likes such.

Yellow Stone Kit[2] has been raising hell here among the Negroes & trying to stir up mob & violence to those who oppose him. Last night at 6 P.M. Rev McEwen received a letter from some col men threatening him & giving him 24 hours to leave town or he would be mobbed.[3] He of course came to me for advice, & I advised him to put the letter for what it was worth in the hands of the Police which he did and since then 5 have been arrested, fined $50.00 & bound over to U.S. Commissioner, *"under act of conspiracy"* & doubtless when they are through they will regret their rash steps to promote *Kits* interest.

There were 25 waiting armed & ready for the attack last night and *I* mounted my horse & rode until nearly day around H. A. Loveless' house (where McEwen boards) to see if any attack would be made & if so to tellephone those in Loveless house of their approach, but for-

tunate for the mob they backed down as "Kit" would not lead them.
I was surprised Prof. to see that some of our ministers viz Dixon,[4]
Weathington & Shepherd have been bribed by such an infamous
Blasphemous man, and refused to sign the ministers Resolutions de-
nouncing him (Kit) because he has given them money, when I see
men supposed to be intelligent taking such a course, I can but say
who can we trust?! & whither are drifting?? The best class of whites
are with us & denounce Kit & his medicine as being a humbug.

Well all else has been going smoother and we hope soon to be rid
of Kit, for the Negros are going wild over him & business is almost
suspended, some of the Negros are so foolish as to want to pick a fuss
with their best friend for him.

Prof Patterson was delighted with his visit up there. Love to all
truly yours

C. N. Dorsette

ALS   Con. 89   BTW Papers   DLC.

[1] Luther Leonidas Hill was a twenty-six-year-old white physician and member of
the Montgomery County Board of Health. Born in Montgomery, Hill attended
Howard College at Marion, New York University Medical School, Jefferson Medical School in Philadelphia, and Kings College in London. In 1884 he began
practicing medicine in Montgomery. By 1887 he was president of the Montgomery
County Medical Association, and in 1897 was president of the Alabama Medical
Association. He wrote many scholarly articles on medicine including a seminal
study, "Retention of the Testicles" (1899). His son Lister was Democratic senator
from Alabama from 1938 to 1969.

[2] Yellowstone Kit was a traveling patent-medicine salesman whose "long curly
hair and foreign marked face . . . easily distinguished [him]." He visited Montgomery for several weeks in January and February 1888. His sales pitch, directed
mainly to blacks, featured a minstrel show and long speeches by Kit. The Montgomery community tolerated him until it was reported that he made "incendiary
speeches to negroes, telling them they ought not to pay yet until their landlords
furnish them better houses and that they are merely eating the crumbs that fall
from the rich men's tables. . . ." "Montgomery people are patient and tolerant,"
noted a letter to the Montgomery *Advertiser*. "They are kind to the stranger within
their gates. They even recognize the right of persons to come here and carry away
the money of the ignorant and credulous, but whenever they abuse the license
afforded them and take advantage of their positions . . . to intermeddle with our
domestic concerns, patience then ceases to be a virtue." Nine Montgomery black
ministers charged in a letter to the Montgomery *Advertiser* that Kit was cheating
"poor illiterate colored people," that by opposing prohibition he "injured the
good name and standing of the colored race," and that "his public harangues in
heaping abuse and ridicule upon the white citizens of Montgomery" bred "bad
blood which may terminate in a war of races." He was arrested on February 11
for offering entertainment without a license. The case was dismissed, ostensibly for

lack of evidence, but probably also because Kit agreed to leave Montgomery. He did so on February 12. (Montgomery *Advertiser,* Feb. 5, 9, 10, 11, 12, 1888.)

[3] Rev. A. N. McEwen, one of the denouncers of Yellowstone Kit, received a note signed by about twenty black followers of Kit: "We give you twenty-four hours to get out of this city, for your expression in your paper about the ladies of this city going to Kit's show, and calling the ladies — and the gentlemen jackasses. And now we give you twenty-four hours to get out of the city." (Montgomery *Advertiser,* Feb. 10, 1888, 4.)

[4] Probably John Dixon, listed in the 1880 census as a fifty-five-year-old black farmer living in Montgomery County.

From James B. Washington

Fayette Sta. W.Va. 2-12-1888

Dear Bro: I rec'd. your letter some time ago, and was truly glad to hear from you. We are all well at present, and hope you and family are well also. I also rec'd the papers you were so kind to send me. I enjoyed reading them so much. Hettie[1] sends regards to both you and your wife and wishes to see you all. Kiss Portia for us. Give my regards to John and his wife. Times are better just now up here than they have been for some time. We have had some very wet weather here for the past few weeks. Of course I will wait until you notify me. I know there is no use changeing your place until you can get a suitable place or a place worth changeing for. I am digging coal at present, and have been all Winter. I will soon be straight now. I am about out of debt now. I would be glad to see you all now as I have not seen you for some time. Booker Jr.[2] is well and can stand alone, he can also walk two steps. I hope by the next time I write to you that he may be walking. I hope to hear from you soon, and hope you are getting along nicely with your school, and I am glad you have such a large enrollment.

It is getting late, and I must close. All send love to you all. Your Brother

Jas. B. Washington

ALS Con. 91 BTW Papers DLC.

[1] Hattie Calloway Washington, James B. Washington's wife.
[2] Booker C[alloway?] Washington, James's son.

From Samuel E. Courtney

Cleveland, Ohio, Feby. 20th 1888

Dear Mr. Washington, After four days hard work, I am *very much* convinced that Cleveland is not the field which you think it is. To say that I am disappointed is putting the matter very light.

I spent Friday and Saturday trying to get before a church on Sunday, and finally had to accept the Unitarian church,[1] providing I would not ask for a collection, or call on any of the parish for help. The ministers are not much in sympathy with us. You can only reach the people through the ministers. Mrs. Matthews does not belong to the Unitarian church, dont know what church she goes to, as there are several families of that name here. Cleveland is a very wealthy city and is chiefly represented in the Episcopalian and Presbyterian churches.

The only fruit of my visit here will be the names of some of the wealthy citizens and the ministers to whom we can send the "Southern Letter," which may prepare the way for a future visit.

I will start South tomorrow. Will stop over a train at Chattanooga to see Mrs. Steel.[2] Will arrive at Tuskegee Thursday night or Friday morning. Regards to all, Very respectfully yours,

S. E. Courtney

ALS Con. 87 BTW Papers DLC.

[1] Courtney wrote to BTW on Jan. 13, 1888 (Con. 87, BTW Papers, DLC): "I find you have written most of the donars in Providence. Still I am very glad that I went, as a few of our friends there were beginning to think that Tuskegee was a Unitarian school. I find many who receive our annual report are thinking the same. Genl. Marshall suggested a remedy for that in our next report, which I will explain to you before the next report comes out."

[2] Mrs. A. S. Steele of Chattanooga was a donor to Hampton and Tuskegee institutes.

To Lemuel Bateman

[Tuskegee, Ala.] February 25 [188]8

Dear Sir: I am very sorry to inform you that we have been compelled to expel your son[1] from school. He has been guilty of striking a student in the dining room. In addition he has made use of and circulated very vulgar and filthy language. We have made the most searching investigation and find that these charges are true beyond a shadow of a doubt although he denies all except the fighting. I have in my possession proof of the most substantial character. The pain at being compelled to take this action cannot be greater to you [than] to me, but our school must be kept clean [and] pure. We cannot keep in school for an instant a student who would be guilty of using [or] circulating the language he has used. My action has not been hasty. I have taken plenty of time to investigate in the matter. You owe the school $13.10 for his board up to the present. This includes $1.65 to pay his way to Montgomery. This I hope you will send at once. Yours Truly,

B. T. Washington

HLpS   Con. 91   BTW Papers   DLC.

¹ William Bateman of Montgomery, Ala., entered the preparatory class at Tuskegee Institute in 1887.

From Celia Smith

Malden, W. Va. March 6th [1888]

Dear Sir. I have not rec'd my box yet. Mr. Parrish has written three or four times for it, and got no answer, only once. He told them to send it to Malden. I have suffered for my clothes. The receipt said *Charlestown.* If it comes back to Ala. let me know. I will have to come to Ala. to see about it if I don't soon hear from it. Give my love to Portia. Tell me where I can find out about my box. I do not want to come there about my box, but I cannot afford to loose it. I am not able to work. I wrote to you a long time ago, have not heard from you. No more,

Celia Smith

P.S. The Depot Agent of Malden sent to me to know who sent it, and to whom it was sent. I told him plain. Write to me at once about it. I am uneasy about it.

ALS   Con. 90   BTW Papers   DLC.

From S. M. Phillips[1]

Natchitoches La. Mar. 10th 1888

Dear Sir: Your letter was received yesterday — the petty salary that you offered amused me, but lo! when I glanced for a second time at the heading of the letter & saw that your school was for the colored race, my chagrin was too great for smiles. Hoping this will terminate our correspondence, I remain   Very Respectfully,

Miss Phillips

ALS   Con. 90   BTW Papers   DLC.

[1] Miss S. M. Phillips, "desirous of securing a situation in some Normal School or College as 'Training' teacher," wrote to BTW on Feb. 26, 1888. (Con. 87, BTW Papers, DLC.) She presented herself as a "teacher of considerable experience," specializing in elocution and educational methods.

From Alice M. Ferribee Lewis

St. Louis. March 12th 1888

Dear Friend and Schoolmate. I have read and heard a great deal of your wonderful success as a leader of our race, and have always felt proud of you as a classmate of mine. I hope that your prosperity may ever continue and that you may live long to do much good before going to receive your great reward in heaven. Maybe you have heard from Mr. Lewis[1] and I from time to time, how we have struggled with helping our people by building up churches and sunday schools.

Mr. Lewis was sent here to secure the deed for a church which none of the former pastors had been able to get, on account of the property having been made over to a man's wife. It has given us lots of trouble and I don't want it said that we were not able to secure the deed. Mr. Hutchins Inge who is a teacher in this city has helped us to raise some money; and I thought I would ask you to do all that you could any amount will be acceptable, but please think how very much we need help and do all you can. I have undertaken to raise one hundred dollars by the first of April.

I hope you and yours are well. There are only three of us my husband my boy of ten summers, Ira John Lewis, and myself. Please be kind enough to answer my letter immediately. Mr. Lewis joins with me in respects to you. I hope to see you again some day. I should like so very much to visit your school. I am so much interested in our work here until I have pushed myself forward and made a request of you, do all you can for me in helping to carry on the work of the Gospel and verily you will in due time reap your reward. From   Your Old Schoolmate

Alice M. Ferribee Lewis

ALS Con. 89 BTW Papers DLC.

[1] Peyton Lewis, a member of the Hampton class of 1875, served as pastor of several Methodist Episcopal churches and in the early 1890s attended Wabash College.

To John Roy Lynch[1]

[Tuskegee, Ala.] Mar. 14 [188]8

Dear Sir: We are exceedingly glad that you can accept our invitation[2] and we shall be willing to bear your expenses from Washington here and return.

In my letter I mentioned Thursday May 24 as the date of our Commencement, but since then we have thought it best to change the date to May 31. But in case you have so arranged your business that you can not be with us on the 31st we will let the date stand as first arranged. As I leave here in a few days for N.Y. I should like the date fixed on before I go so I enclose $1.00 for a reply by telegram stating whether or not you can be with us on the 31.

Rev. F. J. Grimke was with us a few days ago on his annual visit and his conversation concerning you made us all the more desirous to have you deliver the address. Yours Sincerely

B. T. Washington

ALpS Con. 91 BTW Papers DLC.

[1] John Roy Lynch (1847-1939) was born a slave in Louisiana and, like BTW, was a house servant in his youth. He fled slavery during the Civil War and settled in Mississippi. Lynch began what little formal schooling he received in 1866, thanks to northern teachers. Six years later he was speaker of the Mississippi House

of Representatives, having in the meantime mastered photography, served as justice of the peace, and sat for two terms in the Mississippi House. Elected to the U.S. House of Representatives in 1872, he took his seat there at the age of twenty-six. But his days as a publicly elected official were numbered, as the Democrats gained control of the state and by redistricting and intimidation managed by 1876 to emasculate the Republican party. Against even those odds, Lynch won another term in the House in 1880. But in 1882, at the age of thirty-five, when a promising politician would usually try for higher office, he was retired from elective office by the race issue. Instead of hoping for elective office, Lynch had to content himself with the struggle for control of the flagging Mississippi Republican party. He later served as an auditor in the Treasury Department and as a paymaster in the Army. At the time of this letter Lynch was in Mississippi dealing in real estate and running his two plantations. After retiring from public office, he challenged the inaccuracies of Reconstruction history, pointing out in his *The Facts of Reconstruction* (1913) and in other essays that the Reconstruction period was not the era of rape, pillage, and incompetence portrayed by the Dunning school of historians. During his last years he completed his autobiography, *Reminiscences of an Active Life: The Autobiography of John Roy Lynch* (1970).

² In a letter to BTW from Natchez, Mar. 10, 1888 (Con. 2, BTW Papers, ATT), Lynch agreed to deliver an address at the next commencement.

From William D. Floyd¹

Troy, Ala; 3-21-88

Dear principal: If you will get those circulars and other matter concerning the "State Teachers' Institute" here, by Apr. 7th I will be able to see [a] great many of Pike County teachers, as that will be pay day with them.

I can't say at this writing whether I shall be present at the meeting. I will come if we are allowed to vacate during that time.

We have a full school. We have more than two teachers can teach but we have to make out as best we can. J. C. Thomas² has opened an independent school here in Troy. Some did not like it because I whipped their daughters and others because I would not put their children in the highest grade in the school. Thomas tried to get a position in our school but the Board refused to give it to him. So after he found out that he could not get in the "Graded School" he then begin to work against our school, slyly. I was told by some confidential friends that he talked it around that the young lady, that is helping me and myself, did not know enough about teaching, to teach. So he has sided with the kicking crowed and opened an independent school. Mr.

Washington will you write to Thomas and explain to him how important it is to get these people united, and see if he will not close his
school. Don't let on to him as if I have had anything to say in regards
to this matter. It is not from a good motive why he opened this school.
I desire your assistance in this matter.

I've had more trouble since Thomas has been home than any other
time since I have been here.

I received some things from a friend North last week. Yours Truly

W. D. Floyd

ALS   Con. 88   BTW Papers   DLC.

¹ William D. Floyd graduated from Tuskegee in 1887 and taught school in Troy
and Opelika, Ala., until 1894, when he began working for the Southern Express Co.
in Opelika.

² Presumably John C. Thomas, who attended Tuskegee Institute from 1881 to
1885 but did not graduate.

From William Hooper Councill

Huntsville Ala   March 21st 1888

My dear Professor: Please send me a few of the programmes as soon
as published.

I hope that the Association will be a success in every way. I want
you re-elected President. I shall try to be there at the beginning, but if
I am not, I hope that a committee will be appointed who will give us
a good set of officers, as heretofore. I have heard of no opposition to
you, and I am quite sure that your re-election would receive universal
approbation.

I sincerely hope that your family is well and your work prospering
according to your highest wishes. I am very truly

W. H. Councill

ALS   Con. 87   BTW Papers   DLC.

From Warren Logan

Tuskegee, Ala., Mar. 23d 1888

Dear Mr. Washington   I suppose by this time you have reached New York and seen a number of the friends of our work and I trust that they have responded to your appeal with liberal contributions. Please send in the money as fast as you can. We have need, *urgent need* for a good big sum. You remember that we were unable to pay Howard's[1] bill for Feb. supplies, when it fell due. I promised to settle it in 10 or 15 days. The amt. is $314. Besides this, our note for $500. for Mch. supplies and bills amounting to several hundreds for same, fall due in a few days — and must be paid. The students are paying about as well as usual. A great many, by far too many, have not paid anything nor is it likely that they will be able to pay anything. Ours comes as near being a charity school as it is possible to come without being one in fact.

I have been obliged to suspend Thos. Stewart and Frank Rogers[2] from school for the remainder of the year. You will remember that you put these two young men to work until their bills were paid. Well after working for two or three days, they concluded to quit and did so, Rogers on the plea that he was sick, which was false and Stewart because he did not tell you that he would work. I saw Stewart and ordered him to return to his work. Instead of doing this, he went to the town, Rogers going with him. I sent the officer of the day for them and had them brought back to the school. Then I repeated the order that they return to their work. They gave me the understanding that they would do so — but instead of returning to work they went out and packed their trunks and had them hauled to Chehaw and went there themselves with a view of going to Montg'y. on the evening train. When I learned that they had gone, I sent for them to Chehaw & they came back to the school. Through the whole affair they were respectful but determined to have their way. I thought that the least we could do, was to suspend them. Rogers was dropped back into the Junior class. This, however, had nothing to do with his strange conduct as it was not announced until after he had attempted to run away.

Mrs. Washington's lecture last night was much enjoyed. The weather has been quite disagreeable this week. Rains and high cold winds have prevailed. Yours Sincerely,

Warren Logan

ALS Con. 89 BTW Papers DLC.

¹ Probably R. F. Howard and Company, grocers in Tuskegee.
² There is no record that Frank Rogers finished his work at Tuskegee, but Thomas W. Stewart graduated in 1890.

To Warren Logan

102 W. 37 st. [New York] Mar. 24 1888

Dear Mr. Logan: I hasten to send you the enclosed checks¹ for $100 which I know you are wanting.

Hope to send more soon. Yours Sincerely

B. T. Washington

ALS Con. 91 BTW Papers DLC.

¹ On Mar. 26, 1888, BTW sent Logan $25 more, with the comment: "Press down on students about their board bills." (Con. 91, BTW Papers, DLC.)

From Olivia A. Davidson Washington

[Tuskegee, Ala.] Monday. [Mar. 26, 1888]¹

All goes well today darling. I am glad to hear that you are in N.Y. as the sooner you begin the sooner your work there will be over. Rain is falling in *torrents* all day today.

The certificates are found & Mr. Morin² is sending them.

Little Brother³ continues feverish & fretful but I think it is his teeth. Take care of yourself. *Keep your feet dry.* Kisses & love from the children & your loving

Olivia

ALS Con. 87 BTW Papers DLC.

¹ The date is established by the fact that the letter was written on the back of one from Julius Davenport dated Mar. 20, 1888, and the only Monday that

month after Mar. 20 was Mar. 26. The references to New York and the heavy rains tend to confirm this date.

[2] M. Arnold Morin was clerk in the Tuskegee Institute principal's office from 1887 to 1890, and principal's secretary from 1890 to 1893.

[3] BTW Jr.

To Warren Logan

[New York] Mar. 27 1888

Dear Mr. Logan: Enclosed I send check for $.[1]

Am sorry about Stewart and Rogers but think you did right in ~~expelling~~ suspending them. Be sure to give Mr Brown as many boys to work at carpentry as he can take.

Shall try to send more money soon.

I am more than ever satisfied since stopping at Hampton that our course of study should be lowered and simplified. The students have too much to cover in 4 years. Yours Sincerely

B. T. Washington

ALS   Con. 91   BTW Papers   DLC.

[1] BTW omitted the amount.

From Warren Logan

Tuskegee, Ala., Mar. 27th 1888

Dear Mr Washington: I have rec'd. yours of 24th inst. containing checks for $100, which are most welcome. News of the Barnes bequest[1] is very gratifying. Truly the Lord will provide. I trust you are meeting with success in getting money for our work. Please send in the money as fast you can. There are some pretty pressing demands for money being made upon us. We will pull through all right, however, I believe.

Your brother has been ill for the last few days. He is better today and will doubtless, be out in a day or two. It has rained here almost continuously since Sunday morning. We are threatened with another flood like the one we had in '86. Some of the rivers in the State have risen 20 ft in last forty eight hours. Mails and passengers from Tuskegee are being hauled to Chehaw by hacks — there being a wash-out on the R.R. Many students have colds in consequence of getting their feet wet.

Matters are going reasonably smoothly. Yours Sincerely —

Warren Logan

ALS   Con. 89   BTW Papers   DLC.

[1] The estate of the publisher Alfred S. Barnes in New York City gave $1,000 to Tuskegee in 1888. Barnes was earlier a contributor to Hampton Institute.

To Warren Logan

102 W. 37 St. N.Y. Mar. 29 1888

Dear Mr. Logan: The sum $25 I send tonight is not a very encouraging one. Things are all to pieces on Wall St.[1] and that makes money hard to get just now. The people are hoping for a change soon, and so am I. Yours truly

B. T. Washington

ALS   Con. 92   BTW Papers   DLC.

[1] The New York stock market sharply declined in late March 1888, after the announcement of a dividend cut by Jay Gould's Missouri-Pacific Railroad. This was part of a general downward market trend from late 1887 through 1888.

From Warren Logan

Tuskegee, Ala., Mar. 31st 1888

Dear Mr. Washington — Your letters of 26th, 27th & 28th have just been rec'd. — the floods, which were almost equal to those of '86 — delaying them two or three days.[1]

Communication with the outside world was resumed last evening. We feared at one time — a food famine — but we managed to pull through all right. The situation was rendered worse by the sickness of four of the teachers. Altogether, the week has been a hard one.

Matters in general are going about as usual.

Your brother is up and out. Sincerely yours —

Warren Logan

ALS   Con. 89   BTW Papers   DLC.

[1] The Montgomery *Advertiser* of Mar. 27, 1888, reported that the rivers in Macon County had risen more than twenty feet and that the Tuskegee Railroad had been washed out.

To Warren Logan

631 Pine St. Phila. Pa. [March 1888]

Dear Mr. Logan: Enclosed I send check for $25. Sent $210 yesterday in a letter to Mrs. W.

It is my intention to be at home the first of next week. You will perhaps remember that Miss Hunt spoke of two other girls as stealing. Their cases sh'd be looked into and if they are guilty they shd be sent away.

I hope matters are going well. Miss Clark's[1] having to go away is unfortunate. Yours truly

B. T. Washington

ALS   Con. 91   BTW Papers   DLC.

[1] Laura L. Clark taught history and drawing at Tuskegee from 1886 to 1888.

A Speech before the Alabama
State Teachers' Association

[Montgomery, Ala., Apr. 11, 1888]

Opening Address

Ladies and Gentlemen of the State Teachers' Association, of Alabama:

For the seventh time we meet in our annual gathering — a gathering which has so far proven a blessing and honor to the State and race. Coming as you have direct from your fields of labor, perhaps at a sacrifice of time and money, let us at least hope that our meeting shall not only prove restful and refreshing, but that each may go back to his field of labor inspired by a new determination and increased zeal to accomplish more and better work than in the past.

As I look over your faces the question presents itself, for what purpose is this gathering? What end do you have in view in meeting here? Perhaps, if you say education is the end sought after, I would follow this question with another, and ask, what end does education seek to accomplish? I deem it not out of place at the beginning of our meeting to spend a few minutes in considering the subject, "What is the end sought for in education?"

Let us if possible get close up to the question and look it directly in the face. What end are we seeking for in education? Why this annual gathering of teachers from all parts of the State? Why spend so much time and money to attend these meetings?

WORK OF THE FAITHFUL TEACHERS

What is that teacher whose lot is cast in some dark and neglected part of the State with her little school, that is taught in some wreck of a log cabin with slab seats with no backs, seeking to accomplish? What ideal is in her mind as she patiently tries day after day to teach two score of little ones to read and write and spell? What does she expect to gain by working for a salary barely sufficient to clothe and feed the body? What by bearing up under discouragements, accidents and indifference of parents and school officials? What end does she hope to subserve by exposing her body to the cold of winter in poorly built school-houses? Why does she stay month after month in a community where perhaps she is almost completely shut out from intelligent association and from communication with the great busy progressive world? Has this faithful teacher ever paused and considered what in reality will have been accomplished when these boys and girls shall have learned to read and write and cipher? Are these accomplishments and their modifications the great ultimatum sought for?

MONEY AND TIME SPENT

In our higher institutions, our young men and women are spending some of their most precious years in mastering the mysteries of mathematics, science and language, with here and there industrial training added, but when all the mathematics, sciences and languages and industrial arts shall have been mastered (if that be possible) have we reached the goal that we seek through education? Never perhaps in the history of the world has so much money been placed by the hand of the State and private benevolence on the altar of education. What motives have actuated those Christ-like philanthropists in the Northern States who have poured within the last quarter of a century $25,000,-000 into the lap of the South for the education of the Negro? Not satisfied with this, the North has given hundreds of her most gifted and cultivated sons and daughters to the amelioration of the condition of the Negro race, many of whom have suffered ostracism and severe condemnation, but of whom some still cling to this work and have dedicated their entire lives to it, and all for what purpose?

Besides the millions given by the wealthy, the poor widowed mother and decrepit father have given willingly of their dollars that have been earned by days of hard toil over the wash-tub or in the cotton-field; and that have been saved by sacrifices, that they have made with cheerfulness and fortitude, because of what they want to accomplish for their children. Seeking for the same end, we would not forget the generous action of our beloved State in bestowing out of an impoverished treasury, an annuity which combined with the precious savings of parents, the gifts of the wealthy and philanthropic, have produced in a few years results that have not been surpassed in the history of the progress of the world.

Definition of Education

But to recur to the question, what is the great end sought for in education? That powerful something before whose shrine, time, money and even life are freely offered. What did Socrates seek to do when he chose the fatal drug in preference to a cessation of his teaching? What ideal did Plato have in view in devoting his life to the instruction of his fellowmen? What priceless jewel hidden in the human soul did Pestalozzi and Horace Mann bid us seek after?

Is the acquiring of reading, writing and arithmetic education, or do these comprise the great results we seek for in education? These are education so far as they serve as stepping-stones to the rich goal which we seek, but they are not all of education.

Is the ability to master and converse in foreign languages; to travel through the wonderful intricacies of geometry and trigonometry education, or the end we seek for? No; they are but the means to an end. Education is all this, and more, when we have understood all that Newton and Kepler and Tyndall and Edison teach concerning the physical world; when all that Aristotle and Hamilton, and McCosh teach concerning the human soul shall have been comprehended, have we found that which we seek for? Verily, these acquirements are education, but not all nor the end: nor shall the end be reached till every passion, every appetite be controlled, every prejudice, all malice, all jealousy be banished from the heart, and every faculty of the mind be so governed that the united and harmonious action of body, mind and heart shall lead us up, till we live in that atmosphere where God dwells, and that love shall take such complete possession that it may be said of us, it was of him who was greatest of all, that we did no sin but went about doing good.

PROGRESSIVE CENTURY

Clearly the perfect man is to come through a systematic and harmonious development of body, mind and soul. As no generation has ever lived in an age in which the conveniences for the development of perfect men were so great, so the world will expect us to reach a higher degree of perfection in education than has ever been attained. When we contemplate the marvelous progress that has been made during the last century in art, science and letters, we see that the teacher's position is one of supreme importance and of the most weighty responsibility. Ours is an era of progress such as the world never saw before. Review for a moment the progress of the world during the last hundred years.

In 1793 Whitney gave us the cotton gin. Says Dr. Josiah Strong,[1] in "Our Country": "It took Dr. Atkinson eight months to go from New England to Oregon in 1847, but he returned in six days.

"Any one as old as the 19th century has seen a very large proportion of all the progress in civilization made by the race, when seven years old he might have seen Fulton's steamboat on her trial trip up the Hudson. Until twenty years of age he could not have found in all the world an iron plow. At thirty he might have travelled on the first railroad passenger train. He was thirty-eight when steam communication between Europe and America was established. He had arrived at middle age when the first telegram was sent.

"At the close of the 18th century slavery existed almost everywhere — in Russia, Hungary, Prussia, Austria, Scotland, in the British, French and Spanish Colonies, and in North and South America, but this century has seen slavery practically destroyed in all Christendom."

Dr. Strong further adds: "If we reckon time by its results, twenty years of this century may out measure a millennium of olden time."

With such stupendous facts indicating unparalleled progress, crowding themselves upon us; impressing us more and more with our responsibility, the question as to what part education is to play in the wonderful drama of throbbing activity, life and development becomes of the most weighty importance and should cause us to stop, think, reason, refresh ourselves, weigh anchor and take our bearings. This done, let us ask again what is the great end sought for in education?

THREE-FOLD DEVELOPMENT

To obtain the highest and most telling results, the grand trinity composed of the physical, intellectual and spiritual man, must receive due consideration.

Sparta confined her education mainly to the physical man, and as a result, we have a race of athletes skilful in everything where mere muscular force and those qualities that come from confidence in it were the prominent characteristics.

Athens was full of intellect. Students and philosophers filled her streets and public places. "For all the Athenians" says the Testament account, "spent their time in nothing else," but to hear some new thing; and as one result they were as Paul told them, too superstitious; and Paul's spirit was stirred within him when he saw their littleness and short-comings.

In the middle ages we find men on the other hand devoting their time to the development of the spiritual or religious man, and we find monastic life everywhere prevalent. Out of the monasteries at first filled with sincerely religious devotees we have a narrow, bigoted, tyrannical priest-hood developing. In truth, one-side development is not development. It destroys the balance, and to make the most of the

431

man, this must be preserved. No one is truly efficient unless there is harmony throughout his being. In short, unless he is well *poised,* the triune development must go hand in hand.

Physical development makes a man capable of greater exertion, intellectual development makes him keener and better able to utilize his physical force; moral development will enable him to choose right, and hence to direct expenditure of the physical and intellectual strength in higher and purer channels. All these combined will fit a man for great responsibilities and successful work, and nothing less will. To produce such fitness should be the end sought for in the work of our schools of learning.

Use to Be Made of Education

In order to reach the highest results, the use that is to be made of education should be kept constantly in mind. If education is of any practical value it should serve to guide us in living, in other words, to fit us for the work *around* us and demanded by the times in which we live. It should aid us in putting the most into life in the age, country, and into the position we are to fill.

Perhaps all of us agree that training is best which gives the student the broadest and most complete knowledge of the arts, sciences, and literature of all the civilized nations, ancient or modern, but where the want of time and money prevents this broader culture and this choice must be made (and a choice must be made by most), let us choose to give the student that training in his own language in the arts and sciences that will have special bearing on his life, and will thus enable him to render the most acceptable worship to God and the best service to man.

Doing One Thing Well

Too often the educational value of doing well what is done, however little, is overlooked. One thing well done prepares the mind to do the next thing better. Not how much, but how well should be the motto. One problem thoroughly understood is of more value than a score poorly mastered. One language well learned is of more value than six of which we only have a smattering. Show me a youth that is dabbling in all subjects and mastering none, and I will show you a man that will go floundering through life without purpose, without business, without stability, without top or bottom; now here, now there, a complete and disgraceful failure everywhere. There is one specific thing that each can do best and should be the aim of the teacher as far as in his power lies to help the student find that calling and prepare himself for it.

Hitherto, the education of the Negro has too largely failed to produce special men for special work. The jacks-at-all-trades are too numerous.

Give the youth a training that will fit him to do one thing well — better than anybody in the community, and you put his services in demand. The man who is a first grade physician is not a success as a preacher of the gospel. The lady who can teach music in the best manner cannot as a rule teach arithmetic nor dressmaking equally as well. The man who is a first-class carpenter can rarely be a model farmer. Every youth should be helped to find what God meant him to do in the world and get about it as soon as possible.

MADE VALUABLE IN THE AGE AND THE COUNTRY IN WHICH WE LIVE

Common business principles should teach us that if our schools are to turn out students whose education is to be made of use to the world — such that will put the possession in demand and not leave him a drag on the market — the education must be that which can be made most valuable in the age and country in which the student is to live.

One would laugh at the business foresight of a man who would set up a factory for the manufacture of a class and pattern of goods that were in demand a century ago, but which had long since been superseded by more useful and better articles. Equally unwise would he be who should manufacture a merchandise that his imagination led him to believe was going to be in demand a century hence, but while the century is arriving his goods must remain on his hands to become shopworn and an eye-sore. The call for men and women who can take hold of and do some practical thing was never so pressing and loud as now — not for him who can discuss best the way of surveying a field, but him who can take hold of and make the survey; not for him who can go into a learned disquisition as to the best manner to practice law or medicine, but for him who can go into the court and save the innocent from the penitentiary, or the physician who can go into the sick-room and rob death of its intended victim; not for him who can build in the air a model church, but who can give us a real, tangible church that

433

shall be the world's ideal; not for him who can theorize on the best methods of farming, but for him who can show us the actual farm that he has made produce results surpassing all others; not for him who merely by a train of logic convinces us what style of house is the most comfortable and cheapest, but for him who can draw the plans and build the actual house; not for him who can stand off and criticise some school or college that others have built, but for him who can go into a community where no school exists and build a school, that shall bless the world.

UNSELFISHNESS

Above and beyond all, we should ever bear in mind that education should help us to forget ourselves and instill within us the principle, that the highest object for which man can live is to help others. It should teach us to

> "Rise on stepping stones,
> Of our dead selves to higher things."[2]

To

> "Live for the course that needs assistance,
> For the future in the distance;
> For the good that we can do."[3]

CONCLUSION

And now, members of the Association, for three years you have honored me with the presidency of your body. For this honor I sincerely thank you. I have tried with all my strength to serve the best interest of the organization — an organization that for its dignity of manner, devotion to duty and high purpose, is surpassed by few anywhere.

In pursuance of a decision announced at our last meeting I shall ask you to choose another presiding officer. In doing this, it is my earnest wish that your choice may light upon one who shall serve you in a more helpful manner than it has been in my power to do. With a grateful heart I desire to thank you for your earnest support, dignified respect, and unfailing encouragement given me in the performance of my duty.

Adjournment.

Minutes of the Seventh Annual Session, Alabama State Teachers' Association (Montgomery, 1888), 5-9, A-Ar; also see Dd, Shehee Collection, ATT. This speech is not written in BTW's characteristic, plain style. Not only is the sentence structure unusually complex, but the literary reference replaces the anecdote in providing emphasis. Olivia Davidson Washington, who had received a more classical education at Framingham State Normal School, probably helped compose the speech.

¹ Josiah Strong (1847-1916), a social gospel clergyman and expansionist, achieved national prominence in 1885 with the publication of his book, *Our Country: Its Possible Future and Its Present Crisis.* Strong gloried in the material strength of America and in the mission of Anglo-Saxons to bring civil liberty and Christianity to other peoples. He felt, however, that the American promise of world dominance was menaced by the saloon, tobacco, Catholics, immigrants, large cities, socialists, and concentrated wealth. A popular lecturer, he wrote many books and articles warning of the dangers of urbanization.

² Paraphrased from Alfred Lord Tennyson, *In Memoriam A. H. H.* (1850), pt. 1.

³ Paraphrased from *My Aim* by George Linnaeus Banks, an English poet and journalist (d. 1881).

To Timothy Thomas Fortune

[Tuskegee, Ala.] April 15, 1888

Dear Mr. Fortune, I regret that I am some what tardy in [giving] you the information for Miss Hawley.¹

[From what] you say of her cultivation and disposition I am sure she will prove quite an addition to our faculty. There is no end to the amount of good that a thoroughly conscientious teacher can do in this institution. We have a large number of young men and women who will be seeking positions as teachers or in other fields of usefulness. I regret however that the salary we can offer Miss Hawley is not what we wish to have her paid. We can pay $40 per month board and expenses. Our payments are made quarterly. The school year includes 9 calender months.

In regard to the branches to be taught I would say that we prefer to have Miss Hawley teach history — United States and Ancient — and perhaps one or two classes in Geography.

By this mail I send Miss Hawley a catalogue which will give her more general information about the school. The traveling expenses from N.Y. here are about $23.

435

Many excellent workers are prevented, I think, from coming South by the reports of outrages that are committed here. While there are a great many of these reports true still, and there are a great many unpleasant things to undergo, yet I feel that any one who comes here and engages in educational work will become so attached to it that he will feel that the opportunity to educate compensates in a large measure for these other things, and fully makes up for the loss of those privileges he has to give up in leaving the North.

I may be in New York during the latter part of this month, in which case I shall call to see you. Yours Sincerely

B. T. Washington

HLpSr Con. 91 BTW Papers DLC.

[1] Anna C. Hawley taught history, geography, and methods of teaching at Tuskegee from 1888 to 1892.

From Cornelius Nathaniel Dorsette

4/17 88 Montgomery Ala

Dear Prof Washington All seems quiet now. A few have talked to me since you left and all seem to think I showed good judgment in acting as I did. I have been on the go day & night and have not been molested though have met some of the bullies after mid night.

Will write if any trouble. Ever & truly yours

Dorsette

ALS Con. 87 BTW Papers DLC.

From Cornelius Nathaniel Dorsette

Montg — 4/19th 88

Dear Prof Washington Yours rec'd this a.m. please accept my most sincere & heartfelt thanks for the position for my Sister.[1] I did not understand you to say anything regarding a position for her when you were down and so wrote her Monday to that effect, but insisted upon her coming & spending the summer here with me hoping to find an opening somewhere. But can assure you that I prefer her working with *you,* and will see that she fills well what ever position you assign her. Why I have been timid in urging the matter with you was because I did not want my position as trustee & friend of the school to have any weight in the case but wanted Sister to be taken if desired purely on her merit & true worth. She will come here as soon as the school at Bennett Seminary[2] closes and what ever she can do by way of making friends and interesting parents for the school I will see that its done in connection with my own efforts.

Andrew is very anxious indeed for me to return & is indirectly doing all he can to influence others to insist on my coming back. But alas! never again unless he should publish a card correcting the wrong he has done me and I really dont care to if he should, though I know he would not. Things are getting quiet so far as I can see and I pray that they may stay so for I am really tired of this cussed nonsense, yet I have never flinched nor do I intend to even if death stars me in the face.

I am now determined to open a Drugstore if I only have one bottle on the shelves. I have no money but in some way it must come ? for I am more and more convinced that my only safety & stability depends upon my owning something visable and that denotes permanancy, when they see that the cry of "run him off" will cease & not until. I know I will have to face many odds and disadvantages but I am bound to try just as soon as I can rent a store. In going North if you can interest some Drug friend in me it may in time be of good use to me. Will write you daily. Truly your friend

Dorsette

P.S. My baby has been quite ill with bowell trouble but seems better to-night — was much worried last night.

ALS   Con. 87   BTW Papers   DLC.

[1] Cornelia E. Dorsette taught spelling at Tuskegee from 1888 to 1892.

[2] Bennett Seminary (later Bennett College) in Greensboro, N.C., was founded in 1873 by the Freedman's Aid Society of the Methodist Episcopal Church. Originally a coeducational school for training teachers and ministers, it became a women's college in 1926.

From Cornelius Nathaniel Dorsette

[Montgomery, Ala., ca. Apr. 20, 1888]

Dear Prof Washington Yours rec'd & contents noted. I hope all is getting quiet but I cant say for certain yet. I see signs of an undercurrent of sentiment that I dont like and while I hope for the best yet I dare not trust them. However I am here & here to stay unless removed by death. I trust the God that cares for a sparrow will care for me. I dont think an article from you would be of any avail just now. Truly yours

Dorsette

ALS Con. 87 BTW Papers DLC.

From Ward David Newkirk[1]

Talladega, Ala. 4, 23, '88

My dear Teacher: With great pleasure, I write you this letter. It has been several years since you came down south. When you left Hampton, I never once thought that I would be this near you. I have often thought of you and wondered if I would ever be a scholar like you. In an imagination, your picture is often before me. In the year 1881 which was the same period of your departure for the south, I left Hampton. Since that time, I have been engaged as a student under John A. Holt at the Peabody school, Wilmington, N.C. In the year 1884-5, I attended the state Colored Normal School which is situated in the City of Fayetteville, N.C. Prof. E. E. Smith is the principal, a graduate of Shaw University. I was very successful there, for I held the head of my class the whole term. After spending about three years in attendance at Gregory Institute, I finally graduated at the head of ten class-mates. One of the young men who graduated decided to study medicine. He has made his way to Shaw University. Another of the young men who graduated made his choice in being a deciple of the Lord Jesus Christ, therefore, through the advice and persuasion of his good and kind teachers, he has made his way to Talladega. He expects to spend four or five years in the Theological Department at that place.

438

Since I have been here, I have been getting along very well in my studies. I hope that the Lord will prepare me for the work which is before me. There is a great work in this country for each to do. You understand this much better than I. I find this state very mountainous, especially the northern part. ————— I wonder if you can recognize my face. Do you remember of the boys giving a present (a watch chain) to you a few nights before you left for Alabama. I was one of those boys, for you were my teacher. I hope that I may meet you face to face. I heard that you was married. I told the boys that you married a graduate of Hampton for you were courting a young lady when I was there and she had one year in school after you came south. Did you marry that lady or not? I often think of Mr. Hamilton, the music teacher, also Mr. Banks, the book-keeper. I see that Gen. Marshal is gone to Massachusetts. How many of the Hampton graduates are with you at Tuskegee? When will your school close? Will you go north this summer or will you stay at home? You must excuse my poor grammatical expressions and composition, for I have but little time to write. You know something of the school-boy & life. Before I close, let me emplore you to pray for me that God may bless me and the work of which I am preparing, through His grace and strength. Give love to your family. Much love to you all. I remain one of your obedient student at Hampton Va.

Ward D. Newkirk

ALS Con. 89 BTW Papers DLC.

[1] Ward David Newkirk graduated from Talladega College's theological department in 1894 and later served as pastor of Congregational churches in Beaufort, Greensboro, and Mooresville, N.C.

A Speech before the Philosophian Lyceum of Lincoln University

Lincoln University, Pa., Apr. 26, 1888

The South as an Opening for a Career

Gentlemen of the Philosophian Lyceum and Friends:
    What good can I do was the question I considered more than once

before deciding to accept your kind invitation to address you on this occasion; indeed it is with this question before me that I try to decide on every important action of my life. After consideration I decided that perhaps I might say something to you on the subject, "The South as an opening for a Career," that would excite your interest and cause you to think over the possibilities of achievement in that interesting and extensive part of our country.

To be permitted to address an organization that has numbered among its members men who today are counted among America's most worthy citizens, — men who in more than one walk of life are teachers and moulders of public sentiment, in the best and highest sense — brings an honor as well as a serious sense of responsibility.

Out from the classic walls of this venerable institution have gone men who were among the first to prove that God sets no limit on the development of the human intellect, no matter under what color skin it hides itself.

Gentlemen, I am perfectly aware that in your search after knowledge in science, art, and literature, I can be of no service to you. But it has occurred to me that a few minutes spent in considering the resources of that rich and beautiful country — the South — "Where every prospect pleases, and only man is vile,"[1] would not be spent in vain. I come to speak to you of a section of country that has been purchased and paid for ten times over by the sweat and blood of our forefathers. Their two hundred and fifty years of forced and unrequited toil, secured for us an inheritance which at no late day we are going to occupy and enjoy as independent and intelligent citizens.

Perhaps the most important considerations for a successful career are land, men and climate. I would put as the condition of all conditions for success in life, whether it relate to the individual or the race, ownership in the soil — cleavage to mother Earth.

Embracing what are commonly known as the Southern States, we have 877,000 square miles of land that is as well adapted to the sustenance of man as the same sized section found anywhere on the globe. An eminent economist has said that thirty counties in Mississippi properly cultivated could be made to produce last year's cotton crop of 1,200,000 bales. The statement will apply with equal force to other Southern States and to other products.

Can land be secured? Never, I believe, in the history of any state could such valuable property be purchased for so little money as at present in Alabama and other Southern States.

Landed estates which in Antebellum days could not be purchased for $25 per acre can now be had for $4.

Land owners who 20 years ago would not part with their land to the Negro partly because of prejudice and partly because the owners thought that their financial salvation lay in holding on to their lands, are now ready and anxious to sell to black or white, and often it is the old family homestead that has been sacred, where generations of slaveholders have been born and reared that is offered for sale. I do not rejoice at the misfortune of the southern white man, for he is my brother, but I do feel it a duty to urge that his extremity is our opportunity to buy the foundation for a high civilization that is frought with the most favorable conditions.

If the sins of the fathers are visited upon the children to the third and fourth generations, who knows, but what God in His divine goodness means through the enslavers improvidence to repay the enslaved that of which he has been robbed.

The South possesses a soil as rich and productive as that of any country on the globe — a soil that is capable of producing almost every kind of vegetation and of making that section "blossom as the rose" and to become a land of plenty. But one element is wanting and that is brains — every acre of her low lands and hills and valleys needs to be presided over by and impregnated with brains. One Macedonian cry is for brains — brains controlled and directed by religion and conscience. The South is not crowded. Thirty-two inhabitants to every square mile is perhaps the present average population. An increase of 50,000,000 of people in the Southern States could be accommodated and still the population would not be as dense as that of Pennsylvania.

In view of all these facts do you wonder, gentlemen, that even at the risk of disappointing you in my selection I have decided to occupy you in the discussion of a subject so utilitarian?

The time is not far distant when a larger proportion of the educated among us will seek callings outside of the school-room and other professional pursuits and will enter upon careers that will have material gain more directly for their object, and so might it be. It is this aspect of my subject that I shall discuss first.

To the budding capitalists, the lumber resources of the South present a field for financial gain that are presented to but few on the threshold of life in any country. There are in the Southern States perhaps 500,000 square miles of forests as valuable as any and more accessible than in other parts of the country, and these forests can be had for the pittance of $2 per acre. At no distant day the South is to be the lumber mart of the United States. No argument is needed to prove to you that "the products of the soil are the foundations of the wealth of any nation."

If the Vanderbilts, Girards, Peabodys, Peter Coopers started out poverty-stricken with untrained minds and in competition with the shrewd and energetic yankee amassed fortunes what superior opportunities open up before our young men who begin life with a college trained mind and in a locality where competition is at its minimum?

To the rank and file of our aspiring youth seeking an opening in life, to me but two alternatives present themselves as matters now stand — to live a menial in the north or a semi-freeman in the South.

This brings us face to face with Northern competition and Southern prejudice and between them I have no hesitancy in saying that the Negro can find his way to the front sooner through Southern prejudice than through Northern competition. The one decreases, the other increases.

To the really brave, earnest, energetic, ambitious, christian young man the obstacles presented, it seems to me, by prejudice form an apology for not entering this field so weak, so unreasonable as not to *merit* serious consideration, yet prejudice does keep so large and valuable a class of those who are mentally and morally strong from that field that the question must be considered.

The most effective ammunition with which to fight prejudice is men — men such as are before me — men who in every act, word and thought give the lie to the assertion of his enemies North and South that the Negro is the inferior of the white man.

In advocating the South as a field for a career, I have no sympathy with those who would stoop to sacrifice manhood to satisfy unreasonable whims of the South, but would advise you to be there as here a man — every inch a man, and demand with reasonable patience, with proper judgement and in lawful manner every right that God and the constitution have vouchsafed to us as American citizens. I come to you from a seven years' residence in the "Black Belt" of Alabama — the heart of the South — and I speak as one who has given his strength without reserve to the amelioration of the condition of his race and to a consideration on all sides and under all circumstances of the problems that have grown out of his newly acquired citizenship. I do not wish to create the impression that all these problems have been solved yet, and that everything is just right in the South, but out of my own honest opinion that the rate at which prejudice is dying out is so rapid as to justify the conclusion that the Negro will in a quarter of a century enjoy in Alabama every right that he now does in Pennsylvania, a rate such as to furnish occasion for universal gratitude and thanksgiving to Him who controls the destinies of races. As compared with the great question of the race's acquiring education, character and property the question of prejudice, it seems to me, dwindles into insignificance.

Besides, can you afford to put along side the advantage and stimulus that the race will derive from your examples as leaders in the field of letters, professional life, and as financiers such considerations as personal inconveniences and the curtailment of political privileges — considerations which exist but for a day while the good influence that a single one of you may exert in some department of life at this auspicious time may incite the youths of far-off ages to new life and hope by rekindling their faith and aspirations.

One has said "It may be but one colored man in a state has achieved financial independence in a decade, yet that one man is constantly an example to all others, stimulating them to renewed exertion. It may be that in a whole state but two colored men have won their way into the mystic arena of the bar, and even there may be far from encouraging examples of forensic ability, yet never one of them opens his lips in court that his example does not inspire some colored boy that listens to do as he has done."

> "The smallest wave of influence
>   set in motion
> Extends and widens to the
>   eternal shore."

Just so sure as the rays of the sun dispel the frost of winter, so sure will Brains and Property and Character conquer prejudice; just so sure as right in all ages and among all races has conquered wrong, so sure will the time come and at no distant day, when the Negro South shall be triumphant over the last lingering vestige of prejudice. To believe otherwise is to deny the existence of Him who rewards virtue and condemns vice.

It is encouraging to note that there is already an entire absence of hostile feeling against business enterprises of blacks, South. A Negro merchant having a quality of goods that is in demand receives the patronage of both races. This applies in almost all branches of business.

A young man with energy, ambition and foresight can get successfully launched into business there on a capital that would not enable him to pay the first month's rent in a Northern city.

In any business enterprise requiring push, snap, tact, and continual and close attention, the wide awake Negro has an immense advantage, for the Southern white man evades as a rule any occupation that requires early rising or late retiring that removes him very far from a shade tree or the sunless side of a house.

For three hundred years the North has been adding value to value, accumulating wealth and experience in every direction and when we, the freemen of a day, enter into competition with this it is not hard to say who will win and who will lose.

In entering the South for a career, you have the advantage of having a large number of our own kith and kin for whom to work, on whom to depend for support and with whom to cooperate. This is an advantage that perhaps outweighs all others. Notwithstanding many assertions to the contrary, I glean from my experience that the Negro is as loyal to faithful and intelligent leadership, is as ready to cooperate, to stand shoulder to shoulder for the common good as any race with no more experience in self government, whose history we know. Show me a man among us in any walk in life who manifests to those with whom he comes in contact that he is trying to succeed for the welfare of the race as well as for his own good and I will show you a man that is supported, patronized and encouraged by the rank and file.

But as to numbers: we have in the Southern States more than 6,000,000 Negroes — one third of the total population. In eight of these states the Negro population is 48 per cent. of the whole or about 100 Negroes to 108 white men. "In the Black Belt," says Tourgee, "this shows an excess of whites which has already doubtless been neutralized by the greater reproductiveness of the colored race. In three of the Southern states — Mississippi, Louisiana and South Carolina — the Negroes, it should be borne in mind, already outnumber the whites, and in eight of them there is practically one Negro for every white inhabitant."[2]

For reasons which are patent to every thinking observer, in the "Black Belt" the Negro is bound to increase and the white race decrease in relative numbers. Among these reasons one who has given the subject much attention mentions that the proportion of Southern whites who are annually emigrating from their native state is rapidly increasing while the proportion of colored natives who are migrating from the state of their birth is rapidly diminishing.

Outside of a few industrial centers, the white population is receiving no appreciable increase from either Northern or foreign immigration. Now consider the greater reproductiveness of the Negro.

The census of 1880 shows that with no gain in numbers by immigration, he increased thirty-five per cent. while the increase of the whites was only twenty-seven per cent. But Judge Tourgee, whom I regard as the highest authority on this subject, says, that "this shows not merely a percentage of gain, but a greater numerical increase. The 3,500,000 colored inhabitants of eight southern states in 1870 show an actual gain of 98,000 more than the whites although the latter outnumbered the former in 1870, 440,000. In other words, three and a half millions of the colored race are able to give the whites among whom they dwell an odds of over a half million and yet in a decade outstrip them a hundred thousand in numerical strength."[3] Prof. W. W. Gillam,[4] a Southern man, I believe, confirms Tourgee's view in the following statements: Deducting 7% from the rate of increase of the white race for migration he concludes that the white population, increasing at the rate of 20% in ten years, doubles itself in 35 years. The black population, increasing at the rate of 35% in ten years, doubles itself in 20 years; hence in 1900 or 12 years there will be 12,000,000 blacks in the Southern States with only about 15,000 [,000][5] whites to keep them company. In 1920 or 32 years hence there will be 24,000,000 Negroes or twice as many as there are white inhabitants in the Southern States at present. In 1940 or 52 years hence, there will be 48,000,000 while the Southern whites will not reach that number till 1950 or quoting Tourgee again, to give emphasis to these interesting figures, if figures are ever interesting, "In the year 1900 or 12 years hence each of the states lying between Maryland and Texas will have a colored majority within its borders and we shall have eight minor republics of the Union in which the colored race will either rule or a majority will be disfranchised."[6] Every possible view which we have been able to take of the social statistics of these states confirms the conclusion that before the end of the century we shall have a chain of states extending from the Potomac to the Mississippi in every one of which the colored race will have a clear and indisputable majority and in several of which the predominance will be very nearly in the ratio of two to one."[7]

While I cannot agree with Tourgee in his assertion that the Negro must rule or be disfranchised, yet I think his conclusions as to his predominance in numbers are in the main true, and if these figures do not indicate a field where the aspiring colored youth can exercise his talents whether they lay in the direction of science, literature, art, or statesmanship, I am at a loss to know where on the globe one will be found.

A distinguished southern clergyman[8] has compared the Negroes of the South to the Jews as they were led out of Egypt. Says he, "They were then probably as ignorant and degraded as any of our Negroes. They were, like the blacks, suddenly ushered into freedom, and it took 40 years of wandering in the wilderness to fix them for even the pastoral life of the ancients. They are now the leading merchants, financiers, musicians, scholars, and statesmen of the world. If out of such material, God could create such a people, what may he not do with our Southern Blacks?"

In pointing you to this field, I do not do so as one who believes that the Negro must rise at the expense of the Southern white man, for whatever his wrongs to us, he is our neighbor and the divine commandment "Love thy neighbor as thyself" is broad enough to include him with all his shortcomings, and wherever by act or word we can benefit him let us not with-hold our help, but at the same time and under all circumstances show him that we know our rights and that we dare maintain them.

As to climate, I think that an examination of the vital statistics will show that the climate in the South is as conducive to longevity as that of any other part of our country. The range of climate permits the growth of almost the whole of the vegetable kingdom, from the hardiest kind of farm products to the tenderest of tropical fruits.

An examination of the thermal maps of various countries will show that the climatic record of much of our Southern country is very similar to that of oriental countries where civilization and mental development have in past ages reached their zenith.

As to the lines of work, let me be more specific. If you desire school work it seems enough to say that 73% of the colored people south cannot read or write. There is a school population of 2,000,000 but not more than 45% of this number now attend school. There are between 16 and 17 thousand school teachers, but not more than 25% are in any degree competent. We have in the South 99 Normal Schools, academies, and 18 so-called colleges and universities, and 13 schools of law, theology and medicine; hence as regards our higher institutions, the demand is not for an increase in number but in efficiency. They need developing upward and downward.

Let no generation of Negroes ever prove ungrateful to those Christlike workers, the band of noble and heroic northern men and women who have devoted the best years of their lives to building up our schools and colleges south, and at a time when to engage in such work meant for them complete social ostracism and risk of life — but rather let us build, with our earnest and unselfish deeds, monuments to their memories that shall tell succeeding generations from whence we started. But by natural process our Northern friends will gradually withdraw and you will be called upon not only to supply many of their vacant places but to fill new chairs resulting from the great numerical increase of the race. No one should expect or demand or be given a position by virtue of his color but because of his fitness to fill it.

Says one, "What a privilege to have a hand in forming and developing the institutions of today! In 130 years the 6,000,000 Negroes will have grown to 150,000,000 with great universities and renowned scholars, with statesmen and rulers and with honors second to none known to the human race."

But perhaps the most lucrative career is in the line of the professions. What are the chances and opportunities in this field? Let Alabama serve as an example in answering this question. There are in the state 600,000 Negroes. To do the legal business of this number and stand between them and injustice there are but four colored lawyers in the whole state and some of these are far from being brilliant luminaries. Go into any community, examine the deeds (where there are any) of the colored property owners and you will find them of the most defective character, carelessly written by unprincipled lawyers with nothing in view but a fee. Having occasion a short time ago to buy some land from a colored man, I was told by him that a certain white man had a mortgage on it which would have to be paid but on in-

447

vestigating, I found that instead of a mortgage the white man held a deed in fee simple for the land and the hard working Negro had not the scratch of a pen to show his right of possession. Go, if you please, into the jails and penitentiaries and you will find colored men, women, and even boys and girls of tender age serving sentences for crimes of which they have been illegally convicted. Only a few days ago, a colored boy of 15 was found in one of the convict camps of Alabama wearing a chain that had not been taken off his limbs night or day for months and it was so heavy that his legs had swollen twice their natural size. On the same day that this discovery was made the boy had been mercilessly whipped because he did not "jump around fast enough." Often these miserable creatures are sentenced for 12 months but are retained for 15 or 18 months. A perfectly innocent colored man in Alabama was not long ago snatched up in the road and without legal process was taken into Georgia and thrust into a convict camp and kept there six months before opportunity presented itself to inform his friends. I could spend much time in citing similar cases. The white lawyer who will take an interest in his colored client's case farther than to secure his fee is the exception. With such opportunities for work presenting themselves, can those of you who have talent in this direction refrain from going into the South and devoting your lives to seeing that the Negro has justice before the courts? Do this not alone for the financial gain (for there is money to be made by it) but for the real good you can do. In such work you can render acceptable worship to God and high service to man.

Retaining Alabama as an example with 600,000 colored inhabitants there are but six colored physicians in the state. It is my opinion that as a rule the colored physicians have achieved more signal success than any other professional colored men. Patients and money are not long in coming to the dutiful and competent physician. One hundred colored physicians can today earn an independent living in Alabama.

The entrance of a colored physician into a community has a marked and beneficial effect upon the work done by white physicians for colored patients. They soon learn that in order to compete with the colored doctor who is genuinely interested something beyond a three minutes visit, a dose of quinine or blue-mass is necessary. In connection with the practice of medicine there is great opportunity for the most helpful missionary work. Dr. C. N. Dorsette of Montgomery who has,

I think, the largest practice of any colored physician in the country, does as much of this kind of work as a city missionary.

In some cases it may cost the lawyer or physician a severe struggle before a permanent foothold is gained. When this occurs the struggle is but momentary and should not discourage. It is to be accounted for in the peculiar training the Negro has had. For centuries he has been taught by precept and example that everything great has its origin in the white man and that Negro is a synonym for dishonesty, degradation and incapacity. He has been taught that the Devil is black, that the devil's angels are black, that sin is black, and that it is a sin to be black. Success in your practice will undo this false teaching, for as the adage goes, "Nothing succeeds like success."

As to preachers, the numbers to be found in the South would seem to indicate that we are not in very great need. One church near Tuskegee has a total membership of 200 and 18 of them are said to be preachers. But the character of many of these *preachers* may be illustrated by what is told of one. It is said that while he was at work in a cotton field in the middle of July he suddenly stopped, looked up toward heaven and exclaimed, "O, Lord, de work is so hard, de cotton is so grassy, and de sun am so hot, I believe dis darkey am called to preach." The Baptist denomination claims 120,000 communicants in Alabama and there are perhaps 700 ministers of this denomination in charge of churches there, but out of this number of ministers, I question if 50 could be found under whose ministry one could live from year to year and receive benefit thereby. Many of these are grand, faithful characters but they have outlived their time of usefulness. What I have said of the Baptist denomination may be said with almost equal truth of the other prominent denominations. The call for ministers with trained heart and intellect is pressing and loud.

As the colored population grows larger and more wealthy and intelligent a higher and better class of race literature will be in demand. I have no hesitancy in asserting that the time is not far distant when colored men can devote their lives to literature in the South and receive support and encouragement from the race; that the time will come when literature produced by colored men and of the widest scope — from the daily newspaper to the most select and best edited quarterly reviews — will be in paying demand.

But it would be a mistake to attempt to confine our young men to the school room or to professional careers — your services are in de-

449

mand as planters, as merchants, as operators of mines, as manufacturers and as mechanics. The time has come when the Negro should be in a higher sense a producer as well as a consumer, and where can a field more inviting be found? The time is coming when the South will cease to depend on the North for her manufactured wares and when she will cease to keep her smoke houses and corn cribs in the West.

The time to take hold of these enterprises is most opportune because labor is cheap and the manufacturing industries are in their infancy. There is enough unutilized water-power in the state of Alabama to run all the factories in New England. A successful planter or merchant becomes an object lesson to all around and his example results in as much good as the work of the teacher or minister.

Wherever the stars and stripes float, there the sentiment that to be governed implies the right to govern, is cherished and fostered, and this sentiment, like Banquo's ghost, will not down.

I have said that at the close of this century the race will in all probability number twelve millions — twelve million souls,

"With freedom's soil beneath
their feet and
Freedom's banner waving
over them."[9]

Would you tell me that twelve million free people daily growing in wealth, experience and intelligence will long submit to oppression, political disfranchisement and taxation without representation? Will this be submitted to when any considerable number of the masses are intelligent, when schools and colleges exist on every hand, when high-minded, educated and patriotic leaders are in every town and hamlet? No gentlemen, a thousand times — no! Might as well attempt to stop the mighty Mississippi in its onward march to the sea, or to prevent the warmth and moisture of spring from sending forth the flower and fruit of summer.

Ere long you will find positions in the south as clerks of courts, judges, legislators, and even governors — statesmen of the highest order — this is no visionary dream or attempt at poetic....

TMc   In possession of editors.

[1] Paraphrased from the hymn by Reginald Heber (1783-1826) entitled "Missionary Hymn."

[2] Paraphrased from Tourgée, *Appeal to Caesar* (1884), 114-15.

[3] Paraphrased from *ibid.*, 130.

[4] E. W. Gilliam. BTW was drawing here from Tourgée's summary (*ibid.*, 130-35) of Gilliam's article, "The African in the United States," *Popular Science Monthly*, 22 (Feb. 1883), 433-44. Gilliam wrote: "Some home for them [the Negroes] outside of this country must be provided at an early day, or ultimately their presence here will lead to complications and disorders of appalling character."

[5] This is BTW's calculation using Gilliam's formula. It should, however, have been about 17,500,000.

[6] Paraphrased from Tourgée, *Appeal to Caesar*, 135.

[7] Paraphrased from *ibid.*, 183-84.

[8] Probably Atticus Greene Haygood.

[9] From Fitz-Greene Halleck (1790-1867), "The American Flag."

To Warren Logan

Phila. Pa. 631 Pine St. April 28 — 88

Dear Mr. Logan: Enclosed I send check for $45. If I can not arrange other wise you will have to take the $36.34 of this and ch'g to me.

I hope you will do all you can to get every thing in readiness for Commencement. Mr. Frissell[1] will be there and I am very anxious that he sh'd get a favorable impression, especially of the industries. Yours &c

B. T. Washington

ALS   Con. 91   BTW Papers   DLC.

[1] Hollis Burke Frissell.

From Warren Logan

Tuskegee, Ala., May 3d 1888

Dear Mr. Washington   I expected to hear from you today and made promises to several parties to pay them something on their accts. Am sorry to have been obliged to disappoint them. I am receiving bills and accts. every day but have no money with which to pay them. Have you heard anything further in regard to the Barnes' bequest? I have thought that it would have been paid ere this. Mrs. Washington carried Baker to Montg'y day before yesterday. A card from her this morning says that he is very much better. I have no doubt but that the skillful treatment of Dr Dorsette will bring Baker around in a few days.

Matters in general are going with their accustomed smoothness. We have a meeting this evening to select the speakers for Commencement and award class honors. I shall hope to hear from you by the next mail with a good big remittance. Enclosed, I send a number of letters which I think you will want to see and answer.

It continues very dry here. No rain since you left. When may I expect you back? Yours Sincerely

Warren Logan

Check for $45.00 was duly received.

ALS   Con. 89   BTW Papers   DLC.

BTW and Warren Logan
to the Executors of the Alfred S. Barnes Estate

[Tuskegee, Ala.] May 11th [188]8

Gentlemen: As you know, the will of the late Mr Barnes gives $1000 to the "Colored Collegiate Institute at Tuskegee, Miss."

We have reasons to believe that this bequest is intended for our institution. First, because there is no town in Mississippi of the name of Tuskegee nor in any other state, as far as we know, excepting Alabama. Second, our school is variously called "college," "normal school" and "normal institute," although its legal title is "Tuskegee Normal and Industrial Institute." Third, Mr Barnes knew of our school through our dealing with the publishing house of A. S. Barnes & Co. directly or indirectly through its agents. The house donated a number of books to our school library a year or two ago. But it was principally through General Armstrong of the Hampton Institute, that Mr Barnes learned of our school and its work. By permission, we refer you to General

Armstrong for any further information you may desire concerning this school. Yours truly

Booker T. Washington, Prin.
Warren Logan, Treas.

ALpS Con. 91 BTW Papers DLC. Written in Warren Logan's hand.

From Virginia L. Adams

Tallassee, Ala., May 15, 1888

Dear Mr. Washington: I have just recieved your letter asking me to write you concerning my work here.

I have been getting along very nicely this term, and have had a very good school during the term until now. A good many of my pupils have dropped out as this is the very busy season of the year with them. And it is one of the most dificult things that I have to contend with to get the people to keep their children in school long enough to do them some good. Now is the very busy time with the people. I have an average attendance of twenty-five pupils. I have enrolled one hundrend who have been under my care this term. During the winter months my school is very largely attended more than I can well manage alone. There are a good many children who do not attend school at all, but I don't say very much about some attending, because I would have more than I could really manage alone, so I think it is nesessary to have two teachers here another year during the winter months in order that all the children may attend school who have not attended. Of course I tell them all to come but some do not, but if there were two teachers better work could be done here and I think if the people do better with their crops they will be more able next year to help support another teacher. They want to do it and would if they were able, but I can assure you that they are not able to do any more than they have.

We have a very good Sunday School, and have had during the whole term. The children are always very proud of the cards and papers that they get.

My work here has been a very pleasant one. And I feel as if much good has been accomplished this year. I can see a great improvement

453

among the people in their ways and habits. They are very much different from what they were when I came here. My school will colose on the 25th. I remain your earnest worker,

Virginia L. Adams

ALS Con. 87 BTW Papers DLC.

From Cornelius Nathaniel Dorsette

Montgomery, Ala., 5/25th 1888

Dear friend   I telegraphed you this a:m and hope you fully understood me. I have been writing that party[1] regarding the whole status of things and offered my suggestions to him but of course couldnt make it urgent becaus he felt that what ever I said to you you would do and in as much as I was conserned, I know from his conversation & letters that he expected me to save him and abridge this terrible Crisis, which of course I could not do even if I were the victim myself & my own words would save me. But I can assure you its been a matter of no little consern to me from every point of view and has cost me much worry, anxiety, and study, and although I am sure he will resign in the *near future* and may take steps commendable to himself and the situation yet I shall watch all with anxieties for some time yet. I regret these occurance so much as they weigh more heavily upon me than any of my friends realize or I can make them believe, some-how since I have had so much trouble *here,* and too coupled with bereavement & all together I am not the man physically I was e.i. cant pass by these things with ease I did once and I find daily that I must narrow my work & thought down to medicine alone, I am desirous of doing all the good I can and in the broadest way & to the greatest number, but I fear that I get over anxious to do the best in many cases and give advice that in time may seem not the best and too place me in a very bad light of criticism before my friends on both sides. Many ask my advice in matter of business of every kind and when able to I give such advice as I am capable and watch the effect and result and in so doing it cost me a great deal physically and I doubt if the amt. expended is repaid in return. I want to do all for the best and for the best of all, but I know my motives are at times questioned severely. Now in Mr

Brown's[2] case he being a friend of mine and feeling that I should use my position officially to the school in his behalf, and as I did not he has never since felt and acted the same towards me. And so it will be in F's[3] case the same, and while I know I am trying to do the best for both them & the school am I not arraying a lot of enemies for myself??

I gleaned from a statement of Mrs Washingtons when talking to her and trying to show her why I had acted as I had under the circumstances, That she thought the proper thing for me to have done at the moment I know of it to have made a clean breast of the whole matter & let it have been settled openly then & there at any and all cost and that the end would have justified the means. Well you too may feel the same and call into question my actions but I can assure you if it was with my last breath that my whole action in this matter has been first to protect the school, 2ndly one of the parties because of his value to the school, and 3rdly, both school & F. if posible and nothing but that has ever entered my mind I can assure you, and I was stupid enough to think no one could handle it with the same scrutiny & safty as myself and had it been carried out as planned all today would be quiet.

Now Prof Washington allow me in all Love and friendship for you, The *Cause,* and the *school* to ask? Is my relation officially to the school & you worth to you what it cost me in being worried by culprits on the one side to speake and act in their defense, and bound by a sense of honor & position on the other to do the right for the school let it cost what it may to me. Am I not standing in a position to do myself eventually more harm than I do you good? Would not these parties be more careful if they did not think in me they had a friend of defense and too under all circumstances whether wright or wrong they seem to think *I* must use my influence with you for their protection & if I dont then I incur their enmity and ill will. You know & I dont think can doubt my fidelity to the school, and my innumerable efforts quietly for its good and I shall always feel the same, and I want to always work for it as my truest comfort comes in having done some little thing for you & your school yet I hate to be annoyed with those who get into trouble unnecessary to help them out & when I dont & cant be blamed.

Well I must stop its late. Yours truly

Dorsette

P.S. This col. city Band (brass) wants to come up & came & ask me & I have n't given them a reply as I want to hear from you. I dont favor their coming. Tellegraph me if you think well for them to come?

D

ALS Con. 87 BTW Papers DLC.

¹ Henry Clay Ferguson.

² William C. Brown. Born in Virginia in 1857 and graduated from Hampton in 1883, he taught carpentry in Knoxville, Tenn., for over a year and then moved to Tuskegee, where he continued to teach carpentry from 1884 to 1889. He married Ada J. Wallace of the Hampton class of 1882, who was also a teacher at Tuskegee. After leaving Tuskegee they moved to Macon, Ga., where Brown worked as a carpenter.

³ Ferguson's.

To Anna C. Hawley

Tuskegee, Ala. May 26th [188]8

Dear Madam: I am pleased to know that you accept the position and that we shall have the benefit of your services next term.

You state, I think, the conditions on which you are to come correctly, except in one particular.

We shall try to arrange for you to teach history and geography. It may turn out that there will be only two classes in history. We have had three this year.

You understand in a school like this it is very hard for us to judge before hand just the size of the different classes. This term we have had two classes in United States history and ancient history. I think it will be so next term. We shall expect you to teach six classes a day and shall try to confine them to history and geography. It may turn out that in making up the programme we shall have to give you one study outside of Geography or History class but I hope th[at will] not be so.

You understand of course our work is largely of a missionary character. There are a number of things that teachers will be expected to do that I cannot enumerate in a letter. Among them would be teaching Sunday School, taking the girls to walk [once] in a-while and helping make them happy and comfortable. Our lady teachers take turns in keeping evening study hours. This takes, I think, three or four evenings during the month.

Mr Fortune has satisfied me regarding your qualifications, and no examination will be required. I think it best for you to arrange to reach here by the 1st day of September. School opens on the 3rd of that month.

Purchase a ticket via the Piedmont Air Line to Montgomery, Ala. and be sure that it reads via Washington, Danville, Charlotte, Atlanta. After leaving Washington you will have no change of cars to Atlanta. [In] Atlanta take the Western Railroad of Alabama. While your ticket will read through to Montgomery, you will get off 40 miles this side of Montgomery, at a station called Chehaw which is 5 miles from Tuskegee, connected by a shortline railroad. Be sure to tell the conductor in time to have your baggage checked through to Montgomery but it must be put off at Chehaw.

If there are other matters on which you require information I shall be very glad to give it. Yours Truly,

B. T. Washington

HLpS   Con. 91   BTW Papers   DLC.   Addressed to Portland, Me.

From Cornelius Nathaniel Dorsette

Montgomery, Ala., 5/28th 1888

Dear Prof   I have taken the beginning steps to start my Drugstore — have rented the store under my office and hope to get it in readiness by the 15th. But now comes the question I have got to raise at least $200.00 two hundred dolls. and you *must* in some way assist, in some way I must raise that amt. and in a few days. Prof Duncan[1] and I have formed a copartnership and intend to push it for all we can and if close application will make money we are bound to do it. No one else is interested in it and I have thought best not to knowing the tendancy of my people to fuss and dabble when they have a say-so in a thing of that kind. We hope soon to be able if we succeed to secure a good clerk. The firm Name will be Dorsette & Co.

Let me hear from you by return mail. One great object that forces me to start something of the kind is that I see daily if the Negro intends to be permanant & not always being talked of run off he must have some business interest of a visable kind. Yours hastily

Dorsette

ALS   Con. 87   BTW Papers   DLC.

¹ C. H. Duncan.

To Henry Clay Ferguson

[Tuskegee, Ala.] May 29 [188]8

Dear Mr. Ferguson: In accepting your resignation after 5 years of hard service I can not put on paper how deeply I feel that the school is indebted to you for much of its success.¹ Your work for and interest in the school are deeply appreciated by all. No one is unmindful of the sacrifice you have been willing to endure in your work. Those who sacrifice and serve in the difficult and unpleasant beginning of an enterprise should as far as possible, share in the satisfaction and comforts that should come from growth and development.

I do not forget to take into consideration that you have not had the opportunity and conveniences to make your department what you desire. All of these considerations add to the pain of accepting your resignation.

I am free to confess that it will not be an easy task to fill your position indeed if we are ever able to fill it so acceptably as you have filled it. Yours truly

B. T. Washington

ALpS   Con. 91   BTW Papers   DLC.

¹ Hollis Burke Frissell, reporting in June 1888 on his visit to the Tuskegee campus for graduation exercises, had these observations on Ferguson: "The school farmer, a graduate of Hampton, has been of real help to all the community. He has showed them the value of other crops besides cotton. He has instructed them in the raising of fruits, of grapes, of melons. He showed a fine patch of watermelon vines and remarked that there was to be an Association of colored Baptist ministers in Tuskegee later in the summer. He had timed these melons so as to be ripe when the colored brethren met and he was expecting to make a good sum for the school.

He had a brick kiln in operation and I was impressed with the skillful use he made of the students. I found that without definitely appointing them he had made certain ones foremen over the others. I was much pleased with the intelligence which the farm students showed as to the kinds of crops which certain soils could produce, as to the times of planting, and the small details of farm work. They seemed to have been taught to think as well as to work." (*Southern Workman,* 17 [July 1888], 82.)

From William Jenkins

Fisk University, Nashville, Tenn. June 10, 1888

Dear Mr. Washington: I am sorry that I did not get to see you before leaving Tuskegee. I spent three very pleasant days in Montgomery.

While there I visited the examinations of the Alabama University; I also attended the Alumni meeting at the Old Ship.[1] They were both the most miserable excuses that I have ever witnessed. In the latter Paterson occupied most of the time in his usual style of bragadocio and mean insinuations.

Thus far I have been very pleasantly entertained at Fisk. Every body wants to know something of the work at Tuskegee.

I leave for Chicago next Friday. I find that Rev. Mr. Whittaker stands high here. I was out to see him yesterday. I forgot to get the "Story of Tuskegee and its songs"[2] before leaving. I shall be pleased to have you send me a few by return mail.

Remember me to all your household. Sincerely Yours,

William Jenkins

ALS Con. 89 BTW Papers DLC.

[1] Old Ship A.M.E. Zion Church, the oldest black church in Montgomery. In 1852 the Court Street Methodist Episcopal Church, South, gave black Methodists of Montgomery and vicinity a frame building. Several black men including three slaves rolled the 60'-x-45' building on logs to a new location on Holcombe Street. When asked what they were going to name the church, they answered "The Old Ship of Zion." Until 1862 the church was served by white ministers. In 1865 Old Ship joined the A.M.E. Zion denomination and soon became an important center of Negro life. It often served as a meeting house for speeches and celebrations.

[2] Helen Wilhelmina Ludlow, ed., *Tuskegee Normal and Industrial School: Its Story and Its Songs* (Hampton, Va., 1884).

To John Fox Potter[1]

[Tuskegee, Ala.] June 12 [188]8

Dear Sir: In reply to your kind favor of the 5th inst regarding the gift of $300 to this institution from the estate of Augustus Cohen,[2] I would say that I have tried to consider the matter impartially from all sides and have no hesitancy in saying that we shall be *very glad* to receive the money and shall feel as I am sure all persons who know the facts would, that you have made the *right* disposition of it. I feel quite sure that if Mr. Cohen could have a say in it that he would be willing to have it come where it can be made [to] do so much good for his own people. The chances of ever finding heirs seem to me as about one in a thousand.

We are needing very much several buildings for various industries and among them a laundry and sewing room. Of course if *all* the material and work necessary to put up one of these buildings had to [be] paid for in cash the $300 would not go far, but we furnish our own bricks and the students do the labor and I want to ask your opinion about using the money to buy for one of these buildings such material as we can not produce and let the building be called say the "Cohen Laundry." This would be a good monument to him in the land of his birth. It would be hard for you to realize how many good lessons can be taught to our girls through the medium of a first class laundry or sewing room. Many girls come to us who know nothing of washing and ironing, and of course little of cleanliness which must be in all true Christianity.

Enclosed you will find our treasurer's receipt made in the form you suggested. We can use best a draft on Chicago or any bank. Or if you prefer it can be sent through the post office as ours is a money order one and we have "Adams Express Co."

You have our most sincere thanks and gratitude for remembering us in this way and I assure you that we shall try to make every [dollar do all] the good possible for my race. Yours truly

Booker T. Washington

ALpS Con. 91 BTW Papers DLC.

[1] John Fox Potter (1817-99), a lawyer in Mukwonago, Wis., was one of the

founders of the Free Soil party and the Republican party. From 1856 to 1862 he was a congressman and later was consul general in Montreal.

[2] Augustus Cohen, a former slave, had joined the Union Army during Sherman's march through Georgia. After the war he accompanied Captain James Randall to his home in East Troy, Wis. There Cohen worked as a servant, accumulating a few hundred dollars and the respect of the white community before his death in 1873. The state appointed John F. Potter administrator of Cohen's estate. After paying all claims, Potter found that the estate had $300 remaining. He searched unsuccessfully for Cohen's heirs and, reluctant to remand the money to the state, decided to contribute the $300 to Tuskegee Institute in Cohen's name. "It seems to me," Potter wrote to BTW, "that in the absence of heirs, it is a very proper thing to do — to place the money where it will benefit his people and in the section of the country where he lived and was raised. Besides, I am not expecting to live much longer, and I would like that the matter be disposed of while I am living if possible." (Potter to BTW, June 5, 1888, Con. 88, BTW Papers, DLC.)

From George W. Lovejoy

Tuskegee, Ala., June 27, 1888

Dear Sir, I received your letters four or five days a go, but have not aswered them because I was not able to give a satisfactuary answer.

I think from all indications we are not going to be able to get very many letters published.

I think the editors are seeing them as advertisements, and they are not willing to publish them with out pay. You may rest assured that I am going to make all out of it I can.

Mr. Logan and Morain[1] are quite sick with the fever.

Things are going smoothly with us.

I hope to be able to meet Mr. Reid's[2] exspectation.

I am sir your friend trying to do what I can.

Much success to you and your mission. Respectfully yours

G. W. Lovejoy

ALS Con. 89 BTW Papers DLC.

[1] M. Arnold Morin.
[2] William M. Reid.

To Warren Logan

United States Hotel, Portland, Maine   June 30 1888

Dear Mr. Logan: Enclosed I send a check for $100. payable to you on the First National Bank, Portland.

I have been making a call on Miss Hawley who goes to Tuskegee in Sept. She is a very fine teacher and we are very fortunate in securing her. She has taught with great success in the white schools here for several years. Her home is a very cultured and refined one, and I feel sure that she is going to make one of the best teachers we have ever had.

Caution my brother to keep the expenses of the boarding dep't as low as possible. Yours sincerely

B. T. Washington

Mr. C.[1] is still in N.J. sick.

ALS   Con. 86   BTW Papers   DLC.

[1] Samuel E. Courtney. Logan wrote to BTW on June 22, 1888: "I don't see that Mr. Courtney is accomplishing much as far as immediate results are concerned. I have rec'd. no money from him since you went away. He writes that he is ill and thinks it best for him to 'lay off' for a little while." (Con. 89, BTW Papers, DLC.)

From John Henry Washington

Tuskegee, Ala., July 4, 1888

My Dear Brother: I wrote you briefly yesterday about some matters here. I learn from Mr. Brown and Mr. Adams that Mr. Chas. Thompson[1] was raging about the debt that we owe him and went so far as to say if he knew who to sue up here that he would sue for the amt.

We can not afford to have our school to be talked of in that way, as it will make others who we owe become uneasy.

It is a fact that we owe considerable and people are calling for it nearly every day.

Mr. Logan told me before he took sick that school owed about $4,500.00.[2] A great number of the men have been put off so often and long until they have become tired.

It is very hard for us to get provision, even, at Howard and Drake-ford.[3] They charge us an exstreamly high price. Mr. Drakeford charged us 15¢ per Lb. for Lard this week.

We have used nearly all the vegetables and will have more than ever to buy soon.

Matters on the farm are going very well. Mr. Green[4] is making great effort to get in fall vegetables while we are having plenty of rain.

The weather is to bad to make many brick. Mr. Kennedy[5] just sent in his bill for $234.17 and the Cholottville Wooling mill[6] bill is here past due. Mr. Logan is better today and all that have been sick are improving. Your Brother

J. H. Washington

ALS Con. 91 BTW Papers DLC.

[1] Charles Winston Thompson (1860-1904), born near Tuskegee, was a Tuskegee merchant, planter, and president of the Bank of Tuskegee. He served as county school superintendent from 1886 to 1890. In 1896-98 he was on the staff of Governor Joseph F. Johnston, and in 1897 was elected to the Alabama Senate. In 1901 he won a seat in Congress, serving until his sudden death in 1904.

[2] Warren Logan reported that the school owed $1,892 to teachers and $2,278 to "outside parties — not including amts. due Howard & Drakeford." (Logan to BTW, June 22, 1888, Con. 89, BTW Papers, DLC.)

[3] Drakeford and Company, dealers in dry goods, groceries, and plantation supplies.

[4] Charles W. Greene.

[5] A. M. Kennedy of Montgomery, a wholesale dealer in varnish, paint, glass, and other hardware.

[6] Probably the Charlottesville (Va.) Woolen Mills, which made military uniforms for schools.

From Joseph L. Ligon[1]

Montgomery, Ala. July 5th 1888

Dear sir After the men returned home we met at our armory on Monday night as usal and passed a vote of thanks to your teachers & students for their kind hospatality. the men much enjoyed hope to returned again We had this sent in to the press but by neglect failed to come out. Yours

Joseph L. Ligon

ALS Con. 89 BTW Papers DLC.

¹ Joseph L. Ligon, a black forty-year-old captain, commanded the Capital City Guards, a black unit of the Alabama State Troops. He was a hackman. Ligon wrote on the stationery of the Montgomery Greys, a prestigious white unit.

From John W. Whittaker

Nashville, Tenn., July 6, 1888

Dear Sir: After much consideration and prayer, I have made up my mind to give up my present field of labor and accept the position as pastor and teacher in the Tuskegee Normal School. I pray that the change may be for the best for all concerned. For I make the change because I feel that I am going where I am needed and where I shall be able to do a great work for the Lord Jesus Christ. Ever since the call came, my mind has been more and more inclined to enter into the work. So in the name of Jesus I come to labor with you.

Now I would like to know when the school begins, and what time you will expect me to be on the spot to take up my duties.

Now a word in regard to those rooms which I was to have. I would like to have the four rooms on the first floor and if in the partition a door could be made to unite two of the rooms, I think I could get on with them. Let me know if this can be done. Write soon. Very truly,

John W. Whittaker

ALS   Con. 91   BTW Papers   DLC.

To Warren Logan

47 Buckingham St. [Boston] July 8 1888

Dear Mr. Logan: I wrote my brother a few days ago to see you about paying cash for all goods for summer use. Sat. night I telegraphed you to draw on Gen. M.¹ for $500 which I suppose you have done. This I hope will relieve the most pressing debts so that a part of the money I send it can be used in the manner mention[ed].

My brother writes that merchants are charging 15¢ for Lard. This you see is suicidal when lard should be gotten for 10¢. If I do not send in enough money to pay cash let me know and I will borrow it here. I hope you are much better. Yours Sincerely

B. T. Washington

ALS   Con. 86   BTW Papers   DLC.

¹ James Fowle Baldwin Marshall.

From George W. Lovejoy

Tuskegee, Ala., July 8th, 1888

Dear Sir: Your letter received; it found things going well with us.

All the sick ones are able to be up. Mr. Logan went down to Alabama hall to day for the first time in a long while.

All the industrial department seem to be runing smoothly. I hear of no complaints.

I will send you papers that print my communications, from time to time.

I will send a letter to the People's Choice this week.

No sir the Mobile paper has not printed a single letter for me yet; though I do not slight it I send a communication every week.

The New Light of Columbus Miss has printed a letter, which I will send you. I think Miss. is a good field in which to get letters, and I will get as many as I can there.

The Montgomery Herald has not come to us this week. I do not know why. I had a letter in the last isue. Mr. Bedford wrot me that he read it with much interest and ask me to write often.

I will keep you informed from time to time how every thing is going as well as I can.

The children are looking well. Potia was enjoying the little book you sent her very much. She told me that you sent it to her.

I hope you much success on your mission.

I am Sir your friend and laborer.

G. W. Lovejoy

ALS   Con. 89   BTW Papers   DLC.

To Warren Logan

47 Buckingham St. Boston   July 11 1888

Dear Mr. Logan: There should be some definite understanding about the debts we owe to people outside of Tuskegee. Giving them notes may cramp us, but you can easily see that at the end of some month all [of] them might draw on us for the full am't we owe them. If we give a note payable at a certain time we know what to expect, and if we see before these notes fall due that we are not going to be able to pay them there are few of our creditors that will not be willing to accept part payment and a renewal of the note or in case we can pay nothing I think in most cases they would extend the time of payment.

Yours I hope are much better now. Yours Sincerely

B. T. Washington

ALS   Con. 86   BTW Papers   DLC.

From Olivia A. Davidson Washington

Tuskegee, July 12. [1888]

My dear Husband, It is two days since I wrote you. Have been very busy. Mrs. Walker[1] sent me some apples which I have been attending to. I cannot tell you much about things as far as the debts go — John said last night that Mr. Logan had done nothing although he told him of your telegram the day before. I judged by the heading of one of your letters that you were up in the mountains last week, though you said nothing about it. Hope you will succeed in getting Universalist interest.

I received the 80 & $40 checks. Mr. Logan not only does not look *ahead* but puts people off unnecessarily when they do come to him when debts are due.

You ought to be home to see how cute and sweet Brother[2] is. He runs all about and has grown some.

Watermelons are plentiful and Portia is happy. Goodbye dearest,

Olivia

ALS Con. 116 BTW Papers DLC.

[1] Norma E. Walker Carter.
[2] BTW Jr.

From John Henry Washington

Tuskegee, Ala., July 12 1888

Mr. Drakeford, Mr Howard and the Mill[1] have not been paid a cent yet.

Mr. Thompson was paid $50.00 and given an acceptance due in 30 days. While Messrs Howard and Dr Drakeford will not make any noise they want their money badly, the amt. we promised to pay at certain times. I have seen them today. I shall go to Montgomery tomorrow. I asked Mr. Logan about paying Messrs Drakeford, Howard and The Mill Just before writing and he said there were plenty of other bill to pay besides them. Also he said he had to pay the teachers so I did not get any satisfaction about town bills. I dont know why he does not pay them something with out waiting for them to begin to talk. We certainly will have to change from what we are at during the summer. No on knows who to go to get satisfaction about important matters. Your Brother

J H Washington

ALS Con. 91 BTW Papers DLC.

[1] Charlottesville Woolen Mills.

From Warren Logan

Tuskegee, Ala., July 12th 1888

Dear Mr. Washington: I have sufficiently recovered from my attack of fever to be up and to attend to the most of my duties. I hope to be entirely well in a few days. Mr Morin and Mr Terrell[1] are also up and have resumed work. My sickness has thrown me back considerably in my work. I had hoped to be able to wind up everything by Aug. 1st and enter upon my vacation at that time. But now if I get through by the 10th of Aug. I shall account myself fortunate. I am working to this end. I trust that you received my letter sent you just before I was taken ill. In it, you remember, I stated that our indebtedness amounts to something over $4000.00. This, it seems to me, is a very large sum for us to owe. I wish very much that we could pay what we owe then *keep out of debt*. Do you know that the merchants of Tusk. treat us about as they choose when we have no money? We are entirely at their mercy. They charge exorbitant prices for their goods and we are obliged to pay them or go without supplies. Drakeford is charging 15¢ per lb for lard and prices in proportion for other goods. I have tried to use the money that has been sent in to the very best advantage — making it go as far as possible and paying those claims that were most pressing. There is still a number of matters that must receive immediate attention. The $500.00 draft on Gen. Marshall has helped me greatly. If I could get the same amount again in 6 or 8 days, I think that I could do very well. There are at least 100 persons, all told, on the place this summer and these have to be provided for by the school. The expense of this is not inconsiderable.

Matters generally are going smoothly. Mr Green has been here for nearly 3 weeks. He has taken hold well and is running his department in a satisfactory manner. He has not been able to make many brick on account of frequent rains. I trust you keep well and strong. Where is Mr. Courtney now? Sincerely yours

Warren Logan

ALS   Con. 89   BTW Papers   DLC.

[1] Abraham Terrell was assistant instructor in carpentry at Tuskegee from 1888 to 1890.

From John Henry Washington

Tuskegee, Ala., July 13th 1888

My Dear Brother: Mr. Logan paid the mill and Mr. Drakeford $35.00 each today. I told them that we would continue to pay them till they were paid up.

He has not paid Mr. Howard any thing. He is very carless about paying when we get mony. He received two checks today $50.00 each and should have paid some bills.

The business of the school is getting to large to be left during [vacation] as it has been heretofore. There about seventy five students here to be looked after and they have the idea that they can do as they please during vacation. Mr. Brown had to discharge six in his department last saturday about not reporting for work. After they acknowledged their rong he took them back. No matter how important it is for us to get anything and have to get Mr. Logan consent he fails to give any satisfaction.

One of our oxen became tender footed and we either had to stop the team or get one. After waiting a few days I came across a good one for $20.00 and I never could get his consent so I borrowed $5.00 from Mr. Brown to make the first payment.

I go to Montgomery tonight and will write you on my return.

While we owe considerable and I hope will be able to pay it all soon, you need not be uneasy about the town people as I have seen all that we owe any large amount and am satisfied they feel all right.

We shall have to make arrangements about door for Armstrong Hall. Your Brother

J H Washington

ALS Con. 91 BTW Papers DLC.

To Warren Logan

Boston, Mass. July 22–88

Dear Mr. Logan: I want to begin my Northern canvass early next fall and in order to do this it is very necessary that the report be printed early. In buying text books, I wish you would try to arrange with the publishers for a definite time of payment. With the great amount of rivalry among the book publishers I think you can get payments defered till some time in Dec. Even if 6% interest is charged it will pay us to pay that and use the money in getting better terms for groceries &c.

Try to use every effort to make the labor of students this summer as valuable as possible. Yours Sincerely

B. T. Washington

Write to Mr. Fielder[1] about his daughter.

ALS   Con. 86   BTW Papers   DLC.

[1] Probably I. F. Felder of Montgomery, whose daughter Martha entered the night school in 1885. A member of the preparatory class in 1886-88, she did not return in 1888-89. Mrs. Washington wrote Felder on July 27, 1888: "I fear we have done all we can for Martha." (Con. 91, BTW Papers, DLC.)

From Warren Logan

Tuskegee, Ala., July 25th 1888

Dear Mr Washington, I am doing work on the report every day and expect to have it ready for the printer by Aug 15th.

I think satisfactory arrangements can be made with publishers as to payments for school books.

We have considerable paper out that matures between Oct 1st & Dec 1st. These amounts will be due in Aug.: 3/6 $114.86, 8/11 93.82, 15/18 $75.00. Some of the teachers will have to be settled with before they can return to Tuskegee. I am very sorry of this delay in paying the teachers. They are inclined to complain. I don't think the students' labor has been utilized to the best advantage this summer. Very little of the work planned for the summer has been completed. The work on the cottages and Armstrong Hall drags. Nothing at all has been done on the barn. We have just double the number of students here this summer that we had last year, too. I don't understand it. The Steele[1] boys are still here. I wrote Mrs Steele that we could not keep the boys but have heard nothing from her. I will write again if I don't hear this week. Yours Sincerely

Warren Logan

ALS   Con. 89   BTW Papers   DLC.

[1] Mrs. A. S. Steele, a benefactor of Tuskegee, sent five youths to Tuskegee from Chattanooga, Tenn. The boys were all between thirteen and fifteen years of age. Several of them were physically small and Warren Logan felt they were not able to keep up with the summer work and wanted them returned home. (Warren Logan to BTW, June 20, 1888, Con. 89, BTW Papers, DLC.)

From Warren Logan

Tuskegee, Ala., July 30th 1888

Dear Mr. Washington   I hope that the money to pay drafts will be forthcoming. We should have at least $500 in next ten days. I have rec'd. no money from any source for more than a week. Today there is no money at all on hand. I have no idea what the week will bring forth. Mr Courtney has sent in $150.00 since you went North; this amount he sent from Hartford. I wrote you that I had overlooked the scholarship of Brookline church. I trust that the matter is now straight. We are having fever, malarial fever the doctors pronounce it, almost as an epidemic. There have been about 20 cases in all on the school grounds. And the doctors report many cases in the town and country. Lelia Hatcher[1] died last night of a complication of diseases and was buried this morning. Everything in our power was done to prolong her life but without success. Can you not secure the gift from some of the Mass. paper manufacturers of a lot of paper suitable for class use? We will need a lot. Yours Sincerely

Warren Logan

ALS   Con. 89   BTW Papers   DLC.

[1] Lelia P. Hatcher of Charleston, W.Va., was a member of the A middle class in 1887-88.

From William Jenkins

Hotel Lafayette   Minnetonka Beach, Minn., July 31. 1888

Dear Mr. Washington: I have been here about six weeks; and have gained six pounds in weight. I am well pleased with Minnetonka

Beach. The nights are very pleasant, indeed. I have felt the need of an overcoat more than once.

The season has been unusually dull for this place; so they say. But if any more people come here than have come for the last two weeks I shall decrease very much in weight. It is no uncommon thing for us to feed five and six hundred persons at a meal. My trip here was very long and tiresome.

I was much impressed with the beautiful scenery while passing through the state of Illinois. Never before in my life had I seen such fertile and well tilled farms. I saw thousands of bushels of corn piled up in pens along the rail road; too common to be stolen. Chicago is destined to be the greatest city in the world at no distant day. And why shouldn't it? Being situated in the centre of the greatest farming region in the world.

The suburbs of Chicago begin sixteen miles before the city limits are reached. This will all soon be incorporated.

I was not able to remain in the city more than eight hours. Nevertheless, I made the most of my short stay. I visited Lincoln Park & the Museum of Fine Arts.

Our party left Nashville June the 15th, and did not reach St. Paul until June 17th, and Minnetonka Beach the following day. St. Paul at the head of navigation on the Mississippi River is a very pretty and wealthy city. Minneapolis about seven miles west of St. P. is conspicious for its beautiful granite front buildings. Minneapolis, probably, grinds more grain than any other city in the world.

Laborers are well paid here. Hotel waiters earn from twenty five to thirty dollars per month with board and lodgings. Our head waiter receives $100.00 per month.

Our second $75.00 per month. Our third $50 per month.

Several others receive thirty five dollars per month. No waiter at this house receives less than thirty dollars per month and board and lodgings. There are quite a number of colored people in the twin cities S. P. and M. They are principally from the South.

The north west is not entirely free from prejudice against the Negro. And yet, one breathes a little freer here. I have met a few people who seem to be entirely free from prejudice. And others who are southern, in sentiment, to the core. I am sorry that time and space will not admit of a more detailed account of my short experience among these people. The Negroes here are not the kind that I admire.

I am sorry to hear from T.[1] that Treadwell[2] is still there giving trouble.

I may be here for about four weeks longer then I shall probably remain in St. Paul or Chicago until Fisk opens.

Remember me to each one of your family; Miss Campbell[3] included. I shall be pleased to exchange photo's, with you. A few days ago I was in Minneapolis and had some taken, but they have not been sent to me, yet. I have nothing more to say at present. Please excuse penmanship & composition as the young men are making a good deal of noise around me. I am as ever, Your Sincere Friend

William Jenkins

ALS   Con. 89   BTW Papers   DLC.

[1] Tuskegee?

[2] James R. Treadwell.

[3] Probably Mary C. Campbell, who was in charge of the girls' industrial room at Tuskegee in 1886-87.

From Rosa Mason

Poughkeepsie, N.Y. August 1st. 1888

Dear Mr. Washington, As the noise in Ala. Hall was very trying to me last term I would like to board outside next year. Mr. John[1] says that I may board with him, and I would like very much to do so. Have you any objection? I feel that I need a quiet place. In fact I know that I can do better work and will be a great deal stronger if I can have a room alone, and at the same time be away from the noise of the girls.

I do not ask to board outside in order to get rid of any work which may fall to me. My boarding at Mr. John's will not prevent me from assisting with the Study Hours or anything of the kind.

There is another matter which I wish to speak of, and that is my salary next year. I have heretofore worked for less than the most of the other teachers have received, and I *know* that I have done quite as much work as some of them. Is there any reason for the difference?

If not, will I receive as much next year as the other regular lady teachers?

When I am at work the salary has nothing to do with the way in which I do my work. I always do the best I can, but you know I have my living to work for.

I trust that you have had a pleasant vacation and have not worked too hard.

My health has been very good this summer. The study of Elocution has done me a great deal of good physically as well as mentally.

Miss Baright[2] is anxious to have me go to Boston with her this fall and study a few months longer, but I cannot afford it.

Please let me hear from you as soon as possible. Sincerely yours,

Rosa Mason

ALS   Con. 89   BTW Papers   DLC.

[1] John Henry Washington.
[2] Baright was a frequent family name in Poughkeepsie.

Robert Charles Bedford
to Olivia A. Davidson Washington

Montgomery Ala   Aug 4 [1888]

Dear Mrs Washington   Postal note for 70 cts recd. Glad you are pleased with cloth. Am a little disturbed this morning by note in this morning's Advertiser about a letter of Lovejoy's to a Miss paper.[1] What is it? I hope it is nothing that will embarrass you. Personally, I trust you will not apologize for or retract any thing, except what is wrong. There is a future as well as a present in this matter. You have my warmest sympathy in these trying times. I pray God may direct us all. Let me hear the truth, especially inform me if there is any trouble in prospect. Your friend

R C Bedford

ALS   Con. 88   BTW Papers   DLC.

[1] Lovejoy's letter appeared in the Columbus (Miss.) *New Light,* a Negro newspaper, and it was dated Tuskegee Normal School, Tuskegee, Alabama, July 16, 1888. It read in part:

"The white people of our county have caught the spirit of the lynch-law.

"There was a mob being gotten up a few days ago to lynch a negro who was accused of being caught in a white girl's room. The mob was prevented by taking the negro to Montgomery jail.

"There is a vast difference between the spirit of the negro and white man of this country."

Lovejoy compared the treatment of a white man found in a Negro servant girl's quarters and asked to leave with the near lynching of a black man for the same thing. "This is a wide contrast between the two rascals both guilty of the same offense," he charged. He ended the letter by asking students to apply for enrollment at Tuskegee Institute. The Tuskegee *Weekly News* in its headlines offered what could be described as a poem to Lovejoy:

Lying Lovejoy is His Name,
Of Ginger Cake Color,
The Third Dusky Romeo Turned Out to Roam
From the Tuskegee Normal School
That has Ventilated his Spleen and Hate of the White Race.
Is it the Purpose of this School to Breed Such Whelps.

(Tuskegee *Weekly News,* Aug. 2, 1888, 2. See also Montgomery *Advertiser,* Aug. 4, 1888, 1.)

From John Taylor Hollis

Richland Ga., 8-9-88

Dear Friend and Family; I am proud to say that Tuskegee's School is, an Electric Machine, feeding me with energy, courage, up-building, morality and religion. I am proud that out side of my family troubles, I am the same boy I were, when I left your walls in 1885. I have many hindrances. I still go forward in the great work assigned me. My wife has consented to go with me at last. I will come to Tuskegee about December next. My summer school will close the first of October. No Students equal Tuskegee's students in bettering the condition of the Negro race in its broadest term here in this County. Thank God that I still have the greatest confidence in *you* and your *noble* wife! I am anxious to hear from you and other matters. Tell Mr. Dryer & Co.[1] I shall meet them like a man when I come. Write soon. Yours In Christ.

J. T. Hollis

ALS   Con. 88   BTW Papers   DLC.

[1] The Tuskegee dry-goods store of Thomas B. Dryer.

From George W. Lovejoy

Olustee Creek P.O. Pike Co. Ala. August 12th, 1888

My Dear Mr. W: I have not as yet comminced to do any thing. I am now at my mother's. I guess you was shocked to hear of my unfotinate affair.

I am indeed sorry that we have a class citizens that is so ready to miss interpret and always make mountains out of moul hills.

I suppose you have read the letter that caused so much talk and writing.

I might have been a little imprudent but I did not intend to have been.

I have not ask any parden and I do not intend to do so. I do not feel that I have done any wrong.

But I do feel that I have been miserably misrepresented.

I hope the Tuskegee News man will see his mistake some day, for he has mad a miserable one.

I do not care for but one thing and that is involveing the school.

An individual cannot say a thing with out the papers striking at the school.

I left the school because I thought it might be for it's best interest. Had it not been for that I would not have gone.

I have the same interest in the school that I always had and shall ever be found doing what I can for it's interest.

So far as my character and reputation are concern, I think they will bare up the scandolds of the Tuskegee News as a ship will a spider web.

The news could not have called me a lie on but one thing and that was relative to lynching the Negro and the Montgomery Dispatch said attempts were made to lynch him and I was told the same thing by citizens of Tuskegee.

I understand what it all was done for it is not necessary to say any thing more about it.

I hope all the colored people see things on the right side.

I have no inclination to raise race stife, I have nothing a gainst any class of citizens.

I have a little brother[1] a bout the size of Albert[2] I would like very much if you would take him for your office boy. I want to put him in school very much and he is too small to put on the farm yet. He is quick and polite no ways saucy.

I have fixed hem to come and if you will take hem he will be there by the first of Sept.

Our father died last May and Mother has two children she will make any reasonible sacrifice to get in school.

She will not be ready to put but one in school until her crop is gathered. I do not see any chance to go to Portsmouth until next winter. I have not the money to go and cannot borrow it. I think I will be compelled to teach before I will be able to go.

The school ows me $15.00 for writing and I worked on the Brick yard and in the office to gather nearly two months. You paid a debt that I owed McWilliams[3] ($4.00) it was, and I owe you $1.70 for railroad fair from Montgomery to Tuskegee.

I do not know what Mrs. Washington allowed me for office work.

I was writing in the office 7 days. I liked from the second of August until the (12) tweth of August, of working two months on the brick yard, including the time in the office. The school will be in debt to me after it is paid. You may pay your self and if any thing is left I owe Mr. Logan ($5.00) Five dollars. I liked only 4 days working the two months. Allowing the same in the office that was allowed on the Brick Yard.

Including Bickyard and office work the school ows me $16.38 for Brick yard work and $15.00 for newspaper work. Making in the whole $31.38. Mr. Winborn[4] had a bill made for me for the month of June, which was wrong.

He did not allow me but $9.00 per month and I was to have $10.00. I hope you will be able to see through this mixed up affair.

But getting a place for my little brothre is the interesting point with me. Please let me know at once what you can do for him. I am my Dear Sir a devoted friend to the school and all cornected with it.

G. W. Lovejoy

ALS Con. 89 BTW Papers DLC.

[1] Probably Alonzo Lovejoy, who entered Tuskegee's B middle class in 1889. He did not graduate.

[2] George Washington Albert Johnston was the son of BTW's sister, Amanda Johnston. He graduated from Tuskegee in 1893 and later served BTW as his

personal business agent and cashier of the Tuskegee Institute Bank. After 1901 he was an employee of BTW's friend Joseph O. Thompson, U.S. collector of internal revenue for the state of Alabama, in Birmingham.

[3] He may have been referring to a student listed in the 1886-87 Tuskegee catalog as David W. McMillian, a member of the preparatory class from Elba, Ala., or to J. T. McWilliams, a resident of Tuskegee.

[4] Javan F. Winborne was in charge of the sawmill at Tuskegee Institute from 1886 to 1890.

From Robert Charles Bedford

Montgomery Ala   Aug 14 1888

Dear Prof   We are all exceedingly glad you have got home. With all our confidence in Mrs Washington and the other teachers we feel as if a right arm were gone when you are away. I regret Lovejoy's letter very much but still I do not apprehend any injury to the school from it. He is young and inexperienced and any rational person ought readily to understand that his indiscretion came not from his training at school but rather from his want of knowledge of the world and human nature. I trust you will not in any way look upon it as a fault of the school but rather as what often has and often will happen to youth and inexperience.

I do not know what has become of Lovejoy but suppose he has gone home. When he left me last he said if he did not come back he would write to us from wherever he might go. I shall be very glad to see you and hope you will be able to come soon. I go this afternoon to Prattville but return to morrow afternoon. The children are getting along nicely and we are all feeling very well. You need not think the school especially afflicted as there is an unusual amount of sickness here. I have talked with the Dr[1] about it and he says it can readily be traced to natural causes. I will only write a line as I expect soon to see you. Love to Mrs W and all friends. Your bro

R C Bedford

ALS   Con. 87   BTW Papers   DLC.

[1] Cornelius Nathaniel Dorsette.

To the Editor of the Tuskegee *Weekly News*

Tuskegee, Ala. Aug. 14th 1888

Editors News: It has always been and is now the policy of the Normal School to remain free from politics and the discussions of race questions that tend to stir up strife between the races, and when ever this policy is violated it is done without the approbation of those in charge of the school. It seems that the best proof the school can offer as to its character, in this regard, is the fact that during its seven years existence in this community with from three to four hundred students and teachers connected with it, there have been in all not a half dozen acts performed or utterances made at which any one took offense.

During this time no non resident student has ever been charged with violations of law, and the feeling between the races has seemingly been up to this time as pleasant as it well could be. This feeling we hope to have continued and shall do all in our power to that end and any thing that tends to stir up ill feeling is deeply regretted.

B. T. Washington, Prin.

Tuskegee *Weekly News,* Aug. 16, 1888, 3.

From James B. Washington

Fayette Sta [W.Va.] 8-26,–1888

Dear Bro: I rec'd your kind and welcome letter, and was truly glad to hear from you. I have been looking for a letter from you for some time. I am not getting along very well just now. I am going to teach this winter. I wish you would send me some money to get ready to teach. I attended the Institute, and got No. (2).[1] You can see how much I had forgotten. The examination was very rigid indeed. The works are not running more than two days a week. I wish you would be sure and send me some money. If you only lend it to me. I wish you would send me some books. A geography, physiology, and philosophy. Please send them immediately, so that I can be examined again. You are the only one I feel that I can confide my secrets to. You assisted me in the past

479

and I hope you will come to my assistance in the future, or rather now. It seems that when I get straight to do well, something happens. You know how works run during campaigns. Booker it seems that once a year I get in hard luck. I dont see why either, for I can truly say that I work, but you know how it is on Coal works. You have been on works yourself. I have been home once in twelve months, I am going to leave here after this Winter. As Mr Callaway[2] is going to stay here this winter I will leave Hettie and the baby[3] with them. You see coke works have been dull all summer and that threw a great deal of responsibility upon me. If he (Aaron) could have worked on the Coke yard I could have made something, and he cant work in the mines. Booker, can walk and talk, and is just as smart as he can be. Hettie sends much love to you and family. You have never said a word about your boy yet. Kiss the children for me. Mr & Mrs Callaway[4] send their regards to you all, and say you all must come again. I would be glad for you to send the rec'ds to me, and I will try and sell them for you.

Let me know if you are coming home this Fall. I would like much to see you. It has been over two years since I saw you last. Arena and husband send love to you. They lost their little baby since I wrote to you last. Please write me a good long letter, for I enjoy reading your letters more than any others I receive. Dont fail please to send me a little money if it is not more than Five dollars I will pay you when I get to teaching now, trust me once wont you? Your Brother

Jas B. Washington

ALS   Con. 17   BTW Papers   DLC.

[1] A No. 2 teaching certificate.

[2] Aaron Calloway, listed in the 1870 census as a twenty-one-year-old black man who worked as a farm laborer in Fayetteville Township, W.Va.

[3] Booker C[alloway?] Washington.

[4] Mariah Calloway, listed in the 1870 census as a nineteen-year-old mulatto.

To Rosa Mason

Tuskegee, Ala., Sept. 4 1888

Miss Mason: On or before to morrow please give me an answer to the following: the position of Lady Principal is now vacant. Will you accept the position till June 15, 1889, devoting all your time to the general over sight of the girls in their home life; their industrial work and to the over looking of the literary work in the same way the lady principal has always done, this last to include the calling of the rolls &c. You *might* be able to do this and give some time to class work, but I fear you could not and in accepting this work you would be giving up for a time at least one of your cherished plans. But while I feel you would do the school good in carrying out your plans, I am equally sure that in the present organization of the school you would do it far greater service by accepting the position I now tender. I would not think of offering you this position if I had not seen in you a disposition ever since your connection with the school to do what was considered for the best interest of the school.

The salary for the position would be $60 per month.

[B. T. Washington]

AL   Con. 861   BTW Papers   DLC.

From Rosa Mason

[Tuskegee, Ala., Sept. 5, 1888?]

Mr. Washington, Your note received, the contents of which were a great surprise to me after your repeated efforts to secure some one else to fill the position.

I will say in the outset that owing to the responsibilities, I do not want the position of Lady Principal which you have so kindly offered me, but in the present condition of the school I will accept the position as *Acting* Lady Principal until June 15th 1889.

I will try to do what is right and discharge the duties of the position with the best of my ability, and in this I expect your *hearty support*. I will also say I do not wish to be encumbered in the position by outside influences.

While I regret *very much* to give up my class work, I think that the duties of Lady Prin. will require all of my time. Yours,

Rosa Mason

ALS   Con. 89   BTW Papers   DLC.

From John W. Stakely

Union Springs, Ala. Sept. 11, 1888

Dear principal: It has been some time since I wrote you. Yet you have not been forgotten. I have been and am very busy trying to build up a good school house for the colored people of Union Springs. Thus far, we have succeeded in buying the land, contracted for the lumber, and with the carpenter. The lumber is being put on the grounds. Money is being raised through and by the colored and white citizens of our city. I am thankful to state that we shall be aided by the "Peabody Educational Fund" to the amount of three or four hundred dollars. Our building shall be ready for occupancy by the last of October. So you see that I have been very busy. If you can do me any good I shall be very grateful to you. Write a special letter to Capt. W. C. Wilson endorsing me as a worker for the cause of education at once. It will do me considerable good in accomplishing a certain end. My work has met with considerable opposition, but I am going to the front. I have some of your pluck. Remember me kindly to Mrs. Washington & Portia. Yours,

J. W. Stakely

ALS Con. 90 BTW Papers DLC.

To Mrs. G. A. Rumbley[1]

[Tuskegee, Ala.] Sept. 18th–88

Mrs. Rumbley: If you are sure that sarcastic remarks were made about the food at the table today, I wish you would find out for me the words and name of teacher or teachers.

I can not think that we have here a person in the capacity of a teacher who would so far forget themselves as a lady or gentleman to be guilty of such conduct and it is my intention to retain here none but ladies and gentlemen.

B. T. Washington

ALpS Con. 91 BTW Papers DLC.

[1] Mrs. G. A. Rumbley was in charge of the health department at Tuskegee in 1887-88 and the next year was employed also as housekeeper.

To Mrs. G. A. Rumbley

[Tuskegee, Ala.] September 24th [188]8

Mrs. Rumbley: It is very evident that some part of your work is not receiving enough of your present attention. Too much expense is involved in the Teachers' Home to be left so much in charge of students. Miss Mason says you are rarely present at breakfast. I expect you as a rule to give your personal attention to the preparation and over-looking of each meal.

This morning I was present when the breakfast was being prepared and saw that it was left in the hands of the Students. Largely because matters are left so much to students, there is dissatisfaction among the teachers, and the expense of the department goes up to a point where we cannot stand it. For example, one barrel of white sugar lasted one month last time. Now a barrel has been used up in the middle of the month when there have not been more than 3 or 4 more persons in the department during this month than in last term.

I must ask you also to be more careful in your relations to students, that is, what you *say to* and *before* students. In one of the meetings last week, I made some plain remarks about Mittie Avery.[1] In a short time afterwards Mittie came to me knowing what had been said and stated that you told her. I know you have many inconveniences in your work, but the point is to make the best of everything. We are trying as fast as possible to get affairs in better condition.

In the matters that I have referred to a change must be made. It is much better all around to speak plainly than to allow things to go on in an unsatisfactory condition.

B. T. Washington

HLpS Con. 91 BTW Papers DLC.

[1] Mittie Avery was listed in the 1887-88 Tuskegee catalog as a member of the B middle class from Greensboro, Ala.

From Samuel Chapman Armstrong

Hampton, Va., Oct 6th 1888

My dear Washington   Many thanks for the pictures of the Hall. One of them shall be framed & put up in my room. It is the only building anywhere that bears my name and I dont intend that any other one shall.

I will send, framed, in a few days a ~~little~~ photograph of myself for it where you may choose to put it.

I am just back from Dakota — very interesting.

Hope the year will go well with you. Yours Sincerely

S. C. Armstrong

Please remember me kindly to your wife.

ALS   Con. 87   BTW Papers   DLC.

To Moses Pierce

[Tuskegee, Ala.] Oct. 9 [188]8

Kind friend: I have not replied earlier to yours of the 24th of Sept regarding the land for the reasons that I have been unwell and wanted to see some of the Trustees about the matter.

The trustees that I have seen are delighted with the prospect of secur[ing] the land. There is almost no weed on the land — a few small pine trees. It is my opinion that there are about 4 acres that will make brick clay. A portion of it has been planted recently but *very* poorly cultivated. For a number of years the place has been a kind of public pasture as it has no fence around it and the cash outlay for a fence will be about $60. The stream flowing through the land is not the same as the one flowing through the other tract.

As to the conditions now about no whiskey being sold, not selling the land &c. the executive board of our trustees could give you a written promise and have the action confirmed at the regular trustee meeting in May if you think that the best course.

484

As the people in this section are not used to living on small lots I suggest that the lots be 100 ft front and 300 deep instead of 50 front and 150 deep. All the other conditions we will gladly comply with and thank you a thousand times for your generosity. I am sure the arrangement you suggest will help our scholarship fund much. Yours truly

Booker T. Washington

ALpS Con. 91 BTW Papers DLC.

To Mrs. G. A. Rumbley

[Tuskegee, Ala.] October 10th [188]8

Mrs Rumbley: When I made arrangements with you to return this year and take the present work, of course I did not mean that you would be retained in the position throughout the year regardless of the way you perform the service. When I said to you a few days ago that no change would be made to interfere with your plans it was on the supposition that you would do the work properly. When you returned from Mrs Adams' I had a conversation with you in which I told you plainly that the teachers department went more smoothly while you were away, because Miss Jones[1] gave more personal attention to the work. You seemed to see the point and promised to make it go more smoothly. Since then you have not given the attention to the work that I thought you would. For example, you are almost never present to overlook and see to the preparation of the breakfast. It is simply ridiculous to have a teacher in charge of a large boarding department and she not present to watch over so important a meal as the breakfast. My realation to the wellfare of the work here compels me to say to you in the most kindly spirit that unless a change is made within a week in the way you are performing the work I shall be compelled to ask you to give up your position here. When I say a change in the work I mean that you are to be out in the morning in time to see how the meal is prepared and that it is properly served on the table. The one in your position should be pleasant and obliging to teachers, not fractious. I must be assured that you are really interested at heart in your work. Aside from the dissatisfaction arising from the teachers,

485

the school cannot stand the expenses that it is put to, and have the boarding department left to irresponsible students.

Your work needs to be systematized. This can be done by making a study of what will please the teachers. The teachers do not complain of the quality, but it is the way the food is prepared. I still think that you can make a success of your work, but in order to do this you must become interested. In order to make it a success I shall do all in my power to help you in any reasonable way. Yours

B. T. Washington

HLpS Con. 91 BTW Papers DLC.

¹ Alice E. Jones Bailey.

From Thomas McCants Stewart

New York, Oct. 10th., 1888

My Dear Sir: I have secured a final decision in the matter of your application to the executors of the Barnes Estate for the legacy to which you are entitled.

In consequence of the misnomer in the Will, the Executors, through and by advice of their counsel (Lawyer J. Adriance Bush), refuse to pay you the legacy now or at any other time without an order from the Surrogate's Court. They deem this necessary for their protection. They will waive all limitations of time etc. which would ordinarily prevent us from raising the question before the Surrogate at once.

Now, then, please understand, that you must go into Court to get this legacy.

If you wish me to put the matter in shape, I shall expect your check for fifty dollars on account of my fee and certain expenses which we would have necessarily to incur in getting into Court. Yours truly,

T. McCants Stewart

ALS Con. 1 BTW Papers ATT.

To the Executors of the Alfred S. Barnes Estate

[Tuskegee, Ala.] October 27th [188]8

Dear Sirs: We learn with much pain that your counsel advises that you cannot *legally* pay to our institution the sum specified in the will of the late Mr. A. S. Barnes for the colored Collegiate Institution of Tuskegee, Mississippi.

We feel sure for the following reasons that Mr Barnes *intended* the money to come to this institution:

(1) There is no other colored institution in the United States with the name of "Tuskegee" attached to it, nor is there any other post office in the United States by this name.

(2) Our school is variously called "Colored College," "Normal School," "Colored Institute" &c.

(3) Mr Barnes knew of our school from the fact that we have had business dealings with the firm of A. S. Barnes & Co both directly and through their agents, running through a period of seven years and during this time have received a donation of books.

(4) We think it was through his direct knowledge of Gen. S. C. Armstrong of the Hampton Institute that Mr. Barnes learned of this school and its work.

This institution is spoken of as a branch of the Hampton Institute from the fact that most of its teachers are graduates of the Hampton Institute. This school was often spoken of in the "Southern Workman" the organ of the Hampton Institute. This paper was sent to Mr Barnes. Mr Barnes also visited Hampton.

(5) Almost every week mention of this school is made in some missionary magazine, religious or secular paper, and Mr Barnes doubtless kept up to some extent with this school by this means.

If there is any possible way by which Mr Barnes' wish in this matter can be carried out we earnestly trust that it will be, for we are greatly in need of the money and not knowing that we might be debarred on account of the misnomer had really planned to use the money.

In addition to the foregoing I enclose a statement to the executors

487

from Gen. S. C. Armstrong of the Hampton Institute. Respectfully Yours,

B. T. Washington

HLpS Con. 91 BTW Papers DLC.

From William Still[1]

Philadelphia, Nov. 7th, 1888

Dear Sir, The Pennsylvania Society for Promoting the Abolition of Slavery &c., contemplate holding a Quarter-Century Celebration of Freedom, on the 2nd day of Jan. '89, in this City — at this date 25 years of Freedom will have been filled up.

Ought not, therefore, the friends of Freedom, for the enlightenment of this nation, as well as for the encouragement of the Emancipated and their Emancipators, be prepared to present to the world a fitting review of the First 25 years of Freedom, at this juncture?

The condition of the Bondmen, just before and at the time of Emancipation — the First 5 years' struggle under Freedom — the courageous and noble efforts of Northern Philanthropists, to carry Education to those hungering and thirsting for knowledge — the experience and suffering of the race upon first seeking political privileges — the progressions and setbacks on the road — the present status of the colored people of the South and how their elevation may be advanced are themes, that may be made exceedingly interesting and beneficial, on an occasion of this character.

As this is to be the First Quarter Century meeting, we want that full justice shall be done the themes discussed, hence we propose to invite yourself with Hon. Fred. Douglass,[2] Mr. Cable, Rev. J. C. Price, D. D. and Gen'l Armstrong.

With regard to remuneration, all I am prepared to say, at present is, the Society will bear your expenses on this errand.

Now, My Dear Sir, will you come and make us a speech, on this occasion? Pray say, yes, and send me a reply immediately, naming your subject, as we are anxious to arrange matters speedily. Yours Very Truly,

W. Still,
Vice Pres't and
Chair'n Com. of Arrangements

HLS Con. 90 BTW Papers DLC. Still's letterhead advertised the latest edition of his book *The Underground Railroad* and also contained a lengthy endorsement of the book from William Lloyd Garrison, who concluded that "It is a book for every household."

[1] William Still (1821-1902), author of *The Underground Railroad* (1872), was born in New Jersey, the last of eighteen children of former slave parents. His father had purchased his freedom in Maryland and moved to New Jersey and his mother had escaped to follow her husband, leaving two young children behind in bondage. The knowledge that two of his brothers remained slaves prompted Still to become active in the Pennsylvania Society for the Abolition of Slavery in 1847, soon after he had come to Philadelphia, serving as its president from 1851 to 1860. By his own reckoning he helped more than 600 slaves escape. Many of these supplied him with firsthand accounts of their flights, material that served as the basis for his book. Self-educated, Still turned after the Civil War to business and earned a considerable fortune (in excess of $200,000) in the stove and coal business, serving for a time on the Philadelphia Board of Trade. He remained active in Negro affairs, helping in 1867 to press the Pennsylvania legislature to abolish racial discrimination on Philadelphia's streetcars. He was a member of the Freedmen's Aid Commission and became increasingly active in Philadelphia welfare work for blacks in the 1880s. He helped found a YMCA and served on the boards of homes for the aged, orphans, and destitute children. His position on racial matters grew more conciliatory as he grew older, richer, and more famous. In 1885, in an article in the *A.M.E. Church Review,* Still advocated that Negroes should take "less stock in politics and more in education and land" and "make friends with thine adversary." (Quoted in Meier, *Negro Thought in America, 1880-1915,* 35.)

[2] Frederick Douglass (1817?-95), first named Frederick Augustus Washington Bailey, was born a slave near Easton, Md. Unlike BTW, Douglass remained a slave until he reached the age of manhood. Hence the career of Douglass as a slave was more turbulent than that of BTW. While serving under a slave breaker, Douglass fought rather than take a beating, teaching him the utility of resistance. For several years he was a house servant in Baltimore, where, through the kindness of his mistress and his own inventiveness, he learned to read and write. When he returned to the country as a field hand he could no longer tolerate his condition as a slave and planned an escape, but his plan was discovered and thwarted. Later he learned a trade and hired his own time. In 1838 he escaped from slavery, married Anna Murray, a free black woman, and settled in New Bedford, Mass.

In New Bedford Douglass first worked as a common laborer. In 1841 he became interested in the abolitionist movement, attended a meeting, made a speech, and was asked to serve as agent of the Massachusetts Anti-Slavery Society. In this role he became a leading spokesman for abolition. He was so good, in fact, that people began to doubt that he had ever been a slave. To convince people of his past, Douglass in 1845 wrote *Narrative of the Life of Frederick Douglass.* Because his account of his life as a slave was so frank, Douglass feared reenslavement and spent two years in Great Britain and Ireland, where he met many men and women of liberal mind and was impressed with his treatment as an equal. Upon his return to the United States in 1847 English friends bought his freedom. The same year he established a newspaper, *The North Star,* in Rochester, N.Y. Because Douglass was self-assertive and insistent on the equality of blacks, he broke with many of his former abolitionist friends. He favored woman suffrage and was a close friend of John Brown, though he advised against the Harpers Ferry raid. During the Civil War he helped recruit black troops and conferred with President Lincoln about their treatment.

During the Reconstruction years and afterward, Douglass served in several government posts, as marshal and recorder of deeds of the District of Columbia, and as U.S. minister to Haiti. His second marriage in 1884 to a white woman, Helen Pitts, brought him much criticism. By this time Douglass's days of active agitation were on the wane. He maintained a perfunctory relationship with BTW and neither unequivocally endorsed nor condemned the Tuskegean and his conservative approach to race relations. In 1892 Douglass gave the commencement address at Tuskegee Institute. After his death, BTW and some Washington, D.C., friends labored to secure money from black people to save the mortgaged Douglass estate from foreclosure.

To Warren Logan

Boston, Mass   Nov. 8 1888

Dear Mr. Logan: This week I have bought several lots of goods at very low rates. The goods are of the kind that we are constantly dribling out money for there. We must stop buying in small quantities. I have paid cash for a part of the goods, but bills will be sent for most on 30 days. Several times this week parties here have looked up our business standing and in every case have found it good. It is of the utmost importance that it be kept so. It would give us a black eye here to be marked low in a commercial register.

I hope you will plan to give the students a good time Thanksgiving; have a committee of teachers &c on entertainment appointed early.

I am very glad to hear that matters are going so smoothly. Yours truly

B. T. Washington

Political excitement here has been *intense* and is still high. It is seldom that I have seen people rejoice so. Yours t[ruly]

B. T. W.

ALS Con. 1 BTW Papers ATT.

From Rosa Mason

Tuskegee, Ala., Nov. 14, 1888

Dear Mr. Washington, Your letter was received some time ago, would have written before this, but knew that you heard from Tuskegee regularly, and besides I have been busy and not very well.

I am trying to look after the ventilation of the buildings, but we are too much crowded.

There are no serious cases of fever among the girls now. Willie Moore[1] has been very sick and we have been quite anxious about her, but she is better now, and her sister is here with her.

Now that the girls are better the teachers are getting sick. Misses Brown[2] and Benson[3] are quite unwell to-day and Mr. Whittaker has the fever.

I have not been well since you left, but have been keeping up. Yesterday, however, I had to call in the Dr. He says that I will not get any better as long as I stay here, but thinks I will be strong again if I leave the school for three or four weeks and go somewhere where I can have it perfectly quiet. Then he says that Medicine will do me some good. I am going to try to stay here until the other teachers are well and until you return — then I think it will be best for me to give up my work for at least three or four weeks. I think I can arrange it. If I don't stop now I may *have* to stop for good.

Mrs. Pindle[4] says that she has a very little bedding for the girls, and if she does not have more by the time it gets cold that the girls will suffer. I think that you can get covering there cheaper than it can be gotten here. The girls need something to go on the top of their beds. They have nothing now except those common blankets.

Hope that you are well. Respectfully yours,

Rosa Mason

ALS Con. 89 BTW Papers DLC.

[1] Willia A. Moore was a member of the junior class from Eufaula, Ala.

[2] Ellen M. Brown was in charge of the girls' industrial room at Tuskegee during the 1887-88 school year and taught grammar from 1888 through 1892.

[3] Maria A. Benson taught mathematics from 1888 to 1890.

[4] Mrs. Eliza A. Pindle was a matron and in charge of cookery during the 1888-89 school year and continued her matron duties during the following year.

To Warren Logan

New York, N.Y. Nov. 16–88

Dear Mr. Logan: I am here today seeing about Barnes money. The matter seems favorable and the Barnes say that we are reasonably sure of getting it within a few days at any rate by Dec. 1.

They ask though to be remembered in the matter of text books.

What have you found out about a printing press?

I find we can get a good Campell Cylender press[1] for $600 with 18 months to pay for it. What do you think of it?

Write me at Boston. Enclosed I send a check for $50. Yours truly

B. T. Washington

ALS   Con. 1   BTW Papers   ATT.

[1] Andrew Campbell developed the first satisfactory low-priced cylinder press giving perfect register.

Woodie I. McCann[1] to Warren Logan

Lawrence, Mass., Nov. 18–'88

Dear Mr. Logan; Your favor of flattery of 7 inst. received.

I fear you sing to loud for me. A beggar's fortune in New. Eng. is something like its weather — very changeable. I have been very much discouraged within the past few days. The people seem hardened to the appeals of a "poor, unknown beggar." I have but $15 now, and don't see bright prospects of getting many more in Haverhill. I shall not canvass Lawrence at all. The ministers tell me that it will be of no profit. Mr. St. Clair, of Dr. Price's school[2] came here didn't get his expenses but represented his work as being of the same character of Tuskegee "Industrial and Unsectarian" which you know to be false. And I shall wait "till his tracks cool["] before representing Tuskegee.

I shall speak to day in Haverhill — Methodist and Universalist churches.

Hope to get something. I hope you are receiving many donations and wish that she, Tuskegee could secure some millionaire friends; for the northern people are getting tired of many, numerous, innumerable, and constant calls from the south.

My health is good, but I am feeling rather exhausted today.

Remember me kindly to all. I am surprised to hear of Miss Lyman's[3] return. Think it best 'tho.' Your sincere friend,

W. I. McCann

ALS   Con. 89   BTW Papers   DLC.

[1] Woodie I. McCann graduated from Tuskegee in 1887 and raised funds for the school in 1888. Later he taught school in Eagle Lake, Tex.

[2] Livingstone College, of which Joseph Charles Price was president. It was an A.M.E. school.

[3] Eugenia Lyman McCann of Opelika, Ala., graduated from Tuskegee Institute in 1888 and returned to Opelika to teach in 1888-90. She married McCann in 1890 and moved with him to Texas, where she taught and kept house.

To Warren Logan

Boston, Mass. Nov. 29 1888

Dear Mr. Logan: This week I was at Newport and spent considerable time with the Misses Mason[1] talking about the school. They seem more interested than ever in the school and am quite sure they will give as usual though they have set no definite time, but I think one of them will send some thing soon. Miss Ida said hers would be same as last year. To pay the teachers if the Barnes keep their promise we shall have that $1000 and the state money minus what is due Howard & Co. Should neither of the Masons send any thing in time to pay teachers we shall have to devise some means to get the money till their donations are sent.

It is my present intention to start home about the 7th of Dec. I trust all are enjoying Thanksgiving. Yours truly

B. T. Washington

ALS   Con. 1   BTW Papers   ATT.

[1] Ellen Frances and Ida Means Mason.

A Report on the Summer State Teachers' Institutes

Tuskegee, Nov. 1888

HON. SOLOMON PALMER,
    State Superintendent of Education,
        Montgomery, Alabama:

Dear Sir — The State Teachers' Institutes put in my charge were conducted, as last year, by Prof. S. E. Courtney and Miss Adella Hunt.
The Institutes were held at Union Springs, Bullock county, and Greenville, Butler county, August 6th and 13th, respectively, continuing in
session one week at each place. The subjects discussed were Reading,
Language, Writing, Arithmetic, Geography, Grammar, Physiology and
Hygiene. It was the aim to make the Institutes as practical and useful
as possible, so in connection with these exercises a plan of topics on the
various branches was presented and explained, together with simple
means of illustrations.

In the evenings lectures were given on the "Work of the Public
Schools." In the discussion of this subject it was shown that useful
knowledge, a cultivated mind, and a right way of using it, are the
ends to which the Public Schools should direct their attention.

On closing the work in each place a general meeting with the teachers and citizens was held where the subject of the importance of giving
to the schools a generous support, of employing skilled teachers, of
sending the children regularly to school, and of maintaining well constructed school houses was discussed. Exercises of this sort will doubtless produce good results.

The people of the towns where the Institutes were held provided for
them in a generous manner, showing their good will to the teachers.

These Institutes stimulate the teachers to renewed efforts in improving their work.

The attendance at both Institutes was very good.

We thank you again for the privilege of conducting these Institutes.
Respectfully submitted,

B. T. Washington, Conductor of Institute

*Thirty-fourth Annual Report of the Superintendent of Education of the State
of Alabama for the Scholastic Year Ending September 30, 1888* (Montgomery,
1888), 69.

From William Still

Philadelphia, Dec 17th 1888

Dear Sir: Your letter of the 14th inst. arrived safely today indicating that a degree of anxiety was weighing upon your mind relative to the "contemplated celebration," which you had engaged to be at on the 2nd of Jan'y. Of course it is to come off. Today has found me very busy advertising in the weekly papers, and I shall follow up this work in the daily papers quickly. It will be well advertised and I am looking for a meeting of great interest. I will send you a paper or two with Notices & Speakers.

I shall be pleased to have you stop with me. In great haste   Yours truly

W Still

ALS   Con. 90   BTW Papers   DLC.

To Trou City Directory Co.

Tuskegee, Ala., Dec. 27 1888

Dear Sirs: Can you tell me where I can purchase a directory containing only the names of the wealthy of the city of N.Y. Most cities have such a book called the "Blue Book." Yours truly

B. T. Washington

ALS   Con. 91   BTW Papers   DLC. The company's reply was written at the bottom of BTW's letter: "The Directory to which enclosed circular relates includes the names of all people in from moderate to affluent circumstances in NY City and all places within 25 miles thereof."

From Robert Charles Bedford

Montgomery Ala   Dec 27 1888

Dear Prof   Your letter is just recd and I am very sorry to hear of the continued bad condition of Mrs W's throat. I have tried all day to see the Dr[1] and talk with him. Have been to his office once. Dr Sterrs[2] is away so that he is unusually busy. Had you not better have him come up. He can leave here at 12.35 PM and reach here again at 7 PM same day. I feel anxious to do any thing in my power. Please write or telegraph me any thing I can do. I shall look for a card at least every day till you feel more at ease about her condition. I called on Mr Diggs[3] some time ago and will go in again before long. Will also see Mr Alexander[4] soon.

Give my love to Mrs Washington and assure her of our most hearty sympathy. Mr & Mrs Mitchell[5] also join in love & sympathy. Yours truly

R C Bedford

ALS   Con. 87   BTW Papers   DLC.

[1] Cornelius Nathaniel Dorsette.

[2] Willis E. Sterrs, a physician. In 1901 he resided in Decatur, Ala.

[3] John Diggs was reported in the 1880 census as a black grocer in Montgomery, age thirty, unable to read or write.

[4] Probably W. G. Alexander, pastor of St. John's A.M.E. Church in Montgomery.

[5] Possibly Alex Mitchell, reported in the 1880 census as a forty-six-year-old mulatto hackman in Montgomery, and his wife Elmira.

From George W. Lovejoy

Troy, Ala., December 31st, 1888

My Dear Mr. Washington: My school at Flemington has closed and I have just a bout made up my mind to start to Virginia.

I have been thinking all the while that I would teach another three months; but the schools are so devided they do not pay well.

I surpose it will be alright with Mr. Reid for me to go now.

Will there be any chance for me to get my sister[1] in school as a work student now? I am not willing to leave her at home.

If you have any room for her I will try to get her in school by the 8th or 9th of January 1889. I will come by school when I start a way.

There is an other young lady who wishes to enter school as a work student if her father will let her do so. I know the young woman she is all that could be expected of one who has not had any more chance. Please favor her if you can. Her address is —

> Eva Sneed,[2]
> Brundridge P.O.,
> Pike Co. Ala.

Please let me have an answer from you by the 4th of Jan. I am sir a student and Friend.

G. W. Lovejoy

ALS   Con. 92   BTW Papers   DLC.

[1] Louisiana Lovejoy entered the night school in 1889. She did not graduate.
[2] No student of this name was listed in the Tuskegee catalogs of 1888-89 or 1889-90.

A Speech before the Boston Unitarian Club

Boston, 1888

On September 7, 1861, the first Negro school was opened in the South. It was opened by a colored woman at Hampton, Virginia. Out of this beginning grew the Hampton Institute which was opened as a higher institution of learning in 1868. There are doubtless many in this audience and many hundreds in Boston who began with the birth of the Hampton Institute and other Southern institutions, to make investment in the Bank of Negro Education. It is but natural that after the lapse of eighteen years, men should begin enquiring whether or not their investment is a safe and wise one; what interest it is paying. Let examples answer — there are those present who for a number of years have invested Seventy Dollars a year to pay for the teaching of a young man or woman at Hampton. That Seventy Dollars has met strong and worthy young men and women on the half-way ground. As they entered that institution for a four year's course of training, with nothing in many cases but strong muscles and an earnest heart with which to work for their board while there, this seventy dollars has met them and said "You do so much for yourself and I will do so much for you." It met me when I entered that institution fourteen years ago with but fifty cents in my pocket and said, "I'll provide the chance for

497

you to work your way through." It has done more. It has sent one or more of six-hundred earnest, intelligent, Christian young men and women as teachers and mechanics into every Southern state and in some states their influence can be felt in every county and township. It has sent fifteen teachers into the state of Alabama, into the town of Tuskegee, situated in the "Black Belt of Alabama," where there is a dense, degraded and fast increasing Negro population of 15,000 within a radius of ten miles and where, before the war, colored people had a death-like horror of being sent. Fifteen years ago it is said of this town that Northern teachers in the South for the purpose of teaching colored schools were frightened away by the whites. Five years ago the democratic members of the legislature from the town of Tuskegee voluntarily offered and had passed by the General Assembly a bill appropriating $2,000 annually, to help pay the salaries of teachers in a colored normal school to be located in Tuskegee. At the end of the first session of the school, this appropriation was increased by an almost unanimous vote to $3,000 annually. This school was opened in a church where only nine years before three colored men were shot down like brutes when engaged in a religious meeting that the whites thought was a political meeting. About one month ago, one of the white citizens of Tuskegee who had at first looked on the school with cold indifference, said to me, "I have just been telling the white people that the Negroes are more interested in education than we are and are making more sacrifices to educate themselves." At the end of our first year's work some of the whites said, "We are glad the Normal School is here because it draws people and makes labor plentiful." At the end of the second year, several said, "The Normal School is beneficial because it increases the trade of the town." At the close of the last session more than one said, "The Normal School is a good institution; it is making the colored people in the State better citizens." From the opening of the school to the present, the white citizens of Tuskegee have been among its warmest friends. They have not only given of their money, in small sums, it is true, but they are ever ready to suggest and devise plans to build up the school. This institution opened not quite five years ago with one teacher and 275 students from all parts of Alabama, and from other Southern states, with an average age of eighteen and a half years.

Beginning in an old church and one small shanty, owning not a dollar's worth of property or a foot of land, in fact with nothing but the promise of the State to pay $2,000 toward the salary of the teachers, the institution now owns a farm of 500 acres, mostly woodland, and a large four-story brick building erected at a cost of $11,000, besides a half dozen smaller buildings used for various industries. Every one of the 500,000 bricks that went into the brick building, besides many others for outside sale, was made at our own brickyard by our students, and with the exception of a part done on the first story, every dollars' worth of wood-work was done by students. The school-room and bed-room furniture is made in our carpenter shop. Every student entering this institution does so with the understanding that he must work with his hands as well as study. To this end we have such industries as farming, poultry raising, brickmaking, carpentry, painting, printing, blacksmithing and shoemaking, for young men and pla[i]n and fancy sewing, cooking, laundry work and general house-keeping for girls.

The majority of the students are poor and able to pay but little cash for board; consequently the school keeps three points before it. First, to give the student the best mental training; second, to furnish him with labor that will be valuable to the school, and that will enable the student to learn something from the labor *per se;* third, to teach the dignity of labor. A chance to help himself is what we seek to give to every student.

The property of the institution is deeded to a nonsectarian board of trustees, half of whom are Northern and half Southern. The property of the institution is valued at $68,000 and there is not a dollar's debt on it. While the institution owes much of its success to Northern charity, yet it owes much to the noble, earnest hand of students it has gathered around it — noble and earnest (in that) for three years before we were able to provide a comfortable building for any of the young men, they were willing to camp out in shanties, as many are now doing, where the roof and sides of the house let in almost as much wind and cold as they keep out. More than once at midnight in winter have I found these young men hovering around the fire with their blankets wrapped around them, finding that more comfortable than going to bed.

Soon after the beginning of the school, when told that we must have a dining room in which all the students could meet for their meals, but that such a room might be had only by removing many hundreds cubic yards of earth for a basement, day after day when school hours were over did they manfully and willingly work with pick and spade till the earth was removed and the dining room was completed.

But follow the Seventy Dollars further — through Hampton, out from Hampton to Alabama where it produces compound interest at the Tuskegee Normal School in the shape of ten graduates, ten strong intelligent Christian young men and women who went out into the dark places of Alabama to do for Alabama what Hampton graduates do for Virginia. Follow it still further, we find that at a time in the South when Ku Klux Klan made the nights hideous with torture and murder, when the shot gun policy and school house burning prevailed to the extent that no man counted his life safe, when among many it was a question whether to drive the Negro from the country or murder him in the land of his birth, when in politics there was bribery, distrust and uncertainty, and when the better and more friendly class of whites were doubting and debating as to whether or not it were wise for the State to attempt to educate the Negro, and if attempted, whether or not the Negro boy was capable of receiving an education, and if educated whether or not it would make him a better citizen. It was in the midst of this condition of affairs that the Seventy Dollars given to Hampton Institute and other Southern institutions sent out common-sensed, honest, Christian young men and women who by word and action said to the distracted whites, "Peace be still! though yesterday we were master and slave, today we are brothers — sons of the same God. We can live side by side in peace and harmony" — and comparative peace and prosperity came. It has been the example and work of this class of young men and women laboring in conjunction with the younger and better educated southern whites that have brought about a degree of reciprocal confidence, a mutual interest in the affairs of the South, that is exemplified by the fact that notwithstanding that the whites pay eight-tenths of the tax to support the common schools, with the exception of one State, the colored schools share the benefit of the school revenue equally with the whites. This influence is shown further by the fact that the Southern states at almost every session of their legislators, increase their general appropriations for common schools; and there is no Southern state, I think, that does not attempt to provide for either normal or college training for colored youths, and we add to this fact that within the last three years the Southern white Methodist Conferences have established an institution for the education of colored youths, known as the Payne Institute at Augusta, Ga., and that last summer during the sitting of the Alabama Conference located in the "Black Belt" of Alabama, $400 was given at one collection for the support of this institution we find additional cause for hope.

Perhaps nothing will illustrate the change of Southern sentiment toward the Negro more than the following editorial in a leading Alabama paper in condemnation of the recent outrage at Carrotton,[1] Mississippi, and in connection with this it is to be remembered that the Southern press till within a few years has either half applauded such crimes or by silence shown acquiescence in them.

The class of men and women who have been going out for the last twelve or fifteen years from Fisk, Atlanta, Straight, Talladega, and various other Southern institutions, have in many cases bought themselves lots of land in town or small farms in the country and erected on them neat, substantial cottages that are not only homes for themselves but object lessons and centers of light for the surrounding community. Inspired to a large degree by such examples as these, the colored people in the city of Montgomery alone own $500,000 worth of property in the shape of nicely built unpretensious homes. This speaks pretty well for those who twenty-one years ago did not own themselves.

What Seventy Dollars has done at Hampton, a larger or smaller sum has done at other Negro schools. One of these young men helped in this way, went into the city of Montgomery, Alabama as a physician.[2] He was the first to professionally enter the ex-confederate capitol. When his white brother physicians found out by a six day's examination that he had as one of them said, that he had brains enough to pass a better examination than many whites had passed; they gave him a hearty welcome and offered their services to aid him in consultation or in any other way possible and they are standing manfully up to their promise, notwithstanding the fact that the colored doctor gets more practice than any one white physician in the city. Thus the manly, common sense bearing, and almost unparalleled business success of this young man, has forever broken down in that city all barriers that might have prevented a colored man's succeeding in the medical profession. Another young man has done for the legal profession in that city what this one has done for the medical.

Ever since freedom it has been the practice of Southern railroads to crowd colored women and men, no matter how neatly or how poorly dressed, into the white men's smoking car notwithstanding that they have paid for first class tickets. By a quite persistant demand of their rights on business principles, even this damnable and dishonest practice is beginning to give way before the class of young people I have mentioned. Through all the changes, upheavals, and various phases that the Southern Question has assumed, this fact can be traced through the whole, that *brains,* property and character for the Negro settle the question of "Civil Rights," that work along the line that sends out the class of workers to which I have been referring is the only solution — if there is a peculiar solution — of that mysterious, indefinable and misleading term "The Negro Problem." I would not leave the impression that matters are just right in the South yet — on the other hand there is much that is cruelly unjust, unreasonable; much that is hard to bear and at times seemingly dark and discouraging — but I do mean to say that there are more pippings growing in the south than crab apples — more roses than thorns.

There should be no unmanly, cowering or stooping to satisfy unreasonable whims of southern white men, but it is charity and wisdom to keep in mind in dealing with the two races, the two hundred years of schooling in prejudice against the Negro, which the whites are called on to conquer.

Harmony will come in proportion as the black man gets something that the white man wants, whether it be of brains or of material. Let there be in the community a Negro who by virtue of his superior knowledge of the chemistry of the soil, his acquaintance with the most improved tools and best breeds of stock, can raise fifty bushels of corn to the acre while his white neighbor only raises thirty and the white man will come to the black man to learn. Further, they will sit down on the train in the same coach and on the same seat to talk about it. Some of the country whites looked at first with disfavor on the establishing of the rural school at Tuskegee. It turned out that there was no brick yard in the county; merchants wanted to build, but brick must be brought from a distance or they must wait for one house to burn down before they could get brick to build another. The Normal School with student labor started a brick yard. Bricks were successfully made. The whites came for miles around for bricks. From examining bricks they were led to examine the workings of the school. From the discussion of the brick yard came the discussion of Negro education and thus many of the "old masters" have been led to see and become interested in Negro education. In Tuskegee, a Negro mechanic[3] manufactures the best tin ware, the harness, the best boots and shoes, and it is common to see his store crowded with white customers from all over the county. His word or note goes as far as that of the whitest man.

Our institution owns a better printing press for doing job work than that owned by the white printing offices. When the whites want a first class job of printing done, the difference in the color of our skin does not prevent their sending it to our office.

I am aware that there are those both North and South who are inclined to grow impatient at the slow rate at which, to them, the Negro seems to rise. To such I would say, in the words of Frederick Douglass, "The progress of the Negro should not be judged so much by the heights to which he has risen as by the depths from which he has come.["]

In the towns and cities progress is very evident; but to get a true idea of the real condition of the South one should leave the towns and go far into the country on the cotton plantations, miles from any railroad where the majority of the colored people live. On many of these plantations the people are but little in advance of where slavery left them; for before the war the white people lived on the plantations and moved into the towns, leaving the ignorant masses of blacks with neither guide nor example except the preachers, whose number is legion. One church near Tuskegee has total membership of two hundred and eighteen of these are preachers.

The kind of preachers they are may be illustrated by one of whom it is said, that while he was at work in a cotton field in the middle of July he suddenly stopped, lifted his eyes toward heaven and said, "De cotton is so grassy, de work is so hard and de sun am so hot, I believe this darkey am called to preach."

The colored people on these plantations are held in a kind of slavery that is in one sense as bad as the slavery of antebellum days. I mean the Southern mortgage system. This is the curse of the Negro. It is the mortgage system which binds him, robs him of independence, allures him and winds him deeper and deeper in its meshes each year till he is lost and bewildered. The merchant in town says to him "Give me a mortgage on your cotton crop and I will advance you provisions on which to live during the year." For every dollar's worth of provisions advanced, besides the usual percentage of gain on the goods, the Negro farmer is charged 20 to 25 per cent interest.

Naturally at the end of the year he finds hanging over him a debt which he cannot pay. The second year he tries again to free himself, but in addition to the burden of the second year, he finds the first year's debt saddled on to him and thus from year to year many of them struggle. On these plantations the schools are in session on an average of 67 days in the year and the teachers receive an average pay of $22.00 per month. School houses are needed in every township and county. Most schools are at present taught in wrecks of log cabins or under bush harbors. In many school houses rails are used for seats and often the fire is on the outside of the house while they are on the inside and they walk out and in as they get cold and warm. Add to this a teacher who can scarcely write his name, who is as weak morally as mentally and you have a faint idea of the educational condition of the people on the back plantations. It is to this class we seek to send teachers, intelligent farmers and mechanics.

But why this Macedonian cry from the South for the last twenty years and why does it not now cease? Can't the South do more to help itself? The populations of Massachusetts and Alabama are nearly equal. Alabama taxes her citizens as heavily for education as Massachusetts does, but the same taxation gives each school child enrolled in Massachusetts $15.40 and each one in Alabama $2.27 per year. The difference is in the value of the property taxed and the result is what I have attempted to describe. The most encouraging sign in connection with the education of the Negro lies in the fact that as a race they *work*. We know the opposite is often stated, but usually by some white man, lounging around under a shade tree whittling sticks, we know too that like all flocks we have some "black sheep" in ours, but it is unfair to judge us by our worst. True, their labor is unsystematic, misdirected, shiftless and often at the end of the year a jug of whiskey is all they can show as net gain, nevertheless they *work*. The trouble is he does not know how to use the results of that labor. What is the remedy? I have in mind a young lady who went with the proper training about ten months ago into one of these communities to teach where everything was just as dark and discouraging as anything I have mentioned. She began by calling the people together every week. In these meetings she told them how to save their money, how to buy houses, how to stop mortgaging their crops every year, how to put their money into the education of their children instead of spending it for whiskey and snuff. The result of that teacher's year's work is that the people in that community have built and paid for a neat, comfortable school house, and instead of permitting the school to stop when the public school term of three months expired she caused the people to give enough themselves to open for five months. Not till every community gets a teacher like this one can there be rest or letting up.

There is one famous song sung by the colored people which says "Give me Jesus and you may take all the world." The teachings of this they have been trained to follow for a number of years and the result is the Negro has been satisfied with "Jesus" and the white man has gotten all the cotton. But the number of valuable farms and other property that many wide awake colored people have bought and are improving with success and profit, go to show that they have already learned that the way to have the most of Jesus and to have him in the best way is to mix in a little land, and cotton.

But the day is breaking. No one can follow the progress of the Negro from the town of Canterbury in the State of Connecticut when only fifty years ago Prudence Crandall[4] (blessed name) was persecuted and made an outcast for teaching a Negro girl, to the states of Alabama and Georgia where the Southern Methodist Church composed of his former masters is supporting an institution for his Christianization and education, with[out] the feeling that there is abundant cause for hope and encouragement.

TD Speech Collection BTW Papers ATT.

[1] Presumably he meant Carrollton, Miss.

[2] Cornelius Nathaniel Dorsette.

[3] Lewis Adams.

[4] Prudence Crandall Philleo (1803-90) was a schoolteacher in Canterbury, Conn. When she began to take in black girls as pupils in 1833, a bitter controversy developed. The town was outraged and Miss Crandall was boycotted. Townsmen put pressure on merchants not to sell food or other goods to the teacher. At one point vandals wrecked her home. The issue went beyond Canterbury, and the state of Connecticut passed a law denying persons the right to teach nonresident Negroes. Eventually Prudence Crandall was forced to leave town. She married a Baptist minister and settled in Kansas. In her last years, as an elderly widow, the state of Connecticut provided her with a small pension.

From William D. Floyd

Troy, Ala., Jan. 5th 1889

Dear teacher: I am proud to say that my school[1] is progressing very well, I think. My assistant's father died on the 2nd inst. and she is away but will return on or about the 10th inst. I had no trouble in getting the money sent from Boston. My school is much larger now than at the same period last term. Both in finance and number. I find that corporal punishments have to be inflicted quite often. Could you suggest a remedy? If so I would be proud. I am required to keep the exact account of my corporal punishments. I noticed last mo. that my number was very large. In Nov. the same I might say. Remember me to Mrs. Washington. Yours Truly

W. D. Floyd

ALS   Con. 92   BTW Papers   DLC.

[1] Academy Street Colored School.

From George M. Elliott

Selma Ala. Jan. 8th 1889

Dear Sir: The committee on Program has assigned to you the following subject for a paper to be discussed before the coming convention of Alabama teachers: "How to get the Full Amount of Money Appropriated to our Public Schools." Please let us know at once if you can serve; if not who from your school is "up" on that subject and would do well? It is the design of the committee that the writer of such a paper touch on some method of breaking up the abominable habit of St. Superintendents requiring teachers to give them part of their salary.

I thank you for your suggestion concerning Prof. Whittaker. I presume it would be well to allow him to choose his own subject.

I am glad of the hope of getting your band for the meeting. I am sure a good supplement could to [be?] taken up at the convention to aid in defraying expenses. I am anxious that we have a good and full meeting. May we count on most or all of your teachers?

I am thankful for your suggestions. Your letter was received today. If at any time anything profitable for us strikes you please let it be known. Sincerely Yours

G. M. Elliott

P.S. If Dr. Grimke will be visiting Tuskegee about the time of our convention, it is probable we can secure him one night for a lecture. I understood he is to be with you some time this session. Can you make the two occasion[s] conjoin? We should be glad to have him.

G. M. E.

ALS Con. 92 BTW Papers DLC.

From Samuel Chapman Armstrong

Hampton, Va., Jan 8 1888 [1889]

Dear Mr Washington: I was very glad to hear of the kind and helpful intent of your Boston friends in sending a nurse to your wife. I earnestly hope she may go safely through her coming trial.

You have won in a high degree the confidence of people in Boston & richly deserv[e] it.

Your common sense and straight forward way of talking & working has been your strong point.

The Misses Mason were much pleased with your visit to them at Newport & wished me to tell you to talk more of the effect of Tuskegee on the people about as a example.

Get yourself out a little more.

Deeply hoping that all will go well and that a very Happy New Year is before you   I am very sincerely yours

S C Armstrong

ALS Con. 2 BTW Papers ATT.

From Francis J. Grimké

Jacksonville Fla   Jan. 14th 1889

Dear Prof. Washington: Your kind favor reached me a short while
ago, and gave me such pleasure to hear from you. I regret very much
however, to be obliged to say that it will be impossible for me to comply
with your request to be with you this year. I have been away from my
charge here for nearly five months during the epidemic, and as I am
now in the midst of preparations to return to Washington sometime
next month, it will be impossible for me to be absent a single Sunday
between this time and the time of my departure. I regret very much
that it is so, for it has always been to me a source of very great pleasure
to be with you. Mrs. Grimke joins me in kindest regards to yourself and
Mrs Washington. I hope that both of the children are well, and that
Mrs Washington's health has improved. Mrs G's health, I am sorry to
say has been most wretched for months. I return to Washington in the
hope that she may be benefitted by the change.

And now with best wishes, for your continued success in the great
work in which you are engaged, & with the prayer that every blessing
may rest upon you   I am as ever   Your Sincere friend

Francis J. Grimké

ALS   Con. 92   BTW Papers   DLC.

From Moses Pierce

Norwich   Jany 17/89

My dear Sir   Yrs of 14th at hand. I am pleased to learn fr you that
yr Trustees have obtained a deed of the land on which is the clay bed.
May it prove of a good quality and furnish you an abundant supply
for many years. May it add to the profit & success of yr industries, your
Trustees *should now* turn their attention to obtaining a deed of the
large tract of land bought by bargain a long time since. I think it very
important for the future of yr school that you have a good title to that
land. Yours Truly

M Pierce

ALS   Con. 93   BTW Papers   DLC.

From George W. Lovejoy

Auburn   Lee Co. Ala. January 17th, 1889

My Dear Mr. Washington: The people stoped me at Auburn, they seem quite anxious to have me and still the more so because you gave me the letter of introduction.

They said that I was manafactured direcly from your hand.

I have been very unwell since I have been here and have not been able to be out a mong the people but very little as yet; though I can see they are very poor.

All of their public funs have been contracted for except the pol tax. The Town Ship Supt. tells me that will be some where between $25.00 and $40.00; he will not know before the last of March.

The people promis me with the pol tax, let it be little or much, they will make me $25.00 per month clear of all expenses.

If I get any money at all it will be clear. The people board and have my washing done.

I have not seen any children yet who know any thing. I have not met the teacher here yet.

I wanted to have spoken to you about the country schools while with you; but I did not have the time. The schools in the country are not being half taught. Some of our scholars are doing very poor work. My last work was where one of Tuskegee's Graduates taught and in my judgement she did no good, and I am a fraid she is not all.

She was a perfect immorrel wreck.

I have strong reason to be lieve there are others who are doing no better.

They are aiming to get off by fooling the people.

I trust this may reach your family in good health. Best wishes for your success. Your pupil

G. W. Lovejoy

ALS   Con. 92   BTW Papers   DLC.

From Mrs. G. A. Rumbley

Tuskegee, Ala. Jan. 18–/89

Dear Sir. This matter about which I will write is not *strictly speaking mine* and yet I feel that all the teachers who are interested in, and working for the real good of the school; should allow themselves, and should be allowed to speak freely on matters relative to the students welfare. This crowding among the girls i.e five in a room is soonre or later going to bring bad results in several ways. 1st Such close packing will generate diseases in many of these girls of which they can never rid themselves in yrs. to come.

2nd The training that you so much desire to give them cannot be accomplished by any one, in the best manner and to do poor work in this line seems to me worse than no work at all.

3rd One of the greatest evils among the colored people of the South has been the overcrowding in their *poor homes*. It was some time back a necessary evil induced from poverty but long since comfortable homes have been reared for many of them and all over the South things are assuming a more civilized aspect and should we teach them less here?

Crowding girls together as we are doing here brings about a sense of immodesty and indelicacy that is so contrary to all your teachings and instead of reaping a full harvest and having them look back upon these yrs. spent here as the most blissful yrs. of their lives there will be many regrets.

I have heard complaint succeed complaint in regard to this matter among students and others but no one seems to come directly to the front and give an expression. This summer only would have brought you five students from very desirable and monied families but the manner of overcrowding the girls was opposed strongly.

I shall always believe that the continued fever of last summer and fall was brought about by overcrowding and as the experience was such a serious one I trust it wont be forgotten.

Comparisons are always odious but I have heard this matter discussed at large and it has always been decided like this. No! I would not have my children crowded. A great many who come here cannot go anywhere else from the fact of being very poor and a great many more of another class will come if things are made more comfortable.

If these suggestions are worth anything please accept them if not receive them in the spirit of great anxiety I have for the girls. Respectfully

G. A. Rumbley

ALS Con. 93 BTW Papers DLC.

From Robert W. Whiting

Petersburg, Va., Jan. 23rd 1889

Dear Schoolmate & Friend: I well remember the days of '74 & 75. You and Collins[1] and Green[2] as classmates and roommates can never be forgotten.

"Should Cuba be annexed to the U.S.?" I am glad that you have been so successful and that you have made such a grand record for our class and people. I married in 76 and have two children, a boy and girl. Orion, the boy attends the lower classes of the Institute. Our school now numbers 380. Prof. Langston[3] told me that you had not forgotten our class contests while in school.

I shall be glad to hear from you at any time you may have the leisure to write a word to   Yours truly

Robt W. Whiting

ALS Con. 93 BTW Papers DLC.

[1] John W. Collins.
[2] Charles W. Greene.
[3] John Mercer Langston.

To George Washington Cable

Tuskegee, Ala., Feb. 1 1889

Dear Sir: I have kept you waiting in order to get what information I could on the subject of your letter. Within the last year about 1 dozen families in good circumstances have left Montgomery & vicinity and settled in California.

But those [who] are now leaving and have been doing so since Xmas in large numbers are the common plantation hands. I suppose 600 have gone from Montgomery and adjoining counties within the time mentioned. The majority are going to La. and the Mississippi bottoms where flattering inducements are held out by labor agents who are paying the traveling expenses. As to the cause, I feel quite sure it is to be fo[u]nd in the fact that the colored people are tired working hard all the year and getting nothing for it. It is simply impossible under the present mortgage system for them to get ahead — they can not pay 25 & 30 per cent interest on the dollar and many of them have reached the conclusion that no change can make their condition worse.[1]

I have not been able up to this time to get the addresses of but one, Rufus Lewis, Wampoo, Ark, from whom you could get direct information. Yours truly

Booker T. Washington

ALS   George W. Cable Collection   LNHT.

[1] Cable referred to Negro migration from the South in a speech before the Massachusetts Club in Boston, Feb. 22, 1890, published in *The Negro Question* (1890). In that speech Cable suggested a direct causal relationship between the crop lien system and the migration of blacks "by tens of thousands from North and South Carolina to Mississippi and Arkansas." (Cable, *The Negro Question,* 231.)

From Solomon Palmer

[Montgomery, Ala.] Feby 14 [188]9

Dear Sir, In reply to yours of 26th ult will say that I now feel pretty sure I can put at your disposal $150 for institute work. Dr. Curry thinks that an institute for a few days does but little good. For the whites I am inclined to try two or three to continue for two or three weeks each. For your race it is not so essential perhaps as for the whites but I would think you might hold one or two for one or two weeks and do something in the way of real work in the way of showing how school room work should be done. Of this matter I am willing for you to be the judge. I want more earnest work and more attention given to instructors, white and colored, than ever before. *I mean business,* and I want them thoroughly worked up so as to secure large attendance. They can and must be made a power for good.

S. Palmer

ALpS Superintendent of Education Letterbook, 1888-89 A-Ar.

From William Still

Philadelphia, Feb. 19 1889

Dear Friend: Mr. Laing surprised me a few days ago by telling me that you had not received the one hundred dollars voted you on my motion some months back, and promised that he would send me the order in a day or two. To day it reached me, hence I make no delay in forwarding it with his cheque for that sum ($100.) Be good enough to endorse the order and return it at your earliest convenience.

I feel a deep interest in your school and feel highly gratified to think that the work is in the hands of colored men & women, and that the entire enterprise is controled by the intelect and ability of a colored man.

I regreted very much that we could not have you with us at our 1st Quarter Century Celebration. But your excuse being so lawfull we could not complain. Nevertheless we had a great meeting. Such an one as we never had before in some respects. We had a large variety of speakers, and some very able ones — white & colored.

Hoping that Mrs. W. is all right and that the heir is a big bouncing little man. I am very truly Yours

W Still

ALS Con. 93 BTW Papers DLC.

To George Washington Cable

Tuskegee, Ala., February 20th. 1889

Dear Sir: Since writing you the other day I find that at least a dozen families have gone from Montgomery and its vicinity to California.

If you will address Mr. Joe Clinton, Red Bluff, Cal. he can give you the information you desire. Yours truly,

Booker T. Washington

HLS   George W. Cable Collection   LNHT.

Olivia A. Davidson Washington to Warren Logan

Montgomery   Thursday Morn. [ca. February 1889]

Mr. Logan, This check came in the letter forwarded to me. Am sorry you have not had it earlier. I think you need not send me any money just now, but I will ask you to see Miss Hunt and if she wishes it pay her $20. for me. If she does not wish the money you can put that am't on her acc't & ch. to me.

The baby improves slowly — still Dr. D.[1] says he will come out all right. Yours truly

Olivia D. Washington

ALS   Con. 92   BTW Papers   DLC.

[1] Cornelius Nathaniel Dorsette.

From William Jenkins

Nashville Tenn. Mar. 3, 1889

Dear Mr. Washington, Miss Murray[1] is the lady about whom I spoke to you last winter.

She will graduate from the college department next June. *About same age as Miss Mason.*

I think that you would do well to have her among your corps of teachers next winter. Respectfully Yours

Jenkins

ALS   Con. 2   BTW Papers   ATT.

[1] Margaret James ("Maggie") Murray Washington (1861?-1925) became a teacher at Tuskegee in 1889, lady principal in 1890, and BTW's third wife in

1892. There is conflicting evidence on her birth and early life. She said in 1899 that her father was James Murray, an Irish immigrant, and contended that she was born on Mar. 9, 1865. That year was later inscribed on her tombstone. It is certain that she was born in Macon, Noxubee County, Miss., but no James Murray or any other white Murray appeared in the town of Macon in either the 1860 or 1870 census, nor any slaveholder of that name in the county. Her father could, on the other hand, have been a railroad worker, for Lucy Murray, her mother, is reported as head of a household near the railroad yard workers' boardinghouse in Macon in 1870, her occupation being washerwoman. An article by Emmett J. Scott of the Tuskegee staff, presumably written with her approval, reported that her father died when she was seven years old and that she went the next day to live with white Quaker schoolteachers, a brother and sister named Sanders. (Scott, "Mrs. Booker T. Washington's Part in Her Husband's Work," 42.) No one of that name appeared in the 1870 or 1880 census except John W. Sanders, a retail grocer born in England. A few doors away, however, were a white dry-goods merchant, Elijah Sandler, and Eliza Sandler, both born in Alabama.

Whatever the element of truth in Margaret Washington's story, according to the 1870 census Lucy Murray, black, lived with two daughters, Laura, 10, mulatto, and Margaret, 9, mulatto, and two sons, Willis, 7, mulatto, and Thomas, 4, black. Margaret Murray possibly lived with the Sanders or Sandler family, but in 1880 the census reported her as living with her mother, now married to a black man, Henry Brown, a brick mason.

In 1881, deciding that she needed more schooling, Margaret Murray entered Fisk University at the bottom of the preparatory school as a half-rater, that is, working to pay part of her expenses. She progressed through the preparatory and college classes in eight years and was a model pupil, often serving as a monitor for the girls in the lower classes. She may have misstated her age to secure admission to Fisk. One of her fellow students was W. E. B. Du Bois, who remained a lifelong friend despite his ideological differences with BTW.

In 1895 Margaret Washington was president of the National Association of Colored Women's Clubs, and served for many years as president of the Southern Federation of Colored Women's Clubs. She was also active in organizing groups of women for self-help in the town of Tuskegee and at various plantation settlements in the surrounding countryside. She presided at Dorothy Hall on the Tuskegee campus as superintendent of women's industries, and later as dean of women. She continued her work for the school after her marriage, and was hostess to an almost continuous flow of distinguished visitors, black and white. This work absorbed most of her energies. The welfare worker Florence L. Kitchelt, of the New York College Settlement, described Margaret Washington in 1901: "Mrs. Washington is lighter than he and has beautiful features, arched brows, blue (?) eyes, a Grecian nose, and a poise of the head like a Gibson girl. Her hands are white as mine and beautifully shaped. But her hair is kinky." (Florence L. [Cross] Kitchelt, journal entry, Apr. 3, 1901, Sophia Smith Collection, MNS.) She outlived BTW by ten years. She continued active in women's-club work, aided in the establishment of reform schools for black boys and girls in Alabama, and in 1922 was elected president of the International Council of Women of the Darker Races.

To Caleb Davis Bradlee[1]

Tuskegee, Ala., March 12 1889

Dear Sir: I wish to let you know how very grateful I feel for your Sermons which you have been kind enough to send. I appreciate the book because it represents *practical religion.* Yours truly

Booker T. Washington

ALS   Caleb Davis Bradlee Papers   MnHi.

[1] Caleb Davis Bradlee (1831-97), pastor of the Harrison Square Congregational Church in Boston from 1876 to 1892. The book referred to was probably *Sermons for All Sects* (1888). Bradlee's sermons admonished the poor and downcast to accept their lot and fulfill their divine mission by hard work. He wrote: "We can never be just right, nor feel just right, nor stand just right with Almighty God, till we are content to take what is sent, and to receive the gift so meekly, gratefully, patiently, believingly, and triumphantly that it shall reveal its sweet, holy, and gracious benedictions." "All our heroes and our heroines have become distinguished by taking hold of what was directly before them, and by making the best of that; and thus, gradually, but surely, have they ascended to glory, power, and immortality." "How often one says, 'If I had only been this or that!' But let us show what we can do where we are, and not boast of what we are able to do where we are not, and where most likely we shall never be. . . ." (*Sermons for All Sects,* 63, 82, 278.)

From Francis J. Grimké

Washington. D.C. March 17th 1889

Dear Prof. Washington: Your kind favor reached me a short while ago, and gave me much pleasure to hear from you. I did not answer because I gathered from your letter that you would pass through here in a few days, and so I have been looking for you ever since. I shall be glad to see you at any time. I thank you for thinking of me in connection with the Slater Fund. It seems to me however, that it would be very much better, if you could get a man like Dr. Crummell[1] appointed, or Mr. Robert Purvis[2] or Mr. Wm Still. These men are all better known than myself, and I am sure, would be better fitted for the place.[3] I am exceedingly sorry to hear of the poor health of Mrs. Washington, but hope that she is by this time very much improved.

With kindest regards from Mrs. Grimke and myself for you both, and with best wishes I am as ever   Your Sincere friend

Francis J. Grimké

ALS   Con. 1   BTW Papers   ATT.

[1] Alexander Crummell (1819-98), an eloquent spokesman of black nationalism and race regeneration, was born in New York to a free black family. His father, Boston Crummell, was a prominent abolitionist and proponent of industrial education. Alexander Crummell faced the usual difficulties of a free black trying to educate himself. Anti-abolitionist mobs destroyed his grammar school and drove him from another integrated academy at gunpoint. Racial discrimination prevented his admission to the Episcopal General Theological Seminary. In 1840 he began private study with his family minister, and two years later became the second black American ordained as an Episcopal minister.

In the early 1840s Crummell was pastor of several black Episcopal churches. They all failed, and he became convinced that his mission was to solve what he felt to be the black man's chief problems — moral laxity, lack of race pride, and industrial backwardness. In 1847 he went to England to study, and earned a B.A. from Cambridge University in 1853.

Although he had opposed colonization, Crummell went to Liberia in 1853 as a missionary to tribal Africans and agent of the moral and economic improvement of all black men. Crummell believed that God intended the Negro to be a moral example for the regeneration of all mankind, and that Liberia could prove black men worthy of the task. He met only disappointment, however. The Americo-Liberian ruling class regarded itself as superior to native Africans and ignored Crummell's exhortations to unity and race pride. The settlers did not share his vision of African redemption and worked instead toward an economic and social structure patterned after that of America. Crummell's increasing involvement in internal politics resulted in his expulsion from Liberia College and virtual ostracism until, in 1873, he returned to the United States.

In America, Crummell continued to preach race unity from the pulpit of St. Luke's Episcopal Church in Washington, D.C. He had grown disillusioned, however, with industrial and manual training as a means of uplifting black men. He turned instead to the promotion of their intellectual advancement. Foreshadowing W. E. B. Du Bois's concept of the "talented tenth," he advocated training a vanguard of dedicated black intellectuals to lead the race toward equality. In 1896, two years before his death, he founded the American Negro Academy to encourage black writers, artists, scientists, and philosophers.

[2] Robert Purvis (1810-98), a leading black abolitionist, was the son of a wealthy English merchant and a Moorish-Negro mother. He was born free in Charleston, S.C., light-skinned enough to pass for white, and moved with his family to Philadelphia when he was nine. After an education that included time at Amherst, he moved quickly to the center of Philadelphia abolitionist activities. He was one of three black men to sign the original declaration of the American Anti-Slavery Society in 1833, serving afterward as a member of the executive committee, vice-president, and president. He was a leader of the Pennsylvania Anti-Slavery Society, which he helped organize in 1837, and in 1838 became president of the newly established Philadelphia Vigilance Committee, playing a role which earned

him consideration as the father of the Underground Railroad. Byberry, the estate on which he raised prize livestock and poultry after inheriting a fortune from his father, became an important station on the slave escape route north. The committee and its successor, the General Vigilance Committee, in the 1840s reputedly helped more than 300 slaves a year to escape. Purvis preferred biracial to exclusively black organizations for fighting slavery and discrimination. He opposed colonization. Like many other abolitionists, he was interested in a variety of social reforms, supporting woman suffrage, temperance, and the American Reform Society. After the war he remained in the background, reportedly refusing President Johnson's offer in 1867 of the commissionership of the Freedmen's Bureau. He worked with William Still in 1884 to organize a Colored Independent party in Philadelphia. He married Harriet Forten, aunt of Charlotte Forten Grimké. Two of his sons achieved prominence. Henry Purvis was a member of the South Carolina legislature during Reconstruction and Charles B. Purvis was the first black professor at Howard University Medical School.

3 The reference is no doubt to the position of general agent of the Slater Fund, which Atticus Greene Haygood was to vacate in 1890. Jabez Lamar Monroe Curry succeeded him.

From Alfred Haynes Porter

Brooklyn Mch 24/89

Dr Sir: In looking over my Southern Workman this eve'g I learned of the birth of a new Baby[1] in your household for which I desire to offer congratulations! I am sorry to hear of the loss of your Cottage by fire[2] but feel like congratulating again that you were all able to get safely out. My summer cottage was burned in the night three seasons ago, and we just escaped with our lives, loosing furniture, clothing, silver &c, but as I stood out in the night watching the fire I could but say do not condole with me, but congratulate us that we are all safe and not in that burning building. I was insured, but lost 1200 to 1500 dolls, c[l]othing &c not insured. I hope you were more fortunate even than I, but shall be glad to hear from you a few of the particulars, also as to whether Mother and child are doing well after such a fright as the Mother must have had. Trusting you can spare the time to give me a few lines I am with best wishes   Yours Truly

A. H. Porter

ALS Con. 2 BTW Papers ATT.

1 Ernest Davidson ("Dave") Washington (1889-1938), son of BTW and Olivia Davidson Washington, was a delicate child who shared his mother's physical

infirmities as well as her gentle spirit and determination to struggle on. As be-
fitted the youngest child, he was the most lovable. He attended the Tuskegee Institute training school. From the spring of 1904 until December 1905 he attended
Oberlin Academy, Oberlin, Ohio, where John Fisher Peck was principal. He
boarded in town, and made rather low grades. In 1905 he developed serious eye
trouble that caused BTW to consult the best eye physicians in New York and to
withdraw his son from all close use of his eyes for about six months. The eye trouble
continued throughout his life, but he graduated from Tuskegee and in 1910-11
studied at Talladega College in Alabama. From the fall of 1911 to the spring of
1913 he attended Shaw University Medical School but failed to complete the
course, possibly because of his eye trouble. Going to New York City, he enrolled
in the New York School of Secretaries, taking stenography and typing, for which
he had some background through summer work in the principal's office at Tuskegee
Institute. While there, he met and married Edith Merriweather, of an old Washington, D.C., family, a teacher in the Atlantic City, N.J., public schools. On the
advice of his father, he continued his secretarial course through the remainder of
the year, while his wife taught at the Children's House at Tuskegee and made a
closer acquaintance with her parents-in-law. E. Davidson Washington served as
northern financial agent of Tuskegee for many years, and for the last ten years of
his life served the public-relations office of Tuskegee Institute, guiding the thousands of visitors each year through the campus. He edited a compilation of the
speeches of BTW and a shorter volume of his quotations. He died after a year
of failing health, apparently of heart trouble, at the age of forty-nine.

[2] The announcement of the birth of Ernest Davidson Washington, Feb. 6, 1889,
and of a fire two days later that destroyed BTW's house, appeared in the *Southern
Workman,* 18 (Mar. 1889), 25.

From Ellen G. Reveler[1]

Cleveland, O. Mar. 26, 1889

Sir. I thank you for your prompt answer to my letter of inquiry. I am
sorry to say that I have not succeeded as I had expected in being able
to send you a promising teacher. There seems to be a prejudice against
going so far South.

I am greatly interested in the success of your school. Some questions,
as of manual labor, are being solved in the South, out of the necessity
of the case. History will recognize you as leaders in many ways. I enclose a Circular of our school. Yours respectfully

Ellen G. Reveler

ALS Con. 2 BTW Papers ATT.

[1] Ellen G. Reveler was principal of a normal school in Cleveland, Ohio.

From William Jenkins

Nashville Tenn. Mar. 31. 1889

Dear Friend: Since hearing from you I have had a talk with Prof. Morgan[1] who is very much interested in the work at Tuskegee. She asks that I use my influence to get you to visit us at commencement or some other time before school closes. I think that such a visit from you would prove profitable as well as a source of pleasure both to you and us. I do not think that a couple of days spent by you in visiting the various institutions in the city while they are in operation could be other than profitable.

Besides a short stay in the hills of Tennessee might be of inestimable value to Mrs. Washington. Nashville is well supplied with mineral waters such as limestone, iron & sulphur.

I hope that you received the letter which I wrote indorsing Miss Murray.

It is claimed that Nashville has the only high school in the south for Negroes. It is well managed. It gives me great pleasure to know that everything is progressing smoothly at Tuskegee. I am doing well in my studies.

My class is just completing Trigonometry.

In a few days we shall take up surveying. Upon the whole this has been the hardest year of my school life. Some of our studies have been exceedingly difficult. But it is gratifying to know that we have passed the most difficult point in our curriculum. Nothing more at present. Sincerely Yours,

William Jenkins

ALS Con. 2 BTW Papers ATT.

[1] Helen Clarissa Morgan, born in Masonville, N.Y., moved to Oberlin, Ohio, in 1845, when she was twelve years old. After graduation from Oberlin College, she began teaching at Fisk University in 1869. She was professor of Latin, the first woman to hold a professor's chair in an American coeducational university.

From John Wheeler Harding

Longmeadow Mass. April 2. 1889

My dear Mr Washington: We are very sorry to hear of your misfortune, & trust that it will be made up to you in due season.

Mrs Harding has been planning to send you a barrel of miscellaneous goods, reading etc. & is now making it up. Which is the best line to send it by? I have the impression, Savannah Steamer from Boston. Please give me by return of mail the address to put on the barrel, or any information that will expedite its reaching you in the best & cheapest way.

Have you read, Questions of the Day No 67 in Putnams Series "The Plantation Negro as a Freeman" by Philip A. Bruce[1] of Richmond Va. He takes a rather dark view of the future of your people in this country the main feature of which is the growing alienation of the races, and the return of the negro race to its original physical type which he thinks will involve intellectual and moral decadence, and he intimates a growing revulsion between the races and the grim determination of the whites to maintain their political supremacy and if needful thereto by a limitation of the negro franchise. Does it seem to you that there is any real prospect of such a race separation as to create serious civil disturbance? Mr. Bruce admits of a possible deliverance through better education & particularly religious education, but does not seem at all hopeful about it. Do you think Dr Haygood is a thorough friend of the negro as well as a wise peacemaker? I have no reason to doubt it but would like to know your view confidentially expressed. Yours very truly,

John W. Harding

ALS Con. 2 BTW Papers ATT.

[1] Philip Alexander Bruce (1856-1933) was born in Staunton Hill, Va., graduated from the University of Virginia, and received a law degree from Harvard University. In 1889 he published *The Plantation Negro as a Freeman,* a white supremacist statement predicting that Negroes would revert to barbarism because they had been freed from paternal slavery. Bruce became a leading historian, researching seventeenth-century Virginia records and recording the history of the New South. In *The Rise of the New South* (1905) he wrote into history what Henry Grady had earlier offered as myth, that the South had put away its plantation past, entered the industrial era, and solved its race problem.

To Samuel Chapman Armstrong

Tuskegee, Ala., April 4 1889

Dear Gen. Armstrong, I meant to have written you some days ago about a plan we have on foot for summer work. We are planning to take a sextet, composed of 4 students and Messrs Hamilton & Logan through the North giving most of the time to the watering places as in '84. The company will be better trained than before. While we do not expect the direct returns will be great yet I think it will pay in the end.

Can you give us any advice or help in the matter?

The music as far as possible will be confined to that which is peculiar to this part of the South.

School matters go well.

My wife is better but is still far from well. Yours truly

Booker T. Washington

ALS   Business Office   ViHaI.

From Sarah Newlin

Philadelphia, Apr. 4th [1889]

My dear Mr. Washington, My sister gave me one of the enclosed cheques some time ago to send to you when I was ready to send my contribution with it. That time is now so I add my own cheque for a like amount and send both for a scholarship for a *girl* in your school. If too late for this year I suppose you can put them in a bank to draw a little interest for next year. This is one result of the strong endorsement of your school in the "South. Workman."

Do teach your pupils to write on both sides of a sheet of paper. I often get letters from coloured teachers, speaking of great poverty, and using three or four times as much paper for their letters as any other person would. The *habit* of waste never stops at one thing, and this is one.

I hope your school is prospering — I watch its course with much

interest, and have been glad to see its vitality in the missionary committee for the poor around you. That practise & experience is as good
for the pupils as their aid is good for their neighbours. I hope the fire
did your wife no serious harm. Sometimes the sympathy and interest
such need calls forth is worth more than the loss. Truly yours,

S. Newlin

Please acknowledge receipt of cheques.

ALS   Con. 2   BTW Papers   ATT.

To Warren Logan

New York   April 14. 89

If any N.Y. or New England send in money while I am away let
me know so that I will not call on them.

We are getting on well so far.

B. T. W.

ACI   Con. 2   BTW Papers   ATT.

To Warren Logan

Stevens House   New York, April 17 1889

Dear Mr. Logan: Enclosed I send checks for $100.

I left expecting replies from several letters which I hope you will
forward to Boston at once.

Mrs. Washington was much more comfortable when I left her
yesterday. Yours

B. T. Washington

ALS   Con. 2   BTW Papers   ATT.

From Russell Lant Carpenter[1]

Bridport, April 17, 1889

Dear Sir, I am glad that you were pleased with my notice of your school, in the *Inquirer* of Jan. 26. I fear, however, that it has been attended with no pecuniary result. There are so many home claims.

I have however the pleasure of enclosing you a donation of £10., made payable to your Treasurer, Mr. Logan. £5 of it is from myself, and the remaining £5 is from Mrs. Carpenter, who for more than forty years — ever since Mr. F. Douglass's first visit to England — has been a warm friend of your race, as well as earnest in benevolent movements at home. I am very sorry to say that she has, for nearly half a year, been confined to her room by a spinal complaint.

Our donation may be entered as "for general purposes," from *Mr. and Mrs. Russell L. Carpenter, Bridport, England.* Please to see that it is entered properly. In your Report, last year, I am called (p. 6) *George* L. Carpenter; and in your last letter (signed by you) your clerk has written Brid*ford*, instead of Brid*port*.

Bridport is, I believe, the only place of the name: it is the port of the little river Brid (or Brit). It is a small town, with less than 7,000 inhabitants; but it was founded more than 800 years ago; and returned two members to Parliament, till recently. If you hav[e] a tolerable map of England, you will find it on the South coast, in Dorsetshire, a few miles from Devonshire. Th[e] chief trad[e] is in twine, nets, &c. Three or four hundred years ago, it is said to have furnished all the cordage for the English navy — which, at that time, was of course very small! Yours faithfully,

Russell L. Carpenter

ALS   Con. 2   BTW Papers   ATT.

[1] Russell Lant Carpenter, a pastor, was a regular contributor to Tuskegee Institute. Frederick Douglass had been the Carpenters' guest for several days on his first trip to England in 1840.

To Warren Logan

Stevens House   New York, April 18 1889

Dear Mr Logan: Enclosed you will find checks for $65.

I sent a telegram Sunday about subscription books, but have not received them. I want Boston, N.Y. and Philadelphia Subscription books send them care Spencer Tra[s]k & Co. 16 Broad St N.Y.

I return to Boston to night but shall be back here within a day or two. Yours truly

B. T. Washington

ALS   Con. 2   BTW Papers   ATT.

To Warren Logan

Crawford House   Boston, April 19 1889

Dear Mr. Logan: Enclosed I send check for $25.

My wife is more comfortable today but had a hard night last night. Yours truly

B. T. Washington

ALS   Con. 2   BTW Papers   ATT.

To Samuel Chapman Armstrong

25 Beacon St. Boston, Mass. April 21–89

Dear Gen. Armstrong, A week ago I brought my wife here to be treated in the Mass. General Hospital for which friends had kindly arranged. As hard as it is I guess it is best for me to look the matter in the face and say that at present she is not gaining and without a change soon can not last much longer.

Few will ever know what she has done for Tuskegee and for me. Yours faithfully,

Booker T. Washington

ALS   Armstrong Papers   MWiW.

Anonymous to John Henry Washington

Tuskegee, Ala. April 23, 1889

Dear Sir: As I understand, there is some indignation brewing from an immoral source of white and Col. against the school from the act of the suposed student; it would be well to look out for Fires and keep the boys a little closer to the grounds for a while. Your Friend

XXX

AL Con. 2 BTW Papers ATT. Apparently the school officers decided not to worry BTW with this matter in view of his wife's illness and his distance from the scene. None of his letters of the period reflect an awareness of the warning.

To Warren Logan

Boston, April 25, 1889

Dear Mr. Logan; I am very glad to know that you could go with the "Singers" to Columbus, as I know that it gave you an opportunity for a much needed rest.

Mr. McCann[1] is at present down with the measles.

In all I think I have sent you $325.00 since I left. With this I hope you have been able to satisfy matters at the bank.

I expected to have sent in much more by this time, but for the last three or four days have had to give all my time to Mrs. Washington. At present, however, arrangements for her comfort are as comfortable as they can be, and I shall be at liberty to work more for the School.

It seems to me that it will be best to settle with Hobie and Teague[2] with notes.

I think I can send in something pretty often hereafter.

I had written Miss Hawley, the day before receiving your letter, to make whatever arrangements with Miss Rumley[3] she thought best.

I now see that I shall have to leave details with you and my brother, as you are on the ground and can better direct matters than I can at this distance. I am particularly anxious that the brick-yard work shall be pushed. You will have to use your own judgment about the pavilion.

Mrs. Washington I am glad to say is more comfortable; but I fear no stronger. Friends here have spared no expense for her comfort. Yours truly,

B. T. Washington

HLS Con. 2 BTW Papers ATT.

¹ Woodie I. McCann.
² Hobbie and Teague were merchants in Montgomery. John H. Washington wrote them in 1887 asking the price of a carload of lime, which suggests that Hobbie and Teague dealt in fertilizer and possibly other farm items. (John H. Washington to Hobbie and Teague, July 20, 1887, Con. 91, BTW Papers, DLC.)
³ Probably Mrs. G. A. Rumbley.

To Warren Logan

New York. Apr. 26. [1889]

Dear Mr. Logan: Enclosed I send check for $50 and am very sorry it is not more, but I have been compelled to give my time to my wife. She is now so situated that I think I can give more time to money. Just go ahead and make whatever arrangements you think best for Commencement. J. C. Price will deliver address. Invitations should be sent out at once. You can not give too much personal attention to the industrial work.

Mrs. Washington is now more comfortable. Friends in Boston have spared no expense to do every thing for her. Yours Hastily

B. T. Washington

I return to Boston, tomorrow.

ALS Con. 2 BTW Papers ATT.

To Warren Logan

Stevens House   New York, April 27 1889

Dear Mr. Logan, Enclosed I send checks for $125. Shall do my best to send some more next Monday. Shall not be here again for 4 or 5 days.

If Dr. Dorsett thinks it advisable send the Montgomery Capital City Guards[1] a Special invitation to Commencement. They are very anxious to attend again.

I hope lumber enough can be gotten in some way for the pavilion.

Provide all the means you can for the enjoyment of the seniors and teachers during remainder of term.

Mrs. W is more comfortable at present. Yours truly

B. T. Washington

How about the Columbus trips?

ALS   Con. 2   BTW Papers   ATT.

[1] The black unit of the Alabama State Troops commanded by Joseph L. Ligon.

To Warren Logan

New Haven Ct. April 30–89

Dear Mr. Logan: Enclosed I send check for $100 which I know you are badly needing. Shall do my best to send more tomorrow.

I can not be away from Mrs. W. very long. She is a little more comfortable at present but very weak. Every thing possible is being done for her. Yours truly

B. T. Washington

You will find that the more money you can pass through Mr. Campbell's hands the better he will be inclined to treat us in a tight.

ALS   Con. 2   BTW Papers   ATT.

An Article in the *Southern Workman*

[April 1889]

A STABLE AS A CIVILIZER

The Tuskegee Normal and Industrial School, at Tuskegee, Alabama, of which Booker T. Washington is principal, has in process of erection

a stable which, when completed, will be the largest and most con
in the State of Alabama.

There will also be ample room for storing away feed and shelt(
wagons, etc.

The Tuskegee School, being located in the midst of a thickly p(
lated farming district, gives the officers of the school an exception;
good opportunity to know the weak points and needs of the coloi
people.

Scarcely one man in ten exercises any care for the comfort of stoc
The idea that a horse or cow should be protected from the cold, hurtfι
rains enters the minds of but few; and it is very rare to find person
who curry and clean their animals; hence, the animals are weak anc
of a poor quality.

The loss to farmers and others each year resulting from the stealing
of, and damage done to, tools left out over nights and in the field, all
the winter, is very great.

Few colored farmers make any attempt at systematic saving and
making of manure; hence, nothing is returned to the long-worked lands.

The Tuskegee barn will contain a large tool room, where tools can
be cared for in the best way, and students will be required to keep
everything in its place. In short, it will be a constant object lesson in
civilization to the student during his four years course. It would be well
nigh impossible that a student should be in and around a barn for a
number of years where animals are comfortably housed and well-
cleaned tools carefully taken care of, and every effort made to make
and save manure, without receiving lessons which he will put into
practice the remainder of his life.

The barn can be completed for $1,500 cash. It is at present half
completed, all the work having been done by the students, and they
will do all the work necessary to finish the building; but there are
certain cash outlays in the way of material that will amount to $1,500,
and these the school is compelled to ask of its friends. This barn will
be not only a great means of good to students connected with the school,
but a constant teacher for the surrounding country.

B. T. Washington

Southern Workman, 18 (Apr. 1889), 47.

To Warren Logan

[Boston] May 2 1889

Dear Mr. Logan: Mrs. Washington I am glad to say seems to me stronger than when I last wrote and her condition seems a little more encouraging. Unless there is some great change in her condition I do not think you can count on my being at the school except for one or two days before and after Commencement. So you see that I shall have to depend on you for all the arrangements.

Let Mr. Wright[1] examine your system of book keeping.

Please see as soon as you can all the teachers and let me know who of them wish to return another year. These I know about. Mr. Wilson, Miss Williamson,[2] Miss Mason, Miss Dorsette, Mr. Whittaker and I have written to Miss Hawley. Love to all. Yours truly

B. T. Washington

Do all you can to make Mr. Wright's visit interesting. He is going to make a report to the Unitarians.

B. T. W.

ALS   Con. 1   BTW Papers   ATT.

[1] J. Edward Wright was a Unitarian minister in charge of the Church of the Messiah at Montpelier, Vt., and a lifetime member of the American Unitarian Association. His account of his inspection of Tuskegee on behalf of the Unitarians was published in the official Unitarian organ, *The Christian Register,* 68 (July 4, 1889), 430.

[2] Mahala J. Williamson was in charge of the laundry at Tuskegee Institute from 1888 to 1891 and was principal of the night school and librarian during the 1891-92 school year. Born in Wilson County, N.C., in 1864, she graduated from Hampton in 1888.

To Warren Logan

Crawford House   Boston, May 3 1889

Dear Mr. Logan: Enclosed I send check for $25.

Mrs. Washington is brighter today and I think is stronger. Send notices to colored press about Commencement. It is well to send out

invitations to Southern people pretty freely — especially the colored people. Shall try to send some flags and bunting.

Send "S L.["]¹ regularly to

> Mr. Wm. Minot Jr.²
> 39 Court St.
> Boston, Mass.

Better have Florence Taylor's³ father arrange about excursion rates from Pensacola and Mr. Bedford about Montgomery. Mr. Bedford has done it well heretofore. Yours Hastily

B. T. Washington

ALS Con. 2 BTW Papers ATT.

¹ *Southern Letter.*
² William Minot, Jr. (1849-1900) was a Boston lawyer. His brother was the distinguished Harvard biologist Charles Sedgwick Minot (1852-1914).
³ Florence B. Taylor (Mrs. D. J. Cunningham) was an 1889 graduate of Tuskegee who lived in Pensacola, Fla., where she was a housekeeper and a teacher.

The Inscription on the Tombstone of Olivia A. Davidson Washington

[Tuskegee, Ala., May 9, 1889]

Olivia Davidson Washington
June 11, 1854
May 9, 1889
"She lived to the truth."

Tombstone in Tuskegee Institute Cemetery, Tuskegee, Ala.

To Samuel Chapman Armstrong

Tuskegee Alabama. May 18–1889

My dear good friend Gen Armstrong, What a comfort your dear good letter is to me in this hour of my deepest grief. I thank you a thousand times for it.

You have offered to do the very thing that will give me most pleasure and satisfaction. I gladly send the photograph which I hope can be returned as I have only one or two. I never knew till her sickness how dearly she was loved and valued. The Boston people spared no expense or effort to save her life and make her comfortable. They would not let me bear any of the expense. The whole of Tuskegee seems to be in mourning for her.

Few will ever know just what she was to Tuskegee and me. But I can not trust myself to write more now I want to tell you about it all some time.

Many, many thanks to you. I wish you could know how good every body has been to us in this deep, deep affliction. Yours Sincerely

Booker T. Washington

ALS   Armstrong Papers   MWiW.

BIBLIOGRAPHY

THIS BIBLIOGRAPHY gives fuller information on works cited in the annotations and endnotes. It is not intended to be comprehensive of works on the subjects dealt with in the volume or of works consulted in the process of annotation.

Alabama. *Acts of the General Assembly of Alabama, Passed at the Session of 1880-81.* Montgomery, 1881.

———. *Acts of the General Assembly of Alabama, Passed at the Session of 1882-83.* Montgomery, 1883.

———. *Acts of the General Assembly of Alabama, Passed at the Session of 1886-87.* Montgomery, 1887.

———. *Journal of the House of Representatives, Session of 1886-87.* Montgomery, 1887.

———. *Report of H. Clay Armstrong, Superintendent of Education of the State of Alabama, for the Scholastic Year Ending September 30, 1882.* Montgomery, 1882.

———. *Thirty-fourth Annual Report of the Superintendent of Education of the State of Alabama for the Scholastic Year Ending September 30, 1888.* Montgomery, 1888.

Alabama State Teachers' Association. *Fifth Annual Session of the Alabama State Teachers' Association Held at Selma, Alabama, April 21-24, 1886.* Tuskegee, 1887.

———. *Minutes of the First Annual Session, Alabama State Teachers' Association, April 6-7, 1882.* Selma, 1882.

———. *Minutes of the Seventh Annual Session, Alabama State Teachers' Association.* Montgomery, 1888.

Bearss, Edwin C. *The Burroughs Plantation as a Living Historical Farm.* Washington, D.C.: National Park Service, 1969.

Bond, Horace Mann. *Negro Education in Alabama: A Study in Cotton and Steel.* Washington, D.C.: Associated Publishers, Inc., 1939.

Bradlee, Caleb Davis. *Sermons for All Sects.* Boston: W. B. Clarke and Company, 1888.

Bullock, Henry Morton. *A History of Emory University.* Nashville, Tenn.: Parthenon Press, 1936.

Butcher, Philip. "George W. Cable and Booker T. Washington," *Journal of Negro Education,* 17 (Fall 1948), 462-68.

Cable, George W. *The Negro Question.* Arlin Turner, ed. New York: Doubleday and Company, Inc., 1958.

Clarke, James Freeman. *Self-Culture: Physical, Intellectual, Moral and Spiritual, a Course of Lectures.* Boston: J. R. Osgood and Company, 1880.

Collins, Herman LeRoy. *Philadelphia: A Story of Progress.* Philadelphia: Lewis Historical Publishing Company, 1941.

Crofts, Daniel Wallace. "The Blair Bill and the Elections Bill: The Congressional Aftermath to Reconstruction." Ph.D. dissertation, Yale University, 1968.

De Long, Henry C., Walter C. Wright, and Calvin H. Clark. "Mrs. George Luther Stearns," *The Medford Historical Register,* 5 (Jan. 1902), 21-22.

Drake, Richard Bryant. "The American Missionary Association and the Southern Negro, 1861-1888." Ph.D. dissertation, Emory University, 1957.

Dryer, Edmund Hext. *Origin of Tuskegee Normal and Industrial Institute.* Birmingham, Ala.: Roberts and Son, 1938.

Garrett, Mitchell Bennett. *Sixty Years of Howard College, 1842-1902.* Birmingham, Ala.: Howard College, 1927.

Gaston, Paul M. *The New South Creed: A Study in Southern Mythmaking.* New York: Alfred A. Knopf, Inc., 1970.

Gilliam, E. W. "The African in the United States," *Popular Science Monthly,* 22 (Feb. 1883), 433-44.

Hampton Normal and Agricultural Institute. *Twenty-two Years Work of the Hampton Normal and Agricultural Institute at Hampton, Virginia.* Hampton, Va.: Normal School Press, 1893.

Harlan, Louis R. *Booker T. Washington: The Making of a Black Leader.* New York: Oxford University Press, 1972.

Holt, Rackham. *George Washington Carver: An American Biography.* Garden City, N.Y.: Doubleday and Company, Inc., 1946.

James, Jacqueline. "Uncle Tom? Not Booker T.," *American Heritage,* 19 (Aug. 1968), 50-63, 95-100.

Ludlow, Helen Wilhelmina, ed. *Tuskegee Normal and Industrial School for Training Colored Teachers, at Tuskegee, Alabama, Its Story and Its Songs.* Hampton, Va.: Normal School Steam Press, 1884.

McFeely, William S. *Yankee Stepfather: General O. O. Howard and the Freedmen.* New Haven: Yale University Press, 1968.

Mackintosh, Barry. *General Background Studies: The Burroughs Plantation 1856-1865.* Washington, D.C.: National Park Service, 1968.

McPherson, James M. "White Liberals and Black Power in Negro Education, 1865-1915," *American Historical Review,* 75 (June 1970), 1357-79.

Maddex, Jack P., Jr. *The Virginia Conservatives, 1867-1879: A Study in Reconstruction Politics.* Chapel Hill: University of North Carolina Press, 1970.

Marshall, James Fowle Baldwin. "Tuskegee: A Hamptonian's Visit to the Young Hampton," *Christian Register,* 62 (Apr. 5, 1883), 214.

Meier, August. *Negro Thought in America, 1880-1915: Racial Ideologies in the Age of Booker T. Washington.* Ann Arbor: University of Michigan Press, 1963.

Moger, Allen Wesley. *Virginia: Bourbonism to Byrd, 1870-1925.* Charlottesville: University Press of Virginia, 1968.

National Educational Association. *Journal of Proceedings and Addresses of the National Educational Association, Session of the Year 1884, at Madison, Wis.* Boston, 1885.

National Negro Business League. *Proceedings of the Annual Meeting of the National Negro Business League, 1900.* Nashville, Tenn., 1901.

Nixon, Raymond Blalock. *Henry W. Grady: Spokesman of the New South.* New York: Alfred A. Knopf, Inc., 1943.

Olsen, Otto H. *Carpetbagger's Crusade: The Life of Albion Winegar Tourgée.* Baltimore: Johns Hopkins Press, 1965.

Redkey, Edwin S. *Black Exodus: Black Nationalist and Back-to-Africa Movements, 1890-1910.* New Haven: Yale University Press, 1969.

535

Rubin, Louis D., ed. *Teach the Freeman: The Correspondence of Rutherford B. Hayes and the Slater Fund for Negro Education, 1881-1887.* 2 vols. Baton Rouge: Louisiana State University Press, 1959.

Rudolph, Frederick. *Mark Hopkins and the Log: Williams College, 1836-1872.* New Haven: Yale University Press, 1956.

Scott, Emmett J. "Mrs. Booker T. Washington's Part in Her Husband's Work," *Ladies Home Journal,* 24 (May 1907), 42.

Thornbrough, Emma Lou. "The National Afro-American League, 1887-1908," *Journal of Southern History,* 27 (Nov. 1961), 494-512.

Tourgée, Albion Winegar. *An Appeal to Caesar.* New York: Fords, Howard and Hulbert, 1884.

Trotter, James Monroe. *Music and Some Highly Musical People.* Boston: Lee and Shepard, 1878.

United States. Interstate Commerce Commission. *Reports [Court Decisions], May 1887 to June 1888.* Vol. 1. Rochester, N.Y.: Lawyers' Cooperative Publishing Company, 1887 [1888?].

Washington, Booker T. *The Negro in Business* (1907). Reprint. Chicago: Afro-Am Press, 1969.

————. *The Story of My Life and Work.* Naperville, Ill.: J. L. Nichols and Company, 1900.

————, ed. *Tuskegee and Its People: Their Ideals and Achievements* (1905). Reprint. New York: Negro Universities Press, 1969.

————. *Up from Slavery: An Autobiography.* Garden City, N.Y.: Doubleday, Page and Company, Inc., 1901.

Washington, E. Davidson, ed. *Selected Speeches of Booker T. Washington.* Garden City, N.Y.: Doubleday, Doran and Company, Inc., 1932.

INDEX

NOTE: The asterisk indicates the location of detailed identification.

537

The BOOKER T. WASHINGTON *Papers*